T0259812

Lecture Notes in Artificial Intelligence 11793

Subseries of Lecture Notes in Computer Science

More information about this series at http://www.springer.com/series/1244

Christoph Benzmüller · Heiner Stuckenschmidt (Eds.)

KI 2019: Advances in Artificial Intelligence

42nd German Conference on AI
Kassel, Germany, September 23–26, 2019
Proceedings

 Springer

Editors
Christoph Benzmüller 🆔
Freie Universität Berlin
Berlin, Germany

Heiner Stuckenschmidt 🆔
Universität Mannheim
Mannheim, Germany

ISSN 0302-9743   ISSN 1611-3349   (electronic)
Lecture Notes in Artificial Intelligence
ISBN 978-3-030-30178-1   ISBN 978-3-030-30179-8   (eBook)
https://doi.org/10.1007/978-3-030-30179-8

LNCS Sublibrary: SL7 – Artificial Intelligence

This Springer imprint is published by the registered company Springer Nature Switzerland AG
The registered company address is: Gewerbestrasse 11, 6330 Cham, Switzerland

Preface

This volume contains the papers presented at the 42nd German Conference on Artificial Intelligence (KI 2019), held during September 23–26, 2019, in Kassel, Germany.

The German conference on Artificial Intelligence (abbreviated KI for "Künstliche Intelligenz") has developed from a series of inofficial meetings and workshops, organized by the German "Gesellschaft für Informatik" (association for computer science, GI), into an annual conference series dedicated to research on theory and applications of intelligent system technology. While KI is primarily attended by researchers from Germany and neighboring countries, it warmly welcomes international participation.

The KI 2019 conference took place in Kassel, Germany, September 23–26, 2019, and it was held in conjunction with the 49th Annual Conference of the German Computer Science Association (INFORMATIK 2019). Information about the event can be found at www.ki2019.de and informatik2019.de, respectively.

KI 2019 had a special focus theme on "AI methods for Argumentation" and we especially invited contributions that use methods from all areas of AI to understand, formalize, or generate argument structures in natural language. The special focus theme was organized in cooperation with the DFG funded priority program "RATIO: Robust Argumentation Machines". Besides this special focus theme, the conference invited original research papers and shorter technical communications on all topics of AI. Further, we asked for the submission of extended abstracts summarizing papers that had recently been presented at major AI conferences.

KI 2019 received 82 submissions, with authors from 25 countries. Submissions were – except for some special cases – reviewed by three Program Committee members. The Program Committee, comprised of 51 experts from 9 countries, decided to accept 29 papers. Out of these, 16 submissions were accepted as full papers, 10 as short papers and 3 as extended abstracts. The program also included three invited talks:

- Jürgen Altmann (University of Dortmund): Autonomous Weapon Systems – Dangers and Need for an International Prohibition
- Michael Beetz (University of Bremen): Digital Twin Knowledge Bases – Knowledge Representation and Reasoning for Robotic Agent
- Antony Hunter (University College London): Towards Computational Persuasion for Behaviour Change Applications

Two of these presentations are summarized in papers contained in this volume.

Overall, it was a pleasure to organize KI 2019 and we are grateful to our co-organizers, Alexander Steen (Workshops and Tutorials Chair) and Kristina Yordanova (Doctoral Consortium Chair), who provided valuable additional support in organizing the event.

We thank the Program Committee members and all additional reviewers for the effort and time they invested in the reviewing process. Further, we thank the

Organizing Committee of INFORMATIK 2019 who took care of finances and local organization and allowed us to focus on the scientific aspects of the conference. Our appreciation also goes to the developers of EasyChair, which provides great functionalities that helped to organize the reviewing process and to create this volume.

Last but not least, we would like to thank SAP SE for generously sponsoring travel grants for students to attend KI 2019.

July 2019

Christoph Benzmüller
Heiner Stuckenschmidt

Organization

Program Committee

Sebastian Ahrndt	Curamatik UG (haftungsbeschränkt), Germany
Serge Autexier	DFKI, Germany
Franz Baader	TU Dresden, Germany
Christian Bauckhage	Fraunhofer-Gesellschaft, Germany
Christoph Beierle	University of Hagen, Germany
Christoph Benzmüller	Freie Universität Berlin, Germany
Ralph Bergmann	University of Trier, Germany
Philipp Cimiano	Bielefeld University, Germany
Tim Conrad	Freie Universitaet Berlin, Germany
Juergen Dix	Clausthal University of Technology, Germany
Didier Dubois	IRIT, RPDMP Toulouse, France
Anette Frank	University of Heidelberg, Germany
Gerhard Friedrich	Alpen-Adria-Universitaet Klagenfurt, Austria
Johannes Fähndrich	Technische Universität Berlin, DAI Labor, Germany
Holger Giese	Hasso Plattner Institute at the University of Potsdam, Germany
Carsten Gips	Fachhochschule Bielefeld, Germany
Lars Grunske	Humboldt University Berlin, Germany
Malte Helmert	University of Basel, Switzerland
Andreas Herzig	CNRS, IRIT, University of Toulouse, France
Steffen Hölldobler	TU Dresden, Germany
Mateja Jamnik	University of Cambridge, UK
Jean Christoph Jung	Universität Bremen, Germany
Gabriele Kern-Isberner	Technische Universität Dortmund, Germany
Kristian Kersting	TU Darmstadt, Germany
Margret Keuper	University of Mannheim, Germany
Matthias Klusch	DFKI, Germany
Ralf Krestel	Hasso Plattner Institute at the University of Potsdam, Germany
Lars Kunze	Oxford Robotics Institute at the University of Oxford, UK
Thomas Lukasiewicz	University of Oxford, UK
Till Mossakowski	University of Magdeburg, Germany
Maurice Pagnucco	The University of New South Wales, Australia
Heiko Paulheim	University of Mannheim, Germany
Rafael Peñaloza	University of Milano-Bicocca, Italy
Guenter Rudolph	Technische Universität Dortmund, Germany
Matthieu-P. Schapranow	Hasso Plattner Institute at the University of Potsdam, Germany
Stefan Schlobach	Vrije Universiteit Amsterdam, The Netherlands

Ute Schmid	University of Bamberg, Germany
Lars Schmidt-Thieme	University of Hildesheim, Germany
Christoph Schommer	University of Luxembourg, Luxembourg
Lutz Schröder	Friedrich-Alexander-Universität Erlangen-Nürnberg, Germany
Daniel Sonntag	DFKI, Germany
Myra Spiliopoulou	Otto-von-Guericke-University Magdeburg, Germany
Steffen Staab	Institut WeST, University Koblenz-Landau, Germany, and WAIS, University of Southampton, UK
Alexander Steen	University of Luxembourg, Luxembourg
Heiner Stuckenschmidt	University of Mannheim, Germany
Matthias Thimm	Universität Koblenz-Landau, Germany
Paul Thorn	Heinrich-Heine-Universität Düsseldorf, Germany
Ingo J. Timm	University of Trier, Germany
Sabine Timpf	University of Augsburg, Germany
Anni-Yasmin Turhan	TU Dresden, Germany
Carsten Ullrich	DFKI, Germany
Roland Vollgraf	Zalando SE, Germany
Toby Walsh	The University of New South Wales, Australia
Stefan Woltran	Vienna University of Technology, Austria
Kristina Yordanova	University of Rostock, Germany

Additional Reviewers

Ayers, Edward William
Barz, Michael
Biswas, Rajarshi
Boukhers, Zeyd
Brinkmeyer, Lukas
Bundy, Alan
Dimanov, Botty
Diéguez, Martín
Eriksson, Salomé
Finzel, Bettina
Francès, Guillem
Fähndrich, Johannes
Galliani, Pietro
Grüger, Joscha
Heist, Nicolas
Hertling, Sven
Huber, Jakob
Hunter, Anthony
Jawed, Shayan
Klein, Patrick

Kohlhase, Michael
Konev, Boris
Kuijer, Louwe B.
Malburg, Lukas
Neuhaus, Fabian
Nunnari, Fabrizio
Nyrup, Rune
Opitz, Juri
Paul, Debjit
Potyka, Nico
Prange, Alexander
Rabold, Johannes
Schon, Claudia
Shams, Zohreh
Simidjievski, Nikola
Stockdill, Aaron
Sun, Jun
Sztyler, Timo
Wang, Duo

Contents

x   Contents

Autonomous Weapon Systems – Dangers and Need for an International Prohibition

Jürgen Altmann[(✉)]

Experimentelle Physik III, TU Dortmund, 44221 Dortmund, Germany
juergen.altmann@tu-dortmund.de

Abstract. Advances in ICT, robotics and sensors bring autonomous weapon systems (AWS) within reach. Shooting without control by a human operator has military advantages, but also disadvantages – human understanding of the situation and control of events would suffer. Beyond this, compliance with the law of armed conflict is in question. Would it be ethical to allow a machine to take a human life? The increased pace of battle may overburden human understanding and decision making and lead to uncontrolled escalation. An international campaign as well as IT, robotics and AI professionals and enterprises are calling for an international ban of AWS. States have discussed about limitations in the UN context, but no consensus has evolved so far. Germany has argued for a ban of fully autonomous weapons, but has not joined the countries proposing an AWS ban, and is using a problematic definition.

An international ban could comprise a prohibition of AWS and a requirement that each use of force must be under meaningful human control (with very few exceptions). If remotely controlled uninhabited weapon systems remain allowed, a-priori verification that they cannot attack under computer control is virtually impossible. Compliance could be proved after the fact by secure records of all communication and sensor data and the actions of the human operator.

The AI and robotics communities could make significant contributions in teaching and by engaging the public and decision makers. Specific research projects could be directed, e.g., at dual use, proliferation risks and scenarios of interaction between two fleets of AWS. Because of high military, political and economic interests in AWS, a ban needs support by an alert public as well as the AI and robotics communities.

Keywords: Autonomous weapon system · Combat robot ·
Armed uninhabited vehicle · Preventive arms control

1 Introduction

In modern armed forces information and communication technologies (ICT) play an ever increasing and by now central role. Advances in ICT have enabled precision-guided missiles in the 1980s and combat drones in the 2000s that in the attack function up to now are being remotely controlled, even though other functions are often carried out autonomously, by the control software on board. Such armed uninhabited air vehicles (UAVs) have proliferated and are deployed by about 30 countries at present. The next step would be machine autonomy also in the weapon use. Such autonomous

C. Benzmüller and H. Stuckenschmidt (Eds.): KI 2019, LNAI 11793, pp. 1–17, 2019.
https://doi.org/10.1007/978-3-030-30179-8_1

weapon systems (AWS) are the subject of intense research and development (R&D) in several countries. A part of such work is devoted to swarms that promise additional military advantages. Artificial intelligence (AI) is seen as an important enabler. AWS could act in all environments: not only in the air, but also on land, on and under water and principally also in outer space (where the conditions for movement and action are very different).

AWS that would select and engage targets by algorithm, without human control, would pose problems in several areas, from ethics via international law to military stability and international security. Accordingly, a scientific debate as well as discussions among states have unfolded. Much literature exists, exemplary overview works are [1] and [2].

The next Sect. 2 describes the trend from remotely controlled armed UAVs to AWS. Then I take a look at military-technology assessment of AWS. Section 4 covers efforts to raise awareness about the problems and discussions among states. Problems with inappropriate definitions in particular by Germany are discussed in Sect. 5. A possible design of an international AWS ban is presented in Sect. 6. Section 7 is devoted to potential contributions by the AI and robotics communities, and Sect. 8 presents a conclusion.

2 From Remotely Controlled Armed Drones to Autonomous Weapons

Armed UAVs have become prominent with the US attacks in the Middle East since 2001, later expanded to regions in Pakistan and Africa. The number of carriers and operations has increased strongly, as has the number of countries with armed drones – today about 30, partly by indigenous development, partly by imports (with China the biggest exporter) [3, 4]. While these UAVs may have automatic functions – not only for flight and trajectory control, some can take off and land autonomously – the attack function is controlled by a human operator via a communication link. Based on background information and real-time video he or she selects a target and attacks ("engages") it. This requires reliable communication that is not endangered in present, strongly asymmetric conflicts, but could be disturbed or interrupted by a more capable adversary. Purely military arguments speak for AWS, however they would bring serious problems in several areas, as shown below.

There are already weapons that attack on their own, without human control. Mines are a very primitive example; some air- or ship-defence systems have an automatic mode where fast incoming projectiles or missiles are detected by radar and an automatic cannon is directed so that its munitions hit the object, or a target-seeking missile is launched against it. These systems are usually called "automatic". They work at short range, in a restricted environment and against a simple class of objects – nevertheless, even here attacks against wrong targets occurred.[1]

---

[1] Fratricides by US Patriot missiles in the 2003 war against Iraq [53].

Fully autonomous weapons systems, on the other hand, would move in a certain area over a considerable time, search for targets, identify and attack them without human control or oversight. A useful definition was given by the US Department of Defense (DoD):

> "autonomous weapon system. A weapon system that, once activated, can select and engage targets without further intervention by a human operator. This includes human-supervised autonomous weapon systems that are designed to allow human operators to override operation of the weapon system, but can select and engage targets without further human input after activation." [5] (emphasis original)[2]

This sensibly includes immobile systems such as fixed armed guardian robots. Autonomy in other functions, such as trajectory control or co-ordination with other systems, is not considered here. The same meaning is also captured by the International Committee of the Red Cross (ICRC), the institution charged with overseeing international humanitarian law (IHL):

> "The ICRC's working definition of an autonomous weapon system is: 'Any weapon system with autonomy in its critical functions. That is, a weapon system that can select (i.e. search for or detect, identify, track, select) and attack (i.e. use force against, neutralize, damage or destroy) targets without human intervention.'" [6, p. 4]

Often the degree of human control is indicated with respect to the decision loop that is repeated permanently, in US military parlance the "observe, orient, decide, act" (OODA) loop. A human is "in the loop" if he/she commands the attack. If the weapon system acts on its own and the human only supervises the action, possibly with the ability to intervene, the human is "on the loop". If there is no supervision or influence, the human is "out of the loop".[3]

Already remotely controlled uninhabited weapon systems promise several important advantages to armed forces: soldiers are removed from the place where they apply force and thus are much less exposed to danger (however for a competent adversary the control stations are valuable – and legitimate – targets). The endurance of systems is no longer limited by the human need for rest, since remote operators can work in shifts. When human operators no longer need to be accommodated on board, systems can be made smaller, more light-weight and can go beyond human limits e.g. with respect to acceleration, thus can fly narrower curves. And systems could become cheaper (although this can be questioned with respect to the total cost, e.g. [7]). Politically, the decision to apply force in or against another country is easier to take if soldiers need not be sent there and exposed to danger [8].

Proceeding from remotely controlled to autonomous weapon systems would bring additional advantages in combat: without a permanent communication link the systems are more difficult to detect. Reacting to events can be faster since a distant control

---

[2] The US-DoD definition of "semi-autonomous weapon", "a weapon system that is intended to only engage individual targets or specific target groups that have been selected by a human operator" [5] is more problematic in that it does not specify how targets or target groups are to be selected.

[3] For a more differentiated autonomy scale with six steps see [55].

station does not need to be involved – the two-way communication time can be as low as a few seconds, but in a fast-paced battle at short distance such a delay can mean the difference between use or loss of one's systems. Not relying on communication also means that a link cannot be jammed or otherwise disrupted. Personnel can be saved when operators no longer need to observe the situation and control the weapons. Autonomy allows attacks by swarms where human control of the individual elements would be practically impossible.

Given these advantages, it is logical that militaries have a high interest in AWS. However, there are counterarguments from a military view: AWS would reduce predictability and control over events in combat. Also, AWS could be hacked or hijacked.

Several precursors of AWS have been developed and some deployed. The Israeli loitering drone Harpy searches for enemy radars, flies into them and explodes. At the Korean demilitarised zone the immobile guardian robots SGR-1A has an option for autonomous shooting, but it seems not to be used. The range of some fire-and-forget missiles is being expanded greatly so that targets can no longer be designated from the launch position, necessitating search in a wider area. Examples with sensors and algorithms for target recognition are the US-Navy Long Range Anti Ship Missile (LRASM) with several 100 km range or the UK Brimstone missile (35 km).

In the series of its "Roadmaps for Unmanned Systems" that the US DoD has issued from 2007 on it has emphasised autonomy from the beginning as one important strand, stating as a general guideline for processor technology:

> "the ultimate goal is to replace the operators with a mechanical facsimile or equal or superior thinking speed, memory capacity, and responses gained from training and experience." [9, p. 53]

In 2012 the US DoD issued a directive "Autonomy in Weapon Systems" that stated conditions for their deployment and use [5]. Specific emphasis was placed on "rigorous hardware and software V[erification] & V[alidation] and realistic system developmental and operational T[est] & E[valuation], including analysis of unanticipated emergent behavior resulting from the effects of complex operational environments". A regression test of the software is to be applied after changes, using automated tools whenever feasible.

Following the Roadmaps, R&D of AWS is continuing, but for the near-term future the US military focuses on "manned-unmanned" or "human-machine teaming" (e.g. [10, p. 19], [11, p. 31]. Prototypes are being developed and demonstrated in several countries, in the area of jet-engine uninhabited combat air vehicles (UCAV) for example the US X-47B with autonomous aerial refuelling and landing and take-off on an aircraft carrier. The UK Taranis was to provide autonomous combat capability originally, but later human control was emphasised; for the British-French successor Future Combat Air System (FCAS), to be deployed from about 2030, autonomous attack is included as an option. At sea the US Defense Advanced Research Projects Agency (DARPA) has the Sea Hunter demonstrator. US Army, Navy and Air Force have various R&D projects for autonomy in armed unmanned vehicles. The Navy has demonstrated a swarm of motor boats, the Air Force showed a swarm of 103 micro drones released from combat jet aircraft.

Russia is proceeding with armed uninhabited ground vehicles in various sizes and tries to catch up in armed UAVs. Weapons will be under human control for the near future, but autonomous operation by artificial intelligence (AI) is taken into view [12]. In China military R&D aim at intelligent and autonomous weapon systems in all media, with systematic military-civil fusion for fast uses of AI advances in both areas [13]. However, among the three main competitors USA, Russia and China, the latter is the only one that has warned of an arms race and called for a ban on "lethal autonomous weapon systems (LAWS)" [14, pp. 4–7].

3 Military-Technology Assessment of AWS

Questions whether introduction of a new military technology would be good or bad are the subject of military-technology assessment. In this process judgement can be based on the criteria of preventive arms control. They can be arranged in three groups, referring to:

- Existing or intended arms-control treaties; international humanitarian law; weapons of mass destruction.
- Military stability between potential adversaries; arms races; proliferation.
- Human health, environment, sustainable development; societal and political systems; the societal infrastructure.

When a danger in one of these areas is to be feared, considerations about preventive limitations should be done, including methods and means of verification of compliance [15, 16]. AWS raise problems in all fields.

Concerning arms control, existing treaties could be endangered by AWS that would differ from traditional carriers of nuclear or conventional weapons and would thus fall outside of treaty definitions or at least in grey areas, leading to complicated discussions. For example: should small armed UAVs count as combat aircraft under the Treaty on Conventional Armed Forces in Europe (CFE Treaty, 1990)? This problem arises with uninhabited armed vehicles in general, that is already with remotely controlled ones [17].

With respect to the laws of armed conflict, so-called international humanitarian law (IHL), one can state that computer programs will for a long time not be able to reliably discriminate between combatants and non-combatants and to do appropriate assessments of proportionality between damage to civilians or civilian objects on the one hand and the expected military advantage from an attack against a legitimate target on the other. Even the roboticist who did the most research for IHL-compliant AWS-control software wrote of "daunting challenges" that remain.[4] Another roboticist has criticised this work.[5]

Because AWS proper do not exist yet, arms races and proliferation cannot be observed in reality. But one does not need much imagination to extrapolate from the respective developments in remote-control armed UAVs where arms races and proliferation are going on at high speed. Should one important state start fielding AWS, the others will certainly follow suit, and because of the high military interests the qualitative and quantitative arms race and proliferation will likely proceed much faster than with remote-control armed UAVs [18].

Arms racing can be seen as one dimension of deteriorating military stability, working on a time scale of years and decades. The second dimension concerns crisis instability and escalation, working in much shorter time frames. The general military situation between potential adversaries can be called stable if neither side could gain from attacking another. In particular, if in a severe crisis, when the sides assume that war can begin immediately, pressure exists to strike pre-emptively first, because otherwise one would suffer strong losses, this would be referred to as instable. The fear of crisis instability and escalation into war was a central topic of the debate about nuclear weapons and motivated the nuclear arms-control treaties, but similar considerations hold for conventional forces, too.[6] AWS would create specific problems here [18]. The individual systems as well as swarms would be programmed in advance how to act and react. In particular in duel-type situations at short range this would mean to shoot back immediately on indications of being attacked, because waiting a few seconds for a human to assess the situation and send a counter-attack order can mean the loss of one's systems before they could have launched their weapons. In such a situation, false indications of attack – sun glint interpreted as a rocket flame, sudden and

---

[4] "The transformation of International Protocols and battlefield ethics into machine-usable representations ...", "Mechanisms to ensure that the design of intelligent behaviors only provides responses within rigorously defined ethical boundaries", "The development of effective perceptual algorithms capable of superior target discrimination capabilities ...", "The creation of techniques to permit the adaptation of an ethical constraint set and underlying behavioral control parameters that will ensure moral performance ...", "A means to make responsibility assignment clear and explicit for all concerned parties ..." [41, p. 211f.].

[5] "The work ... is, in fact, merely a suggestion for a computer software system for the ethical governance of robot 'behaviour'. This is what is known as a 'back-end system'. Its operation relies entirely on information from systems yet 'to be developed' by others sometime in the future. It has no direct access to the real world through sensors or a vision system and it has no means to discriminate between combatant and non-combatant, between a baby and a wounded soldier, or a granny in a wheelchair and a tank. It has no inference engine and certainly cannot negotiate the types of common sense reasoning and battlefield awareness necessary for discrimination or proportionality decisions. There is neither a method for interpreting how the precepts of the laws of war apply in particular contexts nor is there any method for resolving the ambiguities of conflicting laws in novel situations." [50].

[6] Note that the CFE Treaty in its preamble calls for "establishing a secure and stable balance of conventional forces at lower levels" and for "eliminating disparities detrimental to stability and security". [46] Unfortunately the Treaty is no longer operating with respect to Russia.

unexpected movements of the adversary or a simple malfunction – could trigger escalation. Obviously such interactions could not be tested or trained together beforehand. The outcome of two separate programmed systems interacting with each other cannot be predicted, but if they control armed robots that are directed against each other, fast escalation to actual shooting is plausible. When war would already be occurring, autonomous-weapon interactions could lead to escalation to higher levels, principally up to nuclear-strategic weapons. Similar runaway escalations between different algorithms are being observed in the computer trade at stock exchanges, but after the first severe flash crashes an overarching authority got the possibility to stop the trade, acting as a circuit breaker. No such authority exists in the international system that could interrupt "flash wars".[7]

With respect to the third criteria group, mainly concerned with consequences of new military technology in peace time, the most problematic outcome would be uses of AWS by criminals and in particular terrorists. Such actors could build simple AWS, but not sophisticated ones. The latter would be developed by states, with immensely higher personnel and financial resources, if an AWS arms race between states cannot be prevented. Once built, deployed and exported, however, such systems would probably also get into the hands of non-state actors.

4   Calls, Open Letters and Discussions Among States

Concerned by the increasing use of uninhabited armed systems and by the foreseeable trend to transition to autonomous attack, in 2009 four academics founded the International Committee for Robot Arms Control (ICRAC).[8] In 2012 the international Campaign to Stop Killer Robots was formed that today comprises 106 non-governmental organisations from 54 countries [19]. In 2013 the UN Special Rapporteur on extrajudicial, summary or arbitrary executions for the Office of the High Commissioner for Human Rights called on all states to place a national moratorium on "lethal autonomous robotics" [20]. Many states felt uneasy about the prospect of autonomous killing by machine, so in October 2013 more than 30 countries addressed the problem in the UN General Assembly, and in November 2013 the member states of the Convention on Certain Conventional Weapons (CCW)[9] decided to begin expert discussions on what then became to be called "lethal autonomous weapon systems (LAWS)".

---

[7] Similar unpredictable, but probably escalatory interactions can be foreseen if offensive cyber operations were done under automatic/autonomous/AI control. Combined with AWS operations the problems could intensify each other.

[8] The author was one of the founders. In the meantime the number of members has grown to 33 [52].

[9] The full name is "Convention on Prohibitions or Restrictions on the Use of Certain Conventional Weapons Which May Be Deemed to Be Excessively Injurious or to Have Indiscriminate Effects". This framework convention was concluded in 1980 and has five specific protocols, the most relevant in the present context being Protocol IV that prohibits blinding laser weapons [45]. There are 125 member states, including practically all states with relevant militaries [51].

Such discussions were held regularly since 2014 in Geneva, from 2017 on as a formal Group of Governmental Experts (GGE). Invited talks and extensive discussions were held under topics such as autonomy, IHL, ethics, security, a working definition or characterisation of LAWS. Some progress was made: there is general agreement that some form of human control of the use of force is needed. The notion of "meaningful human control" has gained considerable traction.[10] But strong differences of opinion showed up and could not be bridged. By end-2018 28 countries had spoken out for a legally binding prohibition of AWS and the Non-Aligned Movement has called for prohibitions or regulations. But about a dozen states have declared that they do not support negotiating a ban treaty, among them USA, UK, Russia, Israel, Australia and France [21]. Because a consensus rule is used in the CCW, no decision can be taken if only one member state is opposed. Thus a mandate for negotiations on a prohibition protocol is not to be expected. It is open if sidestepping the CCW and negotiating a separate treaty outside, with the help of benevolent states, would be sensible. This approach had led to the Antipersonnel Mine Convention in Ottawa 1997 and the Cluster Munition Convention in Oslo 2008, but military interests in AWS may be much higher. Achieving an international prohibition probably will need more public pressure in the critical countries.

In this respect, various activities in particular from the robotics and AI community have been helpful. In 2012/13 270 computer scientists, engineers, AI experts, roboticists and professionals from related disciplines called for a prohibition on the development and deployment of AWS [22]. An open letter launched in 2015 arguing against an arms race in AI-enabled weapons got more than 4,500 signatures from AI and robotics researchers and above 26,000 others [23, 24]. Particular attention was raised by the video "Slaughterbots" showing possible future swarms of microdrones that seek out individuals and kill them by a shaped explosive applied to the head; due to cheap series production one could even speak of weapons of mass destruction [25].[11] In a 2018 pledge signed by nearly 250 AI-related organisations, many of them renowned hi-tech firms, and more than 3,200 individuals, the signatories have called on governments to prohibit AWS and, absent that, promise that they "will neither participate in nor support the development, manufacture, trade, or use of lethal autonomous weapons" [26]. In Germany in 2019, the Gesellschaft für Informatik has called for a legal ban on lethal autonomous weapons, in particular for action by the Federal Government [27]. Also the Federation of German Industries (BDI) requests a legally binding ban on fully autonomous weapon systems [28]. Particularly remarkable is the opposition of software developers and other employees in big AI/robotics companies (e.g. [29, 30]).

---

[10] What this can mean in detail is explained in [54].

[11] The Swiss Federal Office for Defence Procurement – armasuisse – has re-enacted the scene and shown that a shaped charge of 3 g explosive can penetrate a skull emulator [47].

5 Problems with Definitions

The discussions about possible limitations hinge on what exactly is meant by an AWS. The understandings of countries differ considerably. The US DoD definition cited in Sect. 2 is succinct and functional. The UK Ministry of Defence (MoD), on the other hand, differentiates between "automatic" and "autonomous" systems:

"Automated system   In the unmanned aircraft context, an automated or automatic system is one that, in response to inputs from one or more sensors, is programmed to logically follow a predefined set of rules in order to provide an outcome. Knowing the set of rules under which it is operating means that its output is predictable. (JDP 0-01.1)

Autonomous system   An autonomous system is capable of understanding higher-level intent and direction. From this understanding and its perception of its environment, such a system is able to take appropriate action to bring about a desired state. It is capable of deciding a course of action, from a number of alternatives, without depending on human oversight and control, although these may still be present. Although the overall activity of an autonomous unmanned aircraft will be predictable, individual actions may not be. (JDP 0-30)" [31, p. 13]

It is very questionable whether the output of a programmed system, logically following predefined rules, will be predictable always. On the one hand, there are the well-known problems from software complexity, on the other there can be changes in the environment and unforeseen actions of an adversary that can lead to unexpected results that have not shown up in testing or training. The requirements given for calling a system autonomous, on the other hand, raise the bar very high. It is thus easy for the MoD to state: "The UK does not possess fully autonomous weapon systems and has no intention of developing them. Such systems are not yet in existence and are not likely to be for many years, if at all." [31, p. 14] The obvious conclusion is that there is no urgency about AWS, and that automatic systems are not problematic.

Similar questionable understandings are found in the German definitions. The draft definition of the Federal Ministry of Defence (BMVg) states:

"Lethal Autonomous Weapon System means a weapon system which is primarily designed to directly cause lethal effects to human beings, and which is designed to sense, rationalize, decide, act, evaluate and learn completely independent from human interaction or control.
…
Lethal (in the context of this definition) means aiming to cause directly death or fatal injury to a single or several human beings.
…
According to this definition, an autonomous system is to be distinguished from a highly/fully automated system which, although not requiring human intervention, operates alone on the basis of a fixed set of inputs, rules, and outputs in a deterministic and largely predictable manner. In particular it is not capable of defining its tasks and goals on its own." [32]

In its proposal at the CCW GGE, the German delegation has used the same understanding:

"Statement delivered by Germany on Working Definition of LAWS/'Definition of Systems under Consideration'

...

Germany rejects autonomous weapon systems which are primarily designed to directly cause lethal effects or other damage to human beings, and which are designed to sense, rationalize, decide, act, evaluate and learn completely independently from human interaction or control.

...

An understanding of autonomy – and its distinction from automatization – for the working purposes of the GGE on LAWS can be built by referring to autonomy as

- the capacity to perceive (sense and interpret) an environment,
- evaluate the circumstances of a changing situation without reference to a set of pre-defined goals,
- reason and decide on the most suited approach towards their realization,
- initiate actions based on these conclusions,
- all of the above being executed without any human involvement once the system has been operationalized.

...

A new quality of technology towards autonomy based on artificial intelligence is reached where systems or individual functionalities have the ability to learn and thus re-define their goals and/or develop new strategies to adapt their respective performance to different situations. Having the ability to learn and develop self-awareness constitutes an indispensable attribute to be used to define individual functions or weapon systems as autonomous.

...

As a consequence Germany does not intend to develop or to acquire weapon systems that completely exclude the human factor from decisions about the employment of weapon systems against individuals." [33] (emphasis original)

The position of Germany is even more problematic than the UK one. 1. Restricting the notion of LAWS[12] to weapon systems primarily directed against human beings exempts all systems designed to attack military objects. 2. What does "completely excluding the human" mean? An interpretation that a human would still be involved if he or she would activate an AWS that then searches targets on its own is at least compatible with that wording. 3. Demanding the ability to learn and develop self-awareness for calling a system autonomous means that autonomy lies far in the future. But it is just systems without these abilities, but programmed to select and engage targets autonomously, that could be developed and deployed in the next five to ten years and would endanger IHL, would bring an arms race and proliferation and would destabilise the military situation – it is these systems that should be prohibited preventively before deployment would begin.

---

[12] In military parlance, "lethal" is mostly understood as "destructive", not explicitly as killing people, as e.g. in military notions of "target kill" or "mission kill". The use of the term LAWS for the CCW expert meetings was not intended for exclusion of weapons against materiél or of non-lethal weapons (personal communication from Ambassador Jean-Hugues Simon-Michel of France, first chair of the expert meetings).

Also, Germany has not joined the 28 countries that in the CCW GGE meetings have called for a legally binding prohibition of AWS [21]. This fact and the AWS definition do not fit to the strong statement of Foreign Minister Maas at the 2018 UN General Assembly:

> "Our common rules must keep pace with technological developments. Otherwise, what currently sounds like science fiction may very soon become deadly reality – autonomous weapons systems, or killer robots, that kill without any human control. I ask that you please support, both here in New York and in Geneva, our initiative to ban fully autonomous weapons – before it is too late!" [34]

If Germany were serious about an AWS ban, it could act accordingly in the CCW GGE meeting and join the group of countries demanding a legally binding prohibition. Unilaterally it could change to a simple AWS definition oriented at the critical functions of target selection an engagement (similar to the US DoD and ICRC definitions cited in Sect. 2), could issue guidelines for the Federal Armed Forces and prescribe meaningful human control for all their weapons; these and other proposals have been made by an international work group [35].

6   Possible Design of an International AWS Ban [17, 36]

In order to prevent violations of IHL, arms races and destabilisation by AWS, a legally binding international prohibition of AWS is needed. Systematically, it would fit best into the CCW, it could be added as Protocol VI to this framework convention. Protocol IV banning the use of laser blinding weapons could serve as a role model, but to be effective in the face of much higher military interests in AWS, the prohibition should be comprehensive, that is, hold not only for use, but also for the earlier stages of deployment, testing and development. This negative obligation should be complemented by a positive requirement that for each use of force the selection of the target and the decision to engage are made by a human being who is responsible and accountable. If consensus about adding such a protocol will be impossible in the CCW, then a separate treaty can be used as discussed above.

If AWS will be banned while remotely controlled uninhabited weapons systems remain allowed, a difficult verification problem arises, since the very same weapons systems could attack under remote control or autonomously – there would be no difference that could be observed from the outside. Thus, from a verification standpoint a complete ban of all armed uninhabited vehicles would be best, since then one could check by on-site inspections whether the uninhabited vehicles (e.g. for reconnaissance) have appliances for weapons, such as a machine-gun mount, a bomb bay or hard points for missiles under wings. However, too many countries have armed UAVs already and more will acquire them; these countries will not be convinced easily to give them up again.

Thus the only difference between remotely controlled and autonomous weapon systems would lie in the software. It is inconceivable that states would open their weapon-control software to international inspection, but even if they would, a new version with autonomous-attack function could be uploaded at any time. Thus, a-priori verification of the inability to attack without human control is practically excluded. The only possibility is to check after the fact that every single attack had been controlled by a human.

To be able to prove this, each warring country would record the sensor and communication data of the remotely controlled combat vehicle and of the ground-control station, as well as the actions of the human operators therein, nationally in a black box. In parallel hash codes of these data would be recorded in a "glass box" and transmitted regularly to a treaty implementing organisation. The organisation would use the hash code to verify that the original data for selected attacks transmitted to it on a later (random or challenge) request are authentic and complete. Because the original data cannot be constructed from the hash code, an adversary could not gain a military advantage even if it had succeeded in getting access to it.

Details of such a method still need to be researched, developed and tested. It would be coupled with inspections and manoeuvre observations and would need more co-operation than customary up to now for inspections, such as under the CFE Treaty. It could provide the necessary transparency for reliable verification but also ensure the needed military secrecy. The effort would not be negligible, but already now similar data are recorded routinely nationally. The glass boxes and corresponding communication would have to be added.

7   Potential Contributions by the AI and Robotics Communities

In the further debate about AWS and about the need for and the possibility of an AWS prohibition, the AI and robotics communities can play an important role. All scientists, engineers and students can follow the national and international developments and discussions and make their voice known – privately as well as with public statements. Whoever has an opportunity to discuss with politicians can use it. Colleagues involved in teaching can include the subject into their curricula. In R&D one can be attentive to potential uses of one's own results for AWS developments.

Some AI or robotics researchers may have the option of devoting a part of their research to the prevention of AWS. Several themes are conceivable, some more interdisciplinary:

- Following general military R&D, dual-use R&D, general AI research with a bearing on AWS.
- Identifying problematic R&D activities, including dual-use research of concern.[13]
- Studying the reliability of machine learning for target recognition, including possible spoofing.
- Looking at the human-machine interface, in particular the concept of explainable AI, for automatic pre-selection of options for human operators.

---

[13] See the respective discussion in the life sciences (e.g. [49]) and the wider German Leopoldina-DFG "Joint Committee for the Handling of Security-Relevant Research" [48].

- How can international-security aspects be incorporated into ethics codes for responsible research, development and use of AI?
- What are the proliferation risks of component technologies?
- What could hobbyists achieve? What degree of AWS sophistication could non-state actors reach by themselves?
- Doing military-technology assessment of AWS in various scenarios.
- Modelling the interaction of two (or more) AWS fleets or AI-controlled battle-management systems.
- Are "circuit breakers" interrupting "flash wars" conceivable – automatic ones or human ones?
- Commonalities and differences between civilian autonomous vehicles and AWS?
- Verification schemes for an AWS ban; doing a test implementation of the secure recording with hash codes. Can blockchain play a role?
- How about societal verification in case of an AWS ban?
- What confidence and security building measures are possible? Can one develop a code of conduct for states?
- Commonalities and differences between AWS and cyber forces?
- Doing military-technology assessment of other potential military AI uses – what would be dangers, could they be limited preventively?

Results in any of these topics could be highly useful in strengthening the conviction that the introduction of AWS would be detrimental in many respects and that a prohibition would serve the interest of humankind best.

8   Conclusion – Preventive AWS Ban Urgently Needed

If developments with AWS will continue without constraints, three trains will race against each other. The US DoD has proclaimed its "Third Offset Strategy": Military-technological superiority is to be maintained with the help of the five building blocks "learning machines, human-machine collaboration, assisted human operations, human-machine combat teaming, and autonomous weapons" [37].[14] In Russia, Kalashnikov has built a "fully automated combat module" [38], the Kronstadt Group works on AI for military and civilian drone swarms [39], and "If the future went as defense experts are now predicting, Putin said, one day 'wars will be concluded when all the drones on one side are destroyed by the drones of another.'" [40] In China "[t]he PLA's [People's Liberation Army] initial thinking on AI in warfare has been influenced by careful analysis of U.S. military initiatives", in particular the US DoD Third Offset strategy. But "its approach could progressively diverge from that of the United States". "The PLA will likely leverage AI to enhance its future capabilities, including in intelligent and autonomous unmanned systems" [13].

---

[14] The Trump administration no longer mentions the offset strategy explicitly, but continues emphasising the need to maintain "decisive and sustained U.S. military advantages" or "overmatch" [56, p. 4] , [43, p. 28].

Beyond AWS AI is seen by all three main military countries as providing the means to lead the world or even rule it.[15] The three countries observe each other's military plans, literature and R&D activities intensely. As in the Cold War – where the situation with only two actors was much simpler – fears of falling behind are strong motives to proceed fast, enhanced by secrecy and worst-case assumptions. When one country would introduce AWS, the other two would fast follow up. The initiating act could, however, also come from a globally less relevant state. The world may have a window of only five to ten years to prevent an AWS arms race. Once it had begun in earnest, it would become extremely difficult to reverse, see the arguments presented above with respect to remotely controlled armed uninhabited vehicles.

Preventing the dangers of an AWS arms race with the destabilisation that would come with it requires the relevant states, first and foremost the USA, to recall the insight that national security can only be ensured sustainably by organising international security. For AWS this means an international prohibition. Because there are strong military, economic and political interests in AWS, achieving it needs intense pressure from an enlightened, critical public and support by benevolent states.[16] In this process, the international AI and robotics communities have started to play an important role, and should intensify their efforts.

References

1. Bhuta, N., Beck, S., Geiß, R., Liu, H.-Y., Kreß, C. (eds.): Autonomous Weapons Systems. Law, Ethics, Policy. Cambridge University Press, Cambridge (2016)
2. Scharre, P.: Army of None: Autonomous Weapons and the Future of War. Norton, New York (2018)
3. New America Foundation (2019). https://www.newamerica.org/in-depth/world-of-drones/3-who-has-what-countries-armed-drones. Accessed 16 July 2019
4. Wezeman, P.D., Fleurant, A., Kuimova, A., Tian, N., Wezeman, S.T.: Trends in international arms transfers, 2018, March 2019. https://www.sipri.org/sites/default/files/2019-03/fs_1903_at_2018.pdf. Accessed 16 July 2019
5. US Department of Defense: Autonomy in Weapon Systems (incorporating Change 1, May 8, 2017), 21 November 2012. http://www.esd.whs.mil/Portals/54/Documents/DD/issuances/dodd/300009p.pdf. Accessed 5 July 2019
6. International Committee of the Red Cross: Ethics and autonomous weapon systems: An ethical basis for human control?, 3 April 2018. https://www.icrc.org/en/download/file/69961/icrc_ethics_and_autonomous_weapon_systems_report_3_april_2018.pdf. Accessed 5 July 2019

---

[15] Russia: "Whoever becomes the leader in this sphere [AI] will become the ruler of the world." (Putin) [42] China: "[T]he PLA intends to 'seize the advantage in military competition and the initiative in future warfare,' seeking the capability to win in not only today's informatized warfare but also future intelligentized warfare, in which AI and related technologies will be a cornerstone of military power." [57, p. 13] The USA is more circumspect: "The Trump Administration's National Security Strategy recognizes the need to lead in artificial intelligence, and the Department of Defense is investing accordingly." [44].

[16] As in the case of the Anti-personnel Land Mine Convention (1997) by Canada and for the Cluster Munitions Convention (2008) by Norway.

7. Walpole, L.: The True Cost of Drone Warfare?, 8 June 2018. https://www.oxfordresearchgroup.org.uk/blog/the-true-cost-of-drone-warfare. Accessed 16 July 2019
8. Sauer, F., Schörnig, N.: Killer drones – the silver bullet of democratic warfare? Secur. Dialogue **43**(4), 353–370 (2012)
9. US Department of Defense: Unmanned Systems Roadmap 2007-2032 (2007). http://www.dtic.mil/cgi-bin/GetTRDoc?Location=U2&doc=GetTRDoc.pdf&AD=ADA475002
10. US Department of Defense: Unmanned Systems Integrated Roadmap FY2013-2038 (2013). http://www.dtic.mil/get-tr-doc/pdf?AD=ADA592015. Accessed 5 July 2019
11. US Department of Defense: Unmanned Systems Integrated Roadmap 2017-2042, 28 August 2018. http://cdn.defensedaily.com/wp-content/uploads/post_attachment/206477.pdf. Accessed 5 July 2019
12. Bendett, S.: Russia Is Poised to Surprise the US in Battlefield Robotics, 25 January 2018. https://www.defenseone.com/ideas/2018/01/russia-poised-surprise-us-battlefield-robotics/145439/. Accessed 8 July 2019
13. Kania, E.B.: Battlefield Singularity: Artificial Intelligence, Military Revolution, and China's Future Military Power, 28 November 2017. https://www.cnas.org/publications/reports/battlefield-singularity-artificial-intelligence-military-revolution-and-chinas-future-military-power. Accessed 9 July 2019
14. Allen, G.C.: Understanding China's AI Strategy – Clues to Chinese Strategic Thinking on Artificial Intelligence and National Security, 6 February 2019. https://www.cnas.org/publications/reports/understanding-chinas-ai-strategy. Accessed 18 February 2019
15. Altmann, J.: Präventive Rüstungskontrolle. Die Friedens-Warte **83**(2–3), 105–126 (2008)
16. Altmann, J.: Nanotechnology and Preventive Arms Control (2005). https://bundesstiftung-friedensforschung.de/wp-content/uploads/2017/08/berichtaltmann.pdf. Accessed 16 July 2019
17. Altmann, J.: Arms control for armed uninhabited vehicles: an ethical issue. Ethics Inf. Technol. **15**(2), 137–152 (2013)
18. Altmann, J., Sauer, F.: Autonomous weapon systems. Survival **59**(5), 117–142 (2017)
19. Campaign to Stop Killer Robots (2019). https://www.stopkillerrobots.org/members/. Accessed 11 July 2019
20. Heyns, C.: Report of the Special Rapporteur on extrajudicial, summary or arbitrary executions, 9 April 2013. http://www.ohchr.org/Documents/HRBodies/HRCouncil/RegularSession/Session23/A-HRC-23-47_en.pdf. Accessed 11 July 2019
21. Campaign to Stop Killer Robots: Country Views on Killer Robots, 22 November 2018. https://www.stopkillerrobots.org/wp-content/uploads/2018/11/KRC_CountryViews22Nov2018.pdf. Accessed 12 July 2019
22. Computing experts from 37 countries call for ban on killer robots – Decision to apply violent force must not be delegated to machines, 15 October 2013. https://www.icrac.net/wp-content/uploads/2018/06/Scientist-Call_Press-Release.pdf. Accessed 12 July 2019
23. Autonomous Weapons: an Open Letter from AI & Robotics Researchers, 28 July 2015. https://futureoflife.org/open-letter-autonomous-weapons. Accessed 12 July 2019
24. The 30717 Open Letter Signatories Include (2019). http://futureoflife.org/awos-signatories/. Accessed 12 July 2019
25. Slaughterbots (Video 7:47), November 2017. https://www.youtube.com/watch?v=9CO6M2HsoIA. Accessed 12 July 2019
26. Future of Life Institute (2019). https://futureoflife.org/lethal-autonomous-weapons-pledge/. Accessed 12 July 2019
27. Gesellschaft für Informatik: Tödliche autonome Waffensysteme (LAWS) müssen völkerrechtlich geächtet werden, February 2019. https://gi.de/fileadmin/GI/Allgemein/PDF/GI-Stellungnahme_LAWS_2019-02.pdf. Accessed 12 July 2019

28. Bundesverband der Deutschen Industrie: Künstliche Intelligenz in Sicherheit und Vertei- digung, January 2019. https://issuu.com/bdi-berlin/docs/20181205_position_bdi_ki. Acces- sed 12 July 2019
29. O'Sullivan, L.: I Quit My Job to Protest My Company's Work on Building Killer Robots. American Civil Liberties Union, 6 March 2019. https://www.aclu.org/blog/national-security/ targeted-killing/i-quit-my-job-protest-my-companys-work-building-killer. Accessed 12 July 2019
30. Conger, K., Metz, C.: Tech Workers Now Want to Know: What Are We Building This For? New York Times, 7 October 2018. https://www.nytimes.com/2018/10/07/technology/tech- workers-ask-censorship-surveillance.html. Accessed 12 July 2019
31. UK Ministry of Defence: Unmanned Aircraft Systems, August 2017. https://www.gov.uk/ government/uploads/system/uploads/attachment_data/file/640299/20170706_JDP_0-30.2_ final_CM_web.pdf. Accessed 13 July 2019
32. Bundesministerium der Verteidigung, Pol II 5. Definitionsentwurf deutsch/englisch: Letales Autonomes Waffensystem. Personal communication (2014)
33. Germany: Statement delivered by Germany on Working Definition of LAWS/Definition of Systems under Consideration, April 2018. https://www.unog.ch/80256EDD006B8954/ (httpAssets)/2440CD1922B86091C12582720057898F/%24file/2018_LAWS6a_Germany. pdf. Accessed 13 July 2019
34. Maas, H. (Minister for Foreign Affairs of Germany): Speech at the general debate of the 73rd General Assembly of the United Nations, 28 September 2018. https://gadebate.un.org/sites/ default/files/gastatements/73/de_en.pdf. Accessed 13 July 2019
35. Amoroso, D., Sauer, F., Sharkey, N., Suchman, L.: Autonomy in Weapon Systems – The Military Application of Artificial Intelligence as a Litmus Test for Germany's New Foreign and Security Policy, 23 May 2018. https://www.boell.de/sites/default/files/boell_autonomy- in-weapon-systems_v04_kommentierbar_1.pdf. Accessed 13 July 2019
36. Gubrud, M., Altmann, J.: Compliance Measures for an Autonomous Weapons Convention, May 2013. https://www.icrac.net/wp-content/uploads/2018/04/Gubrud-Altmann_ Compliance-Measures-AWC_ICRAC-WP2.pdf. Accessed 12 July 2019
37. Work, R.: Deputy Secretary of Defense Speech, 14 December 2015. https://www.defense. gov/News/Speeches/Speech-View/Article/634214/cnas-defense-forum. Accessed 9 July 2019
38. Tucker, P.: Russian Weapons Maker To Build AI-Directed Guns, 14 July 2017. http://www. defenseone.com/technology/2017/07/russian-weapons-maker-build-ai-guns/139452/. Acces- sed 9 July 2019
39. TASS: Russia is developing artificial intelligence for military and civilian drones, 15 May 2017. http://tass.com/defense/945950. Accessed 9 July 2019
40. Sharkov, D.: Vladimir Putin Talks Ruling the World, Future Wars And Life On Mars, 1 September 2017. https://www.newsweek.com/vladimir-putin-talks-ruling-world-future- wars-and-life-mars-658579. Accessed 9 July 2019
41. Arkin, R.C.: Governing Lethal Behavior in Autonomous Robots. Chapman&Hall/CRC, Boca Raton (2009)
42. Russia Today: 'Whoever leads in AI will rule the world': Putin to Russian children on Knowledge Day, 1 September 2017. https://www.rt.com/news/401731-ai-rule-world-putin/. Accessed 29 November 2017
43. President of the USA: National Security Strategy of the United States of America, December 2017. https://www.whitehouse.gov/wp-content/uploads/2017/12/NSS-Final-12-18-2017- 0905.pdf. Accessed 10 July 2019

44. White House: Artificial Intelligence for the American People, 10 May 2018. https://www.whitehouse.gov/briefings-statements/artificial-intelligence-american-people/. Accessed 10 July 2019
45. Protocol on Blinding Laser Weapons (Protocol IV), 13 October 1995. https://www.unog.ch/80256EDD006B8954/(httpAssets)/8463F2782F711A13C12571DE005BCF1A/$file/PROTOCOL+IV.pdf. Accessed 11 July 2019
46. Organization for Security and Co-operation in Europe: Treaty on Conventional Armed Forces in Europe, 19 November 1990. http://www.osce.org/library/14087. Accessed 11 July 2019
47. Drapela, P.: Fake news? Lethal effect of micro drones, 11 April 2018. https://www.ar.admin.ch/en/armasuisse-wissenschaft-und-technologie-w-t/home.detail.news.html/ar-internet/news-2018/news-w-t/lethalmicrodrones.html. Accessed 12 July 2019
48. Scientific Freedom and Scientific Responsibility (2019). https://www.leopoldina.org/en/about-us/cooperations/joint-committee-on-dual-use/. Accessed 12 July 2019
49. World Health Organization: Dual Use Research of Concern (DURC) (2019). https://www.who.int/csr/durc/en/. Accessed 12 July 2019
50. Sharkey, N.E.: The evitability of autonomous robot warfare. Int. Rev. Red Cross **94**, 787–799 (2012)
51. United Nations Office at Geneva: High Contracting Parties and Signatories (2019). https://www.unog.ch/80256EE600585943/(httpPages)/3CE7CFC0AA4A7548C12571C00039CB0C?OpenDocument. Accessed 11 July 2019
52. Members (2019). https://www.icrac.net/members/. Accessed 11 July 2019
53. Report of the Defense Science Board Task Force on Patriot System Performance, January 2005. https://www.acq.osd.mil/dsb/reports/2000s/ADA435837.pdf. Accessed 16 July 2019
54. Sharkey, N.: Staying in the loop. Human supervisory control of weapons. In: Bhuta, N., Beck, S., Geiß, R., Liu, H., Kreß, C. (eds.) Autonomous Weapons Systems. Law, Ethics, Policy, pp. 23–28. Cambridge University Press, Cambridge (2016)
55. US Air Force: Autonomous Horizons – System Autonomy in the Air Force – A Path to the Future, Volume I, Human-Autonomy Teaming, AF/ST TR 15-01. United States Air Force, Office of the Chief Scientist, June 2015. http://www.af.mil/Portals/1/documents/SECAF/AutonomousHorizons.pdf. Accessed 22 July 2019
56. US Department of Defense: Summary of the 2018 National Defense Strategy of the United States of America – Sharpening the American Military's Competitive Edge (2018). https://dod.defense.gov/Portals/1/Documents/pubs/2018-National-Defense-Strategy-Summary.pdf. Accessed 10 July 2019
57. He, L. (vice president of the PLA's Academy of Military Science): Establish a Modern Military Theory System with Chinese Characteristics. Study Times, 19 June 2017. Cited by Kania, E.B., Battlefield Singularity: Artificial Intelligence, Military Revolution, and China's Future Military Power, 28 November 2017. https://www.cnas.org/publications/reports/battlefield-singularity-artificial-intelligence-military-revolution-and-chinas-future-military-power. Accessed 9 July 2019

Towards Computational Persuasion via Natural Language Argumentation Dialogues

Anthony Hunter$^{(\boxtimes)}$, Lisa Chalaguine, Tomasz Czernuszenko,
Emmanuel Hadoux, and Sylwia Polberg

Department of Computer Science, University College London,
London WC1E 6BT, UK
`anthony.hunter@ucl.ac.uk`

Abstract. Computational persuasion aims to capture the human ability to persuade through argumentation for applications such as behaviour change in healthcare (e.g. persuading people to take more exercise or eat more healthily). In this paper, we review research in computational persuasion that incorporates domain modelling (capturing arguments and counterarguments that can appear in a persuasion dialogues), user modelling (capturing the beliefs and concerns of the persuadee), and dialogue strategies (choosing the best moves for the persuader to maximize the chances that the persuadee is persuaded). We discuss evaluation of prototype systems that get the user's counterarguments by allowing them to select them from a menu. Then we consider how this work might be enhanced by incorporating a natural language interface in the form of an argumentative chatbot.

Keywords: Persuasion · Computational models of argument · Chatbots

1 Introduction

Persuasion is an activity that involves one party trying to induce another party to believe or disbelieve something or to do (or not do) something. It is an important and multifaceted human facility. Obviously, it is essential in commerce and politics, but it is equally important in many aspects of daily life. Consider for example, a child asking a parent for a rise in pocket money, a doctor trying to get a patient to enter a smoking cessation programme, a charity volunteer trying to raise funds for a poverty stricken area, or a government advisor trying to get people to avoid revealing personal details online that might be exploited by fraudsters.

Supported by the EPSRC Computational Persuasion grant EP/N008294/1, an EPSRC DTA studentship, and a UCL Summer Reseach Internship.

C. Benzmüller and H. Stuckenschmidt (Eds.): KI 2019, LNAI 11793, pp. 18–33, 2019.
https://doi.org/10.1007/978-3-030-30179-8_2

Table 1. Some examples of potential applications of computational persuasion that could be used to encourage and guide people to change behaviour in healthcare

Issue	Examples
Healthy life-styles	Eating fewer calories, eating more fruit and veg, doing more exercise, drinking less alcohol
Treatment compliance	Undertaking self-management of diabetes, completing a course of antibiotics, completing a course of prophylactics
Treatment reduction	Using alternatives to painkillers for premenstrual syndrome, not requesting antibiotics for viral infections
Problem avoidance	Taking vaccines, taking malaria prophylactics, using safe sex practice
Screening	Participating in breast cancer screening, participating in cervical smear screening, self-screening for prostate cancer, breast cancer, bowel cancer, and melanoma

Arguments are a crucial part of persuasion. They may be explicit, such as in a political debate, or they may be implicit, such as in an advert. In a dialogue involving persuasion, counterarguments also need to be taken into account. Participants may take turns in the dialogue with each of them presenting arguments, some of which may be counterarguments to previously presented arguments. So the aim of the persuader is to change the mind of the persuadee through this exchange of arguments. Since some arguments may be more effective than others in such a dialogue, it is valuable for the persuader to have an understanding of the persuadee and of what might work better with her.

1.1 Persuasion in Behaviour Change

As computing becomes involved in every sphere of life, so too is persuasion a target for applying computer-based solutions. Persuasion technologies have come out of developments in human-computer interaction research (see, for example, the influential work by Fogg [18]) with a particular emphasis on addressing the need for systems to help people make positive changes to their behaviour, particularly in healthcare and lifestyle choices. In recent years, a wide variety of systems has been developed to help users to control body weight, reduce fizzy drink consumption, increase physical exercise, and reduce speeding.

Interestingly, explicit use of argumentation is not central to most current manifestations of persuasion technologies. Either arguments are provided implicitly in the persuasion technology (e.g., through provision of information, or through game playing), or it is assumed that the user has considered the arguments for changing behaviour prior to accessing the persuasion technology (e.g., when using diaries, or receiving email reminders). Explicit argumentation with consideration of arguments and counterarguments is not supported with existing persuasion technologies. Yet, for some tasks in behaviour change, an argument-

Table 2. Simple example of a dialogue between a user and an automated persuasion system (APS). As no natural language processing is assumed, the arguments posted by the user are actually selected by the user from a menu provided by the APS.

Step	Who	Move
1	APS	To improve your health, you could join an exercise class
2	User	Exercise classes are boring
3	APS	For exciting exercise, you could do an indoor climbing course
4	User	It is too expensive
5	APS	Do you work?
6	User	No
7	APS	If you are registered unemployed, then the local sports centre offers a free indoor climbing course
8	APS	Would you try this?
9	User	Yes

based approach could be highly beneficial, particularly when someone is lacking some key information, and/or entertaining misconceptions about a topic.

This creates some interesting opportunities for artificial intelligence, using computational models of argument, to develop persuasion technologies for behaviour change where arguments are central. For reviews of computational models of argumentation, a.k.a computational argumentation, see [3,5,6,52]. Computational models of argument are beginning to offer ways to formalize aspects of persuasion, and with some adaptation and development, they have the potential to be incorporated into computational persuasion tools for behaviour change. For potential applications, see Table 1.

1.2   Automated Persuasion Systems

An automated persuasion system (APS) is a system that can engage in a dialogue with a user (the persuadee) in order to persuade the persuadee to accept a specific argument (the persuasion goal) that encapsulates the reason for a change of behaviour in some specific respect [41]. For example, the persuasion goal might be that the user needs to eat fruit in order to be more healthy, and the system presents supporting arguments (based on evidence, expert opinion, explanation of the fit with the user's goals, etc.) and counter-arguments to correct misconceptions or inconsistencies in the user's opinions. To do this, an APS aims to use convincing arguments in order to persuade the persuadee.

Whether an argument is convincing depends on the context, and on the characteristics of the persuadee. An APS maintains a model of the persuadee to predict what arguments and counterarguments the persuadee knows about and/or believes, and this can be harnessed by the strategy of the APS in order to choose good moves to make in the dialogue.

There have already been some promising studies that indicate the potential of using automated dialogues in behaviour change such as using dialogue games for health promotion [12,19–21], conversational agents for encouraging exercise [7, 44] and for promoting plant-based diets [60], dialogue management for persuasion [1], persuasion techniques for healthy eating messages [58], and tailored assistive living systems for encouraging exercise [22]. However, none of these studies have provided a framework that integrates domain modelling and user modelling for strategic argumentation in behaviour change. In the next section, we review a specific framework that addresses these issues.

2   Framework for Computational Persuasion

In order to provide a framework for computational persuasion, we assume an APS has a domain model, a user model, and a dialogue engine, as components and that these are used by the system to enter into a persuasion dialogue with the user. We will explain these components in more detail below.

In addition, in this section, we assume that the interface for an APS does not accept natural language input from the user. Rather, the system provides a menu of counterarguments, and the user selects those that s/he subscribes to. This therefore avoids the problems of natural language processing. We consider how we may drop this restriction in Sect. 4 by harnessing a simple natural language interface.

2.1   Domain Modelling

The domain model contains the arguments that can be presented in the dialogue by the system, and it also contains the arguments that the user may entertain. The domain model can be represented by a bipolar argument graph [13]. This is a graph where each node is an argument, and each arc denotes a relationship between pairs of arguments. We consider two types of relationship for an arc from A to B. The first is an attack relationship, and so the arc from A to B denotes that A attacks B (i.e., A is a counterargument for B). The second is a support relationship, and so the arc from A to B denotes that A supports B (i.e., A provides further information that supports for B).

In order to have good quality dialogues, it is important that the argument graph has sufficient depth and breadth of coverage of the topic. Each argument is represented by a premise and claim in a natural language statement. The choice of language may be important for particular audiences. The argument graph also needs to have sufficient depth so that the dialogue can proceed with more than one or two exchanges of argument per participant. The arguments for the argument graph can be obtained from literature of the domain. For example, for healthy eating, there is a large medical literature on arguments about healthy eating. However, arguments that the user may wish to play are often more difficult to obtain. For instance, it is more difficult to find argument for not having a healthy diet. Hence, we have investigated various techniques for acquiring argument using crowdsourcing [15,16] and for identifying arguments for behaviour change applications based on for example barriers to change that individuals may perceive [14].

2.2   User Modelling

The user model contains information about the user that can be used by the system for making good choices of move. The information in the user model is what the system believes is true about the user. The key dimensions that we have considered are belief and concerns associated with arguments by users.

Beliefs. Arguments are formed from premises and a claim, either of which may be explicit or partially implicit. An agent can express a belief in an argument based on the agent's belief in the premises being true, the claim being implied by the premises, and the claim being true. There is substantial evidence in the behaviour change literature that shows the importance of the beliefs of a persuadee in affecting the likelihood that a persuasion attempt is successful (see for example the review by Ogden [45]). Furthermore, beliefs can be used as a proxy for fine-grained argument acceptability, the need for which was highlighted by empirical studies conducted in [47,51].

Concerns. Arguments are statements that contain information about the agent and/or the world. Furthermore, they can refer to impacts on the agent and/or the world. These impacts may relate to the concerns of the agent. In other words, some arguments may have significant impacts on what the agent is concerned about. We associate concerns with arguments, and then for a user model, we obtain or predict the user's preferences over the concerns.

To illustrate how beliefs (respectively concerns) arise in argumentation, and how they can be harnessed to improve persuasion, consider Example 1 (respectively Example 2).

Example 1. Consider a student health advisor who wants to persuade a student to join a smoking cessation programme (i.e., a health programme designed to help someone give up smoking). The student may be expressing reluctance to join but not explaining why. Through experience, the advisor might guess that the student believes one of the following arguments.

– Option 1: If I give up smoking, I will get more anxious about my studies, I will eat less, and I will lose too much weight.
– Option 2: If I give up smoking, I will start to eat more as a displacement activity while I study, and I will get anxious as I will put on too much weight.

Based on the conversation so far, the student health advisor has to judge whether the student believes option 1 or option 2. With that prediction, the advisor can try to present an appropriate argument to counter the student's belief in the argument, and thereby overcome the student's barrier to joining the smoking cessation programme. For instance, if the advisor thinks it is argument 1, the advisor can suggest that as part of the smoking cessation programme, the student can join free yoga classes to overcome any stress that the student might feel from nicotine withdrawal symptoms.

Example 2. Consider a doctor in a university health clinic who is trying to persuade a university student to take up regular exercise, and suppose the student says that she does not want to take up a sport because she finds sports boring. The doctor then needs to find a counterargument to the student's argument. Suppose the doctor has two options:

- Option 1: Doing sport will not only help your physical health, but it will help you study better.
- Option 2: Doing sport will get you in shape, and also help you make new friends.

The argument for Option 1 concerns physical health and getting a good degree, whereas the argument for Option 2 concerns physical health and social life. Now suppose the doctor has learnt through the conversation that the student does not prioritize physical health at all, ranks social life somewhat highly, and ranks getting a good degree very highly. In this case, the doctor will regard the argument in Option 1 as being a better counterargument to present to the student, since it appears to have a better chance of convincing the student.

So in Example 1, the student has the same concerns, but different beliefs, associated with the arguments, whereas in Example 2, the student has the same beliefs, but different concerns, associated with the arguments. We therefore see concerns and beliefs as being orthogonal kinds of information that an agent might have about an argument.

We can use crowdsourcing for the acquisition of user models based on concerns [28] and beliefs [36]. To represent and reason with beliefs in arguments, we can use the epistemic approach to probabilistic argumentation [4,32,40,48,56] which has been supported by experiments with participants [47]. In applying the epistemic approach to user modelling, we have developed methods for: (1) updating beliefs during a dialogue [33,34,39]; (2) efficiently representing and reasoning with a probabilistic user model [25]; and (3) modelling uncertainty in the modelling of persuadee beliefs [27,35].

2.3 Dialogue Engine

A **dialogue** is a sequence of **moves** such as asking a query, making a claim, presenting premises, conceding to a premise presented by another agent, etc. The **protocol** specifies the moves that are allowed or required by each participant at each step of a dialogue. There are a number of proposals for dialogues (e.g., [11,17,49,50]). For examples of protocols for persuasion in behaviour change, see [33,34]. The dialogue may involve steps where the system finds out more about the user's beliefs, intentions and desires, and where the system offers arguments with the aim of changing the user's beliefs, intentions and desires. Moves can involve arguments taken from the domain model, and/or they can be queries to improve the user model. In our evaluations (which we review in Sect. 3), we have focused on the system being able to posit arguments, and the user being able to select his/her counterarguments from a menu of options.

In order to optimize a dialogue (i.e. to maximize the probability that the persuasion is successful), the **strategy** chooses the best moves for the persuader to make in response to the moves made by the persuadee. The strategy model consults the user model to select the moves that are allowed by the protocol. There are a number of roles for arguments. For instance, an argument may be a persuasion goal (i.e., an argument that the system wants the user to accept), or a user counterargument (i.e., an argument that the user regards as a counterargument against an argument by the system), or a system counterargument (i.e., an argument that the system regards as a counterargument against an argument by held by the system), or a user supporting argument (i.e., an argument that the user regards as supporting an argument by held the user), or a system supporting argument (i.e., an argument that the system regards as supporting an argument presented by the system).

There are three options for strategies: The **random strategy** which is a non-deterministic choice of move from available moves. It therefore involves no consideration of the user model; The **local strategy** which involves picking the next move from available moves that is maximal according to some measure of quality based on the beliefs and concerns of the user; And the **global strategy** which involves considering all possible dialogues, and picking the dialogue that maximizes a reward function based on the beliefs and concerns of the user.

We illustrate a local strategy in Example 3, and we use this strategy in the evaluation discussed in Sect. 3.1.

Example 3. We can use a local strategy for taking concerns into account. Consider the following user argument:

– Building cycle lanes is too expensive for the city.

Suppose the following are potential counterarguments with concern assignments given in brackets.

1. (CityEconomy) Evidence shows that infrastructures for cyclists favour the local economy generating more taxes for the city to use.
2. (PersonalEconomy) Cycling is cheaper for the citizens than driving or public transportation.

If the following is a ranking over concerns that is predicted to hold for a given user according to the user model,

PersonalEconomy > Time > Comfort > Health > CityEconomy

then counterargument 2 is the best move.

For a global strategy, our approach to making strategic choices of move is to harness decision trees. A **decision tree** represents all the possible combinations

Table 3. Some results from the cycling in the city study regarding the proportion of participants going from a negative belief (resp. positive) to a positive belief (resp. negative) and the average change on the participants who did change (avg. change on a scale from −5 to +5).

	Strategic system	Baseline system
Negative to positive	6%	6%
Positive to negative	0%	4%
Avg. change	0.88	−0.14

of decisions and outcomes of a sequential decision-making problem. In a situation with two agents, and where the agents take turns, a path from the root to any leaf crosses alternately nodes associated with the proponent (called *decision nodes*) and nodes associated with the opponent (called *chance nodes*). In the case of dialogical argumentation, where the proponent (respectively opponent) is a persuader (respectively persuadee), a decision tree represents all possible dialogues. Each path is one possible permutation of the moves permitted by the dialogue protocol *i.e.*, one possible complete dialogue between the two agents. An edge in the tree is the decision (*i.e.*, dialogue move) that has to be taken by the corresponding agent.

Once the decision tree is built, we select, in each decision node, an action to perform (*e.g.*, an argument to posit in each state of the debate) from the point of view of the proponent. This association of a node with the action to perform in this node is called a **policy**. The aim is to compute an **optimal policy**. This is the policy that selects the best action to perform in each decision node. For this, we use a decision rule, composed of two parts: one taking account of the values of all children of a decision node and the other taking account of the values of all the children of a chance node. We can harness decision-theoretic decision rules for optimizing the choice of arguments based on the user model [26,29]. In Sect. 3.2, we discuss the evaluation of system that used a global strategy based on decision theory.

Alternatives to our approach for selecting moves include using planning systems [9,10], minimizing the number of moves [2], selecting a move based on what an agent believes the other is aware of [53], predicting the argument an opponent might put forward based on data about the moves made by the opponent in previous dialogues [24], and using machine learning to predict whether a sequence of dialogue moves would be acceptable to a user [31,54]. See [57] for a review of strategies in multi-agent argumentation.

3   Evaluations with Participants

In order to evaluate our framework, we undertook a number of studies with participants [15,16,28–30,36,47]. In the following we focus on two of these.

3.1 Cycling in the City Study

In this study, we investigated the question of commuting by bicycle in the city [28]. We compiled an argument graph with 51 arguments on the topic of commuting by bicycle in the city and 8 concerns (Health, Fitness, Comfort, Time, Personal Economy, City Economy, Environment, and Safety). We undertook pre-studies to validate key assumptions: (1) Participants tend to agree on assignment of concerns to arguments; (2) Participants give meaningful preferences over types of concern; And (3) Participants play by their preferences over concerns. We ran an APS on the web with 100 crowdsourced participants to persuade them to commute by cycle. Using the strategy given in Example 3, we obtained a statistically significant improvement in persuasion when compared with a baseline system that did not consider concerns (see Table 3). This study shows that incorporating concerns can help an APS make better choices of move.

3.2 University Student Fees Study

In this study, we investigated the question of university student fees in the UK which normally cost over 9K pounds per annum [30]. We had an argument graph with almost 150 arguments on the topic and 10 concerns (Economy, Government finance, Employment, Student finance, Education, Student satisfaction, Student well-being, University management, Commercialization of universities, Fairness, and Society). We crowdsourced assignment of concerns and beliefs to arguments, and preferences over concerns, for the user model from over 400 participants. We compared our APS with a baseline system (that did not access the user model) using 261 crowdsourced participants where for each participant, if they believed the 9K fee should remain (respectively be abolished), we tried to persuade them that it should be abolished (respectively should remain). We obtained a statistically significant increase in belief in a persuasion goal (average +0.15 on a scale from −3 to +3) when compared with the baseline system. By analyzing the dialogues, the difference in performance is attributable to the better choice of moves made by our APS.

4   Towards Natural Language Dialogues

In the evaluation of APSs discussed in Sect. 3, we did not allow users to type their arguments in natural language. Rather, we presented the user with a menu of potential counterarguments to the previous argument by the system, and the user could select those that s/he subscribed to. Whilst using menus has provided a simple interface in our project, it would be better to have a more natural interface. For argumentation, this means having an interface with some natural language understanding capability. Furthermore, within restricted domains, this can be facilitated by some form of chatbot technology.

A chatbot is a software system with limited natural language processing capability [46]. Simple patterns of normal conversation can be used (e.g. pleasantries). A user can give input in natural language, and this is handled using

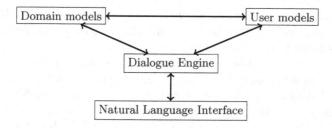

Fig. 1. Extending the framework for computational persuasion with natural language capability. The arcs denote interactions between the components.

one or more of the following: simple pattern matching (e.g. regular expressions); natural language parsing; and machine learning classifiers. By determining the type of the user input, the chatbot can then select an appropriate statement as a reply from the repository, or ask a query, or change tack by switching to another topic. Such an approach was used by Huang and Lin [31] for participating in dialogues with potential customers with the aim of persuading them to offer a higher price for goods.

4.1   First Steps for Argumentative Chatbots

We now briefly discuss how we can harness the approach of chatbots for argumentation using machine learning techniques. For this, we need to acquire arguments on a topic from crowdsourced participants and then cluster them into groups of similar arguments (as done in [15,16]). For example, we might have a cluster with sentences that include the following.

- "I don't exercise because I don't have a lot of free time during the week."
- "I am busy doing university work, which is my top priority."
- "Something always comes up which seems to be more important."
- "I don't have enough time."

An alternative to get a cluster is to start with a domain model (i.e. an argument graph containing all the arguments that the system or user might play). For each argument that the user might play, we can crowdsource linguistic variants of that argument. For this, we present the argument, and ask crowdsourced participants to provide alternative phrasing of the statement. In this way, we can obtain a large number of sentences that contain essentially the same argument (assuming each sentence represents an argument), and we can refer to such a set of sentences as a cluster.

For each cluster (whether obtained by clustering sets of crowdsourced arguments or by obtaining linguistic variants of an argument), we can train a classifier (e.g. a classification tree, a naive Bayes classifier, or a support vector machine) using for instance the SciKit Machine Learning Library for Python. Once trained, the classifier can be applied to user input to determine whether that input belongs to the cluster. For example, if the user types "I work long hours, and there is no space in my schedule for fit in exercise", the classifier might then classify it as being in the above cluster.

We can aim to have a classifier for each type of counterargument that the user might present in a dialogue on a topic. These classifiers can be harnessed by a state-based chatbot. Each state denotes the state of the dialogue from the point of view of the system. In a state, a statement is selected for presentation to the user. In the simplest case, this can be a non-deterministic choice of candidates that are appropriate for that state of the dialogue. Then the transition to the next state depends on the input by the user, and to what cluster this is classified. So each arc to the next state denotes a type of response made by the user.

For example, in the initial state, the chatbot says "Would you like to talk about exercise?", and there are two subsequent states. For the first the classifier recognizes positive answers such as "yes" and for the second, the classifier recognizes negative answers such as "no". At a later stage, the chatbot might give the argument "You need to do more exercise, and so you should consider joining your local gym". For the subsequent states, there might be classifiers to recognize arguments coming from the user such as about time (as in the bullet points above), or about lack of money, or about lack of interest, etc. Once the classifier has recognized the input, an appropriate answer can be provided.

Therefore, by determining the classification of the user argument (i.e. the cluster to which it belongs), the chatbot can select an appropriate counterargument from the repository, or ask a query, or change tack by using another argument to support the persuasion goal. In addition, simple patterns of normal conversation can be used (e.g. pleasantries).

Furthermore, it is straightforward to implement a simple system that trains classifiers, and incorporates them within state models, so as to allow for simple argumentation dialogues to be undertaken with users in natural language on a narrow topic such as given in Table 2.

4.2 Next Steps for Argumentative Chatbots

There are various ways that the classifiers described above could be improved. For our investigations, we used the corpus in [15] which contains clusters of arguments on sufficiently different topics. So for instance arguments about not being able to do exercise because of lack of time can often be discriminated from arguments about not being able to do exercise because of lack of money just by using key words. Indeed, the only features we used for the classifiers were keywords, and synonyms for keywords coming from WordNet in the Python NLTK library [8].

To handle more complex discussions would require more sophisticated discrimination of different arguments. For instance, for the sentence "I am a student, and in my spare time, I prefer to earn money rather than go to the gym", it is likely to be classified as lack to time or as lack of money. Yet, it seems to fall into a third classification. This therefore calls for richer feature sets for training classifiers which in turn calls for use of bigrams or trigrams [43], if there is sufficient data, or the use of natural language processing to identify syntactic or semantic structure in the input. In particular, the identification of negation, and the clause within the scope of negation, is an important aspect of understanding counterarguments. Another issue is the pronoun resolution both within a sentence and between the sentence and previous sentences. This creates many challenges, but potentially offers much higher quality classification. Obviously, there is a large literature in natural language processing that is potentially relevant to developing more sophisticated feature sets that should be harnessed.

The design of more sophisticated interfaces could be influenced by developments in argument mining, which is concerned with identifying components of arguments (e.g. premises, claims), and relationships between them (e.g. support, attack), within free text (for reviews see [42,55]), the use of machine learning to predict the convincingness of arguments [23], and the use of textual entailment to select appropriate responses in an argumentation dialogue [59].

The other aspect of developing argumentation chatbots for persuasion is to hook-up the interface to the dialogue engine so that strategic choices of move can be made based on the domain model and the user model (as illustrated in Fig. 1). This could then allow for the menu of counterarguments from which the user selects his/her choice to be replaced by the chatbot natural language interface.

5 Discussion

In this paper, we have reviewed a framework for computational persuasion based on domain modelling of arguments and counterarguments, user modelling of the beliefs and concerns of persuadees, and optimizing the choice of move in dialogical argumentation by taking into account the user model. We have discussed studies showing that a system based on this framework can outperform a baseline system over a population of participants.

There are various ways that this framework could be further developed including richer domain models (for example using structured arguments), richer user models (for example using epistemic graphs [37,38]), and for better methods for strategic arguments (for example better definitions for reward functions).

Then there is the need to develop natural language interfaces so that we are not restricted to menu-driven input from the user. In this paper, we have briefly described a simple approach to harnessing chatbots, and we have described various ways that this could be developed by harnessing developments in computational linguistics. The combination of computational models of arguments (as underlying the framework for computational persuasion) as presented here with computational linguistics could offer some exciting research with important impact. As part of such an endeavor, it is important to ensure that there are studies with participants. This can help to verify the developments are consistent with how people do actually enter into argumentation dialogues.

References

1. Andrews, P., Manandhar, S., De Boni, M.: Argumentative human computer dialogue for automated persuasion. In: Proceedings of the 9th SIGdial Workshop on Discourse and Dialogue, pp. 138–147 (2008)
2. Atkinson, K., Bench-Capon, P., Bench-Capon, T.: Value-based argumentation for democratic decision support. In: Proceedings of ICAART 2012, pp. 23–32 (2012)
3. Atkinson, K., Baroni, P., Giacomin, M., Hunter, A., Prakken, H., Reed, C., Simari, G.R., Thimm, M., Villata, S.: Towards artificial argumentation. AI Mag. **38**(3), 25–36 (2017)
4. Baroni, P., Giacomin, M., Vicig, P.: On rationality conditions for epistemic probabilities in abstract argumentation. In: Proceedings of COMMA 2014, pp. 121–132 (2014)
5. Baroni, P., Gabbay, D., Giacomin, M., van der Torre, L. (eds.): Handbook of Formal Argumentation. College Publications, London (2018)
6. Besnard, P., Hunter, A.: Elements of Argumentation. MIT Press, Cambridge (2008)
7. BIckmore, T., Schulman, D., Sidner, C.: Automated interventions for multiple health behviours using conversational agents. Patient Educ. Couns. **92**, 142–148 (2013)
8. Bird, S., Klein, E., Loper, E.: Natural Language Processing with Python - Analyzing Text with the Natural Language Toolkit. O'Reilly Media, Sebastopol (2009)
9. Black, E., Coles, A., Bernardini, S.: Automated planning of simple persuasion dialogues. In: Bulling, N., van der Torre, L., Villata, S., Jamroga, W., Vasconcelos, W. (eds.) CLIMA 2014. LNCS (LNAI), vol. 8624, pp. 87–104. Springer, Cham (2014). https://doi.org/10.1007/978-3-319-09764-0_6
10. Black, E., Coles, A., Hampson, C.: Planning for persuasion. In: Proceedings of AAMAS 2017, pp. 933–942 (2017)
11. Caminada, M., Podlaszewski, M.: Grounded semantics as persuasion dialogue. In: Proceedings of COMMA 2012, pp. 478–485. IOS Press (2012)
12. Cawsey, A., Grasso, F., Jones, R.: A conversational model for health promotion on the world wide web. In: Horn, W., Shahar, Y., Lindberg, G., Andreassen, S., Wyatt, J. (eds.) AIMDM 1999. LNCS (LNAI), vol. 1620, pp. 379–388. Springer, Heidelberg (1999). https://doi.org/10.1007/3-540-48720-4_42
13. Cayrol, C., Lagasquie-Schiex, M.C.: Bipolarity in argumentation graphs: towards a better understanding. Int. J. Approx. Reason. **54**(7), 876–899 (2013)
14. Chalaguine, L., et al.: Domain modelling in computational persuasion for behaviour change in healthcare. arXiv (2018). arXiv:1802.10054 [cs.AI]
15. Chalaguine, L., Hamilton, F., Hunter, A., Potts, H.: Argument harvesting using chatbots. In: Proceedings of COMMA 2018, pp. 149–160 (2018)
16. Chalaguine, L., Hamilton, F., Hunter, A., Potts, H.: Impact of argument type and concerns in argumentation with a chatbot. arXiv (2018). arXiv:1905.00646 [cs.AI]
17. Fan, X., Toni, F.: Assumption-based argumentation dialogues. In: Proceedings of IJCAI 2011, pp. 198–203 (2011)
18. Fogg, B.: Persuasive computers. In: Proceedings of CHI 1998, pp. 225–232 (1998)
19. Grasso, F.: Exciting avocados and dull pears - combining behavioural and argumentative theory for producing effective advice. In: Proceedings of CogSci 1998, pp. 436–441 (1998)
20. Grasso, F.: Rhetorical coding of health promotion dialogues. In: Dojat, M., Keravnou, E.T., Barahona, P. (eds.) AIME 2003. LNCS (LNAI), vol. 2780, pp. 179–188. Springer, Heidelberg (2003). https://doi.org/10.1007/978-3-540-39907-0_26

21. Grasso, F., Cawsey, A., Jones, R.: Dialectical argumentation to solve conflicts in advice giving: a case study in the promotion of healthy nutrition. Int. J. Hum Comput. Stud. **53**(6), 1077–1115 (2000)
22. Guerrero, E., Nieves, J., Lindgren, H.: An activity-centric argumentation framework for assistive technology aimed at improving health. Argument Comput. **7**, 5–33 (2016)
23. Habernal, I., Gurevych, I.: Which argument is more convincing? Analyzing and predicting convincingness of Web arguments using bidirectional LSTM. In: Proceedings of ACL 2016, pp. 1589–1599 (2016)
24. Hadjinikolis, C., Siantos, Y., Modgil, S., Black, E., McBurney, P.: Opponent modelling in persuasion dialogues. In: Proceedings of IJCAI 2015, pp. 164–170 (2013)
25. Hadoux, E., Hunter, A.: Computationally viable handling of beliefs in arguments for persuasion. In: Proceedings of ICTAI 2016, pp. 319–326 (2016)
26. Hadoux, E., Hunter, A.: Strategic sequences of arguments for persuasion using decision trees. In: Proceedings of AAAI 2017, pp. 1128–1134 (2017)
27. Hadoux, E., Hunter, A.: Learning and updating user models for subpopulations in persuasive argumentation using beta distributions. In: Proceedings of AAMAS 2018, pp. 1141–1149 (2018)
28. Hadoux, E., Hunter, A.: Comfort or safety? Gathering and using the concerns of a participant for better persuasion. Argument Comput. (2019, in press)
29. Hadoux, E., Hunter, A., Corrégé, J.-B.: Strategic dialogical argumentation using multi-criteria decision making with application to epistemic and emotional aspects of arguments. In: Ferrarotti, F., Woltran, S. (eds.) FoIKS 2018. LNCS, vol. 10833, pp. 207–224. Springer, Cham (2018). https://doi.org/10.1007/978-3-319-90050-6_12
30. Hadoux, E., Hunter, A., Polberg, S.: Strategic argumentation dialogues for persuasion: framework and experiments based on modelling the beliefs and concerns of the persuadee. Technical report, University College London (2019)
31. Huang, S., Lin, F.: The design and evaluation of an intelligent sales agent for online persuasion and negotiation. In: Electronic Commerce Research and Applications, pp. 285–296 (2007)
32. Hunter, A.: A probabilistic approach to modelling uncertain logical arguments. Int. J. Approx. Reason. **54**(1), 47–81 (2013)
33. Hunter, A.: Modelling the persuadee in asymmetric argumentation dialogues for persuasion. In: Proceedings of IJCAI 2015, pp. 3055–3061 (2015)
34. Hunter, A.: Persuasion dialogues via restricted interfaces using probabilistic argumentation. In: Schockaert, S., Senellart, P. (eds.) SUM 2016. LNCS (LNAI), vol. 9858, pp. 184–198. Springer, Cham (2016). https://doi.org/10.1007/978-3-319-45856-4_13
35. Hunter, A.: Two dimensional uncertainty in persuadee modelling in argumentation. In: Proceedings of ECAI 2016, pp. 150–157 (2016)
36. Hunter, A., Polberg, S.: Empirical methods for modelling persuadees in dialogical argumentation. In: Proceedings of ICTAI 2017, pp. 382–389 (2017)
37. Hunter, A., Polberg, S., Potyka, S.: Updating belief in arguments in epistemic graphs. In: Proceedings of KR 2018, pp. 138–147 (2018)
38. Hunter, A., Polberg, S., Thimm, M.: Epistemic graphs for representing and reasoning with positive and negative influences of arguments. arXiv (2018). arXiv:1802.07489 [cs.AI]
39. Hunter, A., Potyka, N.: Updating probabilistic epistemic states in persuasion dialogues. In: Antonucci, A., Cholvy, L., Papini, O. (eds.) ECSQARU 2017. LNCS

(LNAI), vol. 10369, pp. 46–56. Springer, Cham (2017). https://doi.org/10.1007/978-3-319-61581-3_5

40. Hunter, A., Thimm, M.: Optimization of dialectical outcomes in dialogical argumentation. Int. J. Approx. Reason. **78**, 73–102 (2016)

41. Hunter, A.: Towards a framework for computational persuasion with applications in behaviour change, argument and computation. Argument Comput. **9**(1), 15–40 (2018)

42. Lippi, M., Torroni, P.: Argumentation mining: state of the art and emerging trends. ACM Trans. Internet Technol. **16**(2), 10 (2016)

43. Manning, C., Schütz, H.: Foundations of Statistical Natural Language Processing. MIT Press, Cambridge (2000)

44. Nguyen, H., Masthoff, J., Edwards, P.: Persuasive effects of embodied conversational agent teams. In: Jacko, J.A. (ed.) HCI 2007. LNCS, vol. 4552, pp. 176–185. Springer, Heidelberg (2007). https://doi.org/10.1007/978-3-540-73110-8_19

45. Ogden, J.: Health Psychology: A Textbook, 5th edn. Open University Press, Buckingham (2012)

46. Perez-Marin, D., Pascual-Nieto, I. (eds.): Conversational agents and natural language interaction; techniques and effective practices. Information Science Reference (2011)

47. Polberg, S., Hunter, A.: Empirical evaluation of abstract argumentation: supporting the need for bipolar and probabilistic approaches. Int. J. Approx. Reason. **93**, 487–543 (2018)

48. Polberg, S., Hunter, A., Thimm, M.: Belief in attacks in epistemic probabilistic argumentation. In: Moral, S., Pivert, O., Sánchez, D., Marín, N. (eds.) SUM 2017. LNCS (LNAI), vol. 10564, pp. 223–236. Springer, Cham (2017). https://doi.org/10.1007/978-3-319-67582-4_16

49. Prakken, H.: Coherence and flexibility in dialogue games for argumentation. J. Logic Comput. **15**(6), 1009–1040 (2005)

50. Prakken, H.: Formal systems for persuasion dialogue. Knowl. Eng. Rev. **21**(2), 163–188 (2006)

51. Rahwan, I., Madakkatel, M., Bonnefon, J., Awan, R., Abdallah, S.: Behavioural experiments for assessing the abstract argumentation semantics of reinstatement. Cogn. Sci. **34**(8), 1483–1502 (2010)

52. Rahwan, I., Simari, G. (eds.): Argumentation in Artificial Intelligence. Springer, Heidelberg (2009)

53. Rienstra, T., Thimm, M., Oren, N.: Opponent models with uncertainty for strategic argumentation. In: Proceedings of IJCAI 2013, pp. 332–338 (2013)

54. Rosenfeld, A., Kraus, S.: Providing arguments in discussions on the basis of the prediction of human argumentative behavior. ACM Trans. Interact. Intell. Syst. **6**(4), 30:1–30:33 (2016)

55. Stede, M., Schneider, J.: Argumentation Mining. Morgan & Claypool, San Rafael (2019)

56. Thimm, M.: A probabilistic semantics for abstract argumentation. In: Proceedings of ECAI 2012, vol. 242, pp. 750–755 (2012)

57. Thimm, M.: Strategic argumentation in multi-agent systems. Künstliche Intell. **28**, 159–168 (2014)

58. Josekutty Thomas, R., Masthoff, J., Oren, N.: Adapting healthy eating messages to personality. In: de Vries, P.W., Oinas-Kukkonen, H., Siemons, L., Beerlage-de Jong, N., van Gemert-Pijnen, L. (eds.) PERSUASIVE 2017. LNCS, vol. 10171, pp. 119–132. Springer, Cham (2017). https://doi.org/10.1007/978-3-319-55134-0_10

59. Toniuc, D., Groza, A.: Climebot: an argumentative agent for climate change. In: Proceedings of ICCP 2017, pp. 63–70 (2017)
60. Zaal, E., Mills, G., Hagen, A., Huisman, C., Hoeks, J.: Convincing conversations: Using a computer-based dialogue system to promote a plant-based diet. In: Proceedings of the Cognitive Science Conference (CogSci 2017), pp. 3627–3632 (2017)

Analogy-Based Preference Learning with Kernels

Mohsen Ahmadi Fahandar[(✉)] and Eyke Hüllermeier

Heinz Nixdorf Institute and Department of Computer Science,
Intelligent Systems and Machine Learning Group, Paderborn University,
Paderborn, Germany
ahmadim@mail.upb.de, eyke@upb.de

Abstract. Building on a specific formalization of analogical relationships of the form "A relates to B as C relates to D", we establish a connection between two important subfields of artificial intelligence, namely analogical reasoning and kernel-based learning. More specifically, we show that so-called *analogical proportions* are closely connected to kernel functions on pairs of objects. Based on this result, we introduce the *analogy kernel*, which can be seen as a measure of how strongly four objects are in analogical relationship. As an application, we consider the problem of object ranking in the realm of preference learning, for which we develop a new method based on support vector machines trained with the analogy kernel. Our first experimental results for data sets from different domains (sports, education, tourism, etc.) are promising and suggest that our approach is competitive to state-of-the-art algorithms in terms of predictive accuracy.

1 Introduction

In this paper, we establish a connection between analogical reasoning and kernel-based learning, which are two important subfields of artificial intelligence. Essentially, this becomes possible thanks to the observation that a specific formalization of analogical relationships, so-called *analogical proportions* [25,29], defines a kernel function on pairs of objects. This relationship is established by means of generalized (fuzzy) equivalence relations as a bridging concept.

Analogical reasoning has a long tradition in artificial intelligence research, and various attempts at formalizing analogy-based inference can be found in the literature. In this regard, the aforementioned concept of analogical proportion is an especially appealing approach, which has already been used successfully in different problem domains, including classification [7], recommendation [19], preference completion [27], decision making [5], and solving IQ tests [4].

In spite of its popularity in AI in general, analogical reasoning has not been considered very much in machine learning so far. Yet, analogical proportions have recently been used in the context of preference learning [1,6], a branch of machine learning that has received increasing attention in recent years [15]. Roughly speaking, the goal in preference learning is to induce preference models

© Springer Nature Switzerland AG 2019
C. Benzmüller and H. Stuckenschmidt (Eds.): KI 2019, LNAI 11793, pp. 34–47, 2019.
https://doi.org/10.1007/978-3-030-30179-8_3

from observational (or experimental) data that reveal information about the preferences of an individual or a group of individuals in a direct or indirect way; the latter typically serve the purpose of predictive modeling, i.e., they are then used to predict the preferences in a new situation.

Frequently, the predicted preference relation is required to form a total order, in which case we also speak of a *ranking problem*. In fact, among the problems in the realm of preference learning, the task of "learning to rank" has probably received the most attention in the literature so far, and a number of different ranking problems have already been introduced. Based on the type of training data and the required predictions, [15] distinguish between the problems of object ranking [13,21], label ranking [12,17,34], and instance ranking [16].

Building on [1], the focus of this paper is on the problem of object ranking. Given training data in the form of a set of exemplary rankings of subsets of objects, the goal in object ranking is to learn a ranking function that is able to predict the ranking of any new set of objects. Our contribution is a novel approach to this problem, namely a kernel-based implementation of analogy-based object ranking.

The rest of the paper is organized as follows. In the next section, we recall the setting of object ranking and formalize the corresponding learning problem. Section 3 outlines existing methods for the object ranking task, followed by Sect. 4 in which the connection between analogical reasoning and kernel-based learning is established. In Sect. 5, we introduce kernel-based analogical reasoning for the object ranking problem. Finally, we present an experimental evaluation of this approach in Sect. 6, prior to concluding the paper with a summary and an outline of future work.

2   Problem Formulation

Consider a reference set of objects, items, or choice alternatives $\mathcal{X}$, and assume each item $x \in \mathcal{X}$ to be described in terms of a feature vector; thus, an item is a vector $x = (x_1, \ldots, x_d) \in \mathbb{R}^d$ and $\mathcal{X} \subseteq \mathbb{R}^d$. The goal in object ranking is to learn a *ranking function* ρ that accepts any (query) subset $Q = \{x_1, \ldots, x_n\} \subseteq \mathcal{X}$ of $n = |Q|$ items as input. As output, the function produces a ranking $\pi \in \mathbb{S}_n$ of these items, where $\mathbb{S}_n$ denotes the set of all permutations of length n, i.e., all mappings $[n] \longrightarrow [n]$ (symmetric group of order n); π represents the total order

$$x_{\pi^{-1}(1)} \succ x_{\pi^{-1}(2)} \succ \ldots \succ x_{\pi^{-1}(n)}, \tag{1}$$

i.e., $\pi^{-1}(k)$ is the index of the item on position k, while $\pi(k)$ is the position of the kth item x_k (π is often called a *ranking* and π^{-1} an *ordering*). Formally, a ranking function is thus a mapping

$$\rho : \mathcal{Q} \longrightarrow \mathcal{R}, \tag{2}$$

where $\mathcal{Q} = 2^{\mathcal{X}} \setminus \emptyset$ is the *query space* and $\mathcal{R} = \bigcup_{n \in \mathbb{N}} \mathbb{S}_n$ the *ranking space*. The order relation "$\succ$" is typically (though not necessarily) interpreted in terms of preferences, i.e., $x \succ y$ suggests that x is preferred to y. A ranking function ρ is learned on a set of training data that consists of a set of rankings

$$\mathcal{D} = \{(Q_1, \pi_1), \ldots, (Q_M, \pi_M)\}, \tag{3}$$

where each ranking π_ℓ defines a total order of the set of objects Q_ℓ. Once a ranking function has been learned, it can be used for making predictions for new query sets Q. Such predictions are evaluated in terms of a suitable loss function or performance metric. A common choice is the (normalized) *ranking loss*, which counts the number of inversions between two rankings π and π':

$$d_{RL}(\pi, \pi') = \frac{\sum_{1 \leq i,j \leq n} [\![\pi(i) < \pi(j)]\!][\![\pi'(i) > \pi'(j)]\!]}{n(n-1)/2},$$

where $[\![\cdot]\!]$ is the indicator function. The ranking function (2) sought in object ranking is a complex mapping from the query to the ranking space. An important question, therefore, is how to represent a "ranking-valued" function of that kind, and how it can be learned efficiently.

3   Previous Work

Quite a number of approaches to object ranking and related learning-to-rank problems have already been proposed in the literature, most of them based on the idea of representing a ranking function via an underlying (latent) utility function. Depending on the type of training data used for learning such a function, a distinction is often made between so-called pointwise [21,22], pairwise [10,20], and listwise [11] approaches.

In the following, we give a brief overview of the analogy-based approach recently put forward in [1], which is most relevant for us. This approach essentially builds on the following inference pattern: If object a relates to object b as c relates to d, and knowing that a is preferred to b, we (hypothetically) infer that c is preferred to d. This principle is formalized using the concept of analogical proportion [25]. For every quadruple of objects a, b, c, d, the latter provides a numerical degree to which these objects are in analogical relation to each other. To this end, such a degree is first determined for each attribute value (feature) separately, and these degrees are then combined into an overall degree of analogy.

Consider four values a, b, c, d from an attribute domain $\mathbb{X}$. The quadruple (a, b, c, d) is said to be in analogical proportion, denoted by $a : b :: c : d$, if "a relates to b as c relates to d". A bit more formally, the degree of proportion can be expressed as

$$E\big(\mathcal{R}(a, b), \mathcal{R}(c, d)\big), \tag{4}$$

where the relation E denotes the "as" part of the informal description. $\mathcal{R}$ can be instantiated in different ways, depending on the underlying domain $\mathbb{X}$.

In the case of Boolean variables, where $\mathbb{X} = \{0, 1\}$, there are $2^4 = 16$ instantiations of the pattern $a : b :: c : d$, of which only the following 6 satisfy a set of axioms required to hold for analogical proportions: $(0,0,0,0)$, $(0,0,1,1)$, $(0,1,0,1)$, $(1,0,1,0)$, $(1,1,0,0)$, $(1,1,1,1)$. This formalization captures the idea that a differs from b (in the sense of being "equally true", "more true", or "less true", if the values 0 and 1 are interpreted as truth degrees) exactly as c differs from d, and vice versa. In the numerical case, assuming all attributes to be normalized to the unit interval $[0,1]$, the concept of analogical proportion can be generalized on the basis of generalized logical operators [8,14]. In this case, the analogical proportion will become a matter of degree, i.e., a quadruple (a,b,c,d) can be in analogical proportion *to some degree* between 0 and 1. An example of such a proportion, with $\mathcal{R}$ the arithmetic difference $\mathcal{R}(a,b) = a - b$, is the following:

$$v(a,b,c,d) = 1 - |(a-b) - (c-d)|, \qquad (5)$$

if $\operatorname{sign}(a-b) = \operatorname{sign}(c-d)$, and 0 otherwise. Note that this formalization indeed generalizes the Boolean case (where $a,b,c,d \in \{0,1\}$).

To extend analogical proportions from individual values to complete feature vectors, the individual degrees of proportion can be combined using any suitable aggregation function, for example the arithmetic mean:

$$v(\boldsymbol{a},\boldsymbol{b},\boldsymbol{c},\boldsymbol{d}) = \frac{1}{d} \sum_{i=1}^{d} v(a_i, b_i, c_i, d_i).$$

With a measure of analogical proportion at hand, the object ranking task is tackled as follows: Consider any pair of query objects $\boldsymbol{x}_i, \boldsymbol{x}_j \in Q$. Every preference $\boldsymbol{z} \succ \boldsymbol{z}'$ observed in the training data $\mathcal{D}$, such that $(\boldsymbol{z}, \boldsymbol{z}', \boldsymbol{x}_i, \boldsymbol{x}_j)$ are in analogical proportion, suggests that $\boldsymbol{x}_i \succ \boldsymbol{x}_j$. This principle is referred as *analogical transfer* of preferences, because the observed preference for $\boldsymbol{z}, \boldsymbol{z}'$ is (hypothetically) transferred to $\boldsymbol{x}_i, \boldsymbol{x}_j$. Accumulating all pieces of evidence that can be collected in favor of $\boldsymbol{x}_i \succ \boldsymbol{x}_j$ and, vice versa, the opposite preference $\boldsymbol{x}_j \succ \boldsymbol{x}_i$, an overall degree $p_{i,j}$ is derived for this pair of objects. The same is done for all other pairs in the query. Eventually, all these degrees are combined into an overall consensus ranking. We refer to [1] for a detailed description of this method, which is called "analogy-based learning to rank" (able2rank) by the authors.

As an aside, note that an analogy-based approach as outlined above appears to be specifically suitable for *transfer learning*. This is mainly because the relation $\mathcal{R}$ is evaluated separately for "source objects" a and b on the one side and "target objects" c and d on the other side, but never between sources and targets. In principle, one could even think of using different specifications of $\mathcal{R}$ for the source and the target.

4   Analogy and Kernels

The core idea of our proposal is based on the observation that an analogical proportion, by definition, defines a kind of *similarity* between the relation of pairs of objects: According to (4), the analogical proportion $a : b :: c : d$ holds if $\mathcal{R}(a,b)$ is similar to $\mathcal{R}(c,d)$. The notion of similarity plays an important role in machine learning in general, and in kernel-based machine learning in particular. In fact, kernel functions can typically be interpreted in terms of similarity. Thus, a kernel-based approach might be a natural way to incorporate analogical reasoning in machine learning.

More specifically, to establish a connection between kernel-based machine learning and analogical reasoning, we make use of generalized (fuzzy) equivalence relations as a bridging concept. Fuzzy equivalences are weakened forms of standard equivalence relations, and hence capture the notion of similarity. More specifically, a fuzzy equivalence relation E on a set $\mathcal{X}$ is a fuzzy subset of $\mathcal{X} \times \mathcal{X}$, that is, a function $E : \mathcal{X}^2 \longrightarrow [0,1]$, which is reflexive, symmetric, and $\top$-transitive:

- $E(x, x) = 1$ for all $x \in \mathcal{X}$,
- $E(x, y) = E(y, x)$ for all $x, y \in \mathcal{X}$,
- $\top(E(x, y), E(y, z)) \leq E(x, z)$ for all $x, y, z \in \mathcal{X}$,

where $\top$ is a triangular norm (t-norm), that is, a generalized logical conjunction. In our case, the relation E in (4) will play the role of a fuzzy equivalence. The detour via fuzzy equivalences is motivated by the result of [26], who proved that certain types of fuzzy equivalence relations satisfy the properties of a kernel function. Before elaborating on this idea in more detail, we briefly recall some basic concepts of kernel-based machine learning as needed for this paper. For a thorough discussion of kernel methods, see for instance [32,33].

4.1   Kernels

Let $\mathcal{X}$ be a nonempty set. A function $k : \mathcal{X} \times \mathcal{X} \longrightarrow \mathbb{R}$ is a *positive semi-definite kernel* on $\mathcal{X}$ iff it is symmetric, i.e., $k(x, y) = k(y, x)$ for all $x, y \in \mathcal{X}$, and positive semi-definite, i.e.,

$$\sum_{i=1}^{n} \sum_{j=1}^{n} c_i c_j k(x_i, x_j) \geq 0$$

for arbitrary n, arbitrary instances $x_1, \ldots, x_n \in \mathcal{X}$ and arbitrary $c_1, \ldots, c_n \in \mathbb{R}$. Given a kernel k on $\mathcal{X}$, an important theorem by [24] implies the existence of a (Hilbert) space $\mathcal{H}$ and a map $\phi : \mathcal{X} \longrightarrow \mathcal{H}$, such that

$$k(x, y) = \langle \phi(x), \phi(y) \rangle$$

for all $x, y \in \mathcal{X}$. Thus, computing the kernel $k(x, y)$ in the original space $\mathcal{X}$ is equivalent to mapping x and y to $\mathcal{H}$ first, using the *linearization* or *feature map* ϕ, and combining them in terms of the inner product in that space afterward. This connection between a nonlinear combination of instances in the original space $\mathcal{X}$ and a linear combination in the induced feature space $\mathcal{H}$ provides the basis for the so-called "kernel trick", which offers a systematic way to design nonlinear extensions of methods for learning linear models. The kernel trick has been applied to various methods and has given rise to many state-of-the-art machine learning algorithms, including support vector machines, kernel principle component analysis, kernel Fisher discriminant, amongst others [30,31].

4.2 Analogical Proportions as Kernels

Our focus in this paper is the analogical proportion (5), which is a map $v :$ $[0,1]^4 \longrightarrow [0,1]$. In this case, the relation $\mathcal{R}$ is the simple arithmetic difference $\mathcal{R}(a,b) = a - b$, and the similarity relation E is defined as $E(u,v) = 1 - |u - v|$ if both u, v have the same sign, and $E(u,v) = 0$ otherwise. As an aside, we note that, strictly speaking, E thus defined is not a fuzzy equivalence relation. This is due to the thresholding in the case where $\text{sign}(a-b) \neq \text{sign}(c-d)$. Without this thresholding, E would be a $\top_L$-equivalence, where $\top_L$ is the Łukasievicz t-norm $(\alpha, \beta) \mapsto \max(\alpha + \beta - 1, 0)$. For modeling analogy, however, setting E to 0 in the case where b deviates positively from a while d deviates negatively from c (or vice versa) appears reasonable.

We reinterpret v as defined above as a kernel function $k : [0,1]^2 \times [0,1]^2 \longrightarrow [0,1]$ on $\mathcal{X} = [0,1]^2$, i.e., a kernel on pairs of pairs of objects, which essentially means equating k with E:

$$k(a,b,c,d) \mapsto 1 - |(a-b) - (c-d)| \tag{6}$$

if $\text{sign}(a - b) = \text{sign}(c - d)$, and 0 otherwise. In what follows, we show that the "analogy kernel" (6) does indeed define a proper kernel function. The first property to be fulfilled, namely symmetry, is obvious. Thus, it remains to show that k is also positive semi-definite, which is done in Theorem 1 below. As a preparation, we first recall the following lemma, which is proved by [26] as part of his Theorem 11.

Lemma 1. *Let* $\mu_1, \ldots, \mu_n \in [0,1]$, $n \in \mathbb{N}$, *and the matrix* M *be defined by*

$$M_{i,j}^{(n)} = (1 - |\mu_i - \mu_j|).$$

Then M *has a non-negative determinant.*

Theorem 1. *The function* $k : [-1,1]^2 \longrightarrow [0,1]$ *defined as*

$$k(u,v) = \begin{cases} 1 - |u - v| & \text{if } \text{sign}(u) = \text{sign}(v), \\ 0, & \text{otherwise,} \end{cases}$$

is a valid kernel.

Proof. It is easy to see that k is symmetric. Thus, it remains to show that it is positive semi-definite. To this end, it suffices to show that the determinants of all principal minors of every kernel matrix produced by k are non-negative. Thus, consider $\alpha_1, \ldots, \alpha_n \in [-1,1]$, $n \in \mathbb{N}$, and the matrix K defined as

$$K_{i,j}^{(n)} = \begin{cases} 1 - |\alpha_i - \alpha_j|, & \text{if } \text{sign}(\alpha_i) = \text{sign}(\alpha_j), \\ 0, & \text{otherwise,} \end{cases} \tag{7}$$

We need to show that

$$\det\left(K_{i,j}^{(m)}\right) \geq 0,$$

for all $1 \leq m \leq n$. Thanks to the permutation-invariance of determinants, we can assume (without loss of generality) that the values α_i are sorted in non-increasing order, i.e., $\alpha_1 \geq \alpha_2 \geq \cdots \geq \alpha_n$; in particular, note that the positive α_i will then precede all the negative ones. Thus, the matrix K takes the form of a diagonal block matrix

$$K = \begin{pmatrix} A & 0 \\ 0 & B \end{pmatrix},$$

in which the submatrix A contains the values of K for which $\alpha_i, \alpha_j \in [0,1]$, and B contains the values of K where α_i, α_j are negative. According to Lemma (1), $\det(A) \geq 0$. Moreover, since $1 - |u - v| = 1 - |(-u) - (-v)|$ for $u, v \in [0,1]$, the same lemma can also be applied to the submatrix B, hence $\det(B) \geq 0$. Finally, we can exploit that

$$\det(K) = \det(A)\det(B).$$

Since both matrices A and B have non-negative determinant, it follows that $\det(K) \geq 0$, which completes the proof.

The class of kernel functions is closed under various operations, including addition and multiplication by a positive constant. This allows us to extend the analogy kernel from individual variables to feature vectors using the arithmetic mean as an aggregation function:

$$k_A(\boldsymbol{a}, \boldsymbol{b}, \boldsymbol{c}, \boldsymbol{d}) = \frac{1}{d} \sum_{i=1}^{d} k(a_i, b_i, c_i, d_i). \tag{8}$$

Furthermore, to allow for incorporating a certain degree of non-linearity, we make use of a homogeneous polynomial kernel of degree 2,

$$k'_A(\boldsymbol{a}, \boldsymbol{b}, \boldsymbol{c}, \boldsymbol{d}) = \big(k(\boldsymbol{a}, \boldsymbol{b}, \boldsymbol{c}, \boldsymbol{d})\big)^2, \tag{9}$$

which is again a valid kernel.

5   Analogy-Kernel-Based Object Ranking

Recall that, in the setting of learning to rank, we suppose to be given a set of training data of the form

$$\mathcal{D} = \big\{ (Q_1, \pi_1), \ldots, (Q_M, \pi_M) \big\},$$

where each π_ℓ defines a ranking of the set of objects Q_ℓ. If $\boldsymbol{z}_i, \boldsymbol{z}_j \in Q_\ell$ and $\pi_\ell(i) < \pi_\ell(j)$, then $\boldsymbol{z}_i \succ \boldsymbol{z}_j$ has been observed as a preference. Our approach to object ranking based on the analogy kernel, AnKer-rank, comprises two main steps:

– First, for each pair of objects $\boldsymbol{x}_i, \boldsymbol{x}_j \in Q$, a degree of preference $p_{i,j} \in [0,1]$ is derived from $\mathcal{D}$. If these degrees are normalized such that $p_{i,j} + p_{j,i} = 1$, they define a reciprocal preference relation

$$P = \big(p_{i,j}\big)_{1 \leq i \neq j \leq n}. \tag{10}$$

– Second, the preference relation P is turned into a ranking π using a suitable ranking procedure.

Both steps will be explained in more detail further below.

5.1   Prediction of Pairwise Preferences

The first step of our proposed approach, prediction of pairwise preferences, is based on a reduction to binary classification. To this end, training data $\mathcal{D}_{bin}$ is constructed as follows: Consider any preference $x_i \succ x_j$ that can be extracted from the original training data $\mathcal{D}$, i.e., from any of the rankings π_m, $m \in [M]$. Then $z_{i,j} = (x_i, x_j)$ is a positive example for the binary problem (with label $y_{i,j} = +1$), and $z_{j,i} = (x_j, x_i)$ is a negative example (with label $y_{j,i} = -1$). Since these examples essentially carry the same information, we only add one of them to $\mathcal{D}_{bin}$. To keep a balance between positive and negative examples, the choice is simply made by flipping a fair coin.

Note that, for any pair of instances (a, b) and (c, d) in $\mathcal{D}_{bin}$, the analogy kernel (8) is well-defined, i.e., $k_A(a, b, c, d)$ can be computed. Therefore, a binary predictor h_{bin} can be trained on $\mathcal{D}_{bin}$ using any kernel-based classification method. We assume h_{bin} to produce predictions in the unit interval $[0, 1]$, which can be achieved, for example, by means of support vector machines with a suitable post-processing such as Platt-scaling [28].

Now, consider any pair of objects x_i, x_j from a new query $Q = \{x_1, \dots, x_n\}$. Again, the analogy kernel can be applied to this pair and any example from $\mathcal{D}_{bin}$, so that a (binary) prediction for the preference between x_i and x_j can be derived from h_{bin}. More specifically, querying this model with $z_{i,j} = (x_i, x_j)$ yields a degree of support $q_{i,j} = h_{bin}(z_{i,j})$ in favor of $x_i \succ x_j$, while querying it with $z_{j,i} = (x_j, x_i)$ yields a degree of support $q_{j,i} = h_{bin}(z_{j,i})$ in favor of $x_j \succ x_i$. As already said, we assume both degrees to be normalized within the range $[0, 1]$, and define $p_{i,j} = (1 + q_{i,j} - q_{j,i})/2$ as an estimate for the probability of the preference $x_i \succ x_j$. This estimate constitutes one of the entries in the preference relation (10).

5.2   Rank Aggregation

To turn pairwise preferences into a total order, we make use of a rank aggregation method. More specifically, we apply the Bradley-Terry-Luce (BTL) model, which is well-known in the literature on discrete choice [9]. It starts from the parametric model

$$\mathbf{P}(x_i \succ x_j) = \frac{\theta_i}{\theta_i + \theta_j}, \tag{11}$$

where $\theta_i, \theta_j \in \mathbb{R}_+$ are parameters representing the (latent) utility $U(x_i)$ and $U(x_j)$ of x_i and x_j, respectively. Thus, according to the BTL model, the probability to observe a preference in favor of a choice alternative x_i, when being compared to any other alternative, is proportional to θ_i.

Given the preference relation (10), i.e., the entries $p_{i,j}$ informing about the class probability of $x_i \succ x_j$, the parameter $\theta = (\theta_1, \ldots, \theta_n)$ can be estimated by likelihood maximization:

$$\hat{\theta} \in \arg\max_{\theta \in \mathbb{R}^n} \prod_{1 \le i \ne j \le n} \left(\frac{\theta_i}{\theta_i + \theta_j} \right)^{p_{i,j}}.$$

Finally, the predicted ranking π is obtained by sorting the items x_i in descending order of their estimated (latent) utilities $\hat{\theta}_i$.

We note that many other rank aggregation techniques have been proposed in the literature and could principally be used as well; see e.g. [2]. However, since BTL seems to perform very well, we did not consider any other method.

6   Experiments

To study the practical performance of our proposed method, we conducted experiments on several real-world data sets, essentially using the same setup as [1]. As baselines to compare with, we considered able2rank [1], expected rank regression (ERR) [21,22], Ranking SVM (with linear kernel) [20] and RankNet [10].

Table 1. Properties of data sets.

Data set	Domain	# instances	# features	Numeric	Binary	Ordinal	Name
Decathlon	Year 2005	100	10	x	–	–	D1
	Year 2006	100	10	x	–	–	D2
	Olympic 2016	24	10	x	–	–	D3
	U-20 World 2016	22	10	x	–	–	D4
Bundesliga	Season 2015/16	18	13	x	–	–	B1
	Season 2016/17	18	13	x	–	–	B2
	Mid-Season 2016/17	18	7	x	–	–	B3
Footballers	Year 2016 (Streaker)	50	40	x	x	x	F1
	Year 2017 (Streaker)	50	40	x	x	x	F2
FIFA WC	WC 2014 Brazil	32	7	x	–	–	G1
	WC 2018 Russia	32	7	x	–	–	G2
	U-17 WC 2017 India	22	7	x	–	–	G3
Hotels	Düsseldorf	110	28	x	x	x	H1
	Frankfurt	149	28	x	x	x	H2
Uni. Rankings	Year 2015	100	9	x	–	–	U1
	Year 2014	100	9	x	–	–	U2
Volleyball WL	Group 3	12	15	x	–	–	V1
	Group 1	12	15	x	–	–	V2

6.1   Data

We used the same data sets as [1], which are collected from various domains (e.g., sports, education, tourism) and comprise different types of feature (e.g., numeric, binary, ordinal). Table 1 provides a summary of the characteristics of the data sets. For a detailed description of the data, we refer the reader to the source paper. In addition, we include the ranking of the teams that participated in the men's FIFA world cup 2014 and 2018 (32 instances) as well as under-17 in the year 2017 (22 instances) with respect to "goals statistics". This data[1] comprises 7 numeric features such as MatchesPlayed, GoalsFor, GoalsScored, etc.

6.2 Experimental Setup

For the analogy-based methods, an important pre-processing step is the normalization of the attributes in the feature representation $x = (x_1, \ldots, x_d)$, because these attributes are assumed to take values in $[0, 1]$. To this end, we simply apply a linear rescaling

$$x'_k \leftarrow \frac{x_k - \min_k}{\max_k - \min_k},$$

where $\min_k$ and $\max_k$ denote, respectively, the smallest and largest value of the kth feature in the data. This transformation is applied to the training data as well as the test data when a new query Q is received. Since the data from a new query is normally sparse, it might be better to take the minimum and maximum over the entire data, training and test. Yet, this strategy is not recommendable in case the test data has a different distribution. In fact, analogical inference is especially interesting for transfer learning (and indeed, in our experiments, training and test data are sometimes from different subdomains). Therefore, we first conduct a Kolmogorov-Smirnov test [23] to test whether the two parts of the data are drawn from the same distribution. In case the null hypothesis is rejected (at a significance level of $\alpha = 0.05$), normalization is conducted on the test data alone. Otherwise, the training data is additionally taken into account.

We also apply a standard normalization for the other baseline methods (ERR, Ranking SVM and RankNet), transforming each real-valued feature by standardization:

$$x \leftarrow \frac{x - \mu}{\sigma},$$

where μ and σ denote the empirical mean and standard deviation, respectively. Like for the analogy-based methods, a hypothesis test is conducted to decide whether the test data should be normalized separately or together with the training data.

The analogy kernel (9) was used for AnKer-rank. We fixed the cost parameter C of SVM algorithms in an (internal) 2-fold cross-validation (repeated 3 times) on the training data. The search for C is guided by an algorithm[2] proposed by [18], which computes the entire regularization path for the two-class SVM classifier (i.e., all possible values of C for which the solution changes),

---

[1] Extracted from FIFA official website: www.fifa.com.

[2] Publicly available as an R package: http://cran.r-project.org/web/packages/svmpath.

Table 2. Results in terms of loss d_{RL} (averaged over 20 runs) on the test data.

$D_{train} \to D_{test}$	AnKer-rank	able2rank	ERR	Ranking SVM	RankNet
D1 → D2	0.188 ± 0.049(5)	0.055 ± 0.000(4)	0.053(3)	0.014(1)	0.029 ± 0.005(2)
D1 → D3	0.183 ± 0.043(5)	0.072 ± 0.000(4)	0.054(3)	0.040(2)	0.024 ± 0.007(1)
D1 → D4	0.187 ± 0.047(5)	0.119 ± 0.002(4)	0.117(3)	0.095(1)	0.102 ± 0.009(2)
D2 → D1	0.195 ± 0.034(5)	0.090 ± 0.000(4)	0.056(3)	0.015(1)	0.041 ± 0.005(2)
D2 → D3	0.102 ± 0.028(5)	0.082 ± 0.002(4)	0.025(1)	0.032(2)	0.032 ± 0.011(2)
D2 → D4	0.218 ± 0.040(5)	0.143 ± 0.000(4)	0.126(3)	0.104(1)	0.105 ± 0.004(2)
D3 → D1	0.133 ± 0.007(2)	0.150 ± 0.000(4)	0.145(3)	0.096(1)	0.226 ± 0.058(5)
D3 → D2	0.107 ± 0.007(3)	0.106 ± 0.000(2)	0.109(4)	0.082(1)	0.184 ± 0.023(5)
D3 → D4	0.134 ± 0.008(2)	0.144 ± 0.003(4)	0.143(3)	0.126(1)	0.206 ± 0.037(5)
D4 → D1	0.108 ± 0.008(1)	0.156 ± 0.000(4)	0.132(3)	0.119(2)	0.177 ± 0.047(5)
D4 → D2	0.115 ± 0.008(2)	0.144 ± 0.000(5)	0.105(1)	0.118(3)	0.128 ± 0.014(4)
D4 → D3	0.101 ± 0.014(3)	0.099 ± 0.002(1)	0.127(5)	0.101(3)	0.099 ± 0.037(1)
Average ranks	3.58	3.67	2.92	1.58	3.00
B1 → B2	0.018 ± 0.005(1)	0.031 ± 0.006(2)	0.065(4)	0.052(3)	0.104 ± 0.033(5)
B1 → B3	0.011 ± 0.003(1)	0.013 ± 0.000(2)	0.026(4)	0.020(3)	0.056 ± 0.027(5)
B2 → B1	0.001 ± 0.002(1)	0.013 ± 0.005(2)	0.118(5)	0.045(3)	0.096 ± 0.022(4)
B2 → B3	0.000 ± 0.000(1)	0.013 ± 0.000(2)	0.033(4)	0.032(3)	0.043 ± 0.019(5)
B3 → B1	0.000 ± 0.000(1)	0.000 ± 0.000(1)	0.007(3)	0.007(3)	0.053 ± 0.024(5)
B3 → B2	0.000 ± 0.001(1)	0.010 ± 0.003(3)	0.007(2)	0.092(4)	0.092 ± 0.024(4)
Average ranks	1.00	2.00	3.67	3.17	4.67
F1 → F2	0.183 ± 0.027(4)	0.139 ± 0.001(1)	0.314(5)	0.166(2)	0.173 ± 0.006(3)
F2 → F1	0.155 ± 0.003(2)	0.152 ± 0.001(1)	0.293(5)	0.183(4)	0.163 ± 0.009(3)
Average ranks	3.00	1.00	5.00	3.00	3.00
G1 → G2	0.040 ± 0.006(1)	0.061 ± 0.003(3)	0.102(5)	0.053(2)	0.085 ± 0.009(4)
G1 → G3	0.001 ± 0.003(1)	0.012 ± 0.002(3)	0.056(5)	0.004(2)	0.044 ± 0.010(4)
G2 → G1	0.030 ± 0.001(2)	0.026 ± 0.002(1)	0.100(5)	0.037(3)	0.045 ± 0.008(4)
G2 → G3	0.022 ± 0.001(1)	0.025 ± 0.002(3)	0.065(5)	0.022(1)	0.047 ± 0.014(4)
G3 → G1	0.034 ± 0.008(3)	0.042 ± 0.005(4)	0.029(2)	0.023(1)	0.118 ± 0.012(5)
G3 → G2	0.098 ± 0.019(3)	0.106 ± 0.004(4)	0.088(2)	0.052(1)	0.168 ± 0.021(5)
Average ranks	1.83	3.00	4.00	1.67	4.33
H1 → H2	0.065 ± 0.001(2)	0.061 ± 0.000(1)	0.100(5)	0.076(3)	0.083 ± 0.016(4)
Average ranks	2.00	1.00	5.00	3.00	4.00
U1 → U2	0.173 ± 0.018(3)	0.093 ± 0.000(1)	0.245(4)	0.246(5)	0.114 ± 0.012(2)
U2 → U1	0.232 ± 0.005(5)	0.078 ± 0.000(1)	0.218(3)	0.230(4)	0.107 ± 0.010(2)
Average ranks	4.00	1.00	3.50	4.50	2.00
V1 → V2	0.030 ± 0.000(2)	0.030 ± 0.000(2)	0.091(4)	0.002(1)	0.120 ± 0.046(5)
V2 → V1	0.015 ± 0.000(1)	0.038 ± 0.008(3)	0.773(5)	0.015(1)	0.070 ± 0.032(4)
Average ranks	1.50	2.50	4.50	1.00	4.50

with a cost a small (∼3) multiple of the cost of fitting a single model. The following RankNet parameters are adjusted using grid-search and internal cross-validation: The number of units in the hidden layer $(32, 64, 128, 256)$, the batch size $(8, 16, 32)$, the optimizer learning rate $(0.001, 0.01, 0.1)$. Since the data sets are relatively small, the network was restricted to a single hidden layer.

6.3 Results

In our experiments, predictions were produced for certain data set D_{test} of the data, using other parts D_{train} as training data; an experiment of that kind is denoted by $D_{train} \rightarrow D_{test}$ that is considered for all possible combinations within each domain. The averaged ranking loss together with the standard deviation of the conducted experiments (repeated 20 times) are summarized in Table 2, where the numbers in parentheses indicate the rank of the achieved score in the respective problem. Moreover, the table shows average ranks per problem domain.

As can be seen, the relative performance of the methods depends on the domain. In any case, our proposed approach is quite competitive in terms of predictive accuracy, and essentially on a par with able2rank and Ranking SVM, whereas ERR and RankNet show worse performance.

7   Conclusion and Future Work

This paper elaborates on the connection between kernel-based machine learning and analogical reasoning in the context of preference learning. Building on the observation that analogical proportions define a kind of similarity between the relation of pairs of objects, and that kernel functions can be interpreted in terms of similarity, we utilize generalized (fuzzy) equivalence relations as a bridging concept to show that a particular type of analogical proportion defines a valid kernel function. We introduce the analogy kernel and advocate a concrete kernel-based approach for the problem of object ranking. First experimental results on real-world data from various domains are quite promising and suggest that our approach is competitive to state-of-the-art methods for object ranking.

By making analogical inference amenable to kernel methods, our paper depicts a broad spectrum of directions for future work. In particular, we plan to study kernel properties of other analogical proportions proposed in the literature (e.g., geometric proportions [3]).

Besides, various extensions in the direction of kernel-based methods are conceivable and highly interesting from the point of view of analogical reasoning. This includes the use of kernel-based methods other than SVM, techniques such as multiple kernel learning, etc. Last but not least, other types of applications, whether in preference learning or beyond, are also of interest.

References

1. Ahmadi Fahandar, M., Hüllermeier, E.: Learning to rank based on analogical reasoning. In: Proceedings AAAI-2018, 32th AAAI Conference on Artificial Intelligence, New Orleans, Louisiana, USA, pp. 2951–2958 (2018)
2. Ahmadi Fahandar, M., Hüllermeier, E., Couso, I.: Statistical inference for incomplete ranking data: the case of rank-dependent coarsening. In: Proceedings ICML-2017, 34th International Conference on Machine Learning, vol. 70, pp. 1078–1087. PMLR, International Convention Centre, Sydney, Australia (2017)
3. Beltran, W.C., Jaudoin, H., Pivert, O.: Analogical prediction of null values: the numerical attribute case. In: Manolopoulos, Y., Trajcevski, G., Kon-Popovska, M. (eds.) ADBIS 2014. LNCS, vol. 8716, pp. 323–336. Springer, Cham (2014). https://doi.org/10.1007/978-3-319-10933-6_24

4. Beltran, W.C., Prade, H., Richard, G.: Constructive solving of Raven's IQ tests with analogical proportions. Int. J. Intell. Syst. **31**(11), 1072–1103 (2016)
5. Billingsley, R., Prade, H., Richard, G., Williams, M.-A.: Towards analogy-based decision - a proposal. In: Christiansen, H., Jaudoin, H., Chountas, P., Andreasen, T., Legind Larsen, H. (eds.) FQAS 2017. LNCS (LNAI), vol. 10333, pp. 28–35. Springer, Cham (2017). https://doi.org/10.1007/978-3-319-59692-1_3
6. Bounhas, M., Pirlot, M., Prade, H.: Predicting preferences by means of analogical proportions. In: Cox, M.T., Funk, P., Begum, S. (eds.) ICCBR 2018. LNCS (LNAI), vol. 11156, pp. 515–531. Springer, Cham (2018). https://doi.org/10.1007/978-3-030-01081-2_34
7. Bounhas, M., Prade, H., Richard, G.: Analogical classification: a new way to deal with examples. In: Proceedings ECAI-2014, 21th European Conference on Artificial Intelligence, Czech Republic, Prague, pp. 135–140 (2014)
8. Bounhas, M., Prade, H., Richard, G.: Analogy-based classifiers for nominal or numerical data. Int. J. Approx. Reason. **91**, 36–55 (2017)
9. Bradley, R., Terry, M.: The rank analysis of incomplete block designs I. The method of paired comparisons. Biometrika **39**, 324–345 (1952)
10. Burges, C., et al.: Learning to rank using gradient descent. In: Proceedings ICML-2005, 22th International Conference on Machine Learning, Bonn, Germany, pp. 89–96. ACM (2005)
11. Cao, Z., Qin, T., Liu, T.Y., Tsai, M.F., Li, H.: Learning to rank: from pairwise approach to listwise approach. In: Proceedings ICML-2007, 24th International Conference on Machine Learning, pp. 129–136 (2007)
12. Cheng, W., Hühn, J., Hüllermeier, E.: Decision tree and instance-based learning for label ranking. In: Proceedings ICML-2009, 26th International Conference on Machine Learning, pp. 161–168. ACM, New York (2009)
13. Cohen, W.W., Schapire, R.E., Singer, Y.: Learning to order things. J. Artif. Intell. Res. **10**(1), 243–270 (1999)
14. Dubois, D., Prade, H., Richard, G.: Multiple-valued extensions of analogical proportions. Fuzzy Sets Syst. **292**, 193–202 (2016)
15. Fürnkranz, J., Hüllermeier, E.: Preference Learning. Springer, Heidelberg (2011). https://doi.org/10.1007/978-3-642-14125-6
16. Fürnkranz, J., Hüllermeier, E., Vanderlooy, S.: Binary decomposition methods for multipartite ranking. In: Buntine, W., Grobelnik, M., Mladenić, D., Shawe-Taylor, J. (eds.) ECML PKDD 2009. LNCS (LNAI), vol. 5781, pp. 359–374. Springer, Heidelberg (2009). https://doi.org/10.1007/978-3-642-04180-8_41
17. Har-Peled, S., Roth, D., Zimak, D.: Constraint classification: a new approach to multiclass classification. In: Cesa-Bianchi, N., Numao, M., Reischuk, R. (eds.) ALT 2002. LNCS (LNAI), vol. 2533, pp. 365–379. Springer, Heidelberg (2002). https://doi.org/10.1007/3-540-36169-3_29
18. Hastie, T., Rosset, S., Tibshirani, R., Zhu, J.: The entire regularization path for the support vector machine. J. Mach. Learn. Res. **5**, 1391–1415 (2004)
19. Hug, N., Prade, H., Richard, G., Serrurier, M.: Analogy in recommendation. Numerical vs. ordinal: a discussion. In: FUZZ-IEEE-2016, IEEE International Conference on Fuzzy Systems, Vancouver, BC, Canada, pp. 2220–2226 (2016)
20. Joachims, T.: Optimizing search engines using clickthrough data. In: Proceedings of the 8th ACM SIGKDD International Conference on Knowledge Discovery and Data Mining (KDD 2002), pp. 133–142. ACM Press (2002)

21. Kamishima, T., Kazawa, H., Akaho, S.: A survey and empirical comparison of object ranking methods. In: Fürnkranz, J., Hüllermeier, E. (eds.) Preference Learning, pp. 181–202. Springer, Heidelberg (2010). https://doi.org/10.1007/978-3-642-14125-6_9

22. Kamishima, T., Akaho, S.: Supervised ordering by regression combined with thurstone's model. Artif. Intell. Rev. **25**(3), 231–246 (2006)

23. Kolmogorov, A.: Sulla determinazione empirica di una legge di distribuzione. Giornale dell'Istituto Italiano degli Attuari **4**, 83–91 (1933)

24. Mercer, J.: Functions of positive and negative type, and their connection with the theory of integral equations. Philos. Trans. R. Soc. Lond. Ser. A **209**, 415–446 (1909)

25. Miclet, L., Prade, H.: Handling analogical proportions in classical logic and fuzzy logics settings. In: Sossai, C., Chemello, G. (eds.) ECSQARU 2009. LNCS (LNAI), vol. 5590, pp. 638–650. Springer, Heidelberg (2009). https://doi.org/10.1007/978-3-642-02906-6_55

26. Moser, B.: On representing and generating kernels by fuzzy equivalence relations. J. Mach. Learn. Res. **7**, 2603–2620 (2006)

27. Pirlot, M., Prade, H., Richard, G.: Completing preferences by means of analogical proportions. In: Torra, V., Narukawa, Y., Navarro-Arribas, G., Yañez, C. (eds.) MDAI 2016. LNCS (LNAI), vol. 9880, pp. 135–147. Springer, Cham (2016). https://doi.org/10.1007/978-3-319-45656-0_12

28. Platt, J.C.: Probabilistic outputs for support vector machines and comparisons to regularized likelihood methods. In: Advances in Large Margin Classifiers, pp. 61–74. MIT Press (1999)

29. Prade, H., Richard, G.: Analogical proportions and analogical reasoning - an introduction. In: Aha, D.W., Lieber, J. (eds.) ICCBR 2017. LNCS (LNAI), vol. 10339, pp. 16–32. Springer, Cham (2017). https://doi.org/10.1007/978-3-319-61030-6_2

30. Schölkopf, B.: The kernel trick for distances. In: Proceedings NIPS-2000, 13th International Conference on Neural Information Processing Systems, pp. 301–307. MIT Press (2001)

31. Schölkopf, B., Smola, A., Müller, K.R.: Nonlinear component analysis as a kernel eigenvalue problem. Neural Comput. **10**(5), 1299–1319 (1998)

32. Schölkopf, B., Smola, A.J.: Learning with Kernels: Support Vector Machines, Regularization, Optimization, and Beyond. MIT Press, Cambridge (2001)

33. Shawe-Taylor, J., Cristianini, N.: Kernel Methods for Pattern Analysis. Cambridge University Press, New York (2004)

34. Vembu, S., Gärtner, T.: Label ranking algorithms: a survey. In: Fürnkranz, J., Hüllermeier, E. (eds.) Preference Learning, pp. 45–64. Springer, Heidelberg (2011). https://doi.org/10.1007/978-3-642-14125-6_3

Data Acquisition for Argument Search: The args.me Corpus

Yamen Ajjour[1]([⊠]), Henning Wachsmuth[2], Johannes Kiesel[1], Martin Potthast[3], Matthias Hagen[4], and Benno Stein[1]

[1] Bauhaus-Universität Weimar, Weimar, Germany
{yamen.ajjour,johannes.kiesel,benno.stein}@uni-weimar.de
[2] Paderborn University, Paderborn, Germany
henningw@upb.de
[3] Leipzig University, Leipzig, Germany
martin.potthast@uni-leipzig.de
[4] Martin-Luther-Universität Halle-Wittenberg, Halle, Germany
matthias.hagen@informatik.uni-halle.de

Abstract. Argument search is the study of search engine technology that can retrieve arguments for potentially controversial topics or claims upon user request. The design of an argument search engine is tied to its underlying argument acquisition paradigm. More specifically, the employed paradigm controls the trade-off between retrieval precision and recall and thus determines basic search characteristics: Compiling an exhaustive argument corpus offline benefits precision at the expense of recall, whereas retrieving arguments from the web on-the-fly benefits recall at the expense of precision. This paper presents the new corpus of our argument search engine *args.me*, which follows the former paradigm. We freely provide the corpus to the community. With 387 606 arguments it is one of the largest argument resources available so far. In a qualitative analysis, we compare the args.me corpus acquisition paradigm to that of two other argument search engines, and we report first empirical insights into how people search with args.me.

1 Introduction

The web is rife with one-sided documents (marketing, lobbyism, propaganda, hyperpartisan news, etc.), but today's search engines are not well-equipped to deal with such kind of one-sidedness. Ignorant of the fact, they see documents as relevant that match a query's topic. For instance, if a user queries `feminism harms society`, a document that confirms this claim, all other things being equal, will be ranked higher than one denying it. Accordingly, preempting a conclusion on a controversial topic in a query will probably yield strongly biased results towards that conclusion, providing little opportunity to have one's beliefs challenged. Especially for controversial topics, a more nuanced approach may be advisable: *arguments* may be retrieved instead of (one-sided) documents enclosing them, and displayed alongside each other in a pro and con fashion towards a query's

© Springer Nature Switzerland AG 2019
C. Benzmüller and H. Stuckenschmidt (Eds.): KI 2019, LNAI 11793, pp. 48–59, 2019.
https://doi.org/10.1007/978-3-030-30179-8_4

claim. Technologies such as *IBM Debater* [10], *ArgumenText* [14], and our own argument search engine *args.me* [17] are the first such prototypes available. For these technologies, an argument consists of a conclusion together with supporting premises, e.g., "feminism did more good than harm" (conclusion), "since it has contributed a lot to gender equality" (premise).

A search engine typically implements an indexing process and a retrieval process [5]. In the context of argument search, the former acquires arguments (or argumentative documents), assesses their quality, and indexes them to facilitate the recurring execution of the retrieval process. The retrieval process, in turn, retrieves and ranks relevant arguments according to the users' queries [17].

The acquisition of arguments requires the availability of suitable sources, in particular sources which cover the whole range of topics that is of interest to the search engine's users. Depending on the argument acquisition paradigm employed, arguments must be mined from argumentative documents either at indexing time or at retrieval time. Most argument mining approaches are based on dedicated machine learning technology to extract arguments from text, trained on previously annotated corpora [3, 11, 15]. The training corpora available today consist exclusively of samples from specific text genres, such as news editorials, legal text, or student essays. This limits the sources that can be exploited for the still lacking generalizability of these approaches across domains [1, 6].

Despite the fact that argument mining is still in its infancy and hence argument acquisition is limited, it is important to enable the study of the downstream search process. For the three aforementioned argument search engines, their authors pursue different solutions, each having their own advantages and disadvantages (see Sect. 2 for a qualitative analysis). While we introduced our argument search engine args.me and its underlying framework in previous work [17], the focus of this paper is the newly revised and extended argument corpus indexed by args.me, along with the acquisition paradigm it employs. Via distant supervision on dedicated online debate portals, we obtain big amounts of high-quality arguments for a wide range of topics with little to no development overhead. The altogether 387 606 arguments from 59 637 debates constitute one of the largest resources for computational argumentation available so far. We freely provide the complete corpus to the community.[1]

The paper is organized as follows. Section 2 presents background and related work on argument search engines, culminating in a qualitative analysis of three argument acquisition paradigms. Section 3 briefly illustrates the crawling of the debate portals covered by args.me as well as the employed distant supervision heuristics. Section 4 reports key statistics as well as distributions of arguments and debates in our corpus, and Sect. 5 overviews relevant computational argumentation tasks that can be tackled with the corpus. Based on a first log analysis, Sect. 6 provides insights into how people search with args.me.

---

[1] https://webis.de/data/args-me.html or https://doi.org/10.5281/zenodo.3274635.

2   Related Work

Computational argumentation research emanates from different domains and has been motivated by different applications. For example, artificial intelligence studies argumentative agents that persuade humans [13], computational linguistics studies argument mining in the context of writing support [15], and in the field of models for argumentation a web of arguments is envisioned with tools like the AIFdb to unify argument corpora to a standardized argument model [8]. While all these directions can also be relevant to retrieval scenarios, we focus on the specific challenges that argument search poses.

Argument search is a new research area centered around the idea of search engines that retrieve pro and con arguments for a given query. The typical steps include argument acquisition, argument indexing, argument quality assessment [10,14,17]. In the argument acquisition step, the task is to extract arguments from suitable sources, ensuring a wide topic coverage to be able to answer a wide variety of user queries. A key challenge in the acquisition step is to build a robust argument mining method tailored to specific argument sources—a recent study emphasized the difficulty of cross-domain argument mining [6].

The existing argument search prototypes [10,14,17] follow paradigmatically different approaches to argument acquisition: see Fig. 1 for a comparison. The choice of argument sources and mining methods is usually tightly coupled and constitutes a decisive step in designing an argument search engine. The smaller the ratio of explicit arguments to other text in the sources, the more effort needs to be invested to mine high-quality arguments.

ArgumenText (Fig. 1 bottom) follows web search engines in indexing entire web documents. Using a classifier trained on documents from multiple domains, ArgumenText then mines and ranks arguments from topically relevant documents at query time [16]. The advantages of this approach are recall maximization ("everything" is in the index) and the possibility to decide whether a text span is argumentative on a per-query basis. A disadvantage may arise from the aforementioned as of yet unsolved problem of cross-domain robustness [6].

IBM Debater's approach (Fig. 1 center) is to mine conclusions and premises of arguments from recognized sources (such as Wikipedia and high-reputation news portals) with classifiers trained for specific topics [9,10,12]. The arguments are indexed offline (i.e., unlike ArgumenText, the retrieval unit is an argument, not a document)—the complete documents may still be stored in an additional storage. Argument retrieval then boils down to topic filtering and ranking. While the source selection benefits argument quality, recall depends on the effort invested into the training of the classifiers (i.e., human labeling is involved to guarantee the effectiveness of the topic-specific classifiers).

Finally, the approach of args.me is shown in the top Fig. 1. Arguments from debate portals are indexed offline, similar to IBM Debater. However, instead of a classifier-based mining, we harvest arguments using distant supervision, exploiting the explicit debate structure provided by humans (including argument boundaries, pro and con stance, and meta data). This does not only benefit the retrieval precision, but also renders our approach agnostic to topics. A shortcom-

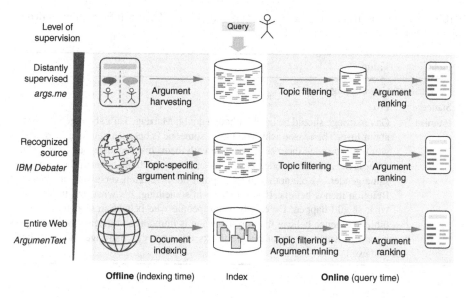

Fig. 1. Comparison of three general argument acquisition paradigms: args.me and IBM Debater index arguments offline, relying on distantly supervised harvesting and on mining from recognized sources respectively. ArgumenText indexes documents and mines online at query time. The *level of supervision* reflects the effort humans spent to create arguments from a source, which in turn implies notable differences regarding index sizes, topic bias, and noise in the data.

ing of our approach is that it needs to decide what is an argument at indexing time, independent of a query. To some extent, this restriction can be overcome in the future through more elaborated topic filtering and ranking algorithms. Besides, the gain of precision comes at the expense of recall as the number of sources qualifying for distantly-supervised argument harvesting is limited. In the next section, we briefly revisit the distant supervision heuristics of args.me underlying the extraction of arguments from debate portals [17].

3   Corpus Acquisition

Debate portals are websites dedicated to *organized* online debate. Not unlike debate clubs, users exchange arguments on controversial issues, allowing their audience to judge their merits. Some portals, such as debate.org, contain dialogical discussions, others, such as debatepedia.org, list arguments with pro and con stance for each covered topic. Both types of portals are largely balanced in terms of the number of pro and con arguments for each topic, allowing users to form opinions in an unbiased manner. Due to the wide range of covered topics and the high average argument quality, many debate portals are a valuable resource often used in computational argumentation research [2,4,7] and form the argument source of args.me [17].

Table 1. Example from the args.me corpus (context and meta information omitted for brevity).

Field	Value
Conclusion	Gay marriage
Stance	Pro
Premise	Gay marriage should be legal without a doubt. Marriage isn't about gender, it is about love. The reason why you marry someone is because you love them and you want to spend the rest of your life with them. Just because your significant other is the opposite gender as you doesn't mean anything, same if they are the same gender. Also, another thing to point out is religion versus gay marriage. Religion means beliefs. If you believe in something, it's what you think, not what should happen. Especially, some people who believe in God follow the bible and hence believe that gay marriage is immoral and disgusting. But just because a small group of people thinks this way, gay marriage shouldn't be outlawed.

In this work, we provide a corpus created from a new, revised crawl of debate portals covering arguments up to May 2019. As different events spark new debates, it is necessary for an argument search engine to provide up-to-date arguments. For args.me, we build software to automatically extract a list of all debate pages from the portals and to store these pages in the standard web archive format (WARC). These web archive files form the raw data for args.me's indexing pipeline. The debate portals contained in our corpus are (1) idebate.org, (2) debatepedia.org, (3) debatewise.org, and (4) debate.org.

As described by Wachsmuth et al. [17], we model an *argument* as a conclusion, a set of one or more premises, and a pro or con stance of each premise towards the conclusion. From each debate's page, we extract its arguments, the context they come from, and some meta information. The *context* of an argument is the text of the debate in which it was used, the title of the debate, and its URL. In terms of *meta information*, we generate a unique ID for each argument as well as a unique ID for the debate (based on the URL of the web page). We also extract the acquisition time of the debate for provenance. Table 1 shows an example of an argument in the args.me corpus.

Based on the structure of the debates, we developed portal-specific heuristics to extract the text of arguments. We briefly revisit these heuristics here, but refer the reader to the original publication for details [17]. A debate in dialogical portals consists mainly of a title and a sequence of argumentative posts by two opposing parties. In most cases, the title is a claim supported by a party (pro) and contested by the other (con). Heuristically, we consider the title to be the conclusion of an argument and each post to be a premise. The stance of the premise towards the conclusion corresponds to the position of the respective party in the debate. Monological portals require different heuristics. While the debate topics usually also are general claims (e.g., "abortion should be banned"),

Table 2. Statistics of the arguments in the args.me corpus, the arguments whose premise is pro and con towards the conclusion respectively, and the debates from each covered debate portal.

Debate Portal	Count of arguments	Count of pro stance	Count of con stance	Count of debates
Debatewise	14 353	8 514	5 839	693
IDebate.org	13 522	6 839	6 683	618
Debatepedia	21 197	15 791	5 406	236
Debate.org	338 534	168 955	169 579	58 090
$\sum$	**387 606**	200 099	187 507	59 637

the individual contributions to a debate should rather be seen as single arguments (i.e., a conclusion with a premise) organized as pro or con towards the debate's topic.

From the extracted arguments, we remove the ones with conclusions formulated as questions (to favor decisive arguments) and we remove commonplace phrases (e.g., "this house believes that" at the start of arguments).

4   The args.me Corpus

The output of the acquisition process above is the *args.me corpus*, which represents the data basis underlying our argument search engine. Table 2 shows the number of arguments and debates from each debate portal included in the corpus. As shown, debate.org is the dominant source among them, but the other three still add up to about 50 000 arguments in total. In general, pro arguments and con arguments are nearly balanced.

Conclusions can be supported or attacked by multiple arguments. The number of existing arguments in our corpus per conclusion gives a lower bound of the number of arguments that may be retrieved for an input conclusion. To obtain this bound, we grouped arguments that have the same conclusion. The average count of arguments per conclusion in the corpus amounts to 5.5. Figure 2a shows a histogram of the conclusions in our dataset using the count of arguments per conclusion. Most of the conclusions are directly addressed in 1 to 10 arguments, whereas only a few conclusions reach more than 20 arguments, the maximum being 2 838.

Our dataset contains around 60 000 debates to which the arguments have a pro or con stance. The average count of arguments per debate in our dataset amounts to 6.5. Figure 2b shows a histogram of the number of arguments over debates in the args.me corpus. Most debates include 6 to 10 arguments. Again, only a few debates reach more than 20 arguments.

Figures 2c and d show two histograms for the count of conclusions and premises over their length in tokens. As can be seen, there is much variance

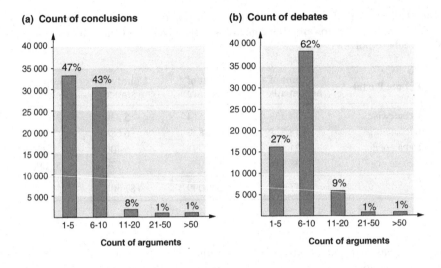

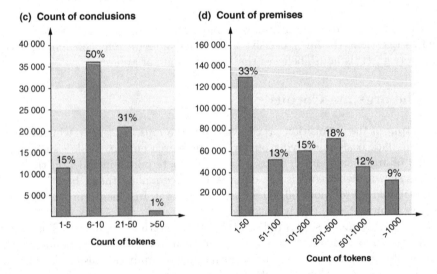

Fig. 2. Histograms illustrating key statistics of the args.me corpus. (a) The number of arguments over conclusions. (b) The number of arguments over debates. (c) The number of conclusions over the count of tokens. (d) The number of premises over the count of tokens.

in the length of both types of argument units. The mean length of conclusions in the corpus is 8.3 tokens, whereas the premises span 293 tokens on average. The high length of the premises in comparison to the conclusions suggests that some of them actually include multiple premises. Since a real argument unit segmentation algorithm is lacking in the args.me framework so far [1], we decided to leave all premises combined, avoiding noise from faulty segmentation.

Table 3. Argument search tasks enabled by the args.me corpus along with their input and output.

Task	Input	Output
Same-side classification	Argument pair	{"same", "opposite"}
Stance classification	{Argument, Topic}	{"pro", "con"}
Argument relation classification	Argument pair	{"support", "attack", "none"}
Argument conclusion generation	Premise	Conclusion

5   Argument Search Tasks

The args.me corpus is meant for studying multiple tasks relevant to argument search in particular, as well as to computational argumentation research in general. While some tasks should be performed online by an argument search engine, others can be performed offline to improve the quality of the corpus or to provide more information to the user. In what follows, we given a brief overview of the tasks for which approaches can be directly developed and evaluated using our corpus, for example, in a supervised machine learning setting. Table 3 lists these tasks along their input and output.

Same-Side Classification. Given two arguments on the same topic, decide whether they have the same or an opposite stance towards it. An argument search engine may address this task at indexing time to reduce noise: For example, if one argument has a clear, unambiguous stance towards a topic, the stance of others may be revised based on a comparison to that argument. Same-side classification can be studied on our corpus, since all its arguments comprise a stance towards their conclusion (i.e., its topic). Using the args.me corpus, we organized the same side stance classification challenge[2] with the goal of fostering the development of classifiers to perform the task.

Stance Classification. Given an argument along with a topic, classify whether the argument is pro or con towards the topic. An argument search engine may address this task online only, when given the topic in the form of a query. This is necessary in order to distinguish pro and con arguments so as to balance bias in the search results. Stance classification can be studied on our corpus similar to same-side classification; any approach to stance classification may also be used for same-side classification.

Argument Relation Classification. Given a pair of arguments, does one argument support or attack the other, or neither. An argument search engine may address this task offline, for instance, to identify counterarguments for a given arguments [18]. Argument relation classification can be studied on our corpus, since the corpus contains arguments whose conclusions represent premises in other arguments.

---

[2] https://sameside.webis.de/.

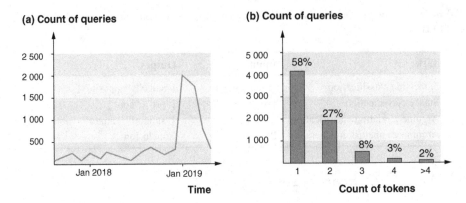

Fig. 3. Statistics of the queries sent to args.me between September 2017 and April 2019: (a) Plot of query distribution over time. (b) Histogram of the queries over their tokens count.

Argument Conclusion Generation. Given the premises of an argument, generate its conclusion. An argument search engine may address this task offline, in order to fill in missing conclusions not available at acquisition time, which may be the case if argument sources other than debate portals are included. Argument conclusion generation can be studied on our corpus, since each argument comes with both a premise and a conclusion.

Naturally, the corpus may also serve several other tasks related to argumentation, but may require additional labels for the arguments. Wachsmuth et al. [17] overview further argument search tasks.

6   First Insights from the args.me Query Log

In this section, we report on an analysis of the args.me query log to provide first insights into what users ask for when looking for arguments. The query log covers all queries that were posted to args.me between September 2017 and May 2019. So far, we assume args.me to be used by researchers mainly, hence the relatively small amount of about 13 000 queries in this period. In addition to the posted free text query, we store for each query an ID derived from the sender's IP address and the query time.

Before our analysis, we removed all queries that originated from our institutes to avoid confusing our analysis with test queries sent during development or presentations of args.me. We also removed all duplicate queries that were sent from the same sender within three seconds, resulting in 7084 queries. Figure 3a shows the distribution of the queries posted to args.me for each month in the covered period. On average, around 393 queries have been submitted per month by external people. The plot shows a peak at the beginning of 2019, where args.me was covered in German news media, suggesting a healthy interest in argument search.

Table 4. (a) Top ten queries found in the args.me query log, and (b) top ten conclusions of arguments in the args.me corpus, each with their absolute and relative frequencies.

(a) Query	Absolute	Relative		(b) Conclusion	Absolute	Relative
climate change	251	3.5%		Abortion	2838	0.7%
feminism	193	2.7%		Gay Marriage	1558	0.4%
abortion	158	2.2%		Rap Battle	1396	0.4%
trump	146	2.0%		Death Penalty	972	0.3%
brexit	128	1.8%		God exists	790	0.2%
death penalty	73	1.0%		Gun control	719	0.1%
google	58	0.8%		Ivf debate	432	0.1%
vegan	57	0.8%		Animal testing	372	0.1%
nuclear energy	56	0.8%		I will not contradict myself	357	0.1%
donald trump	47	0.7%		Euthanasia	331	0.1%

The count of tokens in a query can be seen as an indicator of the specificity and complexity of user information needs. Short queries likely represent a topic, while long queries likely represent a claim or a conclusion. Figure 3b shows the distribution of the queries over their count of tokens. As shown, about 85% of the queries consist of two tokens at most. An example for a topic query is abortion, while a conclusion query may be abortion should be banned. Compared to conclusions which have a specific stance toward a topic, topic queries may indicate that a user seeks to overview both sides' arguments.

We analyzed topic queries sent to args.me in more detail. To identify unambiguous topic queries, we matched the queries in our log with a list of controversial topics extracted from Wikipedia.[3] We found that 20% of the topic queries exactly match one of the Wikipedia topics. The ten most frequently sent queries are listed in Table 4a, along with their absolute count and their relative occurrence among all queries. For comparison, Table 4b lists the ten most frequent conclusions of arguments in the args.me corpus. The comparison between the most frequent queries and conclusions shows some similarities and some divergence between the topics found in our corpus and those that people are interested in. In particular, the top ten queries mostly match controversial topics. Queries such as donald trump, brexit, and global warming are submitted often on args.me, but are not discussed that much in our corpus. Such queries indicate topics for which our corpus should be extended with arguments from other sources in the future.

7   Conclusion

Argument search is a research area that targets the retrieval of arguments (typically "pro" or "con") for queries on controversial topics. Though still in its

---

[3] https://en.wikipedia.org/wiki/Wikipedia:List_of_controversial_issues.

infancy, it has become clear that argument search engines provide a new and effective means to satisfy certain information needs. E.g., an argument search engine can help to compare and assess a user's standpoint since it contrasts both sides of a topic in a probably less biased manner. It can help to effectively close knowledge gaps, among others due do the succinct and concise form of arguments. With args.me, Wachsmuth et al. [17] present such a search engine, which is designed as a pipeline of modular tasks, integrating argument mining, argument matching, and argument ranking.

In this paper we focused on the first step of designing an argument search engine: the acquisition (mining) of arguments. This step includes the choice of argument sources as well as methods to extract the arguments from these sources. We compared the acquisition paradigm of args.me to those of IBM Debater [10] and ArgumenText [14]. The main difference between these approaches can be explained by the following two factors: (1) the level of supervision (high to low: distantly supervised/recognized source/unrestricted web), and (2) the point in time at which important processing steps are executed (offline, at indexing time/online, at query time). Due to the use of distant supervision, args.me can rather easily ensure a high average quality for the indexed arguments—which, however, comes at the price of a restricted recall, since the topics in args.me are limited to those found in debate portals.

We presented the corpus underlying args.me and freely release it for future research. With 387,606 arguments it is (to our knowledge) the currently largest argument resource available for computational argumentation research. Debate portals provide a balanced number of arguments with pro and con stance, a fact that helps to reduce bias in search results. We sketched four standard tasks that can be performed using our corpus and that should be tackled by an argument search engine. The analysis of arg.me's query log reveals that 20% of the queries match well-known controversial topics.

Future research on argument acquisition will focus on finding new argument sources along with tailored extraction methods for them. In this regard, social media and news portals appear promising to us, since they provide a wider and more recent topic coverage than debate portals. However, argument extraction methods for social media and news portals (either automatically or semi-automatically) are largely unexplored as of yet.

References

1. Ajjour, Y., Chen, W.F., Kiesel, J., Wachsmuth, H., Stein, B.: Unit segmentation of argumentative texts. In: Proceedings of the Fourth Workshop on Argument Mining (ArgMining 2017), pp. 118–128
2. Al-Khatib, K., Wachsmuth, H., Hagen, M., Köhler, J., Stein, B.: Cross-domain mining of argumentative text through distant supervision. In: Proceedings of the 15th Conference of the North American Chapter of the Association for Computational Linguistics: Human Language Technologies (NAACL 2016), pp. 1395–1404
3. Al-Khatib, K., Wachsmuth, H., Kiesel, J., Hagen, M., Stein, B.: A news editorial corpus for mining argumentation strategies. In: Proceedings of the 26th International Conference on Computational Linguistics (COLING 2016), pp. 3433–3443

4. Cabrio, E., Villata, S.: Natural language arguments: A combined approach. In: Proceedings of the 20th European Conference on Artificial Intelligence (ECAI 2012), pp. 205–210
5. Croft, W.B., Metzler, D., Strohman, T.: Search Engines - Information Retrieval in Practice. Pearson Education, London (2009)
6. Daxenberger, J., Eger, S., Habernal, I., Stab, C., Gurevych, I.: What is the essence of a claim? Cross-domain claim identification. In: Proceedings of the 2017 Conference on Empirical Methods in Natural Language Processing (EMNLP 2017), pp. 2055–2066
7. Habernal, I., Gurevych, I.: Which argument is more convincing? Analyzing and predicting convincingness of web arguments using bidirectional LSTM. In: Proceedings of the 54th Annual Meeting of the Association for Computational Linguistics (ACL 2016), pp. 1589–1599
8. Lawrence, J., Bex, F., Reed, C., Snaith, M.: AIFdb: Infrastructure for the argument web. In: Proceedings of the Fourth International Conference on Computational Models of Argument (COMMA 2012), pp. 215–516
9. Levy, R., Bilu, Y., Hershcovich, D., Aharoni, E., Slonim, N.: Context dependent claim detection. In: Proceedings of the 25th International Conference on Computational Linguistics: Technical Papers (COLING 2014), pp. 1489–1500
10. Levy, R., Bogin, B., Gretz, S., Aharonov, R., Slonim, N.: Towards an argumentative content search engine using weak supervision. In: Proceedings of the 27th International Conference on Computational Linguistics (COLING 2018), pp. 2066–2081
11. Moens, M.F., Boiy, E., Palau, R.M., Reed, C.: Automatic detection of arguments in legal texts. In: Proceedings of the 11th International Conference on Artificial Intelligence and Law (ICAIL 2007), pp. 225–230
12. Rinott, R., Dankin, L., Perez, C.A., Khapra, M.M., Aharoni, E., Slonim, N.: Show me your evidence – An automatic method for context dependent evidence detection. In: Proceedings of the 2015 Conference on Empirical Methods in Natural Language Processing (EMNLP 2015), pp. 440–450
13. Rosenfeld, A., Kraus, S.: Strategical argumentative agent for human persuasion. In: Proceedings of the 22nd European Conference on Artificial Intelligence (ECAI 2016), pp. 320–328
14. Stab, C., et al.: ArgumentText: searching for arguments in heterogeneous sources. In: Proceedings of 17th Annual Conference of North American Chapter of the Association for Computational Linguistics (NAACL 2018), pp. 2055–2066
15. Stab, C., Gurevych, I.: Identifying argumentative discourse structures in persuasive essays. In: Proceedings of the 2014 Conference on Empirical Methods in Natural Language Processing (EMNLP 2014), pp. 46–56
16. Stab, C., Miller, T., Gurevych, I.: Cross-topic argument mining from heterogeneous sources using attention-based neural networks. In: Proceedings of the 2018 Conference on Empirical Methods in Natural Language Processing (EMNLP 2018), pp. 3664–3674
17. Wachsmuth, H., et al.: Building an argument search engine for the web. In: Proceedings of the Fourth Workshop on Argument Mining (ArgMining 2017), pp. 49–59
18. Wachsmuth, H., Syed, S., Stein, B.: Retrieval of the best counterargument without prior topic knowledge. In: Proceedings of the 56th Annual Meeting of the Association for Computational Linguistics (ACL 2018), pp. 241–251

Monotone and Online Fair Division

Martin Aleksandrov$^{(\boxtimes)}$ and Toby Walsh

Technical University Berlin, Berlin, Germany
{martin.aleksandrov,toby.walsh}@tu-berlin.de

Abstract. We study a new but simple model for online fair division in which indivisible items arrive one-by-one and agents have monotone utilities over bundles of the items. We consider axiomatic properties of mechanisms for this model such as strategy-proofness, envy-freeness and Pareto efficiency. We prove a number of impossibility results that justify why we consider relaxations of the properties, as well as why we consider restricted preference domains on which good axiomatic properties can be achieved. We propose two mechanisms that have good axiomatic fairness properties on restricted but common preference domains.

1 Introduction

Many studies of fair division problems make some simplifying assumptions such as: the problem is offline (i.e. the items and agents are all simultaneously available), and agents have additive utilities over the items. In practice, however, such assumptions may be violated. Recently, Walsh [28] introduced a simple *online* model for the fair division of indivisible items in which, whilst utilities remain additive, the items become available over time and must be allocated to agents immediately. Such an online model has many practical applications. For example, donated kidneys must be allocated to patients as they become available. As a second example, places on university courses open each term and must be allocated before classes begin, and before places open for the following term. As a third example, a charging station might be allocated to a waiting electric car immediately it is freed up. And, as a fourth example, perishable items donated to a food bank might have to be allocated to charities feeding the poor immediately. As a fifth example, when allocating memory to cloud services, we may not know what and how many services are requested in the next moment.

In this paper, we relax this model of online fair division to deal with monotone utilities. There are many settings where utilities might not be additive. For instance, agents may have diminishing returns for multiple copies of an item. You may, for example, gain less utility for a second bicycle. Agents may also have complementarities. You may, for example, get little utility for the cricket bat unless you also get the cricket ball. We thus consider a model of online fair division in which agents have monotone but possibly non-additive utilities. Indeed, monotone utilities are especially challenging in an online setting. As utilities may not be additive, we cannot allocate items independently of previous or, more problematically, of future items. Suppose agent 1 only likes item a in

© Springer Nature Switzerland AG 2019
C. Benzmüller and H. Stuckenschmidt (Eds.): KI 2019, LNAI 11793, pp. 60–75, 2019.
https://doi.org/10.1007/978-3-030-30179-8_5

the presence of item b, whilst agent 2 only likes a in the presence of c. Then the decision to give item a to agent 1 or 2 may depend on whether items b or c will arrive in the future, which we suppose is not known.

We define firstly the model of online fair division with monotone utilities and propose to consider non-wasteful marginal mechanisms for it. We then show that no non-wasteful mechanism can guarantee simple axiomatic properties such as strategy-proofness, envy-freeness (even approximately) or Pareto efficiency under weak conditions, whilst that was possible with additive utilities. We then consider monotone utilities with non-zero marginals. In the offline setting, this is a natural class of restricted preferences in which agents are assumed to prefer always having an item to not having it, supposing that their marginal utility for it could be arbitrarily small. We prove that many axiomatic properties can be achieved in this domain. We also consider a weaker form of strategy-proofness adapted to our online setting that supposes agents only have knowledge of the current item, and not of any future items that might or might not arrive. Finally, we propose two mechanisms - the MINIMUM LIKE and MINIMUM UTILITY mechanisms - and prove that they satisfy this weaker form of strategy-proofness as well as envy-freeness up to some item in common domains with identical utilities.

2   Related Work

Our model of online fair division with monotone utilities generalizes an existing model of online fair division with additive utilities introduced in [28]. Aleksandrov et al. [1] analysed two simple randomized mechanisms for this model, called LIKE and BALANCED LIKE. The LIKE mechanism allocates an incoming item uniformly at random to one of the agents that declares non-zero bid for it. This is strategy-proof and envy-free in expectation. The BALANCED LIKE mechanism allocates an incoming item to an agent with the fewest items currently amongst those that declare non-zero bids for the incoming item. With 0/1 utilities, this bounds the envy of agents, and is strategy-proof for 2 but not more agents. Some other online mechanisms (e.g. MAXIMUM LIKE) that are Pareto efficient ex post and ex ante are considered in [3]. We can extend these to mechanisms for monotone but not necessarily additive utilities by allocating an incoming item to one of the agents that declares a non-zero marginal bid for the item. However, we prove that none of these mechanisms or even any other mechanism is strategy-proof, envy-free or Pareto efficient in our setting with monotone utilities.

Further, for the model with additive utilities, Benade et al. [9] showed that the random assignment of each next item (i.e. LIKE) diminishes the envy over time. By comparison, we prove that approximations of envy-freeness ex post such as EF1 (see [12]) and EFX (see [13]) cannot be satisfied in our monotone setting. On the other hand, we further prove that EF1 can only be satisfied in two restricted but common preference domains of identical utilities. We also contrast our results with similar results in (offline) fair division. For example, it remains an open question if offline EFX allocations exist in general. We prove that no mechanism for online fair division can return such allocations even when they exist. This holds with identical additive utilities in which domain there are offline algorithms that return such allocations [8]. Further, we can show that some other (offline) characterizations (e.g. [10,24]) break in the online setting. In contrast, our results can be mapped to offline settings as online mechanisms can be applied to offline problems by presenting the items in some (perhaps random) order.

There are other related models. For example, Walsh [27] has proposed a different online model in which items are divisible (not indivisible) and agents (not items) arrive over time. Also, Kash, Procaccia and Shah [22] have proposed a dynamic model of fair division in which agents again arrive over time, but there are multiple homogeneous (not heterogeneous) and divisible items. There is also a connection between our consideration of marginal bidding and the one for auctions that has been made by Greenwald and Boyan in [20]. One interesting difference between our work and theirs is that marginal utility bidding is an optimal strategy for sequential auctions whereas, as we prove, it may not be for online mechanisms. Finally, other related works in fair division (e.g. [2,4,18,21]), voting (e.g. [15,19,29]) and kidney exchange (e.g. [16,17]) exist. However, to the best of our knowledge, our results do not follow from any existing results.

3   Monotone and Online Fair Division

We consider an online fair division problem with *agents* from $[n] = \{1, \ldots, n\}$ and *indivisible items* from $O = \{o_1, \ldots, o_m\}$, where $m \in \mathbb{N}_{\geq 1}$. WLOG, we suppose that items arrive one-by-one from o_1 to o_m. Thus, we write O_j for the subset of O of the first j items. We suppose that agents have bundle utilities. We write $u_i(B) \in \mathbb{R}_{\geq 0}$ for the *(private) utility* of $i \in [n]$ for each $B \subseteq O$. We also write $u_i(o)$ for $u_i(\{o\})$. We suppose $u_i(\emptyset) = 0$. We say that the agents have *identical utilities* iff, for each $i, k \in [n]$ and $B \subseteq O$, $u_i(B) = u_k(B)$. In this case, we write $u(B)$ for $u_i(B)$. We further write $u_i(B \cup \{o\}) - u_i(B)$ for the *marginal utility* of $i \in [n]$ for each $B \subset O$ and $o \in O \setminus B$. We say that this marginal utility is *general* iff $u_i(B \cup \{o\}) - u_i(B) \in \mathbb{R}_{\geq 0}$, and *non-zero* iff $u_i(B \cup \{o\}) - u_i(B) \in \mathbb{R}_{>0}$. We write $\pi = (\pi_1, \ldots, \pi_n)$ for an allocation of the items from B to the agents, where $\cup_{i \in [n]} \pi_i = B$ and $\pi_i \cap \pi_j = \emptyset$ for $i, j \in [n]$ with $i \neq j$. And, we let $\Pi_j = \{\pi | \pi \text{ is an allocation with } \cup_{i \in [n]} \pi_i = O_j\}$.

We consider *online* mechanisms that allocate each next item without the knowledge of any future items. We focus on *non-wasteful* mechanisms that allocate items to agents that declare non-zero marginal utility for item o_j, if there are such agents. At round 1, each agent $i \in [n]$ becomes aware of their marginal utility $u_i(o_1)$ for o_1. And, at round jth $(j > 1)$, each agent i becomes aware of their marginal utility $u_i = u_i(\pi_i \cup \{o_j\}) - u_i(\pi_i)$ for o_j where $\pi \in \Pi_{j-1}$ is some allocation of the first $(j-1)$ items. The mechanism firstly asks each $i \in [n]$ for a marginal bid v_i for o_j. Agents may act strategically and bid insincerely, i.e. v_i may be different from u_i. We say that i *likes* o_j if $u_i > 0$. The mechanism secondly shares the probability of 1 for o_j among those who make non-zero marginal bids. If there are no such agents, o_j is allocated at random.

A mechanism thus returns a probability distribution over the allocations in Π_j. We write $\Delta_j = (p(\pi)|\pi \in \Pi_j)$ for it, where $p(\pi) \in [0,1]$ is the probability of $\pi \in \Pi_j$. We have that $\sum_{\pi \in \Pi_j} p(\pi) = 1$. We write $u_i(\pi_k)$ for the *monotone utility* of agent i for the items of agent k in π. We write $\overline{u}_{ik}(\Pi_j)$ for the *expected utility* of agent i for the expected allocation of agent k in Π_j. We have $\overline{u}_{ik}(\Pi_j) = \sum_{\pi \in \Pi_j} p(\pi) \cdot u_i(\pi_k)$. We also write sometime $u_i(\pi)$ for $u_i(\pi_i)$ and $\overline{u}_i(\Pi_j)$ for $\overline{u}_{ii}(\Pi_j)$. Finally, we say that $u_i(\pi_k)$ is *additive* iff it is $\sum_{o \in \pi_k} u_i(o)$. In this case, the expected utility of agent i for the expected allocation of agent k in Π_j is also additive. That is, $\overline{u}_{ik}(\Pi_j) = \overline{u}_{ik}(\Pi_{j-1}) + \sum_{\pi \in \Pi_j} p(\pi) \cdot u_i(o_j)$.

4   Axiomatic Properties

Three fundamental axiomatic properties of mechanisms for our setting concern the incentives of agents to bid strategically for an allocation, the fairness of an allocation and the economic efficiency of an allocation.

Definition 1 (Strategy-proofness, SP). *A mechanism is SP in a problem with m items if, with complete information of o_1 to o_m, no agent i can strictly increase $\overline{u}_i(\Pi_m)$ by misreporting $u_i(\pi_i \cup \{o_j\}) - u_i(\pi_i)$ for one or more item o_j and allocation $\pi \in \Pi_{j-1}$, supposing that every other agent $k \neq i$ bid sincerely their marginal utilities for items o_1 to o_m.*

Definition 2 (Envy-freeness, EF). *A mechanism is EF ex post (EFP) in a problem with m items if, for each $\pi \in \Pi_m$ with $p(\pi) > 0$, no agent i envies another agent k, i.e. $\forall i, k : u_i(\pi_i) \geq u_i(\pi_k)$. It is EF ex ante (EFA) in a problem with m items if no agent i envies another agent k in expectation, i.e. $\forall i, k : \overline{u}_{ii}(\Pi_m) \geq \overline{u}_{ik}(\Pi_m)$.*

Definition 3 (Pareto efficiency, PE). *A mechanism is PE ex post (PEP) in a problem with m items if, for each $\pi \in \Pi_m$ with $p(\pi) > 0$, no $\pi' \in \Pi_m$ is such that $\forall i : u_i(\pi'_i) \geq u_i(\pi_i)$ and $\exists k : u_k(\pi'_k) > u_k(\pi_k)$. It is PE ex ante (PEA) in a problem with m items if, no other probability distribution over the allocations in Π_m gives to each agent i at least $\overline{u}_i(\Pi_m)$ and to some agent k strictly more than $\overline{u}_k(\Pi_m)$.*

We say that a mechanism satisfies a given property **P** iff, for each $m \in \mathbb{N}$, it satisfies **P** on each problem with m items. We are interested in mechanisms for our model that satisfy combinations of these three properties.

5   General Marginal Utilities

We start with general marginal utilities. As we argued earlier, the monotone and online nature of our problem makes it more difficult to achieve nice axiomatic properties. Indeed, we will show that *no* mechanism is strategy-proof, envy-free or Pareto efficient even in very limited utility domains, e.g. monotone utilities with binary marginals, identical monotone utilities, etc.

5.1   Strategy-Proofness

We prove firstly that strategy-proofness is impossible in general. The problem here is that the marginal utility of an agent for an item may depend on their allocation of past items, and thus so is their probability for the item (in a given allocation). We illustrate this in Example 1.

Example 1. *Let us consider the online fair division problem with 2 agents and $O = \{o_1, o_2\}$. Further, let $u_1(\emptyset) = 0, u_1(\{o_1\}) = 2, u_1(\{o_2\}) = 4, u_1(O) = 6$ and $u_2(\emptyset) = 0, u_2(\{o_1\}) = 5, u_2(\{o_2\}) = 2, u_2(O) = 5$. If agent 1 gets o_1, the marginal utilities of agents 1 and 2 for o_2 are 4 (i.e. $u_1(O) - u_1(\{o_1\})$) and 2 (i.e. $u_2(\{o_2\}) - u_2(\emptyset)$). If agent 2 gets o_1, the marginal utilities of agents 1 and 2 for o_2 are 4 (i.e. $u_1(\{o_2\}) - u_1(\emptyset)$) and 0 (i.e. $u_2(O) - u_2(\{o_1\})$).* ◇

It might, therefore, be beneficial for an agent to report strategically a marginal utility of zero for the current item in order to increase their chance for their most favourite bundle of future items. Indeed, for this reason, *no* mechanism is strategy-proof even with very restricted preferences. This contrasts with the case of additive utilities where, for example, the LIKE mechanism is strategy-proof [1].

Theorem 1. *No non-wasteful mechanism for online fair division is strategy-proof, even with identical monotone utilities with 0/1 marginals.*

Proof. Consider agents 1 and 2, items o_1 to o_3 and ordering (o_1, o_2, o_3). The utilities are identical for each $B \subseteq O$. If $|B| = 1$, let $u(B)$ be 1. If $|B| = 2$, let $u(B)$ be 2 if $B = \{o_2, o_3\}$ and 1 otherwise. Also, let $u(O) = 2$. Suppose agents are sincere and the mechanism gives o_1 to agent 1 with $p \in [0, 1]$ and to agent 2 with $(1 - p)$. We consider three cases. In the first case, the mechanism is randomized and $p \in (0, 1)$. If it gives o_1 to agent 1 with p, then it gives o_2 and o_3 to agent 2 with probability 1. If it gives o_1 to agent 2 with $(1 - p) \in (0, 1)$, then it gives o_2 and o_3 to agent 1 with probability 1. Therefore, the expected utility of agent 1 is equal to $(2 - p)$. Suppose next that agent 1 report strategically 0 for o_1. As the mechanism is non-wasteful, it gives o_1 to agent 2 and o_2 and o_3 to agent 1 with probability 1. The (expected) utility of agent 1 is equal to 2. This outcome is strictly greater than $(2 - p)$ as $p \in (0, 1)$. In the second case, the mechanism is deterministic and $p = 0$. The mechanism gives o_1 to agent 2 and o_2 and o_3 to agent 1 with probability 1. The (expected) utility of agent 2 is 1. Suppose next that agent 2 report strategically 0 for o_1. The mechanism gives o_1 to agent 1 and o_2 and o_3 to agent 2 with probability 1. The (expected) utility of agent 2 is 2. This is a strict improvement. Analogously, for the third case when $p = 1$. ◇

5.2   Envy-Freeeness

We next confirm that *no* mechanism exists which is guaranteed to return envy-free allocations even in ex ante sense, supposing agents bid sincerely. The key idea behind this result is that a given agent may like a given bundle of items but not the individual items in the bundle. By comparison, with additive utilities, the LIKE mechanism for example is envy-free ex ante [1].

Theorem 2. *No non-wasteful mechanism for online fair division is envy-free ex post or even ex ante, even with monotone utilities with 0/1 marginals.*

Proof. Let us consider agents 1 and 2, items o_1 and o_2 arriving from (o_1, o_2). Consider $u_1(\emptyset) = u_1(\{o_1\}) = u_1(\{o_2\}) = 0, u_1(O) = 1$ and $u_2(\emptyset) = 0, u_2(\{o_1\}) = u_2(\{o_2\}) = 1, u_2(O) = 2$. We note that an envy-free (offline) allocation gives one item to each agent. However, an online and non-wasteful mechanism gives deterministically both items to agent 2. Hence, agent 1 envies agent 2. ◇

Interestingly, with identical monotone utilities, a distribution of allocations that is envy-free in expectation can always be returned. For example, consider the non-wasteful mechanism that allocates the current item to an agent who makes a non-zero marginal bid for it and so far has been allocated items with the least declared utility.

MINIMUM LIKE: At round $j \in [m]$, given $\pi \in \Pi_{j-1}$, we let Like $= \{i | v_i(\pi_i \cup \{o_j\}) > v_i(\pi_i)\}$ and MinLike $= \{i | i \in \text{Like}, v_i(\pi_i) = \min_{k \in \text{Like}} v_k(\pi_k)\}$. The mechanism gives o_j to some $i \in$ MinLike with probability $(1/|\text{MinLike}|)$ if MinLike $\neq \emptyset$ and, otherwise, to some $i \in [n]$ with probability $1/n$.

Theorem 3. *With identical monotone utilities, the non-wasteful MINIMUM LIKE mechanism is envy-free ex ante.*

Proof. The proof of the result hinges on any pair of agents getting a particular bundle of items with the same probability. Pick agents i, k. We show $\bar{u}_{ii}(\Pi_j) \geq \bar{u}_{ik}(\Pi_j)$ for $j \in [1, m]$. Let $\Delta \bar{u}_{ikj} = \bar{u}_{ii}(\Pi_j) - \bar{u}_{ik}(\Pi_j)$. We have $\Delta \bar{u}_{ikj} = \sum_\pi p(\pi) \cdot u_i(\pi_i) - \sum_\pi p(\pi) \cdot u_i(\pi_k)$ where $\pi \in \Pi_j$. We derive the below expression for $\Delta \bar{u}_{ikj}$.

$$\Delta \bar{u}_{ikj} = \sum_{A \subseteq O, B \subseteq O \setminus A} \left(\sum_{\pi_i = A, \pi_k = B} p(\pi) \cdot u_i(A) + \sum_{\pi_i = B, \pi_k = A} p(\pi) \cdot u_i(B) \right. $$
$$\left. - \sum_{\pi_i = A, \pi_k = B} p(\pi) \cdot u_i(B) - \sum_{\pi_i = B, \pi_k = A} p(\pi) \cdot u_i(A) \right)$$

Pick an allocation $\pi \in \Pi_j$. Let agent i get $A \subseteq O$, agent $k \neq i$ get $B \subseteq O \setminus A$ and each other agent $h \neq i, k$ get π_h in π. By the symmetry of the utilities, there is another allocation, say $\pi' \in \Pi_j$, such that i get B, k get A and h get π_h. With MINIMUM LIKE, $p(\pi') = p(\pi)$. Moreover, with this mechanism, the number of returned allocations that give A to i and B to k is equal to the number of returned allocations that give B to i and A to k. Therefore, we derive $\Delta \bar{u}_{ikj} = 0$ for each $j \in [m]$. ◇

Further, we consider two common approximations of envy-freeness ex post: EF1 and EFX [11,13]. However, many other such approximations that are stronger than EF1 have been studied in the recent years, e.g. GMMS, PMMS, EFL [5–7].

Definition 4 (EF up to some item, EF1). *A mechanism is* EF1 *if, for each* $\pi \in \Pi_m$ *with* $p(\pi) > 0$, *for all* i, k *with* $\pi_k \neq \emptyset$, $\exists o \in \pi_k$ *with* $u_i(\pi_i) \geq u_i(\pi_k \backslash \{o\})$.

Definition 5 (EF up to any item, EFX). *A mechanism is* EFX *if, for each* $\pi \in \Pi_m$ *with* $p(\pi) > 0$, *for all* $i, k, o \in \pi_k$ *with* $u_i(o) > 0$, $u_i(\pi_i) \geq u_i(\pi_k \backslash \{o\})$.

Unfortunately, we cannot guarantee to only return allocations that are even envy-free up to some item. This holds under very strong restrictions on the preference domain. Consequently, there are *no* EF1 (and, therefore, GMMS, PMMS or EFL) mechanisms for our setting in general.

Theorem 4. *No non-wasteful mechanism for online fair division is EF1, even with identical monotone utilities with 0/1 marginals.*

Proof. Consider agents 1 and 2, items o_1 to o_4 and ordering (o_1, o_2, o_3, o_4). Let $B \subseteq O$. If $|B| = 1$, let $u(B) = 1$. If $|B| = 2$ and $o_1 \in B$, let $u(B) = 1$. If $|B| = 2$ and $o_1 \notin B$, let $u(B) = 2$. If $|B| = 3$ and $B = \{o_2, o_3, o_4\}$, let $u(B) = 3$. If $|B| = 3$ and $B \neq \{o_2, o_3, o_4\}$, let $u(B) = 2$. Also, let $u(O) = 3$. By these preferences, a non-wasteful mechanism gives o_1 to agent 1 and o_2, o_3, o_4 to agent 2, or o_1 to agent 2 and o_2, o_3, o_4 to agent 1. WLOG, let agent 1 get o_1 and agent 2 get o_2, o_3, o_4. The utilities of agents 1 and 2 in this allocation are 1 and 3 respectively. The allocation is not envy-free because agent 1 envies agent 2. Moreover, the envy of agent 1 remains even after the removal of any single item from the bundle of agent 2. Consequently, the allocation is not EF1. However, we note that an EF1 (offline) allocation gives two items to each agent. $\diamond$

By Theorem 4, the MINIMUM LIKE mechanism is not EF1. The result in Theorem 4 also contrasts with the offline setting where, with general monotone utilities, an EF1 allocation, bounding the envy from above by the maximum marginal utility of any agent for any item, can always be achieved [23, 26].

5.3 Pareto Efficiency

We lastly consider Pareto efficiency supposing agents bid sincerely. In the offline setting with general monotone utilities, Pareto efficiency is guaranteed [14, 25]. In our setting, we show that there is *no* mechanism that is Pareto efficient, even just ex ante.

Theorem 5. *No non-wasteful mechanism for online fair division is Pareto efficient ex post or even ex ante, even with identical monotone utilities.*

Proof. Consider agents 1 and 2, items o_1 to o_4 and ordering (o_1, o_2, o_3, o_4). The utilities are identical for each $B \subseteq O$. If $|B| = 1$, let $u(B)$ be 2 if $B = \{o_3\}$ or $B = \{o_4\}$, and 1 otherwise. If $|B| = 2$, let $u(B)$ be 1 if $B = \{o_1, o_2\}$ and 2 otherwise. If $|B| = 3$, let $u(B)$ be 3 if $B = \{o_1, o_2, o_4\}$ and 2 otherwise. Also, let $u(\emptyset) = 0$ and $u(O) = 3$. Further, consider below all possible allocations.

$$o_1 \nearrow \overset{p}{} o_2 \overset{1}{-----} o_3 \nearrow \overset{r}{} o_4 \; ------ \; 1 \; (\{o_2,o_4\},\{o_1,o_3\})$$

o_1, p, o_2, o_3, r, o_4, 1 — $(\{o_2, o_4\}, \{o_1, o_3\})$

o_4 — 1 — $(\{o_2, o_3\}, \{o_1, o_4\})$

o_2 — 1 — o_3, q, o_4 — 1 — $(\{o_1, o_4\}, \{o_2, o_3\})$

o_4 — 1 — $(\{o_1, o_3\}, \{o_2, o_4\})$

Key: agent 1-dashed line, agent 2-solid line

Each mechanism induces some probabilities $p, r, q \in [0, 1]$. Such a mechanism allocates deterministically o_2 and o_4 to agents. For example, suppose that agent 2 get o_1 with probability p. Then, agent 1 gets o_2 with probability 1. Suppose that agent 2 gets o_3 with probability r. Then, agent 1 gets o_4 with probability 1. Each agent receives utility of 2 in each of the four allocations. Hence, the agents' (expected) utilities are both equal to 2. These allocations are Pareto dominated by $(\{o_1, o_2, o_4\}, \{o_3\})$ in which agents 1 and 2 get utilities 3 and 2 respectively. The result follows. ◇

6 Non-zero Marginal Utilities

We continue with non-zero marginal utilities. Interestingly, we can achieve most axiomatic properties in this domain. Suppose we are interested in strategy-proofness, Pareto efficiency ex post and ex ante. Consider a simple mechanism that gives deterministically each next item to some fixed agent, say $i \in [n]$. Potentially, agent i may wish to manipule the outcome. However, they then could only receive less items and, therefore, strictly less utility. Consequently, this mechanism is strategy-proof and, for the same reason, it is Pareto efficient even ex ante. Suppose we wish to achieve strategy-proofness, Pareto efficiency ex post and envy-freeness ex ante. Consider a mechanism that picks an agent, say $i \in [n]$, uniformly at random with probability $\frac{1}{n}$ and then gives deterministically each next item to i. This mechanism is strategy-proof and Pareto efficient ex post for the reasons that we mentioned above. It is further envy-free ex ante as it returns a distribution of n allocations (say π^i for $i \in [n]$ that occurs with probability $\frac{1}{n}$ and, WLOG, gives all items to agent i) in which the expected utility of an agent for their own allocation and the allocation of another agent is the same.

Unfortunately, both of the above mechanisms are unappealing because they give all items to some agent. Therefore, they are not EFX or even just EF1. In our online and monotone setting, there are *no* mechanisms that are EF1 even when the utilities are positive and additive, a special case of non-zero marginal utilities.

Theorem 6. *No mechanism for online fair division is EF1, even with positive additive utilities.*

68 M. Aleksandrov and T. Walsh

Proof. Let us consider agents 1 and 2, items o_1 to o_3 and ordering (o_1, o_2, o_3). Further, consider a mechanism and suppose that it is EF1. We consider two cases. In the first one, we assume that it gives o_1 to agent 1 with positive probability. Then, the utilities of agents for items are given in the below table.

	o_1	o_2	o_3
Agent 1	50	100	100
Agent 2	100	50	100

WLOG, we can assume that the mechanism allocates o_1 at the first round. As it is EF1, it gives o_2 to agent 2. Given this partial allocation, there are only two possible allocations of o_3, resulting in $(\{o_1, o_3\}, \{o_2\})$ and $(\{o_1\}, \{o_2, o_3\})$. It is easy to check that none of them is EF1.

In the second case, we assume that the mechanism gives o_1 to agent 2 with probability 1. Then, we consider different utilities of the agents for items o_2 and o_3. These are given in the below table.

	o_1	o_2	o_3
Agent 1	50	40	410
Agent 2	100	200	200

The mechanism gives o_1 to agent 2. As it is EF1, it would then give o_2 to agent 1. Given this partial allocation, the only two possible allocations after the third round are $(\{o_2\}, \{o_1, o_3\})$ and $(\{o_2, o_3\}, \{o_1\})$. It is easy to check that neither of them is EF1. ◇

In contrast, a simple *round-robin* procedure returns an EF1 allocation in the offline setting with general additive utilities [13]. There is some more hope for restricted preference domains on which to achieve EF1. For example, EF1 can be guaranteed in the special case of identical monotone utilities with non-zero marginals.

Theorem 7. *With identical monotone utilities with non-zero marginals, the non-wasteful* MINIMUM LIKE *mechanism is EF1.*

Proof. We use induction on $j \in [m]$. In the base case, the allocation of o_1 is trivially EF1. In the step case, the induction hypothesis requires that $\pi \in \Pi_{j-1}$ with $p(\pi) > 0$ is EF1. Let $1 \in \text{MinLike}$ and the mechanism allocate o_j to agent 1 given π. Consider $\pi' = (\pi'_1, \ldots, \pi'_n)$ where $\pi'_1 = \pi_1 \cup \{o_j\}$ and $\pi'_i = \pi_i$ for each $i \neq 1$. We next show that π' is EF1. We note that the set $\text{Like} = [n]$ as the agents' marginal utilities are non-zero.

Case 1: Suppose $i \neq 1$ and $k \neq 1$. We have $u_i(\pi_i') = u_i(\pi_i)$ and $u_k(\pi_k') = u_k(\pi_k)$ as $\pi_i' = \pi_i$ and $\pi_k' = \pi_k$. By the hypothesis, we have $u_i(\pi_i) \geq u_i(\pi_k \setminus \{o\})$ for some $o \in \pi_k \neq \emptyset$. Hence, $u_i(\pi_i') \geq u_i(\pi_k' \setminus \{o\})$ holds. Or, agent i is EF1 of agent k in π'.

Case 2: Suppose $i \neq 1$ and $k = 1 \in$ MinLike. We have $u_i(\pi_i') = u_i(\pi_i)$ as $\pi_i' = \pi_i$. By the mechanism, we have $u_i(\pi_i) \geq u_1(\pi_1)$. As the utilities are identical, we have $u_1(\pi_1) = u_i(\pi_1)$. Hence, $u_i(\pi_i) \geq u_i(\pi_1)$, or agent i is envy-free of agent 1 in π. We derive $u_i(\pi_i') \geq u_i(\pi_1) = u_i(\pi_1' \setminus \{o_j\})$ as $\pi_1' = \pi_1 \cup \{o_j\}$. Hence, agent i is EF1 of agent 1 in π'.

Case 3: Suppose that $i = 1 \in$ MinLike and $k \neq 1$. We have $u_1(\pi_1') > u_1(\pi_1)$ as $\pi_1' = \pi_1 \cup \{o_j\}$ and the utilities are with non-zero marginals. By the hypothesis, $u_1(\pi_1) \geq u_1(\pi_k \setminus \{o\})$ for some $o \in \pi_k \neq \emptyset$. Hence, $u_1(\pi_1') > u_1(\pi_k \setminus \{o\}) = u_1(\pi_k' \setminus \{o\})$ as $\pi_k' = \pi_k$. Therefore, agent 1 is EF1 of agent k in π'. ◇

By Theorem 3, the MINIMUM LIKE mechanism is envy-free ex ante with identical monotone utilities with non-zero marginals. However, it is not strategy-proof. In fact, *no* other EF1 mechanism satisfies this property.

Theorem 8. *No mechanism for online fair division is EF1 and strategy-proof, even with identical additive utilities.*

Proof. Let us consider two agents, items o_1 and o_2 arriving in (o_1, o_2). Further, let both agents value o_1 with 1 and o_2 with 2. We consider two cases. In the first one, suppose that the mechanism is randomized and allocates o_1 to agent 1 with probability $p \in (0,1)$ supposing agents 1 and 2 declare their sincere utilities for o_1 and o_2. Suppose it gives o_1 to agent 1. As the mechanism is EF1, it must give o_2 to agent 2 with probability of 1. Suppose it gives o_1 to agent 2. As the mechanism is EF1, it must give o_2 to agent 1 with probability of 1. Hence, agent 1 receives expected utility $(2-p)$. If agent 1 report strategically 0 for o_1, then the mechanism gives o_1 to agent 2 and o_2 to agent 1 with probability 1. The expected utility of agent 1 is now 2 which is strictly higher than $(2-p)$ as $p > 0$. Hence, the mechanism is not strategy-proof. In the second case, suppose that the mechanism is deterministic and allocates o_1 to agent 1 with probability 1. Therefore, as it is EF1, it then allocates o_2 to agent 2 again with probability 1. The utility of agent 1 in this returned allocation is 1. If agent 1 report strategically 0 for o_1, then the mechanism swaps the items of the agents. The utility of agent 1 is now 2. This is a strict improvement. We reached contradictions in both cases.◇

By Theorems 3 and 8, we conclude that the MINIMUM LIKE mechanism returns an EF1 and envy-free ex ante allocation with identical additive utilities. In this case, the agents' utilities in each allocation is equal to the total sum of an agent's utilities for the items. For this reason, the mechanism is also Pareto efficient ex post and ex ante in this case. Unfortunately, this no longer holds whenever the utilities are monotone.

Theorem 9. *No mechanism for online fair division is EF1 and Pareto efficient ex post or even ex ante, even with identical monotone utilities with non-zero marginals.*

Proof. Let us consider two agents, items o_1 to o_3 arriving in (o_1, o_2, o_3). The utilities are given in the below table.

	o_1	o_2	o_3	$\{o_1, o_2\}$	$\{o_1, o_3\}$	$\{o_2, o_3\}$	O
Agent 1	1	2	3	4	4	4	5
Agent 2	1	2	3	4	4	4	5

Let us consider a mechanism that gives item o_1 to agent 1 with probability $p \in [0, 1]$. Suppose agent 1 receives item o_1. As the mechanism is EF1, it then gives deterministically item o_2 to agent 2 and item o_3 to agent 1. Hence, the allocation $\pi_1 = (\{o_1, o_3\}, \{o_2\})$ is returned with probability p. Suppose agent 2 receives item o_1. By the symmetry of the preferences, we conclude that the allocation $\pi_2 = (\{o_2\}, \{o_1, o_3\})$ is returned with probability $(1 - p)$. We observe that π_1 is Pareto dominated by $\pi_3 = (\{o_1, o_2\}, \{o_3\})$ and π_2 is Pareto dominated by $\pi_4 = (\{o_3\}, \{o_1, o_2\})$. Hence, the mechanism is not Pareto efficient ex post. Further, with the mechanism, the expected utilities of agents 1 abd 2 are $(2+2 \cdot p)$ and $(4 - 2 \cdot p)$ respectively. For $p \geq [\frac{1}{2}, 1)$, the first of these outcomes is less than 4 and the second one is at most 3. For $p = 1$, they are 4 and 2. These expected allocations are Pareto dominated by π_3 in which agent 1 receive utility 4 and agent 2 receive utility 3. For $p \in (0, \frac{1}{2})$, the first expected outcome is less than 3 and the second one is less than 4. For $p = 0$, they are 2 and 4. These expected allocations are Pareto dominated by π_4 in which agent 1 receive utility 3 and agent 2 receive utility 4. Hence, the mechanism is not Pareto efficient ex ante. ◇

In the offline setting, an EF1 (even EFX) and Pareto efficient ex post (and, therefore, Pareto efficient ex ante) allocation can always be returned with identical monotone utilities whose marginals are non-zero [26]. Further, by Theorem 6, we cannot even hope for mechanisms that satisfy the stronger concept of EFX with positive additive utilities. In fact, this holds even in the more special case of identical utilities. This contrasts with the offline setting [8].

Theorem 10. *No mechanism for online fair division is EFX, even with identical additive utilities.*

Proof. Consider agents 1 and 2, items o_1 to o_3 and (o_1, o_2, o_3). For $i \in \{1, 2, 3\}$, let each agent have utility i for item o_i. We note that two EFX allocations exist: $(\{o_1, o_2\}, \{o_3\})$ and $(\{o_3\}, \{o_1, o_2\})$. Consider a non-wasteful mechanism and suppose that it is EFX. Hence, it would give o_1 and o_2 to different agents because it is online and cannot predict that o_3 will also arrive. WLOG, let agent 1 get o_1 and agent 2 get o_2. Given this allocation, it is easy to see that any allocation of o_3 leads to a violation of EFX. ◇

7 Extensions

In this section, we consider several extensions of our work as a response to our impossibility results in the previous sections, that highlight the technical difficulty of our online and monotone setting.

7.1 Online Strategy-Proofness

In deciding if agents have any incentive to misreport preferences in an online setting, we may consider the past fixed but the future unknown. Indeed, we might not know what items will arrive next, or even if any more items will arrive. This leads to a *new* and weaker form of *online strategy-proofness*.

Definition 6 (Online strategy-proofness, OSP). *A mechanism is* OSP *in a problem with m items if, for each item $o_j \in O$, fixed information of o_1 to o_{j-1} and no information of o_{j+1} to o_m, no agent i can strictly increase $\overline{u}_i(\Pi_j)$ by misreporting $u_i(\pi_i \cup \{o_j\}) - u_i(\pi_i)$ given any allocation $\pi \in \Pi_{j-1}$, supposing that agent i bid sincerely their marginal utilities for o_1 to o_{j-1} and each agent $k \neq i$ bid sincerely their marginal utilities for o_1 to o_j.*

Interestingly, the MINIMUM LIKE mechanism is online strategy-proof. The key idea is that the probability of an agent for each next item given an allocation of the past items is constant for each their positive marginal bid, supposing all other bids are fixed.

Theorem 11. *The non-wasteful* MINIMUM LIKE *mechanism is online strategy-proof.*

Proof. Consider a problem of m items. Let us pick an arbitrary round $j \in [m]$, allocation $\pi \in \Pi_{j-1}$ and agent $i \in [n]$. We consider two cases. In the first one, $i \notin$ MinLike. Then, this agent cannot increase $\overline{u}_i(\Pi_j)$ by misreporting $u_i(\pi_i \cup \{o_j\}) - u_i(\pi_i)$ because, for any such misreported value, they remain outside MinLike. In the second case, $i \in$ MinLike. Hence, they receive o_j with probability $1/|\text{MinLike}|$ supposing they bid $u_i(\pi_i \cup \{o_j\}) - u_i(\pi_i)$ that is positive. In fact, this holds for any other positive marginal bid that they report for this item. However, this probability becomes 0 whenever they report zero marginal bid for the item. We conclude that $\overline{u}_i(\Pi_j)$ cannot increase. ◇

7.2 Wasteful Mechanisms

We say that a mechanism is *wasteful* iff it is not non-wasteful. Clearly, *no* wasteful mechanism is Pareto efficient ex post or even ex ante simply because one can improve the outcome of the mechanism by taking an item that is allocated to an agent who report a zero marginal bid for it and giving it to some other agent who make a positive marginal bid for the item. We, therefore, focus on envy-freeness and strategy-proofness. Let us consider the *uniform mechanism* that gives each next item to an agent with probability $\frac{1}{n}$ given any allocation of past items.

This mechanism is strategy-proof and envy-free ex ante because no agent can increase their own outcome and each agent receives the same probability for a given bundle of items. By Theorem 6, no wasteful mechanism is EF1 in general. However, we can bound the envy ex post with identical monotone utilities. For example, consider the wasteful version of the MINIMUM LIKE mechanism, i.e. the MINIMUM UTILITY mechanism. This one is EF1 in this domain.

MINIMUM UTILITY: At round $j \in [m]$, given $\pi \in \Pi_{j-1}$, we let MinUtil $= \{i|i \in [n], v_i(\pi_i) = \min_{k \in [n]} v_k(\pi_k)\}$. The mechanism gives o_j to some $i \in$ MinUtil with probability $(1/|\text{MinUtil}|)$.

Theorem 12. *With identical monotone utilities, the wasteful* MINIMUM UTILITY *mechanism is EF1.*

Proof. We can use induction on $j \in [m]$ as in the proof of Theorem 7. In the base case, the allocation of o_1 is trivially EF1. In the step case, consider $\pi' = (\pi'_1, \ldots, \pi'_n)$ where $\pi'_1 = \pi_1 \cup \{o_j\}$ and $\pi'_i = \pi_i$ for each $i \neq 1$, supposing that $\pi \in \Pi_{j-1}$ with $p(\pi) > 0$ is EF1. We next show that π' is EF1. Suppose $i \neq 1$ and $k \neq 1$. This follows by Case 1 in Theorem 7. Suppose $i \neq 1$ and $k = 1 \in$ MinUtil. This follows by Case 2 in Theorem 7. Suppose that $i = 1 \in$ MinUtil and $k \neq 1$. We have $u_1(\pi'_1) \geq u_1(\pi_1)$ as $\pi'_1 = \pi_1 \cup \{o_j\}$. As π is EF1, $u_1(\pi_1) \geq u_1(\pi_k \setminus \{o\})$ for some $o \in \pi_k \neq \emptyset$. Hence, $u_1(\pi'_1) \geq u_1(\pi_k \setminus \{o\}) = u_1(\pi'_k \setminus \{o\})$ as $\pi'_k = \pi_k$. Therefore, agent 1 is EF1 of agent k in π'. We conclude that π' is EF1. ◇

It is easy to see that the MINIMUM UTILITY mechanism is online strategy-proof with general utilities and envy-free ex ante with identical utilities. However, by Theorems 8, 9 and 10, we conclude that *no* wasteful mechanism, including MINIMUM UTILITY, is EF1 and strategy-proof or EF1 and Pareto efficient, or just EFX.

As strategy-proofness is possible (e.g. the uniform mechanism), we might wish to achieve even a stronger form of strategic robustness. For example, group strategy-proofness captures the ability of groups of agents to manipulate mechanisms in their joint favor [4].

Definition 7 (Group strategy-proofness, GSP). *A mechanism is* GSP *in a problem with m items if, with complete information of o_1 to o_m, no group of agents G can strictly increase $\sum_{i \in G} \bar{u}_i(\Pi_m)$ by misreporting their marginal bids for one or more item o_j and allocation $\pi \in \Pi_{j-1}$, supposing that every agent $k \notin G$ bid sincerely their marginal utilities for items o_1 to o_m.*

Surprisingly, the (wasteful) uniform mechanism is group strategy-proof in general as the outcome of a given group can only decrease supposing some agents from the group bid strategically marginal zeros for some items, and cannot increase if some of these agents bid strategically any combination of positive bids for some of these items. By comparison, *no* non-wasteful mechanism is group strategy-proof even with two agents who cooperate and have different positive utilities for one item [4]. However, it remains an interesting *open* question if group strategy-proofness is achievable with a non-wasteful mechanism in the case of identical monotone utilities with non-zero marginals, or identical additive utilities. Nevertheless, by Theorem 8, such a mechanism cannot be EF1.

Table 1. Key: ⋈ - impossibility, ✓ - possibility, + - discussion after, − - discussion before.

Property	Non-wasteful mechanisms				Wasteful mechanisms			
	General utilities		Identical utilities		General utilities		Identical utilities	
	Possibly 0 marginals	Non-zero marginals	Possibly 0 marginals	Non-zero marginals	Possibly 0 marginals	Non-zero marginals	Possibly 0 marginals	Non-zero marginals
OSP	✓ [T11]	✓ [T11]	✓ [T11]	✓ [T11]	✓ [T12]$^+$	✓ [T12]$^+$	✓ [T12]$^+$	✓ [T12]$^+$
SP	⋈ [T1]	✓ [T6]$^-$	⋈ [T1]	✓ [T6]$^-$	✓ [T12]$^-$	✓ [T12]$^-$	✓ [T12]$^-$	✓ [T12]$^-$
GSP	⋈ [T1]	⋈ [T12]$^+$	⋈ [T1]	open	✓ [T12]$^+$	✓ [T12]$^+$	✓ [T12]$^+$	✓ [T12]$^+$
EF1	⋈ [T4]	⋈ [T6]	⋈ [T4]	✓ [T7]	⋈ [T6]	⋈ [T6]	✓ [T12]	✓ [T12]
EFX	⋈ [T10]	⋈ [T10]	⋈ [T10]	⋈ [T10]	⋈ [T10]	⋈ [T10]	⋈ [T10]	⋈ [T10]
EFA	⋈ [T2]	✓ [T6]$^-$	✓ [T3]	✓ [T3]	✓ [T12]$^-$	✓ [T12]$^-$	✓ [T12]$^-$	✓ [T12]$^-$
PEP+PEA	⋈ [T5]	✓ [T6]$^-$	⋈ [T5]	✓ [T6]$^-$	⋈ [T12]$^-$	⋈ [T12]$^-$	⋈ [T12]$^-$	⋈ [T12]$^-$

Table 2. Key: × - does not hold, ✓ - holds, + - discussion after, − - discussion before.

Mechanism	SP	OSP	EFA	EF1	EFX	PEA	PEP
	Identical monotone utilities						
MINIMUM LIKE	× [T1]	✓ [T11]	✓ [T3]	× [T4]	× [T10]	× [T5]	× [T5]
MINIMUM UTILITY	× [T8]	✓ [T12]$^+$	✓ [T12]$^+$	✓ [T12]	× [T10]	× [T12]$^-$	× [T12]$^-$
	Identical monotone utilities with non-zero marginals						
MINIMUM LIKE	× [T8]	✓ [T11]	✓ [T3]	✓ [T7]	× [T10]	× [T9]	× [T9]
	Identical additive utilities						
MINIMUM LIKE	× [T8]	✓ [T11]	✓ [T3]	✓ [T7]	× [T10]	✓ [T9]$^-$	✓ [T9]$^-$

8   Conclusions

We consider a model for online fair division in which agents have monotone utilities for bundles of items. We studied common axiomatic properties of mechanisms for this model such as strategy-proofness, envy-freeness and Pareto efficiency. We analysed these properties for several utility domains, e.g. general marginal utilities, non-zero marginal utilities, identical utilities, etc. For non-wasteful mechanisms, most properties cannot be guaranteed. For wasteful mechanisms, most properties can be guaranteed in isolation. However, we also proved some impossibility results for combinations of axiomatic properties. We summarize our results in Table 1. We also proposed two new mechanisms - MINIMUM LIKE and MINIMUM UTILITY - that satisfy a relaxed form of strategy-proofness in general as well as envy-freeness ex ante and ex post up to some item in two domains with identical utilities. We summarize these results in Table 2. Finally, our results hold in offline fair division as well because online mechanisms can be applied to offline problems by picking up an order of the items. In future, we will consider other utility domains such as sub- and super-additive, or sub- and sup-modular utilities. We will also consider other relaxations of the considered properties and other (e.g. not marginal) mechanisms for our model.

References

1. Aleksandrov, M., Aziz, H., Gaspers, S., Walsh, T.: Online fair division: analysing a food bank problem. In: Proceedings of the Twenty-Fourth IJCAI 2015, Buenos Aires, Argentina, 25–31 July 2015, pp. 2540–2546 (2015)
2. Aleksandrov, M., Walsh, T.: Expected outcomes and manipulations in online fair division. In: Kern-Isberner, G., Fürnkranz, J., Thimm, M. (eds.) KI 2017. LNCS (LNAI), vol. 10505, pp. 29–43. Springer, Cham (2017). https://doi.org/10.1007/978-3-319-67190-1_3
3. Aleksandrov, M., Walsh, T.: Most competitive mechanisms in online fair division. In: Kern-Isberner, G., Fürnkranz, J., Thimm, M. (eds.) KI 2017. LNCS (LNAI), vol. 10505, pp. 44–57. Springer, Cham (2017). https://doi.org/10.1007/978-3-319-67190-1_4
4. Aleksandrov, M., Walsh, T.: Pure Nash equilibria in online fair division. In: Sierra, C. (ed.) Proceedings of the Twenty-Sixth International Joint Conference on Artificial Intelligence (IJCAI 2017), pp. 42–48 (2017)
5. Amanatidis, G., Birmpas, G., Markakis, V.: Comparing approximate relaxations of envy-freeness. In: Proceedings of the Twenty-Seventh International Joint Conference on Artificial Intelligence, IJCAI 2018, Stockholm, Sweden, 13–19 July 2018, pp. 42–48 (2018)
6. Aziz, H., Bouveret, S., Caragiannis, I., Giagkousi, I., Lang, J.: Knowledge, fairness, and social constraints. In: AAAI, pp. 4638–4645. AAAI Press (2018)
7. Barman, S., Biswas, A., Murthy, S.K.K., Narahari, Y.: Groupwise maximin fair allocation of indivisible goods. In: AAAI, pp. 917–924. AAAI Press (2018)
8. Barman, S., Krishnamurthy, S.K., Vaish, R.: Greedy algorithms for maximizing nash social welfare. In: Proceedings of the 17th International Conference on Autonomous Agents and MultiAgent Systems, AAMAS 2018, Stockholm, Sweden, 10–15 July 2018, pp. 7–13 (2018)
9. Benade, G., Kazachkov, A.M., Procaccia, A.D., Psomas, C.A.: How to make envy vanish over time. In: Proceedings of the 2018 ACM Conference on Economics and Computation, EC 2018, pp. 593–610. ACM, New York (2018)
10. Brams, S.J., King, D.L.: Efficient fair division: help the worst off or avoid envy? Ration. Soc. 17(4), 387–421 (2005)
11. Budish, E.: The combinatorial assignment problem: approximate competitive equilibrium from equal incomes. J. Polit. Econ. 119(6), 1061–1103 (2011)
12. Budish, E., Cantillon, E.: The multi-unit assignment problem: theory and evidence from course allocation at Harvard. Am. Econ. Rev. 102(5), 2237–2271 (2012)
13. Caragiannis, I., Kurokawa, D., Moulin, H., Procaccia, A.D., Shah, N., Wang, J.: The unreasonable fairness of maximum nash welfare. In: Proceedings of the 2016 ACM Conference on EC 2016, Maastricht, The Netherlands, 24–28 July 2016, pp. 305–322 (2016)
14. Chevaleyre, Y., Endriss, U., Estivie, S., Maudet, N.: Multiagent resource allocation in k-additive domains: preference representation and complexity. Ann. Oper. Res. 163(1), 49–62 (2008)
15. Chevaleyre, Y., Lang, J., Maudet, N., Monnot, J., Xia, L.: New candidates welcome! Possible winners with respect to the addition of new candidates. Math. Soc. Sci. 64(1), 74–88 (2012)
16. Dickerson, J.P., Procaccia, A.D., Sandholm, T.: Dynamic matching via weighted myopia with application to kidney exchange. In: Proceedings of the Twenty-Sixth AAAI Conference on Artificial Intelligence (2012)

17. Dickerson, J.P., Procaccia, A.D., Sandholm, T.: Failure-aware kidney exchange. In: ACM Conference on Electronic Commerce, EC 2013, pp. 323–340 (2013)
18. Freeman, R., Zahedi, S.M., Conitzer, V., Lee, B.C.: Dynamic proportional sharing: a game-theoretic approach. Proc. ACM Meas. Anal. Comput. Syst. **2**(1), 3:1–3:36 (2018)
19. Gibbard, A.: Manipulation of voting schemes: a general result. Econometrica **41**(4), 587–601 (1973)
20. Greenwald, A., Boyan, J.: Bidding under uncertainty: theory and experiments. In: Proceedings of the 20th Conference on Uncertainty in Artificial Intelligence, UAI 2004, pp. 209–216. AUAI Press, Arlington (2004)
21. Hosseini, H., Larson, K., Cohen, R.: Matching with dynamic ordinal preferences. In: Proceedings of the Twenty-Ninth AAAI Conference on Artificial Intelligence, Austin, Texas, USA, 25–30 January, AAAI 2015, pp. 936–943. AAAI Press (2015)
22. Kash, I.A., Procaccia, A.D., Shah, N.: No agent left behind: Dynamic fair division of multiple resources. JAIR **51**, 579–603 (2014). https://doi.org/10.1613/jair.4405
23. Lipton, R.J., Markakis, E., Mossel, E., Saberi, A.: On approximately fair allocations of indivisible goods. In: Proceedings of the 5th ACM Conference on Electronic Commerce (EC-2004), New York, NY, USA, 17–20 May 2004, pp. 125–131 (2004)
24. Manea, M.: Serial dictatorship and Pareto optimality. Games Econ. Behav. **61**(2), 316–330 (2007). https://doi.org/10.1016/j.geb.2007.01.003
25. Nguyen, N., Nguyen, T.T., Roos, M., Rothe, J.: Computational complexity and approximability of social welfare optimization in multiagent resource allocation. Auton. Agent. Multi-Agent Syst. **28**(2), 256–289 (2014)
26. Plaut, B., Roughgarden, T.: Almost envy-freeness with general valuations. In: Proceedings of the Twenty-Ninth Annual ACM-SIAM Symposium on Discrete Algorithms, SODA 2018, New Orleans, LA, USA, 7–10 January 2018, pp. 2584–2603 (2018)
27. Walsh, T.: Online cake cutting. In: Brafman, R.I., Roberts, F.S., Tsoukiàs, A. (eds.) ADT 2011. LNCS (LNAI), vol. 6992, pp. 292–305. Springer, Heidelberg (2011). https://doi.org/10.1007/978-3-642-24873-3_22
28. Walsh, T.: Allocation in practice. In: Lutz, C., Thielscher, M. (eds.) KI 2014. LNCS (LNAI), vol. 8736, pp. 13–24. Springer, Cham (2014). https://doi.org/10.1007/978-3-319-11206-0_2
29. Xia, L., Conitzer, V.: Strategy-proof voting rules over multi-issue domains with restricted preferences. In: Saberi, A. (ed.) WINE 2010. LNCS, vol. 6484, pp. 402–414. Springer, Heidelberg (2010). https://doi.org/10.1007/978-3-642-17572-5_33

A Human-Oriented Term Rewriting System

Edward William Ayers[1]([✉]), William T. Gowers[1], and Mateja Jamnik[2]

[1] DPMMS, University of Cambridge, Cambridge, UK
e.w.ayers@maths.cam.ac.uk
[2] Department of Computer Science and Technology, University of Cambridge,
Cambridge, UK

Abstract. We introduce a fully automatic system, implemented in the Lean theorem prover, that solves equality problems of everyday mathematics. Our overriding priority in devising the system is that it should construct proofs of equality in a way that is similar to that of humans. A second goal is that the methods it uses should be domain independent. The basic strategy of the system is to operate with a subtask stack: whenever there is no clear way of making progress towards the task at the top of the stack, the program finds a promising subtask, such as rewriting a subterm, and places that at the top of the stack instead. Heuristics guide the choice of promising subtasks and the rewriting process. This makes proofs more human-like by breaking the problem into tasks in the way that a human would. We show that our system can prove equality theorems simply, without having to preselect or orient rewrite rules as in standard theorem provers, and without having to invoke heavy duty tools for performing simple reasoning.

1 Introduction

In mathematical proofs one often finds chains of expressions linked by equalities. They are designed to show that the first expression in the chain is equal to the last one, with all the equalities being sufficiently obvious to the reader that no further justification is needed. For example, suppose that one wishes to prove that given a linear map A, its adjoint $A^\dagger$ is linear. To do so one typically provides the following equality chain for all vectors x and all dual vectors u, v:

$$\langle A^\dagger(u+v), x \rangle = \langle u+v, Ax \rangle = \langle u, Ax \rangle + \langle v, Ax \rangle =$$
$$\langle A^\dagger u, x \rangle + \langle v, Ax \rangle = \langle A^\dagger u, x \rangle + \langle A^\dagger v, x \rangle = \langle A^\dagger u + A^\dagger v, x \rangle \quad (1)$$

Here, $\langle \cdot, \cdot \rangle$ is the inner product taking a dual vector and a vector to a real number. The equations that we can compose our reasoning chain from (e.g., $\langle A^\dagger a, b \rangle = \langle a, Ab \rangle$) are called *rewrite rules*.

A central part of automated theorem proving (ATP) is constructing such equality proofs automatically. This can be done with well-researched techniques

C. Benzmüller and H. Stuckenschmidt (Eds.): KI 2019, LNAI 11793, pp. 76–86, 2019.
https://doi.org/10.1007/978-3-030-30179-8_6

from the field of *term rewriting systems* [1]. These techniques take advantage of the fact that computers can perform many operations per second, and large search spaces can be explored quickly, though heuristic functions are still needed to prevent a combinatorial explosion. Many domains – such as checking that two expressions are equal using the ring axioms – also have specialised decision procedures available for them. We will call these approaches to solving equalities *machine-oriented*.

We wish to investigate alternative ways of producing equality proofs. We do not wish to compete with machine-oriented techniques to prove more theorems or prove them faster. Instead, we are motivated by a desire to prove theorems in a different way which better captures the abstract reasoning that seems to occur in the mind of a human.

Why bother finding proofs that are more human-oriented? One answer is purely about efficiency: the runtimes of existing ATP methods do not scale well with the number of competing rules introduced, as one would expect of algorithms that make use of significant amounts of brute-force search. If we can devise new architectures that solve simple equalities with less search, then it may be possible to scale up these techniques to larger problems and improve the efficiency of established ATP methods.

Another reason is that it makes interactive theorem proving easier for the non-specialist. While there is a growing community of mathematicians using formal verification techniques, ATP is met with indifference by the majority of mathematicians [6]. A large part of the reason for this is that the user who wishes to prove a lemma in a proof assistant often has to explicitly provide proofs of intermediate results that would be omitted in a mathematical document. Tools such as Isabelle's Sledgehammer [3] have ameliorated the problem to a large extent, but finding proofs can be slow and the resulting tactics that Sledgehammer recommends are still somewhat cryptic and add clutter. By developing automation that can solve problems that mathematicians find easy, we can contribute to the goal of producing verified proofs that are as easy to read and write as informal ones.

With this in mind, our goals are to create an algorithm which:

- can solve simple equality problems of the kind that an undergraduate might find easy;
- does not encode any domain-specific knowledge of mathematics, that is, it does not invoke specialised procedures if it detects that the problem lies in a particular domain such as Presburger arithmetic;
- is efficient in the sense that it does not store a large state and does not perform a significant search when a human would not.

In this paper we present the `subtask` algorithm which has some success with respect to the above goals. The algorithm is written in Lean 3 [12] and can be found at https://github.com/EdAyers/lean-subtask. In the remainder of the paper we give a motivating example in Sect. 2 followed by a description of the algorithm in Sect. 3. The algorithm is then contrasted with existing approaches in

Sect. 4 and evaluated against the above goals in Sect. 5. Conclusions and further work are contemplated in Sect. 6.

2   Example

Let us begin with the example in elementary linear algebra mentioned above. We have to prove the equality $\langle A^\dagger(u+v), x \rangle = \langle A^\dagger u + A^\dagger v, x \rangle$.

To do this, a human's (not fully conscious) thought process might proceed as follows.

1. I need to create the expression $\langle A^\dagger u + A^\dagger v, x \rangle$.
2. In particular, I need to make the subexpressions $A^\dagger u$ and $A^\dagger v$.
3. The only sensible way I can get these is to use the definition $\langle w, Az \rangle = \langle A^\dagger w, z \rangle$ applied with $w = u$ and v, and presumably with $z = x$.
4. In particular, I'll need to make the subterm Az for some z.
5. I can do that straight away: $\langle A^\dagger(u+v), x \rangle = \langle u+v, Ax \rangle$.
6. Now I'm in a position to obtain the subexpressions $\langle u, Ax \rangle$ and $\langle v, Ax \rangle$ I wanted in step 3, so let me do that using bilinearity: $\langle u+v, Ax \rangle = \langle u, Ax \rangle + \langle v, Ax \rangle$.
7. And now I can get the subexpressions $A^\dagger u$ and $A^\dagger v$ I wanted even earlier in step 2, so let me do that: $\langle u, Ax \rangle + \langle v, Ax \rangle = \langle A^\dagger u, x \rangle + \langle A^\dagger v, x \rangle$.
8. And with one application of bilinearity I'm home: $\langle A^\dagger u, x \rangle + \langle A^\dagger v, x \rangle = \langle A^\dagger u + A^\dagger v, x \rangle$.

The key aspect of the above kind of thought process that we wish to model is the setting of intermediate aims, such as obtaining certain subexpressions when we do not immediately see how to obtain the entire expression. We do this by creating a tree of subtasks.

The tree in Fig. 1 represents what the algorithm does with the additivity-of-adjoint problem. It starts with the subtask $\texttt{CreateAll}(\langle A^\dagger u + A^\dagger v, x \rangle)$. Since it cannot achieve that in one go, it creates some subtasks and then chooses the one that is most promising: later in Sect. 3.1 we shall give details about how it generates and evaluates possible choices. In this case the most promising subtask is $\texttt{Create}(A^\dagger u)$, so it selects that and identifies a rewrite rule – the basic definition of adjoint – that can achieve it. The z that appears is a metavariable that will in due course be set to x. (It will typically also find a number of 'silly' possibilities, not depicted here, which are dismissed by the scoring system.) When it has done that, it has a new subtask which is to create the left-hand side of the rule. It cannot do that in one go, so it creates new subtasks and so on. The process outlined in this example is the one which we want our algorithm to reflect.

3   Design of the Algorithm

The $\texttt{subtask}$ algorithm acts on a tree of *tasks* (as depicted in Fig. 1) and an expression called the *current expression* (CE). A task is any object which implements the following methods:

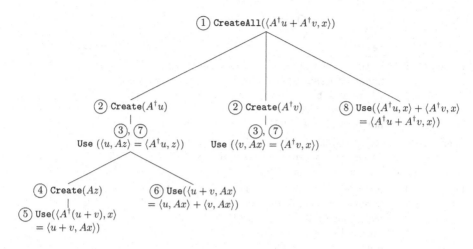

Fig. 1. The subtask tree for solving $\langle A^\dagger(u+v), x\rangle = \langle A^\dagger u + A^\dagger v, x\rangle$. Circled numbers correspond to steps in the above list.

- `refine : task -> list task`
- `test : task -> bool` which returns true when the task is *achieved* for the current expression.
- optionally, `execute : task -> unit` which updates the current expression x to y by providing a proof of x = y. Tasks with `execute` methods are called *strategies*. In this case, `test` returns true when `execute` can be applied successfully.

The main tasks are given in Table 1, however more are added to the software. For example `ReduceDistance`(x, y) will greedily apply any rewrite that causes x and y to be closer in the parse tree. The algorithm is summarised in the pseudocode in Fig. 2.

In the `explore` phase, we take a task X on the tree and `refine` it to produce a list of child tasks $C_1, C_2 \cdots$. We add these to the task tree if they are not already present on it. We then score the strategies $S_1, S_2 \cdots$ in this list – that is, score the children where `execute` is defined. The score is intended to represent the likelihood of the strategy being successful and is determined by heuristics discussed in Sect. 3.1. The reason why the algorithm focusses on strategies before non-strategies is a heuristic that seems to work well in practice. The underlying idea behind the heuristic is that often the first sensible strategy found is enough of a signpost to solve simple problems. That is, once one has found one plausible strategy of solving a simple problem it is often fruitful to stop looking for other strategies which achieve the same thing and to get on with finding a way of performing the new strategy.

If the overall score is above zero then add a backtrack point and take the highest-scoring strategy S.

Table 1. Main tasks

	refine	test	execute
CreateAll(e)	Returns a list of Create(b) subtasks where each b is a minimal subterm of e not present in the CE	True whenever the CE is e	none
Create(e)	Returns a list Use(a = b) subtasks where each e occurs within a	True whenever the CE contains e	none
Use(a = b)	Returns a list of Create(e) subtasks where each e is a minimal subterm of a not present in the CE	True whenever the rule a = b can be applied to the CE	Apply a = b to the CE

```
function explore(X : task) {
  children <- refine(X)
  foreach (C in children) {
    if (C is not on the task tree) {
      add C as a child node of X
    }
  }
  strategies <- children.strategies
  overall_score <- score(strategies)
  if (overall_score > 0) {
    add a backtrack point
    S <- strategies.highest_scoring
    ascend(S)
  } else {
    explore a non-strategy
    child of X or else backtrack
  }
}
```

```
function ascend(X : task) {
  if (X is a strategy) {
    if (test(X)) {
      execute(X)
      ascend(parent(X))
    } else {
      explore(X)
    }
  } else {
    if (test(X)) {
      if (X is the root task) {
        success
      } else {
        ascend(parent(X))
      }
    } else {
      explore(X)
    }
  }
}
```

Fig. 2. Pseudocode for the subtask algorithm.

If test(S) is false then explore S otherwise execute S and ascend S's parents until a task Y is found that can not be achieved then explore Y. Otherwise if the overall score is less than or equal to zero then explore a non-strategy child task of X or backtrack if none exist. The backtracking procedure works by taking the list of backtracking points and choosing the one with the highest overall score if the failed branch is removed.

To find `l = r`, the algorithm is initialised with the tree `CreateAll(r)` and the current expression `l`. We then run `execute(CreateAll(r))` until a timeout is reached or we run out of backtracking points.

3.1   Heuristics

Both lists of strategies and individual strategies are scored using a heuristic to guide the exploration of the tree. The system prioritises strategies if they:

- achieve a task higher in the task tree;
- achieve a task on a different branch of the task tree;
- have a high degree of term overlap with the current expression (this is measured using symbol counting and finding largest common subterms);
- use local hypotheses;
- can be achieved in one rewrite step from the current expression.

The overall score heuristic evaluates sets of strategies. If there is only one strategy then it scores 10. If there are multiple strategies, it discards any scoring less than -5. If there are positive-scoring strategies then all negative-scoring strategies are discarded. The overall score is then set to be 5 minus the number of strategies in the list. The intention of this simple procedure is that we should prefer smaller sets of strategies, even if their scores are bad because it limits choice in what to do next.

4   Related Work

4.1   Term Rewriting

One way to find equality proofs is to perform a graph search using a heuristic. This is the approach of the `rewrite-search` algorithm [8], which uses the heuristic of string edit-distance between the strings two pretty-printed expressions. The `rewrite-search` algorithm does capture some human-like properties in the heuristic, since the pretty printed expressions are intended for human consumption. Our algorithm is different from `rewrite-search` in that we guide search according to achieving sequences of tasks. Since both our software and `rewrite-search` are written in Lean, some future work could be to investigate a combination of both systems.

A term rewriting system (TRS) R is a set of oriented rewrite rules. There are many techniques available for turning a set of rewrite rules in to procedures that check whether two terms are equal. One technique is *completion*, where R is converted into an equivalent TRS R' that is *convergent*. This means that any two expressions a, b are equal under R if and only if repeated application of rules in R' to a and b will produce the same expression. Finding equivalent convergent systems, if not by hand, is usually done by finding decreasing orderings on terms and using Knuth-Bendix completion. When such a system exists, automated rewriting systems can use these techniques to quickly find proofs, but the proofs are often overly long and needlessly expand terms.

Another method is rewrite tables, where a lookup table of representatives for terms is stored in a way that allows for two terms to be matched through a series of lookups.

Both completion and rewrite tables can be considered machine-oriented because they rely on large datastructures and systematic applications of rewrite rules. Such methods are certainly highly useful, but they can hardly be said to capture the process by which humans reason.

Finally, there are many normalisation and decision procedures for particular domains, for example on rings [7]. Domain specific procedures do not satisfy our criterion of generality.

4.2   Proof Planning

As mentioned earlier, our approach is similar to that of proof planning [4]. AI planning in its most general conception [9] is the process of searching a graph G using plan-space rather than by searching it directly. In a typical planning system, each point in plan-space is a DAG of objects called *ground operators* or *methods*, each of which has a mapping to paths in G. Each ground operator is equipped with predicates on the vertices of G called *pre/post-conditions*. Various AI planning methods such as GRAPHPLAN [2] can be employed to discover a partial ordering of these methods, which can then be used to construct a path in G. This procedure applied to the problem of finding proofs is known as proof planning. The main issue with proof planning [5] is that it is difficult to identify sets of conditions and methods that do not cause the plan space to be too large or disconnected. However, in this paper we are not trying to construct plans for entire proofs, but just to model the thought processes of humans when solving simple equalities.

Proof planning in the domain of finding equalities frequently involves a technique called *rippling*, in which an expression is annotated with additional structure determined by the differences between the two sides of the equation that directs the rewriting process. In our system we avoid using rippling because of our concern for generality: for finding chains of equalities, subtasks achieve similar results and are less tied to particular domains.

Our approach also shares properties with Hierarchical Task Networks (HTN) [11,13] used to drive the behaviour of artificial agents such as the ICARUS architecture [10]. Starting tasks are broken down into subtasks, which are then used to find fine-grained methods for achieving the original tasks.

The main difference between our approach and proof planning and hierarchical task networks is that our algorithm is greedier: we generate enough of a plan to have little doubt what the first rewrite rule in the sequence should be, and no more. We believe that this reflects how humans reason for solving simple problems: favouring just enough planning to decide on a good first step, and then planning further only once the step is completed and new information is revealed.

5   Evaluation

Our ultimate motivation is to make an algorithm that behaves as a human mathematician would. We do not wish to claim that we have fully achieved this, but we can evaluate our algorithm with respect to some general goals that we mentioned in Sect. 1.

– Scope: can it solve simple equations?
– Generality: does it avoid techniques specific to a particular area of mathematics?
– Reduced search space: does the algorithm avoid search when finding proofs that humans can find easily without search?
– Straightforwardness of proofs: for easy problems, does it give a proof that an experienced human mathematician might give?

Our method of evaluation is to use the algorithm implemented as a tactic in Lean on a library of thirty or so example problems. This is not large enough for a substantial quantitative comparison with existing methods, but we can still investigate some properties of the algorithm. The source code also contains many examples which are outside the abilities of the current implementation of the algorithm. Some ways to address these issues are discussed in Sect. 6.

Table 2 gives some selected examples. These are all problems that the algorithm can solve with no backtracking.

From this table we can see that the algorithm solves problems from several different domains. We did not encode any decision procedures for monoids or rings. In fact we did not even include reasoning under associativity and commutativity, although we are not in principle against extending the algorithm to do this. The input to the algorithm is simply a list of over 100 axioms and equations for sets, rings, groups and vector spaces which can be found in the file `equate.lean` in the source code. Thus, the algorithm exhibits considerable generality.

All of the solutions to the above examples are found without backtracking, which adds support to the claim that our algorithm requires less search. There are other examples in the source where backtracking occurs, so there is still some work to be done on choosing scoring heuristics here.

Our final criterion is that the proofs are more straightforward than those produced by machine-oriented special purpose tactics. This is a somewhat subjective measure but there are some proxies that indicate that `subtasks` can be used to generate simpler proofs.

To illustrate this point, consider the problem of proving $(x+y)^2 + (x+z)^2 = (z+x)^2 + (y+x)^2$ within ring theory. We choose this example because it is easy for a human to spot how to do it with three uses of commutativity, but it is easy for a program to be led astray by expanding the squares. `subtask` proves this equality with 3 uses of commutativity and with no backtracking or expansion of the squares. This is an example where domain specific tactics do worse than `subtask`, the `ring` tactic for reasoning on problems in commutative rings will

Table 2. subtask's performance on some example problems. "# steps" gives the number of rewrite steps in the final proof. "location" gives the file and declaration name of the example in the source code.

problem	#steps	location
$l\,s : \texttt{list}$ $\textbf{rev}(l +\!\!+ s) = \textbf{rev}(s) +\!\!+ \textbf{rev}(l)$ $\textbf{rev}(a :: l) = \textbf{rev}(l) +\!\!+ [a]$ $\vdash \textbf{rev}(h :: l +\!\!+ s) = \textbf{rev}(s) +\!\!+ \textbf{rev}(h :: l)$	5	datatypes.lean/rev_app_rev
a : monoid element $a^{(m+n)} = a^m * a^n$ $\vdash a^{\mathrm{succ}(m)+n} = a^{\mathrm{succ}(m)} * a^n$	8	groups.lean/my_pow_add
$a\,b$: ring element $a * d = c * b$ $c * f = e * d$ $\vdash d * (a * f) = d * (e * b)$	9	rat.lean
$a\,b$: ring element $\vdash (a + b) * (a + b) = a * a + 2 * (a * b) + b * b$	7	rings.lean/sumsq_with_equate
$A\,B\,C\,X$: set $\vdash X \setminus (B \cup C) = (X \setminus B) \setminus C$	4	sets.lean/example_4

produce a proof by expanding out the squares. The built-in tactics ac_refl and blast in Lean which reason under associativity and commutativity both use commutativity 5 times. If one is simply interested in verification, then such a result is perfectly acceptable. However, we are primarily interested in modelling how humans would solve such an equality, so we want our algorithm not to perform unnecessary steps such as this.

It is difficult to fairly compare the speed of subtask in the current implementation because it is compiled to Lean bytecode which is much slower than native built-in tactics that are written in C++. However it is worth noting that, even with this handicap, subtask takes 1900 ms to find the above proof whereas ac_refl and blast take 600 ms and 900 ms respectively.

There are still proofs generated by subtask that are not straightforward. For example, the lemma $(xz)(z^{-1}y) = xy$ in group theory is proved by subtask with a superfluous use of the rule $e = xx^{-1}$. We hope that some of these defects will be ironed out in future versions of the program.

6   Conclusions and Further Work

In this paper, we introduced a new, task-based approach to finding equalities in proofs and provided a demonstration of the approach by building the subtask tactic in Lean. We show that the approach can solve simple equality proofs with very little search. Our hope is that our work will renew interest in proof planning and spark interest in human-oriented reasoning for at least some classes of problems.

In future work, we wish to add more subtasks and better heuristics for scoring them. The framework we outlined here allows for easy experimentation with such different sets of heuristics and subtasks. In this way, we also wish to make the subtask framework extensible by users, so that they may add their own custom subtasks and scoring functions.

There are times when the algorithm fails and needs guidance from the user. We wish to study further how the subtask paradigm might be used to enable more human-friendly interactivity than is currently possible. For example, in real mathematical textbooks, if an equality step is not obvious, a relevant lemma will be mentioned. Similarly, we wish to investigate ways of passing 'hint' subtasks to the tactic. For example, when proving $x*y = (x*z)*(z^{-1}*y)$, the algorithm will typically get stuck (although it can solve the flipped problem), because there are too many ways of creating z. However, the user – upon seeing subtask get stuck – could steer the algorithm with a suggested subtask such as $\texttt{Create}(x*(z*z^{-1}))$.

Using subtasks should help to give better explanations to the user. The idea of our algorithm is that the first set of strategies in the tree roughly corresponds to the high-level actions that a human would first consider when trying to solve the problem. Thus, the algorithm could use the subtask hierarchy to determine when no further explanation is needed and thereby generate abbreviated proofs of a kind that might be found in mathematical textbooks.

Another potential area to explore is to perform an evaluation survey where students are asked to determine whether an equality proof was generated by our software or a machine.

References

1. Baader, F., Nipkow, T.: Term Rewriting and All that. Cambridge University Press, Cambridge (1999)
2. Blum, A.L., Furst, M.L.: Fast planning through planning graph analysis. Artif. Intell. **90**(1–2), 281–300 (1997)
3. Böhme, S., Nipkow, T.: Sledgehammer: judgement day. In: Giesl, J., Hähnle, R. (eds.) IJCAR 2010. LNCS (LNAI), vol. 6173, pp. 107–121. Springer, Heidelberg (2010). https://doi.org/10.1007/978-3-642-14203-1_9
4. Bundy, A.: The use of explicit plans to guide inductive proofs. In: Lusk, E., Overbeek, R. (eds.) CADE 1988. LNCS, vol. 310, pp. 111–120. Springer, Heidelberg (1988). https://doi.org/10.1007/BFb0012826
5. Bundy, A.: A critique of proof planning. In: Kakas, A.C., Sadri, F. (eds.) Computational Logic: Logic Programming and Beyond. LNCS (LNAI), vol. 2408, pp. 160–177. Springer, Heidelberg (2002). https://doi.org/10.1007/3-540-45632-5_7
6. Bundy, A.: Automated theorem provers: a practical tool for the working mathematician? Ann. Math. Artif. Intell. **61**(1), 3 (2011). https://doi.org/10.1007/s10472-011-9248-8

7. Grégoire, B., Mahboubi, A.: Proving equalities in a commutative ring done right in Coq. In: Hurd, J., Melham, T. (eds.) TPHOLs 2005. LNCS, vol. 3603, pp. 98–113. Springer, Heidelberg (2005). https://doi.org/10.1007/11541868_7

8. Hoek, K., Morrison, S.: Lean-rewrite-search repository (2019). https://github.com/semorrison/lean-rewrite-search

9. Kambhampati, S., Knoblock, C.A., Yang, Q.: Planning as refinement search: a unified framework for evaluating design tradeoffs in partial-order planning. Artif. Intell. 76(1), 167–238 (1995)

10. Langley, P., Choi, D., Trivedi, N.: Icarus user's manual. Institute for the Study of Learning and Expertise 2164 (2011)

11. Melis, E., Siekmann, J.: Knowledge-based proof planning. Artif. Intell. 115(1), 65–105 (1999)

12. de Moura, L., Kong, S., Avigad, J., van Doorn, F., von Raumer, J.: The lean theorem prover (system description). In: Felty, A.P., Middeldorp, A. (eds.) CADE 2015. LNCS (LNAI), vol. 9195, pp. 378–388. Springer, Cham (2015). https://doi.org/10.1007/978-3-319-21401-6_26

13. Tate, A.: Generating project networks. In: Proceedings of the 5th International Joint Conference on Artificial Intelligence, vol. 2, pp. 888–893. Morgan Kaufmann Publishers Inc. (1977)

Mixing Description Logics
in Privacy-Preserving Ontology Publishing

Franz Baader[ID] and Adrian Nuradiansyah[✉][ID]

Theoretical Computer Science, TU Dresden, Dresden, Germany
{franz.baader,adrian.nuradiansyah}@tu-dresden.de

Abstract. In previous work, we have investigated privacy-preserving publishing of Description Logic (DL) ontologies in a setting where the knowledge about individuals to be published is an $\mathcal{EL}$ instance store, and both the privacy policy and the possible background knowledge of an attacker are represented by concepts of the DL $\mathcal{EL}$. We have introduced the notions of compliance of a concept with a policy and of safety of a concept for a policy, and have shown how, in the context mentioned above, optimal compliant (safe) generalizations of a given $\mathcal{EL}$ concept can be computed. In the present paper, we consider a modified setting where we assume that the background knowledge of the attacker is given by a DL different from the one in which the knowledge to be published and the safety policies are formulated. In particular, we investigate the situations where the attacker's knowledge is given by an $\mathcal{FL}_0$ or an $\mathcal{FLE}$ concept. In both cases, we show how optimal safe generalizations can be computed. Whereas the complexity of this computation is the same (ExpTime) as in our previous results for the case of $\mathcal{FL}_0$, it turns out to be actually lower (polynomial) for the more expressive DL $\mathcal{FLE}$.

1 Introduction

Description Logics (DLs) [3] are a well-investigated family of logic-based knowledge representation languages, which are frequently used to formalize ontologies for application domains such as biology and medicine [13]. To define the important notions of such an application domain as formal concepts, DLs state necessary and sufficient conditions for an individual to belong to a concept. For example, in the DL $\mathcal{EL}$ [2], which is, e.g., employed to define the large medical ontology SNOMED CT,[1] the concept of all male patients that are seen by a female doctor working in the oncology department can be formalized as

$$C = Patient \sqcap Male \sqcap \exists seen\_by.(Doctor \sqcap Female \sqcap \exists works\_in.Oncology). \quad (1)$$

When publishing information about an individual (e.g., by stating that it belongs to a concept like C in (1)), one needs to ensure that certain privacy

F. Baader—Partially funded by DFG grant 389792660 as part of TRR 248.
A. Nuradiansyah—Funded by DFG within the Research Training Group 1907 RoSI.

1   see https://www.snomed.org.

C. Benzmüller and H. Stuckenschmidt (Eds.): KI 2019, LNAI 11793, pp. 87–100, 2019.
https://doi.org/10.1007/978-3-030-30179-8_7

constraints are fulfilled. These constraints are encoded as *privacy policies*, and before publishing the information one needs to check whether the information is *compliant* with these policies [5, 11, 12]. For example, when publishing information about hospitals, doctors, and patients, the policy may require that one should not be able to find out who are the cancer patients. This policy can, for instance, be expressed by the $\mathcal{EL}$ concept

$$D = Patient \sqcap \exists seen\_by.(Doctor \sqcap \exists works\_in.Oncology). \qquad (2)$$

The concept C in (1) is not compliant with this policy D since C is subsumed by D (written $C \sqsubseteq D$), i.e., if we know that an individual belongs to C, then we can conclude that is also belongs to D. Thus, part of the information contained in C needs to be removed before it can be published. In [5], we have shown how to compute optimal compliant generalizations of C, i.e., concepts C' such that $C \sqsubseteq C'$ and $C' \not\sqsubseteq D$, where optimal means that C' should be as close to C as possible. In our example, the concept $C' = Male \sqcap \exists seen\_by.(Doctor \sqcap Female \sqcap \exists works\_in.Oncology)$ is such an optimal compliant generalization of C. However, it is *not safe*. In fact, if we publish that John belongs to this concept, and the attacker already knows that John is a patient, then the attacker can still deduce that John belongs to the concept D in (2) since $Patient \sqcap C' \sqsubseteq D$. In general, we say that C' is not safe for the policy D if there is a compliant concept E such that $C' \sqcap E \sqsubseteq D$. Using the algorithm of [5] we can compute the (unique) optimal safe generalization C'' of C in (1) w.r.t. the policy D in (2):

$$C'' = Male \sqcap \exists seen\_by.(Doctor \sqcap Female \sqcap \exists works\_in.\top) \sqcap$$
$$\exists seen\_by.(Female \sqcap \exists works\_in.Oncology).$$

In [5] it was assumed that the information to be published about individuals, the policies, and the attacker's background knowledge are all given by concepts of the DL $\mathcal{EL}$. In the present paper, we investigate how the notion of safety changes if the attacker's knowledge is assumed to be given by concepts formulated in a different DL. More precisely, we consider the DL $\mathcal{FL}_0$, which differs from $\mathcal{EL}$ in that value restrictions $\forall r.C$ are used instead of existential restrictions $\exists r.C$, and the DL $\mathcal{FLE}$, which combines the constructors of $\mathcal{EL}$ and $\mathcal{FL}_0$. If we assume in our example that the attacker's knowledge is given by an $\mathcal{FL}_0$ concept, the concept C'' from above is no longer safe. In fact, we have $C'' \sqcap Patient \sqcap \forall seen\_by.\forall works\_in.Oncology \sqsubseteq D$. An attacker may, for example, gain this knowledge by learning that the individual in question is a patient, but is not seen by any of the doctors working in another department. The results shown in the present paper imply that the concept

$$C''' = Male \sqcap Patient \sqcap \exists seen\_by.(Doctor \sqcap Female)$$

is an optimal safe generalization of C in (1) w.r.t. the policy D in (2) if the attacker's knowledge is assumed to be given by an $\mathcal{FL}_0$ concept.

If, instead, we assume that the attacker's knowledge is given by an $\mathcal{FLE}$ concept, then C''' is no longer safe. In fact, $C''' \sqcap \forall seen\_by.\exists works\_in.Oncology$

$\sqsubseteq D$. In this setting, the results shown in this paper imply that $C'''' = Male$ is the optimal safe generalization of C in (1) w.r.t. the policy D in (2). It may be less intuitive to see how an attacker could gain this additional knowledge. But the assumption in [5,11,12] and in the present paper is that the attacker can gain *any* compliant knowledge that can be formulated in the considered formalism (i.e., $\mathcal{FLE}$ concepts in the last part of our example).

To be more precise, just as in [5], we assume here that all knowledge about individuals (be it the one to be published or the one known by an attacker) is represented using concepts, which corresponds to what is called an instance store in [14]. The restriction compared to general DL-based ontologies is, on the hand, that relations between named individuals cannot be stated. On the other hand, there is no TBox available to state subconcept constraints. One reason for considering this restricted setting is that, when investigating a new inference problem, it is usually quite hard to start with the most general situation. Also note that the work in [11,12] concentrates on a setting where there are relations between individuals, but no instance relationships between individuals and complex concepts can be stated. Our hope is that, by combining our approaches with the ones developed in [11,12], we can make the step from instance stores to general DL ABoxes. A second reason is that, in a medical application that uses SNOMED CT as an ontology, the TBox can be reduced away by expanding concept definitions since SNOMED CT is an acyclic TBox [16]. In addition, patient data are usually annotated with SNOMED concepts, but not with SNOMED roles, which justifies considering an instance store rather than a general ABox. The main difference to our work in [5] is that we assume that the background knowledge of the attacker is formulated in a DL ($\mathcal{FL}_0$ or $\mathcal{FLE}$) different from the one ($\mathcal{EL}$) in which the knowledge to be published and the safety policies are expressed. Using $\mathcal{FL}_0$ concepts for formulating the attacker's knowledge makes sense since in SNOMED CT roles have implicit typing constraints [16], which are not explicitly stated using value restrictions, but which may be known to an attacker. Considering $\mathcal{FLE}$ as well is interesting from an academic perspective since our results illustrate the effect that assuming a more expressive DL for the attacker's knowledge may have on the computation of safe generalizations.

In the next section, we will introduce the DLs $\mathcal{FLE}$, $\mathcal{EL}$, and $\mathcal{FL}_0$, and then define the notions of compliance and safety used in this paper. In Sect. 3, we will investigate the setting where the attacker's knowledge is assumed to be given by an $\mathcal{FL}_0$ concept, and in Sect. 4 we consider the case where $\mathcal{FLE}$ is used instead.

2   Preliminaries

A wide range of DLs of different expressive power has been investigated in the literature [3]. Here, we introduce the DL $\mathcal{FLE}$ and its sublogics $\mathcal{EL}$ and $\mathcal{FL}_0$.

Starting with disjoint sets N_C and N_R of *concept* and *role names*, respectively, the set of $\mathcal{FLE}$ concepts over these names are constructed from concept names using the constructors top concept ($\top$), conjunction ($C \sqcap D$), existential restriction ($\exists r.C$), and value restriction ($\forall r.D$). The sublogic $\mathcal{EL}$ forbids the use of value restrictions, and $\mathcal{FL}_0$ forbids the use of existential restrictions. The *size* of an $\mathcal{FLE}$ concept C is the number of occurrences of $\top$ as well as concept and role names in C, and the *role depth* $\mathrm{rd}(C)$ is the maximal nesting of existential restrictions and value restrictions.

The semantics of $\mathcal{FLE}$ (and thus of $\mathcal{EL}$ and $\mathcal{FL}_0$) is defined through *interpretations* $\mathcal{I} = (\Delta^{\mathcal{I}}, \cdot^{\mathcal{I}})$, where $\Delta^{\mathcal{I}}$ is a non-empty set, called the *domain*, and $\cdot^{\mathcal{I}}$ is the *interpretation function*, which maps every $A \in N_C$ to a set $A^{\mathcal{I}} \subseteq \Delta^{\mathcal{I}}$ and every $r \in N_R$ to a binary relation $r^{\mathcal{I}} \subseteq \Delta^{\mathcal{I}} \times \Delta^{\mathcal{I}}$. This function is extended to arbitrary $\mathcal{FLE}$ concepts by setting

- $\top^{\mathcal{I}} := \Delta^{\mathcal{I}}$ and $(C \sqcap D)^{\mathcal{I}} := C^{\mathcal{I}} \cap D^{\mathcal{I}}$,
- $(\exists r.C)^{\mathcal{I}} := \{\delta \in \Delta^{\mathcal{I}} \mid \exists \eta \in \Delta^{\mathcal{I}}.(\delta, \eta) \in r^{\mathcal{I}} \wedge \eta \in C^{\mathcal{I}}\}$, and
- $(\forall r.C)^{\mathcal{I}} := \{\delta \in \Delta^{\mathcal{I}} \mid \forall \eta \in \Delta^{\mathcal{I}}.(\delta, \eta) \in r^{\mathcal{I}} \Rightarrow \eta \in C^{\mathcal{I}}\}$.

The $\mathcal{FLE}$ concept C is *subsumed by* the $\mathcal{FLE}$ concept D (written $C \sqsubseteq D$) if $C^{\mathcal{I}} \subseteq D^{\mathcal{I}}$ holds for all interpretations $\mathcal{I}$. Strict subsumption (written $C \sqsubset D$) holds if $C \sqsubseteq D$ and $D \not\sqsubseteq C$, and we say that C is *equivalent* to D (written $C \equiv D$) if $C \sqsubseteq D$ and $D \sqsubseteq C$.

Whereas subsumption between concepts (without a TBox) is polynomial in $\mathcal{EL}$ [6] and $\mathcal{FL}_0$ [15], it is NP-complete for $\mathcal{FLE}$ [7]. Fortunately, in the context of this paper, we are not interested in subsumption between two $\mathcal{FLE}$ concepts, but only in deciding whether an $\mathcal{FLE}$ concept is subsumed by an $\mathcal{EL}$ concept. Before we can show that this problem is decidable in polynomial time, we need to introduce some notation.

We call an $\mathcal{FLE}$ concept an *atom* if it is a concept name, an existential restriction, or a value restriction, and we denote the set of atoms occurring in the top-level conjunction of an $\mathcal{FLE}$ concept C with $\mathbf{con}(C)$. For example, if $C = A \sqcap \exists r.(B \sqcap \exists s.A) \sqcap \forall r.\forall s.B$, then $\mathbf{con}(C) = \{A, \exists r.(B \sqcap \exists s.A), \forall r.\forall s.B\}$. Given an $\mathcal{FLE}$ concept C and a role name $r \in N_R$, we define $\mathtt{filler}_r^{\forall}(C) := \{E \mid \forall r.E \in \mathbf{con}(C)\}$.

The following proposition is an easy consequence of the characterization of subsumption between $\mathcal{FLE}$ concepts given in [6] (Theorem 24).

Proposition 1. *Let C be an $\mathcal{FLE}$ concept and D be an $\mathcal{EL}$ concept. Then, $C \sqsubseteq D$ holds iff*

(a.) $A \in \mathbf{con}(D)$ implies $A \in \mathbf{con}(C)$ for every concept name A, and
(b.) for every $\exists r.D' \in \mathbf{con}(D)$, there is $\exists r.C' \in \mathbf{con}(C)$ such that

$$C' \sqcap \bigsqcap \mathtt{filler}_r^{\forall}(C) \sqsubseteq D',$$

where $\bigsqcap \mathtt{filler}_r^{\forall}(C)$ denotes the conjunction of all elements of $\mathtt{filler}_r^{\forall}(C)$.

In particular, subsumption between C and D can be decided in time polynomial in the size of C and D.

By induction on the role depth, it is easy to show that the recursive characterization of subsumption between an $\mathcal{FLE}$ and an $\mathcal{EL}$ concept given in the proposition indeed yields a polynomial-time decision procedure.

We close this section by defining the notions of compliance and safety used in this paper. Following [5], we assume that policies are given not just by one $\mathcal{EL}$ concept, but by a finite set of $\mathcal{EL}$ concepts. We assume that these concepts are not equivalent to $\top$ since otherwise there would not be compliant concepts.

Definition 1. *An $\mathcal{EL}$ policy is a finite set $\mathcal{P} = \{D_1, \ldots, D_p\}$ of $\mathcal{EL}$ concepts that are not equivalent to $\top$. Let C be an $\mathcal{EL}$ concept, $Q \in \{\exists, \forall, \forall\exists\}$, and $\mathcal{L}_\exists = \mathcal{EL}, \mathcal{L}_\forall = \mathcal{FL}_0, \mathcal{L}_{\forall\exists} = \mathcal{FLE}$. We say that*

- *the $\mathcal{L}_Q$ concept C' is compliant with $\mathcal{P}$ if $C' \not\sqsubseteq D_i$ for all $i = 1, \ldots, p$,*
- *the $\mathcal{EL}$ concept C' is*
  - *Q-safe for $\mathcal{P}$ if for all $\mathcal{L}_Q$ concepts C'' that are compliant with $\mathcal{P}$, $C' \sqcap C''$ is also compliant with $\mathcal{P}$, i.e., $C' \sqcap C'' \not\sqsubseteq D_i$ for all $i = 1, \ldots, p$,*
  - *a Q-safe generalization of C for $\mathcal{P}$ if $C \sqsubseteq C'$ and C' is Q-safe for $\mathcal{P}$,*
  - *an optimal Q-safe generalization of C for $\mathcal{P}$ if it is a Q-safe generalization of C for $\mathcal{P}$, and there is no Q-safe generalization C'' of C for $\mathcal{P}$ such that $C'' \sqsubset C'$.*

Let C, C' be $\mathcal{EL}$ concepts, $\mathcal{P}$ be an $\mathcal{EL}$ policy, and $Q \in \{\exists, \forall, \forall\exists\}$. The Q-safety problem asks whether C is Q-safe for $\mathcal{P}$ and the Q-ptimality problem asks whether C' is an optimal Q-safe generalization of C for $\mathcal{P}$.

We call an $\mathcal{EL}$ policy $\mathcal{P}$ *redundancy-free* if $\mathcal{P}$ does not contain distinct concepts D, D' such that $D \sqsubseteq D'$. We can without loss of generality restrict our attention to redundancy-free policies since removing redundant concepts (i.e., concepts $D' \in \mathcal{P}$ such that there is $D \in \mathcal{P} \setminus \{D'\}$ with $D \sqsubseteq D'$) does not change the sets of compliant and safe concepts (see Lemma 2 in [5]).

Compliance for $\mathcal{EL}$ concepts and $\exists$-safety have been investigated in detail in [5]. In the following two sections, we investigate $\forall$-safety and $\forall\exists$-safety.

3   Investigating $\forall$-Safety

In this section, we first characterize $\forall$-safety and prove that this characterization can be decided in polynomial time. Then, we show how to compute optimal $\forall$-safe generalizations of a given $\mathcal{EL}$ concept. Finally, we address the $\forall$-optimality problem.

Characterizing $\forall$-Safety. First, note that a value restriction can never imply an existential restriction. Thus, if C'' is an $\mathcal{FL}_0$ concept and D an $\mathcal{EL}$ concept of role depth > 0, then $C'' \not\sqsubseteq D$. This shows that an $\mathcal{FL}_0$ concept C'' is compliant with any $\mathcal{EL}$ policy that does not contain a concept of role depth 0.

Using this observation and Proposition 1, we can characterize $\forall$-safety for redundancy-free policies as follows.

Proposition 2. *Let C be an $\mathcal{EL}$ concept and $\mathcal{P}$ a redundancy-free $\mathcal{EL}$ policy. Then C is $\forall$-safe for $\mathcal{P}$ iff the following two conditions hold for all $D \in \mathcal{P}$:*

(1.) if $\mathbf{rd}(D) = 0$, then $\mathbf{con}(C) \cap \mathbf{con}(D) = \emptyset$,
(2.) if $\mathbf{rd}(D) > 0$, then there is $\exists r.D' \in \mathbf{con}(D)$ such that
  (a.) if $\mathbf{rd}(D') = 0$, then there is no concept of the form $\exists r.C' \in \mathbf{con}(C)$,
  (b.) if $\mathbf{rd}(D') > 0$, then for all $\exists r.C' \in \mathbf{con}(C)$, C' is $\forall$-safe for $\{D'\}$.

Proof. To show the *if-direction*, assume that C is not $\forall$-safe for $\mathcal{P}$. Then, there is an $\mathcal{EL}$ concept $D \in \mathcal{P}$ and an $\mathcal{FL}_0$ concept C'' that complies with $\mathcal{P}$ such that $C \sqcap C'' \sqsubseteq D$. Since $C \sqcap C''$ is an $\mathcal{FLE}$ concept, Proposition 1 applies to this subsumption. First, we consider the case where $\mathbf{rd}(D) = 0$. Proposition 1 implies that every concept name $A \in \mathbf{con}(D)$ is contained in $\mathbf{con}(C) \cup \mathbf{con}(C'')$. However, since C'' complies with $\mathcal{P}$, we have $C'' \not\sqsubseteq D$, and hence there must be an $A \in \mathbf{con}(D)$ that is not contained in $\mathbf{con}(C'')$. Consequently this A must belong to $\mathbf{con}(C)$, and thus property 1.) above is violated.

Now, consider the case where $\mathbf{rd}(D) > 0$, i.e., there is an existential restriction $\exists r.D' \in \mathbf{con}(D)$. By Proposition 1 and since C is an $\mathcal{EL}$ and C'' an $\mathcal{FL}_0$ concept, $C \sqcap C'' \sqsubseteq D$ implies that there is an existential restriction $\exists r.C' \in \mathbf{con}(C)$ such that $C' \sqcap \prod \mathtt{filler}_r^\forall(C'') \sqsubseteq D'$. If $\mathbf{rd}(D') = 0$, then this clearly violates (2a.). If $\mathbf{rd}(D') > 0$, then (2b.) is violated since $\prod \mathtt{filler}_r^\forall(C'')$ then cannot be subsumed by D', and thus $C' \sqcap \prod \mathtt{filler}_r^\forall(C'') \sqsubseteq D'$ shows that C' is not $\forall$-safe for $\{D'\}$.
To show the *only-if-direction*, we assume that one of the conditions (1.) or (2.) is violated, and prove that this implies that C is not $\forall$-safe for $\mathcal{P}$.

First, assume that (1.) is violated, i.e., there is $D \in \mathcal{P}$ such that $\mathbf{rd}(D) = 0$ and there is $A \in \mathbf{con}(C) \cap \mathbf{con}(D)$. Then, $C'' := \prod(\mathbf{con}(D) \setminus \{A\})$ is an $\mathcal{FL}_0$ concept that complies with D, and satisfies $C \sqcap C'' \sqsubseteq D$. To conclude that C is not $\forall$-safe for $\mathcal{P}$, it remains to show that C'' also complies with all $\hat{D} \in \mathcal{P} \setminus \{D\}$. However, if we assume that $C'' \sqsubseteq \hat{D}$ for some $\hat{D} \in \mathcal{P} \setminus \{D\}$, then the fact that $D \sqsubseteq C''$ implies $D \sqsubseteq \hat{D}$, which contradicts our assumption that $\mathcal{P}$ is redundancy-free.

Second, assume that (2.) is violated. Then there is $D \in \mathcal{P}$ such that $\mathbf{rd}(D) > 0$ and for all $\exists r.D' \in \mathbf{con}(D)$ we have

- if $\mathbf{rd}(D') = 0$, then there is a concept of the form $\exists r.C' \in \mathbf{con}(C)$, and
- if $\mathbf{rd}(D') > 0$, then there is $\exists r.C' \in \mathbf{con}(C)$ such that the concept C' is not $\forall$-safe for $\{D'\}$.

We define the concept C'' as follows: $\underset{(1)}{\prod A} \sqcap \underset{(2)}{\prod \forall r.D'} \sqcap \underset{(3)}{\prod \forall r.F}$, where

(1) $A \in \mathbf{con}(D)$;
(2) $r \in N_R, \exists r.D' \in \mathbf{con}(D)$, and $\mathbf{rd}(D') = 0$;
(3) $r \in N_R, \exists r.D' \in \mathbf{con}(D), \mathbf{rd}(D') > 0$, $\exists r.C' \in \mathbf{con}(C)$, and F is an $\mathcal{FL}_0$ concept complying with D', but satisfying $C' \sqcap F \sqsubseteq D'$.

Note that C'' is an $\mathcal{FL}_0$ concept that is compliant with $\mathcal{P}$. To see the latter, assume that $\hat{D} \in \mathcal{P}$. If $\mathbf{rd}(\hat{D}) > 0$, then $C'' \not\sqsubseteq \hat{D}$ since an $\mathcal{FL}_0$ concept cannot imply an existential restriction. If $\mathbf{rd}(\hat{D}) = 0$, then $C'' \sqsubseteq \hat{D}$ would imply $D \sqsubseteq \hat{D}$, which contradicts our assumption that $\mathcal{P}$ is redundancy-free.

It remains to prove that $C \sqcap C'' \sqsubseteq D$, which we show using Proposition 1. First note that, by the construction of C'', each concept name $A \in \mathbf{con}(D)$ satisfies $A \in \mathbf{con}(C'')$, and thus $A \in \mathbf{con}(C \sqcap C'')$. Second, consider an existential restriction $\exists r.D' \in \mathbf{con}(D)$. If $\mathbf{rd}(D') = 0$, then there is $\exists r.C' \in \mathbf{con}(C)$, but also $\forall r.D' \in \mathbf{con}(C'')$. Thus we have $C' \sqcap \bigsqcap \mathtt{filler}_r^{\forall}(C \sqcap C'') \sqsubseteq C' \sqcap D' \sqsubseteq D'$, as required by Proposition 1. If $\mathbf{rd}(D') > 0$, then we have $\exists r.C' \in \mathbf{con}(C)$ for an $\mathcal{EL}$ concept C' that is not $\forall$-safe for $\{D'\}$. In addition, $\forall r.F \in \mathbf{con}(C'')$, where F is an $\mathcal{FL}_0$ concept such that $C' \sqcap F \sqsubseteq D'$. Consequently, we have $C' \sqcap \bigsqcap \mathtt{filler}_r^{\forall}(C \sqcap C'') \sqsubseteq C' \sqcap F \sqsubseteq D'$. $\square$

Using induction on the role depth, it is easy to show that the characterization of $\forall$-safety stated in the above proposition can be decided in polynomial time.

Theorem 1. *The $\forall$-safety problem is in P.*

Since (1.) and (2.) in Proposition 2 are formulated for each $D \in \mathcal{P}$ separately, the following lemma is an immediate consequence of this proposition.

Lemma 1. *Let C be an $\mathcal{EL}$ concept and $\mathcal{P}$ an $\mathcal{EL}$ policy. Then C is $\forall$-safe for $\mathcal{P}$ iff C is $\forall$-safe for $\{D\}$ for all $D \in \mathcal{P}$.*

In this lemma, we have dispensed with the restriction that $\mathcal{P}$ is redundancy-free. This is admissible since we can first remove redundant elements from $\mathcal{P}$ and then apply the proposition to the redundancy-free policy obtained this way. Note that this fact will become important in the proof of Lemma 3, since there we cannot assume that the policy $\mathcal{P}_i$ defined there is redundancy-free.

Computing Optimal $\forall$-Safe Generalizations. Before we can describe our approach for computing optimal $\forall$-safe generalizations, we need to introduce some notation. Given an $\mathcal{EL}$ concept D such that $\mathbf{rd}(D) > 0$, the set $\mathbf{con}^{\exists}(D)$ consists of the elements of $\mathbf{con}(D)$ that are existential restrictions.

Definition 2. *Let $D_1, \ldots, D_p$ be $\mathcal{EL}$ concepts of role depth greater than zero. We say that $H \subseteq \mathbf{con}^{\exists}(D_1) \cup \ldots \cup \mathbf{con}^{\exists}(D_p)$ is a hitting set of $\mathbf{con}^{\exists}(D_1), \ldots, \mathbf{con}^{\exists}(D_p)$ if $H \cap \mathbf{con}(D_i) \neq \emptyset$ for every $i = 1, \ldots, p$. This hitting set is minimal if, for all $H' \subset H$, H' is not a hitting set.*

We will show that the set defined below contains all optimal $\forall$-safe generalizations of C for $\mathcal{P}$.

Definition 3. *Let C be an $\mathcal{EL}$ concept and $\mathcal{P} = \{D_1, \ldots, D_n\}$ a redundancy-free $\mathcal{EL}$ policy. The set $SSG(C, \mathcal{P})$ of all specific $\forall$-safe generalizations of C for $\mathcal{P}$ consists of the concepts C' that are obtained from C as follows:*

- *If C is $\forall$-safe for $\mathcal{P}$, then $SSG(C, \mathcal{P}) = \{C\}$.*
- *Otherwise, perform the following steps:*
  - *For all concept names $A \in \mathbf{con}(C)$ such that $A \in \mathbf{con}(D)$, where $D \in \mathcal{P}$ and $\mathbf{rd}(D) = 0$, remove A from $\mathbf{con}(C)$.*

- If $D_{j_1}, \ldots, D_{j_p}$ are all concepts in $\mathcal{P}$ such that $\mathbf{rd}(D_{j_\nu}) > 0$, then construct a minimal hitting set H of $\mathbf{con}^\exists(D_{j_1}), \ldots, \mathbf{con}^\exists(D_{j_p})$ and do the following:
  * For all $\exists r.E \in \mathbf{con}(C)$ such that there is a concept of the form $\exists r.D'$ in H with $\mathbf{rd}(D') = 0$, remove $\exists r.E$ from $\mathbf{con}(C)$.
  * For each $\exists r_i.C_i \in \mathbf{con}(C)$ that was not removed in the previous step, consider the set

$$\mathcal{P}_i := \{D' \mid \exists r_i.D' \in H \text{ and } \mathbf{rd}(D') > 0\}.$$

  If $\mathcal{P}_i \neq \emptyset$, then replace $\exists r_i.C_i$ in $\mathbf{con}(C)$ with $\bigsqcap \exists r_i.F$, where $F \in SSG(C_i, \mathcal{P}_i)$. If $\mathcal{P}_i$ is empty, then leave $\exists r_i.C_i$ as it is.

First, we show that the elements of $SSG(C, \mathcal{P})$ are indeed $\forall$-safe generalization.

Lemma 2. *If $C' \in SSG(C, \mathcal{P})$, then C' is a $\forall$-safe generalization of C for $\mathcal{P}$.*

Proof. First, we show that $C \sqsubseteq C'$. This is an easy consequence of the fact that, when constructing C' from C, atoms from the top-level conjunction of C are kept unchanged, removed, or generalized. The only non-trivial case is when $\exists r_i.C_i$ in $\mathbf{con}(C)$ is replaced with $\bigsqcap \exists r_i.F$, where F ranges over the elements of $SSG(C_i, \mathcal{P}_i)$. By induction on the role depth, we know that $C_i \sqsubseteq F$ for all $F \in SSG(C_i, \mathcal{P}_i)$, and thus $\exists r.C_i \sqsubseteq \exists r.F$.

To prove that C' is safe for $\mathcal{P}$, we use the characterization given in Proposition 2. Thus, let $D \in \mathcal{P}$. If $\mathbf{rd}(D) = 0$, then $\mathbf{con}(D)$ is a set of concept names, and each of them has been removed in the construction of C'. Thus, $\mathbf{con}(C') \cap \mathbf{con}(D) = \emptyset$, as required by (1.) in Proposition 2.

If $\mathbf{rd}(D) > 0$, then the minimal hitting H used in the construction of C' contains an existential restriction $\exists r.\hat{D} \in \mathbf{con}(D)$. If $\mathbf{rd}(\hat{D}) = 0$, then all existential restrictions for the role r are removed from the top-level conjunction of C, and thus 2a.) of Proposition 2 is satisfied. Finally, consider the case where $\mathbf{rd}(\hat{D}) > 0$. If $\exists r.E \in \mathbf{con}(C')$, then there is $\exists r_i.C_i \in \mathbf{con}(C)$ such that

$$\mathcal{P}_i = \{D' \mid \exists r_i.D' \in H \text{ and } \mathbf{rd}(D') > 0\} \neq \emptyset,$$

and $r = r_i$ and $E \in SSG(C_i, \mathcal{P}_i)$. Note that $\hat{D} \in \mathcal{P}_i$, and thus $\mathcal{P}_i = \emptyset$ is not possible for an existential restriction $\exists r_i.C_i \in \mathbf{con}(C)$ with $r_i = r$. Induction (over the role depth) yields that E is $\forall$-safe for $\mathcal{P}_i$, and thus for its subset $\{\hat{D}\}$. Hence, (2b.) of Proposition 2 is satisfied. □

However, $SSG(C, \mathcal{P})$ may also contain $\forall$-safe generalizations C' of C for $\mathcal{P}$ that are not optimal, as demonstrated by the following example.

Example 1. Let $C = \exists r_1.(A \sqcap B) \sqcap \exists r_2.B \sqcap \exists r_3.A$ and $\mathcal{P} = \{D_1, D_2\}$, where

$$D_1 = \exists r_1.A \sqcap \exists r_2.\top \quad \text{and} \quad D_2 = \exists r_1.B \sqcap \exists r_3.\top.$$

We have $C \sqsubseteq D_1$ and $C \sqsubseteq D_2$, and thus C is not even compliant, let alone $\forall$-safe, for $\mathcal{P}$. Applying the construction of Definition 3 to C and $\mathcal{P}$, we first construct the minimal hitting set $H_1 = \{\exists r_1.A, \exists r_1.B\}$ of $\mathsf{con}^\exists(D_1)$ and $\mathsf{con}^\exists(D_2)$. Since $\mathsf{rd}(A) = 0 = \mathsf{rd}(B)$ we remove the atom $\exists r_1.(A \sqcap B)$ from $\mathsf{con}(C)$, which yields the concept $C_1' = \exists r_2.B \sqcap \exists r_3.A \in \mathrm{SSG}(C, \mathcal{P})$.

If we take the minimal hitting set $H_2 = \{\exists r_1.A, \exists r_3.\top\}$ instead, then we need to remove the atoms $\exists r_1.(A \sqcap B)$ and $\exists r_3.A$ from $\mathsf{con}(C)$, which yields $C_2' = \exists r_2.B \in \mathrm{SSG}(C, \mathcal{P})$. Since $C_1' \sqsubset C_2'$, the concept C_2' cannot be optimal.

The next lemma states that every $\forall$-safe generalization of C subsumes some element of $\mathrm{SSG}(C, \mathcal{P})$.

Lemma 3. *For all $\forall$-safe generalization C'' of C for $\mathcal{P}$, there is $C' \in \mathrm{SSG}(C, \mathcal{P})$ such that $C' \sqsubseteq C''$.*

Proof. If C is $\forall$-safe for $\mathcal{P}$, then obviously $C \in \mathrm{SSG}(C, \mathcal{P})$ and we have $C \sqsubseteq C''$. Thus, let us assume that C is not $\forall$-safe for $\mathcal{P}$. Since C'' is a $\forall$-safe generalization of C for $\mathcal{P}$, we have $C \sqsubseteq C''$ and C'' satisfies the properties (1.) and (2.) in Proposition 2. Due to (1.), $\mathsf{con}(C'')$ contains no concept name A such that $A \in \mathsf{con}(D)$ for some $D \in \mathcal{P}$ with $\mathsf{rd}(D) = 0$. In addition, for all $D_{j_\nu} \in \mathcal{P}$ such that $\mathsf{rd}(D_{j_\nu}) > 0$, there is $\exists r.G_{j_\nu} \in \mathsf{con}(D_{j_\nu})$ such that (2a.) or (2b.) of Proposition 2 holds. The set $H' := \{G_{j_1}, \ldots, G_{j_p}\}$ is a hitting set of the sets $\mathsf{con}^\exists(D_{j_1}), \ldots, \mathsf{con}^\exists(D_{j_p})$ considered in Definition 3. Thus, there is a minimal hitting set H of $\mathsf{con}^\exists(D_{i_1}), \ldots, \mathsf{con}^\exists(D_{i_q})$ such that $H \subseteq H'$. Let C' be the element of $\mathrm{SSG}(C, \mathcal{P})$ that is constructed by using H. We show that $C' \sqsubseteq C''$ using Proposition 1.

First, consider a concept name $A \in \mathsf{con}(C'')$. Since $C \sqsubseteq C''$, we know that $A \in \mathsf{con}(C)$. In addition, as mentioned above, $\mathsf{con}(C'')$ contains no concept name A such that $A \in \mathsf{con}(D)$ for some $D \in \mathcal{P}$ with $\mathsf{rd}(D) = 0$. Consequently, when constructing C' from C, the concept name A is not removed, which yields $A \in \mathsf{con}(C')$.

Second, consider an existential restriction $\exists r.E \in \mathsf{con}(C'')$. Since $C \sqsubseteq C''$, there is $\exists r.C_i \in \mathsf{con}(C)$ such that $C_i \sqsubseteq E$. If $\exists r.C_i$ is not removed or generalized when constructing C', then $\exists r.C_i \in \mathsf{con}(C')$, and we are done. If $\exists r.C_i$ is removed from $\mathsf{con}(C)$ to construct C', then there is $\exists r.D' \in H \subseteq H'$ such that $\mathsf{rd}(D') = 0$. By the definition of H', we thus know that $\exists r.D'$ must satisfy (2a.) of Proposition 2. But then $\exists r.E \in \mathsf{con}(C'')$ would not be possible.

Finally, if $\exists r.C_i$ is generalized in the construction of C' from C by replacing it with $\bigsqcap_{F \in \mathrm{SSG}(C_i, \mathcal{P}_i)} \exists r.F$, then we know that $\mathcal{P}_i$ is non-empty. Now, consider an element D' of $\mathcal{P}_i$. Then, $\exists r.D' \in H \subseteq H'$ and $\mathsf{rd}(D') > 0$ imply that $\exists r.D'$ satisfies (2b.) of Proposition 2. Since $\exists r.E \in \mathsf{con}(C'')$, we thus know that E is $\forall$-safe for $\{D'\}$. Since this is true for all elements D' of $\mathcal{P}_i$, Lemma 1 yields that E is $\forall$-safe for $\mathcal{P}_i$. Together with $C_i \sqsubseteq E$, this shows that E is a $\forall$-safe generalization of C_i for $\mathcal{P}_i$, and thus induction yields that there is $F \in \mathrm{SSG}(C_i, \mathcal{P}_i)$ such that $F \sqsubseteq E$. Since $\exists r.F \in \mathsf{con}(C')$, this concludes our proof that $C' \sqsubseteq C''$. □

The following proposition states that all optimal $\forall$-safe generalizations of C for $\mathcal{P}$ are contained in $\mathrm{SSG}(C, \mathcal{P})$.

Proposition 3. *Let C be an $\mathcal{EL}$ concept and $\mathcal{P} = \{D_1, \ldots, D_p\}$ a redundancy-free $\mathcal{EL}$ policy. If C'' is an optimal $\forall$-safe generalization of C for $\mathcal{P}$, then $C'' \in SSG(C, \mathcal{P})$ (up to equivalence).*

Proof. Given an optimal $\forall$-safe generalization C'' of C for $\mathcal{P}$, Lemma 3 yields an element $C' \in SSG(C, \mathcal{P})$ such that $C' \sqsubseteq C''$. By Lemma 2, $C \sqsubseteq C'$ and C' is $\forall$-safe for $\mathcal{P}$. Thus, optimality of C'' implies that $C' \equiv C''$. $\qquad\square$

The following theorem is an easy consequence of this proposition and the definition of $SSG(C, \mathcal{P})$.

Theorem 2. *Let C be an $\mathcal{EL}$ concept and $\mathcal{P} = \{D_1, \ldots, D_p\}$ a redundancy-free $\mathcal{EL}$ policy. The cardinality of the set of all optimal $\forall$-safe generalization of C for $\mathcal{P}$ is at most exponential, and each of its elements has at most exponential size. Additionally, the set of all optimal $\forall$-safe generalizations of C for $\mathcal{P}$ can be computed in exponential time.*

Proof. It is sufficient to show that the set $SSG(C, \mathcal{P})$ satisfies the properties stated above. The cardinality of $SSG(C, \mathcal{P})$ is at most exponential since in Definition 3 at most exponentially many minimal hitting sets are considered, and each such set yields exactly one element of $SSG(C, \mathcal{P})$. Moreover, the size of each element C' in $SSG(C, \mathcal{P})$ may become exponential (but not more) since, during constructing C', we may need to compute a conjunction of at most exponentially many existential restrictions, where each of them has at most exponential size (by induction). To compute the set of all optimal $\forall$-safe generalizations of C for $\mathcal{P}$, we need to remove all concepts in $SSG(C, \mathcal{P})$ that are not minimal w.r.t. subsumption. This requires exponentially many (polynomial) subsumption tests on exponentially large concepts. $\qquad\square$

The following example shows that an algorithm for computing all optimal $\forall$-safe generalizations cannot be better than exponential in the worst case.

Example 2. Let $C = \exists r_1.(\exists s_1.\top \sqcap \exists s_2.\top) \sqcap \ldots \sqcap \exists r_n.(\exists s_1.\top \sqcap \exists s_2.\top)$ and $\mathcal{P} = \{\exists r_i.\exists s_1.\top \sqcap \exists r_i.\exists s_2.\top \mid 1 \leq i \leq n\}$. Using Definition 3, we obtain that $SSG(C, \mathcal{P})$ consists of the exponentially many concepts $\exists r_1.\exists s_{j_1}.\top \sqcap \ldots \sqcap \exists r_n.\exists s_{j_n}.\top$, where $j_i \in \{1, 2\}$ for all $i = 1, \ldots, n$. Since these concepts are incomparable w.r.t. subsumption, they are exactly the optimal $\forall$-safe generalization of C for $\mathcal{P}$.

The $\forall$-Optimality Problem. Given $\mathcal{EL}$ concepts C, C' such that $C \sqsubseteq C'$ and an $\mathcal{EL}$ policy $\mathcal{P}$, the $\forall$-optimality problem asks whether C' is an optimal $\forall$-safe generalization of C for $\mathcal{P}$. Since $\forall$-safety is a polynomial, upward-closed property (see Definition 5 in [5]), Theorem 3 in [5] yields the following complexity upper-bound for this problem.

Proposition 4. *The $\forall$-optimality problem is in coNP.*

Similarly to the case of the $\exists$-optimality problem in [5], we do not know whether the $\forall$-optimality problem is also coNP-hard. But we can show that it is at least as hard as the Hypergraph Duality Problem [8], called DUAL. Note that this problem is in coNP, but conjectured to be neither in P nor coNP-hard [9,10].

Proposition 5. DUAL *can be reduced in polynomial time to the $\forall$-optimality problem.*

The proof of this proposition, which is similar to the one of Proposition 7 in [5], is omitted due to the space constraints.

4   Investigating $\forall\exists$-Safety

We now consider the case where the attacker's knowledge is assumed to be given by an $\mathcal{FLE}$ concept. Since $\mathcal{FL}_0$ is a sublogic of $\mathcal{FLE}$, concepts that are $\forall\exists$-safe are also $\forall$-safe, but the opposite need not hold. The following proposition characterizes $\forall\exists$-safety.

Proposition 6. *Let C be an $\mathcal{EL}$ concept and $\mathcal{P} = \{D_1, \dots, D_p\}$ a redundancy-free $\mathcal{EL}$ policy. Then C is $\forall\exists$-safe for $\mathcal{P}$ iff*

(1.) $A \notin \text{con}(C)$ *for all concept names* $A \in \text{con}(D_1) \cup \dots \cup \text{con}(D_p)$, *and*
(2.) for all existential restrictions $\exists r.D' \in \text{con}(D_1) \cup \dots \cup \text{con}(D_p)$, *there is no concept of the form* $\exists r.E$ *in* $\text{con}(C)$.

Proof. First, assume that C is not $\forall\exists$-safe for $\mathcal{P}$. Hence, there is $D_i \in \mathcal{P}$ and an $\mathcal{FLE}$ concept C'' such that C'' complies with $\mathcal{P}$, but $C \sqcap C'' \sqsubseteq D_i$. This subsumption implies that $A \in \text{con}(C) \cup \text{con}(C'')$ holds for all $A \in \text{con}(D_i)$. If there is an $A \in \text{con}(D_i)$ such that $A \in \text{con}(C)$, then property (1.) is violated. Otherwise, all $A \in \text{con}(D_i)$ belong to $\text{con}(C'')$. But then $C'' \not\sqsubseteq D_i$ can only be due to the fact that there is $\exists r.D' \in \text{con}(D_i)$ such that, for all $\exists r.C' \in \text{con}(C'')$, we have $C' \sqcap \text{filler}_r^\forall(C'') \not\sqsubseteq D'$. Applying Proposition 1 again to the subsumption $C \sqcap C'' \sqsubseteq D_i$ thus yields that that there is $\exists r.E \in \text{con}(C)$ such that $E \sqcap \text{filler}_r^\forall(C'') \sqsubseteq D'$. Consequently, property (2.) is violated.

   To show the other direction, assume that condition (1.) or (2.) is violated. If (1.) is violated, then there are $D_i \in \mathcal{P}$ and a concept name A such that $A \in \text{con}(C) \cap \text{con}(D_i)$. We modify D_i to C'' by removing A from the top-level conjunction of D_i. Then C'' is an $\mathcal{EL}$ concept, and thus also an $\mathcal{FLE}$ concept, such that $C'' \not\sqsubseteq D_i$ and $C \sqcap C'' \equiv C \sqcap D_i \sqsubseteq D_i$. Given $D \in \mathcal{P} \setminus \{D_i\}$ we have $C'' \not\sqsubseteq D$ since otherwise $D_i \sqsubseteq C'' \sqsubseteq D$ would contradict our assumption that $\mathcal{P}$ is redundancy-free. Thus C is not $\forall\exists$-safe for $\mathcal{P}$.

   If condition (2.) is violated, then there are $D_i \in \mathcal{P}$ and existential restrictions $\exists r.D' \in \text{con}(D_i)$ and $\exists r.E \in \text{con}(C)$. Let C'' be obtained from D_i by replacing every existential restriction $\exists r.F$ from the top-level conjunction of D_i with the corresponding value restriction $\forall r.F$. To show that $C \sqcap C'' \sqsubseteq D_i$, it is sufficient to show that $C \sqcap C'' \sqsubseteq \exists r.F$ for all $\exists r.F \in \text{con}(D_i)$. This is the case since $C \sqcap C'' \sqsubseteq \exists r.E \sqcap \forall r.F \sqsubseteq \exists r.(E \sqcap F) \sqsubseteq \exists r.F$.

It remains to show that C'' is compliant with $\mathcal{P}$, i.e., for all $D \in \mathcal{P}$ we have $C'' \not\sqsubseteq D$. If D contains an existential restriction for r, then this holds since C'' does not contain an existential restriction for r. In particular, this covers the case where $D = D_i$. If D does not contain an existential restriction for r, then the changes we made when going from D_i to C'' are not relevant for D, i.e., we have $C'' \sqsubseteq D$ iff $D_i \sqsubseteq D$. Since $\mathcal{P}$ is redundancy-free, this yields $C'' \not\sqsubseteq D$. $\qquad\square$

Due to the simplicity of the conditions (1.) and (2.) in this proposition, it is now easy to show that all relevant computation or decision problems for $\forall\exists$-safety are tractable.

Theorem 3. *Given $\mathcal{EL}$ concepts C, C'' and a redundancy-free $\mathcal{EL}$ policy $\mathcal{P}$, we*

- *can decide whether C is $\forall\exists$-safe for $\mathcal{P}$,*
- *can compute the unique optimal $\forall\exists$-safe generalization of C for $\mathcal{P}$, and*
- *can decide whether C'' is an optimal $\forall\exists$-safe generalization of C for $\mathcal{P}$*

in polynomial time.

Proof. First, note that the characterization of $\forall\exists$-safety given in Proposition 6 can obviously be checked in polynomial time. Secondly, to obtain the optimal $\forall\exists$-safe generalization of C for $\mathcal{P}$, we simply remove from $\mathsf{con}(C)$ all concept names A with $A \in \mathsf{con}(D_1) \cup \ldots \cup \mathsf{con}(D_p)$, and all existential restrictions $\exists r.E$ such that $\mathsf{con}(D_1) \cup \ldots \cup \mathsf{con}(D_p)$ contains an existential restriction for the role r. This can clearly be done in polynomial time. Finally, to decide whether C'' is an optimal $\forall\exists$-safe generalization of C for $\mathcal{P}$, apply the procedure just described to C, and check whether the resulting concept C' is equivalent to C''. Since the subsumption problem is polynomial in $\mathcal{EL}$, this yields a polynomial-time decision procedure for the optimality problem. $\qquad\square$

5   Conclusion

We have investigated the notion of safety for a policy in the setting where the knowledge about individuals and the policy are given by $\mathcal{EL}$ concepts, but the attacker's knowledge is assumed to be expressed in $\mathcal{FL}_0$ or $\mathcal{FLE}$. For both cases, we have characterized safety and have shown how to compute optimal safe generalizations of a given $\mathcal{EL}$ concept w.r.t. a given $\mathcal{EL}$ policy. For $\mathcal{FL}_0$, the complexity results proved here are the same as the ones shown in [5] for the case where the attacker's knowledge is assumed to be expressed in $\mathcal{EL}$. Nevertheless, the characterizations of safety and the developed algorithms are, of course, different depending on whether $\mathcal{FL}_0$ or $\mathcal{EL}$ is considered. For the case of $\mathcal{FLE}$, the characterization of safety developed in this paper is considerably simpler, and as a consequence the relevant decision and computation problems become tractable. While this may be seen as an advantage, it is actually due to the fact that, with an assumed stronger capability of the attacker, concepts need to be changed more radically to make them safe. Thus, less knowledge can be preserved when publishing information in a privacy-preserving way.

In the future, we intend to continue this work in several directions. First, we want to extend our framework to a setting where the knowledge about individuals is given by an ABox that contains not only concept assertions, but also role assertions. As mentioned in the introduction, our idea for achieving this is to combine our approaches with the ones developed in [11,12]. In a second step, we intend to add a TBox that constrains the interpretation of concepts. This means that subsumption w.r.t. all interpretations is replaced by subsumption w.r.t. all models of the TBox. Since this subsumption relation is less easy to characterize than the characterization given in Proposition 1 for subsumption without a TBox, this will probably be a quite challenging task. As a starting point, we will also look at the case where the TBox satisfies certain cycle-restrictions (see, e.g., [1]). In addition, we intend to look also at other (combinations of) DLs in these settings.

Another interesting question is how to impose additional constraints on which knowledge is potentially available to an attacker. At the moment, we play it very safe by assuming that any knowledge expressible in the respective DL could be available to the attacker. This may, however, result in very general and uninformative safe generalizations, as in our example in the introduction when we assume the attacker's knowledge is expressed in $\mathcal{FLE}$. It might make sense to restrict the potential knowledge of the attacker about an individual to knowledge that really holds for this individuals (since we are not interested in what follows from lies about the individual), but the question is how to express this restriction formally. One possibility could be to assume that the "real world" is given by a finite interpretation, or by a knowledge base that approximates it.

A different approach for restricting the access to information contained in an ontology has been investigated in [4]. In this work, the axioms of the ontology are labeled with access restrictions, and users can only see (the consequences of) the axioms for which they have the right of access. In contrast, in our work the access restrictions are formulated on the side of the consequences (in the form of policies) rather than on the side of the axioms. In addition, in [4] axioms are removed completely if a user does not have the right to access them, whereas in [5] and in the present work they are weakened appropriately. Nevertheless, it might be interesting to combine the two approaches, e.g., by producing variants of an axiom of different strength, and allowing a user that does not have the right to access the original axiom at least access to an appropriate weakening, which depends on the user's access right.

References

1. Baader, F., Borgwardt, S., Morawska, B.: Extending unification in $\mathcal{EL}$ towards general TBoxes. In: Proceedings of the 13th International Conference on Principles of Knowledge Representation and Reasoning (KR 2012), pp. 568–572. AAAI Press (2012)

2. Baader, F., Brandt, S., Lutz, C.: Pushing the $\mathcal{EL}$ envelope. In: Kaelbling, L.P., Saffiotti, A. (eds.) Proceedings of the Nineteenth International Joint Conference on Artificial Intelligence, IJCAI 2005, pp. 364–369. Morgan-Kaufmann Publishers, Edinburgh (2005)

3. Baader, F., Calvanese, D., McGuinness, D.L., Nardi, D., Patel-Schneider, P.F. (eds.): The Description Logic Handbook: Theory, Implementation, and Applications. Cambridge University Press, New York (2003)

4. Baader, F., Knechtel, M., Peñaloza, R.: Context-dependent views to axioms and consequences of semantic web ontologies. J. Web Semant. **12**, 22–40 (2012)

5. Baader, F., Kriegel, F., Nuradiansyah, A.: Privacy-preserving ontology publishing for $\mathcal{EL}$ instance stores. In: Calimeri, F., Leone, N., Manna, M. (eds.) JELIA 2019. LNCS (LNAI), vol. 11468, pp. 323–338. Springer, Cham (2019). https://doi.org/10.1007/978-3-030-19570-0_21

6. Baader, F., Küsters, R., Molitor, R.: Computing least common subsumers in description logics with existential restrictions. In: Dean, T. (ed.) Proceedings of the 16th International Joint Conference on Artificial Intelligence (IJCAI 1999), pp. 96–103 (1999)

7. Donini, F.M., Lenzerini, M., Nardi, D., Hollunder, B., Nutt, W., Marchetti-Spaccamela, A.: The complexity of existential quantification in concept languages. Artif. Intell. **53**(2–3), 309–327 (1992)

8. Eiter, T., Gottlob, G.: Hypergraph transversal computation and related problems in logic and AI. In: Flesca, S., Greco, S., Ianni, G., Leone, N. (eds.) JELIA 2002. LNCS (LNAI), vol. 2424, pp. 549–564. Springer, Heidelberg (2002). https://doi.org/10.1007/3-540-45757-7_53

9. Fredman, M.L., Khachiyan, L.: On the complexity of dualization of monotone disjunctive normal forms. J. Algorithms **21**(3), 618–628 (1996)

10. Gottlob, G., Malizia, E.: Achieving new upper bounds for the hypergraph duality problem through logic. SIAM J. Comput. **47**(2), 456–492 (2018)

11. Grau, B.C., Kostylev, E.V.: Logical foundations of privacy-preserving publishing of linked data. In: Schuurmans, D., Wellman, M.P. (eds.) Proceedings of the Thirtieth AAAI Conference on Artificial Intelligence, 12–17 February 2016, Phoenix, Arizona, USA, pp. 943–949 (2016)

12. Grau, B.C., Kostylev, E.V.: Logical foundations of linked data anonymisation. J. Artif. Intell. Res. **64**, 253–314 (2019)

13. Hoehndorf, R., Schofield, P.N., Gkoutos, G.V.: The role of ontologies in biological and biomedical research: a functional perspective. Brief. Bioinform. **16**(6), 1069–1080 (2015)

14. Horrocks, I., Li, L., Turi, D., Bechhofer, S.: The instance store: DL reasoning with large numbers of individuals. In: Haarslev, V., Möller, R. (eds.) Proceedings of the 2004 International Workshop on Description Logics (DL 2004), 6–8 June 2004, Whistler, British Columbia, Canada (2004)

15. Levesque, H.J., Brachman, R.J.: Expressiveness and tractability in knowledge representation and reasoning. Comput. Intell. **3**, 78–93 (1987)

16. Suntisrivaraporn, B.: Polynomial-time reasoning support for design and maintenance of large-scale biomedical ontologies. Doctoral thesis, Technische Universität Dresden, Dresden, Germany (2009)

Clustering of Argument Graphs Using Semantic Similarity Measures

Karsten Block⬥, Simon Trumm⬥, Premtim Sahitaj⬥, Stefan Ollinger⬥,
and Ralph Bergmann$^{(\boxtimes)}$⬥

Business Information Systems II, University of Trier, 54296 Trier, Germany
{s4kabloc,s4sitru,sahitaj,ollinger,bergmann}@uni-trier.de
http://www.wi2.uni-trier.de

Abstract. Research on argumentation in Artificial Intelligence recently
investigates new methods that contribute to the vision of developing
robust argumentation machines. One line of research explores ways of
reasoning with natural language arguments coming from information
sources on the web as a foundation for the deliberation and synthesis
of arguments in specific domains. This paper builds upon arguments
represented as argument graphs in the standardized Argument Interchange Format. While previous work was focused on the development of
semantic similarity measures used for the case-based retrieval of argument graphs, this paper addresses the problem of clustering argument
graphs to explore structures that facilitate argumentation interpretation. We propose a k-medoid and an agglomerative clustering approach
based on semantic similarity measures. We compare the clustering results
based on a graph-based semantic measure that takes the structure of the
argument into account with a semantic word2vec measure on the pure
textual argument representation. Experiments based on the Microtext
corpus show that the graph-based similarity is best on internal evaluation measures, while the pure textual measure performs very well for
identifying topic-specific clusters.

Keywords: Argumentation · Argument graph similarity ·
Semantic textual similarity · Text clustering

1 Introduction

As an emerging sub-field in Artificial Intelligence (AI), argumentation includes
research that centers around identifying structures in natural language arguments [1]. In particular, the development of computational methods for extracting arguments and their interrelations from text [13], methods for semantic argument representation, and methods for reasoning with arguments are topics of
current interest. The German Science Foundation (DFG) currently funds the
special research program RATIO[1] which aims at designing robust argumenta-

---

[1] http://www.spp-ratio.de/home/.

© Springer Nature Switzerland AG 2019
C. Benzmüller and H. Stuckenschmidt (Eds.): KI 2019, LNAI 11793, pp. 101–114, 2019.
https://doi.org/10.1007/978-3-030-30179-8_8

tion machines that enable decision making and problem-solving based on arguments. ReCAP [4] as a project within RATIO focuses on the idea of argumentation machines to support researchers, decision- and policy-makers in obtaining a comprehensive overview of topic-related argumentative opinions which enable the development of a sound and credible perspective justified by convincing arguments. ReCAP aims at combining methods from case-based reasoning (CBR), information retrieval (IR), and computational argumentation (CA) to contribute to the foundations of argumentation machines. An argumentation machine can find supporting and opposing arguments for a user's topic or synthesize new arguments for an upcoming, not yet well explored topic. Thereby it could support researchers, journalists, and medical practitioners in various tasks, overcoming the limited support provided by traditional search engines used today.

This paper deals with a core problem that arises in various forms in argumentation machines, namely the clustering of arguments. Argument clustering is useful for deliberation as a method to structure a larger set of arguments dealing with a certain topic. It is also a helpful pre-processing step for the generalization and segmentation of arguments [11] to obtain reuseable patterns for case-based synthesis of new arguments. In our work we build upon arguments represented as argument graphs following the Argument Interchange Format (AIF) developed by the University of Dundee [7]. Argument graphs capture an important part of the semantics of arguments by partitioning them into claims and premises linked by various relations (rules of inference, argumentation schemes) describing how they interact. We propose a k-medoid and an agglomerative method for clustering argument graphs based on a semantic graph-based similarity measure that employs word2vec [15] as a local similarity measure to compare the textual content of claims and premises [3]. The clustering methods are evaluated using the Microtext corpus [17] and compared with pure text-based variants of the cluster methods.

The next section introduces foundations and related work. Section 3 describes the clustering algorithms, while Sect. 4 presents the experimental setup and the results obtained. The paper ends with a conclusion and possible future work.

2   Foundations and Related Work

In argumentation theory an argument consists of a set of premises and a claim together with a rule of inference which concludes from the premises to the claim. A premise can support or oppose a claim as well as an inference step. Together premises, claims, and inference steps form an argument graph. Directed graphs are suitable for formally representing the structure of the individual elements of an argument [5].

2.1   Representing Arguments as Graphs

In our work, we follow the vision of robust argumentation machines which are able to explore natural language arguments from information sources on the web to reason with them on the knowledge level. While argument mining methods [13] aim at converting natural language argumentative texts into argument graphs containing the natural language content, our work aims at supporting the reasoning with such graphs. Thus we do not build our work upon an argumentation framework based on formal logic such Dung's argumentation framework [8] but on a graph representation that encompasses the textual content from the original natural language source of the argument. Therefore we use an argument graph representation based on the Argument Interchange Format (AIF) which was developed by the Argumentation Research Group at the University of Dundee as a standard for representing and exchanging argument graphs [7]. An argument graph can be formally defined as a 5-tuple $W = (N, E, \tau, \lambda, t)$. Here, N describes a set of nodes, $E \subseteq N \times N$ describes a set of edges, $\tau \colon N \to T$ and $\lambda \colon N \to \mathcal{L}$ define functions that map nodes to types T and labels $\mathcal{L}$ respectively. The labels represent the textual content of a node. The set of node types T is declared according to the type ontology used in AIF to represent argumentation schemes. The overall topic of the argument graph is specified by a label $t \in \mathcal{L}$ [3].

Figure 1 illustrates an argument graph in AIF. On a high level perspective, claims and premises are represented as information nodes (I-nodes), depicted as grey rectangular boxes which are related to each other via scheme nodes (S-nodes), depicted as small colored rectangles. In the figure, the information node with the content *"Therefore universities should not charge fees in Germany"* without successor node represents the conclusion of this argument.

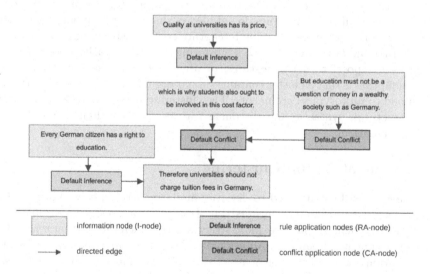

Fig. 1. Example argument graph in AIF (http://www.aifdb.org/diagram/6407.), designed with OVA (http://ova.arg-tech.org). (Color figure online)

In the simplest form applied in this work here, S-nodes can be classified into rule application nodes (RA-nodes, depicted in green color), which denote specific inference relations and conflict application nodes (CA-nodes, depicted in red color), which indicate specific conflict relations. They roughly correspond to the support and attacks relations in other frameworks. However, in general a large variety of different argumentation schemes [21] can be differentiated and represented as type of an S-node. Such argumentation schemes, correspond to archetypical forms of arguments. For example, the supporting argument can of the sub-type *Argument from Positive Consequence*, *Argument from Expert Opinion*, or *Argument from Cause to Effect*. In an other paper [12], we created an ontology consisting of 38 argumentation schemes which are arranged in a taxonomy, which is then used as a more fine grained representation of S-nodes.

2.2 Argument Clustering

In the literature, a few approaches addressing the clustering of arguments can be found. However, they make use of the pure argument text, not considering the representation of arguments in an argument graph. Boltužić and Šnajder [6] identify prominent arguments by using hierarchical clustering based on semantic textual similarity (STS). It was assumed that statements can be grouped into clusters representing abstract arguments by analyzing the degree of semantic similarity between statements. Three methods for semantic textual similarity were evaluated, including word embeddings, weighted bag-of-words and an off-the-shelf STS tool. Hierarchical agglomerative clustering was conducted using complete linkage and Ward's method. Clustering of arguments can be difficult since arguments of different topics do not always share clear boundaries. Further textual similarity might not be able to capture specific aspects of arguments.

Habernal and Gurevych [10] use a clustering of argumentative debate portal sentences and posts to derive features for argument component identification. One assumption is that a cluster contains similar arguments and cluster centroids correspond to prototypical arguments. The clustering-based features outperform other structural, syntactic and discourse features in cross-domain and cross-register evaluation.

3   Argument Graph Clustering

Clustering algorithms are used to discover similarity structures within data by grouping similar objects into clusters [14]. This paper addresses the problem of clustering argument graphs to explore structures that facilitate further reasoning through argument deliberation. Additionally, these structures can be used for the generalization and segmentation of arguments [11] to conduct case-base synthesis of new arguments. In this chapter the used base algorithms for clustering are briefly explained before their application to argument graphs is introduced. In particular the used graph-based similarity measure is described as well as various ways of deriving symmetric variants from this originally asymmetric measure to be used in the clustering algorithms.

3.1   Clustering Algorithms

Clustering algorithms aim at partitioning a data set into clusters of data points. The quality of the result can be determined by the homogeneity of the data points within a cluster and the heterogeneity to data points from other clusters. Clustering algorithms can be classified into flat and hierarchical clustering approaches. In flat clustering, the resulting clusters are without structure or relation to one another. Hierarchical clustering outputs a hierarchy among clusters. These structures are more informative and can be utilized to extract additional insights, such as cluster representatives on multiple levels of granularity. The advantage of a structured result comes at a cost of higher computational effort when compared to flat clustering.

K-medoid is a modified version of the well-known flat clustering algorithm k-means. Its objective is to divide the total quantity of data points into k disjunct clusters. K-means and k-medoid attempt to minimize the distance between data points within a cluster to the respective cluster center [14]. For the k-medoid approach the cluster center is an actual data point which is referred to as medoid. The number of clusters k must be defined prior to the process, the optimal number can be found by varying k. At the beginning of the algorithm random initial medoids are selected and the cluster distribution according to the nearest-neighbor principle is calculated. The cluster distribution is iteratively updated by improving a quality criterion. K-medoid terminates at a local optimum and therefore the cluster quality is dependent on the choice of the randomly initialized cluster centers. K-medoid is less sensitive to noisy data and errors than k-means and similar algorithms.

Agglomerative Nesting (AGNES) is a hierarchical clustering algorithm that iteratively merges previously created sub-clusters bottom-up, starting initially with a cluster for each data point [14]. In each iteration the two clusters are merged that have the smallest distance to one another. There are several alternative criteria that can be used to define closeness of two clusters and thereby the behaviour of the algorithm. In this paper we focus on the following distances measures for clusters: single linkage, complete linkage, average linkage, and Ward's method. Single linkage computes the similarity between two clusters by computing the distance of their respectively closest members. Complete linkage computes the similarity between two clusters by computing the distance of their respectively furthest members. Average linkage computes the similarity between two clusters by computing the average distance of all members. Ward's method reduces the variance within clusters by minimizing the squared error [22].

The resulting agglomerative clustering is a binary cluster tree instead of a set of disjoint clusters as in k-medoid. Although hierarchical clustering algorithms have a high space and time complexity they are suitable since we are interested in the hierarchical structure.

3.2   Similarity Measures for Clustering Argument Graphs

As we aim at clustering argument graphs, the described algorithms require a distance or similarity measure working on argument graphs. We build upon our previous work on similarity-based retrieval of argument graphs [3] in which a graph-based similarity measure for AIF graphs has been developed. This measure is used during retrieval to compare a query in the form of an argument graph with the argument graphs from a corpus.

The general principle of argument graph similarity has been adopted from process-oriented case-based reasoning [2] and follows the local-global principle [19]. The global similarity is computed from local node and edge similarities. The local node similarity $\text{sim}_N(n_q, n_c)$ of a node n_q from the query argument graph QA and a node n_c from the case argument graph CA is computed as follows:

$$\text{sim}_N(n_q, n_c) = \begin{cases} \text{sim}_I(n_q, n_c), & \text{if } \tau(n_q) = \tau(n_c) = \text{I-node} \\ \text{sim}_S(n_q, n_c), & \text{if } \tau(n_q) = \tau(n_c) = \text{S-node} \\ 0, & \text{otherwise} \end{cases}$$

The similarity of I-nodes sim_I is determined using the text contained in the I-nodes, which are typical fragments of sentences. We use a semantic textual similarity approach based on word embeddings. An embedding associates each word with a word vector in a high-dimensional real-valued vector-space. Word vectors capture the semantics of a word, in the sense that similar words have similar word vectors. We use the word2vec skip-gram [15] model to transform each word in the text of an I-node into its vector representation. The embedding vector of the whole I-node is determined by aggregating the word vectors using the weighted mean function. Prior to this, stop-words are removed. Weighting is performed using IDF weighting. Finally, the similarity sim_I is the result of the cosine measure applied to the two mean vectors.

The similarity of the S-nodes sim_S is determined comparing the types of S-nodes. It is 1, if both S-nodes are of the same type (both are RA or both are CA nodes) and 0 otherwise.

The similarity of two edges $\text{sim}_E(e_q, e_c)$ is determined based on the similarity of the nodes at their endpoints l and r respectively:

$$\text{sim}_E(e_q, e_c) = 0.5 \cdot (\text{sim}_N(e_q.l, e_c.l) + \text{sim}_N(e_q.r, e_c.r))$$

To construct a global similarity value, an admissible partial, injective mapping m is applied which maps nodes and edges from QA to CA, such that only nodes of the same type (I-nodes to I-nodes and S-nodes to S-nodes) are mapped. Edges can only be mapped if the nodes they link are mapped as well by m. For a given mapping m let sn_i be the node similarities $\text{sim}_N(n_i, m(n_i))$ and se_i the edge similarities $\text{sim}_E(e_i, m(e_i))$. The similarity for a query graph QA and a case graph CA given a mapping m is the normalized sum of the node and edge similarities (n_N is the number of nodes and n_E is the number of edges in QA).

$$sim_m(QA, CA) = \frac{sn_1 + \ldots + sn_n + se_1 + \ldots + se_m}{n_N + n_E}$$

Finally, the similarity of QA and CA is the similarity of an optimal mapping m, which can be computed using an A^* search [2].

$$sim(QA, CA) = \max_m \{sim_m(QA, CA) \mid m \text{ is admissible}\}$$

This similarity measure computes a similarity by considering the correspondence between the elements of the query argument and case argument. One particular mapping m specifies one possible correspondence which is evaluated by sim_m. In general we are interested only in the best possible correspondence, which is reflected in the overall similarity value. The graph structure of arguments enables the similarity measure to focus on the most relevant elements. When used during retrieval, it determines the best possible matching argument graph in a repository (or a case base in the terminology of case-based reasoning). Given this, it is obvious that this similarity measure is not symmetrical: query graph and case graph have clearly different rôles in these measures. This can be seen easily when the query graph is a sub-graph of the case graph. In that case the query graph can be fully mapped onto the case graph and the similarity will be 1. If instead the case graph is a sub-graph of the query graph, only parts of the query graph can be mapped to the case graph and thus the similarity value will be lower than 1.

3.3 Symmetrization of Graph Similarity Measure

For clustering, a symmetric similarity measure is required to compare two argument graphs from a repository. Thus we need to make the graph similarity measure symmetric. Therefore, we propose and investigate three options in which we apply the similarity measure twice, once in each direction. We can define the symmetric graph similarity value of two argument graphs either as the minimum (1), the maximum (2), or the average (3) of the two similarity values:

$$sim_{min}(x, y) = min\{sim(x, y), sim(y, x)\} \tag{1}$$

$$sim_{max}(x, y) = max\{sim(x, y), sim(y, x)\} \tag{2}$$

$$sim_{avg}(x, y) = \frac{sim(x, y) + sim(y, x)}{2} \tag{3}$$

All symmetrization strategies are used in the evaluation. The resulting similarity measures are referred to in the following as Graph-Min, Graph-Max and Graph-Avg.

3.4 Clustering Based on Topic Vector Similarity

The proposed similarity measure has the advantage that it takes the argument structure defined by the graph into account, but it comes with the disadvantage that it is computationally expensive due to the involved optimization problem. In order to investigate the benefit of using the graph structure over the pure textual representation of the argument, we also investigate the result of the clustering approaches with a simplified similarity measure. Therefore we employ the topic label t defined for each graph (see Sect. 2.1). This topic vector is constructed as the mean of all I-node embedding vectors, thus it is a mean value over the full argument text. Again, stop-words are removed and an IDF-weighting is applied. The topic vector similarity is again computed using the cosine similarity measure. It is already symmetric, thus the proposed symmetrization approaches are not required. Please note that the resulting clustering algorithms resemble those already investigated in the literature (see Sect. 2.2).

4   Experimental Evaluation

We now evaluate the performance of the proposed clustering methods on argument graphs. The evaluation is divided into an internal and an external evaluation. The internal evaluation has the objective to examine the quality of the clustering by using internal evaluation measures, whereas the external evaluation is supposed to determine whether the clustering is able to reconstruct the various topics reflected in a corpus.

4.1   Hypotheses

The following hypotheses are investigated in this evaluation:

- **H1:** The clustering of argument graphs is able to discover the topics contained in the clustered corpus.
- **H2:** The graph similarity measure produces a clustering which is more in line with a human classification compared to the clustering using the topic vector similarity measure.
- **H3:** A coarser topic classification is easier to reproduce by clustering than a more fine-grained classification.

4.2   Argument Corpus and Experimental Setup

As argument corpus for the clustering, an annotated corpus of argumentative microtexts by Peldzsus and Stede [17], the Microtext corpus, will be taken as basis. The corpus consists of 112 short argumentative texts about 18 different topics. One benefit of the corpus is that most texts are pre-classified into those topics. The texts were initially written in German language and then professionally translated into English. We use the English version of the corpus. All texts are annotated as argument graphs, following the scheme proposed in Peldszus and Stede [16]. The corpus is available in the AIFdb[2] in the previously explained AIF graph format (see Fig. 1 for an example). As a kind of data cleaning, a few arguments without relationship to any of the 18 topics have been removed.

---

[2] http://corpora.aifdb.org/.

Table 1. All topics with corresponding cluster number.

Super-Topic	Topic	# Graphs
Education	school_uniforms	3
	increase_weight_of_BA_thesis_in_final_grade	4
	charge_tuition_fees	6
Environment	waste_separation	1
	higher_dog_poo_fines	8
Medicine	health_insurance_cover_complementary_medicine	8
	over_the_counter_morning_after_pill	5
Politics	public_broadcasting_fees_on_demand	7
	stricter_regulation_of_intelligence_services	4
	introduce_capital_punishment	8
	allow_shops_to_open_on_holidays_and_Sundays	8
	buy_tax_evader_data_from_dubious_sources	2
	make_video_games_olympic	3
	EU_influence_on_political_events_in_Ukraine	3
Living	cap_rent_increases	6
	keep_retirement_at_63	6
	partial_housing_development_at_Tempelhofer_Feld	2
	TXL_airport_remain_operational_after_BER_opening	3

To evaluate the effect of coarser-grained topics on the clustering quality, we manually combined the topics to five classes, or super-topics. The goal is to reduce the false classification of graphs with similar topics, for instance, the topics "school uniforms" and "charge tuition fees" were merged into the more general class "education". The generated topic groups are about the same size with the exception of "politics", which is the largest cluster. Table 1 shows all topics of the corpus together with the number of argument graphs and the super-topic. As word representation we used the pre-trained Google News[3] word embeddings for English language.

4.3 Internal Evaluation

In the internal evaluation the quality of the clustering will be evaluated by three measures. The silhouette coefficient utilizes both cohesion and separation into one value from $[-1, 1]$ [20]. Cohesion measures how closely objects in a cluster are related to each other and separation how distinct objects from different clusters are. A high value indicates that objects are well matched within clusters and poorly between clusters whereas a low value corresponds to the opposite. The Dunn index (DI) is a ratio of within cluster and between cluster separations [9].

---
[3] https://code.google.com/archive/p/word2vec/.

DI has values in $[0, \infty]$ and should be maximized as well. Connectivity measures to what extent items are placed in the same cluster as their nearest neighbor with values in $[0, \infty]$. Unlike the other measures lower values correspond to a better clustering quality. For each measure the optimal k is found, which equates the highest value of the respective measure. Evaluation was performed with a varying number k, which ranged from 2 to 18.

Table 2 displays the results for k-medoid clustering using the different similarity measures. In this and the subsequent tables, the best values for the measures are marked in bold font. The best silhouette coefficient is achieved with two clusters. It is notable that topic vectors produce 18 clusters which corresponds to the number of topics in the corpus. Nevertheless, the silhouette coefficient is clearly lower than for the graph similarity, where the value varies from 0.29 to 0.38. This can be interpreted as a weak cluster structure with high separation and low cohesion [11]. DI values are comparable and the number of clusters is relatively high, ranging from 5 to 18 clusters. The connectivity is comparatively low, which is due to the small number of clusters. Topic vectors produce the lowest connectivity score.

Table 2. Cluster results for k-medoid.

	Graph-Min	Graph-Max	Graph-Avg	Topic vectors
Silhouette	**0.38**	0.29	0.35	0.11
Optimal k	2	2	2	18
Dunn index	0.52	0.59	**0.60**	0.57
Optimal k	15	18	5	16
Connectivity	2.96	4.59	7.59	**2.90**
Optimal k	2	3	2	2

The results for AGNES with different linkage methods (SL = single linkage, CL = complete linkage, AL = average linkage, W = Ward's method) are shown in Table 3. The results are quite comparable to the k-medoid clustering, also with regard to the number of clusters. DI comes with a higher k, whereas the silhouette coefficient and connectivity have mostly $k = 2$. The silhouette coefficient varies for the graph similarity from 0.26 to 0.39 and the values for the clustering with topic vectors are much smaller (0.10 to 0.16). The connectivity and DI values are very similar to the values in Table 2 with topic vectors having the overall best values for connectivity.

The internal measures show a weak cluster structure for both similarity methods which could be artificial. For silhouette coefficient and connectivity in most of the configurations the optimal number of clusters is two. However, DI and topic vector cluster analysis for silhouette coefficient prefers a higher number of clusters in k-medoid and AGNES. In comparison, the graph-based similarity measures produce slightly better results for the internal measures.

Clustering of Argument Graphs Using Semantic Similarity Measures   111

Table 3. Cluster results for AGNES.

	Graph-Min				Graph-Max				Graph-Avg				Topic vectors			
	SL	CL	AL	W	SL	CL	AL	W	SL	CL	AL	W	SL	CL	AL	W
Silhouette	**0.39**	0.29	0.36	0.38	0.31	**0.32**	**0.32**	0.26	0.34	0.35	0.35	**0.36**	0.10	0.11	**0.16**	0.12
Optimal k	2	4	2	2	2	2	2	3	2	3	3	2	2	16	2	5
Dunn index	0.52	**0.64**	0.59	**0.64**	**0.72**	**0.72**	**0.72**	0.66	0.53	**0.66**	**0.66**	0.61	0.62	**0.64**	0.60	0.61
Optimal k	9	18	15	18	18	14	14	18	10	17	17	17	5	18	17	16
Connectivity	3.27	12.14	4.39	**2.96**	**2.93**	11.18	5.14	5.88	4.73	4.73	4.73	**2.90**	2.93	10.76	3.03	**2.90**
Optimal k	2	2	2	2	2	2	2	2	2	2	2	2	2	2	2	2

4.4 External Evaluation

The external evaluation focuses on the classification of each graph in relation to their respective topic as shown in Table 1. It is supposed to show whether the clustering complies with the topics and is applicable for further use within the envisioned argumentation machine.

As measures, precision and recall are calculated and combined in the Rand index (RI). RI compares the manual classification (M) and the clustering (C) based on the agreement and disagreement between object pairs in both partitionings [18]. Precision and recall are calculated based on the number of common pairs in both sets (true positives), the number of pairs in C but not in the M (false positives), vice versa (false negatives) and the number of different pairs in both sets (true negatives). For further analysis the resulting classification accuracy is calculated for the clustering with the highest RI.

Table 4 displays the RI values with k equal to the number of classes in the corpus. It shows that all methods achieve very good results, whereas the topic vectors deliver the best value for all configurations. Only AGNES with single linkage leads to significantly lower values.

Table 4. Rand index results $k = 18$.

	k-medoid	AGNES			
		SL	CL	AL	W
Graph-Min	0.86	0.67	0.87	0.82	0.85
Graph-Max	0.87	**0.83**	0.86	0.84	0.87
Graph-Avg	0.89	0.69	0.88	0.85	0.89
Topic vectors	**0.97**	0.60	**0.96**	**0.92**	**0.97**

In order to gain a more detailed insight we evaluated the quality of the clustering for k-medoid with topic vector similarity (k = 18). 11 of 18 topics are perfectly in accordance with the classification, no graph is assigned to a different cluster. Only for two topics no graph is classified correctly, although this affects only three graphs. Furthermore, wrongly classified graphs are often assigned to a cluster with similar content, for example "waste separation" and "higher dog poo fines". 74 of 87 graphs are classified correctly, which leads to an overall classification accuracy of 85%. Hypothesis H1 can therefore be accepted. The graph similarity methods classify only about 25 graphs correctly with a classification accuracy of 29%. The best results are achieved with the topic vector representations and not the graph representations. Hypothesis H2 needs thus to be rejected. This also implies that a high RI does not automatically lead to a good classification. When looking at the parameters of the RI, the pairs of true positives only have a small influence. Thus the reason for the high RI values are true negatives, which have a strong impact on the equation.

Table 5 displays the RI values for the five super-topics. The best result is achieved with topic vectors and k-medoid clustering. AGNES with SL produces very low RI scores. All values are clearly worse than the ones from Table 4. Thus it is shown that cluster analysis with a smaller number of clusters does not automatically lead to better classification.

Table 5. Rand index results for $k = 5$.

	k-medoid	AGNES			
		SL	CL	AL	W
Graph-Min	0.64	0.30	0.59	0.57	0.62
Graph-Max	0.66	**0.34**	0.58	0.49	0.64
Graph-Avg	0.65	0.32	**0.61**	**0.62**	0.62
Topic vectors	**0.82**	0.31	0.60	0.30	**0.66**

The overall classification accuracy of k-medoid with topic vectors is 68%. In comparison to topics, the classification accuracy for the super-topics is lower and only 59 of 87 graphs are correctly clustered instead of 74. The classification for education and environment is perfect. For medicine, the value is nearly perfect (92%). However, the accuracy decreases to 71% or even 0% for the last two super-topics. Negative outlier is the first cluster, where two topics are covered.

Despite this degradation, the topic vector representation still produces the best result. The best graph similarity using max symmetrization classifies only 25 graphs correctly which leads to an accuracy of 28%. This emphasizes the impression that the graph-based similarity measures are not suited for thematic clustering, since the resulting clusters contain argument graphs of different topics. Overall, the results for the more fine-grained topic classification are better for both, RI and classification accuracy. Thus, hypothesis H3 also needs to be rejected.

5   Conclusion

In this paper, we proposed two clustering algorithms for argument graphs which are based on a graph-based similarity measure. The motivation behind this is the hypothesis that the graph structure of the argument provides relevant semantic information about the argument and thus should enable a better clustering as when working on the pure text only. The results, however, show that clustering using the graph-based similarity is only slightly better in the internal evaluation measures, while the clustering based on the topic vector similarity outperforms the graph-based approach in identifying the topics of the arguments. Thus it became obvious that for pure topic discovery the structure of the argument is not really relevant as the words occurring in the text already allow to identify the topic appropriately. Here, the use of the structure seems to distract the clustering process.

However, argument graph clustering shall not only be used to group arguments w.r.t. their topic. In particular for the purpose of generalization, building clusters of graphs with similar structure but different topic is more important as the generalization over different topics is desirable. Further investigation is required to find out whether the proposed clustering approach using the graph-based measure is appropriate for this purpose.

Further, it should be noted that the current evaluation is only performed using a quite small corpus. Thus, more extensive evaluations are necessary, in particular using argument graph corpora automatically mined from text, allowing a larger number of graphs to be used.

During the course of our future work towards argument synthesis with case-based reasoning involving adaptation methods, clustering will play a pivotal role to infer a structure on the case base. Only in the context of this application it will become clear whether the proposed algorithms are able to produce useful clusters.

Acknowledgments. This work was funded by the German Research Foundation (DFG), project 375342983.

References

1. Atkinson, K., et al.: Towards artificial argumentation. AI Mag. **38**(3), 25–36 (2017)
2. Bergmann, R., Gil, Y.: Similarity assessment and efficient retrieval of semantic workflows. Inf. Syst. **40**, 115–127 (2014). https://doi.org/10.1016/j.is.2012.07.005
3. Bergmann, R., Lenz, M., Ollinger, S., Pfister, M.: Similarity measures for case-based retrieval of natural language argument graphs in argumentation machines. In: Proceedings of the 32nd International Florida Artificial Intelligence Research Society Conference, FLAIRS 2019, Sarasota, Florida, USA. AAAI-Press (2019)
4. Bergmann, R., Schenkel, R., Dumani, L., Ollinger, S.: ReCAP - information retrieval and case-based reasoning for robust deliberation and synthesis of arguments in the political discourse. In: Proceedings of the Conference "Lernen, Wissen, Daten, Analysen", LWDA 2018, 22–24 August 2018, Mannheim, Germany, CEUR Workshop Proceedings, vol. 2191. CEUR-WS.org (2018). http://ceur-ws.org/Vol-2191/paper6.pdf
5. Bex, F., Reed, C.: Schemes of inference, conflict and preference in a computational model of argument. Stud. Logic Grammar Rhetoric **23**(36), 39–58 (2011)

6. Boltužić, F., Šnajder, J.: Identifying prominent arguments in online debates using semantic textual similarity. In: Proceedings of the 2nd Workshop on Argumentation Mining, pp. 110–115. Association for Computational Linguistics, June 2015
7. Chesnevar, C., et al.: Towards an argument interchange format. Knowl. Eng. Rev. **21**(4), 293–316 (2006)
8. Dung, P.M.: On the acceptability of arguments and its fundamental role in non-monotonic reasoning, logic programming and n-person games. Artif. Intell. **77**(2), 321–358 (1995)
9. Dunn, J.C.: A fuzzy relative of the ISODATA process and its use in detecting compact well-separated clusters. J. Cybern. **3**(3), 32–57 (1973). https://doi.org/10.1080/01969727308546046
10. Habernal, I., Gurevych, I.: Exploiting debate portals for semi-supervised argumentation mining in user-generated web discourse. In: Proceedings of the 2015 Conference on Empirical Methods in Natural Language Processing, pp. 2127–2137 (2015)
11. Kaufman, L., Rousseeuw, P.J.: Finding Groups in Data - An Introduction to Cluster Analysis. Wiley, New York (1990)
12. Lenz, M., Ollinger, S., Sahitaj, P., Bergmann, R.: Semantic textual similarity measures for case-based retrieval of argument graphs. In: Case-Based Reasoning Research and Development: 27th International Conference, ICCBR 2019, 8–12 September 2019, Otzenhausen, Germany, Proceedings. Springer, Heidelberg (2019, accepted for publication)
13. Lippi, M., Torroni, P.: Argument mining from speech: detecting claims in political debates. In: Schuurmans, D., Wellman, M.P. (eds.) Proceedings of the Thirtieth AAAI Conference on Artificial Intelligence (AAAI 2016), pp. 2979–2985. AAAI Press (2016). http://argumentationmining.disi.unibo.it/publications/AAAI2016.pdf
14. Manning, C.D., Raghavan, P., Schütze, H.: Introduction to Information Retrieval. Cambridge University Press, New York (2008)
15. Mikolov, T., Chen, K., Corrado, G., Dean, J.: Efficient Estimation of Word Representations in Vector Space. arXiv:1301.3781 [cs], January 2013
16. Peldszus, A., Stede, M.: From argument diagrams to argumentation mining in texts. Int. J. Cogn. Inform. Nat. Intell. **7**(1), 1–31 (2013). https://doi.org/10.4018/jcini.2013010101
17. Peldszus, A., Stede, M.: An annotated corpus of argumentative microtexts. In: First European Conference on Argumentation: Argumentation and Reasoned Action, Portugal, Lisbon, June 2015. http://www.ling.uni-potsdam.de/~peldszus/eca2015-preprint.pdf
18. Rand, W.: Objective criteria for the evaluation of clustering methods. J. Am. Stat. Assoc. **66**(336), 846–850 (1971)
19. Richter, M.M., Weber, R.O.: Case-Based Reasoning - A Textbook. Springer, Heidelberg (2013). https://doi.org/10.1007/978-3-642-40167-1
20. Rousseeuw, P.: Silhouettes: a graphical aid to the interpretation and validation of cluster analysis. J. Comput. Appl. Math. **20**(1), 53–65 (1987). https://doi.org/10.1016/0377-0427(87)90125-7
21. Walton, D., Reed, C., Macagno, F.: Argumentation Schemes. Cambridge University Press, Cambridge (2008)
22. Ward, J.H.: Hierarchical grouping to optimize an objective function. J. Am. Stat. Assoc. **58**(301), 236–244 (1963). http://www.jstor.org/stable/2282967

Reducing Search Space of Genetic Algorithms for Fast Black Box Attacks on Image Classifiers

Julius Brandl, Nicolas Breinl, Maximilian Demmler, Lukas Hartmann$^{(\boxtimes)}$, Jörg Hähner, and Anthony Stein

Organic Computing Group, University of Augsburg, Augsburg, Germany
lukas.hartmann@student.uni-augsburg.de,
{joerg.haehner,anthony.stein}@informatik.uni-augsburg.de

Abstract. Recent research regarding the reliability of Deep Neural Networks (DNN) revealed that it is easy to produce images that are completely unrecognizable to humans, but DNNs recognize as classifiable objects with 99.99% confidence. The present study investigates the effect of search space reduction for Genetic Algorithms (GA) on their capability of purposefully fooling DNNs. Therefore, we introduce a GA with respective modifications that is able to fool neural networks trained to classify objects from well-known benchmark image data sets like GTSRB or MNIST. The developed GA is extended and thus capable of reducing the search space without changing its general behavior. Empirical results on MNIST indicate a significantly decreased number of generations needed to satisfy the targeted confidence of an MNIST image classifier (12 instead of 228 generations). Conducted experiments on GTSRB, a more challenging object classification scenario, show similar results. Therefore, fooling DNNs has found not only easily possible but can also be done very fast. Our study thus substantiates an already recognized, potential danger for DNN-based computer vision or object recognition applications.

Keywords: Genetic algorithm · Fooling DNN ·
Search space reduction · Black box attack · Algorithm optimization ·
MNIST · GTSRB

1 Introduction

Recent studies have shown that *Genetic Algorithms* (GA) can fool *Deep Neural Networks* (DNN) with a high degree of confidence [1]. However, the required number of requests to the DNN is still high. Optimization of a GA in order to reduce the number of model queries is the main objective of our study. However, the contribution of this paper is not about the highly domain dependent task of hyperparameter optimization for GAs – it rather investigates novel strategies to reduce a GA's search space and thereby increasing convergence speed. This work

© Springer Nature Switzerland AG 2019
C. Benzmüller and H. Stuckenschmidt (Eds.): KI 2019, LNAI 11793, pp. 115–122, 2019.
https://doi.org/10.1007/978-3-030-30179-8_9

Default	Grayscale	Black-And-White	DCVR	Resolution 8x8	Combined Methods
51 Generations	38 Generations	3 Generations	11 Generations	3 Generations	2 Generations
Stop Sign	Speed Limit 100	Speed Limit 50	Speed Limit 100	Road Works	Right Of Way

Fig. 1. Fooling images with 99% confidence on GTSRB

originates from the participation at the InformatiCup challenge 2019 hosted by the *Gesellschaft für Informatik* (GI)[1], whose topic has been set to adverserial attacks on black box models for this year's edition. The remainder of this paper is organized as follows: Sect. 2 provides a brief overview of relevant related work. In Sect. 3 we present our theoretical approach, followed by evaluations in Sect. 4. Finally in Sect. 5, our work is summarized and put into perspective for future developments.

2   Related Work

Papernot et al. [2,3] show that fooling images can be created with a substitute model approach. Therefore, a substitute DNN is trained by querying the black box to be fooled. The full access to the substitute model then can be used to generate adversarial images with gradient based approaches. Their approach requires initial queries to the black box in order to train the substitute model.

Hu et al. [4] use a *Generative Adversarial Network* (GAN) in order to bypass black box malware detectors with generated adversarial examples. The GAN's discriminator is a substitute model as proposed by [2,3]. Their experimental results show that the approach achieves better true positive rates on adversarial examples than gradient based approaches. However, they only applied the attack on adversarial malware. This approach still remains to be executed and evaluated on image classifiers. As in [2,3], initial queries are required to train the substitute model. In the work presented in this paper, a GA is utilized which does not rely on initial querying.

GAs have been first proposed by Holland [5] and then widely extended in various works [6–9]. GAs are used for a variety of tasks in machine learning, some of which being improved placement of wind turbines [10], fuzzy system design stages integration [11], urban bus transit route network design [12] and electromagnetic optimization [13]. Nguyen et al. [1] use GAs to fool image classifier DNNs with both direct and indirect encoding. Direct encoding evolves the pixels of an image independently. The indirect encoding evolves a compositional pattern-producing network (CPPN), which is an artificial neural network that takes a pixel's coordinates as an input and returns a color. Contrary to our approach, these methods do not pay attention to reducing the search space in order

---

[1] https://gi.de/.

to increase efficiency. An approach that actually focuses on search space reduction is the one-pixel attack proposed by Su et al. who make use of differential evolution [14].

3   Proposed Approach

Attacking a black box implies that the attacker, here the GA, only has access to its input and output. As an example we consider the specific case of fooling a DNN-based image classifier for GTSRB. The input is given by a 24-bit (3 color channels) 64×64 pixel RGB image, and the output are the corresponding confidences for all classes computed by the black box.

In order to validate our proposed approach we use a GA based on Mitchell's work [[15], p. 251]. Algorithm 1 displays the GA that is used throughout the further course of this study. This does not necessarily mean that our methods do not work with different GA structures. At first, a population of random images is created and their fitness value is evaluated. The evaluation is done by querying the image to the black box. The returned confidence(s) of the black box are assigned to the fitness value of the image. Selection, crossover, mutation and evaluation are repeatedly executed until at least one of the images exceeds the given fitness threshold Θ. We use a tournament selection and uniform crossover from [[15], pp. 255–256], furthermore we use a gaussian mutation from [16].

Algorithm 1. Structure of the proposed GA.

Initialization: Initialize population P with random images;
Evaluation: Evaluate fitness f for each image p in P;
while $\max_p f(p) < \Theta$ **do**
  Selection: Use tournament selection to create subset P' of P;
  Crossover: Create offsprings using uniform crossover, add offsprings to P';
  Mutation: Perform gaussian mutation on P';
  P $\longleftarrow$ P';
  Evaluation: Evaluate fitness of images in P;
end
return $\max_p f(p)$

Since the search space S of the GA is very large ($|S| = (256^3)^{64*64}$) numerous iterations (generations or evolutionary cycles) are needed until a termination criterion (here target confidence) is met. Thus, one obvious approach to cope with this challenge is to seek ways to reduce the search space. This work proposes three approaches to accomplish this reduction: (1) In a first attempt, the resolution of input images is reduced, what essentially results in fewer pixels. It has to be explicitly noted that the decreased resolution is only used within the GA – the actual query images are rescaled to fit the black box' requirements. (2) Reduction of the incorporated three, i.e. RGB, channels toward only one leads to grayscale images. (3) As a third approach, a coarser resolution for each of the individual color channels is applied. This procedure is referred to as *Discrete Color Values Reduction* (DCVR).

Those three approaches can either be applied individually or in combination. With a combination of the latter two approaches *Black-And-White* (BAW) images are created. By means of mixing the abovementioned capabilities, the search space is drastically reduced to only a small fraction of the original one, more precisely to $|S| = (2^1)^{8*8}$. Thereby the expected number of generations until an appropriately selected termination criterion is met is assumed to be significantly decreased. The visual outcome of our search space reduction methods can be seen in Fig. 1.

4   Evaluation

In the following we present results from conducted experiments that corroborate the hypothesized benefits of the proposed methods – fast convergence of a GA evolving fooling images that are misclassified by the attacked DNN-based blackbox with high confidence. The experiments are conducted based on *Convolutional Neural Networks* (CNN) trained on the well-known MNIST and GTSRB data sets. The networks are regarded as black boxes, thus, the GA only has access to the networks' input and output. Targeted attacks target one specific classification class to fool the black box on, untargeted attacks aim at fooling the black box on any class. The stochastic nature of GAs can cause large deviations regarding the results for individual measurements. Therefore, all results represent the averages over repeated measurements.

MNIST - Black Box Description: The MNIST database is a collection of 60,000 images of handwritten digits from 0 to 9. As black box we used a CNN[2] with multiple max pooling and dropout layers. Input to the black box are grayscaled images with a size of 28 × 28 pixels, output are the confidences (real values ranging from 0 to 1) for each class (0–9). After 12 epochs of training, the CNN achieves an accuracy of 99.15% on the test dataset.

GTSRB - Black Box Description: The GTSRB database provides more than 50,000 images of traffic signs that can be categorized into 43 different classes. In contrast to MNIST, the images used as input to the black box are colored (RGB encoded) and of bigger size (64 × 64). Again, the network's output are real numbers between 0 and 1 (confidence) for all 43 classes. We trained a CNN with several max pooling and dropout layers and used it as a black box. After 30 epochs of training, it achieved 97.32% accuracy on test data, which is close to human performance (estimated at 98.81%, [17]).

4.1   Results on MNIST

The following analysis was carried out with a population size of 30 individuals and with digit 1 as the target class to be fooled. Note that untargeted or else

---

[2] Keras CNN Model: https://keras.io/examples/mnist_cnn/.

targeted attacks can lead to results of different scale but with similar overall patterns. We selected digit 1 because it has empirically been found to be one of the most difficult target classes for the GA.

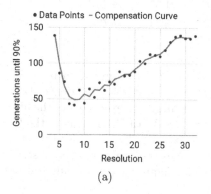 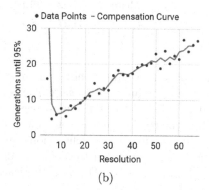

(a)   (b)

Fig. 2. Effect of resolution on MNIST (a) and GTSRB (b). 20 repetitions on data points.

Reduced Resolution: Figure 2 depicts the effects of changing the resolution of images. During the process, the resolutions always stay quadratic. The final input to the black box remains a 28×28 pixel sized image. Lowering the resolution leads to a reduction of the search space as discussed in Sect. 3. Hence, the required number of generations to reach 90% confidence decreases from 137.60 to 41.45 – considering the global minimum (8×8 px) in contrast to the default resolution (28×28 px). Further reducing the resolution has been found to lower the convergence speed (in this context 'speed' refers to the number of queries sent to the black box). This effect is expected to occur since the search space lacks a sufficient number of solution candidates.

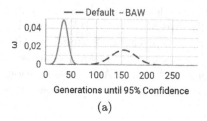 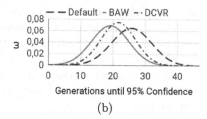

(a)   (b)

Fig. 3. Effect of BAW on MNIST (a) and GTSRB (b). Mean and SD are shown in Table 1.

Black-And-White Images: Reducing the number of discrete color values from 256 (default) to only 2 reduces images to BAW representations, clearly decreasing

Table 1. Mean and SD in 100 iterations for each method.

Method	Default	BAW	Default	DCVR	BAW
Target	MNIST	MNIST	GTSRB	GTSRB	GTSRB
Mean	154.02	**35.81**	25.7	21.55	**19.1**
SD	24.27	**8.18**	6.19	5.34	**5.78**

the size of S. Figure 3 shows the normal distribution of termination probabilities ω for the number of generations needed to achieve 95% confidence. BAW and default (grayscaled) images are compared. During the execution of the algorithm, the resolution was constantly set to 28×28. With BAW images, the GA terminates after 35.81 generations on average (mean). This is more than four times faster compared to using the default images. Furthermore, the observed standard deviation (SD) drops, indicating that the approach is not only fast but also reliable.

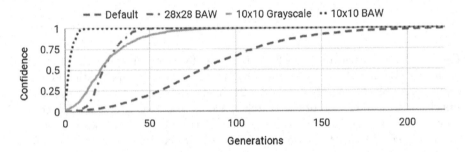

Fig. 4. Combined methods - effect of lowering resolution and color channels on MNIST. 20 repetitions on data points

Combining Methods: The previous results only demonstrated the capabilities of our approaches when applied individually. We also tested BAW with low resolutions (see Fig. 4). With these settings, the GA reaches 99% confidence after only 12 generations on average. This is more than three times faster in contrast to using reduced resolutions only (41 generations) and using BAW representations only (39 generations). The GA terminates after 228 generations on average with default settings.

4.2 Results on GTSRB

Because of its colored images with bigger sizes, the GTSRB image collection provides a different and more challenging benchmark than MNIST. Due to the vast search space, we slightly increased the population size to 50 individuals for the following experiments. The class 'Maximum Speed (100)' is targeted in all cases, this again constitutes one of the more difficult scenarios.

Reduced Resolution: Lowering the resolution proves to be effective for this scenario as well. The overall outcomes (see Fig. 2) are comparable with the results obtained for MNIST.

Black-And-White Images: As proposed in Sect. 3 we lowered the number of channels from 3 to 1, converting colored images to grayscaled ones. In addition to that, rendering images BAW implies DCVR. The BAW method still improves convergence speed, but the impact is noticeably lower when compared to MNIST. One explanation for this difference is that digits have hard edges and are easy to display in black-and-white. Images of traffic signs have various colors and smoother transitions. The low impact of BAW images also suggests that the black box CNN has learned strong relations between colors of different pixels. Images obtained by using DCVR still contain colors and therefore show improvements. These approaches were compared to default images in Fig. 3.

5 Concluding Remarks

The methods outlined in this paper lead to fast convergence (low number of queries to the black box). As well, performing attacks against MNIST and GTSRB indicated promising properties regarding generalized application and scalability for our approaches. Our GA-based approach is not dependent on initial queries to the black box in contrast to the substitute model attack as proposed by Papernot et al., what renders it more difficult to recognize an adversarial attack. In summary, the utilization of GAs bears the potential of creating fast and hardly recognizable adversarial images for fooling a wide range of black box types.

DNN-based image classification is used in security- and safety-critical tasks such as filtering illegal contents in social networks, authentication (e.g. face recognition) or for vision purposes in autonomous driving. Authentication applications could be bypassed efficiently with search space reduction. Thus, there is a high potential risk for machine learning based recognition applications. A viable approach to protect a black box is to hide the exact confidence values. Confidence values are needed as fitness measure in order to compare images and, thus, are indispensable for the GA. In future work, we aim at applying our search space reduction approach on other domains than image classification.

References

1. Nguyen, A., Yosinski, J., Clune, J.: Deep Neural Networks are Easily Fooled: High Confidence Predictions for Unrecognizable Images. arXiv:1412.1897 [cs], December 2014

2. Papernot, N., McDaniel, P., Goodfellow, I., Jha, S., Celik, Z.B., Swami, A.: Practical black-box attacks against machine learning. In: Proceedings of the 2017 ACM on Asia Conference on Computer and Communications Security, ASIA CCS 2017, pp. 506–519. ACM, New York (2017). ISBN 978-1-4503-4944-4

3. Papernot, N., McDaniel, P., Jha, S., Fredrikson, M., Celik, Z.B., Swami, A.: The limitations of deep learning in adversarial settings. In: 2016 IEEE European Symposium on Security and Privacy (EuroS P), March 2016, pp. 372–387 (2016)

4. Hu, W., Tan, Y.: Generating Adversarial Malware Examples for Black-Box Attacks Based on GAN. In: CoRR abs/1702.05983 (2017). arXiv:1702.05983

5. Holland, J.H.: Adaptation in Natural and Artificial Systems: An Introductory Analysis with Applications to Biology, Control and Artificial Intelligence. MIT Press, Cambridge (1992). ISBN 0262082136

6. Whitley, D., Starkweather, T.: GENITOR II: a distributed genetic algorithm. J. Exp. Theoret. Artif. Intell. 2(3), 189–214 (1990). ISSN 0952–813X

7. Srinivas, M., Patnaik, L.M.: Adaptive probabilities of crossover and mutation in genetic algorithms. IEEE Trans. Syst. Man Cybern. 24(4), 656–667 (1994). ISSN 0018–9472

8. Michalewicz, Z.: Genetic Algorithms + Data Structures = Evolution Programs. Springer, Heidelberg (2013). Google-Books-ID: JmyrCAAAQBAJ. ISBN 978-3-662-03315-9

9. Muhlenbein, H., Schomisch, M., Born, J.: The parallel genetic algorithm as function optimizer. Parallel Comput. 17(6), 619–632 (1991). ISSN 0167–8191

10. Grady, S.A., Hussaini, M.Y., Abdullah, M.M.: Placement of wind turbines using genetic algorithms. Renew. Energy 30(2), 259–270 (2005). ISSN 0960–1481

11. Lee, M.A., Takagi, H.: Integrating design stages of fuzzy systems using genetic algorithms, pp. 612–617 (1993)

12. Pattnaik, S.B., Mohan, S., Tom, V.M.: Urban bus transit route network design using genetic algorithm. J. Transp. Eng. 124(4), 368–375 (1998)

13. Rahmat-Samii, Y., Michielssen, E.: Electromagnetic Optimization by Genetic Algorithms, November 1999. English

14. Su, J., Vargas, D.V., Kouichi, S.: One pixel attack for fooling deep neural networks. arXiv:1710.08864 [cs, stat], October 2017

15. Mitchell, T.M.: Machine Learning, 1st edn. McGraw-Hill Inc., New York (1997). ISBN 0070428077, 9780070428072

16. Bäck, T., Schwefel, H.-P.: An overview of evolutionary algorithms for parameter optimization. Evol. Comput. 1(1), 1–23 (1993)

17. German Traffic Signs Benchmark. http://benchmark.ini.rub.de/?section=gtsdb&subsection=dataset. Accessed 26 Apr 2019

An Empirical Study of the Usefulness of State-Dependent Action Costs in Planning

Sumitra Corraya[1], Florian Geißer[2], David Speck[1],
and Robert Mattmüller[1(✉)]

[1] University of Freiburg, Freiburg im Breisgau, Germany
{corrayas,speckd,mattmuel}@informatik.uni-freiburg.de
[2] Australian National University, Canberra, Australia
florian.geisser@anu.edu.au

Abstract. The vast majority of work in planning to date has focused on state-independent action costs. However, if a planning task features state-dependent costs, using a cost model with state-independent costs means either introducing a modeling error, or potentially sacrificing compactness of the model. In this paper, we investigate the conflicting priorities of modeling accuracy and compactness empirically, with a particular focus on the extent of the negative impact of reduced modeling accuracy on (a) the quality of the resulting plans, and (b) the search guidance provided by heuristics that are fed with inaccurate cost models. Our empirical results show that the plan suboptimality introduced by ignoring state-dependent costs can range, depending on the domain, from inexistent to several orders of magnitude. Furthermore, our results show that the impact on heuristic guidance additionally depends strongly on the heuristic that is used, the specifics of how exactly the costs are represented, and whether one is interested in heuristic accuracy, node expansions, or overall runtime savings.

Keywords: Planning · State-dependent costs · Heuristic accuracy

1 Introduction and Background

State-dependent action cost (SDAC) models can provide more compact representations of planning tasks than unit-cost or constant-cost models [7]. Among many other applications, they are useful to model state-dependent penalties for unsupplied power lines in the power supply restoration domain [14]. Research has been done in an attempt to plan with state-dependent action costs both using explicit-state search [6–8,15] and symbolic search [17].

Geißer et al. [6,7] studied compilations of tasks with state-dependent costs into tasks with state-independent costs. The exponential compilation replaces each action with a collection of actions, including one action for each possible valuation of the state variables on which the original action cost function depends.

C. Benzmüller and H. Stuckenschmidt (Eds.): KI 2019, LNAI 11793, pp. 123–130, 2019.
https://doi.org/10.1007/978-3-030-30179-8_10

The EVMDD-based compilation, which uses edge-valued multi-valued decision diagrams [2] to represent action cost functions, also replaces each action with a collection of actions, which in this case encode a simulation of the evaluation of the original cost function, using as few new actions as possible. Both compilations preserve plan costs, and both are worst-case exponential in the number of relevant state variables. The EVMDD-based compilation is often smaller, though, whereas the exponential compilation is necessarily exponential.

Previous work mostly focused on the representational power of the EVMDD-based compilation and on the question to what extent heuristic values are preserved under this compilation [6]. The question of how bad it is to ignore state-dependent costs altogether was not in the focus of that work. In the present paper, we will address this question, or more specifically, two sub-questions: in Sect. 2, we empirically study the plan suboptimality caused by ignoring state-dependent costs, and in Sect. 3, we study the impact of various ways of dealing with state-dependent costs, including ignoring them, on heuristic quality and related measures such as node expansions and search time.

Related work includes literature on diverse action costs [4]. Note that planning tasks with diverse and with state-dependent action costs both induce edge-weighted transition systems and differ only in their compact representations – diverse costs are a special case of state-dependent costs. For the former, Fan et al. [4] proved a no-free-lunch theorem stating that, depending on the specifics of the task, diverse costs can be either beneficial or harmful for search. Our empirical results in Sect. 3 confirm their result empirically in the setting of state-dependent costs. Our results are also in line with those of Ivankovic et al. [14], who use a different encoding of state-dependent costs and additionally support state constraints.

2   Sub-optimality of Ignoring SDAC During Search

For a formal definition of planning tasks with state-dependent costs, we refer the reader to the literature [7]. For this exposition, suffice it to say that every planning task comes with a cost function $c : A \times S \to \mathbb{Q}_{\geq 0}$ that maps every action $a \in A$ and every state $s \in S$ to a value $c(a, s)$, the cost of a in s. Let $u : A \times S \to \mathbb{Q}_{\geq 0}$ be the *unit-cost function* with $u(a, s) = 1$ for each $a \in A$ and $s \in S$. The cost $\mathcal{C}^c(\pi)$ of a plan π is the sum of action costs along the execution trace of π, where c is the cost function that is used to evaluate the cost of each plan step. Furthermore, let $OPT^c(\Pi)$ be the set of cost-optimal plans for task Π, where optimality is with respect to cost function c. Unit-cost optimal plans are not necessarily optimal for other cost functions, i.e. $\mathcal{C}^c(\pi') \geq \mathcal{C}^c(\pi)$ for all $\pi' \in OPT^u(\Pi)$ and $\pi \in OPT^c(\Pi)$, where c is the original cost function of Π. Clearly, for some Π the inequality can be strict. Note that $\mathcal{C}^c(\pi)$ is identical for all $\pi \in OPT^c(\Pi)$, since the same cost function c is used both in determining optimality and in the evaluation of $\mathcal{C}^c(\pi)$. Therefore, if c is the original cost function of Π, we also refer to this value as $\mathcal{C}^*(\Pi)$, or $\mathcal{C}^*$, if Π is clear from context. By contrast, $\mathcal{C}^c(\pi')$ is *not* necessarily identical for all $\pi' \in OPT^u(\Pi)$, since plan optimality is with respect to unit costs, whereas evaluation is with respect to the true original costs. An extreme case where this happens is the TRAVELLING SALESMAN domain. Here, the planner has to solve a travelling salesman problem and the cost function to move between cities is based on the Manhattan distance. There can be a unique optimal plan with respect to the true cost function c, whereas all $n!$ orders of visiting the n cities are optimal under the assumption of unit costs u. For this reason, in the empirical results presented below, there may be more than one data point per planning task: there is one data point for each $\pi' \in OPT^u(\Pi)$, relating $C^c(\pi')$ to $C^*(\Pi)$. Treating the cost of unit-cost optimal plans as a random variable depending on Π, we also refer to $C^c(\pi')$ as $\mathcal{U}^*(\Pi)$, or just $\mathcal{U}^*$, below. Notice that in the TRAVELLING SALESMAN domain, the relative error $C^c(\pi')/C^*(\Pi)$ for $\pi' \in OPT^u(\Pi)$ can be made arbitrarily large by choosing large enough distance between cities on suboptimal tours, as those distances determine the costs c of moving between cities.

Whereas all of the above is clear *theoretically*, the purpose of this section is to study *empirically* how large the relative error becomes in the benchmark domains used in planning with state-dependent action costs. All plans in this section were computed using the planning system SYMPLE[1] [17,18], which performs symbolic bidirectional breadth-first search. For our evaluation, we used 206 tasks from eight domains introduced by Speck et al. [17][2]. All experiments were run on a 3.3 GHz machine with 16 GB memory limit, with a runtime limit of 30 min.

Before studying the relative error, let us discuss why one would want to plan under a unit-cost assumption instead of using the true cost function in the first place. An argument might be that, by planning under the assumption of unit costs, one is able to solve more tasks. The question is whether the original state-dependent action costs guide the search to the goal or not. Depending on the domain, this is indeed the case. Whereas coverage is unaffected by the unit-cost transformation in the domains ASTERIX (30 vs. 30 in 30 problems solved), PEG SOLITAIRE-08 (27 vs. 27 in 30) and PEG SOLITAIRE-11 (17 vs. 17 in 20), and even slightly decreases in OPENSTACKS-08 (15 vs. 12 in 30), OPENSTACKS-11 (20 vs. 16 in 20), and OPENSTACKS-14 (7 vs. 4 in 20), it increases in COLORED GRIPPER (10 vs. 12 in 30), and, most pronouncedly it doubles in TRAVELLING SALESMAN (13 vs. 26 in 26). This makes intuitively sense, as ignoring state-dependent costs in TRAVELLING SALESMAN essentially turns an optimization problem into a satisfaction problem, which makes it easy to solve.

The relative error introduced by ignoring state-dependent costs is depicted in Fig. 1. Each dot represents a pair $(C^*(\Pi), \mathcal{U}^*(\Pi))$ for one task Π solved in both configurations. The error bars in the $\mathcal{U}^*(\Pi)$ dimension are owed to the above-mentioned fact that different optimal plans under the assumption of unit costs can have different true costs under the original state-dependent cost function. The dots represent the mean values, the error bars the standard deviations. Wherever possible, to compute means and standard deviations, we took all plans

---

[1] https://gkigit.informatik.uni-freiburg.de/dspeck/symple.
[2] https://gkigit.informatik.uni-freiburg.de/dspeck/SDAC-Benchmarks.

$\pi' \in OPT^u(\Pi)$ into account. If, the cardinality of $OPT^u(\Pi)$ grew prohibitively, we resorted to a representative sample from $OPT^u(\Pi)$.

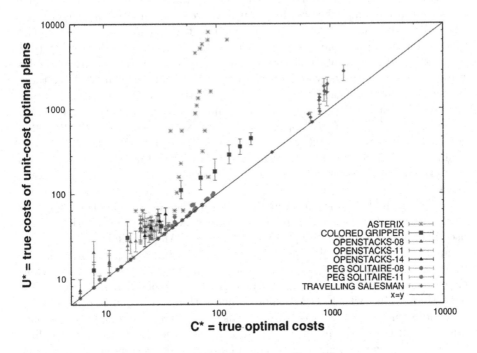

Fig. 1. Scatter plot relating $\mathcal{C}^*$ to $\mathcal{U}^*$.

Generally, the results indicate that sometimes, ignoring state-dependent costs is largely unproblematic in terms of optimality (PEG SOLITAIRE), whereas in OPENSTACKS, COLORED GRIPPER, and TRAVELLING SALESMAN we see errors of an order of magnitude. In the ASTERIX domain, the worst-case error ranges up to three orders of magnitude and is clearly not negligible.

3   Sub-optimality of Ignoring SDAC in Heuristics

While searching for unit-cost optimal plans leads to arbitrarily suboptimal plans, computing heuristics based on unit-cost cost functions preverves plan optimality, as long as the heuristic is still admissible [5,16]. In this section, we investigate therefore the effects of different ways of dealing with state-dependent costs on the informativeness of several goal-distance heuristics and on the guidance they provide to the search (in terms of numbers of node expansions). As different ways of dealing with state-dependent costs we consider: (a) the exponential compilation [6], (b) the EVMDD-based compilation [6], (c) replacing all costs by u, and (d) replacing all costs $c(a, s)$ by $\min_{s' \in S} c(a, s')$. Transformation (d), to which we will also refer as the *minimum transformation*, is similar in simplicity to (c), but unlike in (c), different actions can still have different constant costs, and as a consequence of taking minimal costs, admissibility of heuristics is preserved under transformation (d). This is not generally guaranteed with transformation (c) if the task contains actions with cost less than one. Notice that (a) and (b) are "lossless", where as (c) and (d) are "lossy" transformations. This section complements Geißer's study [6], which investigated invariance of various heuristics under transformations (a)–(d) theoretically and empirically, by considering additional heuristics not studied there. In particular, we considered (a) the maximum heuristic $h^{\max}$ [1], (b) the incremental pattern database heuristic h^{iPDB} [9], (c) the merge-and-shrink heuristic $h^{\text{M\&S}}$ [12], and (d) the landmark-cut heuristic $h^{\text{LM-cut}}$ [11]. We chose those four heuristics as all of them are implemented in the FAST DOWNWARD [10] planner that we use in this experiment, and all of them are admissible.

For the sake of brevity, in the following, we will focus on the results for one specific heuristic, $h^{\text{M\&S}}$, exemplarily. Recall that $h^{\text{M\&S}}$ is an abstraction heuristic that builds the abstract transition system that is used for goal-distance estimation incrementally, starting with atomic abstractions, one per state variable, and keeps *merging* abstract transition systems into larger ones until a critical size has been reached. Merging is done by computing synchronized products of the involved transition systems and leads to finer, more informative, abstractions. Once the critical size has been reached, abstractions get *shrunk*, i.e., abstractions are made coarser, hence less informative, by lumping abstract states together.

Since the EVMDD-based and the exponential compilation preserve plan costs, $h^{\text{M\&S}}$ computed on either of those compilations is still admissible with respect to the original cost function. Similarly, since the minimum transformation only leads to underestimation of the true actions costs, $h^{\text{M\&S}}$ computed on the minimum transformation also remains admissible. Hence, plans computed by A* search in all $h^{\text{M\&S}}$ configurations are still optimal. The only configuration that is not guaranteed to be optimal is $h^{\text{M\&S}}$ together with the unit-cost transformation, in case the original task contains actions with costs less than one in some states. This is the case with the OPENSTACKS domain, where actions have a cost of zero in some states. Indeed, $h^{\text{M\&S}}$ with the unit-cost transformation leads to slightly suboptimal plans. Note that we used "standard" merge-and-shrink, not the version with delta cost partitioning of Fan et al. [3].

To assess how informative $h^{\text{M\&S}}$ is combined with the four task transformations, we first measured the initial heuristic values in all cases. The exponential compilation tends to lead to the most informative heuristic values, especially in the TRAVELLING SALESMAN domain. However, informative heuristic values are only a means to another end: few node expansions, and ultimately low runtime and high coverage. Numbers of node expansions are depicted in Fig. 2. As can be seen, the exponential compilation often leads to the fewest node expansions, especially in the TRAVELLING SALESMAN domain. Yet, overall, the exponential compilation solves the fewest tasks, since the compiled task is often too large to be generated. The unit-cost transformation tends to lead to slightly fewer node expansions than the minimum-cost transformation and the EVMDD-based compilation, but this comes at the cost of suboptimality of some plans. The two transformations without those obvious flaws (unacceptable problem size increase, inadmissibility of heuristic), the minimum-cost transformation (simple, but lossy) and the EVMDD-based compilation (complicated, but lossless), are remarkably similar in terms of node expansions. The minimum transformation does better in a few OPENSTACKS tasks, whereas the EVMDD-based compilation does better in the smaller TRAVELLING SALESMAN tasks. There, the resulting heuristic of the initial state is almost perfect. Only in the larger TRAVELLING SALESMAN instances the performance tends to degrade, as the M&S abstractions get shrunk and shortcuts are introduced in the abstract transition systems.

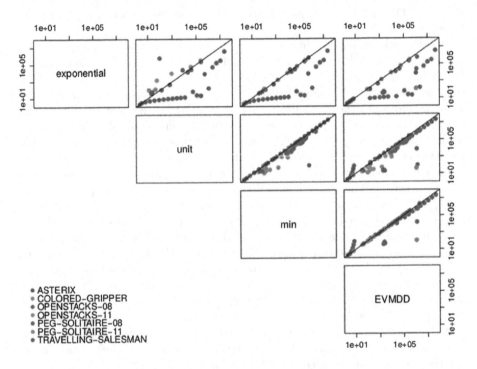

Fig. 2. Matrix of scatter plots showing comparison of node expansions with M&S heuristic under different transformations. All axes denote node expansions.

The difference in complexity of computing the various transformations (exponential is most costly, followed by EVMDD-based, minimum-cost, and unit-cost) and in informativeness of the compilations (exponential is most informative, usually followed by EVMDD-based, minimum-cost, and unit-cost) also results in different overall numbers of solved tasks: 41 (exponential), 87 (EVMDD-based), 88 (minimum-cost), and 91 (unit-cost). The picture is similar with the other heuristics we investigated. While these results give the impression that more complex transformations do not pay off, we have to note that at least in the classical setting some of the domains are not a good indicator for heuristic performance [13]. This might also be the case for their state-dependent counter part. Furthermore, without adaptation none of the presented heuristics is invariant under any of the presented transformations except exponential compilation. This motivates further research into whether it is worth to make these heuristics invariant.

4   Conclusion

In this paper, we have empirically investigated the benefits of planning when state-dependent action costs are supported or ignored. Our first experiment showed that supporting them during search is usually beneficial in that it leads to better plans. Depending on the domain, ignoring costs can positively or negatively affect search guidance. Our second experiment investigated how beneficial it is to reflect state-dependent cost within goal-distance heuristics. Again, results are mixed. The more accurately costs are represented within the heuristic, the more informative the heuristic values can become, provided that the simplification that underlies the heuristic computation is compatible with the way costs are represented in the heuristic (which is not necessarily the case—i.e., auxiliary predicates and actions introduced to represent cost functions may also "confuse" the heuristic). More informative heuristic values may or may not, in turn, lead to fewer node expansions, as discussed by, e.g., Fan et al. [4], and this may or may not translate into lower runtimes and more solved problems. Even if the heuristic is accurate, but expensive, heuristic values may be informative and node expansions low, but runtime can still be prohibitively large.

Acknowledgments. David Speck was supported by the German National Science Foundation (DFG) as part of the project EPSDAC (MA 7790/1-1). Florian Geißer was supported by ARC project DP180103446, "On-line planning for constrained autonomous agents in an uncertain world".

References

1. Bonet, B., Geffner, H.: Planning as heuristic search: new results. In: Biundo, S., Fox, M. (eds.) ECP 1999. LNCS (LNAI), vol. 1809, pp. 360–372. Springer, Heidelberg (2000). https://doi.org/10.1007/10720246_28
2. Ciardo, G., Siminiceanu, R.: Using edge-valued decision diagrams for symbolic generation of shortest paths. In: Proceedings of the Fourth International Conference on Formal Methods in Computer-Aided Design (FMCAD), pp. 256–273 (2002)
3. Fan, G., Müller, M., Holte, R.: Additive merge-and-shrink heuristics for diverse action costs. In: Proceedings of the Twenty-Sixth International Joint Conference on Artificial Intelligence (IJCAI), pp. 4287–4293 (2017)
4. Fan, G., Müller, M., Holte, R.: The two-edged nature of diverse action costs. In: Proceedings of the Twenty-Seventh International Conference on Automated Planning and Scheduling (ICAPS), pp. 98–106 (2017)
5. Geffner, H., Bonet, B.: A Concise Introduction to Models and Methods for Automated Planning. Morgan & Claypool Publishers, San Rafael (2013)

6. Geißer, F.: On planning with state-dependent action costs. Ph.D. dissertation, Albert-Ludwigs-Universität Freiburg (2018)
7. Geißer, F., Keller, T., Mattmüller, R.: Delete relaxations for planning with state-dependent action costs. In: Proceedings of the 24th International Joint Conference on Artificial Intelligence (IJCAI), pp. 1573–1579 (2015)
8. Geißer, F., Keller, T., Mattmüller, R.: Abstractions for planning with state-dependent action costs. In: Proceedings of the 26th International Conference on Automated Planning and Scheduling (ICAPS), pp. 140–148 (2016)
9. Haslum, P., Botea, A., Helmert, M., Bonet, B., Koenig, S.: Domain-independent construction of pattern database heuristics for cost-optimal planning. In: Proceedings of the 22nd AAAI Conference on Artificial Intelligence, pp. 1007–1012 (2007)
10. Helmert, M.: The fast downward planning system. J. Artif. Intell. Res. **26**, 191–246 (2006)
11. Helmert, M., Domshlak, C.: Landmarks, critical paths and abstractions: what's the difference anyway? In: Proceedings of the 19th International Conference on Automated Planning and Scheduling (ICAPS) (2009)
12. Helmert, M., Haslum, P., Hoffmann, J.: Flexible abstraction heuristics for optimal sequential planning. In: Proceedings of the 17th International Conference on Automated Planning and Scheduling (ICAPS), pp. 176–183 (2007)
13. Helmert, M., Röger, G.: How good is almost perfect? In: Proceedings of the Twenty-Third AAAI Conference on Artificial Intelligence (AAAI 2008), pp. 944–949 (2008)
14. Ivankovic, F., Haslum, P., Gordon, D.: Planning with global state constraints and state-dependent action costs. In: Proceedings of the 29th International Conference on Automated Planning and Scheduling (ICAPS) (2019)
15. Keller, T., Pommerening, F., Seipp, J., Geißer, F., Mattmüller, R.: State-dependent cost partitionings for Cartesian abstractions in classical planning. In: Proceedings of the Twenty-Fifth International Joint Conference on Artificial Intelligence (IJCAI), pp. 3161–3169 (2016)
16. Pearl, J.: Heuristics: Intelligent Search Strategies for Computer Problem Solving. Addison-Wesley Longman, Boston (1984)
17. Speck, D., Geißer, F., Mattmüller, R.: Symbolic planning with edge-valued multi-valued decision diagrams. In: Proceedings of the Twenty-Eighth International Conference on Automated Planning and Scheduling (ICAPS), pp. 250–258 (2018)
18. Speck, D., Geißer, F., Mattmüller, R.: SYMPLE: symbolic planning based on EVMDDs. In: Ninth International Planning Competition (IPC-9): Planner Abstracts, pp. 91–94 (2018)

Strong Equivalence for Argumentation Frameworks with Collective Attacks

Wolfgang Dvořák[iD], Anna Rapberger[✉][iD], and Stefan Woltran[iD]

Institute of Logic and Computation, TU Wien, Vienna, Austria
arapberg@dbai.tuwien.ac.at

Abstract. Argumentation frameworks with collective attacks are a prominent extension of Dung's abstract argumentation frameworks, where an attack can be drawn from a set of arguments to another argument. These frameworks are often abbreviated as SETAFs. Although SETAFs have received increasing interest recently, the notion of strong equivalence, which is fundamental in nonmonotonic formalisms to characterize equivalent replacements, has not yet been investigated. In this paper, we study how strong equivalence between SETAFs can be decided with respect to the most important semantics and also consider variants of strong equivalence.

1 Introduction

Abstract argumentation frameworks (AFs) as introduced by Dung [6] are a core formalism in formal argumentation. A popular line of research investigates extensions of Dung AFs that allow for a richer syntax (see, e.g. [5]). In this work we consider SETAFs as introduced by Nielsen and Parsons [12] which generalize the binary attacks in Dung AFs to collective attacks such that a set of arguments B attacks another argument a but no proper subset of B attacks a. As discussed in [12], there are several scenarios where arguments interact and can constitute an attack on another argument only if these arguments are jointly taken into account. Representing such a situation in Dung AFs often requires additional artificial arguments to "encode" the conjunction of arguments.

SETAFs have received increasing interest in the last years. For instance, semi-stable, stage, ideal, and eager semantics have been adapted to SETAFs in [8,10]; translations between SETAFs and other abstract argumentation formalisms are studied in [14]; and the expressiveness of SETAFs is investigated in [7]. [17] observed that for particular instantiations, SETAFs provide a more convenient target formalism than Dung AFs.

The notion of strong equivalence is recognized as a central concept in non-monotonic reasoning [11,15,16] and provides means for the replacement property. In terms of AFs, strong equivalence (with respect to a semantics σ) between two frameworks F and G holds, if for any further AF H, $\sigma(F \cup H) = \sigma(G \cup H)$. Hence, replacing a subframework F by a strongly equivalent AF G in any context does not alter the extensions. In other words, the notion of strong equivalence

C. Benzmüller and H. Stuckenschmidt (Eds.): KI 2019, LNAI 11793, pp. 131–145, 2019.
https://doi.org/10.1007/978-3-030-30179-8_11

allows for simplifying a part of an argumentation framework without looking at the rest of the framework; a method that has been recently applied in a practical setting in terms of preprocessing Dung AFs [9].

For Dung AFs, strong equivalence and variants thereof have been extensively studied in the literature [1–4,13]. The main results reveal that strong equivalence can be decided by syntactic identity of so-called kernels of the AFs to be compared. In these kernels, depending on the actual semantics, certain inactive attacks need to be removed. Up to date, similar investigations for SETAFs have not been undertaken and it remained open how the concept of inactive attacks can be generalized to the richer attack structure SETAFs provide.

In this paper, we provide characterizations of strong equivalence between SETAFs with respect to admissible, complete, stable, preferred, semi-stable and stage semantics. We do so by generalizing the notion of kernels to SETAFs. Moreover, we show that strong equivalence for the semantics under consideration coincides with weaker notions of equivalence, where we disallow certain context frameworks H in the definition of the equivalence relation. Our results confirm that SETAFs are a natural generalization of AFs in the sense that the appealing concept of kernels also is applicable to SETAFs.

Some proofs are omitted but are provided in a technical report available at www.dbai.tuwien.ac.at/research/report/dbai-tr-2019-116.pdf.

2   Preliminaries

Throughout the paper, we assume a countably infinite domain $\mathfrak{A}$ of possible arguments.

Definition 1. *A SETAF is a pair $F = (A, R)$ where $A \subseteq \mathfrak{A}$ is finite, and $R \subseteq (2^A \setminus \{\emptyset\}) \times A$ is the attack relation. SETAFs (A, R), where for all $(S, a) \in R$ it holds that $|S| = 1$, amount to (standard Dung) AFs. In that case, we usually write (a, b) to denote the set-attack $(\{a\}, b)$. Moreover, for a SETAF $F = (B, S)$, we use $A(F)$ and $R(F)$ to identify its arguments B and respectively its attack relation S.*

Given a SETAF (A, R), we write $S \mapsto_R b$ if there is a set $S' \subseteq S$ with $(S', b) \in R$. Moreover, we write $S' \mapsto_R S$ if $S' \mapsto_R b$ for some $b \in S$. We drop subscript R in $\mapsto_R$ if there is no ambiguity. For $S \subseteq A$, we use S_R^+ to denote the set $\{b \mid S \mapsto_R b\}$ and define the range of S (w.r.t. R), denoted $S_R^\oplus$, as the set $S \cup S_R^+$.

The notions of conflict and defense naturally generalize to SETAFs.

Definition 2. *Given a SETAF $F = (A, R)$, a set $S \subseteq A$ is conflicting in F if $S \mapsto_R a$ for some $a \in S$. A set $S \subseteq A$ is conflict-free in F, if S is not conflicting in F, i.e. if $S' \cup \{a\} \not\subseteq S$ for each $(S', a) \in R$. cf(F) denotes the set of all conflict-free sets in F.*

Definition 3. *Given a SETAF $F = (A, R)$, an argument $a \in A$ is defended (in F) by a set $S \subseteq A$ if for each $B \subseteq A$, such that $B \mapsto_R a$, also $S \mapsto_R B$. A set T of arguments is defended (in F) by S if each $a \in T$ is defended by S (in F).*

The semantics we study in this work are the admissible, stable, preferred, complete, stage and semi-stable semantics, which we will abbreviate by *adm*, *stb*, *pref*, *com*, *stage* and *sem* respectively [8,10,12].

Definition 4. *Given a SETAF $F = (A, R)$ and a conflict-free set $S \in cf(F)$. Then,*

- *$S \in adm(F)$, if S defends itself in F,*
- *$S \in stb(F)$, if $S \mapsto a$ for all $a \in A \setminus S$,*
- *$S \in pref(F)$, if $S \in adm(F)$ and there is no $T \in adm(F)$ s.t. $T \supset S$,*
- *$S \in com(F)$, if $S \in adm(F)$ and $a \in S$ for all $a \in A$ defended by S,*
- *$S \in stage(F)$, if $\nexists T \in cf(F)$ with $T_R^\oplus \supset S_R^\oplus$, and*
- *$S \in sem(F)$, if $S \in adm(F)$ and $\nexists T \in adm(F)$ s.t. $T_R^\oplus \supset S_R^\oplus$.*

The relationship between the semantics has been clarified in [8,10,12] and matches with the relations between the semantics for Dung AFs, i.e. for any SETAF F:

$$stb(F) \subseteq sem(F) \subseteq pref(F) \subseteq com(F) \subseteq adm(F) \subseteq cf(F) \qquad (1)$$

$$stb(F) \subseteq stage(F) \subseteq cf(F). \qquad (2)$$

The following property also carries over from Dung AFs: For any SETAF F, if $stb(F) \neq \emptyset$ then $stb(F) = sem(F) = stage(F)$.

3 Notions of Strong Equivalence and Basic Concepts

We define the notion of strong equivalence for SETAFs along the lines of [13]. Given SETAFs F, G we define the union of F and G as $F \cup G = (A(F) \cup A(G), R(F) \cup R(G))$.

Definition 5. *Two SETAFs F and G are strongly equivalent to each other wrt. a semantics σ, in symbols $F \equiv_s^\sigma G$, iff for each SETAF H, $\sigma(F \cup H) = \sigma(G \cup H)$ holds.*

By definition, we have that $F \equiv_s^\sigma G$ implies $\sigma(F) = \sigma(G)$, i.e. standard equivalence between F and G wrt. σ. However, no matter which of the considered semantics we choose for σ, the converse direction does not hold in general (cf. [13]).

We consider two weakenings for Definition 5 by restricting the potential context SETAF H. First, we let H to be only an AF instead of a SETAF. We consider this an interesting restriction in the sense of whether an AF is sufficient to reveal the potential difference between the compared SETAFs in terms of strong equivalence. Another weakening has first been proposed in [1] under the name *normal expansion equivalence*. Here the framework H is not allowed to add attacks between "existing" arguments (in F or G), and thus better reflects that in dynamic scenarios new arguments may be proposed but the relation between given arguments remains unchanged.

Definition 6. *Let F and G be SETAFs and σ be a semantics. Moreover, let $B = A(F) \cup A(G)$. We write*

- *$F \equiv_n^\sigma G$, iff for each SETAF H with $R(H) \cap (2^B \times B) = \emptyset$, $\sigma(F \cup H) = \sigma(G \cup H)$.*
- *$F \equiv_{sd}^\sigma G$, iff for each AF H, $\sigma(F \cup H) = \sigma(G \cup H)$.*
- *$F \equiv_{nd}^\sigma G$, iff for each AF H with $R(H) \cap (B \times B) = \emptyset$, $\sigma(F \cup H) = \sigma(G \cup H)$.*

Results for strong equivalence between AFs (i.e. $\equiv_{sd}^\sigma$ in our notation) rely on so-called kernels that remove attacks that do not contribute to the computation of the extensions of an AF F, no matter how the AF is extended to $F \cup H$. This is best illustrated in terms of stable semantics. Consider an attack (a, b) where a is self-attacking. Then, removing (a, b) from the attacks has no effect since (i) the conflicts remain the same (note that a is never part of a conflict-free set, due to the self-attack), (ii) if b needs to be attacked by a stable extension, this cannot happen due to attack (a, b) (again, since a will never part of a stable extension due to its conflict). In [13], it has been shown that removal of such *inactive attacks* is sufficient to decide strong equivalence w.r.t. stable semantics: given an AF F, define its stable kernel as

$$F^{sk} = (A(F), R(F) \setminus \{(a, b) \in R(F) \mid a \neq b, (a, a) \in R(F)\}).$$

For AFs F, G it holds that $F \equiv_{sd}^\sigma G$ iff $F^{sk} = G^{sk}$. For other semantics, the notion of kernel needs to be further restricted; intuitively, an attack (a, b) with self-attacking a might still be responsible for defending b against a.

However, as we will show in the next section, kernels can be defined for SETAFs as well. Before doing so, we first consider the concept of redundant attack and show that they are also redundant when testing for strong equivalence. Then, we generalize the concept of inactive attacks to SETAFs.

Definition 7. *Let $F = (A, R)$ be a SETAF. An attack $(S, a) \in R$ is called* redundant *in F if there exists $(S', a) \in R$ with $S' \subset S$.*

As shown in [14] we can remove redundant attacks of SETAF F without changing its semantics. When removing all redundant attacks from F the resulting SETAF G is called *minimal form* of F.

Lemma 1. *For a SETAF F and its minimal form G we have $F \equiv_s^\sigma G$ for $\sigma \in \{adm, stb, pref, com, stage, sem\}$.*

Proof. Let R be the set of redundant attacks in F and consider an arbitrary SETAF H. The attacks in R are also redundant in the SETAF $F \cup H$ and thus, by [14][1], $\sigma(F \cup H) = \sigma((F \cup H) \setminus R) = \sigma(G \cup H)$. Now as $\sigma(F \cup H) = \sigma(G \cup H)$ for each SETAF H we obtain that $F \equiv_s^\sigma G$. $\square$

---

[1] *sem* and *stage* are not considered in [14] but the result immediately extends to those semantics.

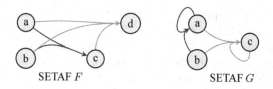

Fig. 1. A SETAF F with active attack $(\{a,b\},c)$ and inactive attack $(\{a,b,c\},d)$ and a SETAF G with active self-attack $(\{a,b\},a)$ and inactive self-attack $(\{a,b,c\},c)$.

We have that two SETAFs are strongly equivalent iff their minimal forms are strongly equivalent. Thus in the remainder of the paper we will assume that SETAFs tested for strong equivalence are in minimal form, i.e. have no redundant attacks.

A crucial role in the definition of kernels plays the concept of an inactive attack which we define right now.

Definition 8. *Let $F = (A, R)$ be a SETAF. An attack $(S, a) \in R$ is called inactive in F if (i) $a \notin S$ and there exist $S' \subseteq S$ and $b \in S$ such that $(S', b) \in R$, or (ii) $a \in S$ and there exist $S' \subset S$ and $b \in S$ such that $(S', b) \in R$. An attack that is not inactive in F is said to be* active *in F.*

Figure 1 illustrates the different notions of inactive attacks. An example of an inactive attack according to case (i) in Definition 8 is given by the SETAF F; here, the source-set $S = \{a, b, c\}$ is conflicting and attacks an argument $d \notin S$. Case (ii) covers inactive self-attacks; note that in this case, the set S' is required to be a proper subset of S. This subtile difference ensures the existence of active self-attacks since the source-set of each self-attack is conflicting by definition. The SETAF G in Fig. 1 provides an example; here, the active self-attack $(\{a, b\}, a)$ deactivates the self-attack $(\{a, b, c\}, c)$. Note that in terms of AFs Definition 8 boils down to the situation discussed above for binary attacks (a, b) with $a \neq b$: $(\{a\}, b)$ is inactive iff a attacks itself. We conclude this section with a technical result.

Lemma 2. *Let $F = (A, R)$ be a SETAF and $(S, a) \in R$ be inactive in F. Then there exists an attack $(S', b) \in R$ with $S' \subseteq S$ and $b \in S$ that is active in F.*

Proof. Towards a contradiction let $(S, a) \in R$ be an attack violating the condition of the lemma such that all inactive attacks $(T, b) \in R$ with $|S \cup \{a\}| > |T \cup \{b\}|$ satisfy the condition, i.e. (S, a) is minimal in this respect. By inactivity of (S, a) either (i) $a \notin S$ and there exist $S' \subseteq S$ and $b \in S$ such that $(S', b) \in R$, or (ii) $a \in S$ and there exist $S' \subset S$ and $b \in S$ such that $(S', b) \in R$. By assumption, (S', b) is inactive in F.

In case (i) we have $|S' \cup \{b\}| < |S \cup \{a\}|$, and, by the minimality of (S, a), we obtain that there is an active attack $(S'', c) \in R$ with $S'' \subseteq S' \subseteq S$ and $c \in S' \subseteq S$.

The same reasoning applies in case (ii) if $|S' \cup \{b\}| < |S \cup \{a\}|$. Thus assume that $|S' \cup \{b\}| = |S \cup \{a\}|$, i.e. $S' = S \setminus \{b\}$, $b \in S$. By assumption (S', b) is inactive and thus there exist $S'' \subseteq S'$, $c \in S'$ such that $(S'', c) \in R$. But then $|S'' \cup \{c\}| < |S \cup \{a\}|$ and, by the minimality of (S, a), we obtain that there is an active attack $(S''', d) \in R$ with $S''' \subseteq S'' \subseteq S$ and $d \in S'' \subseteq S$.   □

4   Characterizations of Strong Equivalence

In this section we characterize strong equivalence as well as its variants (cf. Definition 6) for all semantics under consideration by introducing three different kernels for the different semantics. We will show that two SETAFs are strongly equivalent iff they have the same kernel of a particular type. We start with the result for stable and stage semantics. In the corresponding kernel all inactive attacks have to be removed. For the two remaining kernels, the situation is slightly different and towards our results for admissible, semi-stable, preferred, and complete semantics we will introduce an additional normal form for SETAFs to handle this situation.

4.1   Stable Kernel

The main idea of the stable kernel is that for stable semantics only active attacks are relevant. However, for self-attacks (i.e. attacks (S, a) such that $a \in S$) additional care is needed, since self-attacks (S, a) and (S, b) turn out to be indistinguishable. This is due to the fact that self-attacks never contribute to the range of a stable extension and thus only the information that the set S is conflicting is relevant. For example consider the SETAFs $F = (\{a, b\}, \{(\{a, b\}, a)\})$ and $G = (\{a, b\}, \{(\{a, b\}, b)\})$. The two SETAFs have different active attacks but as we argue next, $F \equiv_s^{stb} G$ holds. Let H be an arbitrary SETAF and let $S \in stb(F \cup H)$. Then S cannot contain both a and b. If $a, b \notin S$, then S attacks (in $F \cup H$) both a and b via attacks in H. Otherwise, wlog let $a \in S$. Then S attacks b via an attack in H. In both cases S is stable in $G \cup H$. That is, for active self-attacks (S, a) only the set S but not the concrete attacked argument $a \in S$ is significant. For conflicting S, we thus add (S, b) for all $b \in S$ to the kernel. An illustrative example is provided in Fig. 2.

Definition 9. *For a SETAF $F = (A, R)$ in minimal form, we define the stable kernel of F as $F^{sk} = (A, R^{sk})$ with*

$$R^{sk} = \{(S, a) \in R \mid (S, a) \text{ active in } F\} \cup \{(S, b) \mid (S, a) \text{ active in } F, a \in S, b \in S\}.$$

The stable kernel of an arbitrary SETAF F is the stable kernel of the minimal form of F.

In a first step we show that the stable, and stage respectively, extensions of a SETAF F coincide with the stable, and stage respectively, extensions of its stable kernel F^{sk}. The following result suffices in this endeavor.

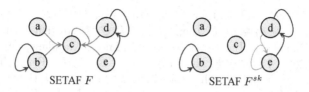

Fig. 2. Example illustrating the stable kernel of a SETAF F. Active attacks in blue; inactive in red. Newly introduced self-attacks appear in green. (Color figure online)

Lemma 3. *For any SETAF in minimal form F (1) $cf(F) = cf(F^{sk})$ and (2) for each $S \in cf(F)$, $S_{R(F)}^{\oplus} = S_{R(F^{sk})}^{\oplus}$.*

Proof. (1) $cf(F) \subseteq cf(F^{sk})$: Consider $T \in cf(F)$ and towards a contradiction assume $T \notin cf(F^{sk})$. Thus there is $(S,b) \in R^{sk}$ such that $S \cup \{b\} \subseteq T$. If (S,b) would be an active attack in F then $T \notin cf(F)$ and thus we have that $b \in S$ and there is an $a \in S$ such that $(S,a) \in R(F)$. As $S \subseteq T$ this is in contradiction to our initial assumption $T \in cf(F)$. For $cf(F) \supseteq cf(F^{sk})$, let $T \in cf(F^{sk})$ and (S,a) be any attack in F that is not present in F^{sk}. We have to show that $S \cup \{a\} \not\subseteq T$. From Lemma 2 there exists $(S',b) \in R$ with $S' \subseteq S$ and $b \in S$ that is active in F and thus contained in $R(F^{sk})$. Since $T \in cf(F^{sk})$, $S' \cup \{b\} \not\subseteq T$ and $S \cup \{a\} \not\subseteq T$ follows.

(2) Let $S \in cf(F)$. $S_{R(F)}^{\oplus} \supseteq S_{R(F^{sk})}^{\oplus}$: Notice that no attack in the set $\{(S,b) \mid (S,a)$ active in $F, a \in S, b \in S\}$ contributes to the range of a conflict-free set and as $R(F) \supseteq R^{sk} \setminus \{(S,b) \mid (S,a)$ active in $F, a \in S, b \in S\}$ we obtain that $S_{R(F)}^{\oplus} \supseteq S_{R(F^{sk})}^{\oplus}$. For $S_{R(F)}^{\oplus} \subseteq S_{R(F^{sk})}^{\oplus}$, let (S',a) be any attack in F that is not present in F^{sk}, i.e. (S',a) is inactive in F. As (S',a) is inactive we have that $S' \not\subseteq S$ and thus the attack does not contribute to the range of S. $\square$

Given the above semantical correspondence between SETAFs and their kernels we show that SETAFs with the same kernel are strongly equivalent on a purely syntactic level. That is, we show that if two SETAFs F, G have the same stable kernel then also their expansions with the same SETAF H have the same kernel.

Lemma 4. *Let F and G be SETAFs in minimal form such that $F^{sk} = G^{sk}$. Then, $(F \cup H)^{sk} = (G \cup H)^{sk}$ for all SETAFs H.*

Proof. Notice, that $F \cup H$ (and likewise $G \cup H$) might not be in minimal form. However, by definition, we remove redundant attacks before constructing the kernel. It suffices to show $R((F \cup H)^{sk}) \subseteq R((G \cup H)^{sk})$ as $R((F \cup H)^{sk}) \supseteq R((G \cup H)^{sk})$ then follows by symmetry. Let $(S,a) \in R((F \cup H)^{sk})$. We show that $(S,a) \in R((G \cup H)^{sk})$ by considering two cases.

(1) Assume that (S,a), $a \notin S$, is active and non-redundant in $F \cup H$, i.e. there is no attack $(S',b) \in R(F \cup H)$ such that (i) $S' \subseteq S$, $b \in S \cup \{a\}$ and $(S,a) \neq (S',b)$. We show that (S,a) is active and non-redundant in $G \cup H$, i.e.

(a) $(S,a) \in R(G \cup H)$ and (b) there is no attack $(S',b) \in R(I)$, $I \in \{H,G\}$ which satisfies (i). (a) If $(S,a) \in R(H)$, then $(S,a) \in R(G \cup H)$ by definition. Otherwise, if $(S,a) \in R(F)$, then, as the attack is active and non-redundant, we can conclude that $(S,a) \in R(F^{sk}) = R(G^{sk})$ and thus $(S,a) \in G \cup H$. (b) For $R(H)$ this holds by the fact that there is no such attack in $R(F \cup H)$. Notice that as there is no such attack in $R(F)$ there is also no such attack in $R(F^{sk}) = R(G^{sk})$. Towards a contradiction assume that there is an attack $(S',b) \in R(G)$ satisfying (i). Then, by Lemma 2, there is an active attack (T,c) with $T \subseteq S'$ satisfying (i). Thus $(T,c) \in R(G^{sk}) = R(F^{sk})$ and thus $(S,a) \notin R(G^{sk}) = R(F^{sk})$, a contradiction. By (a) and (b) we can conclude that $(S,a) \in R((G \cup H)^{sk})$.

(2) Assume that (S,a) is such that $a \in S$ and there is a non-redundant active attack $(S,b) \in R(F \cup H)$ with $b \in S$. If $(S,b) \in R(F)$ then, by the assumption $F^{sk} = G^{sk}$, there is an active and non-redundant attack $(S,c) \in R(G)$ with $c \in S$. Now, as (S,b) is active in $F \cup H$, there is no $(S',d) \in R(H)$ with $S' \subset S$ and $d \in S$ and thus (S,c) is active in $F \cup H$. Hence, $(S,a) \in R((G \cup H)^{sk})$.

Now assume there is no such $(S,b) \in R(F)$. Then $(S,b) \in R(H)$ and thus $(S,b) \in R(G \cup H)$. Towards a contradiction assume (S,b) is redundant or inactive.

- If (S,b) is redundant, i.e. there is $S' \subset S$ with $(S',b) \in R(G \cup H)$ and (S',b) non-redundant. As (S,b) is non-redundant in $F \cup H$ we have that $(S',b) \in R(G)$. If (S',b) is inactive in G then there is an attack (S'',c) with $S'' \cup \{c\} \subseteq S'$ active in G. By $F^{sk} = G^{sk}$, there is an active attack (S''',d) in F with $S''' \cup \{d\} = S'' \cup \{c\}$. But now again (S,b) is inactive in $F \cup H$, a contradiction. Otherwise if (S',b) is active in G then, by $F^{sk} = G^{sk}$, there is an active attack (S'',c) in F with $S'' \cup \{c\} = S' \cup \{b\}$. Hence (S,b) is inactive in F, a contradiction.
- If (S,b) is inactive, i.e. there is $S' \subset S, c \in S$ with $(S',c) \in R(G \cup H)$ and (S',c) active. As (S,b) is active in $F \cup H$ we have that $(S',a) \in R(G)$. By $F^{sk} = G^{sk}$, there is an active attack (S'',d) in F with $S'' \cup \{d\} = S' \cup \{c\}$. Thus (S,b) is inactive in F, a contradiction.

We obtain that (S,b) is active and non-redundant and thus $(S,a) \in R((G \cup H)^{sk})$.   □

While the previous lemmas enable us to show that two SETAFs with the same kernel are strongly equivalent it remains to show that this condition is necessary. We do so in the next theorem by providing constructions for a (SET)AF H that shows that two SETAFs are not strongly equivalent if they have different kernels. Moreover, we extend our results to the other notions of equivalence.

Theorem 1. *For any AFs F and G and $\sigma \in \{stb, stage\}$ the following are equivalent: (a) $F \equiv_s^\sigma G$; (b) $F \equiv_n^\sigma G$; (c) $F \equiv_{sd}^\sigma G$; (d) $F \equiv_{nd}^\sigma G$; (e) $F^{sk} = G^{sk}$.*

Proof. By definition (a) implies (b) and (c). Likewise, (b) implies (d) and (c) implies (d). It remains to show (1) $F^{sk} = G^{sk}$ implies $F \equiv_s^\sigma G$ and (2) $F^{sk} \neq G^{sk}$ implies $F \not\equiv_{nd}^\sigma G$. By Lemma 1 we can assume that F and G are in minimal form.

(1) Suppose $F^{sk} = G^{sk}$ and let H, S such that $S \in \sigma(F \cup H)$. We show $S \in \sigma(G \cup H)$. By Lemma 3, $S \in \sigma((F \cup H)^{sk})$ and we get $S \in \sigma((G \cup H)^{sk})$ from Lemma 4. Thus, $S \in \sigma(G \cup H)$, again by Lemma 3. By symmetry and definition of strong equivalence, we get $F \equiv_s^\sigma G$.

(2) First, we consider the case $A(F^{sk}) \neq A(G^{sk})$. This implies $A(F) \neq A(G)$. W.l.o.g. let $a \in A(F) \setminus A(G)$. We use $B = (A(F) \cup A(G)) \setminus \{a\}$, and c as a fresh argument. Consider $H = (B \cup \{c\}, \{(c, b) \mid b \in B\})$. Note that H is conform with the definition of $\equiv_{nd}^\sigma$, i.e. it is a simple AF not changing the relation between existing arguments. Suppose now, a is contained in some $S \in \sigma(F \cup H)$. Then, we are done since a cannot be contained in any $S' \in \sigma(G \cup H)$, since $a \notin A(G \cup H)$. Otherwise, we extend H to $H' = H \cup (\{a\}, \emptyset)$. Then, $\{a, c\}$ is the unique stable extension (and thus unique stage extension) of $G \cup H'$. On the other hand, observe that $F \cup H' = F \cup H$, hence by assumption, a is not contained in any $S \in \sigma(F \cup H')$. In both cases, we get $F \not\equiv_s^\sigma G$. Now suppose $A(F^{sk}) = A(G^{sk})$ but $R(F^{sk}) \neq R(G^{sk})$. W.l.o.g. assume there exists some $(S, a) \in R(F^{sk}) \setminus R(G^{sk})$ such that there is no $(S', a) \in R(G^{sk})$ with $S' \subset S$ (otherwise exchange the roles of F and G). We distinguish the two cases of attacks that constitute the stable kernel: (1) $(S, a) \in R$ is active in F with $a \notin S$; (2) (S, a) with $a \in S$, such that there is some $(S, d) \in R$ with $d \in S$ active in F.

(1) For fresh arguments c, t, we define $H = (A(F) \cup \{c, t\}, R_H)$ with

$$R_H = \{(t, c), (c, t)\} \cup \{(c, b) \mid b \in A(F) \setminus (S \cup \{a\})\} \cup \{(t, b) \mid b \in A(F)\}.$$

First, by construction we have that $\{t\} \in stb(F \cup H)$ and $\{t\} \in stb(G \cup H)$ and thus stable and stage semantics coincide in both $F \cup H$ and $G \cup H$. Thus we can restrict ourselves to stable semantics. We have $S \cup \{c\} \in stb(F \cup H)$, since $S \cup \{c\}$ is conflict-free and attacks all arguments $b \notin S$ either collectively via S or via the newly introduced argument c. However, $S \cup \{c\} \notin stb(G \cup H)$ as by the assumption there is no $(S', a) \in R(G^{sk})$ with $S' \subseteq S$ and thus $S \cup \{c\}$ does not attack a.

(2) Notice that, by construction, whenever $(S, a) \in R(F^{sk})$ then also $(S, b) \in R(F^{sk})$ for all $b \in S$. W.l.o.g we can assume that there is no $(S', b) \in R(G^{sk})$ with $S' \cup \{b\} \subseteq S$ (otherwise we exchange the roles of F and G as $(S', b) \notin R(F^{sk})$). For a fresh argument c, we define

$$H = (A(F) \cup \{c\}, \{(c, b) \mid b \in A(F) \setminus S\}).$$

We have $S \cup \{c\} \notin stb(F \cup H)$ and $S \cup \{c\} \notin stage(F \cup H)$, since (S, a) is a conflict within the set $S \cup \{c\}$. However, for $G \cup H$ we have that $S \cup \{c\}$ is conflict free and attacks all argument outside the set, i.e. $S \cup \{c\} \in stb(G \cup H)$ and thus also $S \cup \{c\} \in stage(G \cup H)$.

In both cases we have found a witness H for $F \not\equiv_{nd}^\sigma G$.   □

4.2   SETAFs in Normal Form

We next turn to admissible based semantics, i.e. *adm*, *com*, *pref*, and *sem* semantics, and define the respective kernels. While for stable semantics we can ignore

SETAF F SETAF G

Fig. 3. Given that $(\{a, b\}, c)$ is inactive it is equivalent to $(\{a, b, c\}, c)$ for all semantics under our considerations. We call the attack $(\{a, b, c\}, c)$ in F reducible and G the normal form of F.

inactive attacks they are significant for admissible-based semantics as one has to defend arguments also against inactive attacks. We first identify equivalent inactive attacks and introduce a corresponding normal form of SETAFs.

Definition 10. *Let $F = (A, R)$ be a SETAF. We call an attack (S, a) with $a \in S$ reducible in F if there exists $S' \subseteq S \setminus \{a\}$ and $b \in S$ such that $(S', b) \in R$.*

First note that a reducible attack (S, a) is inactive since the set S is conflicting; thus S will never appear in a conflict-free set T. Moreover, each conflict-free set T which defends the argument a attacks some argument in $S \setminus \{a\}$, otherwise T would be conflicting. We introduce a normal form of a SETAF F which is given by its minimal form where each reducible attack (S, a) is replaced by the attack $(S \setminus \{a\}, a)$. Figure 3 shows a SETAF F and its normal form G. Here, $(\{a, b, c\}, c)$ is reducible in F; the attack is replaced by $(\{a, b\}, c)$ in G.

Definition 11. *Let $F = (A, R)$ be a SETAF. We define the normal form G of F as the minimal form of $(A, R \cup \{(S \setminus \{a\}, a) \mid (S, a) \text{ reducible in } F\})$.*

The next lemma states that replacing reducible attacks (S, a) with $(S \setminus \{a\}, a)$ preserves the semantics. The modification does not affect conflict-free sets; furthermore, the argument a is defended by the same conflict-free sets in both SETAFs F and its normal form G. Moreover, modifying inactive attacks does not affect stable and stage extensions. This follows directly from Lemma 3 and the fact that inactive attacks are deleted in the stable kernel.

Lemma 5. *Let $F = (A, R \cup \{(S, a)\})$ and let (S, a) be reducible in F. Let $G = (A, R \cup \{(S \setminus \{a\}, a)\})$. Then $\sigma(F) = \sigma(G)$ for $\sigma \in \{adm, pref, sem, com, stb, stage\}$.*

It follows that each SETAF F and its normal form G are also strongly equivalent. Indeed, consider an extension $F \cup H$ where H is arbitrary. The repetitive application of Lemma 5 yields $\sigma(F \cup H) = \sigma(G \cup H)$ for all considered semantics σ.

Proposition 1. *For a SETAF F and its normal form G, $F \equiv^\sigma_s G$ for $\sigma \in \{adm, pref, sem, com, stb, stage\}$.*

4.3   Admissible and Complete Kernel

We start this section by introducing the kernel for complete semantics. The complete kernel F^{ck} consists of all active attacks and inactive attacks (S, a) such that a is not attacked by any $S' \subset S \cup \{a\}$. Notice that whenever there is such an attack (S', a) the argument a is only defended by a complete extension E if E attacks $S' \setminus \{a\}$ and thus also S, i.e. whenever a is defended against (S', a) it is also defended against (S, a). We thus do not include such attacks (S, a) in the kernel. It turns out that all the remaining inactive attacks influence whether the argument a is defended by a set E or not for certain expansions H.

Definition 12. *For a SETAF $F = (A, R)$ in normal form, we define the complete kernel of F as $F^{ck} = (A, R^{ck})$ with*

$$R^{ck} = \{(S, a) \in R \mid (S, a) \, is \, active \, in \, F\} \cup$$
$$\{(S, a) \in R \mid \not\exists S' \subset S \cup \{a\} : a \in S', (S', a) \in R\}.$$

The complete kernel of an arbitrary SETAF F is the complete kernel of the normal form of F.

For admissible semantics, we extend the complete kernel by additionally removing inactive attacks (S, a) where the attacked argument a defends itself against S. Notice that self-defense is not sufficient for removing an inactive attack in the complete kernel since inactive attacks must be additionally taken into account for determining whether arguments outside of an admissible set T are defended by this set T.

Definition 13. *For a SETAF $F = (A, R)$ in normal form, we define the admissible kernel of F as $F^{ak} = (A, R^{ak})$ with*

$$R^{ak} = \{(S, a) \in R \mid (S, a) \, is \, active \, in \, F\} \cup$$
$$(\{(S, a) \in R \mid \not\exists S' \subset S \cup \{a\} : a \in S' \, and \, (S', a) \in R\} \cap$$
$$\{(S, a) \in R \mid \not\exists b \in S \, such \, that \, (\{a\}, b) \in R\}).$$

The admissible kernel of an arbitrary SETAF F is the admissible kernel of the normal form of F.

Example 1. Consider the SETAF $F = (A, R)$ from Fig. 4, which shows F together with its complete and its admissible kernel. Attacks which are colored in red are inactive. The complete kernel F^{ck} is constructed by removing the inactive attack $(\{d, e\}, c)$ since c is attacked by $\{c, d\}$, i.e. by a subset of $\{c, d, e\}$. In the admissible kernel F^{ak} also the attack $(\{a, b\}, c)$ can be removed, since c defends itself by attacking the argument a. Observe that the set $\{e\}$ is admissible and complete in both F and F^{ck} but $\{e\}$ is not complete in F^{ak} since c defends c in F^{ak}.

Before showing our characterisation for strong equivalence we clarify the relation between the introduced kernels. Observe that $F^{ak} \subseteq F^{ck}$ by definition.

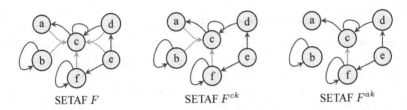

SETAF F SETAF F^{ck} SETAF F^{ak}

Fig. 4. Complete and the admissible kernel of a SETAF F. Active attacks in blue. Inactive in red. (Color figure online)

Lemma 6. *For any two SETAFs F, G in normal form, (a) $F^{ak} = G^{ak}$ implies $F^{sk} = G^{sk}$ and (b) $F^{ck} = G^{ck}$ implies $F^{ak} = G^{ak}$ and $F^{sk} = G^{sk}$.*

Proof. We will show (a) and omit the proof of (b) due to space limits. Assume that $F^{ak} = G^{ak}$. We show that $F^{sk} \subseteq G^{sk}$, the other direction is by symmetry. Let $(S, a) \in R(F^{sk})$. We show that $(S, a) \in R(G^{sk})$.

Towards a contradiction, assume $(S, a) \notin R(G^{sk})$. First note that we can assume that (S, a) is active in F. In the case $(S, a) \in \{(S, b) \mid \exists (S, c)$ active in $F, b, c \in S\}$, there is an active attack $(S, b) \in R(F)$, $b \in S$, and $(S, b) \notin R(G^{sk})$ (otherwise there is an active attack $(S, c) \in R(G)$, $c \in S$, and therefore $(S, a) \in R(G^{sk})$, contradiction).

By definition of F^{ak}, we get that $(S, a) \in F^{ak}$, and therefore $(S, a) \in R(G^{ak})$ by assumption. Thus $(S, a) \in R(G)$ and (S, a) is inactive (since $(S, a) \notin R(G^{sk})$). By Lemma 2, there is an active attack $(S', b) \in R(G)$ such that $S' \subseteq S$, $b \in S$. Thus we conclude that $(S', b) \in R(G^{ak})$ (by definition of the admissible kernel) $(S', b) \in R(F^{ak})$ (by assumption $F^{ak} = G^{ak}$) and therefore $(S', c) \in R(F)$, making the attack (S, a) inactive in F, contradiction. $\square$

Two SETAFs are strongly equivalent w.r.t. *com* semantics iff their complete kernels coincide. Likewise two SETAFs are strongly equivalent w.r.t. *adm, pref,* or *sem* semantics iff their admissible kernels coincide. The proofs proceed in a similar way as for stable kernels.

Lemma 7. *For any SETAF $F = (A, R)$, $com(F) = com(F^{ck})$, and $\sigma(F) = \sigma(F^{ak})$ for $\sigma \in \{adm, pref, sem\}$.*

The next lemma states that if two SETAFs have the same kernel then their extensions with an arbitrary SETAF H will also agree on their kernels.

Lemma 8. *Let F, G be SETAFs in normal form. For all SETAFs H, (a) if $F^{ck} = G^{ck}$ then $(F \cup H)^{ck} = (G \cup H)^{ck}$ and (b) if $F^{ak} = G^{ak}$ then $(F \cup H)^{ak} = (G \cup H)^{ak}$.*

Using the previous lemmas one can show that two SETAFs F, G are strongly equivalent w.r.t. complete semantics iff their complete kernels coincide. It can be shown that the conditions are also necessary and characterize other notions of equivalence as well.

Theorem 2. *For any two SETAFs F, G, the following are equivalent: (a) $F \equiv_s^{com} G$; (b) $F \equiv_n^{com} G$; (c) $F \equiv_{sd}^{com} G$; (d) $F \equiv_{nd}^{com} G$; (e) $F^{ck} = G^{ck}$.*

Similarly, any two SETAFs F, G with the same admissible kernel are strongly equivalent w.r.t. admissible, preferred and semi-stable semantics.

Theorem 3. *For any two SETAFs F, G and for $\sigma \in \{adm, pref, sem\}$, the following are equivalent: (a) $F \equiv_s^\sigma G$; (b) $F \equiv_n^\sigma G$; (c) $F \equiv_{sd}^\sigma G$; (d) $F \equiv_{nd}^\sigma G$; (e) $F^{ak} = G^{ak}$.*

Due to space limits, we shall omit the proofs of the above theorems. Instead, we highlight central constructions and sketch the main arguments. The proofs proceed in the same way as the proof of Theorem 1, i.e. first we use the Lemmas 7 and 8 to show $(e) \Rightarrow (a)$. To show $\neg(e) \Rightarrow \neg(d)$, we assume that the kernels of F and G differ and then construct an AF H such that $\sigma(F \cup H) \neq \sigma(G \cup H)$. This again requires a case study where the crucial new arguments are for the cases where the argument sets of the kernels coincide but there is an inactive attack (S, a) which is just present in the kernel of F but not in the kernel of G (or vice versa). W.l.o.g. we can assume that (S, a) is a minimal such attack. We sketch the case where $a \notin S$ below. There we use the following AF

$$H = (A(F) \cup \{c, d\}, \{(c, b) \mid b \in A(F) \setminus (S \cup \{a\})\} \cup$$
$$\{(d, d), (d, b) \mid b \in S\}).$$

Note that, as (S, a) is inactive, S contains an attack (S', b) for some $S' \subseteq S$, $b \in S$. For admissible kernels the set $\{a, c\}$ is not admissible in $F \cup H$ as the argument a is not defended against S. On the other hand, it can be shown that $\{a, c\}$ is admissible in $G \cup H$: Clearly, $\{a, c\}$ is conflict-free; moreover, the argument c defends a in $G \cup H$ against every attack where the source-set contains arguments from $A(F) \setminus (S \cup \{a\})$. It can be shown that there is no attack (T, a) with $T \subseteq S \cup \{a\}$ using the definition of admissible kernels and the fact that (S, a) is minimal among the attacks in the symmetric difference of the kernels F and G. For complete kernels, $\{c\}$ is complete in $F \cup H$ as a is not defended against S. On the other hand, we have that $\{c\}$ is not complete in $G \cup H$ since one can show that c defends a using the definition of complete kernels and the fact that the kernels of F and G coincide on smaller attacks. That is, for both kernels the AF H is a witness of $F \neq_{nd}^\sigma G$ for the corresponding semantics σ.

5 Conclusion

In this work we considered strong equivalence for SETAFs under admissible, complete, preferred, stable, semi-stable and stage semantics. Strong equivalence between SETAFs can be characterized by computing so-called kernels and comparing them on a syntactical level. By that, strong equivalence for the considered semantics can be tested in polynomial time. Moreover, the SETAF kernels are generalizations of the respective kernels in the AF setting, in the sense that when applied to AFs our kernels coincide with the ones from [13]. Given the relations between kernels for SETAFs F, G we obtain that the strong equivalence notions of the different semantics coincide as follows: $F \equiv_s^{stb} G \Leftrightarrow F \equiv_s^{stage}$; and $F \equiv_s^{adm} G \Leftrightarrow F \equiv_s^{pref} G \Leftrightarrow F \equiv_s^{sem} G$. Moreover, (a) whenever $F \equiv_s^{com} G$ then also $F \equiv_s^{\sigma} G$ for all $\sigma \in \{adm, pref, stb, sem, stage\}$, and (b) whenever $F \equiv_s^{\tau} G$ for $\tau \in \{adm, pref, sem\}$ then also $F \equiv_s^{\sigma} G$ for all $\sigma \in \{stb, stage\}$.

One finding based on the kernels is that strongly equivalent SETAFs necessarily coincide w.r.t. their set of arguments, which is in accordance with the results for Dung AFs. However, we identified classes of attacks that can be removed without affecting strong equivalence. Notice that this goes beyond the notion of redundant attacks in SETAFs from [14]. In particular a significant difference between the SETAF setting and the AF setting appears when we consider frameworks without self-attacks. For AFs without self-attacks the kernels coincide with the initial AFs while for SETAFs the kernels, even in absence of self-attack, remove (certain) inactive attacks. The reason for this is that the only way to deactivate an attack in AFs is to make the source argument self-attacking while in SETAFs there several ways to produce a conflict in the source set of an attack.

One direction for future work is to extend our results to further semantics as ideal, eager and grounded semantics. Notice that although grounded semantics is closely related to admissible and complete semantics neither the admissible nor the complete kernel are suitable to characterize strong equivalence w.r.t. grounded semantics. This is immediate by the corresponding results of AFs where the grounded kernel is different from all the other kernels [13]. Another direction for future research are generalizations of alternative notions of equivalence that have been investigated for AFs, e.g. the recently introduced notion of C-relativized equivalence [4].

Acknowledgments. This research has been supported by FWF through projects I2854, P30168 and W1255-N23.

References

1. Baumann, R.: Normal and strong expansion equivalence for argumentation frameworks. Artif. Intell. **193**, 18–44 (2012)
2. Baumann, R.: Characterizing equivalence notions for labelling-based semantics. In: Baral, C., Delgrande, J.P., Wolter, F. (eds.) Principles of Knowledge Representation and Reasoning: Proceedings of the Fifteenth International Conference, KR 2016, 25–29 April 2016, Cape Town, South Africa, pp. 22–32. AAAI Press (2016)
3. Baumann, R., Brewka, G.: The equivalence zoo for Dung-style semantics. J. Log. Comput. **28**(3), 477–498 (2018)
4. Baumann, R., Dvořák, W., Linsbichler, T., Woltran, S.: A general notion of equivalence for abstract argumentation. In: Sierra, C. (ed.) Proceedings of the Twenty-Sixth International Joint Conference on Artificial Intelligence, IJCAI 2017, 19–25 August 2017, Melbourne, Australia, pp. 800–806 (2017)
5. Brewka, G., Polberg, S., Woltran, S.: Generalizations of Dung frameworks and their role in formal argumentation. IEEE Intell. Syst. **29**(1), 30–38 (2014)

6. Dung, P.M.: On the acceptability of arguments and its fundamental role in non-monotonic reasoning, logic programming and n-person games. Artif. Intell. **77**(2), 321–358 (1995)
7. Dvořák, W., Fandinno, J., Woltran, S.: On the expressive power of collective attacks. In: Modgil, S., Budzynska, K., Lawrence, J. (eds.) Computational Models of Argument - Proceedings of COMMA 2018, 12–14 September 2018, Warsaw, Poland. Frontiers in Artificial Intelligence and Applications, vol. 305, pp. 49–60. IOS Press (2018)
8. Dvořák, W., Greßler, A., Woltran, S.: Evaluating SETAFs via answer-set programming. In: Thimm, M., Cerutti, F., Vallati, M. (eds.) Proceedings of the Second International Workshop on Systems and Algorithms for Formal Argumentation (SAFA 2018) Co-located with the 7th International Conference on Computational Models of Argument (COMMA 2018), 11 September 2018, Warsaw, Poland. CEUR Workshop Proceedings, vol. 2171, pp. 10–21. CEUR-WS.org (2018)
9. Dvořák, W., Järvisalo, M., Linsbichler, T., Niskanen, A., Woltran, S.: Preprocessing argumentation frameworks via replacement patterns. In: Calimeri, F., Leone, N., Manna, M. (eds.) JELIA 2019. LNCS (LNAI), vol. 11468, pp. 116–132. Springer, Cham (2019). https://doi.org/10.1007/978-3-030-19570-0_8
10. Flouris, G., Bikakis, A.: A comprehensive study of argumentation frameworks with sets of attacking arguments. Int. J. Approx. Reason. **109**, 55–86 (2019)
11. Lifschitz, V., Pearce, D., Valverde, A.: Strongly equivalent logic programs. ACM Trans. Comput. Logic **2**(4), 526–541 (2001)
12. Nielsen, S.H., Parsons, S.: A generalization of Dung's abstract framework for argumentation: arguing with sets of attacking arguments. In: Maudet, N., Parsons, S., Rahwan, I. (eds.) ArgMAS 2006. LNCS (LNAI), vol. 4766, pp. 54–73. Springer, Heidelberg (2007). https://doi.org/10.1007/978-3-540-75526-5_4
13. Oikarinen, E., Woltran, S.: Characterizing strong equivalence for argumentation frameworks. Artif. Intell. **175**(14–15), 1985–2009 (2011)
14. Polberg, S.: Developing the abstract dialectical framework. Ph.D. thesis, TU Wien, Institute of Information Systems (2017)
15. Truszczynski, M.: Strong and uniform equivalence of nonmonotonic theories - an algebraic approach. Ann. Math. Artif. Intell. **48**(3–4), 245–265 (2006)
16. Turner, H.: Strong equivalence for causal theories. In: Lifschitz, V., Niemelä, I. (eds.) LPNMR 2004. LNCS (LNAI), vol. 2923, pp. 289–301. Springer, Heidelberg (2003). https://doi.org/10.1007/978-3-540-24609-1_25
17. Yun, B., Vesic, S., Croitoru, M.: Toward a more efficient generation of structured argumentation graphs. In: Modgil, S., Budzynska, K., Lawrence, J. (eds.) Computational Models of Argument - Proceedings of COMMA 2018, 12–14 September 2018, Warsaw, Poland. Frontiers in Artificial Intelligence and Applications, vol. 305, pp. 205–212. IOS Press (2018)

Developing Fuzzy Inference Systems from Qualitative Interviews for Travel Mode Choice in an Agent-Based Mobility Simulation

Klaas Dählmann[✉], Ute Samland, and Jürgen Sauer

Department of Computing Science, Carl von Ossietzky Universität Oldenburg,
Oldenburg, Germany
{klaas.daehlmann,ute.samland,juergen.sauer}@uni-oldenburg.de

Abstract. Both qualitative and quantitative research are integral parts for the understanding of traffic systems, yet it can be difficult to formalize and execute qualitative research results in a technical simulation system in an understandable and flexible manner. This paper presents an approach to systematically construct fuzzy inference systems from socio-scientific data for the application as a decision making component in an agent-based mobility simulation. A general fuzzy inference concept is presented and subsequently applied to statements about travel mode choice and common activities from semi-structured interviews on mobility behavior. It is shown that the inference concept can be used to determine both fuzzy rule base and the linguistic variables and terms from the interviews and that such an inference system can be used successfully in an agent-based mobility simulation.

Keywords: Agent-based model · Decision making · Fuzzy inference · Mobility simulation · Modal choice

1 Introduction

Simulating and forecasting mobility and traffic behavior is a difficult endeavor. Common traffic simulation systems such as ALBATROSS [2], FEATHERS [4], TASHA [17], MatSIM-T [3], TAPAS [8], C-TAP [12], PCATS, AMOS [9], or SAMS [10] use so-called activity-based or tour-based approaches [14] to generate and execute plausible, logically coherent sets of trips throughout a time period of interest. Such systems usually consist of different components, e.g. population synthesis [13] for the generation of a representative population, the creation of their individual daily/weekly activities [5], as well as identification and decision making on suitable modes of transport for the pursued activities, e.g. by using suitable decision trees [2] or multinomial logit models [3,8]. The more recent of those systems pair activity/tour-based approaches with agent-based models [19] to further improve the simulation quality on the microscopic individual or household level [2–4,8,12,17]. While therefore technically agent-based

© Springer Nature Switzerland AG 2019
C. Benzmüller and H. Stuckenschmidt (Eds.): KI 2019, LNAI 11793, pp. 146–153, 2019.
https://doi.org/10.1007/978-3-030-30179-8_12

microsimulations, these systems are often intended for the analysis and explanation of large-scale traffic systems such as larger cities or entire regions/counties with their decision making component usually based on socio-economic distributions in the area to be modeled and simulated. Applying such systems to small-scale situations, e.g. the ex ante simulation of policy changes or changes in the public transport in small, rural villages, can be problematic as those places tend to be the areas where the explanatory power of the system is less reliable. Moreover, modeling individual behavior in such microscenarios requires in-depth knowledge of the subtleties of local mobility practices often obtained through social research [7].

In this paper, we present and apply an approach to make results from qualitative, socio-scientific field research executable in a decision making component that is designed on the principle of fuzzy inference [15, 16] for application in an agent-based mobility simulation. This allows for the development of heterogeneous agents and agent classes that make their travel mode decisions not only easily quantifiable socio-economic parameters such as age or gender but also on soft factors such as individual, subjective feelings and normative beliefs based on contextual information on the options at hand.

In Sect. 2, we describe the general concept of our fuzzy inference system and then apply the concept in Sect. 3, where we first illustrate how to determine both rule base and fuzzy variables from qualitative data and then use these findings in three example activities in an agent-based simulation. In the subsequent conclusion in Sect. 4, we reflect the approach presented in this paper and outline the future application.

2   General Fuzzy Inference Concept

The general fuzzy inference concept described in this section serves as a template to systematically create and implement fuzzy inference systems for the calculation of the utility of competing travel mode decision options. A more detailed description of the general inference concept and its particular requirements can be found in [6].

Initially, all available input values to the decision making are fuzzified using suitable linguistic input variables and terms. These input values may be socio-economic attributes of the agent, information on the decision option at hand (e.g. distances, durations, departure and arrival times), information about the pursued activity, or global parameters such as the weather. After the fuzzification, a three-step process leads from the fuzzified inputs to a single, normalized utility score for comparison with other travel mode options. These three steps reduce the complexity of designing a controller that would otherwise immediately map input values to the utility of the entire decision option. By introducing these intermediate steps, it becomes easier to formulate and organize fuzzy rules based on input data from interviews or questionnaires, as will be shown by the application in Sect. 3. This concept uses the principle of Takagi-Sugeno inference [18], as all output variables in each of the three steps merely use singleton terms: In this work, −1 denotes a negative attitude or rejection, 1 implies a positive attitude or acceptance of the concept represented by that particular output variable. These values represent the lower and upper bound of the utility score.

The optional first step is the operationalization of latent information not immediately available from the fuzzified input values. Operationalization is the process of making a latent or diffuse construct measurable. For example, the perceived feeling of safety is an important factor for some travel mode choice situations such as dynamic ride sharing offers [1], yet, it is no clear simulation parameter and therefore has to be operationalized based on the context of the decision option. This is done by mapping input values to the singleton terms of the fuzzy variable representing the latent construct, e.g. safety.

The second step is the individual evaluation of each mode of transport required for the travel mode option at hand, such as walking, biking, the car, or the bus. This is especially important for intermodal options that consist of more than one mode of transport, e.g. park and ride, where one part of the trip might be evaluated favorably yet the other part is negatively evaluated. This evaluation is based on the initial or subsequently operationalized fuzzy inputs. After this step, each mode of transport has been individually evaluated.

The third and last step is the aggregation of those individual evaluation towards a single, normalized utility score that allows comparison of the decision option with other, competing options. The utility is calculated based on the weighted average of the activation degree of each singleton term in the output variables of the second step, a defuzzification as required for e.g. Mamdani inference [11] is therefore not necessary. By using the weighted average, it can be ensured that the utility score remains within the predefined range from −1 to 1. For other applications, using the weighted sum instead of the weighted average or increasing the values of the singleton terms used may be a worthwhile consideration.

3   Example Application

To evaluate the approach described in Sect. 2, we use the information from two separate, one hour-long, semi-structured interviews of the same person, the first interview in 2016, the second in 2019. The interviewee was a female university student, age 24 at the time of the first interview, living in a large city in northern Germany. Subject of the interviews were the general mobility practices as well as modal choice behavior regarding common activities of the interviewees. To illustrate the utilization of the qualitative information from these interviews, we first detail the process of determining the rule base and linguistic variables and terms from the interview transcripts and then apply the newly constructed fuzzy inference system in a simulation to compare the simulated modal choice behavior with the stated behavior of the interviewee regarding three of her typical activities. The full interviews contain significantly more activities and related behavior, but for this paper, we reduce the rule base and variables to only those needed for the three example activities examined in the evaluation in Sect. 3.2.

3.1 Determining Rule Base and Linguistic Variables

With regard to typical distances, the interviewee stated that she *rather does not like walking one kilometer at all*. Moreover, she mentioned that *three to four kilometers is the limit for biking*. Yet, she stated that she often runs *errands at the grocery store around the corner [note: about half a kilometer from her apartment] by bike or sometimes by foot*. We therefore determined the following four fuzzy rules, the terms of their related linguistic variables are based on the ranges mentioned by the interviewee, as shown in Fig. 1.

```
IF walking_distance IS short THEN walking IS 1;
IF walking_distance IS long THEN walking IS -1;
IF biking_distance IS short THEN biking IS 1;
IF biking_distance IS long THEN biking IS -1;
```

The interviewee voiced her liking of public transport because she *owns a student ticket for public transport* and *the bus is for free, is not wasting any gas, and is comfortable*. The corresponding fuzzy rule favors using public transport when a student ticket is available, its respective variable mimics a simple boolean variable with an input value of 1 representing the possession of a student ticket (Fig. 1).

```
IF student_ticket IS available THEN public_transport IS 1;
```

Although she favors taking the bus, the interviewee mentioned that lateness can be problematic *because it is annoying to take the bus when you have to wait for a long time*. She later substantiated this statement by recalling a situation where she took the car whenever possible because she otherwise *would have been there half an hour early*. Moreover, she stated that she cannot take the train to work *because it would arrive two minutes late*. The rules to those statements are as follows, the hard constraint regarding arrival and departure time at work is respected through a significantly increased rule weight:

```
IF lateness IS convenient THEN public_transport IS 1;
IF lateness IS inconvenient THEN public_transport IS -1;
IF purpose IS work AND lateness IS late_arrival
   OR lateness IS early_departure
   THEN public_transport IS -1 WITH 100.0;
```

The variable for the lateness ranges from -30 min (earliness) to 30 min (tardiness) and represents the shift in convenience depending on ideal and actual arrival or departure time, the terms for late arrival and early departure are offset by one minute from an input value of 0 to depict the cases of coming too late or leaving too early. The variable for purpose distinguishes between work and shopping, which is needed for the next set of rules (Fig. 1).

The interviewee mentioned that she, although normally walking or using the bike when going to buy groceries, tends to *rather use the car when it is already dark outside* and that it *depends on the feeling in the particular situation*. In this case, the operationalization of the feeling of safety from the information about the decision option becomes necessary. For this particular example, we defined rules that estimate the overall perceived safety based on the combination of the time of day and the length of the day within a year. The perceived safety is then used in a rule to decide on the preferred mode of transport when going shopping:

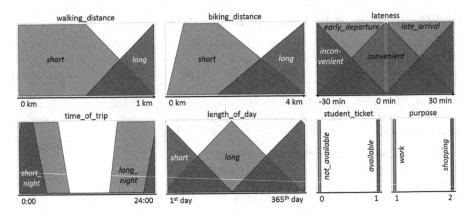

Fig. 1. Graphical representation of the fuzzy variables determined from the interviews.

```
IF time_of_trip IS long_night AND length_of_day IS short
   THEN perceived_safety IS -1;
IF time_of_trip IS short_night AND length_of_day IS long
   THEN perceived_safety IS -1;
IF perceived_safety IS -1 AND purpose IS shopping
   THEN walking IS -1 AND biking IS -1 AND car IS 1;
```

The respective fuzzy variable for the time of trip models the duration of the night during a 24 h day. With regard to the particular city of the interviewee, the dusk on the longest day in summer lasts from 22:00 to 0:30, the dawn lasts from 2:30 to 5:00. On the shortest day in winter, the dusk lasts from 16:00 to 17:30 and the dawn last from 7:00 to 9:00. The variable for the length of day linearly maps the day of the trip in the year (1 to 365) to the membership towards the duration of the daytime on the given day, with the maximum membership of the term long being June 21 (day 172) and the maximum membership of the term short being December 21 (day 355) (Fig. 1). The output variable for the perceived safety consists of two singleton terms to model bad (−1) and good (1) feeling of safety, as described in Sect. 2.

3.2   Evaluation of the Fuzzy Inference System

The fuzzy inference System determined in Sect. 3.1 has been used on three example activities of the interviewee within an agent-based mobility simulation. These three activities are of particular interest because the interviewee changed her modal choice based on changing contextual situations. The travel mode options within the simulation were generated using the Google Directions API[1]. As our simulation is a tour-based system [14], the decision making of the agent is based on the sum of the utilities of both the outward and the return trip of a tour.

---

[1] developers.google.com/maps/documentation/directions.

Activity 1: Going to and from Work at Previous Job. During her time as an university student, the interviewee worked at a place about 13 km aerial distance away from her apartment. Work began at 8:00 and lasted until 13:00. She stated that she had to take the bus, which unfortunately was about 30 min early because the train would have arrived just 5 min late. The way home was equally problematic with a waiting time of almost 40 min until the bus arrived. Therefore, she took the family car whenever she had an opportunity to, although she owned a student ticket for the entire time while working at that particular job.

Within our simulation, the three most feasible options for the outward trip where indeed a bus trip arriving 35 min early and requiring a walk of 810 m, a train trip arriving just 2 min too late and needing a walk of 1560 m, or the private car. For the trip back home, the API suggested either a bus trip departing with a delay of 38 min and a walk of 820 m or again the private car. These five individual trip options lead to three options for the entire tour: Outward and return trip by bus with a total utility of -0.173, outward trip by train and return trip by bus with a utility of -1.055, and both trips by car with a utility of 0. The agent representing the interviewee therefore picked the car when it was given access to a car, otherwise the bus trip was chosen. This behavior of the agent is similar to the stated behavior of the interviewee.

Activity 2: Going to and from Work at Current Job. Since finishing her university degree, the interviewee works at a place about 15 km aerial distance away from her apartment. Work begins at 7:30 and lasts until 13:00. She stated that she used to take the bus until her student ticket expired, at which point she started going by car.

Using the simulation, the two most feasible outward trip options were on the one hand the bus with a scheduled arrival time 7 min before work and a walk with a total distance of 770 m and on the other hand the car. For the return trip, the simulation also suggested either the bus with a departure time 36 min after work ends and a walk of 770 m or the car. When the simulation agent was given access to a student ticket, the combined utility of the outward and return bus trip was 0.457 while the total utility of the car tour was 0. Yet when the agent did not possess a student ticket, the total utility of the bus tour dropped to -0.313. The agent therefore only used the bus for as long as it had a student ticket, the same behavior as stated by the interviewee.

Activity 3: Going Grocery Shopping. When running errands, the interviewee stated that she usually goes to the same grocery store, 550 m away from her apartment. As mentioned above, she changes her modal choice from walking or biking to the car depending on her situational feeling. Since we cannot showcase all combinations of trip time and length of day, we will instead give the tour utilities at the longest and shortest day as well as the days at which the utilities of the bike and car tour break even. The time of the shopping activity is fixed at 20:00.

Using the simulation, the decision options given to the agent were walking, biking and going by car. On the longest day of the year, June 21, the total utility of going by bike is 2 followed by a utility of 1.6 for walking, the car is scored with a utility of 0. On the shortest day, December 21, the total utility for the bike is 0, for walking it is -0.2, and for the car it is 2. Based on this simulation, walking is never chosen as its total utility always stays slightly below the utility of biking. On April 7 (day 97) and September 5 (day 248), the bike and car options break even at a combined utility of 0.828 for each decision option. With the actual sunset being at 20:10 on both of these days, the decision of the agent to switch between bike and car seems plausible.

4 Conclusion

We presented a fuzzy inference concept to systematically formalize the modal choice behavior of real persons based on their own descriptions, beliefs and needs regarding individual modes of transport. The three steps of the conceptual framework simplified the formulation of the rule base by separating latent constructs, individual modes of transport, and total utility of a travel mode option. The feasibility was demonstrated through the creation of a simple inference system and the application of said system to three representative modal choice situations based on information from qualitative interviews. Of course, the fuzzy inference system determined in this work is a very basic one and is by no means a comprehensive decision model for travel mode choice. Rather, it is intended to illustrate the inference concept itself as well as the method of determining a functional fuzzy inference system from qualitative interview data. To increase the quality of future decision models developed with this concept, interviewees should be asked about the perceived importance of the factors causing their decisions, as such statements could be easily interpreted as weights to the corresponding fuzzy rules. Another way of improving models is to identify more accurate fuzzy terms than the simple linear functions used in this work.

The next steps in this ongoing work are the design of agent archetypes that represent typical traffic participants with their heterogeneous decision making and reasoning as well as the application of said agents in a multi-agent mobility simulation for the exploration of acceptance or rejection of dynamic ride sharing offers in rural regions in Germany.

Acknowledgments. This work is part of the project "NEMo – Sustainable satisfaction of mobility demands in rural regions". The project is funded by the Ministry for Science and Culture of Lower Saxony (Germany) and the Volkswagen Foundation (VolkswagenStiftung) through the "Niedersächsisches Vorab" grant programme (grant number VWZN3122).

References

1. Amey, A., Attanucci, J., Mishalani, R.: Real-time ridesharing: opportunities and challenges in using mobile phone technology to improve rideshare services. Transp. Res. Rec.: J. Transp. Res. Board **2217**, 103–110 (2011)

2. Arentze, T.A., Timmermans, H.J.P.: ALBATROSS - a learning-based transportation oriented simulation system. Transp. Res. Part B: Methodol. **38**(7), 613–633 (2004)
3. Balmer, M., Meister, K., Rieser, M., Nagel, K., Axhausen, K.W.: Agent-based simulation of travel demand: Structure and computational performance of MatSIM-T. In: 2nd TRB Conference on Innovations in Travel Modeling (2008)
4. Bellemans, T., Kochan, B., Janssens, D., Wets, G., Arentze, T.A., Timmermans, H.J.P.: Implementation framework and development trajectory of FEATHERS activity-based simulation platform. Transp. Res. Rec. **2175**(1), 111–119 (2010)
5. Charypar, D., Nagel, K.: Generating complete all-day activity plans with genetic algorithms. Transportation **32**(4), 369–397 (2005)
6. Dählmann, K., Sauer, J.: A hybrid fuzzy controller for human-like decision making in modal choice situations. In: Bungartz, H.J., Kranzlmüller, D., Weinberg, V., Weismüller, J., Wohlgemuth, V. (eds.) Adjunct Proceedings of the 32nd EnviroInfo Conference, pp. 281–286 (2018)
7. Gustafson, P.: Roots and routes: exploring the relationship between place attachment and mobility. Environ. Behav. **33**(5), 667–686 (2001)
8. Heinrichs, M., Krajzewicz, D., Cyganski, R., von Schmidt, A.: Disaggregated car fleets in microscope travel demand modelling. Procedia Comput. Sci. **83**, 155–162 (2016)
9. Kitamura, R., Fujii, S.: Two computational process models of activity-travel behavior. In: Gärling, T., Laitila, T., Westin, K. (eds.) Theoretical Foundations of Travel Choice Modeling, pp. 251–279. Emerald Group Publishing Limited (1998)
10. Kitamura, R., Pas, E.I., Lula, C.V., Lawton, T.K., Benson, P.E.: The sequenced activity mobility simulator (SAMS): an integrated approach to modeling transportation, land use and air quality. Transportation **23**, 267–291 (1996)
11. Mamdani, E.H., Assilian, S.: An experiment in linguistic synthesis with a fuzzy controller. Int. J. Man-Mach. Stud. **7**(1), 1–13 (1975)
12. Märki, F., Charypar, D., Axhausen, K.W.: Agent-based model for continuous activity planning with an open planning horizon. Transportation **41**, 905–922 (2014)
13. Müller, K.: A generalized approach to population synthesis. Ph.D. thesis, ETH Zürich (2017)
14. Ortúzar, J.D.D., Willumsen, L.G.: Modelling Transport, 4 edn. Wiley, Hoboken (2011)
15. Passino, K.M., Yurkovich, S.: Fuzzy Control. Addison Wesley Longman, Boston (1998)
16. Pedrycz, W.: Fuzzy Control and Fuzzy Systems. Wiley, Hoboken (1993)
17. Roorda, M.J., Miller, E.J., Habib, K.M.N.: Assessing transportation policy using an activity based microsimulation model of travel demand. ITE J. **54**, 4378–4381 (2006)
18. Sugeno, M.: Industrial Applications of Fuzzy Control. Elsevier Science, Amsterdam (1985)
19. Wooldridge, M.: An Introduction to MultiAgent Systems. Wiley, Hoboken (2009)

Monte-Carlo Search for Prize-Collecting Robot Motion Planning with Time Windows, Capacities, Pickups, and Deliveries

Stefan Edelkamp[1], Erion Plaku[2], and Yassin Warsame[1(✉)]

[1] King's College London, London, UK
{stefan.edelkamp,yassin.warsame}@kcl.ac.uk
[2] Catholic University of America, Washington, D.C., USA
plaku@cua.edu

Abstract. Logistics operations often require a robot to pickup and deliver objects from multiple locations within certain time frames. This is a challenging task-and-motion planning problem as it intertwines logical and temporal constraints about the operations with geometric and differential constraints related to obstacle avoidance and robot dynamics. To address these challenges, this paper couples vehicle routing over a discrete abstraction with sampling-based motion planning. On the one hand, vehicle routing provides plans to effectively guide sampling-based motion planning as it explores the vast space of feasible motions. On the other hand, motion planning provides feasibility estimates which vehicle routing uses to refine its plans. This coupling makes it possible to extend the state-of-the-art in multi-goal motion planning by also incorporating capacities, pickups, and deliveries in addition to time windows. When not all pickups and deliveries can be completed in time, the approach seeks to minimize the violations and maximize the profit.

1 Introduction

We are seeing nowadays an emergent need to enhance the capabilities of mobile robots deployed in factories, warehouses, and other logistics operations. In these settings, robots are often required to pickup and deliver objects from multiple locations within certain time windows. This gives rise to challenging task-and-motion planning problems as it intertwines logical and temporal constraints about the operations with geometric and differential constraints related to obstacle avoidance and robot dynamics. Robot dynamics, which are often high-dimensional and nonlinear, constrain the feasible motions, making it difficult to generate trajectories that enable the robot to complete its tasks. Moreover, due to the limited capacity, a robot may have to deliver some objects before picking up others, causing the robot to travel longer, which could violate temporal constraints. When the problem is oversubscribed, the robot also has to decide

© Springer Nature Switzerland AG 2019
C. Benzmüller and H. Stuckenschmidt (Eds.): KI 2019, LNAI 11793, pp. 154–167, 2019.
https://doi.org/10.1007/978-3-030-30179-8_13

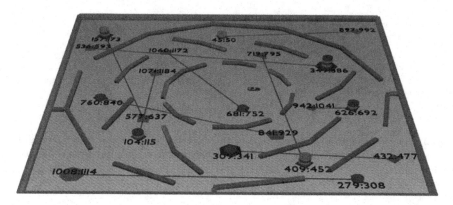

Fig. 1. Example of a multi-goal motion-planning problem with time windows and capacity constraints. The vehicle is required to pickup items, without exceeding its capacity, and deliver them to the corresponding locations within the specified time windows. Videos of solutions obtained by our approach can be found anonymously at https://bit.ly/2Ef7HMQ.

which tasks to abandon, while seeking to complete as many of the remaining tasks as possible.

To address these challenges, we build upon the burgeoning body of research on task-and-motion planning. In a discrete setting, which ignores the obstacles and robot dynamics, there has been significant progress in solving challenging vehicle routing problems that often include time windows, pickups, deliveries, capacities, or premium service requests [1,2,4,7,10,14]. In a continuous setting, sampling-based motion planning has shown great success in dealing with constraints imposed by collision avoidance and robot dynamics [3,5,11,12,15]. Sampling-based motion planning has even been coupled with TSP solvers to effectively solve multi-goal motion-planning problems [16]. Temporal reasoning has also been integrated to allow for time windows [6].

We advance research on task-and-motion planning by developing an effective approach that solves significantly more complex problems. While related work can solve multi-goal motion planning with time windows [6], this paper develops the first effective approach that also incorporates pickups, deliveries, and capacities. Another contribution is that our approach is able to deal with oversubscription by generating collision-free and dynamically-feasible trajectories that enable the robot to pickup and deliver as many objects as possible within the specified time windows. This is made possible by first developing an effective discrete solver based on Monte-Carlo search to quickly generate low-cost tours. Central to our approach is an effective coupling of vehicle-routing solvers in a discrete setting with sampling-based motion planning in a continuous setting that accounts for obstacles and robot dynamics. On the one hand, vehicle routing provides low-cost tours to effectively guide sampling-based motion planning as it explores the vast space of feasible motions. On the other hand, motion

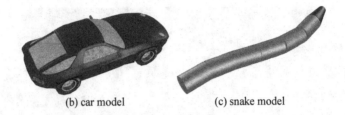

(b) car model   (c) snake model

Fig. 2. Vehicle models and scenes used in the experiments (scene 1 shown in Fig. 1). Figures (b) and (c) also show roadmaps constructed by our approach to facilitate navigation.

planning provides feasibility estimates which vehicle routing uses to refine its plans. To deal with oversubscription, our approach associates costs with the travel and benefits with fulfilling pickups and deliveries, seeking to minimize the temporal violations and maximize the net benefit. Experiments with nonlinear vehicle models show the efficiency and scalability of the approach as we increase the complexity of the operations.

2   Problem Formulation

Robot dynamics are expressed as differential equations

$$\dot{s} \leftarrow f(s, a), s \in \mathcal{S}, a \in \mathcal{A}, \tag{1}$$

where $\mathcal{S}$ and $\mathcal{A}$ denote the state space and action space, respectively. As an example, the dynamics of the car model (Fig. 2) used in the experiments are defined as

$$\dot{x} = v\cos(\theta)\cos(\psi), \dot{y} = v\sin(\theta)\cos(\psi), \tag{2}$$
$$\dot{\theta} = v\sin(\psi), \dot{v} = a_{\mathrm{acc}}, \dot{\psi} = a_{\omega}, \tag{3}$$

where the state $(x, y, \theta, \psi, v) \in \mathcal{S}$ defines the position, orientation, steering angle, and velocity; the action $(a_{\mathrm{acc}}, a_{\omega}) \in \mathcal{A}$ defines the acceleration and steering rate. As another example, a snake model (Fig. 2) can be obtained by attaching several trailers to the car and augmenting f as

$$\dot{\theta}_i = (v/H)(\sin(\theta_{i-1}) - \sin(\theta_0))\textstyle\prod_{j=1}^{i-1}\cos(\theta_{j-1} - \theta_j), \tag{4}$$

where $\theta_0 = \theta$, N is the number of trailers, θ_i is the orientation of the i-th trailer, and H is the hitch distance [11].

When applying an action $a \in \mathcal{A}$ to a state $s \in \mathcal{S}$, the robot changes state according to its dynamics. The new state $s_{\mathrm{new}} \in \mathcal{S}$ is computed by a function

$$s_{\mathrm{new}} \leftarrow \mathrm{SIMULATE}(s, a, f, dt), \tag{5}$$

which numerically integrates f for one time step dt. Applying a sequence of actions $\langle a_1, \ldots, a_{i-1} \rangle$ gives rise to a dynamically-feasible motion trajectory ζ : $\{1, \ldots, i\} \rightarrow \mathcal{S}$, where $\zeta(1) \leftarrow s$ and $\forall j \in \{2, \ldots, i\}$:

$$\zeta(j) \leftarrow \text{SIMULATE}(\zeta(j-1), a_{j-1}, f, dt). \tag{6}$$

Multi-Goal Motion Planning with Time.Windows, Pickups, Deliveries, and Capacities: The world contains obstacles, pickup regions $\{\mathcal{R}_1, \ldots, \mathcal{R}_k\}$, and delivery regions $\{\mathcal{R}_{k+1}, \ldots, \mathcal{R}_{n=2k}\}$. Each $\mathcal{R}_i \in \mathcal{R} = \{\mathcal{R}_1, \ldots, \mathcal{R}_n\}$ is associated with a load $\ell_i \in \mathbb{Z}$ and a time interval $[t_i^{\text{start}}, t_i^{\text{end}}]$ during which the pickup or delivery can be made. For each pickup-delivery pair $\langle \mathcal{R}_i, \mathcal{R}_{i+\lfloor \frac{n}{2} \rfloor} \rangle$, it holds that $\ell_i = -\ell_{i+\lfloor \frac{n}{2} \rfloor} \geq 0$. The robot has a maximum capacity $C_{\max} \in \mathbb{N}$.

Let $\mathcal{G} = \{\mathcal{G}_1, \ldots, \mathcal{G}_n\}$ denote the goals, where $\mathcal{G}_i = \langle \mathcal{R}_i, [t_i^{\text{start}}, t_i^{\text{end}}], \ell_i \rangle$. Let GOALS$(\zeta)$ denote the goals completed by the robot as it moves according to a trajectory ζ. A pickup goal $\mathcal{G}_i$ is completed only when the robot reaches $\mathcal{G}_i$ within its time window $[t_i^{\text{start}}, t_i^{\text{end}}]$ and has sufficient remaining capacity to add the load ℓ_i. The robot makes a delivery only when the region is reached within its time window and the corresponding load has already been picked up.

Given an initial state $s_{\text{init}} \in \mathcal{S}$, the objective is then to compute a collision-free and dynamically-feasible trajectory ζ that enables the robot to complete all the goals, i.e., GOALS$(\zeta) = \mathcal{G}$. When this is not possible, the objective is to reduce the number of missed goals $|\mathcal{G} \setminus \text{GOALS}(\zeta)|$.

3 Discrete Problem Solving

As mentioned, our approach relies on vehicle routing over a discrete abstraction to guide sampling-based motion planning. The discrete solver is required to solve a variant of TSP that includes prizes, time windows, and capacity constraints for pickup and delivery tasks. The discrete solver is invoked numerous times by the approach. While the initial call requires the discrete solver to find a solution involving all pickups and deliveries, subsequent calls involve only a subset of the original problem as some goals may have already been reached. This makes the problem more challenging since the discrete solver has to deal with partial problems where some orders have already been completed and some items have already been picked up and are still on the vehicle.

We now define the discrete problem and then describe a specialized solver based on Monte-Carlo search and a general PDDL3 planner. Section 4 describes how the discrete solvers are integrated within the overall framework.

Definition 1. *(Prize-Collecting TSP with Time Windows, Pickups, and Deliveries, and Capacity Constraints) Given*

- *a graph $G = (V, E, T)$ with $V = \{v_{\text{start}}, g_1, \ldots, g_m\}$, $E = V \times V$, and times $T = \{t_{(v', v'')} : (v', v'') \in E\}$*
- *goals $\{\langle g_1, t_1^{\text{start}}, t_1^{\text{end}}, \ell_1, p_1 \rangle, \ldots, \langle g_m, t_m^{\text{start}}, t_m^{\text{end}}, \ell_m, p_m \rangle\}$*

Algorithm 1. Rollout for the NRPA MC discrete solver.

Input: discrete problem as in Definition 1
Output: a valid tour σ

1: $\text{visits}_0 \leftarrow 1$; $\text{tour}_0 \leftarrow 0$; $z \leftarrow 1$; $\text{cost} \leftarrow 0$; $\text{node} \leftarrow 0$
2: $\text{prev} \leftarrow \text{mspan} \leftarrow \text{cap} \leftarrow \text{violations} \leftarrow \text{profit} \leftarrow 0$
3: **while** $z < N$ **do**
4: $\quad$ $\text{sum} \leftarrow s \leftarrow 0$
5: $\quad$ **for** $i = 0 \ldots N-1$ **do**
6: $\quad\quad$ **if** $\text{visits}_i = 0$ **and** $\text{delivery}_i \Rightarrow \text{pickup}_{\text{link}_i}$ **then**
7: $\quad\quad\quad$ $\text{moves}_s \leftarrow i$; $s \leftarrow s+1$
8: $\quad\quad\quad$ **for** $j = 0 \ldots N-1$ **and** $i \neq j$ **do**
9: $\quad\quad\quad\quad$ **if** $\text{visits}_j = 0$ **and** $l_i > r_j \vee \text{mspan} + d_{\text{node},i} > r_j$ **then** $\{s \leftarrow s-1; \textbf{break}\}$
10: $\quad$ **if** $s = 0$ **then**
11: $\quad\quad$ **for** $i \leftarrow 0 \ldots N-1$ **do**
12: $\quad\quad\quad$ **if** $\text{visits}_i > 0$ **and** $\text{delivery}_i \Rightarrow \text{pickup}_{\text{link}_i}$ **then**
13: $\quad\quad\quad\quad$ $\text{moves}_s \leftarrow i$; $s \leftarrow s+1$
14: $\quad$ $i \leftarrow \textsc{RouletteWheel}(\text{sum}, \text{policy})$
15: $\quad$ $\text{node}' \leftarrow \text{moves}_i$; $\text{prev}' \leftarrow \text{node}$
16: $\quad$ $\text{span}' \leftarrow \text{span}' + d_{\text{prev}',\text{node}'} > \ell_{\text{node}'}$?
$\quad\quad\quad$ $\text{span}' + d_{\text{prev}',\text{node}'} : \ell_{\text{node}'}$
17: $\quad$ $\text{visits}_{\text{node}'} \leftarrow \text{visits}_{\text{node}'} - 1$
18: $\quad$ **if** $\text{cap} + w_{\text{node}'} > C_{\max} \vee \text{mspan}' > r_{\text{node}'}$ **then**
19: $\quad\quad$ $\text{violations} \leftarrow \text{violations} + 1$
20: $\quad\quad$ $\text{tour}_z \leftarrow -1$; $z \leftarrow z+1$; **continue**
21: $\quad$ **if** $\text{isDelivery}(\text{node}')$ **then** $\text{profit} \leftarrow \text{profit} + w_{\text{node}'}$
22: $\quad$ $\text{prev} \leftarrow \text{prev}'$; $\text{node} \leftarrow \text{node}'$; $\text{tour}_z \leftarrow \text{node}$; $z \leftarrow z+1$
23: $\quad$ $\text{cost} \leftarrow \text{cost} + d_{\text{prev},\text{node}}$;
24: $\quad$ $\text{span} \leftarrow \text{mspan}'$; $\text{cap} \leftarrow \text{cap} + w_{\text{node}}$
25: **return** $a * \text{violations} + b * \text{profit} + \text{cost}$

- $[t_i^{\text{start}}, t_i^{\text{end}}]$ *is the time interval to visit* g_i
- $\ell_i \in \mathbb{Z}$ *represents the load associated with* g_i
- $p_i \in \mathbb{R}$ *is the profit gained by visiting* g_i

– *orders* $O = \{\langle p_1, d_1 \rangle, \ldots, \langle p_k, d_k \rangle\}$ *of pickup* $P = \{p_1, \ldots, p_k\}$ *and delivery* $D = \{d_1, \ldots, d_k\}$ *tasks*

- $P \cup D = \{g_1, \ldots, g_n\}$ *(mutually disjoint)*
- *if* p_i *is empty (denoted by* $p_\perp$*), then* $\langle p_i, d_i \rangle$ *is a* delivery-only *order*
- *otherwise, the load for* p_i *must be positive and match the negative value of the load for* d_i

– *maximum capacity* $C_{\max}$ *that exceeds the preload, i.e.,* $C_{\max} \geq C_{\text{pre}} = -\sum_{p_i \in P, p_i = p_\perp} \text{load}(d_i)$

compute a path $\sigma = \sigma_1, \ldots, \sigma_k$ *over* $G = (V, E, T)$ *and start times* $\langle t_1, \ldots, t_{|\sigma|} \rangle$ *such that (i)* σ *starts at* v_{start}*; (ii) each goal* σ_i *is reached within its time window; (iii) pickups are visited before corresponding deliveries; (iv) capacity is respected; and (v) maximize the accrued net benefit* $\text{payoff}(\sigma) - a \cdot \text{travelcost}(\sigma) + b \cdot$ $\text{goalsvisited}(\sigma)$ *where* a *and* b *are user-defined constants.*

This objective function allows for oversubscription, making it possible to generate partial tours. We have implemented a solver based on Monte-Carlo search and another on PDDL3.

Monte-Carlo Solver. Monte-Carlo search [19] is a randomized reinforcement learning strategy that utilizes random rollouts. Nested rollout policy adaptation (NRPA) [17] was introduced as a way to use gradient ascent rather than navigating the tree directly. The algorithm starts with nested level L and performs a sequential call to $L-1$, $L-2$, and if they reach the lowest recursion level, the rollout occurs, which could find a better solution.

Pseudocode for the rollout function developed for our discrete problem is shown in Algorithm 1. Rollout incrementally constructs the tour, penalizing for capacity constraint violations, and rewarding for making deliveries. To handle the fact the vehicle has to wait when it arrives early at a goal, we use two different variables, one for makespan and one for distance.

An important principle of NRPA is to bias rollouts through learning by weighting possible actions. The weights for the actions are updated in each step of the algorithm to prioritize the movements of the best routing sequence found. In addition, each simulation state is coded differently to prevent the policy of the simulation state from affecting the selection of subsequent simulation state steps. The choices of the simulation steps are random, but the probability is not the same in each step. Policy adaptation adds value to the action of the best sequence and decreases the weight of other actions.

PDDL3 Planner. Preferences are soft constraints on logical expressions. In PDDL3 [8], we compute the quality of a plan based on how many preferences

```
(:durative-action execute_task_pickup
 :parameters (?v - vehicle ?wp - waypoint ?t - task)
 :duration ( = ?duration (taskduration ?t))
 :condition (and
    (at start (at ?v ?wp)) (at start (located ?t ?wp))
    (at start (todo ?t))
    (at start (<= (+ (customer ?wp) (cap ?v)) (max_cap ?v)))
    (at start (is-pickup ?wp)) (at start(tw_open ?t)))
 :effect (and
    (at start (not (todo ?t))) (at end (visited ?wp))
    (at end (increase (cap ?v) (customer ?wp)))
    (at end (decrease (profit ?v) (customer ?wp)))
    (at end (completed ?t))))
(:durative-action execute_task_delivery
 :parameters (?v - vehicle ?wp1 ?wp2 - waypoint ?t - task)
 :duration ( = ?duration (taskduration ?t))ov
 :condition (and
    (at start (at ?v ?wp1)) (at start (located ?t ?wp1))
    (at start (todo ?t)) (at start (is-delivery ?wp1))
    (at start (and (visited ?wp2) (link ?wp2 ?wp1)))
    (at start (tw_open ?t)))
 :effect (and
    (at start (not (todo ?t))) (at end (visited ?wp1))
    (at end (increase (cap ?v) (customer ?wp1)))
    (at end (decrease (profit ?v) (customer ?wp1)))
    (at end (completed ?t))))
```

Fig. 3. Two actions in PDDL3 domain.

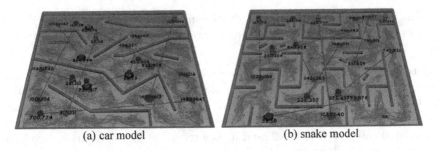

(a) car model   (b) snake model

Fig. 4. Vehicle models and scenes used in the experiments (scene 1 shown in Fig. 1). Figures (b) and (c) also show roadmaps constructed by our approach to facilitate navigation.

are satisfied. We transform the routing problem of Definition 1 into a PDDL3 planning domain and task description, and call a domain-independent planner to generate a feasible plan. We use OPTIC [2], which allows the handling of preferences and uses CPLEX as the backend MILP solver.

Two main PDDL3 actions are shown in Fig. 3. For pickup and delivery tasks, we split the durative action execute task into one for pickups and one for the delivery, and one that executes a delivery-only task, based on some preload value.

4 Overall Approach

Our approach enhances the framework for integrating temporal reasoning into motion planning [6]. The main components are as follows: (i) construct a roadmap to provide a suitable discrete abstraction, (ii) expand a tree in the vast state space of feasible motions and partition the motion tree into equivalence classes, and (iii) use discrete solvers to guide the expansion of the equivalence classes.

We make significant technical contributions to enhance these components, namely: (a) develop an efficient discrete solver based on Monte-Carlo search, (b) develop effective notions of equivalence classes that account for pickups, deliveries, and capacities, and (c) enable guidance of the motion-tree expansion by partial tours to handle oversubscription.

Pseudocode is shown in Algorithm 2. The rest of the section describes the components and their interplay in more detail.

Discrete Abstraction. As in [6], the discrete abstraction is obtained by constructing a roadmap RM to capture the connectivity of the environment. As in PRM [9], the roadmap is obtained by sampling collision-free configurations and connecting neighboring configurations. This process continues until all the regions in $\mathcal{R}$ are connected. Figure 4 shows some examples.

After constructing the roadmap, Dijkstra's shortest-path algorithm is invoked from each region $\mathcal{R}_i$ to compute minimum cost paths to every roadmap vertex. As an enhancement to [6], in order to generate paths that are not so close to the

Algorithm 2. Framework for the proposed approach.

Input: multi-goal motion planning problem with time windows, pickups, deliveries, capacities, as defined in Section 2
Output: collision-free and dynamically-feasible trajectory ζ that seeks to maximize GOALS(ζ)

1: $RM \leftarrow$ CONSTRUCTROADMAP($\mathcal{O}, \mathcal{G}$)
2: $\Xi \leftarrow$ SHORTESTPATHS($RM, \mathcal{G}$)
3: $\mathcal{T} \leftarrow$ INITIALIZEMOTIONTREE(s_{init})
4: $\mathcal{X} \leftarrow$ INITIALIZEEQUIVALENCECLASSES(s_{init})
5: **while** TIME() $< t_{\max}$ **and** not solved **and** not converged **do**
6:    $\mathcal{X}_{\text{key}} \leftarrow$ SELECTEQUIVALENCECLASS($\mathcal{X}$)
7:    $\mathcal{X}_{\text{key}}.\sigma \leftarrow$ DISCRETESOLVER(RM, Ξ, key)
8:    EXPANDMOTIONTREE($\mathcal{T}, \mathcal{X}_{\text{key}}.\sigma$)
9:    UPDATEEQUIVALENCECLASSES($\mathcal{X}$)
10: **return** trajectory ζ in $\mathcal{T}$ that maximizes GOALS(ζ)

obstacles, we add a clearance component to the cost of each roadmap edge, i.e., COST(q_i, q_j) $= ||q_i - q_j|| / \min(\text{CLEAR}(q_i), \text{CLEAR}(q_j))$, where CLEAR($q_i$) denotes the separation from the obstacles. These paths will be used by the discrete solver when computing tours.

Motion Tree and Equivalence Classes. A motion tree $\mathcal{T}$ is incrementally expanded by adding new vertices and edges. Each vertex v is associated with a collision-free state, denoted by $v.s$. Each edge (v_i, v_j) is labeled with a control action a and represents a collision-free and dynamically-feasible motion from $v_i.s$ to $v_j.s$, i.e., $v_j.s \leftarrow$ SIMULATE($v_i.s, a, f, dt$).

Let $\zeta_{\mathcal{T}}(v)$ denote the trajectory from the root of $\mathcal{T}$ to the vertex v. If GOALS($\zeta_{\mathcal{T}}(v)$) $= \mathcal{G}$, then $\zeta_{\mathcal{T}}(v)$ constitutes a solution since all goals would have been completed. As $\mathcal{T}$ is expanded, our approach keeps track of the vertex v that minimizes $|\mathcal{G} \setminus \text{GOALS}(\zeta_{\mathcal{T}}(v))|$, using the time duration of $\zeta_{\mathcal{T}}(v)$ to break ties. The tree expansion continues until a solution is found, a runtime limit is reached, or a convergence criterion is met (no improvement in best v after numerous iterations). At the end, the approach returns the best trajectory $\zeta_{\mathcal{T}}(v)$.

How should $\mathcal{T}$ be expanded from v? Since $\zeta_{\mathcal{T}}(v)$ has already completed GOALS($\zeta_{\mathcal{T}}(v)$), the objective is to complete as many of the remaining goals as possible. This is where the discrete solver comes into play as it can provide tours to visit the remaining goals, while accounting for time windows, pickups, deliveries, and capacity constraints. Since the discrete solver operates over the roadmap, we must also map $v.s$ to the roadmap, e.g., by selecting the nearest roadmap configuration to $v.s$. Let then $v.t$ denote the time duration of $\zeta_{\mathcal{T}}(v)$, v.rem the remaining goals, i.e., $v.\text{rem} = \mathcal{G} \setminus \text{GOALS}(\zeta_{\mathcal{T}}(v))$, and $v.q$ the mapping from $v.s$ to a roadmap configuration. The discrete solver can then be invoked to provide a tour over the roadmap that starts from $v.q$ at time $v.t$ and completes as many of the remaining goals v.rem as possible.

It is infeasible, however, to call the discrete solver for every vertex since $\mathcal{T}$ can have tens of thousands of vertices. For this reason, $\mathcal{T}$ is partitioned into equivalence classes, which group together vertices that provide the same discrete information. A new vertex v_{new} is added to an equivalence class $\mathcal{X}_v$ only if it has the same remaining goals (hence, the same remaining capacity, pickups, and deliveries), maps to the same roadmap configuration, and the tour associated with v (denoted by $v.\sigma$) is compatible with the start time of v_{new}, i.e.,

$$\mathcal{X}_v = \{v_{\text{new}} \in \mathcal{T} : v.q = v_{\text{new}}.q \wedge v.\text{rem} = v_{\text{new}}.\text{rem} \wedge$$
$$\text{COMPATIBLETOUR}(v.\sigma, v_{\text{new}}.t)\}$$

When a new vertex v_{new} is added to $\mathcal{T}$, it is also checked if it can be added to an existing equivalence class. If not, a new equivalence class $\mathcal{X}_{v_{\text{new}}}$ is created. At this point, the discrete planner is invoked to compute the tour associated with $\mathcal{X}_{v_{\text{new}}}$.

Putting it All Together: Guided Search

As shown in Algorithm 2, the overall approach starts by constructing a roadmap RM, computing shortest paths in RM, and then initializing the motion tree $\mathcal{T}$ and the equivalence classes $\mathcal{X}$. The core loop is driven by two procedures: (i) selecting an equivalence class $\mathcal{X}_v$ and (ii) expanding the motion tree $\mathcal{T}$ along the temporal plan $\mathcal{X}_v.\sigma$. The equivalence classes are continually updated each time a vertex is added to $\mathcal{T}$. These procedures are invoked repeatedly until a solution is found, a runtime limit is reached, or the convergence criterion is met.

Selecting an Equivalence Class. A weight is defined for each equivalence class $\mathcal{X}_v \in \mathcal{X}$ as

$$w(\mathcal{X}_v) = \frac{\alpha^{\text{NRSELECTIONS}(\mathcal{X}_v)}}{\beta^{\text{DURATION}(\mathcal{X}_v.\sigma)} + \gamma^{|\mathcal{X}_v.\sigma|} + \delta^{|\mathcal{X}_v.\text{rem}| - |\mathcal{X}_v.\sigma|}}. \tag{7}$$

and the equivalence class with maximum weight is then selected for expansion. The term $\beta^{\text{DURATION}(\mathcal{X}_v.\sigma)}$, $\beta > 1$, increases the weight when the temporal plan $\mathcal{X}_v.\sigma$ is short. The term $\gamma^{|\mathcal{X}_v.\sigma|}$, $\gamma > 1$, increases the weight when the tour has only a few goals. The term $\delta^{|\mathcal{X}_v.\text{rem}| - |\mathcal{X}_v.\sigma|}$, $\delta > 1$, is essential to deal with oversubscription (which was not considered in [6]). Note that $\mathcal{X}_v.\text{rem}$ denotes the goals that have to be reached; so $\mathcal{X}_v.\sigma$ is a partial or complete tour over these goals. The term essentially penalizes temporal plans that miss goals. We recommend setting $\delta \gg \gamma \gg \beta$ so that the weight is dominated by how many goals a temporal plan missed, followed next by the number of goals, and lastly by the plan duration. The term $\alpha^{\text{NRSELECTIONS}(\mathcal{X}_v)}$, $0 < \alpha < 1$, decreases the weight over repeated selections. This is to avoid selecting $\mathcal{X}_v$ when repeated expansions from $\mathcal{X}_v$ fail due to constraints imposed by the obstacles and the robot dynamics.

Expanding the Equivalence Class. After selecting $\mathcal{X}_v$, the approach seeks to expand $\mathcal{T}$ to complete the pickup and delivery goals of the temporal plan $\mathcal{X}_v.\sigma$. To reach the first goal $\mathcal{G}_1$ in $\mathcal{X}.\sigma$, the approach retrieves the minimum cost path $\langle q_1, \ldots, q_k \rangle$ in the roadmap from $v.q$ to $\mathcal{G}_1$ and attempts to expand $\mathcal{T}$ along this path. A proportional-derivative-integrative controller [18] is used to expand $\mathcal{T}$ toward $\langle q_1, \ldots, q_k \rangle$ in succession by turning and then moving the

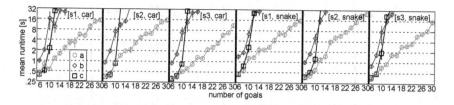

Fig. 5. Runtime results when varying the discrete planner in our approach: (a) MC (b) Optic (c) Random.

vehicle toward each target. Intermediate collision-free states are added to $\mathcal{T}$ as new vertices. The expansion stops when a collision occurs or $\mathcal{G}_1$ is reached. Once the expansion stops, the approach updates the equivalence classes and their weights to account for the new vertices added to $\mathcal{T}$ and goes back to the core loop to select perhaps another equivalence class. When the approach has difficulty expanding $\mathcal{T}$, it penalizes the edges so that in the next iteration the expansion could be attempted along a different path. This allows the approach to discover alternative paths to reach each goal.

5   Experiments and Results

Experiments are conducted using challenging logistics scenarios, where a vehicle with nonlinear dynamics (car or snake) has to navigate in obstacle-rich environments (Figs. 1 and 4) to pickup and deliver items from numerous locations within specified time windows. The efficiency and scalability of the approach is evaluated by increasing the number of goals, tightening the time windows, and reducing the vehicle capacity.

Discrete Solvers. We use *Monte-Carlo* as the specialized solver and *Optic* [2] as the general temporal planner. We also use a *Random* solver as a baseline for small problem instances. *Random* iterates in a random order over all the possible permutations with n goals (then with $n-1, \ldots, 1$), stopping as soon as it finds a valid tour.

Benchmark Instances. We extended the benchmark generator in [6] to incorporate loads and capacity constraints. Specifically, 30 instances were generated for each combination of a scene S and number of goals n, denoted by $\mathcal{I}_{\langle S,n\rangle}$. Each instance is generated by randomly placing the goals and the vehicle until there are no collisions. Each goal $\mathcal{G}_i$ is assigned a random load (from 1 to 5) and a random assignment is then used to create pickup-delivery pairs. Time bounds are generated by first computing a random tour with the constraint that a pickup must appear before its corresponding delivery. The time window for goal $\mathcal{G}_i$ is set to $[(1-\epsilon)t_i, (1+\epsilon)t_i]$, where t_i is the time to reach $\mathcal{G}_i$ in the tour when traveling along the shortest paths in the roadmap, using the expected velocity to convert distances to time. The parameter ϵ is used to tighten the time window (default is 0.2).

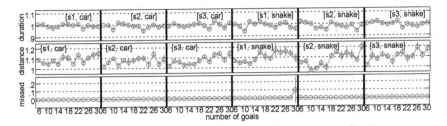

Fig. 6. Quality of the dynamically-feasible and collision-free solution trajectories computed by the approach as measured by the time duration, distance traveled, and goals missed. The results are normalized with respect to the tour obtained from the initial location over the discrete abstraction. Results are shown for our approach using the *Monte-Carlo* discrete solver.

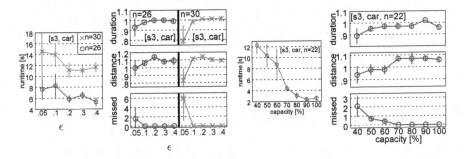

Fig. 7. (left) Results when adjusting the time window $[(1-\epsilon)t_i, (1+\epsilon)t_i]$. (right) Results when adjusting the vehicle capacity as a percentage of the sum of the loads.

The vehicle capacity, by default, is set to 100% of the sum of the loads. Even in such cases, it may be difficult or even impossible to reach all the goals due to constraints imposed by the time windows, obstacles, and dynamics. Experiments are also conducted with reduced capacity.

For each combination of parameters, the planner is run over all instances. Results report mean runtime, distance traveled, time duration, and goals missed. The mean is computed after dropping runs that are below the first quartile or above the third quartile to avoid the influence of outliers. Runtime measures everything from reading the input until finding a solution or reaching the runtime limit (set to 40 s per run).

Results: Increasing the Number of Goals. Figure 5 shows the efficiency and scalability of the approach as the number of goals is increased from 6 to 30. Even when coupled with *Random*, the approach is still able to quickly solve problems with up to 10 goals. The approach has similar performance when using *Optic*, which provides generality but is not as fast as specialized solvers. Indeed, the approach achieves the best results when coupled with the *Monte-Carlo* discrete solver, scaling up to 30 goals in a matter of a few seconds.

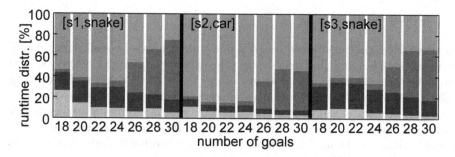

Fig. 8. Runtime distribution as a percentage of the total runtime (bottom to top): (1) roadmap construction and shortest paths, (2) collision checking and SIMULATE, (3) discrete solver, and (4) other.

Figure 6 shows results on the quality of the solution trajectories in terms of the time duration, distance traveled, and goals missed. The results are normalized with respect to the tour obtained from the initial location (tour associated with $\mathcal{X}_{v_{\text{init}}}$). The results show that our approach produces high-quality solutions. Note that in some cases our approach is able to find even shorter solutions than those associated with the initial tour. This could be due to the vehicle traveling faster than the expected velocity used in the tour calculations or taking smoother turns when following tour edges.

Results: Adjusting the Time Windows. Figure 7 (left) shows the results when varying $\epsilon \in \{0.05, 0.1, 0.2, 0.3, 0.4\}$ to adjust the time window $[(1-\epsilon)t_i, (1+\epsilon)t_i]$ for each goal $\mathcal{G}_i$. Note that the approach is quite efficient even for small values. As expected, when ϵ is too small, e.g., $\epsilon = 0.05$, it becomes quite difficult to find solutions, causing the approach to miss some goals (which is also why the reported solutions are shorter).

Results: Adjusting the Vehicle Capacity. Figure 7 (right) summarizes the results when varying the vehicle capacity from 100% of the sum of the loads down to 40%. The results show that the approach is quite efficient even when the vehicle capacity is considerably reduced. When the capacity becomes too small, the problem becomes significantly more difficult, which in some cases causes our approach to miss some goals.

Results: Runtime Distribution. Figure 8 summarizes the runtime distribution. As the problems increase in complexity so does the time taken by the discrete solver. Recall that the discrete solver is invoked numerous times during each run to compute tours for each equivalence class that is created during the motion-tree expansion. The discrete solver enables our approach to focus the expansion along promising directions, thus saving valuable computational time.

6 Discussion

We have developed an effective and scalable approach to solve challenging multi-goal motion-planning problems with time windows, pickups, deliveries, and capacity constraints. A crucial aspect of our approach is the use of a discrete solver over a suitable abstraction to effectively guide sampling-based motion planning. We expect our framework to benefit even more from advances in discrete planning. A natural but involved research direction is minimizing energy consumption, e.g., by adding recharging stations. Another direction is to enable more expressive PDDL tasks. We also expect to progress this work towards cooperative motion planning of several robots [13].

References

1. Abdo, A., Edelkamp, S., Lawo, M.: Nested rollout policy adaptation for optimizing vehicle selection in complex VRPs. In: IEEE Conference on Local Computer Networks LCN, pp. 213–221 (2016)
2. Benton, J., Coles, A.J., Coles, A.: Temporal planning with preferences and time-dependent continuous costs. In: ICAPS, vol. 77, pp. 2–10 (2012)
3. Choset, H., et al.: Principles of Robot Motion: Theory, Algorithms, and Implementations. MIT Press, Cambridge (2005)
4. Coltin, B., Veloso, M.: Online pickup and delivery planning with transfers for mobile robots. In: Workshops at the Twenty-Seventh AAAI Conference on Artificial Intelligence (2013)
5. Şucan, I.A., Kavraki, L.E.: A sampling-based tree planner for systems with complex dynamics. IEEE Trans. Robot. 28(1), 116–131 (2012)
6. Edelkamp, S., Lahijanian, M., Magazzeni, D., Plaku, E.: Integrating temporal reasoning and sampling-based motion planning for multi-goal problems with dynamics and time windows. IEEE Robot. Autom. Lett. 3, 3473–3480 (2018)
7. Edelkamp, S., Gath, M., Cazenave, T., Teytaud, F.: Algorithm and knowledge engineering for the TSPTW problem. In: 2013 IEEE Symposium on Computational Intelligence in Scheduling (SCIS), pp. 44–51. IEEE (2013)
8. Gerevini, A., Haslum, P., Long, D., Saetti, A., Dimopoulos, Y.: Deterministic planning in the fifth international planning competition: PDDL3 and experimental evaluation of the planners. Artif. Intell. 173(5–6), 619–668 (2009)
9. Kavraki, L.E., Švestka, P., Latombe, J.C., Overmars, M.H.: Probabilistic roadmaps for path planning in high-dimensional configuration spaces. IEEE Trans. Robot. Autom. 12(4), 566–580 (1996)
10. Kiesel, S., Burns, E., Wilt, C., Ruml, W.: Integrating vehicle routing and motion planning. In: Twenty-Second International Conference on Automated Planning and Scheduling (2012)
11. LaValle, S.M.: Planning Algorithms. Cambridge University Press, Cambridge (2006)
12. LaValle, S.M.: Motion planning: the essentials. IEEE Robot. Autom. Mag. 18(1), 79–89 (2011)
13. Le, D., Plaku, E.: Cooperative, dynamics-based, and abstraction-guided multi-robot motion planning. J. Artif. Intell. Res. 63, 361–390 (2018)

14. Nenchev, V., Belta, C., Raisch, J.: Optimal motion planning with temporal logic and switching constraints. In: 2015 European Control Conference (ECC), pp. 1141–1146. IEEE (2015)
15. Plaku, E.: Region-guided and sampling-based tree search for motion planning with dynamics. IEEE Trans. Robot. **31**, 723–735 (2015)
16. Plaku, E., Rashidian, S., Edelkamp, S.: Multi-group motion planning in virtual environments. Comput. Anim. Virtual Worlds (2016, in press)
17. Rosin, C.D.: Nested rollout policy adaptation for Monte Carlo tree search. In: IJCAI, pp. 649–654 (2011)
18. Spong, M.W., Hutchinson, S., Vidyasagar, M.: Robot Modeling and Control. Wiley, Hoboken (2005)
19. Winands, M.H., Björnsson, Y., Saito, J.T.: Monte-carlo tree search solver. Comput. Games **5131**, 25–36 (2008)

Automated Robot Skill Learning from Demonstration for Various Robot Systems

Lisa Gutzeit[1]([✉]), Alexander Fabisch[2], Christoph Petzoldt[1,3],
Hendrik Wiese[2], and Frank Kirchner[1,2]

[1] Robotics Research Group, University of Bremen, Bremen, Germany
{lisa.gutzeit,christoph.petzoldt}@uni-bremen.de
[2] German Research Center for Artificial Intelligence (DFKI GmbH),
Robotics Innovation Center, Bremen, Germany
{alexander.fabisch,hendrik.wiese,frank.kirchner}@dfki.de
[3] BIBA - Bremer Institut für Produktion und Logistik GmbH
at the University of Bremen, Bremen, Germany
ptz@biba.uni-bremen.de

Abstract. Transferring human movements to robotic systems is of high interest to equip the systems with new behaviors without expert knowledge. Typically, skills are often only learned for a very specific setup and a certain robot. We propose a modular framework to learn skills that is applicable on different robotic systems without adaptations. Our work builds on the recently introduced BesMan Learning Platform, which comprises the full workflow to transfer human demonstrations to a system, including automatized behavior segmentation, imitation learning, reinforcement learning for motion refinement, and methods to generalize to related tasks. For this paper, we extend this approach in order that different skills can be imitated by various systems in an automated fashion with a minimal amount of configuration, e.g., definition of the target system and environment. For this, we focus on the imitation of the demonstrated movements and show their transferability without movement refinement. We demonstrate the generality of the approach on a large dataset, consisting of about 700 throwing demonstrations. Nearly all of these human demonstrations are successfully transferred to four different robot target systems, namely Universal Robot's UR5 and UR10, KUKA LBR iiwa, and DFKI's robot COMPI. An analysis of the quality of the imitated movement on the real UR5 robot shows that useful throws can be executed on the system which can be used as starting points for further movement refinement.

Keywords: Behavior learning · Learning from demonstration · Behavior segmentation · Imitation learning · Transfer learning · Manipulation · Robotics

L. Gutzeit, A. Fabisch and C. Petzoldt have contributed equally as first authors.

C. Benzmüller and H. Stuckenschmidt (Eds.): KI 2019, LNAI 11793, pp. 168–181, 2019.
https://doi.org/10.1007/978-3-030-30179-8_14

1 Introduction and Related Work

Implementing new behaviors for robotic systems is tedious work. In recent years more and more often machine learning has been used to simplify this problem. By using learning from demonstration techniques, intuitive knowledge from humans is leveraged to initialize a refinement process that has to be done on the real system. For this purpose we recently proposed the BesMan Learning Platform that automatizes the process of transferring relevant motion segments from human motion capture data to a robotic platform in a format that can be refined by standard policy search algorithms [7]. Most steps of this learning process, like the segmentation of the movement demonstration and the imitation learning, are already automatized. Manual work remains in defining a reward function to refine the skill.

In this work, we present our general approach to imitate human demonstrations proposed in [7] in more detail, evaluate it on a bigger dataset and show that demonstrated behaviors can be transferred to different robotic systems. To automatize imitation learning for different systems, poses of certain keypoints of the human body have to be mapped to poses of elements of the robotic system. This is a special case of the correspondence problem [14]. That means, demonstrated end effector trajectories have to be changed in a way that they are executable on the target system.

This process, which is also called motion retargeting, is a well-known problem in the computer graphics and animation community [5]. In practice it is often solved manually. In the context of imitation learning for robots it has been explored by [12,16] with a fixed mapping. Similar work on automating the embodiment mapping has been published by [11]. Our approach to this problem has been presented briefly in [7] but not systematically analyzed so far. Our approach is more restricted: we do not integrate task-specific constraints in the optimization process (e.g., collision penalties for external objects, via-points) and we do not modify the shape of the trajectory. The benefit is twofold: our approach is more modular, which allows us to use any standard black-box optimization method to optimize the embodiment, and do task-specific adaptation with standard reinforcement learning algorithms. Furthermore, no model of the environment is needed at this stage. The only prior knowledge that is needed is a kinematic model of the robot. In this paper we particularly examine if this restricted approach already generates useful trajectories in the workspace of the robot. We build upon previous work [7] and evaluate the applicability of the learning platform to several different robotic target systems. The main focus lies on the automation of the embodiment mapping to map human movement recordings to a trajectory which is executable on the system.

In Sect. 2, the general learning platform, including automatized movement segmentation and our approach to solve the correspondence problem in a general and easily configurable way, are described. In Sect. 3, we present the experiments in which approx. 700 throwing motions have been recorded and transferred to the target system to evaluate the approach. The results of these experiments are presented and discussed in Sect. 4 before we give a conclusion.

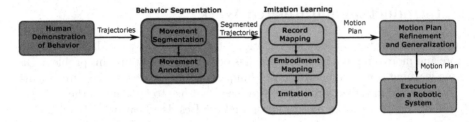

Fig. 1. Overview of the learning platform. In this paper the focus is on the first three modules: recording of human demonstration and automatized movement segmentation and imitation.

2 Generic Learning Platform

The BesMan Learning Platform is designed to cover the whole workflow of teaching robotic systems new behavior from human demonstrations. It provides utilities for human motion recording, behavior segmentation, imitation learning as well as motion refinement and generalization in a single framework [7].

In this paper we focus on the first part of the learning platform dealing with segmentation of human demonstrations and imitation learning. A general overview is shown in Fig. 1.

Human demonstrations of the movements that will be transferred are recorded, automatically segmented into movement building blocks, and labeled according to known movement classes, as described in more detail in Sect. 2.1. Afterwards, the segmented trajectories are mapped to the robot workspace and imitated, as described in Sect. 2.2.

In this work, the learning process presented in [7] is automatized for learning behaviors on various new robotic systems or environments by just requiring a minimal amount of configuration to integrate the available prior knowledge about the robot target system or the scenario, respectively. This is possible due to the modular design of the approach. Demonstrations of the same task can be transferred to different systems by configuring general robot related properties, like kinematic structure of the robot, type of gripper and default joint configuration (home position) and definition of a rotation matrix to map the robot's end effector rotation to the human hand orientation.

We summarize the methods used to automatically identify the relevant movement in the human demonstrations in the following section. Afterwards, methods for the transformation and optimization are presented, which are needed to make the movements executable on a robotic system. These methods are applicable on different robotic systems by just defining the robot configuration as described above.

2.1 Movement Segmentation

The learning platform allows for learning complex skills which cannot be learned monolithically. By splitting complex movements into simpler sub-tasks, learning of these tasks becomes feasible. Previously learned sub-tasks can be reused in other related tasks. In the learning platform, this process is automatized using the segmentation and classification approach presented in [8]. Human manipulation movements follow a characteristic bell-shaped velocity pattern of the hand [13]. We use these bell-shaped profiles to identify building blocks of manipulation movements using an unsupervised segmentation algorithm, called *velocity-based Multiple Change-point Inference (vMCI)*, introduced in [18]. To generate labels for the identified movement building blocks, we use a supervised approach based on 1-Nearest Neighbor (1-NN) classification. By transforming recorded trajectories of several positions of the demonstrator's arm to a coordinate frame relative to the back of the human, and interpolating the identified segments to the same length, simple 1-NN classification shows good classification results on several manipulation tasks with small training set sizes [7,8]. Using the unsupervised movement segmentation algorithm vMCI in combination with 1-NN classification, the relevant movement parts of the demonstrations that shall be learned by the system can be selected. Benefits of the approach are that the movements can be performed naturally by the demonstrator, and no manual segmentation procedure is required. Furthermore, the same approach works for different manipulation movement without the need for adaptations. This has already been evaluated on ball-throwing and pick-and-place movements in our previous work [6,8]. In this work, we additionally evaluate this approach on a bigger dataset, containing approximately 700 stick-throwing demonstrations.

2.2 Imitation Learning

It is not easily possible to directly transfer behaviors between humanoids (e.g. humans, humanoid robots, or robots which are similar to parts of humans) due to the correspondence problem [14]. To circumvent this problem, a record mapping is needed which maps marker trajectories of human demonstrations to a sequence of actions or system states, as well as an embodiment mapping, which maps the recorded sequence to a trajectory that is executable on the target system [1]. In this section we present solutions for the record and embodiment mapping as well as an optimization of the embodiment mapping which is applicable on different robotic systems.

Record Mapping. We assume that the demonstrator's state-action sequence can be discretized with

$$\tau^D = \left(s_0^D, a_0^D, \dots, s_{T-1}^D, a_{T-1}^D, s_T^D \right), \tag{1}$$

and that there is some underlying policy that has been used to generate τ^D, which is fully defined by a probability density function $\pi^D(s,a)$. τ^D cannot be directly observed because neither the actions $a_t^D, t \in \{0, \dots, T-1\}$ (e.g., muscle contractions of a human) can be observed directly, nor can the states $s_t^D, t \in \{0, \dots, T\}$ be observed in their entirety (e.g. configurations of all joints of a human). Instead, $g^R(s^D, a^D) = \left(s^R, a^R \right)$ can be observed and recorded, where information can be lost (e.g., some joint configurations, muscle states, etc.) in the *record mapping* $g^R : S^D \times A^D \to S^R \times A^R$. In our case, marker positions on the human's body are captured by a motion capture system and represented in the motion capture system's world coordinate system. The information about the state of the human is limited by the amount of markers that are attached to the body, and we cannot measure joint angles directly because we attach markers exclusively to the skin and clothes of the human, hence poses can change slightly over time without any actual joint movement. From these markers, hand pose trajectories can be extracted and represented relative to the pose of the human's back.[1] Our setup allows to easily add tracking of dual-hand motions as well. Hence, we extract a sequence τ^R that contains poses of end effectors.

Embodiment Mapping. We assume that in the ideal case all states and actions can be recorded perfectly; that is, g^R is the identity. We would like to infer the policy π^D based on the collected data $\tau^R = \left(s_0^R, a_0^R, \ldots, s_{T-1}^R, a_{T-1}^R, s_T^R\right)$. However, it is often not possible to reach all states or execute all actions. For example, if a movement from a human shall be transferred to a humanoid robot, it might be the case that the robot has not as many degrees of freedom as the human and thus cannot execute a similar, smooth trajectory within the workspace. It might be impossible to reach several states because they are not in the robot's workspace, the robot might be too weak or slow to execute the desired motions, or it might be to stiff and heavy to generate the same sequence of states. Actions are ignored for this discussion. They can be generated by position or velocity controllers on the real system. That means, an *embodiment mapping* $g^E : S^R \times A^R \to S^E \times A^E$ is required, which maps the recorded data to states and actions that are executable on the target system. g^E is not given like g^R, but instead has to be constructed either manually, from data, or both. As in Sect. 2.3.2 of [7], we propose to use simple black-box optimization to find g^E.

Optimization of Embodiment Mapping. In our work, we observe sequences of end effector poses (trajectories) from, e.g., a human teacher. Thus, an embodiment mapping has to be obtained that maps these trajectories to the workspace of the robot such that they are reachable and there are no discontinuities in joint space. We propose a parameterized linear mapping of the form

$$g^E(x_t, y_t, z_t, \alpha_t, \beta_t, \gamma_t) = \begin{pmatrix} R_{\alpha,\beta,\gamma}\left((1-s)\begin{pmatrix}x_0\\y_0\\z_0\end{pmatrix} + s\begin{pmatrix}x_t\\y_t\\z_t\end{pmatrix}\right) \\ \alpha + \alpha_t \\ \beta + \beta_t \\ \gamma + \gamma_t \end{pmatrix} + b, \quad (2)$$

where $s \in [0,1]$ is a scaling factor, $\theta = \alpha, \beta, \gamma$ are Euler angles (rotation around x-, y'- and z"-axis) that define a rotation, and b is an offset vector. s, θ, b will be selected to maximize the objective

---

[1] We use `pytransform3d` to calculate these transformations [4].

$$f(s, \boldsymbol{\theta}, \boldsymbol{b}) = \exp \left(\frac{10}{T+1} \sum_t r(g^E(\boldsymbol{p}_t)) \right)$$

$$-w_{vel} \sum_t \dot{\boldsymbol{q}}(g^E(\boldsymbol{p}_t)) - w_{acc} \sum_t \ddot{\boldsymbol{q}}(g^E(\boldsymbol{p}_t)) - w_{jrk} \sum_t \dddot{\boldsymbol{q}}(g^E(\boldsymbol{p}_t))$$

$$-w_{coll} \sum_t c(\boldsymbol{q}_t) - w_{dist} \|\boldsymbol{p}_T\|$$

$$+w_{height} \sum_t \boldsymbol{p}_{3,t} + w_{size} \sum_{d=1}^{3} \max_t \boldsymbol{p}_{d,t} - \min_t \boldsymbol{p}_{d,t}, \tag{3}$$

where $t \in \{0, \ldots, T\}$ is the time step, $r(\boldsymbol{p})$ is 1 if $\boldsymbol{p}$ is a reachable end effector pose and 0 otherwise, $c(\boldsymbol{q})$ is 1 if the configuration results in self-collision and 0 otherwise, $\boldsymbol{p}_t$ is an end effector pose and $\boldsymbol{q}_t$ are corresponding joint angles at step t. The objective maximizes reachability, while minimizing the risk of getting too close to singularities, avoiding self-collisions, and maximizing exploitation of the robot's workspace. To maximize f any black-box optimizer can be used. We decided to use covariance matrix adaptation evolution strategies (CMA-ES; [9]) for this paper. The weights have to be configured appropriately. Depending on the target system, an analytic solution to inverse kinematics, a numerical solution, or even an approximation of a numerical solution [3] can be used if it is difficult to find a mapping that fits the trajectory into the workspace of the robot. In this paper we use both a numerical solution and an approximation, and take the solution that yields the best result. In addition, the resulting trajectory is smoothed with a mean filter in Cartesian space and in joint space (positions and accelerations) to avoid infeasibly high accelerations.

Imitation Learning. After mapping the recorded trajectory to the robot's workspace, a suitable representation that can be used for further adaptation and refinement is needed. A popular class of policy representations that has been used to learn movement primitives for robotic manipulation are Dynamical Movement Primitives (DMPs; [10,15]). There are numerous advantages of DMPs in comparison to other policy representations for our purposes, among them: (1) They are stable trajectory representations. Slight errors in execution of the trajectory will not result in error accumulation like in general function approximators. (2) To reproduce a demonstrated movement, a one-shot learning algorithm can be used that determines the weights of the forcing term θ_i. Hence, imitation learning with DMPs is much simpler than it is for more general function approximators. (3) Movements can be easily adapted (even during execution): the goal of the movement can be changed and obstacles can be avoided.

3   Experiments

In this section, we evaluate the proposed configurable learning platform on a Touhu scenario.

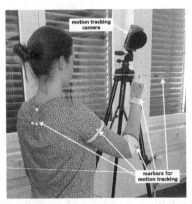 

(a) Setup to record the human arm motion with markers attached to the back, arm and hand.

(b) To record the stick position, a marker is attached to the tip of the stick. The movement of the robotic arm UR5 is tracked with a marker attached to the end effector

Fig. 2. Motion recording setup.

Touhu, also known as *pitch-pot*, is a throwing game that is traditionally played in Eastern Asia. The goal is to throw a stick from a given distance into a pot. We use this scenario to evaluate the transferability of throwing movements to different robotic systems using their kinematic models.

Additionally, the quality of the transferred movements is evaluated in a second experiment, where the trajectory and goal position of the stick thrown by humans is compared to the one thrown by a real UR5 robot.

3.1 Experimental Setup

The throwing motions demonstrated by the human subject are recorded with a marker based-motion capturing system. The position of infrared light reflecting markers attached to the human body are recorded by several cameras at 500Hz. To record the throwing motions, markers are attached to the hand, elbow, shoulder and back of the subject to track these positions. To determine the record mapping as described in Sect. 2.2, additionally to the position of the back, its orientation is also needed. Thus, we attached three markers to the back instead of one, relative to each other in a well-known setup. The setup allows for determining the orientation of the markers. The same applies to the hand to allow for tracking the hand pose including its orientation. The complete marker setup can be seen in Fig. 2.

In the second experiment, in addition to the human movement, likewise the position of the stick is of interest. With it, the trajectories of the thrown stick from the demonstration can be compared to the resulting trajectories after imitation of the throwing motion on the real system. Thus, a maker is placed on one end of the stick. Additionally, the movement of the robotic arm UR5 is captured by placing a marker at the end effector (see again Fig. reffig:setupspstuho). The recorded demonstrations were down-sampled to 30Hz and automatically segmented into movement building blocks with a bell-shaped velocity profile of the hand using the vMCI algorithm as described in Sect. refsec:segmentation. Using 1-NN classification, the movement segments were classified into the classes *strike_out*, *throw*, *swing_out* and *idle*. To transfer the recorded demonstrations to the four robotic systems, the embodiment mapping has been optimized with the following weights in the objective function: $w_{coll} = 100, w_{vel} = 100, w_{acc} = 10, w_{jrk} = 1, w_{dist} = 0.1, w_{height} = 50, w_{size} = 100$. These weights have been determined empirically. The optimization was limited to the Cartesian translation of the trajectory within the workspace of the robot. Orientation and scaling remained unchanged.

3.2 Transfer in Simulation

Throwing motions of seven different subjects, each performing between 41 and 246 throws, were recorded to evaluate the generality of our approach. In total, 697 Touhu demonstration were recorded. With this large dataset, we are able to evaluate the generality of the movement segmentation as well as the transfer to different robotic systems, namely Universal Robots' UR5 and UR10, KUKA LBR iiwa and DFKI's COMPI [2]. To evaluate the movement classification, a stratified cross-validation repeated 100 times was performed with a fixed number of examples per class in the training data. Segments which could not be clearly assigned to one of the movement classes were removed from this evaluation. Furthermore, the number of successfully transferred movements as well as the difference between the position of the hand in the demonstrations and the end effector position of the systems are analyzed.

3.3 Transfer to a Real System

In the second part of the Touhu experiment, we additionally recorded 34 throwing movements of three subjects, in which also the position of the stick was recorded. Three subjects performed 10, 11 and 13 throws respectively. These demonstrations were transferred to the real UR5 robotic arm. We analyzed the number of successful throws, the stick position during the throw and its goal position. The transferability of the demonstrated throws on the UR5 robot is evaluated with respect to the following aspects: Does the robot inadvertently collide with anything including the stick? Does the stick fall out of the stick holder while the robot approaches the starting pose of the trajectory? Does the stick leave the holder during the throwing motion? If any of these aspects are evaluated negatively, the trajectory is considered not transferable. To evaluate the quality of the transferred throws, we compare the stick trajectories of the demonstrated throws and the recordings of the throws transferred to the UR5. Since the motion capture system sometimes returned noisy stick position measurements, the trajectories had to be interpolated. A quadratic model was

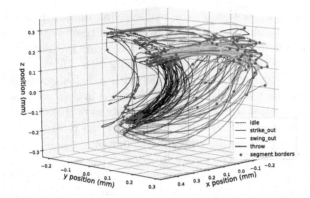

Fig. 3. Throwing trajectories of subject 5. The position of the hand is shown for one set consisting of 41 Touhu-throws. Green dots mark the result of the vMCI segmentation. The resulting segment trajectories were labeled with 1-NN classification. Different line styles mark the different classes. Throwing segments are visualized as straight lines with a different color for each throw. (Color figure online)

used for interpolation. The same model has been used to extrapolate both the demonstrated and the reproduced stick trajectory until the stick hit the ground. Before this, we aligned the demonstrated trajectory with the start position of the transferred one. Thus, the distance between ground contact points as well as the similarity of the the stick trajectories can be determined. We use the average dynamic type warping (DTW; [17]) distance, i.e., the DTW distance divided by the maximum number of steps of the two time series, to compare the trajectories.

4 Results

4.1 Transfer in Simulation

The automatic segmentation of 697 demonstrated throws resulted in 2913 identified segments with a bell-shaped velocity profile. Although some throwing demonstrations showed just a small decrease of the velocity of the hand between throw and swing out phase of the movement, most of the throwing segments were successfully segmented. As an example result, a demonstration of one subject containing 41 throws is visualized in Fig. 3.

2233 segments were used to evaluate the annotation. The number of training examples per class was varied between 1 and 20. With 4 examples per class a mean classification accuracy of 90% could be achieved. 95% could be achieved with 9 examples per class. Thus, a training data set with 9 examples per class was created, which contains the first three throwing demonstration of three different subjects. Using this training data, the segments of all recorded demonstration were classified. The movement class *throw* could be detected with an accuracy of 99%, with 623 correctly detected throwing movements, 13 false negatives and 2 false positives. In Fig. 3, different colors indicate the resulting labels of subject 5.

The segments of this subject were classified with an accuracy of 98%, with 24 segments that had to be removed from evaluation. This result shows that the approach to identify the relevant parts in the demonstrations also generalizes to larger datasets. A small number of labeled training data was sufficient to annotate the automatically derived segments. The throwing trajectories mapped into the workspace of the robotic system UR5, UR10, KUKA LBR iiwa and COMPI, are shown in Fig. 4a and b. 682 trajectories were transferred to the workspaces of all target systems. We can see that most trajectories easily fit in the workspace of UR10 (arm radius: 1300 mm) and KUKA LBR iiwa 7 (arm radius: 1266mm), while many trajectories have to be distorted or are close to

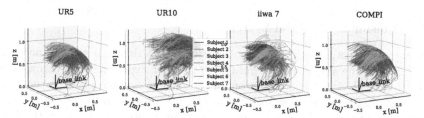

(a) All recognized throwing movements transferred to the workspace of the four robots. Trajectories from the same subject are shown in the same color

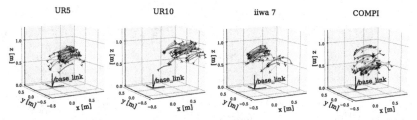

(b) All throwing movements of subject 5. Colors indicate the indices of the throws and correspond to the colors in Figure 3. The frames of the robots' base links are shown.

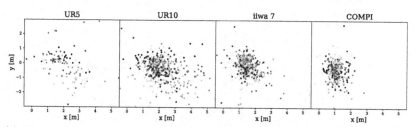

(c) Throwing results in simulation. We display the distribution of ground contact points of the sticks. Colors of the points indicate the index of the transferred throwing trajectory

Fig. 4. End-effector trajectories of throwing movements in robots' workspaces and corresponding ground contact points of the sticks. (Color figure online)

the borders of the workspace of UR5 (arm radius: 850 mm) and COMPI (arm radius: 940 mm). Throwing movements often tend to be close to the borders of the human's workspace. Hence, the skill that we selected is quite challenging for smaller robots. The middle row of Fig. 4 shows the demonstration of subject 5 visualized in Fig. 3 transferred to the robotic arms. The different colors match the colors of the throwing segments in Fig. 3.

Figure 4 shows the ground contact points of sticks for the presented throwing trajectories from simulation. It can be seen that on average the UR10 has the widest distribution as it has the largest workspace. We quantify how well the throwing trajectories can be transferred to the real UR5 robot, as it is one of the more challenging robotic systems due to the more restricted workspace.

4.2 Transfer to the Real System

In this experiment, the throwing motions have been detected with an accuracy of 97%, using the same training data as in the first experiment. 33 throws were correctly detected and one was wrongly assigned to another class by the 1-NN classification. 27 out of these segments could be transferred to the real UR5. A comparison of the stick trajectories can be seen in Fig. 5a, in which the best,

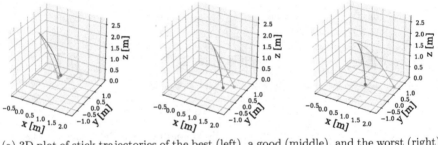

(a) 3D plot of stick trajectories of the best (left), a good (middle), and the worst (right) result. The orange trajectory indicates how the stick was thrown in the demonstration and the blue trajectory is the reproduction by the UR5

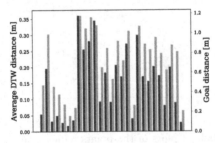

(b) Average dynamic time warping distances and distances of goal positions.

Fig. 5. Analysis of the execution of throws on the real UR5 (Color figure online)

a good and the worst result in visualized. The mean average DTW distance is 0.15m (standard deviation: 0.1m), and the mean goal distance is 0.72m (standard deviation: 0.31m). The full error distribution is shown in Fig. 5. The results show, that it is possible to automatically imitate demonstrated throws and that most of these throws are executable on the real system. Furthermore, the executed movements show useful throws. However, the goal positions of the demonstrated throws are not reached by the system.

5 Conclusion

This work is built on our previous work about the platform for learning robot skills from humans, presented in [7]. We described how this approach can be used in a more general way, applicable to multiple systems with little configuration overhead. Throwing trajectories are automatically extracted from human demonstrations, and transferred to four robotic target systems. We show that the embodiment mapping, which is needed to map human movement trajectories into the robot workspace, can be automized for a dataset of 697 throws. Throwing is a challenging skill for these robots because it has high acceleration and velocities and is close to the border of the workspace of humans. Nonetheless, most of the demonstrated throws could be transferred to the systems using our approach. Furthermore, we evaluate the difference of stick trajectories and ground contact points between demonstrated throws and reproductions of those on a real UR5. Although the demonstrated throwing motions could be successfully executed on different systems, there is still a significant gap between the outcome of demonstrated throws and their reproductions.

Furthermore, this approach does not work well for arbitrary types of robot skills. To transform demonstrated trajectories to the robot's workspace, the trajectories sometimes have to be modified. Long trajectories may have to be scaled down to completely fit into the workspace. Fast trajectories may have to be slowed down to be executable by the system. Often, trajectories have to be translated with respect to the synchronization frame in the workspace of the robot. This conflicts with trajectories that require, for example, that certain poses, such as viapoints and goals, are reached. For these type of task it is required that these particular poses are reachable by the end effector, relative to given reference frames. These constraints are not integrated in the objective of our embodiment mapping and will be completely ignored. Thus, even though the human may have demonstrated a successful reaching behavior, the robot might not be able to solve the same task because the trajectory has been shifted by the embodiment mapping. The goal of our embodiment mapping is to generate a good initial motion that is executable and can later be refined for a specific task and target system. As proposed earlier [7], a solution to this problem would be to use reinforcement learning to refine the motion.

Acknowledgements. This work was supported through grants from the German Federal Ministry for Economic Affairs and Energy (BMWi, No 50RA1703, No 50RA1701), one grant from the European Union's Horizon 2020 research and innovation program (No H2020-FOF 2016 723853), and part of the work was done in a collaboration with Intel Labs China. We would like to thank Intel Corp. for financial support.

References

1. Argall, B.D., Chernova, S., Veloso, M., Browning, B.: A survey of robot learning from demonstration. Robot. Auton. Syst. **57**(5), 469–483 (2009)
2. Bargsten, V., de Gea Fernández, J.: Compi: Development of a 6-DOF compliant robot arm for human-robot cooperation. In: Proceedings of the 8th International Workshop on Human-Friendly Robotics. Technische Universitaet Muenchen (TUM) (2015)
3. Fabisch, A.: A Comparison of Policy Search in Joint Space and Cartesian Space for Refinement of Skills. In: Berns, K., Görges, D. (eds.) RAAD 2019. AISC, vol. 980, pp. 301–309. Springer, Cham (2020). https://doi.org/10.1007/978-3-030-19648-6_35
4. Fabisch, A.: pytransform3d: 3D transformations for python. J. Open Source Softw. **4**, 1159 (2019). https://doi.org/10.21105/joss.01159
5. Gleicher, M.: Retargetting motion to new characters. In: Proceedings of the 25th Annual Conference on Computer Graphics and Interactive Techniques, SIGGRAPH 1998, pp. 33–42. ACM, New York (1998). https://doi.org/10.1145/280814.280820
6. Gutzeit, L., Otto, M., Kirchner, E.A.: Simple and robust automatic detection and recognition of human movement patterns in tasks of different complexity. In: Physiological Computing Systems. Springer (2019, submitted)
7. Gutzeit, L., et al.: The BesMan learning platform for automated robot skill learning. Front. Robot. AI **5**, 43 (2018). https://doi.org/10.3389/frobt.2018.00043
8. Gutzeit, L., Kirchner, E.A.: Automatic detection and recognition of human movement patterns in manipulation tasks. In: Proceedings of the 3rd International Conference on Physiological Computing Systems (2016)
9. Hansen, N., Ostermeier, A.: Completely derandomized self-adaptation in evolution strategies. Evol. Comput. **9**, 159–195 (2001)
10. Ijspeert, A.J., Nakanishi, J., Hoffmann, H., Pastor, P., Schaal, S.: Dynamical movement primitives: learning attractor models for motor behaviors. Neural Comput. **25**(2), 328–373 (2013)
11. Maeda, G.J., Ewerton, M., Koert, D., Peters, J.: Acquiring and generalizing the embodiment mapping from human observations to robot skills. IEEE Robot. Autom. Lett. (RA-L) **1**(2), 784–791 (2016). https://doi.org/10.1109/LRA.2016.2525038
12. Michieletto, S., Chessa, N., Menegatti, E.: Learning how to approach industrial robot tasks from natural demonstrations. In: 2013 IEEE Workshop on Advanced Robotics and its Social Impacts, pp. 255–260, November 2013. https://doi.org/10.1109/ARSO.2013.6705538
13. Morasso, P.: Spatial control of arm movements. Exp. Brain Res. **42**, 223–227 (1981)
14. Nehaniv, C.L., Dautenhahn, K., Dautenhahn, K.: Imitation in Animals and Artifacts. MIT Press, Cambridge (2002)

15. Pastor, P., Hoffmann, H., Asfour, T., Schaal, S.: Learning and generalization of motor skills by learning from demonstration. In: IEEE International Conference on Robotics and Automation, pp. 763–768 (2009)
16. Pollard, N.S., Hodgins, J.K., Riley, M.J., Atkeson, C.G.: Adapting human motion for the control of a humanoid robot. In: Proceedings 2002 IEEE International Conference on Robotics and Automation (Cat. No. 02CH37292). vol. 2, pp. 1390–1397, May 2002. https://doi.org/10.1109/ROBOT.2002.1014737
17. Sakoe, H., Chiba, S.: Dynamic programming algorithm optimization for spoken word recognition. IEEE Trans. Acoust. Speech Sig. Process. **26**(1), 43–49 (1978). https://doi.org/10.1109/TASSP.1978.1163055
18. Senger, L., Schröer, M., Metzen, J.H., Kirchner, E.A.: Velocity-based multiple change-point inference for unsupervised segmentation of human movement behavior. In: Proceedings of the 22th International Conference on Pattern Recognition (ICPR2014), pp. 4564–4569 (2014). https://doi.org/10.1109/ICPR.2014.781

Learning Gradient-Based ICA by Neurally Estimating Mutual Information

Hlynur Davíð Hlynsson[✉] and Laurenz Wiskott

Ruhr University Bochum, 44801 Bochum, Germany
hlynurd@gmail.com

Abstract. Several methods of estimating the mutual information of random variables have been developed in recent years. They can prove valuable for novel approaches to learning statistically independent features. In this paper, we use one of these methods, a mutual information neural estimation (MINE) network, to present a proof-of-concept of how a neural network can perform linear ICA. We minimize the mutual information, as estimated by a MINE network, between the output units of a differentiable encoder network. This is done by simple alternate optimization of the two networks. The method is shown to get a qualitatively equal solution to FastICA on blind-source-separation of noisy sources.

Keywords: Adversarial training · Deep learning · Independent component analysis

1 Introduction

Independent component analysis (ICA) aims at estimating unknown *sources* that have been mixed together into an *observation*. The usual assumptions are that the sources are statistically independent and no more than one is Gaussian [16]. The now-cemented metaphor is one of a cocktail party problem: several people (sources) are speaking simultaneously and their speech has been mixed together in a recording (observation). The task is to unmix the recording such that all dialogues can be listened to clearly.

In linear ICA, we have a data matrix S whose rows are drawn from statistically independent distributions, a mixing matrix A, and an observation matrix X:

$$X = AS$$

and we want to find an unmixing matrix U of A that recovers the sources up to a permutation and scaling:

$$Y = UX$$

The general non-linear ICA problem is ill-posed [9,14] as there is an infinite number of solutions if the space of mixing functions is unconstrained. However,

© Springer Nature Switzerland AG 2019
C. Benzmüller and H. Stuckenschmidt (Eds.): KI 2019, LNAI 11793, pp. 182–187, 2019.
https://doi.org/10.1007/978-3-030-30179-8_15

post-non-linear [22] (PNL) ICA is solvable. This is a particular case of non-linear ICA where the observations take the form

$$X = f(AS)$$

where f operates componentwise, i.e. $X_{i,t} = f_i \left(\sum_n^N A_{i,n} S_{n,t} \right)$. The problem is solved efficiently if f is at least approximately invertible [24] and there are approaches to optimize the problem for non-invertible f as well [15]. For signals with time-structure, however, the problem is not ill-posed even though it is for i.i.d. samples [6,21].

To frame ICA as an optimization problem, we must find a way to measure the statistical independence of the output components and minimize this quantity. There are two main ways to approach this: either minimize the mutual information between the sources [2,4,8], or maximize the sources' non-Gaussianity [5,13].

There has been an interest in combining neural networks with the principles of ICA for several decades [17]. Our work can be categorized with methods where the objective is optimized by means of playing a minimax game: In Predictability Maximization [19], a game is played where one agent tries to predict the value of one output component given the others, and the other tries to maximize the unpredictability. More recently, Deep InfoMax (DIM) [12], Graph Deep InfoMax [23] and Generative adversarial networks [11], utilize the work of Brakel et al. [7] to deeply learn ICA. Our work differs from these adversarial training methods in the rules of the minimax game being played to achieve this: one agent directly minimizes the lower-bound of the mutual information, as derived from the Donsker-Varadhan characterization of the KL-Divergence [18], as the other tries to maximize it.

2   Method

We train an encoder E to generate an output $(z_1, z_2, \ldots, z_M)$ such that any one of the output components is statistically independent of the union of the others, i.e. $P(z_i, z_{-i}) = P(z_i)P(z_{-i})$, where

$$z_{-i} := (z_1, \ldots, z_{i-1}, z_{i+1}, \ldots, z_M)$$

The statistical independence of z_i and z_{-i} can be maximized by minimizing their mutual information

$$I(Z_i; Z_{-i}) = \int_z \int_{z_{-i}} p(z_i, z_{-i}) \log \left(\frac{p(z_i, z_{-i})}{p(z_i)p(z_{-i})} \right) dz_i dz_{-i} \qquad (1)$$

This quantity is hard to estimate, particularly for high-dimensional data. We therefore estimate the lower bound of Eq. (1) using a mutual information neural estimation (MINE) network M [3]:

$$I(Z_i; Z_{-i}) \geq L_i = \mathbb{E}_\mathbb{J} \left[M(z_i, z_{-i}) \right] - \log \left(\mathbb{E}_\mathbb{M} \left[e^{M(z_i, z_{-i})} \right] \right) \qquad (2)$$

where $\mathbb{J}$ indicates that the expected value is taken over the joint and similarly $\mathbb{M}$ for the product of marginals. During training, the expectations are replaced with the empirical samples of E's outputs or by shuffling z_i vs. z_{-i} along the batch axis. The expectation inside the log is handled by calculating the mean of the empirical samples and passing it to the Nesterov momentum ADAM optimizer [10]. The networks E and M are parameterized by θ_E and θ_M. The encoder takes the observations as input and the MINE network takes the output of the encoder as an input.

The E network minimizes $L = \max_{\theta_M} \sum_i L_i$ in order for the outputs to have low mutual information and therefore be statistically independent. In order to get a faithful estimation of the lower bound of the mutual information, the M network maximizes L. Thus, in a push-pull fashion, the system as a whole converges to independent output components of the encoder network E. In practice, rather than training the E and M networks simultaneously it proved useful to train M from scratch for a few iterations after each iteration of training E, since the loss functions of E and M are at odds with each other. When the encoder is trained, the MINE network's parameters are frozen and *vice versa* (Fig. 1).

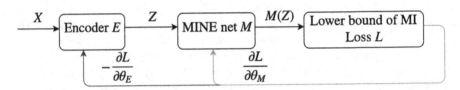

Fig. 1. The system learns statistically independent outputs by alternate optimization of an encoder E and a MINE network M parameterized by θ_E and θ_M. The MINE objective (Eq. 2) is minimized with respect to θ_E for weight updates of the encoder but it is *maximized* with respect to θ_M for weight updates of the MINE network.

3   Results

We validate the method[1] for linear noisy ICA example [1]. Three independent, noisy sources—sine wave, square wave and sawtooth signal (Fig. 2a)—are mixed linearly (Fig. 2b):

$$Y = \begin{bmatrix} 1 & 1 & 1 \\ 0.5 & 2 & 1 \\ 1.5 & 1 & 2 \end{bmatrix} S$$

The encoder is a single layer neural network with linear activation with a differentiable whitening layer [20] before the output. The whitening layer is a key component for performing successful blind source separation for our method. Statistically independent random variables are necessarily uncorrelated, so whitening the output by construction beforehand simplifies the optimization problem significantly.

---

[1] Full code for the results is available at github.com/wiskott-lab/gradient-based-ica/bl ob/master/bss3.ipynb.

The MINE network M is a seven-layer neural network. Each layer but the last one has 64 units with a rectified linear activation function. Each training epoch of the encoder is followed by seven training epochs of M. Estimating the exact mutual information is not essential, so few iterations suffice for a good gradient direction.

Since the MINE network is applied to each component individually, to estimate mutual information (Eq. 2), we need to pass each sample through the MINE network N times—once for each component. Equivalently, one could conceptualize this as having N copies of the MINE network and feeding the samples to it in parallel, with different components singled out. The N copies have shared weights to allow for potential feature re-use over the output variable pairs. Thus, for sample $(z_1, z_2, \ldots, z_N)$ we feed in $(z_i; z_{-i})$, for each i. Both networks are optimized using Nesterov momentum ADAM [10] with a learning rate of 0.005.

For this simple example, our method (Fig. 2c) is equivalently good at unmixing the signals as FastICA (Fig. 2d), albeit slower. Note that, in general, the sources can only be recovered up to permutation and scaling.

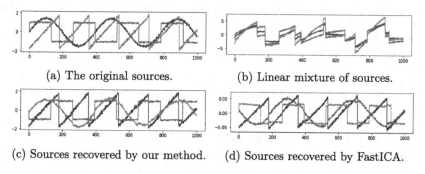

(a) The original sources.   (b) Linear mixture of sources.

(c) Sources recovered by our method.   (d) Sources recovered by FastICA.

Fig. 2. Three independent, noisy sources (a) are mixed linearly (b). Our method recovers them (c) to the same extent as FastICA (d).

4   Summary

We've introduced a proof-of-concept implementation for training a differentiable function for performing ICA. The method consists of alternating the optimization of an encoder and a neural mutual-information neural estimation (MINE) network. The mutual information estimate between each encoder output and the union of the others is minimized with respect to the encoder's parameters. Although this work is in a very preliminary stage, further investigation into the method is warranted. The general non-linear ICA problem is ill-posed, but it is an interesting question whether this method can work for non-linear problems with low complexity. We can constrain the expresiveness of our encoder by limiting for example the number of layers or number of hidden units in the neural network, thus constraining the solution space of the method. The method is also trivially extended for over- or undercomplete ICA by changing the number of output units. Higher dimensional and real-world data can also be tested.

As this method can be used for general neural network training, it should be investigated whether useful representations can be learned while solving the ICA task. This method blends nicely into deep learning architectures and the MINE loss term can be added as a regularizer to other loss functions. We imagine that this can be helpful for methods such as deep sparse coding to enforce independence between features and disentangle factors of variation.

References

1. Blind source separation using FastICA. https://scikit-learn.org/stable/auto_examples/decomposition/plot_ica_blind_source_separation.html. Accessed 24 Feb 2019
2. Amari, S.i., Cichocki, A., Yang, H.H.: A new learning algorithm for blind signal separation. In: Advances in Neural Information Processing Systems, pp. 757–763 (1996)
3. Belghazi, M.I., et al.: MINE: mutual information neural estimation. arXiv preprint arXiv:1801.04062 (2018)
4. Bell, A.J., Sejnowski, T.J.: A non-linear information maximisation algorithm that performs blind separation. In: Advances in Neural Information Processing Systems, pp. 467–474 (1995)
5. Blaschke, T., Wiskott, L.: CuBICA: independent component analysis by simultaneous third-and fourth-order cumulant diagonalization. IEEE Trans. Sig. Process. **52**(5), 1250–1256 (2004)
6. Blaschke, T., Zito, T., Wiskott, L.: Independent slow feature analysis and nonlinear blind source separation. Neural Comput. **19**(4), 994–1021 (2007)
7. Brakel, P., Bengio, Y.: Learning independent features with adversarial nets for non-linear ICA. arXiv preprint arXiv:1710.05050 (2017)
8. Cardoso, J.F.: InfoMax and maximum likelihood for blind source separation. IEEE Sig. Process. Lett. **4**(4), 112–114 (1997)
9. Darmois, G.: Analyse générale des liaisons stochastiques: etude particulière de l'analyse factorielle linéaire. Revue de l'Institut international de statistique, pp. 2–8 (1953)
10. Dozat, T.: Incorporating Nesterov momentum into ADAM (2016)
11. Goodfellow, I., et al.: Generative adversarial nets. In: Advances in Neural Information Processing Systems, pp. 2672–2680 (2014)
12. Hjelm, R.D., Fedorov, A., Lavoie-Marchildon, S., Grewal, K., Trischler, A., Bengio, Y.: Learning deep representations by mutual information estimation and maximization. arXiv preprint arXiv:R1808.06670 (2018)
13. Hyvärinen, A., Oja, E.: Independent component analysis: algorithms and applications. Neural Netw. **13**(4–5), 411–430 (2000)
14. Hyvärinen, A., Pajunen, P.: Nonlinear independent component analysis: existence and uniqueness results. Neural Netw. **12**(3), 429–439 (1999)
15. Ilin, A., Honkela, A.: Post-nonlinear independent component analysis by variational Bayesian learning. In: Puntonet, C.G., Prieto, A. (eds.) ICA 2004. LNCS, vol. 3195, pp. 766–773. Springer, Heidelberg (2004). https://doi.org/10.1007/978-3-540-30110-3_97

16. Jutten, C., Karhunen, J.: Advances in nonlinear blind source separation. In: Proceedings of the 4th International Symposium on Independent Component Analysis and Blind Signal Separation (ICA2003), pp. 245–256 (2003)
17. Karhunen, J.: Neural approaches to independent component analysis and source separation. In: ESANN, vol. 96, pp. 249–266 (1996)
18. McAllester, D., Statos, K.: Formal limitations on the measurement of mutual information. arXiv preprint arXiv:1811.04251 (2018)
19. Schmidhuber, J.: Learning factorial codes by predictability minimization. Neural Comput. **4**(6), 863–879 (1992)
20. Schüler, M., Hlynsson, H.D., Wiskott, L.: Gradient-based training of slow feature analysis by differentiable approximate whitening. arXiv preprint arXiv:1808.08833 (2018)
21. Sprekeler, H., Zito, T., Wiskott, L.: An extension of slow feature analysis for non-linear blind source separation. J. Mach. Learn. Res. **15**(1), 921–947 (2014)
22. Taleb, A., Jutten, C.: Source separation in post-nonlinear mixtures. IEEE Trans. Sig. Process. **47**(10), 2807–2820 (1999)
23. Veličković, P., Fedus, W., Hamilton, W.L., Liò, P., Bengio, Y., Hjelm, R.D.: Deep graph InfoMax. arXiv preprint arXiv:1809.10341 (2018)
24. Ziehe, A., Kawanabe, M., Harmeling, S., Müller, K.R.: Blind separation of post-nonlinear mixtures using linearizing transformations and temporal decorrelation. J. Mach. Learn. Res. **4**(Dec), 1319–1338 (2003)

Enhancing Explainability of Deep Reinforcement Learning Through Selective Layer-Wise Relevance Propagation

Tobias Huber$^{(\boxtimes)}$ [iD], Dominik Schiller, and Elisabeth André [iD]

Universität Augsburg, Universitätsstraße 6a, 86159 Augsburg, Germany
{huber,schiller,andre}@hcm-lab.de
http://www.hcm-lab.de

Abstract. Modern deep reinforcement learning agents are capable of achieving super-human performance in tasks like playing Atari games, solely based on visual input. However, due to their use of neural networks the trained models are lacking transparency which makes their inner workings incomprehensible for humans. A promising approach to gain insights into the opaque reasoning process of neural networks is the layer-wise relevance propagation (LRP) concept. This visualization technique creates saliency maps that highlight the areas in the input which were relevant for the agents' decision-making process. Since such saliency maps cover every possible cause for a prediction, they are often accentuating very diverse parts of the input. This makes the results difficult to understand for people without a machine-learning background. In this work, we introduce an adjustment to the LRP concept that utilizes only the most relevant neurons of each convolutional layer and thus generates more selective saliency maps. We test our approach with a dueling Deep Q-Network (DQN) agent which we trained on three different Atari games of varying complexity. Since the dueling DQN approach considerably alters the neural network architecture of the original DQN algorithm, it requires its own LRP variant which will be presented in this paper.

1 Introduction

Reinforcement learning addresses the problem of optimizing a long-term reward that an agent receives while interacting with an environment. Deep reinforcement learning (DRL) describes the combination of those methods with deep neural networks (DNN) by using a DNN as decision function of the agent.

One of the first successful applications of DRL was the deep Q-Network (DQN) developed by Mnih et al. [12]. This approach was able to achieve high-level performance across a set of 49 games for the Atari 2600 console, using the same hyperparameters and network architecture for all games, while only receiving the pixels of the game screen and the game score as input.

© Springer Nature Switzerland AG 2019
C. Benzmüller and H. Stuckenschmidt (Eds.): KI 2019, LNAI 11793, pp. 188–202, 2019.
https://doi.org/10.1007/978-3-030-30179-8_16

For a long time, DRL research only focused on optimizing the performance of DRL agents, but recent years saw an increasing interest in making the decision process of DRL agents more explainable [7,9,19,21,23]. One problem with explaining the actions of a DRL agent is that the inner workings of the underlying DNNs are incomprehensible to humans, making it difficult to identify the parts of the input on which the agent bases its decision. A common approach to tackle this challenge is the generation of saliency maps that visualize the relevance of each input pixel for the output of the network [1].

While such saliency map algorithms are already well established and were even used to improve classification models [15], they are usually developed with experienced machine learning practitioners in mind. This can make the generated explanations difficult to interpret for beginners or users who are unrelated to the field of machine learning. Weitz et al. [22], for example, found that traditional saliency maps are too fine-granular for humans to easily detect relevant features for the classification. In a recent meta-study, Miller [11] explored the explanation process between humans to derive new design paradigms for explainable artificial intelligence algorithms that can help to make such methods more accessible to non-expert users. One major finding of this study was that people usually prefer selected explanations that focus on specific evidence instead of showing every possible cause of a decision. Based on this insight, we aim to adjust an existing saliency map approach to be more focused on the parts of the input that are most relevant for the decision-making process of a system.

We base our approach on layer-wise relevance propagation (LRP): A promising concept for generating saliency maps, which visualizes how much each pixel of the input picture contributed to the output based on the activations of each neuron during the forward pass. In contrast to most other approaches, LRP offers the benefit of conserving the certainty of the prediction throughout its process, which provides the user with additional useful information. Furthermore, LRP concepts do not contain contradictory evidence, because they do not generate negative relevance values [13]. Our adjustment uses an *argmax* function to follow only the most contributing neurons of each convolutional layer, which enables us to filter out the most relevant information. Therefore we can create selective and more focused saliency maps while maintaining the advantageous properties of LRP mentioned above.

Modern DQN variants, like the rainbow algorithm [8], are employing dueling DQN systems which use two separate estimators to measure the value of the current state and the advantage of each action the agent can take in that state. To test our approach with state-of-the-art dueling DQN algorithms, we introduce a slightly adapted version of LRP that can handle the dueling DQN architecture without losing its advantageous properties. Since no other improvement of the DQN algorithm considerably changes the underlying neural network architecture, this extension allows us to use LRP on any DQN based DRL algorithm without any further adjustments.

We test our approach on three Atari 2600 games of varying complexity using the OpenAi gym and baselines libraries [4,5]. The Atari game domain is well suited for testing and introducing new RL algorithms because it offers a wide array of different tasks in similar environments.

2   Related Work

In this section, we look at successful applications of saliency maps for DNNs and DRL. Because saliency maps work best on visual input data, those methods focus on increasing the explainability of CNNs which are most often used on visual input data.

One of the first methods used to measure the relevance of pixels of visual input data is to see how much a change in that pixel impacts the prediction of the CNN. If a pixel is relevant for the decision of the model, then even small changes of the pixel will greatly impact the output of the model. This local rate of change with respect to certain inputs of the CNN can be calculated by using partial derivatives. Simonyan et al. [17] for example use the derivative of the neural network with respect to an input pixel to determine the relevance of that input pixel. To get this derivative they use the backpropagtion algorithm also used during the training of the neural network. The deconvolution [24] and guided backpropagation [18] approaches are based on the same theory but use modified versions of the backpropagation algorithm to get relevance values for the input pixels. Another similar approach is Grad-CAM [16], which uses partial derivatives of the fully connected part of a CNN with respect to the output of the last convolutional layer to identify regions inside the input, which were relevant for the specific prediction of the CNN. Guided backpropagation and Grad-CAM can be combined by computing the component-wise product of the attention maps created by the different approaches. The result is called guided Grad-CAM and creates a fine granular but class specific saliency map [16].

In contrast to those gradient-based saliency maps Bach et al. [3] proposed a method that directly uses the activations of the neurons during the forward pass to calculate the relevance of the input pixels. This is computationally efficient compared to gradient-based methods because they can reuse the values of the forward pass. Instead of calculating how much a change in an input pixel would impact the prediction, Bach et al. investigate the contribution of the input pixels to prediction. For this purpose, they do not only describe a single specific algorithm but introduce a general concept which they call layer-wise relevance propagation (LRP). This concept has two advantageous properties which gradient-based saliency maps lack. The first is the conservation property which says that the sum of all relevance values, generated by LRP, is equal to the value of the prediction. This ascertains that the relevance values reflect the certainty of the prediction. The second property is positivity which states that all relevance values are non-negative. This ascertains that the generated saliency maps do not contain contradictory evidence [13]. Some gradient-based approaches achieve positivity by squaring the partial derivatives, but this only masks the negativity for the viewer.

Another approach that uses the activations of each neuron during the forward pass was proposed by Mopuri et al. [14]. Instead of measuring the relevance of each input pixel, they search for the position of all input pixels that contributed positively to the prediction. While doing so they only track the most contributing neuron in each convolutional layer. We aim to combine this idea with the LRP concept to get a more focused version of LRP which still contains relevance values.

So far we only covered methods to generate saliency maps for deep neural networks in general. From this point on we look at implementations of saliency maps which focused on DRL. Because many DRL algorithms utilize CNNs it is possible to directly use the methods we just covered on DRL agents. Zahavy et al. [23] and Wang et al. [20] for example used gradient-based saliency maps similar to [17] on traditional and Dueling DQN algorithms. Weitkamp et al. [21] tested Grad-CAM on an Actor-Critic DRL algorithm. LRP has been used to visualize DRL in [10] but, to our knowledge, it has not been used to visualize the Dueling DQN architecture yet.

Iyer et al. [9] proposed a completely new visualization algorithm for DRL. They use template matching to identify objects in each input image and use this information as additional channels of the input to retrain the DRL agent. Given an agent trained in this way, they can measure the relevance of an identified object by comparing the prediction of the input image containing that object with the prediction for the same input image without this specific object.

Greydanus et al. [7] also propose a new algorithm, where they selectively blur regions of the input image and measure how much this changes the output of the DRL agent. The idea behind this is to introduce uncertainty to the blurred area and to see how much the DRL agent is influenced by the loss of information in that area.

The approaches of Iyer et al. and Greydanus et al. both lack the conservation property of LRP.

3   Saliency Maps

In this section, we revisit the foundations of LRP and show how to use it on the original DQN. Then we propose an adjustment to this algorithm which generates more focused saliency maps. In the last subsection, we introduce a way to apply those LRP algorithms to the Dueling DQN architecture.

3.1   Foundations

LRP does not describe a specific algorithm but a concept which can be applied to any classifier f that fulfills the following two requirements. First, f has to be decomposable into several layers of computation where each layer can be modeled as a vector of real-valued functions. Secondly, the first layer has to be the input x of the classifier containing, for example, the input pixels of an image and the last layer has to be the real-valued prediction of the classifier $f(x)$. Any DRL agent fulfills those requirements if we only consider the output value that corresponds to the action we want to analyze.

For a given input x, the goal of any method following the LRP concept is to assign relevance values R_j^l to each computational unit j of each layer of computation l in such a way that R_j^l measures the local contribution of the unit j to the prediction $f(x)$. A method of calculating those relevance values R_j^l is said to follow the LRP concept if it sets the relevance value of the output unit to be the prediction $f(x)$ and calculates all other relevance values by defining

$$R_j^l := \sum_{k \in \{j \text{ is input for neuron } k\}} R_{j \leftarrow k}^{l,l+1}, \tag{1}$$

for **messages** $R_{j \leftarrow k}^{l,l+1}$, such that

$$R_k^{l+1} = \sum_{j \in \{j \text{ is input for neuron } k\}} R_{j \leftarrow k}^{l,l+1}. \tag{2}$$

In this way a LRP variant is determined by choosing messages $R_{j \leftarrow k}^{l,l+1}$. Through definition 1 it is then possible to calculate all relevance values R_j^l in a backward pass, starting from the prediction $f(x)$ and going towards the input layer. Furthermore Eq. 2 gives rise to

$$\sum_k R_k^{l+1} = \sum_k \sum_{j \in \{j \text{ is input for neuron } k\}} R_{j \leftarrow k}^{l,l+1}$$
$$= \sum_j \sum_{k \in \{j \text{ is input for neuron } k\}} R_{j \leftarrow k}^{l,l+1} = \sum_j R_j^l. \tag{3}$$

This ensures that the relevance values of each layer l are a linear decomposition of the prediction

$$f(x) = \cdots = \sum_{j=1}^{dim(l)} R_j^l = \cdots = \sum_{j=1}^{dim(input)} R_j^{input}. \tag{4}$$

Such a linear decomposition is easier to interpret than the original classifier because we can think of positive values R_j^l to contribute evidence in favor of the decision of the classifier and of negative relevance values to contribute evidence against the decision.

To use LRP on a DQN agent we first have to look at its network architecture. The DQN f, as introduced by Mnih et al. [12], consists of three convolutional layers $conv_1, ..., conv_3$ followed by two fully connected layers fc_1 and fc_2. For an input x we write $fc_i(x)$ and $conv_i(x)$ for the output of the layers fc_i and $conv_i$ respectively during the forward pass that calculates $f(x)$.

In this notation, the Q-Values (i. e. the output of the whole DQN) are $fc_2(x)$.

Following the LRP notation, we denote the relevance value of the j-th neuron in the layer l with R_j^l. As seen before we have to define messages $R_{j \leftarrow k}^{l,l+1}$ for any two consecutive Layers $l, l+1$ to determine a LRP variant. For now we assume that $l+1$ is one of the fully connected layers fc_i. The convolutional case works analogously and will be covered in more detail in the next chapter. $R^{l,l+1}_{j \leftarrow k}$ should measure the contribution of the j-th neuron of fc_{i-1} to the k-th neuron of fc_i, therefore we have to look at the calculation of $fc_i(x)_k$. The fully connected layer fc_i uses a weight matrix W_i, a bias vector b_i and an activation function σ_i as parameters for its output. Let W_i^k be the k-th row of W_i and b_i^k the k-th entry of b_i. Then the activation of the k-th neuron in $fc_i(x)$ is

$$\sigma_i(W_i^k \cdot fc_{i-1}(x) + b_i^k), \tag{5}$$

where $\cdot$ denotes the dot product and fc_0 is the flattened output of $conv_3$.

Usually the ReLU function $\sigma(x) = max(0, x)$ is used as activation function σ_i in the DQN architecture. Bach et al. [3] argue that any monotonous increasing function σ with $\sigma(0) = 0$, like the ReLU function, conserves the relevance of the dot product $W_i^k \cdot fc_{i-1}(x)$. Newer LRP variants, like the one used by Montavon et al. [13], also omit the bias when defining $R^{l,l+1}_{j \leftarrow k}$. With those two assumptions the relevance of each neuron of fc_{i-1} to $fc_i(x)_k$ is the same as their contribution to the dot product $W_i^k \cdot fc_{i-1}(x) = \sum_j w_{jk} fc_{i-1}(x)_j$. This is a linear decomposition, so we can use $w_{jk} fc_{i-1}(x)_j$ to measure the contribution of the j-th neuron of fc_{i-1}.

Since we want to find the parts of the input that contributed evidence in favor of the decision of the DQN agent, we restrict ourself to the positive parts of that sum. That is we set

$$z^+_{jk} := \begin{cases} w_{jk} fc_{i-1}(x)_j & \text{if } w_{jk} fc_{i-1}(x)_j > 0 \\ 0 & \text{if } w_{jk} fc_{i-1}(x)_j \leq 0 \end{cases}. \tag{6}$$

With this, we define the messages as $R^{l,l+1}_{j \leftarrow k} := \frac{z^+_{jk}}{\sum_j z^+_{jk}} R^{l+1}_k$. This method is called z^+-rule (without bias) and satisfies the LRP Eq. 2.

3.2 An Argmax Approach to LRP

In this subsection, we introduce our adjustment to an LRP variant called z^+-rule which we revisited in the last subsection. Recent work [6,9] indicates that DRL agents mainly focus on whole objects, for example cars or balls, within the visual input. With our approach, we aim to generate saliency maps that reflect this property by focusing on the most relevant parts of the input instead of giving too many details. For this purpose, we propose to use an *argmax* function to find the most contributing neurons in each convolutional layer.

This idea is inspired by Mopuri et al. [14], who generated visualizations for neural networks solely based on the positions of neurons that provide evidence in favor of the prediction. During this process, they follow only the most contributing neurons in each convolutional layer. Our method adds relevance values to the positions of those neurons and therefore expands the approach of Mopuri et al. by an additional dimension of information. Since those relevance values follow the LRP concept, they also possess the advantageous properties of the LRP concept like conservation of the prediction value.

As we have seen in the foundations Sect. 3.1, a LRP method is defined by its messages $R_{j\leftarrow k}^{l,l+1}$ which propagate the relevance from a layer $l+1$ to the preceding layer l. If $l+1$ is a fully connected layer fc_i of the DQN (see Sect. 3.1 for our notation of the DQN architecture), we use the same messages that are used in the z^+-rule. In the case that l and $l+1$ are convolutional layers $conv_{i-1}$ and $conv_i$, we propose new messages based on the $argmax$ function. To define those messages we analyze how the activation of a neuron $conv_i(x)_k$ was calculated during the forward pass.

Let W and A denote the weight kernel and part of $conv_{i-1}(x)$ respectively that were used to calculate $conv_i(x)_k$ during the forward pass. If we write W and A in appropriate vector form, we get

$$conv_i(x)_k = \sigma(\sum_j w_j a_j + b), \tag{7}$$

where σ denotes the activation function of $conv_i$ and b the bias corresponding to W. Analogously to the z^+-rule we assume that the activation function and the bias can be neglected when determining the relevance values of the inputs a_i. We propose to use an $argmax$ function to find the most relevant input neurons by defining the messages in the following way

$$R_{j\leftarrow k}^{l,l+1} := \begin{cases} R_k^{l+1} & \text{if } j = argmax\{w_j a_j\} \\ 0 & \text{if not.} \end{cases} \tag{8}$$

This definition satisfies the LRP condition given by Eq. 2 because the only non vanishing summand of the sum

$$\sum_{j\in\{j \text{ is input for neuron } k\}} R_{j\leftarrow k}^{l,l+1} \tag{9}$$

is R_k^{l+1}.

If we use the same $argmax$ approach to propagate relevance values from $conv_1$ to the input $conv_0$, then we get very sparse saliency maps where only a few neurons are highlighted. If we highlight the whole areas of the input $conv_0$ that were used to calculate relevant neurons of $conv_1$, then we lose information about the relevance values inside those areas. Therefore we draw inspiration from the guided Grad-CAM approach introduced in [16]. Guided Grad-CAM uses one throughout relevance analysis for the neurons of the last convolutional layer to get relevant areas for the specific prediction and another throughout relevance calculation for the input pixels to get fine granular relevance values inside those areas. We already did a throughout analysis of the neurons of the last convolutional layer by using the z^+-rule on the fully connected layers. By following the most relevant neurons through the convolutional layers we keep track of the input areas that contributed the most to those values. Mimicking the second throughout analysis of the Guided Grad-CAM approach we propose to use the z^+-rule to propagate relevance values from $conv_1$ to $conv_0$. This generates fine granular relevance values inside the areas identified by following the most

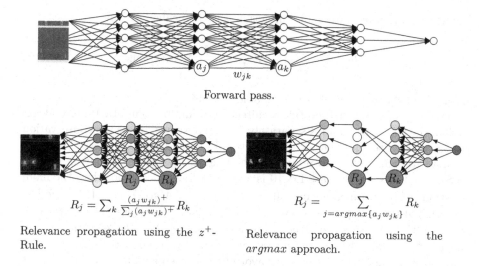

Forward pass.

$$R_j = \sum_k \frac{(a_j w_{jk})^+}{\sum_j (a_j w_{jk})^+} R_k$$

$$R_j = \sum_{j=argmax\{a_j w_{jk}\}} R_k$$

Relevance propagation using the z^+-Rule.

Relevance propagation using the $argmax$ approach.

Fig. 1. A visualization of how our $argmax$ approach differs from the z^+ Rule.

contributing neurons and ascertains that those relevance values follow the LRP concept.

Figure 1 visualizes the differences between our $argmax$ approach and the z^+-rule. We implemented our proposed algorithm for the OpenAi baselines library [5] and plan to integrate it in the iNNvestigate framework [2].

3.3   LRP on Dueling Q-Networks

The dueling Q-network is a neural network architecture first introduced by Wang et al. in [20] as an improvement of the neural network architecture used in the DQN algorithm [12]. Because it is only changing the architecture of the neural network, it is independent of the training algorithm. Therefore it can easily be combined with other improvements of the DQN algorithm. This can be seen in the rainbow algorithm, the current state of the art deep Q-learning algorithm [8], which combines many different improvements of the DQN algorithm. We chose Dueling DQN because the LRP concept only depends on the neural network architecture. Therefore applying LRP to the Dueling DQN architecture suffices to apply LRP on all currently used versions of the DQN algorithm.

Instead of using a single fully connected network after the convolutional part of the DQN, the Dueling DQN architecture uses two fully connected networks A and S which both use the output of the last convolutional layer as input. These two fully connected networks share the same architecture apart from their output layer. For an input state s, the state value network S has only one single output neuron $S(s)$ which measures the value of the state s. The network A has an output neuron $A(s, a)$ for each action a which describes the advantage of choosing the action a in the state s. The Q-Value (the prediction of the whole model) for an input state s and an action a is then calculated by

$$Q(s,a) = S(s) + A(s,a) - \frac{1}{N} \sum_{i=1}^{N} A(s,a_i), \tag{10}$$

where N denotes the number of available actions a_i.

One way of using LRP on this architecture would be to use LRP methods on each of the networks S and A separately, but then we would lose the conservation property because the relevance values would not add up to $Q(s,a)$. Therefore we have to define a way to propagate the relevance value of the output $Q(s,a)$ to $S(s)$ and $A(s,a)$. Because Eq. 10 is already a linear decomposition, the main question is how we handle the summand $-\frac{1}{N}\sum_{i=1}^{N}A(s,a_i)$. For this we follow the original thought process of Wang et al. in [20], where they treat $(A(s,a) - \frac{1}{N}\sum_{i=1}^{N}A(s,a_i))$ as the modified contribution of $A(s,a)$ to $Q(s,a)$. Analogously to the z^+-rule we only propagate those values if they are positive since we want to exclusively highlight evidence in favor of the chosen action a . That is we set

$$S(s)^+ := max(0, S(s)) \tag{11}$$

$$A(s,a)^+ := max\Big(0, A(s,a) - \frac{1}{N} \sum_{i=1}^{N} A(s,a_i)\Big). \tag{12}$$

If we would use these values as LRP messages, then the LRP Eq. 2 would not hold if either of $S(s)$ or $A(s,a)$ are negative. Therefore we set the LRP messages analogously to the z^+-rule as:

$$R_{S(s)\leftarrow Q(s,a)} := \frac{S(s)^+}{S(s)^+ + A(s,a)^+} Q(s,a) \tag{13}$$

$$R_{A(s,a)\leftarrow Q(s,a)} := \frac{A(s,a)^+}{S(s)^+ + A(s,a)^+} Q(s,a). \tag{14}$$

If both $S(s)$ and $A(s,a)$ are negative, then there is no evidence in favor of the prediction. Consequently, it is justified that we do not propagate any relevance values in this case.

4   Results and Discussion

In order to verify that our *argmax* approach, described in Sect. 3.2, creates more selective saliency maps then the r^+-rule (see Sect. 3.1), we tested our approach on three different Atari 2600 games and will present the results of those experiments in this section. For all games, we trained an agent using the DQN implementation of the OpenAi baselines framework [5]. Since this implementation utilizes the Dueling DQN architecture [20], we used the approach described in 3.3 to apply LRP to this architecture.

We keep track of which relevance values correspond to the state value and the action advantage values and differentiate them by coloring them red and

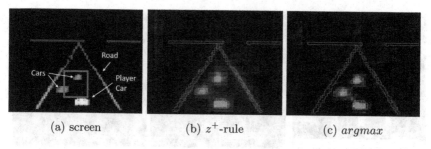

(a) screen   (b) z^+-rule   (c) $argmax$

Fig. 2. A comparison of action advantage analysis: The left image (a) shows a screen from the Atari game Enduro with additional descriptions. The red area was identified as relevant by gradient-based saliency maps in [20]. While the z^+-rule (b) highlights the cars and the edge of the road even though it is not important in this situation, our $argmax$ approach (c) selects only the relevant cars. (Color figure online)

green respectively. This allows us to compare our saliency maps with the ones generated by gradient-based methods in [20] for a Duelling DQN agent trained on the Atari game Enduro. In this simple driving game, the Player controls a car and has to avoid hitting other cars while overtaking as many of them as possible. The left image of Fig. 2 shows a screen from this game in the preprocessed form that the agent received. The area that was identified as relevant for the action advantage value in similar game-states by the gradient-based saliency maps in [20] is marked in red. To facilitate readability, we added descriptions of the important game objects and cut off the lower part of the screen which only contains the score. The middle and right images show saliency maps generated by the z^+-rule and our $argmax$ approach respectively for the game-state shown in the left image. All three saliency maps identified the area in front of the player car as the most relevant area. The gradient-based saliency map in [20] focused strongly on this region but was not fine-grained enough to select individual cars. The z^+-rule, on the other hand, emphasizes all the relevant cars but does not focus on the area in front of the agent. Instead, it also highlights the general course of the road which is not particularly important in this situation. Our $argmax$ approach is the most selective and only highlights the relevant cars inside the area which was also identified by the gradient-based approach.

The second game we trained our agent on is called Space Invaders. In this game, the agent controls a cannon, which can move horizontally along the bottom of the screen, and has to destroy descending waves of aliens. Additionally, the player needs to evade incoming projectiles fired from the aliens or to take cover behind three floating obstacles. In contrast to purely reactive games like Enduro, Space Invaders requires the agent to develop long-term strategies, as it has to determine an order in which it destroys the aliens in each wave and also has to decide when to hide behind obstacles.

While this does not necessarily imply that the game is harder to learn for an agent, analyzing the trained model might lead to a better understanding of an optimal strategy to solve this game.

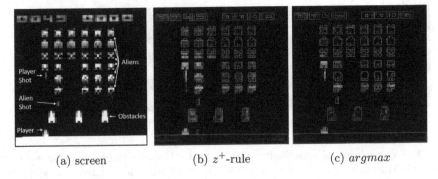

| (a) screen | (b) z^+-rule | (c) $argmax$ |

Fig. 3. The first image (a) shows a screen of the Atari game Space Invaders with additional descriptions. The saliency map created for this game-state by the z^+-rule (b) highlights most of the aliens and all the obstacles while our $argmax$ approach (c) focuses on the first row of aliens which the agent can actually hit.

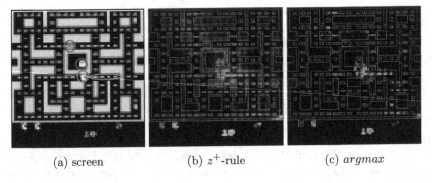

| (a) screen | (b) z^+-rule | (c) $argmax$ |

Fig. 4. The left image (a) shows a screen of Pacman. The player (green circle) has to collect pellets (blue area) while avoiding ghosts (red circles). The saliency map created for this game-state by the z^+-rule (b) highlights a huge area as relevant while our $argmax$ approach (c) focuses on the vicinity of the player. (Color figure online)

Figure 3 shows a comparison of the two different saliency map approaches for a specific game-state of space invaders. Both the z^+-rule, as well as the $argmax$ approach are showing that the agent mostly considers the aliens positioned on the outline of the grid as relevant. However the $argmax$ approach does so more clearly by only highlighting aliens on the outline of the grid. This selection makes sense since the other enemies cannot be hit by the agent.

Our selective $argmax$-rule further shows that the agent is not paying attention to the obstacles. Given a certain performance level of our model, this suggests that they might not be a necessary component of an optimal strategy for Space Invaders.

In this way, our selective saliency maps enable us not only to find errors in our model but also to pass on the learned knowledge to human players.

The last game we used to verify our approach is MsPacman, where the player has to navigate through a maze and collect pellets while avoiding enemy ghosts. Because this game contains many important objects and gives the agent a huge variety of possible strategies, DQN agents struggle in this environment and perform worse than the average human player [12]. Transparency methods are especially desirable in environments like this, where the agent is struggling because they help us to understand where the agent had difficulties. The saliency map created by the z^+-rule (see Fig. 4 b) reflects the complexity of MsPacman by showing that the agent tries to look at nearly all of the objects in the game. This information might be helpful to optimize the DRL agent, but it also distracts from the areas which influenced the agents' decision the most. Figure 4 shows that the saliency map created by the *argmax* approach is more focused on the vicinity of the agent and makes it clearer what the agent is focusing on the most. Figure 4 further illustrates that a fine-granular saliency map in the vicinity of the agent is necessary to see that the agent will most likely decide on moving to the right as his next action.

For the sake of completeness, we want to mention that a similar selective effect can be obtained by using the z^+-rule and implementing some kind of threshold, for example only showing the highest 1% of all relevance values. However, this approach comes with its own set of challenges. While a threshold might be suited for one environment it might be too high or low for other environments, presenting too much or too less information (see for example Fig. 5). Our proposed approach is independent of the environment which eliminates the need to empirically determine a specific threshold for each new problem. Furthermore, the conservation property of LRP is lost by simply removing relevance values.

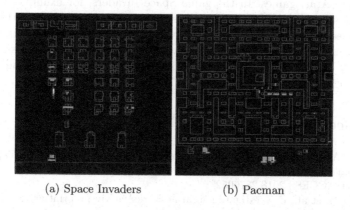

(a) Space Invaders   (b) Pacman

Fig. 5. Only showing the top 42 relevance values created by the z^+-rule produces a saliency map (a) which is similar to the one created by our *argmax*-approach for Space Invaders in Fig. 3(c). Using the same threshold for Pacman (b) we lose some relevant information since, in contrast to 4(c), the position of the player is no longer highlighted.

Therefore the generated saliency maps are not proportional to the prediction which makes it harder to compare different saliency maps.

In total, our experiments have shown that our approach can be used on three games, each of which presents a different challenge, and that it generates informative saliency maps that are more selective than the ones generated by the z^+-rule.

5 Conclusion

In this paper, we presented two adjustments to the LRP concept which enable compatibility with state of the art deep reinforcement learning approaches and increase the selectivity of the generated saliency maps while maintaining all desired properties of the original algorithm. For one, we have shown a way to use LRP on the Dueling DQN architecture, which makes it possible to use LRP on all current versions of the DQN algorithm. Secondly, we introduced an adjustment to an existing LRP variant, which generates saliency maps that focus more on the important objects inside the input image.

We tested our approach on three different Atari 2600 games and verified that the saliency maps generated by our system are more selective than the ones created by existing LRP methods, while still including the information expected from visual explanations. Since this selectiveness is an important property of inter-human explanations we argue that our approach might prove beneficial, when it comes to explain the actions of a trained agent to people without a machine-learning background. Understanding an agents reasoning process is especially interesting since DQN agents are already outperforming human players in many Atari games. In the game Space Invaders, for example, the analysis of our selective saliency maps helped us to formulate the hypothesis that the obstacles, which protect the agent from enemy projectiles, are not relevant for an optimal strategy. In the future, we would like to further investigate the potential of our approach to impart the learned knowledge, which leads to such achievements, to a human user.

References

1. Adadi, A., Berrada, M.: Peeking inside the black-box: a survey on explainable artificial intelligence (XAI). IEEE Access **6**, 52138–52160 (2018). https://doi.org/10.1109/ACCESS.2018.2870052
2. Alber, M., et al.: iNNvestigate neural networks! arXiv preprint arXiv:1808.04260 (2018)
3. Bach, S., Binder, A., Montavon, G., Klauschen, F., Müller, K.R., Samek, W.: On pixel-wise explanations for non-linear classifier decisions by layer-wise relevance propagation. Plos One **10**(7), e0130140 (2015). https://doi.org/10.1371/journal.pone.0130140
4. Brockman, G., et al.: Openai gym. arXiv preprint arXiv:1606.01540 (2016)
5. Dhariwal, P., et al.: Openai baselines (2017). https://github.com/openai/baselines

6. Goel, V., Weng, J., Poupart, P.: Unsupervised video object segmentation for deep reinforcement learning. In: Advances in Neural Information Processing Systems 31: Annual Conference on Neural Information Processing Systems 2018, NeurIPS 2018, Montréal, Canada, 3–8 December 2018, pp. 5688–5699 (2018). http://papers.nips.cc/paper/7811-unsupervised-video-object-segmentation-for-deep-reinforcement-learning
7. Greydanus, S., Koul, A., Dodge, J., Fern, A.: Visualizing and understanding atari agents. In: Proceedings of the 35th International Conference on Machine Learning, ICML 2018, Stockholmsmässan, Stockholm, Sweden, 10–15 July 2018, pp. 1787–1796 (2018). http://proceedings.mlr.press/v80/greydanus18a.html
8. Hessel, M., et al.: Rainbow: combining improvements in deep reinforcement learning. In: Proceedings of the 32nd Conference on Artificial Intelligence, AAAI 2018, pp. 3215–3222 (2018)
9. Iyer, R., Li, Y., Li, H., Lewis, M., Sundar, R., Sycara, K.P.: Transparency and explanation in deep reinforcement learning neural networks. In: Proceedings of the 2018 AAAI/ACM Conference on AI, Ethics, and Society, AIES 2018, New Orleans, LA, USA, 02–03 February 2018, pp. 144–150 (2018). https://doi.org/10.1145/3278721.3278776
10. Lapuschkin, S., Wäldchen, S., Binder, A., Montavon, G., Samek, W., Müller, K.R.: Unmasking clever hans predictors and assessing what machines really learn. Nat. Commun. **10**(1), 1096 (2019)
11. Miller, T.: Explanation in artificial intelligence: insights from the social sciences. Artif. Intell. **267**, 1–38 (2019). https://doi.org/10.1016/j.artint.2018.07.007
12. Mnih, V., et al.: Human-level control through deep reinforcement learning. Nature **518**(7540), 529–533 (2015)
13. Montavon, G., Samek, W., Müller, K.: Methods for interpreting and understanding deep neural networks. Digit. Sig. Process. **73**, 1–15 (2018). https://doi.org/10.1016/j.dsp.2017.10.011
14. Mopuri, K.R., Garg, U., Babu, R.V.: Cnn fixations: an unraveling approach to visualize the discriminative image regions. IEEE Trans. Image Process. **28**(5), 2116–2125 (2019)
15. Schiller, D., Huber, T., Lingenfelser, F., Dietz, M., Seiderer, A., André, E.: Relevance-based feature masking: Improving neural network based whale classification through explainable artificial intelligence. In: 20th Annual Conference of the International Speech Communication Association INTERSPEECH (2019, in press)
16. Selvaraju, R.R., Cogswell, M., Das, A., Vedantam, R., Parikh, D., Batra, D.: Grad-cam: visual explanations from deep networks via gradient-based localization. In: IEEE International Conference on Computer Vision, ICCV 2017, Venice, Italy, 22–29 October 2017, pp. 618–626 (2017). https://doi.org/10.1109/ICCV.2017.74
17. Simonyan, K., Vedaldi, A., Zisserman, A.: Deep inside convolutional networks: visualising image classification models and saliency maps. CoRR abs/1312.6034 (2013)
18. Springenberg, J.T., Dosovitskiy, A., Brox, T., Riedmiller, M.A.: Striving for simplicity: the all convolutional net. CoRR abs/1412.6806 (2014)
19. Such, F.P., et al.: An atari model zoo for analyzing, visualizing, and comparing deep reinforcement learning agents. CoRR abs/1812.07069 (2018)
20. Wang, Z., Schaul, T., Hessel, M., van Hasselt, H., Lanctot, M., de Freitas, N.: Dueling network architectures for deep reinforcement learning. In: Proceedings of the 33nd International Conference on Machine Learning, ICML 2016, New York City,

NY, USA, 19–24 June 2016, pp. 1995–2003 (2016). http://jmlr.org/proceedings/papers/v48/wangf16.html

21. Weitkamp, L., van der Pol, E., Akata, Z.: Visual rationalizations in deep reinforcement learning for atari games. CoRR arXiv:1902.00566, February 2019

22. Weitz, K., Hassan, T., Schmid, U., Garbas, J.U.: Deep-learned faces of pain and emotions: elucidating the differences of facial expressions with the help of explainable AI methods. tm-Technisches Messen **86**(7–8), 404–412 (2019). https://doi.org/10.1515/teme-2019-0024

23. Zahavy, T., Ben-Zrihem, N., Mannor, S.: Graying the black box: Understanding DQNs. In: Proceedings of the 33nd International Conference on Machine Learning, ICML 2016, New York City, NY, USA, 19–24 June 2016, pp. 1899–1908 (2016). http://jmlr.org/proceedings/papers/v48/zahavy16.html

24. Zeiler, M.D., Fergus, R.: Visualizing and understanding convolutional networks. In: Fleet, D., Pajdla, T., Schiele, B., Tuytelaars, T. (eds.) ECCV 2014. LNCS, vol. 8689, pp. 818–833. Springer, Cham (2014). https://doi.org/10.1007/978-3-319-10590-1_53

A Crow Search-Based Genetic Algorithm for Solving Two-Dimensional Bin Packing Problem

Soukaina Laabadi[1](✉), Mohamed Naimi[2], Hassan El Amri[1],
and Boujemâa Achchab[2]

[1] Laboratory of Mathematics and Applications, ENS - Hassan II University,
Casablanca, Morocco
soukainalaabadi@gmail.com
[2] Laboratory of Analysis, Modeling Systems and Decision Support,
ENSA - Hassan I University, Berrechid, Morocco

Abstract. The two-dimensional bin packing problem (2D-BPP) consists of packing, without overlapping, a set of rectangular items with different sizes into smallest number of rectangular containers, called "bins", having identical dimensions. According to the real-word requirements, the items may either have a fixed orientation or they can be rotated by 90°. In addition, it may or not be subjugate to the guillotine cutting. In this article, we consider the two-dimensional bin packing problem with fixed orientation and free cutting. In fact, we propose a hybrid approach by combining two bio-inspired algorithms that are the crow search algorithm (CSA) and the genetic algorithm (GA) to solve the considered problem. So, the main idea behind this hybridization is to expect reaching a sort of cooperative synergy between the operators of the two combined algorithms. That is, the CSA is discretized and adapted to the 2D-BPP context, while using genetic operators to improve individuals (i.e. crows) adaptation. The average performance of the proposed hybrid approach is evaluated on the standard benchmark instances of the considered problem and compared with two other bio-inspired algorithms having closely similar nature; namely standard genetic algorithm and binary particle swarm optimization algorithm. The obtained results are very promising.

Keywords: Two-dimensional bin packing problem · Bio-inspired algorithms · Crow search algorithm · Genetic algorithm · Hybridization

1 Introduction

The bin packing problem belongs to the family of cutting and packing (C&P) problems [1]. It occupies an important place in the literature of C&P problems, as it can be encountered in several fields, such as logistics [2], industry [3], and Cloud computing [4]. In this paper, we consider the bin packing problem of rectangles, called two-dimensional bin packing problem (2D-BPP). Given a finite number of small rectangles (*items*), and an undetermined number of large and identical rectangles (*bins*). The aim is to allocate all items, without overlapping, to a minimum number of bins. Formally,

© Springer Nature Switzerland AG 2019
C. Benzmüller and H. Stuckenschmidt (Eds.): KI 2019, LNAI 11793, pp. 203–215, 2019.
https://doi.org/10.1007/978-3-030-30179-8_17

204 S. Laabadi et al.

we have a set of n items; each item j is characterized by a width w_j and a height $h_j (j = 1, \ldots, n)$, additionally to an unlimited number of bins, each bin has a width W and a height H. The goal is to minimize the number of used bins to pack all items by respecting the loading capacity $(W \times H)$ of each used bin. The items are packed with their edges parallel to those of bins. In addition, each item must be packed in one and only one bin. We assume, without loss of generality, that all input data are positive integers satisfying $h_j \leq H$ and $w_j \leq W$, for all $j \in \{1, \ldots, n\}$. No further restriction is present: The items cannot be rotated by 90°, and we do not impose the so-called guillotine cutting, which means that the items are obtained through a sequence of edge-to-edge cuts parallel to the edges of the bin.

Several variants of 2D-BPP exist in the literature. In most cases, they are classified into four categories according to two criteria: whether or not the items could be rotated by 90° and whether or not a guillotine cutting is required. The reader is referred to [5] for more details. The availability of information about items is another aspect to distinguish two other different categories of 2D-BPP, which are online and offline 2D-BPP. Online version means that items arrive one by one and we don't have any information about the complete items sequence [6]. Offline version means that all items are known before they are packed. This latter is the standard version of 2D-BPP. Other extensions of 2D-BPP depend on the fragility of items [7, 8], priority of items [9], and compatibility between items. Indeed, in some fields, items may be incompatible, and have to be separated by a safety distance when they are packed in the same bin [10] or they must be packed totally in different bins [11].

The 2D-BPP is NP-hard in the strong sense [5] since it is a generalization of the well-known one-dimensional bin packing problem (1D-BPP). Exact methods cannot calculate optimal solutions in reasonable runtime for such problems, especially in large-scale instances. So, heuristics and metaheuristics are the methods of choice. Traditional heuristic methods for solving 2D-BPP include level-oriented heuristics are proposed in [12]. Other heuristics dedicated to different variants of 2D-BPP are introduced in [5]. In [13], the authors have proposed a set-covering-based heuristic approach. Recently, the authors in [14], have designed a multi-start algorithm based on probabilistic version of Wang and Lee's heuristic [15]. To enhance the search ability hoping to find high-quality solutions, the recent studies are widely focalized on metaheuristic approaches. In [5], the authors have incorporated their proposed heuristics in Tabu search algorithm which is proved to be effective for solving 2D-BPP. In [16], a new Greedy Randomized Adaptive Search Procedure (GRASP) is designed, in which the constructive phase is based on maximal-space heuristic (see [17]), while in the improvement phase, several new moves are combined with Variable Neighborhood Descent (VND). Moreover, the authors in [18], have proposed a new random-key genetic algorithm (RKGA) that uses the maximal-space concept to manage free space in bins. We note that RKGA is a genetic algorithm in which the chromosomes are represented as vectors of randomly generated real numbers in the interval [0, 1]. In [19], the authors have proposed an improved genetic algorithm and a simulated annealing method to solve 2D-BPP. In [20], the authors have developed an evolutionary algorithm by combining it with Wang and Lee's heuristic. Nevertheless, only few researchers have been interested by swarm intelligence algorithms to solve 2D-

BPP. An improved version of particle swarm optimization algorithm (PSO) is proposed in [21], wherein they used a second global best position of all particles additionally to the global and the personal best positions. Otherwise, an evolutionary PSO dealing with multi-objective 2D-BPP is introduced in [22].

The remainder of the paper is organized as follows. In Sect. 2, we give briefly the principles of CSA and GA. Our proposed CSA based on genetic operators, called CSGA, is described in Sect. 3. The results reached by the proposed algorithm are presented and analyzed in Sect. 4. Finally, we give some conclusions in Sect. 5.

2 Background

In this section, we will briefly review genetic algorithm and crow search algorithm.

2.1 Genetic Algorithm Principle

GA is a bio-inspired algorithm developed from the natural reproduction process. In general, GA maintains a population with a certain number of encoded individuals. Each member is encoded as a *chromosome* that represents a candidate solution, and it is composed of *genes* that correspond to decision variables of the optimization problem. The quality of chromosomes is evaluated with a fitness function. In fact, GA starts with an initial population of chromosomes and then conducts selection, crossover, and mutation operators to improve its population generation by generation until satisfying the stopping criterion (*i.e.* a maximum number of generation or a fixed amount of time). For more details about GA, one can refer to [23]. A conventional GA works as follows:

- Generate randomly an initial population of chromosomes.
- Repeat until the stopping criterion is met:
    - Execute selection operation in the whole population. The selected chromosomes (parents) will participate to reproduction.
    - Recombine pairs of parents with a probability p_c to breed offspring chromosomes, by applying a crossover operator.
    - Mutate the offspring chromosomes with a probability p_m to avoid the classical problem of GA; that is premature convergence.
    - Replace the population of parents with the generated offspring chromosomes thanks to a replacement strategy.
- Return the best chromosome as a global optimum of the considered problem.

2.2 Crow Search Algorithm Principle

CSA is a recent bio-inspired algorithm developed from the crows' behavior for hiding food and finding it later if needed. CSA maintains a swarm with N crows. Each crow is encoded by its position (hiding place) in d-dimensional environment $x_i(G) = \left(x_i^1(G), x_i^2(G), \ldots, x_i^d(G) \right)$, where $i \in \{1, \ldots, N\}$ and G is the generation number. Each crow position corresponds to a feasible solution in search space. Each crow i has a memory $m_i(G)$, at the generation G, where it memorizes its best hiding place. The quality of positions is measured by a fitness or objective function of the optimization problem.

The CSA starts with initial positions of crows and sets the memory of crows to their initial positions, and then iteratively updates the position and the memory of crows according to the following formulas:

$$x_i(G) = \begin{cases} x_i(G-1) + r_i \times FL \times (m_j(G-1) - x_i(G-1)) & \text{if } r_j \geq AP \\ a \text{ random position} & \text{otherwise} \end{cases} \quad (1)$$

$$m_i(G) = \begin{cases} x_i(G) & \text{if } f(x_i(G)) \geq f(m_i(G-1)) \\ m_i(G-1) & \text{otherwise} \end{cases} \quad (2)$$

In fact, at each generation, each crow i selects randomly a crow j from the swarm in order to follow it aiming to steal its food. If the crow j knows about the presence of crow i, the former fools the latter by moving towards a random position. We note that FL is the crows flight length, AP is the awareness probability, $f(.)$ is the fitness function, while r_i and r_j are uniform distributed random numbers in the interval $[0, 1]$.

The CSA terminates when a maximum number of generations is met. Then, it picks out the overall best memory in the swarm as a global optimum of the problem.

For more details, we invite the readers to refer to the original paper of CSA [24].

3   Crow Search-Based Genetic Algorithm

It is worth mentioning that the CSA cannot be directly applied to binary-valued optimization problems. To the best of our knowledge, [25] was the first work to deal with a binary version of CSA, in which the authors have applied a v-shaped binarization technique to resolve the feature selection problem. In this paper, we propose a hybrid approach to solve 2D-BPP. Our approach combines GA with CSA, and we call it Crow Search-based Genetic Algorithm (CSGA). That is, we are first motivated by the smart behavior of crows in CSA and then by the evolutionary behavior of individuals in GA. Besides, the GA operators can be easily and even directly adapted in binary search spaces. In comparison with GA, in the CSGA each member of the population participates with its own information to crossover operation. So, the crossover probability is not considered and the algorithm doesn't need a replacement strategy to create the upcoming generations. In comparison with CSA, in the CSGA each crow i selects one of the crows in the swarm as direction to follow it using a selection operator. In addition, a mutation operator is applied with a mutation probability, in order to increase the population diversity. The following subsections will elaborate the full process of our proposed CSGA.

3.1   Building Initial Population

The positions of crows in d-dimensional environment are elaborated by allocating a given item or not to a given bin. So, each position is considered as a potential solution of the problem. It is encoded as a $n \times d$ matrix, where n is the number of items to be packed into bins, and d is regarded as the number of available bins. The representation of each solution i, in a population having N crows, is shown below:

$$X^i = \left(x^i_{jk}\right) \in \{0,1\}^{n \times d}; \quad for \, i \in \{1, \ldots, N\} \tag{3}$$

For all i, the decision variable x^i_{jk} takes the value 1 if the j-th item is packed in the k-th bin, and it is equal to 0 otherwise. For the sake of clarity, an item is allocated to one and only one bin, then it is immediately removed from the list of items. Moreover, the packing of each item might respect the Bottom-Left strategy that consists of placing an item in the lowest and the left-most position of a given bin (see [12]).

The memory matrix M^i has the same dimensions as the position matrix X^i of each crow i. In the initial stage, the position matrix coefficients are generated randomly and the position matrix coincides with memory matrix of each crow i.

3.2 Evaluating Feasibility and Quality of Solutions

On one hand, the random process used at the initial stage can generate infeasible solutions. A solution is regarded as infeasible whether it violates the capacity constraint (see Eq. (4)) of at least one of the used bins:

$$for \, i \in \{1, \ldots, N\} : \sum_{j=1}^{n} w_j \times h_j \times x^i_{jk} \leq W \times H \times y_k; \forall k \in \{1, \ldots, d\} \tag{4}$$

Where

$$y_k = \begin{cases} 1 & \text{if the bin } k \text{ is used} \\ 0 & \text{otherwise} \end{cases} \tag{5}$$

Notice that the bin k is considered as a used bin, if $\sum_{j=1}^{n} x^i_{jk} \geq 1$, i.e. it contains at least one item, while it is not considered whether $\sum_{j=1}^{n} x^i_{jk} = 0$.

Meanwhile, to restore the feasibility of infeasible solutions. A repair operator is applied that consists of removing items from exceeded bins iteratively until the capacity of the corresponding bins will be respected, then inserting the removed items in the former well-filled bins that can accommodate them.

On the other hand, we use the following fitness function to assess the quality of feasible solutions:

$$f = \frac{1}{\sum_{k=1}^{d} y_k} \tag{6}$$

The Eq. (6) corresponds to reverse of the cost function of the 2D-BPP, which means that the fewer the bins used to pack all items, the higher the fitness value.

3.3 Updating Crows Position and Memory

The GA operators and the CSA process are applied in order to update the crows position. Henceforth, we consider crow positions as chromosomes. Each column of the position matrix corresponds to a gene of the chromosome, while such a gene is encoded by a binary vector of n alleles. Figure 1 shows the structure of a chromosome.

$$\begin{pmatrix} 1 & 0 & 0 & 0 \\ 0 & 0 & 1 & 0 \\ 0 & 0 & 0 & 1 \\ 1 & 0 & 0 & 0 \\ 1 & 0 & 0 & 0 \end{pmatrix}$$

Fig. 1. Representation of a chromosome with $(n = 5)$ and $(d = 4)$

Selection Operation. In this stage, each crow i selects a crow j from the population, by using a binary tournament selection. In fact, the binary tournament selection consists of choosing at random two crows from the population and making a competition between them. The winner is a crow with highest fitness value. So, the crow i chooses the winner as a target to follow. That is, the position of the crow i is updated.

Crossover Operation. Crossover is the process of exchanging genes between individuals in order to create new ones. Its main goal is to exploit more the search space of solutions. In this stage, we combine the CSA rules with crossover strategy in order to update positions as follows. If $r_j \geq AP_j$, we cross the position of crow i with the position of the selected crow j. Else, the position of crow i is crossed with its memory. A PMX crossover operator developed by Goldberg and Lingle [26], is applied to recombine two positions, or even position and memory. The example in Fig. 2 explains how we adapt it in our context. Indeed, we choose at random a bin from the first parent position (for instance, bin 1), and we replace its content {item 2, item 3} in the offspring at the same bin ID. The other bins inherits their contents from the second parent. The duplicate items are replaced by items packed in the bin 1 of the second parent by respecting the same order. In our example, items 2 and 3 are packed respectively in bins 3 and 2 of the second parent. So, we replace the item 2 with item 4 and the item 3 by the item 5. We note that the sign «$\otimes$» indicates the crossover operation.

$$\begin{pmatrix} 0 & 0 & 0 & 0 \\ 1 & 0 & 0 & 0 \\ 1 & 0 & 0 & 0 \\ 0 & 1 & 0 & 0 \\ 0 & 0 & 1 & 0 \end{pmatrix} \otimes \begin{pmatrix} 0 & 1 & 0 & 0 \\ 0 & 0 & 0 & 1 \\ 0 & 1 & 0 & 0 \\ 1 & 0 & 0 & 0 \\ 1 & 0 & 0 & 0 \end{pmatrix} = \begin{pmatrix} 0 & 1 & 0 & 0 \\ 1 & 0 & 0 & 0 \\ 1 & 0 & 0 & 0 \\ 0 & 0 & 0 & 1 \\ 0 & 1 & 0 & 0 \end{pmatrix}$$

Fig. 2. An example of crossover operation with $(n = 5)$ and $(d = 4)$

Once the crossover strategy has finished, the feasibility of offspring positions is evaluated. If it is necessary, the above-mentioned repair operator is applied for restoring the feasibility of solutions.

Mutation Operation. Besides crossover operation, the mutation operator is used to explore more regions of solution search space hopping to find new better solutions. We mutate some generated offspring by using the split bin mechanism proposed in [22]. It consists of choosing randomly one used bin and split its content into two bins. In our algorithm, we have applied this mechanism according to the following manner. The first part of items is kept in its original bin and the second part of items is merged into other bin that can bear it without violating the constraint capacity. If no used bin can pack it, a new one is opened.

Update of Crow Memory. After mutation, the quality of each offspring position is investigated using the fitness function, and compared with the memory of each crow. If the offspring position is better than the so far memorized position, the crow updates then its memory with the offspring position. Otherwise, it keeps its former memory.

3.4 The Framework of CSGA

The overall algorithm is summarized as follows.

Step1. Initialize the population with N crows, and set the control parameters, such as, maximal generation number G, flight length of crows and their awareness probability. For each crow i, set $M^i(G = 1) = X^i(G = 1)$.
Step 2. Evaluate the feasibility of solutions, and restore the feasibility of infeasible solutions by the proposed repair operator. Then, calculate their fitness value.
Step 3. For each crow i, apply a binary tournament selection to select the crow j.
Step 4. Update the position of each crow i using the following equations:

$$\text{If } r_j \geq AP_j, \text{then } X^i(G+1) = X^i(G) \otimes X^j(G) \tag{7}$$

$$\text{Else}, X^i(G+1) = X^i(G) \otimes M^i(G) \tag{8}$$

Step 5. Restore the feasibility of infeasible offspring positions.
Step 6. Apply mutation strategy to generated offspring positions with probability p_m.
Step 7. Calculate the fitness function for each offspring position, and update the memory of each crow by the Eq. (2).
Step 8. Loop to Step 3 until a maximum number of generations is satisfied and then output the best found memory as an optimal solution of 2D-BPP.

4 Simulation

4.1 Simulation Design

The proposed CSGA is coded in JAVA on a PC with an Intel Core i5 with 2.5 GHz and 4.0 GB of RAM, running on 64-bits Windows 7 operating system. The performance of CSGA is examined on various test instances of the 2D-BPP available at the URL [27]. We should note that the considered test data are divided into different classes. Ten classes are generated randomly by varying the capacity of bins as well as the range of item' sizes. The first six classes were introduced by Berkey and Wang [12], while the last four classes were proposed by Martello and Vigo [28]. In each class, identical bins are considered while the items are characterized by different sizes that are uniformly generated in a same interval of values. Each class is also divided into five subclasses according to the number of available items ($n = 20, 40, 60, 80, 100$), whereas each subclass is divided into ten problem instances which gives a total of 50 problem instances for each class. During the experiments, four problem classes are undertaken (see Table 1). Three classes that seem to be representative are chosen from Berkey and Wang classes, while only one class is selected from Martello and Vigo classes to represent its colleagues. Meanwhile, we considered just three subclasses having $n = 20, 60, 100$ that corresponds, respectively, to small, medium and large size problem.

Table 1. Information about test instances used in experiments

Class problem	Bin capacity	Item height	Item width
Class 1	$W = H = 10$	[1, 10]	[1, 10]
Class 3	$W = H = 40$	[1, 35]	[1, 35]
Class 5	$W = H = 100$	[1, 100]	[1, 100]
Class 9	$W = H = 100$	70% in $[1/2H, H]$ and 10% in $[2/3H, H]$, $[1, 1/2H]$	70% in $[1/2W, W]$ and 10% in $[2/3W, W]$, $[1, 1/2W]$

To validate the efficiency of CGSA, this later is compared against the binary particle swarm optimization algorithm (BPSO) proposed by Kennedy and Eberhart [29], and the standard genetic algorithm (GA). We should note that the BPSO has undergone minor modifications in order to adapt it to the 2D-BPP context, especially, in encoding scheme which is similar to that of CSGA, and in the fact that it incorporates the abovementioned repair operator in order to meet the capacity constraint of bins. Moreover, the standard GA uses the same genetic operators as used by CSGA (see Subsect. 3.3). The control parameters of each algorithm are reported in Table 2. That is; *Popsize* means the population size, *Maxgen* indicates the maximum number of generations, BTS-*size* indicates the size of binary tournament selection. Furthermore, w_{min} and w_{max} denote respectively the minimum and maximum inertia weight, while c_1 and c_2 denote the acceleration coefficients. Finally, V_{min} and V_{max} refer to the minimum and maximum velocity of particles. It is worth mentioning that the parameters of CSGA are set based upon many preliminary independent experiences, while the BPSO parameters are chosen according to the experiences of other authors.

Table 2. Parameter settings

Algorithms	Parameter values
CSGA	*Popsize* = 100; FL = 2; AP = 0,01; p_m = 0,10; *Maxgen* = 100
GA	*Popsize* = 100; BTS-*size* = 2; p_c = 0,95; p_m = 0,01; *Maxgen* = 100
BPSO	*Popsize* = 100; w_{min} = 0,4; w_{max} = 0,9; c_1 = c_1 = 1,5; V_{min} = −2; V_{max} = 2; *Maxgen* = 100

4.2 Simulation Results

All test cases of CSGA as well as the comparative algorithms were evaluated by 30
independent runs, and the average results are retained. To assess our results, in terms of
fitness values, we apply Wilcoxon test that is used in order to determine whether the
average fitness values of CSGA compared with those of BPSO and GA are significantly different or not. The confidence level is fixed at 0,95, and the obtained results of
p-value are shown in Table 3. We use the SPSS statistics 22 for statistical testing. If the
p-value is less than 0,05, we reject the null hypothesis that assumes there is no significant difference between two compared algorithms. Otherwise, we accept the
alternative hypothesis that assumes there is a significant difference between them. The
value of R− (respectively, R+) in Table 3 indicates the sum of the ranks corresponding
to negative (respectively, positive) difference. In fact, the sum of ranks is the absolute

Table 3. Wilcoxon test results on average fitness value of CSGA against other algorithms

Problem class	Number of items	Compared algorithms	R+	R−	*p*-value	*s*
Class 1	20	CSGA - GA	55	0	0,005	1
		CSGA - BPSO	18,5	2,5	0,093	0
	60	CSGA - GA	55	0	0,005	1
		CSGA - BPSO	27,5	27,5	1,000	0
	100	CSGA - GA	55	0	0,005	1
		CSGA - BPSO	55	0	0,005	1
Class 3	20	CSGA - GA	55	0	0,004	1
		CSGA - BPSO	2	13	0,136	0
	60	CSGA - GA	55	0	0,005	1
		CSGA - BPSO	0	55	0,005	−1
	100	CSGA - GA	55	0	0,005	1
		CSGA - BPSO	2	53	0,009	−1
Class 5	20	CSGA - GA	55	0	0,005	1
		CSGA - BPSO	4	41	0,028	−1
	60	CSGA - GA	55	0	0,005	1
		CSGA - BPSO	0	55	0,005	−1
	100	CSGA - GA	55	0	0,005	1
		CSGA - BPSO	0	55	0,005	−1

Table 4. Comparative results of CSGA versus GA and BPSO using instances with 40 items

Test instance	LB*	CSGA		GA		BPSO	
		Used bins	CPU time	Used bins	CPU time	Used bins	CPU time
Instance1	25	29	**0,067**	37	2,013	34	4,346
Instance2	32	29	**0,066**	36	1,916	35	4,383
Instance3	29	29	**1,914**	35	1,914	34	4,386
Instance4	31	28	**0,063**	35	2,085	34	4,472
Instance5	27	27	**0,064**	33	1,993	29	4,382
Instance6	29	29	**0,067**	36	2,030	35	4,393
Instance7	24	26	**0,068**	32	1,920	29	4,421
Instance8	26	28	**0,063**	35	2,006	34	4,676
Instance9	21	25	**0,062**	33	1,995	30	4,389
Instance10	34	**30**	**0,064**	38	2,028	39	4,423
Average	**27,8**	28	**0,250**	35	1,990	33,3	4,427

value of the difference between results of two algorithms. The value of s in Table 3 shows the statistical result of pairwise comparison: $s = 1$ indicates that the first algorithm is significantly better than the latter; $s = -1$ indicates that the first algorithm is significantly worse than the latter. Both values -1 and 1 means there is a significant difference. Whereas $s = 0$ indicates that there is no significant difference between the two compared algorithms. From Table 3, we can then observe that CSGA is superior to the standard GA. However, it is sometimes nearly equivalent to BPSO and sometimes it is outperformed by BPSO.

Tables 4, 5 and 6 report the empirical results of CSGA, GA and BPSO in terms of average used bins obtained over 30 runs, and the average execution time. These tests are performed on class 9. In each table, the first column indicates the test instances of

Table 5. Comparative results of CSGA versus GA and BPSO using instances with 80 items

Test instance	LB*	CSGA		GA		BPSO	
		Used bins	CPU time	Used bins	CPU time	Used bins	CPU time
instance1	59	60	**0,264**	70	7,816	65	34,436
instance2	58	59	**0,271**	69	7,718	66	39,465
Instance3	57	59	**0,252**	70	8,001	66	34,008
Instance4	53	60	**0,263**	69	7,753	65	37,740
Instance5	62	**61**	**0,259**	74	7,772	72	32,446
Instance6	62	**59**	**0,251**	71	7,576	68	31,868
Instance7	59	**59**	**0,262**	70	7,833	66	39,240
Instance8	58	**58**	**0,264**	71	7,902	68	32,110
Instance9	49	54	**0,261**	59	40,232	59	34,454
Instance10	60	61	**0,274**	74	7,575	71	32,291
Average	**57,7**	59	**0,262**	69,7	11,018	66,6	34,806

Table 6. Comparative results of CSGA versus GA and BPSO using instances with 100 items

Test instance	LB*	CSGA		GA		BPSO	
		Used bins	CPU time	Used bins	CPU time	Used bins	CPU time
instance1	**71**	75	**0,377**	87	11,755	81	63,273
instance2	**64**	69	**0,371**	86	11,785	81	64,554
Instance3	68	**61**	**0,384**	82	11,767	71	65,076
Instance4	78	**76**	**0,372**	92	11,872	88	62,890
Instance5	**65**	73	**0,388**	84	11,892	76	74,067
Instance6	**71**	74	**0,381**	78	64,425	78	73,664
Instance7	**66**	69	**0,380**	87	12,084	81	64,983
Instance8	74	**73**	**0,375**	90	11,859	86	62,992
Instance9	**66**	**66**	**0,379**	85	12,039	78	73,892
Instance10	**72**	75	**0,384**	84	64,165	84	65,849
Average	**69,5**	71,1	**0,379**	85,5	22,364	80,4	67,124

class 9. The second column records the benchmark lower bounds of 2D-BPP (see URL [27]). The last columns represent the obtained average results of the three compared algorithms.

From Tables 4, 5 and 6, we can see that the number of used bins obtained by CSGA, in each instance, is nearest or equal to corresponding lower bound, and sometimes even better than the latter. Furthermore, the proposed algorithm yields better results in less computational time, in comparison with both BPSO and GA. We note that best results are in bold and the computation time is expressed in seconds.

4.3 Results Analysis

From Table 3, the outcomes of experiments tested on classes 1, 3 and 5 have shown that the average results of CSGA are better than GA and worse than BPSO. For these test classes the difficulty grows quite regularly with the number of available items (see [28]). However, from Tables 4, 5 and 6 in which class 9 is used as data test instances, the computations prove that CSGA allocates the available items to a smallest number of bins when it is compared against GA and BPSO, and even LB*. In class 9, the generated data set seems to be easy than the sub-mentioned problem classes. This is because there are a high percentage of large items, thereby having few free areas to be managed. Such instances illustrate real-life situations [5].

It is interesting to see that CSGA has a better performance in comparison with GA independently of whatever the type of instances. Nevertheless, it has generally a worst performance against BPSO in difficult instances (classes 1, 3 and 5), but it performs better than BPSO in more realistic situations as test instances of class 9 and yields results of high quality in few amount of time.

5 Conclusions

In this paper, we proposed a crow search algorithm based on genetic operators for solving the 2D-BPP. We used various benchmark tests to examine the performance of the proposed algorithm. In addition, we compared our algorithm with two state-of-the-art algorithms that have the same nature (*i.e.* bio-inspired algorithms). The experimental results showed that the proposed approach gives good results against that of GA regardless the type of instances. However, our algorithm is outperformed by BPSO in difficult instances, but it performs well than BPSO in more realistic instances. In addition, our algorithm is quite fast than both comparative algorithms in easy instances as well as in difficult instances. These results are very encouraging. They prove the efficiency of the CSGA. Since our algorithm incorporates the genetic operators in the core idea of CSA, it can be applied to solve, as the GA, several optimization problems that work in discrete search space, as well as continuous search space. So, in future research, we hope to exploit that in 2D-BPP which takes into account the guillotine constraint and/or allows rotation of items by 90°, in addition to other important real-world applications coming from different fields.

References

1. Wäscher, G., Haußner, H., Schumann, H.: An improved typology of cutting and packing problems. Eur. J. Oper. Res. **183**, 1109–1130 (2007)
2. Crainic, T.G., et al.: Bin packing problems with uncertainty on item characteristics: An application to capacity planning in logistics. Procedia-Soc. Behav. Sci. **111**, 654–662 (2014)
3. Wee, T.S., Magazine, M.J.: Assembly line balancing as generalized bin packing. Oper. Res. Lett. **1**, 56–58 (1982)
4. Song, W., et al.: Adaptive resource provisioning for the cloud using online bin packing. IEEE Trans. Comput. **63**, 2647–2660 (2014)
5. Lodi, A., Martello, S., Vigo, D.: Heuristic and metaheuristic approaches for a class of two-dimensional bin packing problems. INFORMS J. Comput. **11**, 345–357 (1999)
6. Epstein, L., Van Stee, R.: Optimal online algorithms for multidimensional packing problems. SIAM J. Comput. **35**, 431–448 (2005)
7. Laabadi, S.: A new algorithm for the Bin-packing problem with fragile objects. In: 3rd International Conference on Logistics Operations Management, pp. 1–7. IEEE, Fez (2016)
8. Bansal, N., Liu, Z., Sankar, A.: Bin-packing with fragile objects and frequency allocation in cellular networks. Wirel. Netw. **15**, 821–830 (2009)
9. Shakhsi, N.M., Joulaei, F., Razmi, J.: Extending two-dimensional bin packing problem: consideration of priority for items. J. Ind. Syst. Eng. **3**, 72–84 (2009)
10. Hamdi-Dhaoui, K., Labadie, N., Yalaoui, A.: Algorithms for the two dimensional bin packing problem with partial conflicts. RAIRO-Oper. Res. **46**, 41–62 (2012)
11. Khanafer, A., Clautiaux, F., Talbi, E.G.: Tree-decomposition based heuristics for the two-dimensional bin packing problem with conflicts. Comput. Oper. Res. **39**, 54–63 (2012)
12. Berkey, J.O., Wang, P.Y.: Two-dimensional finite bin-packing algorithms. J. Oper. Res. Soc. **38**, 423–429 (1987)
13. Monaci, M., Toth, P.: A set-covering-based heuristic approach for bin-packing problems. INFORMS J. Comput. **18**, 71–85 (2006)

14. Baumgartner, L., Schmid, V., Blum, C.: Solving the two-dimensional bin packing problem with a probabilistic multi-start heuristic. In: Coello, C.A.C. (ed.) LION 2011. LNCS, vol. 6683, pp. 76–90. Springer, Heidelberg (2011). https://doi.org/10.1007/978-3-642-25566-3_6
15. Wong, L.: Heuristic placement routines for two-dimensional rectangular bin packing problems. Ph.D. thesis, Universiti Putra Malaysia (2009)
16. Parreño, F., et al.: A hybrid GRASP/VND algorithm for two-and three-dimensional bin packing. Ann. Oper. Res. **179**, 203–220 (2010)
17. Lai, K.K., Chan, J.W.: Developing a simulated annealing algorithm for the cutting stock problem. Comput. Ind. Eng. **32**, 115–127 (1997)
18. Gonçalves, J.F., Resende, M.G.: A biased random key genetic algorithm for 2D and 3D bin-packing problems. Int. J. Prod. Econ. **145**, 500–510 (2013)
19. Soke, A., Bingul, Z.: Hybrid genetic algorithm and simulated annealing for two-dimensional non-guillotine rectangular packing problems. Eng. Appl. Artif. Intell. **19**, 557–567 (2006)
20. Blum, C., Schmid, V.: Solving the 2D bin packing problem by means of a hybrid evolutionary algorithm. Procedia Comput. Sci. **18**, 899–908 (2013)
21. Shin, Y.B., Kita, E.: Solving two-dimensional packing problem using particle swarm optimization. Comput. Assist. Methods Eng. Sci. **19**, 241–255 (2017)
22. Liu, D.S., et al.: On solving multiobjective bin packing problems using evolutionary particle swarm optimization. Eur. J. Oper. Res. **190**, 357–382 (2008)
23. Reeves, C., Rowe, J.E.: Genetic Algorithms: Principles and Perspectives: A Guide to GA Theory. Springer, New York (2002). https://doi.org/10.1007/b101880
24. Askarzadeh, A.: A novel metaheuristic method for solving constrained engineering optimization problems: crow search algorithm. Comput. Struct. **169**, 1–12 (2016)
25. De Souza, R.C.T., et al.: A V-shaped binary crow search algorithm for feature selection. In: IEEE Congress on Evolutionary Computation, pp. 1–8. IEEE, Rio de Janeiro (2018)
26. Goldberg, D., Lingle, R.: Alleles, loci, and the travelling salesman problem. In: First International Conference on Genetic Algorithms and their Applications, pp. 154–159. Lawrence Erlbaum Associates, Hillsdale (1985)
27. http://or.dei.unibo.it/library/two-dimensional-bin-packing-problem
28. Martello, S., Vigo, D.: Exact solution of the two-dimensional finite bin packing problem. Manag. Sci. **44**, 388–399 (1998)
29. Kennedy, J., Eberhart, R.C.: A discrete binary version of the particle swarm algorithm. In: International Conference on Systems, Man, and Cybernetics. Computational Cybernetics and Simulation, vol. 5, pp. 4104–4108 (1997)

Extracting Reasons for Moral Judgments Under Various Ethical Principles

Felix Lindner[✉] and Katrin Möllney

Computer Science Department, Foundations of Artificial Intelligence,
University of Freiburg, 79110 Freiburg im Breisgau, Germany
{lindner,moellnek}@informatik.uni-freiburg.de

Abstract. We present an approach to the computational extraction of reasons for the sake of explaining moral judgments in the context of an hybrid ethical reasoning agent (HERA). The HERA agent employs logical representations of ethical principles to make judgments about the moral permissibility or impermissibility of actions, and uses the same logical formulae to come up with reasons for these judgments. We motivate the distinction between sufficient reasons, necessary reasons, and necessary parts of sufficient reasons yielding different types of explanations, and we provide algorithms to extract these reasons.

Keywords: Machine ethics · Explainable AI · Reasons

1 Introduction

Artificial Intelligence technology is currently making huge impact on society. Many important questions arise on how we want to design technology to the benefit of humans, how we can build systems that are in line with our ethical values, and how we can build systems that we can trust. The approach taken by the machine-ethics community [5,18,19] to building systems that align with ethical values is to represent these values formally within these systems and thus enable artificial systems to explicitly take ethical values into account during reasoning and decision making. One such attempt to explicitly formalize ethics is undertaken in the HERA (Hybrid Ethical Reasoning Agents)[1] project [2]. The HERA software library currently provides a suite of philosophically founded and practically usable machine ethics tools for implementation in physical and virtual moral agents such as social robots [1]. Until recently, it was not possible to ask the HERA agent for the reasons why a situation is judged morally permissible or impermissible according to a given ethical principle. It has recently been argued that the capability to explain decisions to humans is an important ingredient for human-robot interaction to ensure trust and transparency [6], and for AI in general [7,12]. Earlier versions of HERA could not address this requirement in a satisfying way. In this article, we report how, once a moral judgment has

---

[1] www.hera-project.com.

© Springer Nature Switzerland AG 2019
C. Benzmüller and H. Stuckenschmidt (Eds.): KI 2019, LNAI 11793, pp. 216–229, 2019.
https://doi.org/10.1007/978-3-030-30179-8_18

been computed, reasons can be extracted based on the logical representations of ethical principles.

The paper is structured as follows: First, the moral-judgment component of HERA is briefly reviewed. We then propose an explanation component which relies on computing sufficient and necessary reasons that explain a moral judgment. We relate the problem of computing sufficient and necessary reasons to the problem of computing prime implicants and prime implicates of a Boolean formula. We discuss a connection to the INUS condition [9] and problematize cases of overdetermination. We then point out connections to related work in the eXplainable AI community (XAI).

2 Hybrid Ethical Reasoning Agents

2.1 Causal Agency Models

Causal agency models were introduced by Lindner, Bentzen and Nebel [2] as a variant of causal models in the tradition of Pearl and Halpern [3]. Causal agency models are particularly designed to capture ethically relevant aspects of a situation. These include the set of actions available to the agent in that situation, the causal chains of consequences of each action, the intended consequences of each action, as well as a utility function which assigns a numeric value to actions and consequences representing how good or bad that action or consequence is. Definition 1 introduces causal agency models formally.

Definition 1 (Causal Agency Model). *A causal agency model M is a tuple (A, C, F, I, u, W), where A is the set of action variables, C is a set of consequence variables, F is a set of modifiable Boolean structural equations, $I = (I_1, \ldots, I_n)$ is a list of sets of intentions (one for each action), $u : A \cup C \to \mathbb{Z}$ is a mapping from actions and consequences to their individual utilities, and W is a set of Boolean interpretations of A.*

A pair $\langle M, w_\alpha \rangle$ with $w_\alpha \in W$ constitutes the *situation* which results from performing action α according to model M. Intuitively, each Boolean interpretation $w \in W$ of the variables in A corresponds to an *option* available to the agent. The interpretation w_α denotes the interpretation where action α has been chosen, i.e., α has the Boolean value *True*. By assumption, all other actions get the value *False*. Given some w_α, the value of each of the variables in C can be uniquely determined as long as the dependence graph induced by F in situation $\langle M, w_\alpha \rangle$ is recursive (cycle-free), cf., [3]. Subsequently, we will assume that this is always the case.

Symmetric Trolley Problem. As a running example throughout this paper we consider a symmetric trolley problem: A trolley has gone out of control and threatens to kill a person (called "person 1"). However, a bystander has the chance to pull a lever and thereby direct the trolley onto the second track. Unfortunately, there is a second person (called "person 2") standing on the second track and who will die in case the lever gets pulled.

The situation is represented as a causal agency model M like this:

$$A = \{a_1, a_2\}$$
$$C = \{d_1, d_2\}$$
$$F = \{f_{d_1} := \neg a_1, f_{d_2} := a_1\}$$
$$I = (I_{a_1} = \{a_1, \neg d_1\}, I_{a_2} = \{a_2\})$$
$$u(a_1) = u(a_2) = 0, u(d_1) = u(d_2) = -1, u(\neg d_1) = u(\neg d_2) = 1$$
$$W = \{\{a_1 \to T, a_2 \to F\}, \{a_1 \to F, a_2 \to T\}\}$$

The action a_1 represents the pulling of the lever, action a_2 is an extra action variable representing refraining from action. This special action will never appear in structural equations, hence, refraining never causes anything. This way, causal agency models can express the distinction between causing and letting happen (cf., [2]). Consequence variables d_1, d_2 represent the deaths of person 1 and person 2, respectively. The structural equation f_{d_1} models that in case of not pulling the lever, person 1 will die. The structural equation f_{d_2} models that the effect of pulling the lever is that person 2 will die. The set I captures that by pulling the lever the agent intends to actually pull the lever (i.e., pulling is a voluntary action) and that the agent intends to rescue person 1's life. In case of refraining, only the refraining itself is supposed to be intended. The death of either of the two persons is considered a bad consequence, their survival is considered good. This is represented by the utility function u.

The symmetric trolley problem so defined does not give rise to the usual tension between utilitarian and non-utilitarian reasoning. However, it still constitutes a case of choosing between causing harm and letting harm happen, and thus different ethical theories will yield different judgments. The overall approach to ethical reasoning presented in [2] can also handle utilitarian reasoning in the classical trolley dilemma (5 persons versus 1 person). For the principles considered in this paper, more persons on the track would not make any difference and would not contribute to the demonstration of the new explainability feature.

For the remainder of the paper, we use $\langle M, w_{a_1} \rangle$ to refer to the situation of the symmetric trolley problem where the agent pulls the lever, and $\langle M, w_{a_2} \rangle$ for the situation where the agent refrains from pulling the lever.

2.2   Causal Agency Logic

A logical language is defined to talk about causal agency models. Particularly, the logic is employed for the specification of moral permissibility according to various ethical principles.

Language. The language L of causal agency logic is recursively defined as follows:

- Let $Lit_p = \{p, \neg p \mid p \in A \cup C\} \subset L$ be the set of propositional variables denoting actions and consequences and their negations.

- For all actions or consequences $p, q \in Lit_p$ formula $Causes(p, q)$ is in L.
- For all $p \in Lit_p$ formulae $Good(p), Bad(p), Neutral(p) \in L$.
- For all $p \in Lit_p$ formula $I(p) \in L$.
- If $\phi, \psi \in L$, then $\neg\phi, \phi \wedge \psi, \phi \vee \psi, \phi \to \psi \in L$.

The language is kept simple in various ways: First, it only allows to talk about causation between literals. A more expressive logic would allow to also speak about combinations of actions and consequences being the cause of some consequence. Second, the logic can express that some consequence or action is good, bad, or neutral, but one cannot arbitrarily compare the utility of consequences and actions.

Semantics. The semantics of L is defined over situations $\langle M, w_\alpha \rangle$ as follows:

- $\langle M, w_\alpha \rangle \models p$ iff p is an action and $p = \alpha$, or if p is a consequence and the structural equation f_p evaluates to True under $\langle M, w_\alpha \rangle$.
- $\langle M, w_\alpha \rangle \models Causes(p, q)$ iff $\langle M, w_\alpha \rangle \models p \wedge q$ and $\langle M_{\neg p}, w_\alpha \rangle \models \neg q$, where $M_{\neg p}$ is the model where the structural equation of p is substituted by the complement of the truth value that p has in $\langle M, w_\alpha \rangle$. This is in accordance with the but-for definition of causality [3].
- $\langle M, w_\alpha \rangle \models Good(p)$ iff $u(p) > 0$.
- $\langle M, w_\alpha \rangle \models Bad(p)$ iff $0 < u(p)$.
- $\langle M, w_\alpha \rangle \models Neutral(p)$ iff $0 = u(p)$.
- $\langle M, w_\alpha \rangle \models I(p)$ iff $p \in I_\alpha$.
- $\langle M, w_\alpha \rangle \models \neg\phi$ iff $\langle M, w_\alpha \rangle \not\models \phi$.
- $\langle M, w_\alpha \rangle \models \phi \wedge \psi$ iff $\langle M, w_\alpha \rangle \models \phi$ and $\langle M, w_\alpha \rangle \models \psi$.
- $\langle M, w_\alpha \rangle \models \phi \vee \psi$ iff $\langle M, w_\alpha \rangle \models \phi$ or $\langle M, w_\alpha \rangle \models \psi$.
- $\langle M, w_\alpha \rangle \models \phi \to \psi$ iff $\langle M, w_\alpha \rangle \not\models \phi$ or $\langle M, w_\alpha \rangle \models \psi$.

2.3   Making Moral Judgments

The moral-judgment component of HERA employs model checking: Ethical principles are formulae written in the causal agency logic introduced above. A causal agency model together with an interpretation which sets one action (the performed action) to true is a representation of the situation to be judged from the perspective of a particular ethical principle. The performed action is permissible according to the ethical principle if and only if the situation satisfies the ethical principle.

For brevity we will only introduce the deontological principle and the do-no-harm principle, but many other ethical principles can be formulated (cf., [2]) and handled likewise. The deontological principle is a non-consequentialist ethical principle. Accordingly, all that matters is the intrinsic value of an action rather than the consequences it will bring about.

Definition 2 (Deontological Principle). *Action α in situation $\langle M, w_\alpha \rangle$ is morally permissible according to the deontological principle if and only if the action α is morally good or neutral, i.e., $\langle M, w_\alpha \rangle \models \neg Bad(\alpha)$.*

Thus, in the trolley problem modeled earlier in the text, both pulling the lever and refraining from doing so are permissible from the perspective of the deontological principle, because their intrinsic values are neutral. To verify this, the formulae $\phi_{deon}^{\langle M, w_{a_1} \rangle} = \neg Bad(a_1)$ and $\phi_{deon}^{\langle M, w_{a_2} \rangle} = \neg Bad(a_2)$ have to be checked for truth in the situations $\langle M, w_{a_1} \rangle$ and $\langle M, w_{a_2} \rangle$, respectively.

We note that the resulting judgment is not in line with many textbooks that claim deontology forbids pulling the lever in the trolley problem. This judgment could be reproduced in our model by assigning negative utility to the pull action. Doing so is justified if the modeler advocates the moral view that pulling the lever and causing the death of the one person is actually the same and should not be distinguished from each other. This shows that, generally, moral judgment is a matter of both moral principles and conceptualizations and (mental) models of moral situations.

The do-no-harm principle is a consequentialist principle. Consequentialists do not believe that actions bear intrinsic value which cannot be reduced to the consequences they bring about. The do-no-harm principle renders exactly those actions morally permissible which do not cause harmful consequences. That is, it may be acceptable that harm exists in the situation, however, this harm should not be due to the action performed by the agent. Definition 3 captures the do-no-harm principle formally.

Definition 3 (Do-No-Harm Principle). *An action α in situation $\langle M, w_\alpha \rangle$ is morally permissible according to the do-no-harm principle if and only if none of the bad consequences is caused. Formally, $\langle M, w_\alpha \rangle \models \bigwedge_c (Bad(c) \to \neg Causes(\alpha, c))$.*

Unlike the deontological principle, the do-no-harm principle forbids pulling the lever. This is, because in the situation resulting from pulling the lever person 2 dies, and person 2 would not have died if the lever had not been pulled, i.e., the pulling is a but-for cause for the person's death. Therefore, both $Bad(d_2)$ and $Causes(a_1, d_2)$ hold in situation $\langle M, w_{a_1} \rangle$. However, refraining is permitted by the do-no-harm principle: It is true that person 1 dies when a_2 is set to $True$, but setting a_2 to $False$ does not help person 1. Only in the case of pulling the lever, the harm can be avoided by doing less, and thus the harm counts as caused.

We refer to [2] for a more complete presentation of the HERA approach to ethical reasoning. Next, we make a new contribution by outlining an approach to computing explanations for moral judgments.

3   Generating Sufficient and Necessary Reasons

Given a judgment about the moral (im-)permissibility of some action in a situation, we want to compute reasons that explain why the judgment was made. One naïve way of doing so would consist in just citing the whole formula that was proven to be true in the given situation and which thus is necessary and sufficient for the permissibility judgment, and therefore explains it. For the symmetric trolley dilemma, one could just cite Formula (1) stating the whole necessary and sufficient condition for the permissibility of refraining in situation $\langle M, w_2 \rangle$.

$$\phi_{\text{DoNoHarm}}^{\langle M, w_{a_2} \rangle} = \tag{1}$$
$$(Bad(d_1) \rightarrow \neg Causes(a_2, d_1)) \wedge (Bad(d_2) \rightarrow \neg Causes(a_2, d_2)) \wedge$$
$$(Bad(\neg d_1) \rightarrow \neg Causes(a_2, \neg d_1)) \wedge (Bad(\neg d_2) \rightarrow \neg Causes(a_2, \neg d_2))$$

Hence, there are eight different literals and their logical connectives to be reported. As the models grow bigger, the formulae representing permissibility also grow in size. There is hope that not the whole of these formulae has to be verbalized to produce a comprehensible explanation. We therefore now turn to the problem of pinpointing subformulae of the ethical principles that were responsible for the moral permissibility judgment in a particular situation.

3.1   Preliminaries

We briefly recall some basic terminology of propositional logic. Every propositional variable and its negation is called a *literal*. An *interpretation* w assigns a Boolean value to every propositional variable of a formula. If the formula is true under w, then w is called a *model*. We also think of a model as the set of literals true under w. A conjunction of literals m (a *monomial*) is called a *prime implicant* of formula ϕ if and only if m entails ϕ, and no proper part of m entails ϕ. A disjunction of literals (a *clause*) c is called a *prime implicate* of ϕ if and only if ϕ entails c, and no proper part of c is already entailed by ϕ.

As an example consider formula $\phi = (x_1 \wedge x_2) \vee (x_1 \wedge x_2 \wedge x_3) \vee (x_1 \wedge x_3)$. The monomial $m_1 = (x_1 \wedge x_2)$ is a prime implicant of ϕ, because the truth of m_1 implies the truth of ϕ and no subformula of m_1 does. The monomial $m_2 = (x_1 \wedge x_2 \wedge x_3)$ is not a prime implicant of ϕ, because removing x_3 results in m_1, which already is a prime implicant. The clause x_1 is a prime implicate of ϕ, because a model that satisfies ϕ will also make x_1 true. The other prime implicate is $x_2 \vee x_3$.

Regarding causal agency logic, not every Boolean model corresponds to a causal agency model. For example, consider $Good(a) \wedge Bad(a)$, which has the propositional model $\{Good(a), Bad(a)\}$ while it is unsatisfiable in causal agency logic. We therefore implemented a theory solver which filters those models that are actual models of causal agency logic respecting the logic's specific constraints: Given a Boolean model w, then if $Good(x) \in w$, then $Neutral(x) \notin w$ and $Bad(x) \notin w$ (and analog constraints for $Neutral$ and Bad); if $Causes(x, y) \in w$, then $\neg x, \neg y \notin w$, $Causes(x, \neg y) \notin w$, $Causes(\neg x, y) \notin w$, and $Causes(y, x) \notin w$ (if $x \neq y$); and $\neg Causes(x, x) \notin w$; if $I(x) \in w$, then $I(\neg x) \notin w$.

3.2   How Principles Give Rise to Reasons

As a starting point of our analysis we take a deeper look at the properties of the formulae which represent the ethical principles. Each such formula is grounded in a particular situation. This means they are built from the action and consequence variables specified in the given situation via the causal agency model. Thus, the domain of quantification is fixed. Formula (1) is such a formula grounded in situation obtained from pulling the lever in the causal agency model defined in Subsect. 2.1. Usually, the permissibility judgment depends on further properties of actions and consequences—such as being bad or being caused. Some combinations of such properties already entail the permissibility judgment. For instance, in the trolley dilemma from the introduction, nothing being caused by refraining entails the formula that represents the do-no-harm principle: Because nothing is caused, all other properties (being good or bad) have no impact on the judgment. Hence, nothing being caused is a *sufficient reason* for the permissibility of refraining. Counterfactually, had refraining caused the death of person 1, then refraining would have been judged impermissible. Hence, the fact that person 1's death is not caused is a *necessary reason* for the permissibility of refraining.

We anticipate that sufficient reasons give a good idea about the regularities that underlie a judgment, while necessary reasons give an idea about what should have been different to prevent that judgment. Hence, an agent can learn from necessary reasons for future actions. As will become apparent by the end of this section, there are also reasons that are both sufficient and necessary. These types of reasons are often very concise and straight to the point.

Sufficient Reasons. We take a *sufficient reason* to be a minimal conjunctive term which entails the permissibility judgment. More formally, a conjunctive term ψ is a sufficient reason for the permissibility of α in model M according to principle P iff $\langle M, w_\alpha \rangle \models \phi_p^{\langle M, w_\alpha \rangle} \wedge \psi$ (actuality), $\psi \models \phi_p^{\langle M, w_\alpha \rangle}$ (sufficiency), and no sub-term of ψ is already sufficient. Hence, asking for a sufficient reason is the same as asking for a prime implicant of the (grounded) ethical principle formula. To compute all prime implicants of $\phi_p^{\langle M, w_\alpha \rangle}$, HERA employs a SAT solver [15] to compute all models of $\phi_p^{\langle M, w_\alpha \rangle}$, and a theory solver to pick those models which are also models of causal agency logic (see note in Subsect. 3.1). Each of the models so found is an implicant. To obtain prime implicants we search for inclusion-minimal parts of the implicants, *sub*, already sufficient for the truth of $\phi_p^{\langle M, w_\alpha \rangle}$, i.e., for which $sub \rightarrow \phi_p^{\langle M, w_\alpha \rangle}$ is a tautology. All inclusion-minimal parts sufficient for the truth of $\phi_p^{\langle M, w_\alpha \rangle}$ are kept.

The set of prime implicants of Formula (1), $\phi_{\text{DoNoHarm}}^{\langle M, w_{a_2} \rangle}$, is listed as Formulae (2–5) below.

$$\neg Causes(a_2, d_1) \wedge \neg Causes(a_2, \neg d_2) \tag{2}$$

$$\neg Causes(a_2, d_1) \wedge \neg Bad(\neg d_2) \tag{3}$$

$$\neg Causes(a_2, \neg d_2) \wedge \neg Bad(\neg d_1) \tag{4}$$

$$\neg Bad(d_1) \wedge \neg Bad(\neg d_1) \tag{5}$$

Thus, if we only knew the HERA agent used formula $\phi_{\text{DoNoHarm}}^{\langle M, w_{a_2} \rangle}$ to evaluate the situation and that the agent came to the judgment that the situation was permissible, then we can conclude that the HERA agent believes in at least one of the four formulae (2) to (5). In the depicted case, we learn that to be permissible, the situation has to be such that either the action does not cause any consequences (2), or no consequence is bad (5), or one consequence is not caused (so it does not matter if it is bad) and the other is not bad (so it does not matter if it is caused).

Next, the HERA agent can state its beliefs about the causal relationships in the situation and its beliefs about moral badness or goodness by citing those prime implicants that are consistent with these beliefs as an explanation for its judgment. For the case of refraining from pulling the lever in the trolley problem (Subsect. 2.1), the agent can thus cite formulae (2) and (3) as sufficient reasons: "Refraining is permissible, because the death of person 1 is not caused nor is the survival of person 2." and "Refraining is permissible, because the death of person 1 is not caused, and the survival of person 2 is not bad."

Necessary Reasons. We take a *necessary reason* for a permissibility judgment to be a minimal property whose negation would result in an impermissibility judgment, thus, literally, the truth of this property is necessary for the permissibility. Thus, a necessary reason for the truth of $\phi_p^{\langle M, w_\alpha \rangle}$ is a minimal formula ψ such that the falsehood of ψ implies the falsehood of $\phi_p^{\langle M, w_\alpha \rangle}$. That is, ψ is a necessary reason for the truth of $\phi_p^{\langle M, w_\alpha \rangle}$ (and therefore for the permissibility of α according to principle p), iff $\models \neg\psi \rightarrow \neg\phi_p^{\langle M, w_\alpha \rangle}$ holds. This is equal to requiring that $\models \phi_p^{\langle M, w_\alpha \rangle} \rightarrow \psi$ holds. Hence, ψ is a necessary reason iff ψ is a prime implicate of $\phi_p^{\langle M, w_\alpha \rangle}$. For the computation of prime implicates, we make use of the relationship between prime implicates and prime implicants [16]: The prime implicates of a formula ϕ are just the negations of the prime implicants of $\neg\phi$; and we have already seen above how prime implicants can be computed. The prime implicates of $\neg\phi_{\text{DoNoHarm}}^{\langle M, w_{a_2} \rangle}$ are given in Eqs. (6) and (7).

$$\neg Causes(a_2, d_1) \vee \neg Bad(d_1) \tag{6}$$

$$\neg Causes(a_2, \neg d_2) \vee \neg Bad(\neg d_2) \tag{7}$$

Consequently, the permissibility of refraining implies that both (6) and (7) are true: Either the death of person 1 is not true or it is not bad, and either the death of survival is not caused or it is not bad. Hence, if the negation of any of the prime implicates (6) or (7), viz., (8) or (9), were satisfied in the situation, refraining would be impermissible according to the do-no-harm principle.

$$Causes(a_2, d_1) \wedge Bad(d_1) \tag{8}$$

$$Causes(a_2, \neg d_2) \wedge Bad(\neg d_2) \tag{9}$$

Some of the conjuncts of the negated prime implicates may already be satisfied in the given situation and therefore be no convincing reasons when talking about the concrete situation. For example, $Bad(d_1)$ is true in the causal agency model representing the symmetric trolley problem, and it may sound strange to state that had the death of person 1 been bad and caused, then refraining would have been impermissible (although this is, of course, correct). Therefore, we decide that $Bad(d_1)$ can be removed leaving $Causes(a_2, d_1)$ as the interesting part of this implicate. Indeed, if it were (additionally) the case that $Causes(a_2, d_1)$ were true in the situation, then the action would be impermissible. A second way of altering the judgment would require two changes to the situation: the survival of person 2 must be caused and its survival must be morally bad. We hence end up with Formulae (10) and (11).

$$Causes(a_2, d_1) \tag{10}$$

$$Causes(a_2, \neg d_2) \wedge Bad(\neg d_2) \tag{11}$$

In accordance to necessity, we take the perspective that conditions (10) and (11) to *not* be true was necessary for the permissibility judgment, i.e., $\neg Causes(a_2, d_1)$ and $\neg(Causes(a_2, \neg d_2) \wedge Bad(\neg d_2))$ are necessary reasons for the permissibility of action a_2. This leads to (12) and (13).

$$\neg Causes(a_2, d_1) \tag{12}$$

$$\neg Causes(a_2, \neg d_2) \vee \neg Bad(\neg d_2) \tag{13}$$

Formulae (12) and (13) correspond to the actual output of the HERA agent: For refraining to be permissible, it was necessary that the death of person 1 was not caused, and it was necessary that it was not the case that the survival of person 2 was bad and caused.

Necessary Parts of Sufficient Reasons. Mackie [9] has proposed the INUS condition, according to which causal explanations are *Insufficient but Necessary parts of a condition which is itself Unnecessary but Sufficient.*

Indeed, for the symmetric trolley problem, we find exactly one such INUS reason, viz., $\neg Causes(a_2, d_1)$. However, for the deontology principle, there is no INUS reason, because the only fact that explains the permissibility of the action is its not being bad, and this reason is both sufficient and necessary. We could either decide that no INUS reasons exists in this case, or we can decide to weaken the INUS condition a bit and identify those reasons which are necessary parts of sufficient reasons. Under this condition, we still get only $\neg Causes(a_2, d_1)$ as the reason for the permissibility of refraining in the symmetric trolley problem under the do-no-harm principle, and we also get $\neg Bad(a_2)$ as the reason under the deontology principle. In the actual HERA implementation, we have decided to go for the weakened version of the INUS condition.

The computation of INUS reasons is straightforward: For each necessary reason c (a clause), we check if there is a sufficient reason m (a monomial), such that every literal in c is also a literal in m.

Using the concept of a necessary part of a sufficient reason, the HERA agent is able to say: "Refraining is permissible (according to the do-no-harm principle), because refraining does not cause the death of person 1." and "Refraining is permissible (according to deontology), because refraining is not morally bad."

Impermissibility. We finally turn to explaining impermissibility judgments. In case of impermissibility, the formula $\phi_p^{\langle M, w_\alpha \rangle}$ is false in the given situation. For instance, pulling the lever in the symmetric trolley problem is impermissible according to the do-no-harm principle, because $\phi_{\text{DoNoHarm}}^{\langle M, w_{a_1} \rangle}$ is false in $\langle M, w_{a_1} \rangle$. To find out the reasons for the formula not to be satisfied, we reduce the computation of sufficient and necessary reasons for impermissibility judgments to reason computation for permissibility judgments. First, $\phi_p^{\langle M, w_\alpha \rangle}$ is negated, and then the necessary and sufficient reasons for the truth of $\neg \phi_p^{\langle M, w_\alpha \rangle}$ are computed just in the same way as outlined above. For the trolley problem example, we thus start with the formula $\neg \phi_{\text{DoNoHarm}}^{\langle M, w_{a_1} \rangle}$:

$$\neg \phi_{\text{DoNoHarm}}^{\langle M, w_{a_1} \rangle} = \tag{14}$$
$$(Bad(d_1) \wedge Causes(a_1, d_1)) \vee (Bad(d_2) \wedge Causes(a_1, d_2)) \vee$$
$$(Bad(\neg d_1) \wedge Causes(a_1, \neg d_1)) \vee (Bad(\neg d_2) \wedge Causes(a_1, \neg d_2))$$

In this case, each conjunct is a prime implicant. One of them is true in $\langle M, w_{a_1} \rangle$:

$$Bad(d_2) \wedge Causes(a_1, d_2) \tag{15}$$

Hence, there is one sufficient reasons for the impermissibility of pulling the lever: "Pulling the lever is impermissible, because the death of person 2 is bad and pulling causes the death of person 2."

Each of the conjuncts of Formula 15 is a necessary reason. In fact, both these reasons are also reasons according to the INUS condition (and its weakened version). As they refer to the salient feature of the situation (the death of person 2), the formulations "Pulling the lever is impermissible, because the death of person 2 is bad" and "Pulling the lever is impermissible, because pulling the lever causes the death of person 2" sound reasonable.

4   Discussion

We have proposed three types of explanations: those based on sufficient reasons, those based on necessary reasons, and those based on necessary reasons that are part of a sufficient reason. One problem that all these reasons may suffer from is that they do not explicitly take the knowledge status of the hearer into account, a factor which is known to be essential for explanations to be comprehensible [8]. Consider, for example, the reason $Causes(a_1, d_2)$, which is a necessary part of a sufficient reason for the impermissibility of pulling the lever (a_1). A hearer of this explanation who is not aware of the do-no-harm principle or who does not know that d_2 is morally bad, may ask "Why is causing the death of person 2 (d_2) a reason for impermissibility?" We leave it as an open question, how such questions could be addressed by including more information or by a dialogue with the HERA agent.

Moreover, it is questionable if principle-based reasons are appropriate moral reasons in all possible application domains. Stocker [24] gives the example of visiting a friend in a hospital. Neither "I visit you, because visiting is not bad" nor "I visit you, because doing so does not cause harm" seem appropriate—instead the explanation should cite care for that person as reason.

A more technical problem explanations have to deal with is the problem caused by overdetermination. Overdetermination occurs in theories of causation whenever two or more conditions are sufficient for one effect to occur, cf., [10]. Under such circumstances, it is not possible to point out single causes. In our case, overdetermination comes into play when more than one condition is sufficient for the (im-)permissibility judgment. Consider the situation when pulling the lever causes the death of two persons: person 1 and person 2. The causing of one of the two deaths is already sufficient for the impermissibility judgment. The two sufficient reasons are:

$$Bad(d_1) \wedge Causes(a_1, d_1) \tag{16}$$
$$Bad(d_2) \wedge Causes(a_1, d_2) \tag{17}$$

The necessary reasons are:

$$Bad(d_1) \vee Causes(a_1, d_2) \tag{18}$$
$$Bad(d_2) \vee Causes(a_1, d_1) \tag{19}$$
$$Bad(d_1) \vee Bad(d_2) \tag{20}$$
$$Causes(a_1, d_1) \vee Causes(a_1, d_2) \tag{21}$$

In this case, we cannot find any necessary reason which is part of a sufficient reason. This is because it is necessary for the action to be permissible to change conditions with respect to both caused deaths, viz., either make them morally acceptable or avoid causing them. However, the sufficient reasons only talk about individual deaths, because each of these deaths is sufficient on its own. For now, we just take this as a proof that INUS reasons do not always exist, even under the weakened definition. Thus, subsequent procedures, like natural-language generation, should be prepared to make use of the other two types of reasons in case the set of INUS reasons is empty.

The runtime performance of the current implementation is not suited for real-time use. As dilemmas become more complex or more complex principles (such as the Pareto principle [4] or the principle of double effect [2]) are used, reason generation becomes time consuming. For instance, while explaining permissibility of refraining in the symmetric trolley problem is very fast, explaining under the double effect principle already takes several minutes on a usual desktop machine. This is due to the fact that finding an prime implicant is a NP-hard problem, and our procedure enumerates all (potentially exponentially many) of them. In future, we plan to employ more sophisticated approaches to prime implicant enumeration, e.g., those described in [16,23]. Moreover, some of our principles are actually Horn formulas or even representable as 2-CNF formulas (e.g., do-no-harm principle). Thus, in future we will exploit the complexity class of the satisfiability problem of the logical fragment actually needed for the description of the ethical principle at hand, and use more specialized algorithms for prime implicant and prime implicate generation.

5   Related Work

Explainable AI has recently gained new interest due to the broad success of AI. This section only very briefly summarizes some recent developments that cut cross statistical and logics-based approaches to AI.

Dannenhauer and colleagues [11] propose an architecture for enabling agents to explain why they chose not to adopt a goal. In their approach, when the agent rejects a goal, the agent proves that it could not find a plan that achieves that goal without violating a hard constraint. In contrast, HERA agents evaluate actions not goals. Another difference is that HERA agents employ ethical principles which do not necessarily reason about alternatives. Explanations that involve contrastive arguments referring to alternatives (e.g., the action is permissible, because the other ones are even worse) are not always what we are after. Russell [13] proposes a method for generating counterfactual explanations of outputs of arbitrary classifiers. The method solves this problem as an integer program which finds a data-point which is maximally similar to the original input but results in another classification. The difference between the original datapoint and the chosen one can be cited as a counterfactual reason. This is closely related to our necessary reasons, whose negations also denote minimal conditions under which the judgment would have been different. Shih and colleagues [14] take a similar approach in the context of Bayesian classifiers. Apart from data points which lead to changes in the classifier's output (necessary reasons), the authors also consider parts of input that always lead to the classifier's output no matter how the other parts of the input look like (sufficient reasons).

The aforementioned approaches are located outside the domain of logic-based AI. However, they are less far away than one might expect: Our setting can also be conceptualized as a classifier (viz., the formula representing the conditions for moral permissibility of the action in that situation) classifying input (viz., the situation as given as a causal agency model together with an option) as either permissible or not. By finding out which parts of the input are sufficient or necessary for the classification, we compute sufficient and necessary reasons.

Another closely related approach is presented by Baum and colleagues [18]. Here, a robot's moral decision making is modeled as a utilitarian decision function, which judges an action possibility A as more, less, or equally morally permissible than another action possibility B. The authors propose a means to algorithmically derives arguments for the robot's judgments which can be presented to humans as rationalizations of the robot's actions. Borgo and colleagues [22] propose a system for explaining action plans to users. The user of the system can propose an alternative plan to the one generated by an AI planner. The explanation module then generates an explanation by comparing features of the user's and the AI planner's suggested plans. The type of explanation generated then can be categorized as consisting of necessary reasons, i.e., "the AI planner has generated that plan, because the alternative plan is more costly." Finally, logic programming has been employed for machine ethics in [19,20]. The authors also capture notions of causality for moral reasoning using logics. Future work should explore how approaches to explanation generation for logic programs [21] could be applied to machine ethics.

Interestingly, we are the only ones to explicitly point out INUS reasons and the problem of overdetermination in explanation. We expect both concepts to be important aspects when computing comprehensible explanations. None of the mentioned approaches really investigates the production of linguistic explanation. In the context of a navigating robot, Rosenthal an colleagues [17] propose different types of explanations along the dimensions of abstractness and granularity. However, they do not address the distinction between sufficiency and necessity. We see it as a limitation of the current state of the art that the algorithmic problem of reason computation and linguistic aspects of explanation generation have not been considered together.

6   Conclusions

The HERA architecture got extended with a module for the extraction of reasons for the sake of generating explanations for judgments about the moral permissibility or impermissibility of actions. The approach operates on the formulae that represent the ethical principle used for the judgment—no additional knowledge engineering is necessary. The procedure is based on computing prime implicants and prime implicates of the ethical-principle formulae. We take prime implicants and prime implicates to correspond to sufficient reasons and necessary reasons for the (im-)permissibility judgments. Further, a (weakened) version of the INUS condition was proposed to serve as a definition of a third type of reasons. It identifies necessary reasons that are part of sufficient reasons as constituents of explanations. However, we have seen that such reasons do not always exist like in the case of overdetermination. We are currently working towards linguistically framing explanations. This work will investigate which type of reasons are best suited for communicating different aspects of the situation. INUS reasons seem to be quite concise and straight to the point. Sufficient reasons seem to give a good idea about the regularities that underlie the judgment. And necessary reasons give an idea about what should have been different in order to enforce a different judgment, thus, they provide the basis for contrastive explanations. A user study to investigate these questions is underway.

Acknowledgments. We would like to thank the three anonymous reviewers for their constructive comments.

References

1. Lindner, F., Bentzen, M.M.: The hybrid ethical reasoning agent IMMANUEL. In: HRI 2017, pp. 187–188 (2017)
2. Lindner, F., Bentzen, M.M., Nebel, B.: The HERA approach to morally competent robots. In: IROS 2017, pp. 6991–6997 (2017)
3. Halpern, Y.: Causality. MIT Press, Cambridge (2016)

4. Kuhnert, B., Lindner, F., Bentzen, M.M., Ragni, M.: Perceived difficulty of moral dilemmas depends on their causal structure: a formal model and preliminary results. In: CogSci 2017, pp. 2494–2499 (2017)
5. Anderson, M., Anderson, S.L.: Machine Ethics. Cambridge University Press, Cambridge (2011)
6. Wachter, S., Mittelstadt, B., Floridi, L.: Transparent, explainable, and accountable AI for robotics. Sci. Robot. **2**(6) (2017)
7. Mittelstadt, B., Russel, C., Wachter, S.: Explaining explanations in AI. In: FAT* 2019, pp. 279–288 (2019)
8. Miller, T.: Explanation in artificial intelligence: insights from the social sciences. Artif. Intell. **267**, 1–38 (2019)
9. Mackie, J.L.: Causes and conditions. Am. Philos. Q. **12**, 245–65 (1965)
10. Lewis, D.: Causation. J. Philos. **70**, 556–567 (1973)
11. Dannenhauer, D., Floyd, M.W., Magazzeni, D., Aha, D.W.: Explaining rebel behavior in goal reasoning agents. In: ICAPS 2018 Workshop on Explainable Planning, pp. 12–18 (2018)
12. Langley, P., Meadows, B., Sridharan, M., Choi, D.: Explainable agency for intelligent autonomous systems. In: Twenty-Ninth Annual Conference on Innovative Applications of Artificial Intelligence, pp. 4762–4763 (2017)
13. Russell, C.: Efficient search for diverse coherent explanations. In: FAT* 2019, pp. 20–28 (2019)
14. Shih, A., Choi, A., Darwiche, A.: A symbolic approach to explaining Bayesian network classifiers. In: IJCAI/ECAI 2018 Workshop on Explainable Artificial Intelligence (XAI), pp. 144–150 (2018)
15. Ignatiev, A., Morgado, A., Marques-Silva, J.: PySAT: a Python toolkit for prototyping with SAT oracles. In: Beyersdorff, O., Wintersteiger, C.M. (eds.) SAT 2018. LNCS, vol. 10929, pp. 428–437. Springer, Cham (2018). https://doi.org/10.1007/978-3-319-94144-8_26
16. Jabbour, S., Marques-Silva, J., Sais, L., Salhi, Y.: Enumerating prime implicants of propositional formulae in conjunctive normal form. In: Fermé, E., Leite, J. (eds.) JELIA 2014. LNCS (LNAI), vol. 8761, pp. 152–165. Springer, Cham (2014). https://doi.org/10.1007/978-3-319-11558-0_11
17. Rosenthal, S., Selvaraj, S. P., Veloso, M.: Verbalization: narration of autonomous robot experience. In: IJCAI 2016, pp. 862–868 (2016)
18. Baum, K., Hermanns, H., Speith, T.: From machine ethics to explainability and back. In: International Symposium on Artificial Intelligence and Mathematics (ISAIM 2018) (2018)
19. Hölldobler, S.: Ethical decision making under the weak completion semantics. In: Proceedings of the Workshop on Bridging the Gap Between Human and Automated Reasoning, pp. 1–5 (2018)
20. Pereira, L.M., Saptawijaya, A.: Programming Machine Ethics. Springer, Cham (2016). https://doi.org/10.1007/978-3-319-29354-7
21. Shanahan, M.: Prediction is deduction but explanation is abduction. In: IJCAI 1989, pp. 1055–1060 (1989)
22. Borgo, R., Cashmore, M., Magazzeni, D.: Towards providing justifications for planner decisions. In: Proceedings of IJCAI 2018 Workshop on Explainable AI (2018)
23. Previti, A., Ignatiev, A., Morgado, A., Marques-Silva, J.: Prime compilation of non-clausal formulae. In: IJCAI 2015, pp. 1980–1987 (2015)
24. Stocker, M.: The schizophrenia of modern ethical theories. J. Philos. **73**(14), 453–466 (1976)

Gaussian Lifted Marginal Filtering

Stefan Lüdtke[1]([✉]), Alejandro Molina[2], Kristian Kersting[2], and Thomas Kirste[1]

[1] Institute of Visual and Analytic Computing, University of Rostock,
Rostock, Germany
{stefan.luedtke2,thomas.kirste}@uni-rostock.de
[2] Computer Science Department, TU Darmstadt, Darmstadt, Germany
{molina,kersting}@cs.tu-darmstadt.de

Abstract. Recently, *Lifted Marginal Filtering* has been proposed, an efficient Bayesian filtering algorithm for stochastic systems consisting of multiple, (inter-)acting agents and objects (entities). The algorithm achieves its efficiency by performing inference jointly over groups of *similar* entities (i.e. their properties follow the same distribution).

In this paper, we explore the case where there are no entities that are directly suitable for grouping, which is typical for many real-world scenarios. We devise a mechanism to identify entity groups, by formulating the distribution that is described by the grouped representation as a *mixture* distribution, such that the parameters can be fitted by Expectation Maximization. Specifically, in this paper, we investigate the Gaussian mixture case. Furthermore, we show how Gaussian mixture merging methods can be used to prevent the number of groups from growing indefinitely over time. We evaluate our approach on an activity prediction task in an online multiplayer game. The results suggest that compared to the conventional approach, where all entities are handled individually, decrease in prediction accuracy is small, while inference runtime decreases significantly.

Keywords: Lifted inference · Probabilistic inference ·
Bayesian filtering · Probabilistic Multiset Rewriting System ·
Gaussian mixture · Activity recognition

1 Introduction

Many AI tasks like Human Activity Recognition (HAR) or network analysis involve modeling stochastic systems that consist of multiple, interacting agents or objects. Recently, a novel inference approach (Lifted Marginal Filtering [7]) has been devised, that performs efficient inference in such systems. It models system states as *multisets*, and the system dynamics as a *Probabilistic Multiset Rewriting System* (PMRS) [2]. The algorithm is efficient when the system consists of groups of entities that are *similar*, i.e. whose properties follow the same distribution, and that have the same capabilities to interact. In this case, inference complexity only depends on the number of groups, but not on the number of entities per group.

© Springer Nature Switzerland AG 2019
C. Benzmüller and H. Stuckenschmidt (Eds.): KI 2019, LNAI 11793, pp. 230–243, 2019.
https://doi.org/10.1007/978-3-030-30179-8_19

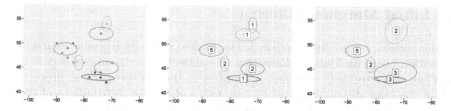

Fig. 1. Proposed approach for efficient inference multi-entity scenarios, illustrated by the multiplayer game domain from Example 1. Different colors denote different players. Left: Actual village positions are shown by dots. We do not use the actual positions, but Gaussian mixture components of village locations, shown by ellipses. Center: Example of state after several conquer actions occurred. Right: New mixture model, after merging of mixture components (to avoid growing the state space indefinitely). (Color figure online)

Many Bayesian filtering problems consist of such interacting entities, but often, it is not immediately clear which entities are suitable for grouping – because all of them may have distinct properties. For example, consider the online multiplayer game we are concerned with in this paper (Fig. 1), whose system dynamics can be conveniently described by a PMRS: Players own villages arranged on a grid map, and can perform actions like conquering other players' villages. The task is to estimate the distribution over future game states (i.e. to perform Bayesian filtering). However, initially, all entities (villages) have distinct properties (the position on the map), and thus Bayesian filtering in this system quickly leads to a very large number of possible states.

In this paper, we investigate methods to find groups of entities that can be handled jointly. The basic observation is that in many cases, some of the entities show almost the same behavior, despite having different properties. The idea is to approximate their properties by a single parametric distribution, such that the entities can be handled as a group. We call the state representation where entities are grouped *lifted state*[1]. Ideally, the lifted state still contains the relevant information to compute the posterior state distribution. Furthermore, we show how methods from Gaussian mixture merging [12] can be used to prevent the number of groups (and thus inference complexity) from growing indefinitely over time.

The empirical results in the online game domain show that our approach is much faster than the conventional approach of working with distinct entities (as done for the same game by [15]). Additionally, in this domain, the approximation that is performed to arrive at a lifted state representation has only marginal influence on the prediction accuracy.

---

[1] Based on the connections to our approach to lifted probabilistic inference [5], as outlined in [7].

2   Lifted Marginal Filtering

In this section, we briefly introduce LiMa, a lifted recursive Bayesian estimation algorithm based on Multiset Rewriting. We show how distributions over multisets can be factorized, such that (i) entities in the multisets whose properties follow the same distribution can be grouped, and (ii) the distributions of those properties are represented on the parametric rather than on the instance level. We then show how recursive Bayesian estimation can be performed directly on this lifted representation, without computing the original, much larger ground representation first.

2.1   Problem Statement

We are concerned with a *recursive Bayesian estimation* task (also called *Bayesian filtering*). That is, the goal is to estimate the posterior distribution $p(X_t|y_{1:t})$ of the *hidden* system state x_t at time t from the previous posterior $p(X_{t-1}|y_{1:t-1})$ and an observation y_t. We assume that the system dynamics is a first-order Markov chain (i.e. it can be described by a *transition model* $p(X_{t+1}|x_t)$), and that the observation y_t only depends on the state x_t. Then, the computation can be decomposed into two steps: The *prediction* step calculates the distribution after applying the transition model, i.e. $p(X_{t+1}|y_{1:t}) = \int_{x_t} p(X_{t+1}|X_t=x_t)\, p(X_t=x_t|y_{1:t})\, dx_t$. Afterwards, the posterior distribution is computed by employing the *observation model* $p(y_{t+1}|X_{t+1})$:

$$p(X_{t+1}|y_{1:t+1}) = \frac{p(y_{t+1}|X_{t+1})\, p(X_{t+1}|y_{1:t})}{p(y_{t+1}|y_{1:t})} \tag{1}$$

In LiMa, the states x_t are *multisets*, i.e. functions of *entities* to *multiplicities* (natural numbers). We use *structured* entities here, i.e. entities are key-value maps. The transition model $p(X_{t+1}|x_t)$ is modeled as a *Probabilistic Multiset Rewriting System*, introduced in more detail in Sect. 2.3. The following example illustrates how system states can be modeled as multisets.

Example 1. Consider the situation depicted in Fig. 1 (left): There are three players, each one having multiple villages. Each village is represented as a separate entity, containing owner and position information, for example:

$$c_1 = \langle \text{Player: } Red, \text{Pos: } (-72, 54) \rangle$$
$$c_2 = \langle \text{Player: } Red, \text{Pos: } (-84, 46) \rangle$$
$$\dots$$
$$c_{15} = \langle \text{Player: } Green, \text{Pos: } (-74, 43) \rangle$$

The state is a multiset of those entities, each entity having a multiplicity of one:

$$x = [\![\, 1c_1, 1c_2, \dots, 1c_{15} \,]\!]$$

Modeling a distribution over such multisets naively as a categorical distribution (i.e. a set of tuples (x_i, p_i)) quickly becomes infeasible, due to the combinatorial explosion in the number of tuples with respect to the number of entities. When m different types of entities (species) can exist in the system, and n entities are present at a given time, the maximum number of states is $\binom{m+n-1}{n} = \frac{(m+n-1)!}{n!(m-1)!}$, i.e. the number of multisets of cardinality n, with elements chosen from a set of cardinality m. Note that enumeration becomes impossible when entities can contain continuous values, e.g. from $\mathbb{R}$.

2.2 Lifted Representation

Lifted Marginal Filtering (LiMa) uses a more efficient representation for such distributions over structured multisets. Specifically, LiMa can efficiently represent situations where multiple entities are similar, i.e. their properties follow the same distribution, and efficiently perform inference in such domains. The idea is that in these cases, the distribution of properties can be represented *parametrically*, and the similar entities can then be grouped in the multiset. To make this more clear, consider the following example.

Example 2. For the online game domain introduced in Example 1, consider the situation where the *Red* player owns two villages, and we are uncertain about whether they are at location 1 or location 2 (both villages could be either at 1 or 2 with uniform probability). Using the representation above, this requires 3 distinct ground states

$$x_1 = [\![\, 2\langle \text{P: } \textit{Red}, \text{Pos: } 1\rangle \,]\!]$$
$$x_2 = [\![\, 1\langle \text{P: } \textit{Red}, \text{Pos: } 1\rangle, 1\langle \text{P: } \textit{Red}, \text{Pos: } 2\rangle \,]\!]$$
$$x_3 = [\![\, 2\langle \text{P: } \textit{Red}, \text{Pos: } 2\rangle \,]\!]$$

with probabilities $p(x_1) = p(x_3) = 0.25$ and $p(x_2) = 0.5$. However, by using a *parametric distribution* to represent the location of both entities, we can represent the same situation as:

$$s = [\![\, 2\langle \text{P: } \delta_{\text{Red}}, \text{Pos: } \mathcal{C}(0.5{:}1, 0.5{:}2)\rangle \,]\!]$$

Here, $\mathcal{C}(0.5{:}1, 0.5{:}2)$ represents the categorical distribution, where both 1 and 2 are drawn with probability 0.5, and δ_{Red} represents the singleton distribution with value *Red*.

We call such a multiset, which contains entitites that map properties to representations of a distribution, a *lifted state*. The number of lifted states that are required to represent a distribution can be much lower than the number of ground states, as each lifted state already describes a distribution of *multiple* ground states. In general, it is also possible to maintain factors that represent joint distributions over values of multiple entities, see [7] for more details.

A lifted state s represents a distribution of ground states x by the following generative process: Fix an order of the entities in s (e.g. lexicographically), denote the i-th entity as s_i. For simplicity of the definitions, identical entities are repeated here. Denote the overall number of entities in s and x as n. The k-th distribution in s_i is called $p_{s_i}^{(k)}$. Then, for each distribution $p_{s_i}^{(k)}$, sample a value and replace the representation of $p_{s_i}^{(k)}$ in s by the sampled value. Finally, all entities created this way are collected in a multiset x.

For example, the lifted state $[\![\,2\langle \text{P: } \delta_{\text{Red}}, \text{Pos: } \mathcal{C}(0.5{:}1, 0.5{:}2)\rangle\,]\!]$ represents the distributions $p_{s_1}^{(1)} = p_{s_2}^{(1)} \sim \delta_{\text{Red}}$ and $p_{s_1}^{(2)} = p_{s_2}^{(2)} \sim \mathcal{C}(0.5{:}1, 0.5{:}2)$. Suppose we sample the value Red from both $p_{s_1}^{(1)}$ and $p_{s_2}^{(1)}$, 2 from $p_{s_1}^{(2)}$ and 1 from $p_{s_2}^{(2)}$. The resulting ground state is $x = [\![\,1\langle \text{P: } Red, \text{Pos: } 1\rangle, 1\langle \text{P: } Red, \text{Pos: } 2\rangle\,]\!]$. Note that the same ground state is also obtained by sampling 1 from $p_{s_1}^{(2)}$ and 2 from $p_{s_2}^{(2)}$. This is due to the fact that both x and s are multisets, where the entities do not have an order.

Next, we give a closed-form expression of the ground distribution $p(x|s)$ that is described by a lifted state. This will allow us to describe the relationship of the distribution to mixture models in more detail in Sect. 3. Assume we can fix an order of the entities in x (e.g. lexicographically), and call the j-th entity x_j. First, each lifted entity s_i describes a distribution $p(x_j|s_i)$ of ground entities. According to the sampling process, this is simply

$$p(x_j|s_i) = \prod_{k=1}^{K} p^{(k)}(x_j^{(k)}|s_i), \tag{2}$$

i.e. all distributions contained in a lifted entity s_i are independent. There are multiple ways how a given ground state x can be sampled from a lifted state s (i.e. which entity in x has been sampled from which entity in s). Thus, we need to consider all possible associations. Each association between entities from x and entities from s can be described by a permutation σ of $1, \ldots, n$: Given a permutation σ, the probability of the entity x can be defined as:

$$p(x|s, \sigma) = p(x_1, \ldots, x_n|s_1, \ldots, s_n, \sigma) = \prod_{j=1}^{n} p(x_j|s_{\sigma(j)}) \tag{3}$$

Finally, the distribution of ground states x is obtained by marginalizing over all permutations:

$$p(x|s) = \sum_{\sigma} p(x|s, \sigma)\, p(\sigma), \tag{4}$$

where $p(\sigma) = 1/n!$, i.e. a uniform distribution over permutations.

2.3   System Dynamics

The system dynamics, i.e. the transition model $p(s_t|s_{t-1})$ is described by a *Probabilistic Multiset Rewriting System* (PMRS). Notably, the transition model can be applied directly to a distribution of *lifted states*, without generating all ground states first: This is possible when the actions are *homogeneous* with respect to the lifted states s, i.e. all ground states x described by s are manipulated in the same way by the action, such that the posterior can again be represented by a lifted state s'.

An *action* a is a triple (c, f, w), where c is a list of preconditions, f is an effect function and w is a weight. It is useful to formulate the preconditions as *constraints*, i.e. boolean functions on the lifted entities. An action a is compatible to a sequence $i = (i_1, \ldots, i_n)$ of entities when each constraint is satisfied by the corresponding entity. We call a pair of action and a compatible sequence of entities an *action instance*. An action instance can be applied to a lifted state s when all entities are contained in the state. The posterior state s' of applying an action instance is obtained by removing the entities from s, and inserting the results of the effect function f (applied to the entities): $s' = \text{apply}(s, (a, i)) = (s \uplus i) \uplus f(i)$.

An example of such an action in the multiplayer domain is the $\text{conquer}(c_1, c_2)$ action, describing that a village c_2 is conquered by an attack starting from a village c_1. The precondition of this action is that the owners of c_1 and c_2 are different (a player cannot conquer a city of himself). Note that the preconditions are *positional* – the action instance $\text{conquer}(c_1, c_2)$ is different from $\text{conquer}(c_2, c_1)$.

Probabilistic MRSs assign a *weight* w_{ai} to each action instance ai. This weight is based on the property values of the bound entities. For example, the weight of a specific instance of the conquer action depends on the distance of the locations of c_1 and c_2. In the scenarios we are concerned with, all entities can act simultaneously between observations. For example, multiple players can conquer villages in a single time step. Formally, this is expressed by a *maximally parallel* MRS [2] (MPMRS). In such a system, each state transition is described by a parallel executed of a multiset of action instances, called *compound action*.

We use a generalization of MPMRSs to model this behavior: We distinguish between *exclusive* constraints, where the entity that is bound to such a constraint cannot participate in any other action, and *non-exclusive* constrains. For example, in the multiplayer domain, the same entity can conquer multiple other entities, but can only be conquered once per timestep. A compound action is applied to a state s by applying all of its action instances to s. A compound action is *valid* in a state s when all exclusiveness conditions are satisfied.

Given a state s, each valid compound action k can be assigned a weight, based on its *multiplicity* $\mu_s(k)$ (the number of ways the entities in k can be chosen from s), and the weights of its action instances: $w_s(k) = \mu_s(k) \prod_{ai \in k} w_{ai}$. The distribution of valid compound actions is the normalized weight: $p(k|s) = w_s(k) / \sum_{k_i \in K_s} w_s(k_i)$, where K_s is the set of all valid compound actions in s. As the number of valid compound actions can quickly become very large, we use the MCMC method proposed in [8] to approximate $p(k|s)$ here. Finally, the transition model (i.e. the distribution of successor states of a given state s_t) is obtained as:

$$p(s_{t+1}|s_t) = \sum_{\{k | s_{t+1} = apply(s_t, k)\}} p(k|s_t) \tag{5}$$

The transition semantics is illustrated by the following example.

Example 3. Consider the entities $e_1 = \langle$P: Red, Pos: $\mathcal{N}(\mu_1, \Sigma_1)\rangle$, $e_2 = \langle$P: Red, Pos: $\mathcal{N}(\mu_2, \Sigma_2)\rangle$ and $e_3 = \langle$P: $Green$, Pos: $\mathcal{N}(\mu_3, \Sigma_3)$, and the lifted state $s = [\![\, 2e_1, 1e_2, 5e_3\,]\!]$. The only action is the conquer action described above. There are four action instances: $a_1 = \text{conquer}(e_1, e_3)$, $a_2 = \text{conquer}(e_3, e_1)$, $a_3 = \text{conquer}(e_2, e_3)$ and $a_4 = \text{conquer}(e_3, e_2)$. This results in a number of valid compound actions. For illustration, consider the compound action $k = [\![\, 2a_1, 1a_4\,]\!]$. The resulting successor state is

$$s = [\![\, 2\langle\text{P: } Red, \text{Pos: } \mathcal{N}(\mu_1, \Sigma_1)\rangle, 1\langle\text{P: } Green, \text{Pos: } \mathcal{N}(\mu_2, \Sigma_2)\rangle,$$
$$3\langle\text{P: } Green, \text{Pos: } \mathcal{N}(\mu_3, \Sigma_3)\rangle, 2\langle\text{P: } Red, \text{Pos: } \mathcal{N}(\mu_3, \Sigma_3)\rangle\,]\!],$$

and its probability can be computed as shown in Eq. 5 (specific values are not given in this example).

Afterwards, the probability $p(s_{t+1}|y_{1:t})$ of each posterior state s_{t+1} is reweighed by the observation likelihood $p(y_{t+1}|s_{t+1})$. The observations y can be continuous or discrete random variables, and $p(y_{t+1}|s_{t+1})$ can be any distribution, as long as we are able to compute its value, given a state s_{t+1} and an observation y_{t+1}. Note that this operation does not increase the representational complexity (as it is simply reweighing the probability of each state s_{t+1}. In this paper, we are only concerned with the *prediction* step (Eq. 5), which can increase the representational complexity.

An important aspect to note here is that the number of compound actions (and thus the cardinality of the posterior distribution) depends on the number of action instances, and thus on the number of *different* entities. Thus, the lifted state representation is more efficient for two reasons: (i) The number of states is lower (each lifted state represents a distribution of ground states), and (ii) the number of successor states per lifted state is lower (as fewer compound actions can be applied).

3   Gaussian Lifted Marginal Filtering

In the following, we show how a lifted state representation can be obtained, given data of ground entities. Furthermore, we discuss how the representational size of the distribution can be prevented from growing indefinitely over time.

3.1   Lifting by Mixture Fitting

Given a ground state, the goal is to find a lifted state that approximates the ground states as close as possible, but has fewer different entities. Specifically, the goal is to find s such that the likelihood of s for the ground state x, i.e. $p(x|s)$, is maximized. Thus, we need to devise a maximum likelihood estimator for $p(x|s)$.

Consider again how $p(x|s)$ has been defined in Sect. 2.2: Overall, $p(x|s)$ is a sum over permutations, i.e. ways to associate the entities in x and in s. This is due to the fact that given a sample x (a ground state) from a lifted state s, we do not know which entity has been sampled from which entity in s. Instead of attempting to directly perform maximum likelihood estimation for the distribution $p(x|s)$, we instead make the following simplification: Instead of considering all *permutations* of $1, \ldots, n$, we consider all *tuples* $\tau \in T_n$ of length n, with elements chosen from $1, \ldots, n$. In other words, we omit the constraint that we sample exactly once from each distribution in s. This way, the likelihood becomes

$$\tilde{p}(x|s) = \sum_{\tau} p(\tau) \prod_{j=1}^{n} p(x_j | s_{\tau(j)}) \qquad (6)$$

i.e. it sums over even more terms. Again, $p(\tau)$ is a uniform distribution over all $\tau \in T_n$, i.e. $p(\tau) = 1/n^n = \prod_{j=1}^{n} 1/n$. Then, by using the identity $\sum_{\tau} \prod_{j=1}^{n} a_{j,\tau(j)} = \prod_{j=1}^{n} \sum_{i=1}^{n} a_{ij}$, we obtain

$$\tilde{p}(x|s) = p(x_1, \ldots, x_n | s) = \prod_{j=1}^{n} \sum_{i=1}^{n} \frac{1}{n} p(x_i | s_j). \qquad (7)$$

Finally, remember that in s, there are multiple identical entities. Denote the multiplicity of entity s_j by n_j, and the number of different entities by m. Thus, the distribution can be written as

$$\tilde{p}(x|s) = p(x_1, \ldots, x_n | s) = \prod_{j=1}^{n} \sum_{i=1}^{m} \frac{n_j}{n} p(x_i | s_j). \qquad (8)$$

This distribution describes a sequence of i.i.d. samples from a mixture, where $p(\cdot|s_j)$ are the mixture components and n_j/n is the weight of each mixture. The likelihood $\tilde{p}(x|s)$ can be maximized by standard mechanisms to fit mixture distributions. Specifically, for the online game domain, each distribution $p(\cdot|s_j)$ is a product of a singleton distribution (to encode the owner of a village), and a normal distribution (to encode the location of the distribution). Thus, for each value of the singleton distributions (i.e. for each player), a Gaussian mixture needs to be fitted, which can be done efficiently using Expectation Maximization (EM) [4].

The lifted state is constructed by generating one entity for each mixture component, with a value distribution according to that component. The multiplicity of each of those entities is the number of ground entities associated with this mixture component. As an example, consider Fig. 1, showing the original village locations, and the estimated mixture components per player (and thus entities in the lifted state).

3.2 Merging Entities

Over time, the lifted representation that has been obtained can degenerate in multiple ways. First, the number of *states* typically increases over time due to the system dynamics, as each state can have multiple successor states, and some operations can require *splitting* a lifted states into multiple partitions (see [7] for more details). To prevent the representational size of the distribution from growing indefinitely, an operation that reduced the number of lifted states is required (e.g. by identifying multiple lifted states that can be represented by a single lifted state). Solving this problem in general is a topic for future work.

Here, we consider a closely related problem: The number of *distinct entities* (species) can also be increased due to the system dynamics, which in turn also leads to an increased number of posterior states. This is illustrated in Example 3. In other contexts, this problem is well-known: In a mixture Kalman filter [1], the number of mixture components grows exponential over time. For this method, *merging* procedures have been developed: Given a Gaussian mixture, they compute a mixture with fewer components that has a minimal distance to the original mixture.

For our approach, we employ the same concepts: After each transition, we apply a merging procedure that reduces the number of different entities (i.e. mixture components). Specifically, we employ the procedure described in [12]: Let s_i and s_j be two entities in a state s, with multiplicities n_i and n_j. Assume that they have associated value distributions $p_i \propto \mathcal{N}(\mu_i, \Sigma_i)$ and $p_j \propto \mathcal{N}(\mu_j, \Sigma_j)$. The Gaussian mixture of p_i and p_j is $p_m = w_i\,p_i + w_j\,p_j$, where $w_i = n_i/n$ and $w_j = n_j/n$. The parameters of the normal $p_{ij} \propto \mathcal{N}(\mu_{ij}, \Sigma_{ij})$ with minimal Kullback-Leibler divergence to p_m are calculated as follows:

$$w_{ij} = w_i + w_j, \qquad w_{i|ij} = \frac{w_i}{w_i + w_j}, \qquad w_{j|ij} = \frac{w_j}{w_i + w_j}$$

$$\mu_{ij} = w_{i|ij}\mu_i + w_{j|ij}\mu_j$$

$$\Sigma_{ij} = w_{i|ij}\Sigma_i + w_{j|ij}\Sigma_j + w_{i|ij}w_{j|ij}(\mu_i - \mu_j)(\mu_i - \mu_j)^T \tag{9}$$

The weight of the new component p_{ij} is w_{ij}, and the multiplicity of the new entity is $n_i + n_j$. Given a mixture, it is possible to find the *optimal* components to merge, i.e. those producing the smallest change in Kullback-Leibler divergence of the mixtures before and after merging. This is done by calculating the bound $B(i,j) = \frac{1}{2}[w_{ij}\log|\Sigma_{ij}| - w_i\log|\Sigma_i| - w_j\log|\Sigma_j|]$ for all combinations of components p_i and p_j and selecting the two components for which $B(i,j)$ is minimal. This operation is repeated, until either the minimal bound $B(i,j)$ exceeds a threshold (meaning that merging the mixture further would lead to a larger error), or the desired number of mixture components is reached. An example of this procedure is shown in Fig. 1 (right).

4   Experimental Evaluation

We evaluated the proposed approach on a prediction task in the large-scale massively multiplayer online strategy game Travian[2]. Travian is a strategy game, consisting of a grid map. Players own one or multiple villages located on the

---

[2] www.travian.com.

Table 1. Factors and levels of experimental design.

Factor	Levels	Description
Entities per player	1,3,5,∞ (ground representation)	Maximum number of entities per player, i.e. mixture components
Timesteps	2,...,5	Prediction horizon
Players	3,...,10	Number of players per state
Merging	Yes, no	Gaussian mixture reduction
Dataset	1,...,10	Random subset of complete data

map. They harvest resources from the environment, improve their village, build military units and attack other players' villages (possibly conquering them). In the following, we will focus on the high-level aspects of the game, namely village ownership and attacks. The same application scenario has already been investigated by Thon et al. [15], using a ground state representation.

The factors of the experimental design are shown in Table 1. We logged the state of a game server over 5 days and recorded high-level data (position and affiliation of villages). The data was collected once every 24 hours. The data contains more than 6400 villages and 1400 players.

We evaluated our approach on a subset of this data, that has been extracted in the same way as done by Thon et al. [15]: From the complete data, sequences of *local* game world states were sampled. Each sequence contains the game state for a small set of players (3 to 10 players).

The goal of the experiments is to evaluate the performance of the proposed approach, regarding prediction accuracy and runtime. Specifically, we compare the lifted state representation to the conventional ground state representation. Multiple prediction steps (up to 5) are performed, without incorporating observations. After each prediction step, either Gaussian mixture merging is performed to the maximally allowed number, or no merging is performed (to investigate the effect of the merging operation on runtime and accuracy). The prediction accuracy is assessed by computing receiver operating characteristic (ROC) curves, regarding whether each conquer event did or did not occur in the transition, and by calculating the area under the curve (AUC). In all experiments, we used the MCMC-based algorithm to compute compound actions described in [8] with 100 samples, and performed 10 runs for each factor configuration. We use a prototypical implementation of our approach in R, and use the R package `mclust` [14] for fitting Gaussian mixtures by Expectation Maximization.

5   Results

Results of the evaluation are shown in Fig. 2. The upper left plot shows exemplary ROC curves for the subsets containing 3 players. AUC is substantially greater than 0.5, indicating that all models capture some of the characteristics of the true system dynamics. As expected, the AUC is lowest when only a single mixture

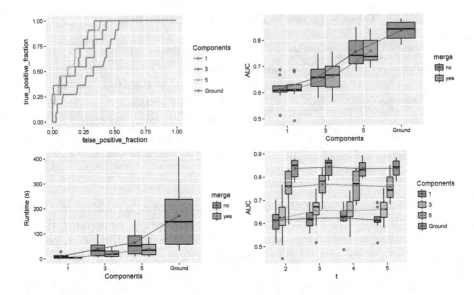

Fig. 2. Results for the Travian scenario for 5-timestep prediction. Top left: Exemplary ROC curves (3 players). Top right: AUC for different numbers of mixture components per player (aggregated over all runs and numbers of players). Bottom left: Runtime for different number of mixture components per player. Bottom right: AUC for different prediction horizons (aggregated over all runs and numbers of players).

component is allowed per player, as this is the broadest approximation of the true village locations. The more components are allowed, the more information about the true village locations is preserved, resulting in a more accurate prediction.

Figure 2 (top right) shows the mean AUC (aggregated over all experiments of 3 to 10 players) for different numbers of mixture components, and a prediction horizon of 2. Allowing more components in general leads to a higher AUC, as discussed above. The obtained AUC values for the ground version of our approach are comparable to results reported by [15] (approximately 0.8 in both cases). Their approach is similar to the *ground* version of our approach, except that the transition model they use considers additional factors like history of players and alliances. Interestingly, the AUC for 5 components over all numbers of players is not significantly lower than the AUC of the ground model ($p > 0.12$ using Wilcoxon signed rank test, $n = 80$). Furthermore, for each number of mixture components, there is no significant difference in AUC between the runs where Gaussian mixture merging was performed or not performed.

Figure 2 (bottom left) shows the average runtime of computing the prediction. More components lead to an increased algorithm runtime (as the number of action instances increases). The ground model has by far the highest runtime. In contrast to the AUC, the runtime of the lifted models is significantly lower than runtime of the ground model ($p < 10^{-10}$ using Wilcoxon signed rank test, $n = 80$), and Gaussian mixture merging also leads to a significantly lower runtime.

To summarize, the results suggest that the lifted model can achieve an AUC that is not significantly lower than the AUC of the ground model (given a sufficiently large number of mixture components per entity), but needs a significantly lower runtime.

6   Related Work

The concept of factorizing the state distribution, and handling some factors analytically, is prominently and successfully used in the Rao-Blackwellized particle filter (RBPF) [3]. In the RBPF, the distribution of the variables that are not handled analytically is estimated by a particle filter. The distribution of these remaining variables has a lower dimensionality and smaller support. Thus fewer particles are necessary to provide a good approximation. In contrast to the RBPF, in our approach, the factorization has an additional advantage: The remaining object is a *multiset*, where more elements can be grouped, and inference on this multiset (using multiset rewriting) can be performed more efficiently.

There are a number of other approaches that use a computational language to describe system dynamics (just as we use a MRS), known as Computational State Space Models (CSSM) [6,11]. We are not aware of any CSSM that uses a factorized state representation, as done by Lifted Marginal Filtering. Stochastic Relational Processes (SRP) [15] are a specific instance of CSSMs that describe states by logical interpretations, and state dynamics by a probabilistic logic. Their approach is conceptually similar to the *ground* version of our approach (although the semantics of parallel actions is different in detail).

The concept of grouping entities that are not exactly identical in a multiset is known as *super-individuals* [10,13] in the modeling and simulation community. The idea is to maintain not all individual entities, but typical representatives, that each represent a large number of actual entities. In contrast to our approach, each of the super-individuals has *specific* property values (i.e. it its assumed that each of the entities represented by the super-individual has the same property values), whereas LiMa is able to represent (and manipulate) the *distribution* of property values. A further difference of LiMa to these approaches is that it directly estimates state *distributions*, instead of repeatedly drawing sample trajectories, which allows to incorporate observations and thus recursive Bayesian estimation.

7   Conclusion

In this paper, we investigated how Lifted Marginal Filtering (LiMa) can be applied to situations without exactly identical entities. The central idea is to formulate the distribution described by a lifted state as a mixture distribution, which allows to use Expectation Maximization to estimate the parameters of the mixture (i.e. of the lifted state). Inference can then be performed directly on this compact representation of the distribution, which is much more efficient than inference on the instance level. Specifically, in this paper we considered the special case where the value distributions are assumed to be normal distributions, and showed how methods for fitting Gaussian mixtures can be used to find a suitable grouping. The evaluation on an online multiplayer game suggests that using this approach, prediction accuracy decreases only marginally, while runtime is significantly lower.

The ideas developed in this paper can be extended in several directions: First, other parametric or non-parametric distributions (instead of normal distributions) could be used for the value distribution. Second, a more general approach to estimate the parameters of such mixtures – that include different types of distributions – is needed. Both of these requirements can potentially be satisfied by using the recently proposed *Mixed Sum-Product Networks* (MSPNs) [9]. An MSPN is a general density estimator, that allows to fit a hierarchical probabilistic model, consisting of layers of mixtures and factorization. Using MSPNs, we do not need any prior knowledge about which property values to approximate by distributions, or about the parametric form of the distribution.

A further direction for future work is concerned with keeping the representation of the posterior distribution small, by identifying *groups* of lifted states whose ground distribution can be represented (approximately) by a single lifted state. Finally, the experimental evaluation could be extended by integrating (partial) state observations (thus performing full Bayesian Filtering, the original task Lifted Marginal Filtering was developed for), a more elaborate transition model (for example based on the transition model used by [15]), or by investigating more complex application domains, like sensor-based human activity recognition.

References

1. Alspach, D., Sorenson, H.: Nonlinear Bayesian estimation using Gaussian sum approximations. IEEE Trans. Autom. Control **17**(4), 439–448 (1972)
2. Barbuti, R., Levi, F., Milazzo, P., Scatena, G.: Maximally parallel probabilistic semantics for multiset rewriting. Fundamenta Informaticae **112**(1), 1–17 (2011). https://doi.org/10.3233/FI-2011-575
3. Doucet, A., De Freitas, N., Murphy, K., Russell, S.: Rao-Blackwellised particle filtering for dynamic Bayesian networks. In: Proceedings of the Sixteenth Conference on Uncertainty in Artificial Intelligence, pp. 176–183. Morgan Kaufmann Publishers Inc. (2000)
4. Fraley, C., Raftery, A.E.: Model-based clustering, discriminant analysis, and density estimation. J. Am. Stat. Assoc. **97**(458), 611–631 (2002)
5. Gogate, V., Domingos, P.: Probabilistic theorem proving. Commun. ACM **59**(7), 107–115 (2016). https://doi.org/10.1145/2936726
6. Krüger, F., Nyolt, M., Yordanova, K., Hein, A., Kirste, T.: Computational state space models for activity and intention recognition. A feasibility study. PLoS ONE **9**(11), e109381 (2014). https://doi.org/10.1371/journal.pone.0109381
7. Lüdtke, S., Schröder, M., Bader, S., Kersting, K., Kirste, T.: Lifted filtering via exchangeable decomposition. In: Proceedings of the 27th International Joint Conference on Artificial Intelligence (2018)

8. Lüdtke, S., Schröder, M., Kirste, T.: Approximate probabilistic parallel multiset rewriting using MCMC. In: Trollmann, F., Turhan, A.-Y. (eds.) KI 2018. LNCS (LNAI), vol. 11117, pp. 73–85. Springer, Cham (2018). https://doi.org/10.1007/978-3-030-00111-7_7

9. Molina, A., Vergari, A., Di Mauro, N., Natarajan, S., Esposito, F., Kersting, K.: Mixed sum-product networks: a deep architecture for hybrid domains. In: Proceedings of the Thirty-Second AAAI Conference on Artificial Intelligence (2018)

10. Parry, H.R., Evans, A.J.: A comparative analysis of parallel processing and super-individual methods for improving the computational performance of a large individual-based model. Ecol. Model. **214**(2–4), 141–152 (2008)

11. Ramírez, M., Geffner, H.: Goal recognition over POMDPs: inferring the intention of a POMDP agent. In: Proceedings of the 22nd IJCAI, pp. 2009–2014. AAAI Press (2011)

12. Runnalls, A.R.: Kullback-Leibler approach to Gaussian mixture reduction. IEEE Trans. Aerosp. Electron. Syst. **43**(3), 989–999 (2007)

13. Scheffer, M., Baveco, J., DeAngelis, D., Rose, K., van Nes, E.: Super-individuals a simple solution for modelling large populations on an individual basis. Ecol. Model. **80**(2–3), 161–170 (1995)

14. Scrucca, L., Fop, M., Murphy, T.B., Raftery, A.E.: mclust 5: clustering, classification and density estimation using Gaussian finite mixture models. R J. **8**(1), 289 (2016)

15. Thon, I., Landwehr, N., De Raedt, L.: Stochastic relational processes: efficient inference and applications. Mach. Learn. **82**(2), 239–272 (2011). https://doi.org/10.1007/s10994-010-5213-8

An Introduction to AnyBURL

Christian Meilicke[(✉)], Melisachew Wudage Chekol, Daniel Ruffinelli,
and Heiner Stuckenschmidt

University of Mannheim, Mannheim, Germany
christian@informatik.uni-mannheim.de

1 Introduction

Current research on knowledge graph completion is often concerned with latent approaches that are based on the idea to embed a knowledge graph into a low dimensional vector space. At the same time symbolic approaches have attracted less attention [13]. However, such approaches have a big advantage: they yield an explanation in terms of the rules that trigger a prediction. In this paper we propose a bottom-up technique for efficiently learning logical rules from large knowledge graphs inspired by classic bottom-up rule learning approaches as Golem [8] and Aleph [10]. Our approach is called AnyBURL (**A**nytime **B**ottom-**U**p **R**ule **L**earning). We report on experiments where we evaluated AnyBURL on datasets that have been labelled as hard cases for simple (rule-based) approaches. Our approach performs as good as and sometimes better than most models that have been proposed recently. Moreover, the required resources in terms of memory and runtime are significantly smaller compared to latent approaches. This paper is an extended abstract of an IJCAI 2019 paper [6].

2 Language Bias and Algorithm

A small subset of a knowledge graph is shown in Fig. 1. Suppose that we are interested in finding rules that explain why Ed speaks Dutch, which corresponds to the fact $speaks(ed, d)$. To construct useful rules, we look at all paths of length n that start at ed or d. Note that we allow a path to be constructed by following in- and outgoing edges. We have marked three paths starting at ed in Fig. 1. Two of these paths are acyclic paths ending somewhere in the knowledge graph, while the third path is, together with $speaks(ed, d)$, cyclic. On the left side of the figure these paths are shown in terms of their corresponding bottom rules.

In [6] we argued that any useful rule, that can be generalized from such a bottom rule, must belong to a certain type of rule. Thus, we can directly instantiate these types instead of building up a complete generalization lattice. We list in the following all rules that result from generalizing the second and the third bottom rule. We use upper-case letters to refer to variables.

© Springer Nature Switzerland AG 2019
C. Benzmüller and H. Stuckenschmidt (Eds.): KI 2019, LNAI 11793, pp. 244–248, 2019.
https://doi.org/10.1007/978-3-030-30179-8_20

$$speaks(ed, d) \leftarrow born(ed, a)$$
$$speaks(ed, d) \leftarrow mar(ed, lisa), born(lisa, a)$$
$$speaks(ed, d) \leftarrow lives(ed, nl), lang(nl, d)$$

Fig. 1. Three paths sampled from a knowledge graph

$$speaks(X, d) \leftarrow married(X, A_2), born(A_2, a) \tag{1}$$
$$speaks(X, d) \leftarrow married(X, A_2), born(A_2, A_3) \tag{2}$$
$$speaks(X, Y) \leftarrow lives(X, A_2), lang(A_2, Y) \tag{3}$$
$$speaks(X, d) \leftarrow lives(X, A_2), lang(A_2, d) \tag{4}$$
$$speaks(ed, Y) \leftarrow lives(ed, A_2), lang(A_2, Y) \tag{5}$$

The main algorithm of AnyBURL samples random paths of length n and generalizes them to rules as the ones shown above. Then AnyBURL computes confidence and support of each rule. If the rule fulfils a quality criteria defined by the user, e.g., being above minimal support or confidence threshold, it is stored. AnyBURL checks how much new rules are learned within a certain interval. If the fraction of new rules learned within this interval is below a threshold it increases n and continues to search for longer rules.

Given a completion task as $r(a, ?)$, we have to compute a ranking of the top-k candidates that can substitute the question mark. It would be straight forward to create such a ranking based on the rules that have been learned, if each entity would be generated by at most one rule. We could just order the proposed entities by the confidence values of the rules that suggested them. However, an entity is usually suggested by several rules. If we would assume that these rules are independent, we could use a Noisy-Or aggregation. However, the assumption that the rules are independent is often not valid. In [6] we report also about experiments that support this claim. Instead of that we apply a rather simple but efficient approach. We order the candidates via the maximum of the confidences of all rules that have generated the candidates. If the maximum score of several candidates is the same, we order these candidates via the second best rule that generates them, and so on, until we find a rule that makes a difference. The results of this approach can be computed without grounding all relevant rules.

3   Results

In our experiments we have used the standard knowledge base completion evaluation datasets FB15k and WN18 [1] plus their harder variants FB15-237 [11] and

Table 1. Comparing our approach against current state of the art

Approach	WN18			WN18RR			FB15			FB15-237		
	h@1	h@10	MRR	h@1	h@10	MRR	h@1	h@10	MRR	h@1	h@10	MRR
SimplE [4]	93.9	94.7	94.2				66.0	83.8	72.7			
ConvE [2]	93.5	95.5	94.2	39	48	46	67.0	87.3	74.5	23.9	49.1	31.6
ComplEx-N3 [5]		96	95		57	48		91	86		56	37
R-GCN+ [9]	69.7	96.4	81.9				60.1	84.2	69.6	15.1	41.7	24.9
CrossE [14]	74.1	95.0	83.0				63.4	87.5	72.8	21.1	47.4	29.9
AMIE+ [3]	87.2	94.8		35.8	38.8		64.7	85.8		17.4	40.9	
AnyBURL, 10 s	94.2	94.9	≥94	43.2	52.7	≥46	79.6	83.8	≥81	13.4	25.9	≥17
AnyBURL, 100 s	94.6	95.9	≥95	44.5	54.9	≥48	80.8	87.6	≥83	19.6	41.0	≥26
AnyBURL, 1000 s	93.9	95.6	≥95	44.6	55.5	≥48	80.4	89.0	≥83	23.0	47.9	≥30
AnyBURL, 10000 s	93.5	95.4	≥94	44.1	55.2	≥47	79.6	88.7	≥82	23.3	48.6	≥31

WN18RR [2]. The first block in Table 1 lists the results of current state of the art completion techniques. We selected five models, which achieved very good results published within the last year at top conferences. AnyBURL achieves after a 1000 seconds learning phase results that are at the same level and sometimes slightly better than most of these models. AnyBURL has, for example, better hits@1, hits@10, and MMR results[1] than ConvE [2] on all datasets except FB15-237, where the results of AnyBURL are only slightly worse. AnyBURL outperforms SimplE [4] already when using the rules that have been learned after 10 s.

Exceptionally, the ComplEx-N3 model proposed in [5], originally introduced in [12], achieves better results than any other model including AnyBURL. While we ran AnyBURL on a standard laptop, the ComplEx-N3 runtimes are based on the use of a Quadro GP100 GPU. Moreover, AnyBURL runtimes are significantly lower.

In line six we present results for the rule learner AMIE+. These results have been reported in [7] in an environment similar to ours. AMIE+ does not have an anytime behaviour, however, the parameters have been chosen dataset specific to exploit a time frame of 10 h as good as possible. Thus, the results are roughly comparable to the 10000 s results of AnyBURL. AnyBURL generates significantly better results than AMIE+ on all datasets.

4   Conclusion

AnyBURL generates in short time results that are as good and better than many recent state of the art techniques, while using only limited resources (both in

---

[1] As in [1] we compute filtered hits@k. We omit the adjective filtered. Since AnyBURL cannot compute a complete ranking efficiently, we assume that any candidate ranked at a position >k is not a correct prediction. We use this assumption to compute a lower bound for the MRR.

terms of memory and computational power). Compared to latent representation models AnyBURL has several advantages in common with other rule based approaches: (1) The candidate ranking can be explained in terms of the rules that generated this ranking. (2) The generated model (= rule set) can be reused for a dataset using the same predicates and an overlapping set of (important) constants. (3) A rule based approach does not require to learn dataset specific hyper parameters. In the future we plan to extend the language bias of Any-BURL. AnyBURL is implemented as a Java program without any dependencies. It is available at http://web.informatik.uni-mannheim.de/AnyBURL/.

References

1. Bordes, A., Usunier, N., Garcia-Duran, A., Weston, J., Yakhnenko, O.: Translating embeddings for modeling multi-relational data. In: Advances in Neural Information Processing Systems, pp. 2787–2795 (2013)
2. Dettmers, T., Minervini, P., Stenetorp, P., Riedel, S.: Convolutional 2D knowledge graph embeddings. In: Thirty-Second AAAI Conference on Artificial Intelligence (2018)
3. Galárraga, L., Teflioudi, C., Hose, K., Suchanek, F.M.: Fast rule mining in ontological knowledge bases with AMIE+. VLDB J.- Int. J. Very Large Data Bases 24(6), 707–730 (2015)
4. Kazemi, S.M., Poole, D.: Simple embedding for link prediction in knowledge graphs. In: Advances in Neural Information Processing Systems, pp. 4289–4300 (2018)
5. Lacroix, T., Usunier, N., Obozinski, G.: Canonical tensor decomposition for knowledge base completion. In: ICML, pp. 2869–2878 (2018)
6. Meilicke, C., Chekol, M.W., Ruffinelli, D., Stuckenschmidt, H.: Anytime bottom-up rule learning for knowledge graph completion. In: Proceedings of the Twenty-Eighth International Joint Conference on Artificial Intelligence (IJCAI 2019) (2019)
7. Meilicke, C., Fink, M., Wang, Y., Ruffinelli, D., Gemulla, R., Stuckenschmidt, H.: Fine-grained evaluation of rule- and embedding-based systems for knowledge graph completion. In: Vrandečić, D., et al. (eds.) ISWC 2018. LNCS, vol. 11136, pp. 3–20. Springer, Cham (2018). https://doi.org/10.1007/978-3-030-00671-6_1
8. Muggleton, S.H., Feng, C.: Efficient induction of logic programs. In: Proceedings of the First Conference on Algorithmic Learning Theory, pp. 368–381 (1990)
9. Schlichtkrull, M., Kipf, T.N., Bloem, P., van den Berg, R., Titov, I., Welling, M.: Modeling relational data with graph convolutional networks. In: Gangemi, A., et al. (eds.) ESWC 2018. LNCS, vol. 10843, pp. 593–607. Springer, Cham (2018). https://doi.org/10.1007/978-3-319-93417-4_38
10. Srinivasan, A.: The aleph manual. Technical report, Computing Laboratory, Oxford University (2000)
11. Toutanova, K., Chen, D.: Observed versus latent features for knowledge base and text inference. In: Proceedings of the 3rd Workshop on Continuous Vector Space Models and their Compositionality, pp. 57–66 (2015)
12. Trouillon, T., Welbl, J., Riedel, S., Gaussier, É., Bouchard, G.: Complex embeddings for simple link prediction. In: International Conference on Machine Learning, pp. 2071–2080 (2016)

13. Wang, Q., Mao, Z., Wang, B., Guo, L.: Knowledge graph embedding: a survey of approaches and applications. IEEE Trans. Knowl. Data Eng. **29**(12), 2724–2743 (2017)
14. Zhang, W., Paudel, B., Zhang, W., Bernstein, A., Chen, H.: Interaction embeddings for prediction and explanation in knowledge graphs. In: Proceedings of the Twelfth ACM International Conference on Web Search and Data Mining, pp. 96–104. ACM (2019)

Simplifying Automated Pattern Selection for Planning with Symbolic Pattern Databases

Ionut Moraru[1], Stefan Edelkamp[1(✉)], Santiago Franco[2], and Moises Martinez[1]

[1] Informatics Department, Kings College London,
London, UK
{ionut.moraru,stefan.edelkamp,moises.martinez}@kcl.ac.uk
[2] Department of Computer Science, Royal Holloway University of London,
Egham, UK
santiago.francoaixela@rhul.ac.uk

Abstract. Pattern databases (PDBs) are memory-based abstraction heuristics that are constructed prior to the planning process which, if expressed symbolically, yield a very efficient representation. Recent work in the automatic generation of symbolic PDBs has established it as one of the most successful approaches for cost-optimal domain-independent planning. In this paper, we contribute two planners, both using *bin-packing* for its pattern selection. In the second one, we introduce a greedy selection algorithm called *Partial-Gamer*, which complements the heuristic given by bin-packing. We tested our approaches on the benchmarks of the last three International Planning Competitions, optimal track, getting very competitive results, with this simple and deterministic algorithm.

Keywords: Heuristic search · Cost-optimal planning · Bin packing

1 Introduction

The automated generation of search heuristics is one of the holy grails in AI, and goes back to early work of Gaschnik [11], Pearl [25], and Prieditis [27]. In most cases, lower bound heuristics are problem relaxations: each plan in the original state space maps to a shorter one in some corresponding abstract one. In the worst case, searching the abstract state spaces at every given search nodes exceeds the time of blindly searching the concrete search space [30]. With pattern databases (PDBs), all efforts in searching the abstract state space are spent prior to the plan search, so that these computations amortize through multiple lookups.

Initial results of Culberson and Schaeffer [3] in sliding-tile puzzles, where the concept of a pattern is a selection of tiles, quickly carried over to a number of combinatorial search domains, and helped to optimally solve random instances of the Rubik's cube, with non-pattern labels being removed [22]. When shifting

© Springer Nature Switzerland AG 2019
C. Benzmüller and H. Stuckenschmidt (Eds.): KI 2019, LNAI 11793, pp. 249–263, 2019.
https://doi.org/10.1007/978-3-030-30179-8_21

from breadth-first to shortest-path search, the exploration of the abstract state-space can be extended to include action costs.

The combination of several databases into one, however, is tricky [13]. While the maximum of two PDBs always yields a lower bound, the sum usually does not. Korf and Felner [23] showed that with a certain selection of disjoint (or additive) patterns, the values in different PDBs can be added while preserving admissibility. Holte et al. [18] indicated that several smaller PDBs may outperform one large PDB. The notion of a pattern has been generalized to production systems in vector notation [19], while the automated pattern selection process for the construction of PDBs goes back to the work of Edelkamp [6].

Many planning problems can be translated into state spaces of finite domain variables [15], where a selection of variables (pattern) influences both states and operators. For disjoint patterns, an operator must distribute its original cost, if present in several abstractions [20,31].

During the PDB construction process, the memory demands of the abstract state space sizes may exceed the available resources. To handle large memory requirements, symbolic PDBs succinctly represent state sets as binary decision diagrams [5]. However, there are an exponential number of patterns, not counting alternative abstraction and cost partitioning methods. Hence, the automated construction of informative PDB heuristics remains a combinatorial challenge. Hill-climbing strategies have been proposed [13], as well as more general optimization schemes such as genetic algorithms [6,9]. The biggest area of research in this area remains the quality evaluation of a PDB (in terms of the heuristic values for the concrete state space) which can only be estimated. Usually, this involves generating the PDBs and evaluating them [7,22].

In this paper, we bring forth two methods based on the CPC method [9] in which we concentrate on the bin packing subroutine of the heuristic creation. Planning-PDBs introduces two bin packing methods which replace the multi-arm bandit selection methods from CPC. Greedy-PDB is a reinterpretation of CPC, using bin packing to create a diverse group of patterns which will complement a PBD created with partial-Gamer [21]. This later method greatly simplifies the CPC heuristic, while maintaining very good results.

2   Background

There are a variety of planning formalism. Fikes and Nilson [8] invented the propositional specification language STRIPS, which inspired PDDL [24]. Holte and Hernádvölgyi [19] invented the production system vector notation (PSVN), with uses focused on permutation games. Bäckström [1] prefers the SAS$^+$ formalism, which is a notation of finite-domain state variables over partial states and operators with pre-, (prevail-,) and postconditions. Depending on the formalism chosen, the definition of a pattern changes. In the rest of this paper, we will be focusing on SAS$^+$.

Definition 1 (SAS$^+$ Planning Task). *is a quadruple $\mathcal{P} = \langle \mathcal{V}, \mathcal{O}, s_0, s_* \rangle$, where $\mathcal{V} = \{v_1, \ldots, v_n\}$ is the set of finite-domain variable; $\mathcal{O}$ are the operators which consist of preconditions and effects. The remaining two, s_0 and s_* are states. A (complete) state $s = (a_1, \ldots, a_n) \in \mathcal{S}$ assigns a value a_i to every $v_i \in \mathcal{V}$, with a_i in a finite domain D_i, $i = 1, \ldots, n$. For partial states $s^+ \in \mathcal{S}^+$, each $v_i \in \mathcal{V}$ is given an extended domain $D_i^+ = D_i \cup \{\sqcup\}$. We have $s_0 \in \mathcal{S}$ and $s_* \in \mathcal{S}^+$.*

A state space abstraction ϕ is a mapping from states in the original state space $\mathcal{S}$ to the states in the abstract state space $\mathcal{A}$.

Let an abstract operator $o' = \phi(o)$ be defined as $pre' = \phi(pre)$, and $post' = \phi(post)$. For planning task described above, the corresponding abstract task is $\langle \mathcal{V}, \mathcal{O}', s_0', s_*' \rangle$ with $s_0' \in \mathcal{A}$, $s_*' \in \mathcal{A}^+$, The result of applying operator $o' = (pre', post')$ to an abstract state $a = s'$ satisfying pre', sets $s_i' = post_i' \neq \sqcup$, for all $i = 1, \ldots, n$.

A cost is assigned to each operator. In the context of cost-optimal planning, the aim is to minimize the total cost over all plans that lead from the initial state to one of the goals.

The set of reachable states is generated on-the-fly, starting with the initial state by applying the operators. In most state-of-the-art planners, lifted planning tasks are grounded to SAS$^+$. A STRIPS domain with states being subsets of propositional atoms can be seen as a SAS$^+$ instance with a vector of Boolean variables. The core aspect of grounding is to establish invariances, which minimizes the SAS$^+$ encoding.

Definition 2 (State-Space Homomorphism). *A homomorphic abstraction ϕ imposes that if s' is the successor of s in the concrete state space we have $\phi(s')$ is the successor of $\phi(s)$ in abstract one. This suggests abstract operators $\phi(o)$ leading from $\phi(s)$ to $\phi(s')$ for each $o \in \mathcal{O}$ from s of s'.*

As the planning problem spans a graph by applying a selection of set of rules, the planning task abstraction is generated by abstracting the initial state, the partial goal state *and* the operators. Plans in the original space have counterparts in the abstract space, but not vice verse. Usually, the planning task of finding a plan from $\phi(s_0)$ to $\phi(s_*)$ in $\mathcal{A}$ is computationally easier than finding one from s_0 to s_* in $\mathcal{P}$.

Pattern Databases
Planning is a PSPACE-complete problem [2], heuristic search has proven to be one of the best ways to find solutions in a timely manner.

Definition 3 (Heuristic). *A heuristic h is a mapping of the set of states in $\mathcal{P}$ to positive reals $R_{\geq 0}$. A heuristic is called admissible, if $h(s)$ is a lower bound of the cost of all goal-reaching plans starting at s. Two heuristics h_1 and h_2 are additive, if h defined by $h(s) = h_1(s) + h_2(s)$ for all $s \in \mathcal{S}$, is admissible. A heuristic is consistent if for all operators o from s to s' we have $h(s') - h(s) + c(o) \geq 0$.*

For admissible heuristics, search algorithms like A* [12] will return optimal plans. If h is also consistent, no states will be reopened during search. This is the usual case for PDBs.

Definition 4 (Pattern Database). *Is an abstraction mapping for states and operators and a lookup table that for each abstract state a provides the (minimal) cost value from a to the goal state.*

The minimal cost value is a lower bound for reaching the goal of the state that is mapped to a in the original state space. PDBs are generated in a backwards enumeration of the abstract state space, starting with the abstract goal. They are stored in a (perfect) hash table for explicit search, and in the form of a BDD with all abstract states of a certain h value while in symbolic search.

Showing that PDBs yield consistent heuristics is trivial [7,14], as shortest path distances satisfy the triangular inequality. It has also been shown that for PDBs the sum of heuristic values obtained via *projection* to a disjoint variable set is admissible [7]. The projection of state variables induces a projection of operators and requires *cost partitioning*, which distributes the cost $c(o)$ of operators o to the abstract state spaces [26]. We will discuss more about cost partitioning in the following section.

For ease of notation, we identify a pattern database with its abstraction function ϕ. As we want to optimize PDBs via genetic algorithms, we need an objective function.

Definition 5 (Average Fitness of PDB). *The average fitness f_a of a PDB ϕ (interpreted as a set of pairs $(a, h(a))$) is the average heuristic estimate $f_a(\phi) = \sum_{(a,h(a))\in\phi} h(a)/|\phi|$, where $|\phi|$ denotes the size of the PDB ϕ.*

There is also the option of evaluating the quality of PDB based on a sample of paths in the original search space.

Definition 6 (Sample Fitness of PDB). *The fitness f_s of a PDB ϕ wrt. a given sample of (random) paths $\pi_1, \ldots, \pi_m$ and a given candidate pattern selection $\phi_1, \ldots, \phi_k$ in the search space is determined by whether the number of states with a higher heuristic value (compared to heuristic values in the existing collection) exceeds a certain threshold C, i.e.,*

$$\sum_{i=1}^{m}[h_\phi(last(\pi_i)) > \max_{j=1}^{k}\{h_{\phi_j}(last(\pi_i))\}] > C,$$

where $[cond] = 1$, if cond is true, otherwise $[cond] = 0$, and $last(\pi)$ denotes the last state on π.

Definition 7 (Pattern Selection Problem). *Is to find a collection of PDBs that fit into main memory, and maximize the average heuristic value[1].*

---

[1] The average heuristic value has shown empirically that it is a good metric. While it is not the solution to evaluating the pattern selection problem perfectly, it is a good approximation up to this point.

Symbolic Pattern Databases

In symbolic plan search, we encode each variable domain D_j of the SAS$^+$ encoding, $j = 1, \ldots, n$, in binary. Then we assign a Boolean variable x_i to each i, $0 \leq i < \lceil \log_2 |D_1| \rceil + \ldots + \lceil \log_2 |D_n| \rceil$. This eventually results in a characteristic function $\chi_S(x)$ for any set of states S. The ordering of the variables is important for a concise representation, so that we keep finite domain variables as blocks and move inter-depending variables together. The optimization problem of finding such best linear variable arrangement among them is NP-hard. It is also possible to encode operators as Boolean functions $\chi_o(x, x')$ and to progress (and regress) a set of states to accelerate this (pre)image, the disjunction of the individual operators images could be optimized. For action costs, always expanding the set attached to the minimum cost value yields optimal results [5]. As symbolic search is available for partial states (which denote sets of states), both the forward and the backward symbolic exploration in plan space become similar.

There has been considerable effort to show that PDB heuristics can be generated symbolically and used in a symbolic version of A* [5]. The concise representation of the Boolean formula for these characteristic functions in a binary decision diagram (BDD) is a technique to reduce the memory requirement during the search. Frequently, the running time for the exploration often reduces as well.

3 Pattern Selection and Cost Partitioning

Using multiple abstraction heuristics can lead to solving more complex problems, but to maintain optimality, we need to distribute the cost of an operator among the abstractions. One way of doing this is present in [28]. Saturated Cost Partitioning (SCP) has shown benefits to simpler cost partitioning methods. Given an ordered set of heuristics, in our case PDBs, SCP relies on only using those costs which each heuristic uses to create an abstract plan. The remaining costs are left free to be used by any subsequent heuristic. However, considering the limited time budget, this approach is more time consuming compared to other cost partitioning methods [29].

One such method is 0/1 cost partition, which zeroes any cost for subsequent heuristics if the previous heuristic has any variables affected by that operator. Both SCP and 0/1 allow heuristics values to be added admissibly. SCP dominates 0/1 cost partitioning (given a set of patterns and enough time, SCP would produce better heuristic values), but it is much more computationally expensive than 0/1 cost partitioning.

Franco et al. [9] shows that, in order to find good complementary patterns, it is beneficial to try as many pattern collections as possible. As such, we implemented 0/1 cost partitioning in our work. We tested using the canonical cost partitioning [13] method as well whenever we added a new PDB, but this resulted in a very pronounced slow down which increased the more PDBs have already been selected. This was the reason we adopted a hybrid combination approach, where 0/1 cost partition is used on-the-fly to generate new pattern collections, and, only after all interesting pattern collections have been selected, we run the canonical combination method, slightly extended to take into account that each pattern has its own 0/1 cost partition.

Given a number of PDBs in the form of pattern collections (sets of individual patterns, each associated with a cost partitioning function), *canonical pattern databases* will select the best admissible combination of PDB maximization and addition. The computation of the canonical PDB is still expensive, so we execute it only once, right before search starts.

There are many alternatives for automated pattern selection based on bin packing such as random bin packing (PBP), causual dependency bin packing (CBP), which could be refined by a genetic algorithm Franco et al. [9].

Greedy Selection

Franco et al. [9] compared the pattern selection method to the one of Gamer [21], which tries to construct one single best PDB for a problem. Its pattern selection method is an iterative process, starting with all the goal variables in one pattern, where the causally connected variables who would most increase the average h value of the associated PDB are added to the pattern.

Following this work, we devised a new *Gamer-style* pattern generation method, which behaves similarly, but that adds the option of *partial pattern database* generation to it. By partial we mean that we have a time and memory limit for building each PDB. If the PDB building goes past this limit, we truncate it in the same way we would do with a perimeter PDB, i.e., any unmapped real state has the biggest h value the PDB building was at when it was interrupted.

An important difference with the Gamer method is that we do not try every possible pattern resulting of adding a single causally connected variable to the latest pattern.

Genetic Algorithm Selection

A *genetic algorithm* (GA) is a general optimization method in the class of *evolutionary strategies* [17]. It refers to the recombination, selection, and mutation of *genes* (states in a state-space) to optimize the *fitness* (objective) function. In a GA, a population of candidate solutions is sequentially evolved to generate a better performing population of solutions, by mimicking the process of evolution. Each candidate solution has a set of properties which can be mutated and recombined. Traditionally, candidate solutions are bitvectors, but there are strategies that work on real-valued state vectors.

An early approach for the automated selection of PDB variables by Edelkamp [6] employed a GA with genes representing state-space variable patterns in the form of a 0/1 matrix G, where $G_{i,j}$ denotes that state variable i is chosen in PDB j. Besides flipping and setting bits, mutations may also add and delete PDBs in the set.

The PDBs corresponding to the bitvectors in the GA have to fit into main memory, so we have to restrict the generation of offsprings to the ones that represent a set of PDB that respect the memory limitation. If time becomes an issue, we stop evolving patterns and invoke the overall search (in our case progressing explicit states) eventually. An alternative, which sometimes is applied as a subroutine to generate the initial population for the GA, is to use bin packing.

Bin Packing

The bin packing problem (BPP) is one of the first problems shown to be NP-hard [10]. Given objects of integer size $a_1, \ldots, a_n$ and maximum bin size C, the problem is to find the minimum number of bins k so that the established mapping $f : \{1, \ldots, n\} \rightarrow \{1, \ldots, k\}$ of objects to bins maintains $\sum_{f(a)=i} a \leq C$ for all $i \leq k$. The problem is NP-hard in general, but there are good approximation strategies such as first-fit and best-fit decreasing (being at most $11/9$ off the optimal solution [4]).

In the PDBs selection process, however, the definition of the BPP is slightly different. We estimate the size of the PDB by computing the product (not the sum) of the variable domain sizes, aiming for a maximum bin capacity M imposed by the available memory, and we find the minimum number of bins k, so that the established mapping f of objects to bins maintains $\prod_{f(a)=i} a \leq M$ for all $i \leq k$. By taking the logs on both sides, we are back to sums, but the sizes become fractional. In this case, $\prod_{f(a)=i}$ is an upper bound on the number of abstract states needed.

Taking the product of variable domain sizes is a coarse upper bound. In some domains, the abstract state spaces are much smaller. Bin packing chooses the memory bound on each individual PDB, instead of limiting their sum. Moreover, for symbolic search, the correlation between the cross product of the domains and the memory needs is rather weak. However, because of its simplicity and effectiveness, this form of bin packing currently is chosen for PDB construction.

By limiting the amount of optimization time for each BPP, we do not insist on optimal solutions, but we want fast approximations that are close-to-optimal. Recall, that suboptimal solutions to the BPP do not imply suboptimal solutions to the planning problem. In fact, *all* solutions to the BPP lead to admissible heuristics and therefore optimal plans.

For the sake of generality, we strive for solutions to the problem that do not include problem-specific knowledge but still work efficiently. Using a general framework also enables us to participate in future solver developments. Therefore, in both of the approaches we present in this paper, we focus on the first-fit algorithm.

First-Fit Increasing (FFI), or Decreasing (FFD), is a fast on-line approximation algorithm that first sorts the objects according to their sizes and, then, starts placing the objects into the bins, putting an object to the first bin it fits into. In terms of planning, the variables are sorted by the size of their domains in increasing/decreasing order. Next, the *first* variable is chosen and packed at the same bin with the rest of the variables which are related to it if there is space enough in the bin. This process is repeated until all variables are processed.

4   Symbolic PDB Planners

Based on the results from [9], we decided to work only with Symbolic PDBs. Further experiments suggested that PDBs heuristic performs well when it is complemented with other methods. One good combination was using our method to complement a symbolic perimeter PDB, method that we used in the first of the planners we present. The selected method to be complemented first generates a symbolic PDB up to a fixed time limit and memory limit. One advantage of seeding our algorithm with such a perimeter search is that if there is an easy solution to be found in what is basically a brute force backwards search, we are finished before even creating a PDB. Secondly, we combined the Partial-Gamer with bin packing and saw very good results in how they complemented each other. In Fig. 1 we see that each method gives good results on their own, Bin-Packing solving 434 and Partial-Gamer 457, but when used together they increase to 475.

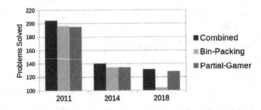

Fig. 1. Coverage of Bin Packing, Partial-Gamer and of both combined on three latest cost-optimal IPC benchmark problems.

In our work, however, we decided to use a hybrid, keeping the forward exploration explicit-state, and the PDBs generated in the backward exploration symbolic. Lookups are slightly slower than in hash tables, but they are still in time linear to the bitvector length.

In this section, we will present two symbolic planners, Planning-PDB and GreedyPDB, based on the Fast-Downward planning framework [16]. The two differ in the pattern selection methods that we use in each of them.

GreedyPDB

We encountered that greedily constructed PDBs outperform the perimeter PDB, which we decided not to use. The two construction methods do not complement well, on the extreme case greedy PDBs will build a perimeter PDB after adding all the variables. There is a significant amount of overlapping between both methods. The collection of patterns received from bin packing, however, complements well the greedily constructed PDBs. One reason for this is that in domains amenable to cost-partitioning strategies, i.e. alternative goals are easily parallelized into a complementary collection of PDBs, bin packing can do significantly better than the single PDB approach. Evaluation is based on the

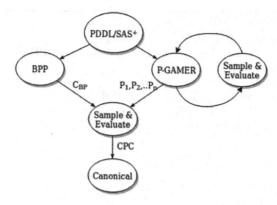

Fig. 2. High level architecture of GreedyPDB

definition of sample fitness. The sample is redrawn each time an improvement was found.

Algorithm 1 shows how Greedy PDBs combines two bin packing algorithms with a greedy selection method called Partial Gamer. The two bin packing algorithms use First Fit Decreasing (FFD) and First Fit Increasing (FFI), same used in BP-PDB. For FFD we set a limit of 50 s, while for FFI we used a limit of 75 s (both limits were found empirically to give the best results). To evaluate (EM) if the generated pattern collections should be added to our selection ($\mathcal{P}_{sel}$), we used as an evaluation method a random walk. If enough of the sampled states heuristic values are improved, the pattern is selected.

Partial Gamer greedily grows the largest possible PDB by adding causally connected variables to the latest added pattern. If a pattern is found to improve, as defined by the evaluation method, then we add it to the list of selected pattern collections as a pattern collection with a single PDB. Note that we are using symbolic PDBs with time limits on PDB construction, hence a PDB which includes all variables of a smaller PDB does not necessarily dominate it since the smaller PDB might reach a further depth.

An important difference with the Gamer method is that we do not try every possible pattern resulting of adding a single causally connected variable to the latest pattern. As soon as a variable is shown to improve the pattern, we add it and restart the search for an even larger improving pattern. We found this to work better with the tight time limits required by combining several approaches. All the resulting pattern database collections are combined by simply maximizing their individual heuristic values. The PDBs inside each collection were combined using zero-one cost partitioning. The rationale behind the algorithm is that some domains are more amenable to using several patterns where costs are distributed between each patterns, while other domains seem to favour looking for the best possible single pattern.

Algorithm 1. Greedy PDBs Creation

1: **function** GREEDYPDBS(M,T,S_{min},S_{max},EM) :
Require: time and memory limits T and M, min and max PDB size S_{min} ad S_{max},
    evaluation method EM.
2:     $SelPDBs \leftarrow \emptyset$
3:     $\mathcal{P}_{sel} \leftarrow \mathcal{P}_{sel} \cup Packer(FFD, S_{min}, M, T, EM)$
4:     $\mathcal{P}_{sel} \leftarrow \mathcal{P}_{sel} \cup Packer(FFI, S_{min}, M, T, EM)$
5:     $\mathcal{P}_{sel} \leftarrow \mathcal{P}_{sel} \cup PartialGamer(M, T, EM)$
6:     **Return** $\mathcal{P}_{sel}$
7: **end function**
8:
9: **function** PACKER($Method,S_{min}, M, T,EM$) :
10:     $SizeLim \leftarrow S_{min}$
11:     **while** ($t < T$) **and** ($m < M$) **do**
12:         GENERATE_$\mathcal{P}(Method,SizeLim)$
13:         **if** $EM(\mathcal{P})$ **then**
14:             $\mathcal{P}_{sel} \leftarrow \mathcal{P}$
15:         **end if**
16:         $Size \leftarrow Size * 10$
17:     **end while**
18:     **Return** $\mathcal{P}_{sel}$
19: **end function**
20:
21: **function** PARTIALGAMER($M, T,EvalMethod$) :
22:     $InitialPDB \leftarrow$ all goal variables
23:     $SelPDBs \leftarrow InitialPDB$
24:     **while** ($t < T$) **and** ($m < M$) **do**
25:         generate all $CandidatePatterns$ resulting of adding one casually connected
        variable to latest $P \in \mathcal{P}_{sel}$
26:         **for all** $P \in CandidatePatterns$ **do**
27:             **if** $EM(\mathcal{P})$ **then**
28:                 $\mathcal{P}_{sel} \leftarrow P$
29:                 break
30:             **end if**
31:         **end for**
32:     **end while**
33:     **Return** $\mathcal{P}_{sel}$
34: **end function**

BP-PDB

In *BP-PDBs*, we start with the construction of the perimeter PDB, and continue by using two bin-packing methods to create a collection of PDBs. The first method uses first-fit increasing, while the second being first-fit decreasing. Bin-packing for PDBs creates a small number of PDBs which use all available variables. Even though reducing the number of PDBs used to group all possible variables does not guarantee a better PDB, by having a smaller PDB collections, it is less likely to miss interactions between variables due to them being placed on different PDBs. The bin packing algorithms used ensures that each PDB has a least one goal variable.

If no solution is found after the perimeter PDB has been finished, the method will start generating pattern collections stochastically until either the generation time limit or the overall PDB memory limit are reached. We then decide whether to add a pattern collection to the list of selected patterns if it is estimated that adding such PDB will speed up search. We optimize the results given by the bin-packing algorithm giving it to a GA. It then resolve operator overlaps in a 0/1 cost partitioning. To evaluate the fitness function, the corresponding PDBs is built—a time-consuming operation, which nevertheless payed off in most cases. Once all patterns have been selected, the resulting canonical PDB combination is used as an admissible heuristic to do A* search.

5   Experiments

Following is an ablation-type study were we analyze which components worked best. We run different configurations on the competition benchmarks on our cluster that utilized Intel Xeon E5-2660 V4 with 2.00 GHz processors. We compare GreedyPDB Planner and Planning-PDB with other pattern database and symbolic planners that competed in the 2018 International Planning Competition in the most prestigious and attended deterministic cost-optimal track.

Table 1. Overall coverage of PDB-type planners across different International Planning Competitions for cost-optimal planning.

Year/Method	2011	2014	2018	Total
GreedyPDB	**204**	140	**131**	475
Planning-PDBs	190	131	123	444
Scorpion	190	118	104	412
SymBiDir	174	129	114	417
Comp1	185	111	123	419
Comp2	**204**	**155**	124	**483**
Oracle	227	171	143	541

Looking at the results of various cost-optimal planners across all domains from the IPC competitions from 2011 to 2018 in Table 1, we get a good overall picture on the PDB planner performance. Symbolic bidirectional search (417 problems being solved) is almost on par with Scorpion (412) and Complementary1 (419), while Planning-PDB performs slightly better (444). The overall top two planning systems are GreedyPDB (475) and Complementary2 (483). We deduce that with GreedyPDB we have a simple automated pattern selection strategy in a PDB planning system that is competitive with the state-of-the-art.

Table 2. Coverage of PDB-type planners on the 2018 International Planning Competition for cost-optimal planning

Domain/Method	Agr	Cal	DN	Nur	OSS	PNA	Set	Sna	Spi	Ter	Total
GreedyPDB	13	**12**	**14**	**15**	**13**	16	8	13	11	16	**131**
Planning-PDBs	6	12	14	12	**13**	**19**	8	11	12	16	123
Scorpion	1	**12**	**14**	12	**13**	0	**10**	13	**15**	14	104
SymBiDir	**14**	9	12	11	**13**	**19**	8	4	6	**18**	114
Complementary1	10	11	**14**	12	12	18	8	11	11	16	123
Complementary2	6	**12**	13	12	**13**	18	8	**14**	12	16	124
Oracle	14	12	14	15	13	19	10	14	15	18	142

On the 2018 benchmark, likely the most challenging one featuring a wide range of expressive application domain models, GreedyPDB would have actually won the competition (Table 2). This indicates that for several planning problems, the best option is to keep growing one PDB with the greedy pattern selector, and compare and merge the results with a PDB collection based on bin packing.

6   Related Work

Pattern Databases have become very popular since the 2018 International Planning Competition showed that top five planners employed the heuristic in their solver. However, the topic has been vastly researched prior to this competition, a lot of work going in the automated creation of a PDB, with the best know being the iPDB of Haslum et al., [13] and the GA-PDB by Edelkamp [6]. The first performs a hill-climbing search in the space of possible pattern collections, while the other employs a bin-packing algorithm to create initial collections, that will be used as an initial population for a genetic algorithm. iPDB evaluates the patterns by selecting the one with the higher h-value in a selected sample set of states, while the GA of the GA-PDB uses the average heuristic value as its fitness function.

Another two approaches related to our work is Gamer [21] and CPC [9]. The first is in the search of only one best PDB, starting with all the goal variables, and adding the one that it will increase the average heuristic value. CPC is a *revolution* of the GA-PDB approach, aiming to create pattern collections with PDBs that are complementary to eachother. It also employs a GA and its evaluation is based on Stratified Sampling.

7   Conclusion and Discussion

The 2018 International Planning Competition in cost-optimal planning revealed that symbolic PDB planning probably is the best non-portfolio approach. In fact, five of the top six IPC planners were based on heuristic search with PDB and/or symbolic search, while the winning portfolio used such a planner (namely SymBA*, the winner of IPC 2014) for more than half of its successful runs.

In this paper, we present two methods building on top of the CPC approach by Franco et al., [9], one incremental on an existing work (Planning-PDBs) and one that is a reformulation of how it creates complementary pattern collections (GreedyPDB), by combining it with an adapted version of the Gamer approach [21]. In both we have only one bin-packing solver, removing the multi-armed bandit algorithm to select its packing algorithm. In GamerPDB, we also removed the optimization done with a GA over the pattern collections, seeing that bin-packing and partial-gamer complement already very well each other. Overall, the structure of GamerPDB in comparison with CPC is very much simplified, with a small loss of coverage on the problem set of the IPC 2014.

Using different pattern generators to complement the two seeding heuristics was extremely successful. It improved our overall results for all the methods we tested compared to simply using the seeding heuristics. One of the best performing method is the combination of an incremental pattern selection with advanced bin packing. When combining both pattern selection methods, the results are greatly improved, and GreedyPDB would have won the last IPC even ahead of the best portfolio planners (solving 5 more problems), thus contributing a new state-of-the-art in cost-optimal planning.

It is probable that using SCP instead of canonical would improve results. It is also likely that if we used SCP online, i.e., for evaluating whether to add a PDB to the current selected set, instead of the current 0/1 approach a PDB is evaluated, would significantly reduce the total number of patterns we can try given the IPC time limit. How to navigate the trade-off between SCP's better heuristic values vs 0/1's faster computational time is future research.

However, as seen with the impressive results of Complementary2 in the 2011 and 2014 competition benchmark, there is no free lunch. Which pattern generator method is best depends on the benchmark domain it is applied to. By the obtained diversity in the individual solutions, an oracle deciding which pattern selector to take would have solved more problems, so that a portfolio planner could exploit this.

References

1. Bäckström, C.: Equivalence and tractability results for SAS+ planning. In: KR, pp. 126–137 (1992)
2. Bylander, T.: The computational complexity of propositional STRIPS planning. Artif. Intell. **69**(1–2), 165–204 (1994)
3. Culberson, J.C., Schaeffer, J.: Pattern databases. Comput. Intell. **14**(4), 318–334 (1998)
4. Dósa, G.: The tight bound of first fit decreasing bin-packing algorithm is FFD(i) ≤ 11/9opt (i)+ 6/9. In: Chen, B., Paterson, M., Zhang, G. (eds.) ESCAPE 2007. LNCS, vol. 4614, pp. 1–11. Springer, Berlin (2007). https://doi.org/10.1007/978-3-540-74450-4_1
5. Edelkamp, S.: Symbolic pattern databases in heuristic search planning. In: AIPS, pp. 274–283 (2002)

6. Edelkamp, S.: Automated creation of pattern database search heuristics. In: Edelkamp, S., Lomuscio, A. (eds.) MoChArt 2006. LNCS (LNAI), vol. 4428, pp. 35–50. Springer, Heidelberg (2007). https://doi.org/10.1007/978-3-540-74128-2_3

7. Edelkamp, S.: Planning with pattern databases. In: Sixth European Conference on Planning (2014)

8. Fikes, R.E., Nilsson, N.J.: STRIPS: a new approach to the application of theorem proving to problem solving. Artif. Intell. **2**(3–4), 189–208 (1971)

9. Franco, S., Torralba, A., Lelis, L.H., Barley, M.: On creating complementary pattern databases. In: Proceedings of the 26th International Joint Conference on Artificial Intelligence, pp. 4302–4309. AAAI Press (2017)

10. Garey, M.R., Johnson, D.S.: Computers and Intractibility, A Guide to the Theory of NP-Completeness. Freeman & Company, New York (1979)

11. Gaschnig, J.: A problem similarity approach to devising heuristics: first results, pp. 434–441 (1979)

12. Hart, P.E., Nilsson, N.J., Raphael, B.: A formal basis for the heuristic determination of minimum cost paths. IEEE Trans. Syst. Sci. Cybern. **4**(2), 100–107 (1968)

13. Haslum, P., Botea, A., Helmert, M., Bonet, B., Koenig, S.: Domain-independent construction of pattern database heuristics for cost-optimal planning, pp. 1007–1012 (2007)

14. Haslum, P., Bonet, B., Geffner, H., et al.: New admissible heuristics for domain-independent planning. In: AAAI, vol. 5, pp. 9–13 (2005)

15. Helmert, M.: A planning heuristic based on causal graph analysis, pp. 161–170 (2004)

16. Helmert, M.: The fast downward planning system. J. Artif. Intell. Res. **26**, 191–246 (2006)

17. Holland, J.: Adaption in natural and artificial systems. Ph.D. thesis, University of Michigan (1975)

18. Holte, R., Newton, J., Felner, A., Meshulam, R., Furcy, D.: Multiple pattern databases, pp. 122–131 (2004)

19. Holte, R.C., Hernádvölgyi, I.T.: A space-time tradeoff for memory-based heuristics. In: AAAI/IAAI, pp. 704–709. Citeseer (1999)

20. Katz, M., Domshlak, C.: Optimal additive composition of abstraction-based admissible heuristics. In: ICAPS, pp. 174–181 (2008)

21. Kissmann, P., Edelkamp, S.: Improving cost-optimal domain-independent symbolic planning. In: Twenty-Fifth AAAI Conference on Artificial Intelligence (2011)

22. Korf, R.E.: Finding optimal solutions to Rubik's cube using pattern databases, pp. 700–705 (1997)

23. Korf, R.E., Felner, A.: Disjoint pattern database heuristics. In: Chips Challenging Champions: Games, Computers and Artificial Intelligence, pp. 13–26. Elsevier (2002)

24. McDermott, D.: The 1998 AI planning systems competition. In: AI Magazine, pp. 35–55 (1998)

25. Pearl, J.: Heuristics: Intelligent Search Strategies for Computer Problem Solving. Addison-Wesley, Boston (1984)

26. Pommerening, F., Helmert, M., Röger, G., Seipp, J.: From non-negative to general operator cost partitioning. In: Twenty-Ninth AAAI Conference on Artificial Intelligence (2015)

27. Preditis, A.: Machine discovery of admissible heuristics. Mach. Learn. **12**, 117–142 (1993)

28. Seipp, J., Helmert, M.: Counterexample-guided Cartesian abstraction refinement for classical planning. J. Artif. Intell. Res. **62**, 535–577 (2018)

29. Seipp, J., Keller, T., Helmert, M.: A comparison of cost partitioning algorithms for optimal classical planning. In: Twenty-Seventh International Conference on Automated Planning and Scheduling (2017)
30. Valtorta, M.: A result on the computational complexity of heuristic estimates for the A* algorithm. Inf. Sci. **34**, 48–59 (1984)
31. Yang, F., Culberson, J., Holte, R., Zahavi, U., Felner, A.: A general theory of additive state space abstractions. J. Artif. Intell. Res. **32**, 631–662 (2008)

ALICA 2.0 - Domain-Independent Teamwork

Stephan Opfer[(✉)], Stefan Jakob, Alexander Jahl, and Kurt Geihs

Distributed Systems Research Group, University of Kassel,
Wilhelmshöher Allee 73, Kassel, Germany
{opfer,jakob,jahl,geihs}@vs.uni-kassel.de

Abstract. We present a new version of ALICA - "A Language for Interactive Cooperative Agents". The ALICA framework is a highly reactive multi-agent framework and comprises three components for working with multi-agent plans: a specification language, an execution engine, and a graphical modelling tool. The framework automatically coordinates teams, allocates tasks to team members, and compensates execution failures in a fully distributed manner. In a major redesign, we extended the description language and re-implemented the execution engine and graphical modelling tool. As a result, the second version of ALICA encompasses fewer dependencies, is domain independent, and adaptable to different environments.

Keywords: Multi-agent systems · Dynamic coordination ·
Robotic teams

1 Introduction

In multi-robot domains like autonomous cars, automated guided vehicles in logistics, or service robotics the involved autonomous agents need to cooperate swiftly in many ways. They need to distribute tasks, share knowledge, coordinate their execution progress, resolve conflicts, incorporate unknown agents, assign roles among them, and keep track of the current team. The ALICA framework specifically addresses such domains and provides highly dynamic solutions for the aforementioned research problems.

ALICA has been broadly published [27–30,35] and forms the basis for ongoing research [9,16,18–20]. Its application domains involve practical use cases like space exploration [26], robotic soccer [1], autonomous driving [34], service-oriented architectures addressed by the DFG project PROSECCO[1], and is used by Rapyuta Robotics for cloud robotic solutions in warehouse logistics. Furthermore, ALICA has been successfully used in the Space Bot Cup and the Audi Autonomous Driving Cup.

---

[1] http://www.uni-kassel.de/eecs/fachgebiete/vs/research/prosecco.html [accessed on May, 9th 2019].

We would like to thank Rapyuta Robotics for the continuous stream of pull requests!

© Springer Nature Switzerland AG 2019
C. Benzmüller and H. Stuckenschmidt (Eds.): KI 2019, LNAI 11793, pp. 264–272, 2019.
https://doi.org/10.1007/978-3-030-30179-8_22

In the next section, we introduce the ALICA framework focussing on the improvements of the second version. In Sect. 3, a short overview of similar frameworks is given. Section 4 summarises our contributions and ongoing research efforts.

2   ALICA 2.0

The central part of the ALICA framework[2] is its language for describing hierarchical multi-agent plans. A graphical modelling tool, denoted as Plan Designer, allows to create those plans. Finally, the ALICA execution engine implements the operational semantics for executing the plans by a team of agents. The next subsections explain the components and our corresponding improvements.

2.1   Language

The ALICA language it used to specify hierarchical multi-agent plans similar to hierarchical task networks [25]. The service robot plans shown in Fig. 1 are examples for such plans. A plan, like *Clean Up*, comprises several concurrently executable finite state machines (FSM), that together are necessary for achieving the implicit goal of a plan. Each initial state, like Z_0 and Z_3 in plan *Clean Up*, is annotated by a task, a minimum and a maximum cardinality, and the information whether the FSM needs to be successfully completed for a successful plan execution. In order to be successful, FSMs need at least one success state, like Z_2 of the *CleanUp* plan.

The ALICA language defines three different types of conditions, i.e. pre-, runtime, and postconditions. While postconditions are expected to hold, after a successful execution of, e.g., a plan, pre- and runtime conditions need to hold in order to start a plan or to move over a transition from one state to another. A state contains an arbitrary number of other plans, behaviours, or sets of alternative plans, denoted as plan types. For example, the *Transport* plan type in Z_1 of the *Clean Up* plan includes one transport plan for heavy and one for light objects. Agents occupying a state execute all elements within the state, if possible according to the pre- and runtime conditions of the elements, but they execute only one plan of each plan type at a time. As plans can contain other plans within their states, a plan hierarchy is build. This hierarchy must form a Directed-Acyclic Graph (DAG), as shown in Fig. 2, in order to avoid unlimited recursions in the plan hierarchy. The annotations of the edges denote the task, state, and plan type along another plan or atomic behaviour is reachable in the plan hierarchy.

At runtime, the DAG of the plan hierarchy is interpreted as a tree with behaviours forming its leaves, i.e. each plan or behaviour in Fig. 2 is instantiated once per path from the root plan to it. Otherwise, failing agents would influence each other, although working on potential different sub-goals of the plan hierarchy. Behaviours are considered as domain specific and can only start, stop, fail,

---

[2] The source code [6,7] is available under the MIT License.

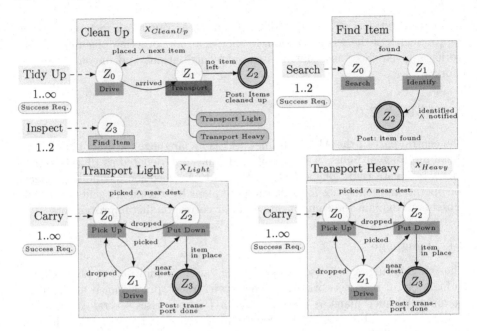

Fig. 1. Hierarchy of plans for service robots

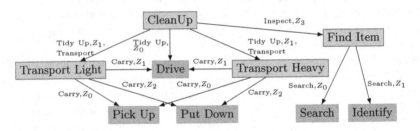

Fig. 2. Directed-acyclic graph for plans in Fig. 1

or be successful from the execution engines' perspective. The implementation of the behaviours is up to the domain expert. The same holds for conditions, making ALICA applicable in a potential unlimited number of different domains. An enhancement to ALICA 2.0 is the ability to directly attach conditions to behaviours, while this had to be modelled in the original ALICA version via an extra plan level encapsulating the behaviour in a single state and increasing the complexity of the plan hierarchy.

Our main improvement with regard to the ALICA language is its extension by a general solver interface [19]. The former ALICA version included a solver for the problem domain of continuous non-linear constraint satisfaction and optimization problems [35] hardwired to its language, modelling tool, and execution engine. We separated this solver and instead provided an interface to arbitrary solvers. As a result, ALICA gained domain independence and an increasing set of solvers [9,20,35].

Through variables, like $X_{CleanUp}$ of the *Clean Up* plan, agents can query corresponding solvers for solutions. The range of solutions is narrowed by constraints attached at pre- and runtime conditions in ALICA. This way, solutions may change depending on the progress of the agents within a plan. For example, the $X_{CleanUp}$ variable of the *Clean Up* plan only offers a solution, if an agent found a transportable item to be cleaned up by executing the *Find Item* plan. Concurrently, the *Drive* behaviour stops the agent until a solution for the $X_{CleanUp}$ variable tells it where to drive. According to the capabilities of the agent occupying Z_1, either the *Transport Light* or the *Transport Heavy* plan is chosen. In both cases, the variable $X_{CleanUp}$ is bound to the variable of the child plan and its solution is further constrained, e.g., to items that are either lightweight or heavy, but with a proper handle attached.

2.2 Execution Engine

The most important design feature of the ALICA Execution Engine is to run distributed with one instance on each agent. No central coordinator, registry or any kind of extra role is necessary, making ALICA robust against network delay, packet loss, and failures of other agents. Figure 3 shows the architecture of the engine with its three layers. The task layer includes modules for assigning roles and tasks to agents and a module that handles conflicts about these assignments between team members. Tasks, for example, are assigned according to the utility functions of each plan, valuating different assignments. According to the taxonomy presented in [14], the task allocation module belongs to the group of distributed optimisation-based approaches and solves multi-robot, multi-task, instantaneous assignment problems. Details are given in Chapter 5.8 of [29]. The team layer manages the information about existing and cooperating agents. Its service is used in all other modules. Since ALICA 2.0, it is also able to dynamically incorporate unknown agents at runtime, as the developer cannot be expected to know all potentially running agents a priori.

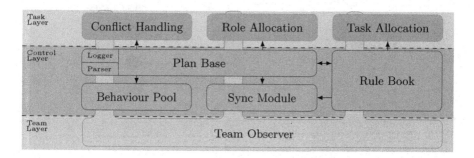

Fig. 3. ALICA execution engine architecture

Finally, the control layer incorporates the core of the engine. It is responsible for the progress in executing plans, parsed from the JSON files of the Plan Designer. It triggers corresponding modules like solvers, task allocation, or rule book accordingly. The rule book implements the operational semantics of ALICA via a prioritised list of rules. They determine when and how to, e.g., follow transitions, restart plans, trigger the task allocation, handle or propagate plan execution failures, and observe the truth value of annotated conditions and constraints. Especially with regard to conditions, constraints, and task allocations, the engine follows a locality principle that forbids references in the runtime representation of the plan tree to siblings of the current context. For example, the precondition of a plan is not allowed to depend on the execution state of another plan that is a sibling in the plan tree. Due to the locality principle, the execution engine is, for example, able to reallocate all tasks in a plan tree with 30 Hz. Such reactivity makes the ALICA Execution Engine applicable in highly dynamic domains.

Our re-implementation in C++ avoids performance problems due to memory management and makes it easier for domain experts to integrate ALICA with the low level control and sensor layers of robotic application domains. A further design decision that makes the new ALICA version easier to integrate in existing frameworks or adapt to new application domains is its communication- and time-agnostic implementation. The only assumption the execution engine makes about communication, is that it is somehow possible to send messages to other team members. Furthermore, the engine does not directly depend on the system clock, instead it is possible to provide a simulated time that runs faster or slower than real-time for instance in a simulated environment.

2.3 Plan Designer

The Plan Designer, implemented in Java, is the graphical modelling tool for the ALICA language. Figure 4 shows its user interface of the re-implemented version for ALICA 2.0.

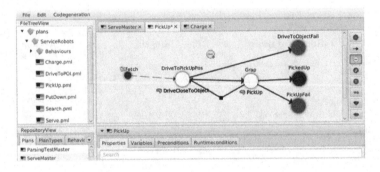

Fig. 4. Plan designer - the graphical modelling tool for ALICA

The previous version of the Plan Designer was based on the Eclipse Rich Client Platform [32] and included dependencies on huge frameworks like the Eclipse Modelling Framework [31], the Graphical Editing Framework [24], and the Open Architecture Ware system [10].

The output of the Plan Designer is twofold, on the one hand it serialises the modelled plans into some machine readable format. On the other hand it generates stubs of source code for the domain expert to implement behaviours, conditions, and constraints. The former Plan Designer version serialised the plans into XML files and generated C# source code. The re-implemented Plan Designer now serialises to JSON files, since it encodes information more efficiently. Furthermore, the Plan Designer generates the stubs for different languages on demand. Currently C++ stubs are available and Java and Python are work in progress. In order to support the different solvers, we introduced a plug-in system that allows to offer a specific UI and code generation for the constraints of each solver. The only dependencies of the re-implemented version are Java, including JavaFX [33], and Jackson [8], in order to stay platform-independent.

3   Related Work

The related work can be divided into five main categories. The first category comprises the underlying runtime structure. Hierarchical Finite (Concurrent) State Machines are used by ALICA, HFSM-IC [15], CABSL [23], XABSL [17], CPL [2], and LRP [4]. GOL [12] utilises Tactical Instruction Boards while RAFCON [3] relies on Hierarchical Flow Control. The remaining four categories are shown in Table 1. Category *Exchange* considers the ability to change behaviours at runtime, which is supported by [3,4,17], since they rely on reflection and interpreted languages. *Concurrency* is the capability to run multiple behaviours simultaneously. A graphical modelling *Tool* is supported by most frameworks. Finally, the explicit support for *Teams* of agents is, among the presented frameworks, only available in ALICA. There exist a lot more languages [5,11,22] based on the Belief Desire Intention Theory and teamwork approaches [13,21,36] that

Table 1. Framework comparison

	Exchange	Concurrency	Teams	Tool
ALICA	✗	✓	✓	✓
CABSL [23]	✗	✗	✗	✓
XABSL [17]	✓	✗	✗	✓
CPL [2]	✗	✓	✗	✗
GOL [12]	✗	✗	✗	✓
LRP [4]	✓	✗	✗	✓
RAFCON [3]	✓	✓	✗	✓
HFSM-IC [15]	✗	✓	✗	✗

we cannot discuss within this paper due to lack of space, but ALICA supports most of their features like joint intentions and shared plans, too.

4   Conclusion

The new improved version of the framework ALICA that comprises a partially extended description language and re-implementations of the execution engine and the graphical modelling tool. The presented re-implementation reduces the dependencies of ALICA, improves its domain independence, and increases its adaptability to different environments. Our current research aims at the implementation and combination of execution engines in different programming languages and to exchange behaviours at runtime.

References

1. Amma, T., et al.: Carpe Noctem 2013. In: CD Proceedings of RoboCup Symposium (2013)
2. Beetz, M., Mösenlechner, L., Tenorth, M.: CRAM - a cognitive robot abstract machine for everyday manipulation in human environments. In: 2010 IEEE/RSJ International Conference on Intelligent Robots and Systems (IROS), pp. 1012–1017. IEEE (2010)
3. Brunner, S.G., Steinmetz, F., Belder, R., Dömel, A.: RAFCON: a graphical tool for engineering complex, robotic tasks. In: 2016 IEEE/RSJ International Conference on Intelligent Robots and Systems (IROS), pp. 3283–3290. IEEE (2016)
4. Campusano, M., Fabry, J., Bergel, A.: Live programming in practice: a controlled experiment on state machines for robotic behaviors. Inf. Softw. Technol. **108**, 99–114 (2019)
5. Dastani, M., van Riemsdijk, M.B., Dignum, F., Meyer, J.-J.C.: A programming language for cognitive agents goal directed 3APL. In: Dastani, M.M., Dix, J., El Fallah-Seghrouchni, A. (eds.) ProMAS 2003. LNCS (LNAI), vol. 3067, pp. 111–130. Springer, Heidelberg (2004). https://doi.org/10.1007/978-3-540-25936-7_6
6. Distributed Systems Research Group, University of Kassel: ALICA GitHub Repository (2019). https://github.com/dasys-lab/alica. Accessed 10 May 2019
7. Distributed Systems Research Group, University of Kassel: Plan Designer GitHub Repository (2019). https://github.com/dasys-lab/alica-plan-designer-fx. Accessed 10 May 2019
8. Friesen, J.: Processing JSON with Jackson. In: Friesen, J. (ed.) Java XML and JSON, pp. 323–403. Apress, Berkeley (2019). https://doi.org/10.1007/978-1-4842-4330-5_11
9. Geihs, K., Witsch, A.: Decentralized decision making in adaptive multi-robot teams. it-Inf. Technol. **60**(4), 239–248 (2018)
10. Haase, A., Völter, M., Efftinge, S., Kolb, B.: Introduction to openArchitectureWare 4.1. 2. In: MDD Tool Implementers Forum (2007)
11. Hindriks, K.V., Meyer, J.-J.C.: Agent logics as program logics: grounding KARO. In: Freksa, C., Kohlhase, M., Schill, K. (eds.) KI 2006. LNCS (LNAI), vol. 4314, pp. 404–418. Springer, Heidelberg (2007). https://doi.org/10.1007/978-3-540-69912-5_30

12. Hofmann, M., Gürster, F.: GOL-a language to define tactics in robot soccer. In: Proceedings of the 10th Workshop on Humanoid Soccer Robots, in Conjunction with the IEEE-RAS International Conference on Humanoid Robots (HUMANOIDS) (2015)

13. Jennings, N.R.: Controlling cooperative problem solving in industrial multi-agent systems using joint intentions. Artif. Intell. **75**(2), 195–240 (1995)

14. Khamis, A., Hussein, A., Elmogy, A.: Multi-robot task allocation: a review of the state-of-the-art. In: Koubâa, A., Martínez-de Dios, J.R. (eds.) Cooperative Robots and Sensor Networks 2015. SCI, vol. 604, pp. 31–51. Springer, Cham (2015). https://doi.org/10.1007/978-3-319-18299-5_2

15. Kim, R., Kwon, H.T., Chi, S., Yoon, W.C.: A Coordination model for agent behaviors using hierarchical finite state machine with inter-level concurrency. In: International Conference on Information and Communication Technology Convergence (ICTC), pp. 359–364, October 2016

16. Kirchner, D., Geihs, K.: Adaptive model-based monitoring for robots. In: Menegatti, E., Michael, N., Berns, K., Yamaguchi, H. (eds.) Intelligent Autonomous Systems 13. AISC, vol. 302, pp. 43–56. Springer, Cham (2016). https://doi.org/10.1007/978-3-319-08338-4_4

17. Loetzsch, M., Risler, M., Jüngel, M.: XABSL-a pragmatic approach to behavior engineering. In: IROS, pp. 5124–5129 (2006)

18. Neuber, D.: Planning of autonomous and mobile robots in dynamic environments. Ph.D. thesis, University of Kassel (2018)

19. Opfer, S., Jakob, S., Geihs, K.: Reasoning for autonomous agents in dynamic domains. In: van de Herik, J., Rocha, A.P., Filipe, J. (eds.) 9th International Conference on Agents and Artificial Intelligence (ICAART), pp. 340–351 (2017)

20. Opfer, S., Jakob, S., Geihs, K.: Reasoning for autonomous agents in dynamic domains: towards automatic satisfaction of the module property. In: van den Herik, J., Rocha, A.P., Filipe, J. (eds.) ICAART 2017. LNCS (LNAI), vol. 10839, pp. 22–47. Springer, Cham (2018). https://doi.org/10.1007/978-3-319-93581-2_2

21. Pynadath, D., Tambe, M.: Multiagent teamwork: analyzing the optimality and complexity of key theories and models. In: Proceedings of the 1st Conference of Autonomous Agents and Multiagent Systems (AAMAS), pp. 873–880. ACM (2002)

22. Rao, A.S.: AgentSpeak(L): BDI agents speak out in a logical computable language. In: Van de Velde, W., Perram, J.W. (eds.) MAAMAW 1996. LNCS, vol. 1038, pp. 42–55. Springer, Heidelberg (1996). https://doi.org/10.1007/BFb0031845

23. Röfer, T.: CABSL – C-based agent behavior specification language. In: Akiyama, H., Obst, O., Sammut, C., Tonidandel, F. (eds.) RoboCup 2017. LNCS (LNAI), vol. 11175, pp. 135–142. Springer, Cham (2018). https://doi.org/10.1007/978-3-030-00308-1_11

24. Rubel, D., Wren, J., Clayberg, E.: The Eclipse Graphical Editing Framework (GEF). Eclipse Series, vol. 1. Addison-Wesley Professional and Addison-Wesley, Boston (2011)

25. Sacerdoti, E.D.: The nonlinear nature of plans. Technical report, Stanford Research Institute, Menlo Park, CA (1975)

26. Saur, D., Geihs, K.: IMPERA: integrated mission planning for multi-robot systems. Robotics **4**(4), 435–463 (2015)

27. Skubch, H., Wagner, M., Reichle, R., Geihs, K.: A modelling language for cooperative plans in highly dynamic domains. Mechatronics **21**(2), 423–433 (2011)

28. Skubch, H., Wagner, M., Reichle, R., Triller, S., Geihs, K.: Towards a comprehensive teamwork model for highly dynamic domains. In: Filipe, J., Fred, A., Sharp, B. (eds.) Proceedings of the 2nd International Conference on Agents and Artificial Intelligence, vol. 2, pp. 121–127. INSTICC Press, January 2010
29. Skubch, H.: Modelling and Controlling of Behaviour for Autonomous Mobile Robots. Springer, Berlin (2013). https://doi.org/10.1007/978-3-658-00811-6
30. Skubch, H., Saur, D., Geihs, K.: Resolving conflicts in highly reactive teams. In: 17th GI/ITG Conference on Communication in Distributed Systems (KiVS). Schloss Dagstuhl-Leibniz-Zentrum für Informatik (2011)
31. Steinberg, D., Budinsky, F., Paternostro, M., Merks, E.: EMF: Eclipse Modeling Framework. Eclipse Series, 2nd edn. Addison-Wesley Professional, Boston (2008)
32. Vogel, L.: Eclipse Rich Client Platform: The Complete Guide to Eclipse Application Development, 3rd edn. Vogella, Hamburg (2015)
33. Weaver, J., Gao, W., Chin, S., Iverson, D., Vos, J.: Pro JavaFX 8: A Definitive Guide to Building Desktop, Mobile, and Embedded Java Clients. Apress, New York (2014)
34. Witsch, A., Opfer, S., Geihs, K.: A formal multi-agent language for cooperative autonomous driving scenarios. In: International Conference on Connected Vehicles & Expo (ICCVE). IEEE, Vienna, November 2014
35. Witsch, A., Skubch, H., Niemczyk, S., Geihs, K.: Using incomplete satisfiability modulo theories to determine robotic tasks. In: International Conference on Intelligent Robots and Systems (IROS). IEEE, Tokyo, November 2013
36. Yen, J., Yin, J., Ioerger, T.R., Miller, M.S., Xu, D., Volz, R.A.: CAST: collaborative agents for simulating teamwork. In: Proceedings of the 17th International Joint Conference on Artificial Intelligence (IJCAI) - Volume 2, pp. 1135–1142. Morgan Kaufmann Publishers Inc., San Francisco, USA (2001)

Extending Modular Semantics for Bipolar Weighted Argumentation (Extended Abstract)

Nico Potyka$^{(\boxtimes)}$ (iD)

Institute of Cognitive Science, University of Osnabrueck,
Osnabrück, Germany
npotyka@uos.de

Abstract. This extended abstract summarizes the key results from [10].

Keywords: Weighted bipolar argumentation · Algorithms

1 Introduction

Weighted bipolar argumentation frameworks allow modeling arguments and their relationships in order to decide which arguments can be accepted. Arguments have an initial weight that is adapted based on the strength of their attackers and supporters [2,4,7,8,11]. Applications include decision support [3,11], social media analysis [1,5,6] and information retrieval [12].

A simple example is shown in the upper left of Fig. 1. In this scenario, we have stocks of a company and want to decide if we should buy additional stocks or perhaps sell our stocks. Different arguments attack and support these choices. Attack relations are denoted by solid edges, support relations by dashed edges. Weights (and final strength values) can be values between 0 and 1. Intuitively, 0 (1) means that we completely reject (accept) the argument. We are initially indifferent between our choices, so we just set their initial weights to 0.5. The initial weight of the remaining arguments can be set based on the reputation of their sources. In our example, every argument may correspond to a different expert and the initial weight may be their historical success rate.

When designing the argumentation graph, we weigh arguments independently and do not consider their relationships. The weights should then be adapted automatically such that certain common-sense postulates are satisfied [2]. For example, if attackers and supporters of an argument are 'equally strong', then the weight should remain unchanged. Otherwise, if the attackers (supporters) are 'stronger than' the supporters (attackers), the strength should decrease (increase). The remaining graphs in Fig. 1 show the final strength values computed under different weighted argumentation approaches, namely *DF-QuAD* [11], the *Euler-based semantics* [2] and the *quadratic energy model* [8].

A discussion of the exact semantic properties of these semantics can be found in [2,8,11]. One thing to note here is that some semantics are more and

© Springer Nature Switzerland AG 2019
C. Benzmüller and H. Stuckenschmidt (Eds.): KI 2019, LNAI 11793, pp. 273–276, 2019.
https://doi.org/10.1007/978-3-030-30179-8_23

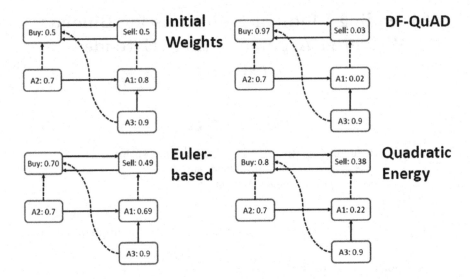

Fig. 1. Weighted bipolar argumentation framework.

some are less conservative. For example, for the Euler-based semantics, the final strength of A1 is still very close to the original weight even though it has two strong attackers (A2 and A3). For DF-QuAD and the quadratic energy model, the final strength is significantly smaller.

2   Open Problems and Contributions

One central problem in weighted argumentation is computing the final strength values of arguments. The final strength values are usually defined in an operational way by an iterative procedure. Most semantics can be characterized by an *aggregation function* that aggregates the strength of attackers and supporters and a *combination function* that combines this aggregate with the initial weight of an argument in order to compute a new strength value. These functions are then applied repeatedly until the strength values converge. While it is easy to show that convergence is guaranteed in acyclic graphs, convergence in cyclic graphs is not very well understood.

Mossakowski and Neuhaus gave recently first divergence examples and provided sufficient conditions under which the strength values are guaranteed to converge [7]. Figure 2 shows a simple divergence example. Initially ($t = 0$), argument B has a strong attacker, but only a weak supporter and so will have a significantly lower strength after the first iteration ($t = 1$). For A, the situation is inverted. In the next iteration, A and B switch roles. In the function graph in the middle of Fig. 2, we can see that the strength values start jumping between a state where A is accepted and B is rejected and a state where B is accepted and A is rejected. We applied DF-QuAD in Fig. 2, but similar examples can be constructed for other semantics [7]. However, in [7], also sufficient conditions for convergence are given. Roughly speaking, the general conditions are as follows: The strength values are guaranteed to converge if

- the strength of attackers and supporters is aggregated using addition or maximum and
- the combination function is differentiable and the derivative is bounded.

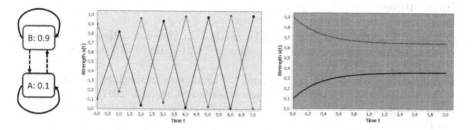

Fig. 2. Divergence example.

In the work summarized here [10], the results from [7] have been extended in several directions. First, the convergence guarantees in [7] turn out to be a special case of the contraction principle. This observation can be used to generalize the convergence guarantees to more general Lipschitz-continuous aggregation and combination functions that grow sufficiently slowly [10]. In this way, in particular, new convergence guarantees for DF-QuAD and the quadratic energy model can be derived. We can also show that the number of iterations until convergence increases only linearly with respect to the desired accuracy.

Second, we found that strong convergence guarantees are bought at the cost of *open-mindedness*. That is, semantics for which we can derive stronger convergence guarantees, tend to stay close to the initial weights no matter how strong attackers and supporters are. The notion of Lipschitz-continuity is again helpful to analyze the tradeoff between convergence guarantees and open-mindedness [10]. Interestingly, we can avoid this tradeoff by replacing the discrete iterative procedures that we discussed before with continuous procedures [8]. These continuous procedures can be automatically derived from the aggregation and combination functions [10]. We can show that whenever our convergence conditions are met, the continuous procedure cannot converge to another limit than the discrete one. That is, we do not affect any semantical properties. In particular, if the discrete procedure defined an open-minded semantics, the corresponding continuous procedure still defines the same open-minded semantics. Furthermore, we can give examples in which the discrete procedures diverge, but the continuous procedures still converge to a meaningful limit. The function graph on the right in Fig. 2 demonstrates this for our previous example.

Finally, all semantical building blocks and algorithms have been implemented in the Java library Attractor[1] [9]. They can be applied without any knowledge

---

[1] https://sourceforge.net/projects/attractorproject.

about discrete or continuous update procedures. New models can be added and continuized by just implementing new aggregation or combination functions. Furthermore, if these functions are Lipschitz-continuous, we can immediately derive information about the convergence guarantees and open-mindedness of the corresponding semantics [10].

References

1. Alsinet, T., Argelich, J., Béjar, R., Fernández, C., Mateu, C., Planes, J.: Weighted argumentation for analysis of discussions in Twitter. Int. J. Approximate Reasoning **85**, 21–35 (2017)
2. Amgoud, L., Ben-Naim, J.: Evaluation of arguments in weighted bipolar graphs. In: Antonucci, A., Cholvy, L., Papini, O. (eds.) ECSQARU 2017. LNCS (LNAI), vol. 10369, pp. 25–35. Springer, Cham (2017). https://doi.org/10.1007/978-3-319-61581-3_3
3. Baroni, P., Romano, M., Toni, F., Aurisicchio, M., Bertanza, G.: An argumentation-based approach for automatic evaluation of design debates. In: Leite, J., Son, T.C., Torroni, P., van der Torre, L., Woltran, S. (eds.) CLIMA 2013. LNCS (LNAI), vol. 8143, pp. 340–356. Springer, Heidelberg (2013). https://doi.org/10.1007/978-3-642-40624-9_21
4. Baroni, P., Romano, M., Toni, F., Aurisicchio, M., Bertanza, G.: Automatic evaluation of design alternatives with quantitative argumentation. Argument Comput. **6**(1), 24–49 (2015)
5. Cocarascu, O., Rago, A., Toni, F.: Extracting dialogical explanations for review aggregations with argumentative dialogical agents. In: International Conference on Autonomous Agents and MultiAgent Systems (AAMAS), pp. 1261–1269 (2019)
6. Leite, J., Martins, J.: Social abstract argumentation. In: International Joint Conferences on Artificial Intelligence (IJCAI), vol. 11, pp. 2287–2292 (2011)
7. Mossakowski, T., Neuhaus, F.: Modular semantics and characteristics for bipolar weighted argumentation graphs. arXiv preprint arXiv:1807.06685 (2018)
8. Potyka, N.: Continuous dynamical systems for weighted bipolar argumentation. In: International Conference on Principles of Knowledge Representation and Reasoning (KR), pp. 148–157 (2018)
9. Potyka, N.: A tutorial for weighted bipolar argumentation with continuous dynamical systems and the Java library attractor. In: International Workshop On Non-Monotonic Reasoning (NMR) (2018)
10. Potyka, N.: Extending modular semantics for bipolar weighted argumentation. In: International Conference on Autonomous Agents and MultiAgent Systems (AAMAS), pp. 1722–1730 (2019)
11. Rago, A., Toni, F., Aurisicchio, M., Baroni, P.: Discontinuity-free decision support with quantitative argumentation debates. In: International Conference on Principles of Knowledge Representation and Reasoning (KR), pp. 63–73 (2016)
12. Thiel, M., Ludwig, P., Mossakowski, T., Neuhaus, F., Nürnberger, A.: Web-retrieval supported argument space exploration. In: ACM SIGIR Conference on Human Information Interaction and Retrieval (CHIIR), pp. 309–312. ACM (2017)

Epistemic Multi-agent Planning
Using Monte-Carlo Tree Search

Daniel Reifsteck⬤, Thorsten Engesser⬤, Robert Mattmüller[(✉)]⬤,
and Bernhard Nebel⬤

Institut für Informatik, Albert-Ludwigs-Universität Freiburg,
Freiburg im Breisgau, Germany
daniel.reifsteck@googlemail.com,
{engesser,mattmuel,nebel}@informatik.uni-freiburg.de

Abstract. Coordination in multi-agent systems with partial and non-uniform observability is a practically challenging problem. We use Monte-Carlo tree search as the basis of an implicitly coordinated epistemic planning algorithm which is capable of using the knowledge distributed among the agents to find solutions in problems even with a large branching factor. We use Dynamic Epistemic Logic to represent the knowledge and the actual situation as a state of the Monte-Carlo tree search, and epistemic planning to formalize the goals and actions of a problem. Further, we describe the required modifications of the Monte-Carlo tree search when searching over epistemic states, and make use of the cooperative card game Hanabi to test our planner on larger problems. We find that the approach scales to games with up to eight cards while maintaining high playing strength.

Keywords: Epistemic planning · Monte-Carlo tree search ·
Multi-agent systems · Hanabi

1 Motivation

In many situations where multiple agents have to work together, the agents have only limited information about the current state of the world. Nevertheless, they have to coordinate their plans and share certain information with other agents to guarantee the successful execution of their plans and to reach their goals. Now, the problem is how to achieve this implicit coordination in multi-agent systems with partial and non-uniform observability.

Dynamic Epistemic Logic (DEL) [6] provides the possibility to represent the knowledge every agent has both about the world and about other agents' knowledge, and can serve as the basis of epistemic planning. In this setting, we can distinguish between centralized approaches and decentralized ones such as *implicit coordination* [7], where agents, when planning, *take the perspectives* of the other agents involved when reasoning about the other agents' potential contributions to the plan. In the present paper, we are interested in studying this form of

C. Benzmüller and H. Stuckenschmidt (Eds.): KI 2019, LNAI 11793, pp. 277–289, 2019.
https://doi.org/10.1007/978-3-030-30179-8_24

implicitly coordinated multi-agent epistemic planning from an *algorithmic* point of view. So far, algorithmic support for this notion of plans has been limited to poorly scaling algorithms like breadth-first search over epistemic states. In order to improve over that, in partially observable situations with many possible actions for every agent, we need a method which is able to find implicitly coordinated plans while not having to explore the whole search tree. The Monte-Carlo tree search (MCTS) approach [5] is a method which was already proved successful in achieving good results in large problems despite large branching factors in non-epistemic settings. Although MCTS does not necessarily find optimal plans, in many cases, the plans are of sufficient quality. The contribution of this paper is the development of an MCTS variant based on DEL models. More precisely, we use MCTS as the planning algorithm, where the states of the MCTS are epistemic states which contain the actual situation and the knowledge of the various agents, including higher-order knowledge. We benchmarked our MCTS algorithm on a simplified version of the game *Hanabi*, which is a cooperative card game with imperfect information for every agent. Hanabi is an interesting problem because the agents have to cooperate to achieve a common goal and have only limited possibilities to share information with each other. They strongly rely on getting information from other agents in order to be able to successfully complete the game. The need for implicit coordination and a large branching factor make Hanabi a suitable testbed for epistemic planning in general, and for our MCTS algorithm in particular.

To our knowledge, the combination of MCTS and DEL for solving Hanabi has not been investigated before. Still, we want to discuss a few papers from the literature which either have built up essential basics of our work or examined related topics recently. One of the first attempts to solving Hanabi was presented by Osawa [10], where average results were achieved by knowledge-based strategies. A recent paper by Bard et al. [1] proposes Hanabi as a new challenge at the "frontier of AI research". While Hanabi-specific solvers can play almost perfectly, especially when playing in groups of identical players and allowed to reason under the assumption that exactly that is the case, performance is typically much worse if either of those premises is violated. Coming up with competitive *general* game playing engines that are also good at Hanabi, without handcrafted Hanabi knowledge, is still challenging, and so is *ad-hoc team play*, where different players have to adapt to each other without making too many prior assumptions about how the other participants will play [1]. The work of Bolander and Andersen [2] and Engesser et al. [7] in epistemic planning provides the foundation of our proposed algorithm, as we use their definitions of epistemic planning, perspective shifts, and implicit coordination.

2   Theoretical Background

2.1   The Rules of Hanabi

Before we discuss the theoretical basics of DEL and MCTS, we first want to give a short explanation of the game Hanabi. Hanabi is a cooperative card game for two to five players, each holding four or five cards, depending on the number of players. Each card has a color (red, green, blue, white, or yellow) and a number (1 to 5). Cards not dealt to any player are initially located on a replenishment stack. The players have to hold their cards in such a way that they cannot see their own cards, but that the other players can see them. This ensures that each player initially only knows the cards of the other players but not their own hand. The objective of the game is to build up a stack of cards for each color, where the cards have to be played in increasing order, so the red 2 has to be played before the red 3, and so on. Since players can only play their cards in a reasonable way if they know about the colors and numbers of their cards, other players have to provide them with the necessary information. In order to limit information exchange, there are eight hint tokens that can be used up when giving hints, and earned back by irreversibly discarding cards. The game ends if either (a) all five stacks have been completed, (b) the players made three mistakes in playing their cards, or (c) the replenishment stack is depleted. The resulting score is the total number of successfully played cards, or zero if the game ended with too many mistakes made by the players. In each turn, the player whose turn it is has to choose one out of three possible actions: first she can play one of her cards which will be put on the stack of the same color if the number of the card is by one higher than the number of the topmost card of the stack. If the card has a non-fitting number, then this counts as one mistake, and the card will be discarded. In both cases the player has to replenish her hand. The second possible action is to discard a card to get a hint token back. In this case, the hand of the player has to be replenished, too. The third action is to give a hint to another player by pointing at all cards with a certain number or color, for example all cards with the number 4 or all cards with the color red. In this case, the players have to pay one hint token which cannot be used anymore until a card is discarded later on.

As mentioned before, we use a simplified version of Hanabi with fewer cards and no limitation of hints. We can also scale the number of agents and cards, on the hand and in total, to be more flexible in evaluating.

2.2 Dynamic Epistemic Logic and Epistemic Planning

In this paper, we use the conventions and definitions of Bolander and Andersen [2] and Engesser et al. [7]. We start with the definition of the basic epistemic language.

Definition 1. *The language $\mathcal{L}_K$ of epistemic formulas is generated by the following grammar, where $p \in P$ is an atomic proposition, and $i \in A$ an agent:*

$$\varphi ::= p \mid \neg\varphi \mid \varphi \wedge \varphi \mid K_i\varphi.$$

The modality $K_i\varphi$ means that agent i knows that the formula φ holds. Adding common knowledge ($C\varphi$) is straightforward, but we omit it here for brevity. Abbreviations ($\top, \bot, \vee, \rightarrow, \dots$) can be introduced as usual. Epistemic formulas are evaluated in epistemic models, defined next.

Definition 2. *An* epistemic model M *is a tuple* $(\dot{W}, (\sim_i)_{i \in A}, V)$, *where*

- W *is a non-empty finite set of* worlds, *called the* domain *of* M,
- $\sim_i \subseteq W \times W$ *is the* indistinguishability relation *for agent* i, *an equivalence relation, and*
- $V : W \to 2^P$ *is a function which assigns to each world* w *the set of atomic propositions that are true in* w.

An *(epistemic) state* is a pair $s = (M, W_d)$ consisting of an epistemic model $M = (W, (\sim_i)_{i \in A}, V)$ and a subset $W_d \subseteq W$ of its worlds, the *designated worlds*. If W_d only contains a single world w, the state is called *global*, with w as actual world. A state s is called *local* for an agent i if W_d is closed under agent i's indistinguishability. We depict epistemic states as graphs, where the nodes correspond to worlds and the edges correspond to the indistinguishability relations. Worlds are labeled with the propositions that are true in them. We usually omit world names as well as edges that are implied by reflexivity or transitivity. We mark designated worlds with a circle. E.g., consider the following simplified Hanabi state where each agent has only one card and cards do not have a color:

$$s_0 = \quad \underset{\substack{\text{alice-has-2} \\ \text{bob-has-1}}}{\odot} \!\!\overset{\text{bob}}{\rule{2cm}{0.4pt}}\!\! \underset{\substack{\text{alice-has-2} \\ \text{bob-has-3}}}{\bullet}$$

The global state contains two possible worlds, one in which Bob has a 1 (the actual world) and one in which he has a 3. Since Alice can distinguish both worlds and Bob cannot, the state is local for Alice but not for Bob. Truth of epistemic formulas in epistemic states is defined as follows:

$M, w \models p$	iff	$p \in V(w)$ for $p \in P$
$M, w \models \neg\varphi$	iff	$M, w \not\models \varphi$
$M, w \models \varphi \wedge \psi$	iff	$M, w \models \varphi$ and $M, w \models \psi$
$M, w \models K_i\varphi$	iff	$M, v \models \varphi$ for all v such that $w \sim_i v$.

Moreover, $M, W_d \models \varphi$ iff $M, w \models \varphi$ for all $w \in W_d$. E.g, in our example we can see that $s_0 \models K_{\text{alice}}(\text{alice-has-2} \wedge \text{bob-has-1}) \wedge \neg K_{\text{bob}}\text{bob-has-1}$. In order to perform actions on states, we define *event models*.

Definition 3. *An* event model $\mathcal{E}$ *is a tuple* $(E, (\sim_i)_{i \in A}, \text{pre}, \text{eff})$, *where*

- E *is a non-empty finite set of* events,
- $\sim_i \subseteq E \times E$ *is the* indistinguishability relation *for agent* i, *an equivalence relation,*
- $\text{pre} : E \to \mathcal{L}_K$ *defines the* precondition *of every event, and*
- $\text{eff} : E \to \mathcal{L}_K$ *defines the* effect *of every event. Formulas* $\text{eff}(e)$ *for* $e \in E$ *must be conjunctions of literals over* P.

An *(epistemic) action* a is a pair $(\mathcal{E}, E_d)$ consisting of an event model $\mathcal{E}$ and a non-empty set $E_d \subseteq E$ of *designated events*, and is only applicable in a state s if for every designated world in s, there exists a designated event in E_d with precondition satisfied in s. Note that actions are nondeterministic if they contain two different designated events with consistent preconditions.

Epistemic actions are depicted analogously to epistemic states, except that the nodes now correspond to events, and that they are labeled with preconditions and effects. The following action a_0 is for publicly announcing that Bob has the card 1. In action a_1, Bob's card is put onto the table (which works regardless of whether the card is a 1, 2, or 3 and regardless of whether Bob knows his card):

$$a_0 = \quad \bullet \qquad\qquad a_1 = \quad \bullet \qquad\qquad \bullet \qquad\qquad \bullet$$

pre: bob-has-1   pre: bob-has-1   pre: bob-has-2   pre: bob-has-3
eff: $\top$ eff: stack-1∧   eff: stack-2∧   eff: stack-3∧
                   ¬bob-has-1   ¬bob-has-2   ¬bob-has-3

The result of applying an action in a state is defined by the *product update*.

Definition 4. *Given an epistemic state s and an epistemic action a as above, the product update $s \otimes a$ of s and a is defined as the epistemic state $(M', W'_d) = ((W', (\sim'_i)_{i \in A}, V'), W'_d)$ with*

- $W' = \{(w, e) \in W \times E \mid M, w \models pre(e)\}$,
- $\sim'_i = \{((w, e), (w', e')) \in W' \times W' \mid w \sim_i w' \text{ and } e \sim_i e'\}$,
- $V'((w, e)) = \{p \in P \mid eff(e) \models p \text{ or } (M, w \models p \text{ and } eff(e) \not\models \neg p)\}$, *and*
- $W'_d = \{(w, e) \in W' \mid w \in W_d \text{ and } e \in E_d\}$.

We can see that for our previously defined state and actions the product update works as expected. If at first, Alice announces to Bob that his card is a 1, then this becomes common knowledge. Then Bob can put down its card onto the stack.

$$s_1 = s_0 \otimes a_0 = \quad \bullet \qquad\qquad s_2 = s_1 \otimes a_1 = \quad \bullet$$

alice-has-2   alice-has-2
bob-has-1   stack-1

Finally, Bob can draw a new card from the replenishment stack:

$$s_2 \quad \otimes \quad \bullet \xrightarrow{\text{bob}} \bullet \xrightarrow{\text{bob}} \bullet \quad = \quad \bullet$$

pre: ¬stack-1∧   pre: ¬stack-2∧   pre: ¬stack-3∧   alice-has-2
¬alice-has-1   ¬alice-has-2   ¬alice-has-3   bob-has-3
eff: bob-has-1   eff: bob-has-2   eff: bob-has-3   stack-1

Since it is common knowledge that card 2 is already owned by Alice and card 1 is on the table, it is clear that Bob will draw the 3. However, if we use this type of actions to draw the initial cards for Bob and Alice, we first get a state with three worlds containing all three possible cards for Bob, and then a state with six worlds consisting of all combinations of two cards for Bob and Alice.

We use these types of DEL states and actions in our Hanabi player to model the game states and the available moves for the agents. In contrast to the example, we additionally have to keep track of which of the players' turn it is and we also have to make sure to end the game given a mistake is made.

To choose an appropriate action for a given state, agents have to take into account that everyone tries to maximize the common score, but from their own imperfect knowledge about the world. Our approach is related to the notion of *subjectively strong policies* by Engesser et al. [3,7]: After planning to execute an action owned by itself, the agent has to consider the potential local perspectives of the next agent to decide on the potentially best follow-up moves for this agent.

E.g., in our example, Alice should announce Bob's card, because she can be sure that afterwards Bob will know from his own perspective that the best course of action is to put his card onto the stack. This works even if Alice is still uncertain about her own card (which might be a 2 or a 3).

In DEL, we can shift perspective to the next agent j by simply closing the set of designated worlds under the indistinguishability relation of agent j. Since the resulting local state can contain multiple distinguishable classes of worlds for agent j, we can branch over these classes to get all the potential local states that the next agent j might actually see after the action application.

E.g., if Alice is uncertain about her own card when announcing Bob's 1, we branch over one local state for Bob where Alice actually has the 2 and one where she has the 3. In both cases, Bob knows that he has the 1.

2.3 Monte-Carlo Tree Search

Monte-Carlo tree search (MCTS) [5] is an algorithm that uses randomized simulations to generate a search tree and find the best action. The search tree is generated by repeating the four steps *selection, expansion, simulation* and *backpropagation* until a certain termination condition is met, in our case until a certain number of simulations are executed. Before we explain the individual steps, we show the basic structure of MCTS as pseudo-code below.

```
def MonteCarloTreeSearch(root)
    Searchtree.create(root)
    while root.simulations < max_simulations:
        vertex = select()
        expand(vertex)
        for child in vertex.get_children():
            result = simulate(child)
            backpropagate(child, result)

    return root.get_best_child().get_action()
```

Selection. The selection step decides which leaf node of the search tree is explored further in the current repetition of the four steps. To select a vertex to be simulated, the selection step always chooses a child of the current vertex until reaching a leaf, beginning from the root. As the strategy for choosing a child we use the UCT (Upper Confidence Bound applied to Trees) formula [8] which selects a child i of the vertex e with maximal value of the UCT formula $v_i + c \cdot \sqrt{(\ln n_e)/n_i}$, where n_i is the number of simulations of a vertex i, v_i the average result of the simulations of a vertex i and c a coefficient, the exploration parameter. UCT generally leads to a decent tradeoff between exploration and exploitation.

Expansion. In the expansion step, for every action that is applicable in the state of the selected leaf vertex, a child vertex is generated and inserted into the search tree.

Simulation. The simulation step executes one simulation per child node that was inserted during the expansion step, starting in the newly generated states. Executing a simulation means that random applicable actions are performed until either (a) the termination criterion of the planning task has been satisfied, (b) no action is applicable any more, or (c) a predefined horizon has been reached. The last case is used to bound the simulation lengths. Upon termination of a simulation, the value of the final state is either known, or, in case (c), approximated by a knowledge-based heuristic.

Backpropagation. The results computed in the simulation step are now propagated back through the search tree so that the expected value of a vertex is always the average score of all simulations executed on its children. Additionally, the number of executed simulations of every visited vertex is increased, as this statistic is needed in the UCT formula.

Action Selection. After a certain number of simulations have been executed, MCTS has to select the next action to be played. In this work, we select the action leading to the most robust child of the root vertex, because we want to minimize the risk of choosing a poor action.

3 Dynamic Epistemic Logic in a Monte-Carlo Tree Search

As mentioned in the introduction, we now want to combine MCTS with a DEL-based state representation in order to find implicitly coordinated plans in larger planning tasks such as the game Hanabi. For this purpose, we use epistemic states to represent the actual situation in the game and the information of the different agents. Furthermore, we have epistemic actions that represent the actions in the game and which can cause changes to the game state and the agents' knowledge. But before we can use DEL in an MCTS, it is necessary to modify several steps of the search, in particular the selection, expansion and simulation step. After explaining our modifications, we present two possibilities of how to improve the efficiency of our MCTS.

3.1 Modifications

For the expansion step, it is not sufficient to consider the product updates of the current local state with each action. Instead, we have to look at all potential successor states from the perspective of the agent who will act next. We expand a local state (M, W_d) in two steps:

1. For each applicable action a, we first generate the successor state $(M^a, W_d^a) = (M, W_d) \otimes a$, which is still local for the agent who has performed the action.
2. We *split* each of those successor states into the set of global states $\{(M^a, w) \mid w \in W_d^a\}$ that the agent who performed the action actually considers possible. We then immediately shift the perspective of these global states further to the agent who has to act next. Thus for each action, we obtain the set of successor states $\{(M^a, \{w' \mid w \sim_{ag(M^a)} w'\}) \mid w \in W_d^a\}$, where $ag(M^a)$ is the agent who acts in M^a. Notice that, up to perspective shifting, this split corresponds to branching over possible probabilistic action outcomes or over possible observations in (partially observable) probabilistic planning.

This approach leads to a search tree with two different types of vertices. We call the vertices generated by a product update *action vertices* and the vertices generated by a split *split vertices*. These types of vertices must be handled differently in MCTS, in particular in the selection step.

If MCTS has to select an action vertex in the selection step, the vertex with the highest UCT value is chosen, which is a common approach in MCTS. The problem is now that we cannot use the UCT formula for selecting a split vertex, because we do not know which designated world is the actual world. E.g., the world with the highest UCT value is not necessarily the actual world and should not be simulated more often than other designated worlds. Given that split vertices are very similar to chance nodes in Monte-Carlo search trees for MDPs, we assume every designated world to be the actual world with a certain probability so that we can compute the expected result of the parent vertex. In our simplified version of Hanabi, every designated world is the actual world with the same probability, so we can select a world uniformly at random in every step. It is more difficult if we want to use our MCTS in other problems, because in general, we do not know with which probability a designated world is the actual world. So, for general problems, we make a worst-case assumption and minimize. After every designated world has been simulated at least once, the selection step always selects the split vertex with the lowest average score in the simulations. In this way, the expected result of the parent vertex converges to the average result of the worst designated world with a growing number of simulations. This ensures that MCTS chooses low-risk actions to avoid losses in Hanabi, or unsolvable or poor states in general. In summary, the selection step of our MCTS always selects the action vertex with the maximum UCT value and the split vertex with the minimum expected value.

The simulation step does not require large modifications, because we do not use a sophisticated simulation strategy. In every turn of a simulation, MCTS selects a random action to perform on the current state before one random designated world is chosen to be the current world for the next turn. So, the simulation step in our MCTS is basically the same as in every MCTS with a random simulation strategy. In the case that we would have a different simulation strategy for selecting action and split vertices in the simulations, it would be necessary to modify the simulation step, because selecting action and split vertices other than uniformly requires different strategies.

3.2 Efficiency Improvements

We implemented two enhancements to improve the efficiency of our MCTS. The enhancements can be activated separately or in combination and are compatible with each other.

Search Tree Reuse. In the standard case, a new search tree has to be generated after MCTS has computed an action and executed it. With this enhancement, MCTS can reuse a part of the old search tree and its results to reduce the number of simulations in the current turn. To reuse the old search tree, we prune the actions which were not executed from the tree and set the vertex representing the current state as new root. The simulations which were executed from the new root in the previous turn count for this turn so that MCTS does not have to do so many simulations any more. This is expected to lead to an improvement of the run-time of MCTS.

State Heuristic. MCTS can be improved with a knowledge-based heuristic which is used to further direct the search by selecting good actions in the selection and simulation steps. We evaluate states by taking the current score (i.e., the number of successfully played cards so far). We then multiply this value with a constant and add it to the UCT value of the search node.

4 Evaluation

4.1 Experimental Results

We benchmarked our variant of MCTS on a simplified version of Hanabi with different numbers of cards and agents and different combinations of our proposed improvements. Figure 1 shows the average runtimes of our MCTS variant compared to those of a random strategy and a simple knowledge-based strategy.

The runtimes of our MCTS variant are higher than those of the baseline approaches, which was expected due the fact that the baselines do not perform any search at all. Furthermore, as Fig. 2(a) shows, we can reduce the runtime of MCTS by using our proposed efficiency enhancements. The scores of all combinations were still nearly optimal, so our efficiency enhancements have no negative influence on the scores.

We furthermore tested our MCTS with three instead of two agents to find out the effect of adding more agents to the model. Overall, we discovered two major effects of additional agents in Hanabi. First, they increase the runtime of the MCTS as shown in Fig. 2(b) due to the increased number of applicable actions and the larger models. Furthermore, we have shown that an additional agent may increase the runtime, but also improves the scores achieved by MCTS. In all benchmark problems with three agents, MCTS not only achieved the maximum score, but also avoided useless hints to other agents in nearly every solution. This may be because the uncertainty about the own cards decreases with each additional agent as each agent sees more cards with more other agents around.

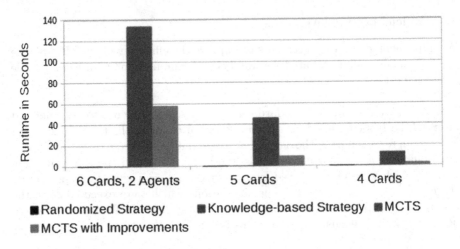

Fig. 1. Runtimes of our MCTS variant and baseline strategies

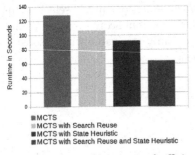

(a) Different combinations of efficiency enhancements

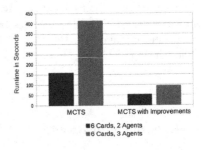

(b) Models with two and three agents

Fig. 2. Runtime results for enhancements and for varying numbers of agents

In this case, our efficiency enhancements are more effective, especially the reuse of the search trees, because the agents often found good plans already at the start and reused them in every turn.

Table 1 shows that the achieved scores were nearly optimal for MCTS and the knowledge-based strategy due to the small size of the benchmarked models. The scores are the numbers of successfully played cards plus one extra point if all cards were played successfully, so the optimal score for a model with n cards is $n + 1$.

4.2 Limitations

Before we move on to the conclusion, we briefly want to discuss some limitations of our work and point out some problems of this method.

Table 1. Scores of our MCTS variant and baseline strategies

Model	Random	Knowledge-based	MCTS	MCTS + improvements
4 cards	1.4	5.0	5.0	5.0
5 cards	0.0	6.0	6.0	6.0
6 cards	0.4	6.9	5.8	5.9

There are three main types of limitations we had to handle in MCTS, (a) the limitations of our model, (b) the time-consuming simulations and (c) the high memory consumption of the epistemic states. First, our model of Hanabi is not complete, so we have no possibility to limit the number of hints or to discard cards, which is necessary in situations where no agent can play a card successfully. These limitations of our model were introduced to reduce the complexity, but are hindering in larger problems.

Another limitation is the runtime of the simulations in MCTS for which mainly the time-consuming product updates are responsible. The runtime of a single simulation increases with the size of the model, and in order to solve larger problems with higher branching factors, we need to execute more simulations to achieve a solution.

The last and most impactful limitation is the memory consumption of the epistemic states. MCTS has to store all epistemic states in the search tree, the number and size of which drastically increase with the total number of cards n, the number of cards on each hand h, and the number of agents a. The number of total worlds scales in the order of $O(n^{a \cdot h})$, while the number of designated worlds from an agent's perspective at the start of a game scales in the order of $O((n-a \cdot h)^h)$ for $n > h \cdot a$. Some concrete numbers exemplifying the exponential increase in a and h can be seen in Table 2.

Table 2. Size of different Hanabi models

Model	Size	Total worlds	Designated worlds
$n = 6, a = 2, h = 2$	123 KB	360	12
$n = 8, a = 2, h = 2$	497 KB	1680	30
$n = 8, a = 2, h = 4$	15951 KB	40320	24
$n = 8, a = 4, h = 2$	21559 KB	40320	2

5   Conclusion and Future Work

We introduced and implemented a new method for implicitly coordinated cooperative online epistemic planning, where the objective is to maximize the expected reward. We used (a) DEL models to represent the epistemic aspect of the problem, (b) perspective shifts to assure implicit coordination, and (c) MCTS over our DEL models with such perspective shifts and with branching over non-determinism and partial observability as a search algorithm that works online, can focus on promising regions of the search space, and is geared towards maximizing the expected reward. In this way, agents can plan in a decentralized manner without the necessity to explore the entire search space. We benchmarked this variant of MCTS in the Hanabi game and showed that it is able to find implicitly coordinated plans in small but non-trivial game instances. We identified the size of the DEL models to be the reason why our method is not able to solve larger problems.

There are different directions of further research. First, the efficiency has to be improved, which mainly means that the epistemic models have to be optimized. This can include lossless optimizations such as improved bisimilarity contractions or lazy state representations, or lossy optimizations that trade off some accuracy in the representation of higher-order knowledge for runtime and space.

Second, we might give up some of the generality of the proposed algorithm and add domain-specific optimizations. For instance, knowledge-based heuristics for a simulation or selection strategy could be used [4]. In particular, the simulations would be much more efficient if there is a strategy which relies on domain knowledge instead of choosing random actions.

Furthermore, the possibility to take the perspectives of other agents is successfully used in our planning algorithm to find implicitly coordinated plans, but the question is now how effectively it works in non-cooperative situations. In situations where different agents want to achieve different goals, it might be useful to find out which actions the other agents intend to execute.

Finally, the empirical work presented here needs to be complemented by a more elaborate theory. The concept of implicit coordination is reasonably well-understood for *reachability goals* to be achieved cooperatively, both for non-branching and for branching plans [7]. Playing Hanabi is an optimization problem, though. We still lack a formal definition of what it means for a group of agents to implicitly coordinate themselves towards maximizing the expected reward. Such a definition is indispensable when attempting, e.g., to prove that a search algorithm like the one presented in this paper converges towards an optimal implicitly coordinated solution after sufficiently many simulations. Algorithmically, it is an open question whether it is preferable to handle the probabilistic aspect of the problem in the Monte-Carlo tree search or using a probabilistic variant of DEL [9].

References

1. Bard, N., et al.: The Hanabi challenge: a new frontier for AI research. CoRR abs/1902.00506 (2019)
2. Bolander, T., Andersen, M.B.: Epistemic planning for single and multi-agent systems. J. Appl. Non-classical Logics **21**(1), 9–34 (2011)

3. Bolander, T., Engesser, T., Mattmüller, R., Nebel, B.: Better eager than lazy? How agent types impact the successfulness of implicit coordination. In: Proceedings of the Sixteenth International Conference on Principles of Knowledge Representation and Reasoning (KR), pp. 445–453 (2018)
4. Chaslot, G.M.J.B., Winands, M.H.M., van den Herik, H.J., Uiterwijk, J.W.H.M., Bouzy, B.: Progressive strategies for Monte-Carlo tree search. New Math. Nat. Comput. 4(3), 343–357 (2008)
5. Coulom, R.: Efficient selectivity and backup operators in Monte-Carlo tree search. In: van den Herik, H.J., Ciancarini, P., Donkers, H.H.L.M.J. (eds.) CG 2006. LNCS, vol. 4630, pp. 72–83. Springer, Heidelberg (2007). https://doi.org/10.1007/978-3-540-75538-8_7
6. van Ditmarsch, H., van der Hoek, W., Kooi, B.: Dynamic Epistemic Logic. SYLI, vol. 337. Springer, Berlin (2008). Synthese Library
7. Engesser, T., Bolander, T., Mattmüller, R., Nebel, B.: Cooperative epistemic multi-agent planning with implicit coordination. In: Proceedings of the Ninth Workshop on Methods for Modalities (M4M) (2017)
8. Kocsis, L., Szepesvári, C.: Bandit based Monte-Carlo planning. In: Fürnkranz, J., Scheffer, T., Spiliopoulou, M. (eds.) ECML 2006. LNCS (LNAI), vol. 4212, pp. 282–293. Springer, Heidelberg (2006). https://doi.org/10.1007/11871842_29
9. Kooi, B.: Probabilistic dynamic epistemic logic. J. Logic Lang. Inf. 12(4), 381–408 (2003)
10. Osawa, H.: Solving Hanabi: estimating hands by opponent's actions in cooperative game with incomplete information. In: Computer Poker and Imperfect Information: Papers from the 2015 AAAI Workshop (2015)

Towards Intuitive Robot Programming Using Finite State Automata

Lukas Sauer[1]([✉]), Dominik Henrich[1], and Wim Martens[2]

[1] Lehrstuhl Angewandte Informatik 3 (Robotik und Eingebettete Systeme),
Universität Bayreuth, Bayreuth, Germany
lukas.sauer@uni-bayreuth.de
[2] Lehrstuhl Angewandte Informatik 7 (Theoretische Informatik),
Universität Bayreuth, Bayreuth, Germany

Abstract. This paper describes an approach to intuitive robot programming, with the aim of enabling non-experts to generate sensor-based, structured programs. The core idea is to generate a variant of a finite state automaton (representing the program) by kinesthetic programming (physically guiding the robot). We use the structure of the automaton for control flow (loops and branching according to conditions of the environment). For programming, we forgo a visual user interface completely to determine to what extent this is viable. Our experiments show that non-expert users are indeed able to successfully program small sample tasks within reasonable time.

Keywords: Robotics · Finite state automata · Programming

1 Introduction

While robots are used most in large scale industry, their future use is expected to comprise fields where no expert programmers are available, e.g. small and medium-sized enterprises, workshops, or private households. We describe an approach extending playback programming (*guiding* in [13]) by simple means of program structuring, based on the model of finite state automata, thus taking an automata theory point of view to robot programming. It aims to enable intuitive programming of sensor-based, structured robot programs by non-expert users. Furthermore, we do not use a textual or graphical user interface. This means that no monitor is required, reducing the amount of necessary hardware both to acquire and to set up in the workspace. While personal devices like smartphones are present for many users, these are generally too small for more complex interfaces and program representations. Interaction in our approach takes place solely

This work has partly been supported by the Deutsche Forschungsgemeinschaft (DFG) under grant agreement He2696/15 INTROP. We acknowledge Katharina Barth, who developed a preliminary version of the presented work and code base upon which we could build.

© Springer Nature Switzerland AG 2019
C. Benzmüller and H. Stuckenschmidt (Eds.): KI 2019, LNAI 11793, pp. 290–298, 2019.
https://doi.org/10.1007/978-3-030-30179-8_25

via the robot (and a small number of hardware buttons, similar to the controls of a media player). Our hypothesis is that, for programming a task known to the user, the visible state of robot and environment is sufficient. In that case, the absence of a textual or graphical interface allows the user to focus exclusively on the robot. The user especially does not need to switch between devices, and always has both hands available to interact with the robot. In the experiments, we explore the viability of such a system.

Robot programming is a well-known field of research, surveys of which can be found in [4,13,20]. In programming by demonstration (PbD), the user guides the robot through tasks. Overviews can be found in [2,5]. Kinesthetic programming as employed here (guiding the robot directly, in a real environment, while it compensates for its weight) has been used in numerous works, e.g. [1,12,15,17]. Finite state automata (FSA) have been used in robotics repeatedly, but mostly at other levels of abstraction. Some applications are [6,10,14]. In all of these, states represent more abstract properties of the system, while here, they are associated directly with robot configurations. An exception, [18] can also employ states like we do. But their automaton as a whole is generated in an automatic fashion rather than explicitly by the user. Generalizing demonstrated behaviour is typical for PbD, found e.g. in [8,21]. This is applied to FSA in [11,23] in the strongest extent, where the automata are evolved via genetic algorithms.

Most works about simplified robot programming use extensive visual user interfaces, as [7,16,26,28]. This includes approaches commercially available like the Franka Emika Desk interface [9], the Artiminds Robot Programming Suite [3], the TechMan software TMflow [27], Universal Robots' PolyScope [29], or the Rethink Robotics Intera software for their Baxter or Sawyer robots [22]. An approach close to ours in terms of program structuring is [24], with basic loops and branches. But there, too, a visual representation of the program (in the vein of Gantt charts) is essential for the concept.

To summarize, robot programming (by demonstration or using FSA) is and has been an active field of research. But, to the best of our knowledge, this approach of explicitly generating structured, sensor-based programs (represented as automata) without a visual interface has not been explored so far.

2   Programming Concept

Our model is a variation of FSA that we refer to as *Robot State Automata (RSA)*.

Definition 1. *An RSA is given as a tuple $M = (Q, \Sigma, C, \delta, \varphi, q_s, E)$ where*

- Q *is the finite set of states,*
- Σ *is the finite input alphabet,*
- C *is the space of robot joint configurations,*
- $\delta : Q \times \Sigma \cup \{\varepsilon\} \to Q$ *is the state transition function,*
- $\varphi : Q \to C$ *is the function mapping states to robot joint configurations,*

- $q_s \in Q$ *is the initial state, and*
- $E \subseteq Q$ *is the set of terminal states.*

A *(robot joint) configuration* $c \in C$ is a tuple of positions of all joints of the robot, also including gripper opening. States $q \in Q$ are mapped to configurations by φ. The input alphabet Σ is the set of *stimuli* the robot perceives via its sensors. This can be as simple as a color space (e.g. represented as $[0, 255]^3$), when a single stimulus is the average color of a camera image. But it is also possible to use entire images (in which case Σ is the set of $n \times m$ matrices of color values for image dimensions $n \times m$) and use an image-based similarity measure to compare stimuli. Another option is extracting information about objects in the image, with stimuli being vectors of properties. Note that Σ will, generally, be a large set, and that it is neither practical nor necessary to ever list it explicitly.

The partial function δ determines the possible state transitions, i.e. if the RSA is in $q \in Q$ and the robot perceives a stimulus $s \in \Sigma$, it will move to $\delta(q, s)$ if defined. By $\varepsilon \notin \Sigma$ we denote, as in FSA, an empty input sequence. We need this for transitions where the robot does not read a stimulus and the RSA directly moves from q to $\delta(q, \varepsilon)$, called *spontaneous transitions*. We require RSA to be deterministic, i.e., if $\delta(q, \varepsilon)$ is defined, then $\delta(q, s)$ must be undefined $\forall s \in \Sigma$. As a consequence, Q can be partitioned as $Q_\varepsilon \uplus Q_b$ where $Q_b = \{q \in Q \mid \exists s \in \Sigma : \delta(q, s) \text{ defined}\}$ are *branching states* and $Q_\varepsilon = Q \setminus Q_b$ are states with spontaneous transitions. In branching states, the automaton can branch into several possible transitions. Figure 1 provides a visualization of branching in a robot program. Spontaneous transitions are, by definition, always uniquely determined.

In execution, the RSA starts in q_s, the robot in $\varphi(q_s)$. In each step, the current state q is either in Q_ε or in Q_b. If $q \in Q_\varepsilon$, the RSA changes state to $q' = \delta(q, \varepsilon)$ and the robot moves from $\varphi(q)$ to $\varphi(q')$. If $q \in Q_b$, the RSA makes the robot take a stimulus $s \in \Sigma$. If $q' = \delta(q, s)$ is defined, the RSA changes state to q' and the robot moves from $\varphi(q)$ to $\varphi(q')$. Otherwise, the RSA remains in q and makes the robot take another stimulus s. This keeps repeating until a stimulus s with a defined transition is perceived. Execution stops when the new state is in E.

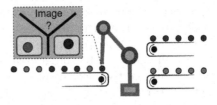

Fig. 1. Example: parts arriving on the left are sorted onto different conveyor belts. Sensors measure the color of objects (different $s_i \in \Sigma$) to select a branch in the branching state. (Color figure online)

We now explain how an RSA is created in our approach. User interaction consists of guiding the robot and using three *command inputs*. Note that command inputs (triggering a command, e.g. by pushing a button) and recorded stimuli (elements $s \in \Sigma$, e.g. observed color values) are different. Command inputs are used to program the robot, as explained below. We start with $Q = \{q_s\}$, no transitions, and $\varphi(q_s)$ as configuration. Then, incrementally, new states are generated. In the default interaction, the user (physically) guides the robot, while the system records its configuration in fixed time intervals Δ. So, with the RSA in q at time t, the system automatically adds a state q' to Q at $t + \Delta$, defines $\delta(q, \varepsilon) = q'$, and sets $\varphi(q') = c$, where c is the configuration at $t + \Delta$.

The first command input is for *branching*. When triggered in some state q, this makes the robot record a stimulus s. When the user then continues to guide the robot, the next transition is set as $\delta(q, s) = q'$, where q' is a newly generated state. Note that this is not an ε-transition and will require the same stimulus s to be executed. After this transition, the system goes back to recording the guided trajectory.

The second command input is for *recurrence transitions* from a current state q to an already existing state q'. For this, the user moves the robot back to the configuration $\varphi(q')$ and triggers the command input. This generates a new ε-transition $\delta(q, \varepsilon) = q'$. Then, the robot starts executing spontaneous transitions from q' until reaching a branching state, where the user can take control again to add a new branch. To introduce a new branch in the branching state, the first command input is used again, just as above.[1] To make recurrence transitions easier to use, it can be decided to only allow branching states as targets (greatly reducing the number of potential targets to keep in mind).

The third command input is used to define terminal states. Triggering it while in state q adds q to the set of terminal states E.

These command inputs and guiding the robot are the only interactions necessary. No display is used, and mapping the command inputs to physical buttons installed on the robot itself allows the user to only interact with the manipulator.

So the user generates the robot program (i.e. the RSA) step by step in *programming mode*. In *execution mode*, this program controls the robot. These two modes are interwoven. When reaching a terminal or a previously known state in programming mode, the system switches to execution mode. Then, the automaton is executed from the initial or current state, respectively. When execution reaches a branching state, the robot executes known branches for corresponding stimuli, or the user can expand the program with a new transition. If they record a new transition, the system switches back to programming mode. This interwoven process of programming and execution has the benefit that the automaton can be expanded on demand, even after executing it a number of times.

3   Expressiveness of the Approach

Different approaches to robot programming can express programs of different complexity. For our approach, this is the class of FSA. By construction, generated programs are RSA. We can reduce a given RSA to an FSA by removing the excess components (C and φ). By these steps, generated programs can be mapped to FSA. We argue the reverse to be true as well: any given FSA can be (mapped to an RSA and then) generated in the proposed approach.

---

[1] Note that looping back is not the only way to reach a branching state for adding new branches. The system can also be programmed up to a terminal state, then executed from the beginning, until reaching the branching state again, as detailed below.

First, if we cut away all unreachable states of an FSA, the result will be functionally equivalent to the original, so we use such a reduced FSA as basis. We then need to specify a mapping from FSA to RSA. The components Q, Σ, δ, q_s and E can be adopted directly. We demand $\varphi(q_s)$ to be a known, fixed start position, and $\varphi(q_e) = \varphi(q_s) \forall q_e \in E$. Configurations $\varphi(q)$ for all other $q \in Q$ can be chosen freely (assuming they do not generate collisions with the environment and targets for recurrence transitions have different configurations). Transitions correspond to movements of the robot (possibly degenerate ones from and to the same position), which also need to be collision-free. With some convex region of free space including $\varphi(q_s)$, we can guarantee this e.g. by spacing evenly over that region all states with more than one incoming transition and one additional position for all other non-start and non-end states. This mapping leads to an RSA that satisfies the conditions: All linking targets can be distinguished from each other, and all configurations and movements are in the free space.

It remains to show that any legal RSA can be programmed. We can trivially generate branches and recurrence transitions, and a state that is visited for the first time is generated automatically. So to generate a given RSA, we can choose a sequence of runs of that RSA (each a sequence of states with legal transitions between them) with the conditions that each run must cover at least one state or transition not covered before, and over all runs we must cover all states and transitions in the (reduced) automaton. Since the number of states and transitions is finite, we can do this in a finite number of runs.

Together, this shows that arbitrary FSA can be both represented as RSA and, in the proposed approach, generated in terms of program structure.

4   Experimental Evaluation

The prototype setup used in the experiments consisted of a Kuka LWR IV, with a Robotiq three-finger gripper and an IDS uEye color camera as eye-in-hand, as depicted in Fig. 2. Command inputs were given via buttons on a keyboard. For the prototype, recording a stimulus consisted of taking the average color value over a central area of pixels in the camera image.

Experiments were structured as follows: First, an introductory briefing of approximately five minutes was held to detail the programming system. Then, participants were asked to program three small pick-and-place tasks with colored wooden cubes aimed to use the features of the approach, sketched in Fig. 3. In the first task, a branching state with two branches was programmed, testing the color of a block. Green and red blocks were placed in respective target areas. In the second task, a second layer of branches was programmed. Blocks were placed in their target area only if a mat of the same color was present. In the third task, recurrence transitions were used. Green or red blocks were picked up and placed on a blue block, when the latter was present. Blue blocks detected were placed as basis. The states after picking up red and green blocks were linked to program the rest of those branches only once. An automaton for the first task is depicted in Fig. 4, omitting most non-branching states.

 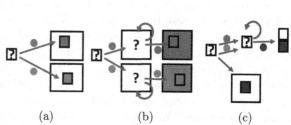

(a)   (b)   (c)

Fig. 2. The robot setup as used in the experiments.

Fig. 3. Task sketch used in the experiments for explanation. First a simple sorting task, using a branching state (a). The second requires a second layer of branching to check the presence of the correct mat (b). The third makes use of recurrence transitions, uniting the branches for green and red (c). (Color figure online)

These were conducted with five non-expert participants. Programming times are given in Fig. 5. Overall, the concept was deemed comprehensible by the participants and 12 out of 15 tasks were successfully programmed. The main problem in failed attempts was the camera implementation (small misplacements sometimes led to a wrong color value). The robot also deviated from its position in some configurations (due to imperfect calibration). Apart from these issues, which are orthogonal to the programming concept, participants were found to cope well with this concept of RSA programming, despite having no prior knowledge of finite state automata.

Of the twelve successful tasks, ten were programmed in less than five minutes. Recalling that the study involved non-expert users with a briefing of roughly five minutes, we feel this demonstrates that the approach can be adopted quickly and efficiently, despite not using a visual interface.

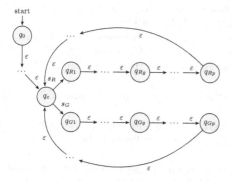

Parti-cipant	Task		
	1	2	3
1	131s	160s	
2	134s	290s	285s
3	106s	253s	413s
4	112s	234s	
5	127s		368s
average	122s	234s	355s

Fig. 4. Automaton for the first task. States go from q_0 to branching state q_c, to grasp states $q_{\alpha g}$ for picking up blocks ($\alpha \in \{R, G\}$), to placement states $q_{\alpha p}$, then return to q_c.

Fig. 5. Programming times. Missing values indicate failed tasks.

5   Conclusion

We have outlined an approach to intuitive programming via robot state automata and presented the results of experiments on the implemented prototype. The approach aims to enable non-expert users to easily generate sensor-based structures, without the feedback of a visual interface. The experiments confirm that this is indeed possible: Users completely new to robotics were able to program the example pick-and-place tasks quickly and with only a short introduction to the system. More complex tasks and programs are expressible in the system and its underlying formalism. Whether it is also practically feasible to program such tasks in this manner will require further study.

In future work, the automata model can be expanded, allowing for tasks other than pick-and-place with absolute positioning. Here, states correspond to robot configurations, but they could be generalized e.g. to positions relative to perceived objects. This could provide solutions for problems such as placing blocks next to each other, for an variable number of blocks. Different models for perceiving and recording stimuli could be tried and evaluated, especially such that extract more high-level information about the objects in view. Motion planners could be employed to cope with dynamically placed objects. Furthermore, on an interface level, the problems of dealing with errors in programming and of debugging robot programs should be considered. Finally, to compare directly to other approaches, user studies with a larger number of participants should be conducted, with the same tasks being programmed on different systems.

References

1. Akgun, B., et al.: Trajectories and keyframes for kinesthetic teaching. In: Proceedings of the Seventh Annual ACM/IEEE International Conference on Human-Robot Interaction, pp. 391–398. IEEE (2012)
2. Argall, B.D., et al.: A survey of robot learning from demonstration. Robot. Auton. Syst. 57(5), 469–483 (2009)
3. ArtiMinds Robotics GmbH: Artiminds Robot Programming Suite. https://www.artiminds.com/artiminds-rps/. Accessed 5 July 2019
4. Biggs, G., MacDonald, B.: A survey of robot programming systems. In: Proceedings of the Australasian Conference on Robotics and Automation (2003)
5. Billard, A., et al.: Survey: robot programming by demonstration. In: Handbook of Robotics, chap. 59 (2008)
6. Brooks, R.A.: A robust layered control system for a mobile robot. IEEE J. Robot. Autom. **RA–2**(1), 14–23 (1986)
7. Brunner, S.G., et al.: RAFCON: a graphical tool for engineering complex, robotic tasks. In: IEEE International Conference on Intelligent Robots and Systems, pp. 3283–3290 (2016)
8. Calinon, S., et al.: A task-parameterized probabilistic model with minimal intervention control. In: Proceedings - IEEE International Conference on Robotics and Automation, pp. 3339–3344 (2014)

9. Franka Emika GmbH: Franka Emika Panda Capabilites. https://www.franka.de/capability. Accessed 5 July 2019
10. Grollman, D.H., Jenkins, O.C.: Can we learn finite state machine robot controllers from interactive demonstration? Motor Learn. Interact. Learn. Robots **264**, 407–430 (2010)
11. König, L., Mostaghim, S., Schmeck, H.: Decentralized evolution of robotic behavior using finite state machines. Int. J. Intell. Comput. Cybern. **2**(4), 695–723 (2009)
12. Kormushev, P., et al.: Imitation learning of positional and force skills demonstrated via kinesthetic teaching and haptic input. Adv. Robot. **25**(5), 581–603 (2011)
13. Lozano-Perez, T.: Robot programming. Proc. IEEE **71**(7), 821–841 (1983)
14. Marino, A., et al.: Behavioral control for multi-robot perimeter patrol: a finite state automata approach. In: Proceedings - IEEE International Conference on Robotics and Automation, pp. 831–836 (2009)
15. Montebelli, A., et al.: On handing down our tools to robots: single-phase kinesthetic teaching for dynamic in-contact tasks. In: Proceedings - IEEE International Conference on Robotics and Automation, pp. 5628–5634. IEEE (2015)
16. Nguyen, H., et al.: ROS Commander (ROSCo): behavior creation for home robots. In: Proceedings - IEEE International Conference on Robotics and Automation, pp. 467–474 (2013)
17. Orendt, E.M., et al.: Robot programming by non-experts: intuitiveness and robustness of one-shot robot programming. In: IEEE International Symposium on Robot and Human Interactive Communication (2016)
18. Orendt, E.M., Henrich, D.: Control flow for robust one-shot robot programming using entity-based resources. In: 18th International Conference on Advanced Robotics, pp. 68–74 (2017)
19. Ott, C., et al.: A passivity based Cartesian impedance controller for flexible joint robots - part I: torque feedback and gravity compensation. In: Proceedings of the 2004 IEEE International Conference on Robotics and Automation, vol. 3, pp. 2666–2672 (2004)
20. Pan, Z., et al.: Recent progress on programming methods for industrial robots. Robot. Comput.-Integr. Manuf. **28**(2), 87–94 (2012)
21. Park, D.H., et al.: Movement reproduction and obstacle avoidance with dynamic movement primitives and potential fields. In: 8th IEEE-RAS International Conference on Humanoid Robots, pp. 91–98 (2008)
22. Rethink Robotics GmbH. Intera. https://www.rethinkrobotics.com/intera. Accessed 9 July 2019
23. Riano, L., McGinnity, T.M.: Automatically composing and parameterizing skills by evolving finite state automata. Robot. Auton. Syst. **60**(4), 639–650 (2012)
24. Riedl, M., Orendt, E.M., Henrich, D.: Sensor-based loops and branches for playback-programmed robot systems. In: Ferraresi, C., Quaglia, G. (eds.) RAAD 2017. MMS, vol. 49, pp. 183–190. Springer, Cham (2018). https://doi.org/10.1007/978-3-319-61276-8_21
25. Schraft, R.D., Meyer, C.: The need for an intuitive teaching method for small and medium enterprises. In: VDI Berichte 1956, p. 95 (2006)
26. Steinmetz, F., et al.: RAZER - a HRI for visual task-level programming and intuitive skill parameterization. IEEE Robot. Autom. Lett. **3**(3), 1362–1369 (2018)
27. TechMan Robot Inc.: Software Manual TMflow. https://assets.omron.eu/downloads/manual/en/v1/tm_flow_software_manual_installation_manual_en.pdf. Accessed 5 July 2019

28. Thomas, U., et al.: A new skill based robot programming language using UML/P statecharts. In: Proceedings - IEEE International Conference on Robotics and Automation, pp. 461–466. IEEE (2013)
29. Universal Robots A/S: Polyscope Manual. https://s3-eu-west-1.amazonaws.com/ur-support-site/53076/Software_Manual_en_Global.pdf. Accessed 9 July 2019

Improving Implicit Stance Classification in Tweets Using Word and Sentence Embeddings

Robin Schaefer[(✉)] and Manfred Stede

Applied Computational Linguistics, University of Potsdam, Potsdam, Germany
{robin.schaefer,stede}@uni-potsdam.de

Abstract. Argumentation Mining aims at finding components of arguments, as well as relations between them, in text. One of the largely unsolved problems is implicitness, where the text invites the reader to infer a missing component, such as the claim or a supporting statement. In the work of Wojatzki and Zesch (2016), an interesting implicitness problem is addressed on a Twitter data set. They showed that implicit stances toward a claim can be found with some success using just token and character n-grams. Using the same dataset, we show that results for this task can be improved using word and sentence embeddings, but that not all embedding variants perform alike. Specifically, we compare fastText, GloVe, and Universal Sentence Encoder (USE); and we find that, to our knowledge, USE yields state-of-the-art results for this task.

Keywords: Argumentation mining · Social media · Stance classification

1 Introduction

Argumentation mining can be defined as the task of automatically identifying argument components and their relations in text. While the majority of prior work has been focused on well-structured text genres, e.g. persuasive essays [19] or legal texts [14], a more recent branch of research has concentrated on argumentation mining in social media, like Twitter messages [9,12].

One mainly unsolved issue in argumentation mining is the implicitness of a core component of the argumentation. This is especially the case for social media where claims and their premises tend to be incomplete, which is also due to the often short nature of social media texts. In addition, messages are often conveyed using incorrect language leading to noisy textual data [18]. This leads to increased demands for the argument detection system.

Following [20] (henceforth WZ16), we approach the issue of implicit argument detection by reconsidering a part of argumentation mining as a stance classification problem. This is based on the assumption that a claim can be reformulated as a stance toward the topic at hand, which allows us to infer the

© Springer Nature Switzerland AG 2019
C. Benzmüller and H. Stuckenschmidt (Eds.): KI 2019, LNAI 11793, pp. 299–307, 2019.
https://doi.org/10.1007/978-3-030-30179-8_26

implicit claim from the data. For instance, in example (1) a tweet on atheism is given containing an explicit premise toward the claim (2) to be inferred. (3) shows the claim reformulated as an implicit stance, which could be the output of a stance classifier taking (1) as input.

(1) Bible: that infidels are going to hell! (explicit premise) [WZ16]
(2) *Therefore, atheism is to be rejected. (implicit claim)*
(3) *I am against atheism. (implicit claim reformulated as implicit stance)* [WZ16]

In this paper, we will replicate the classification results of WZ16 with our own implementation. Afterward, we will show that different variants of word and sentence embeddings considerably surpass the n-gram-based results reported in WZ16.[1]

We structure this paper as follows: Sect. 2 gives an overview of the related research including WZ16, which is the basis for our work. Section 3 describes the data set. Section 4 describes the applied method including the embedding variants that we used. Section 5 presents the results before we conclude in Sect. 6 with a discussion and a short outlook.

2   Related Work

[4] present a preliminary pipeline for argumentation mining in Twitter data. This pipeline consists of different sub-steps like separating argumentative from non-argumentative parts and defining argumentative relations between tweet pairs. Their work is based on DART [3], a Twitter data set containing tweets annotated for their argumentative relations. While this work presents an interesting approach to argumentation mining in tweets, it is ignoring implicit components of argumentation which renders it less relevant for our work.

[2] use features based on textual entailment (following [5]) and semantic textual similarity in order to automatically detect arguments in online debates. This task is motivated by the assumption that argument detection improves the classification of stances toward the debate topic. Like WZ16, the authors recognize implicitness as a central issue of argumentation mining. However, unlike WZ16, [2] approach this issue using features that are somewhat more semantic in nature than n-grams. We follow this idea by using pre-trained word embeddings.

WZ16 propose to reformulate an implicit claim as a stance toward the given topic, thereby modeling argumentation mining as a stance classification problem. As the actual implicit claim is hard to extract, classifying a newly formulated implicit stance can help approximating it. In addition, WZ16 created the Atheism Stance Corpus (ASC), which is based on the Twitter data set provided for the first shared task on automatic stance detection (Task 6, SemEval 2016) [15]. They annotated the tweets according to their stances toward a predefined set

---

[1] The code can be downloaded from https://github.com/RobinSchaefer/tweet-stance-classification.

of topics (see Table 1), one of which is the implicit stance to the overall topic *atheism*. They further implemented a linear Support Vector Machine (SVM) and used different sizes of token and character n-grams as features. This model achieved an F1 score of 0.66. In order to investigate the full potential of implicit stance classification using explicit stances toward subtopics, WZ16 create an oracle condition utilizing the manually annotated explicit stances as features. With respect to (1), this could mean a positive stance toward the topic *Christianity*. This model achieved an F1 score of 0.88. In this work, we will compare our results both to the results elicited by the n-gram model and to the more 'artificial' oracle results.

3 Data

In this work, we use the ASC from WZ16, which contains 715 tweets from the *atheism* sub-part of the SemEval data set. It has been annotated for *the implicit stance toward the debate topic*, i.e. the tweet being pro/contra atheism, and for *the explicit stances toward a set of derived topics*. These topics include the subtopics *Christianity* and *supernatural power*. A full list including their annotations in percentages is given in Table 1.

Table 1. The topics and their annotations in percentages

Topic	Pro	Contra	None
Atheism (debate stance)	**20**	**49**	**31**
Christianity	27	04	69
Conservatism	01	01	98
Freethinking	04	–	96
Islam	04	02	94
Life after death	01	01	98
No evidence	01	–	99
Religious freedom	01	–	99
Same-sex marriage	02	–	98
Secularism	03	–	97
Supernatural power	39	08	53
USA	04	–	96

4 Method

In this work we investigate the applicability of different feature types to solve the task of implicit stance classification. Specifically, we make use of n-grams and different variants of word and sentence embeddings (fastText, GloVe and USE).

To begin with, we present our implementation of the processing pipeline reported in WZ16 using the scikit-learn library [16][2] in Python. For preprocessing we apply the Tweet NLP tokenizer [10]. We further implement certain text cleaning and normalization steps: tokens are turned to lowercase; stopwords and punctuation[3] are removed; the Snowball Stemmer[4] is applied. We report results for different processing pipelines which will give insights regarding the most promising ways to approach this task.

We classify our data using a linear SVM with the C hyperparameter set to 1. We further apply 10-fold cross-validation and report F1 scores for all models.

4.1   N-Grams

Following WZ16, we derive n-grams from the data, which we treat as a baseline for the word and sentence embedding models. We use a binary bag-of-n-gram representation (existent/nonexistent). Apart from stopword and punctuation removal, we do no restrict our set of tokens. This contrasts with WZ16 who only use the 1000 most frequent tokens. However, this leads to an arbitrary set of tokens due to the majority of tokens occurring only once. We further experiment with different token n-gram sizes and their combinations.

4.2   fastText Embeddings

We use pre-trained 300-dimensional fastText [11] word vectors that have been trained on Wikipedia and Common Crawl data. For training, an extension of the CBOW model has been used. Thus, a word vector is created based on a prediction of the respective word given the context it appears in. In addition, the model makes use of subword information, i.e. each word vector is the result of the summation of the underlying subword vectors. Also, position weights are incorporated in order to weigh the impact of the context words.

In order to obtain a vector for a whole tweet we create document vectors by averaging the respective word vectors for the words used in the tweet. If a word is not included in the set of word vectors it is discarded.

4.3   GloVe Embeddings

In addition, we apply pre-trained 200-dimensional GloVe [17] word vectors. These vectors have been trained on tweets which may have a positive impact on the results. However, in order to directly compare results based on differences in

---

[2] Note that WZ16 apply the DKPro Core [6] and DKPro TC frameworks [8].

[3] Note that during punctuation removal #'s are ignored in order to maintain hashtags, which we assume to be meaningful for our task.

[4] The Snowball Stemmer is implemented using NLTK [13].

algorithms and not on differences in dimensions we also apply pre-trained 300-dimensional GloVe word vectors trained on Common Crawl.

In contrast to fastText, GloVe incorporates global statistics using matrix factorization. Also, the model has been trained on words instead of subwords, meaning that it has issues processing unseen words.

To receive the final tweet vectors we follow the same steps as for the fastText vectors.

4.4   USE Embeddings

Finally, we apply the pre-trained language-agnostic USE model based on English as the source language and German as the target language [7]. The model has been trained via a dual-encoder architecture that consisted of different monolingual and cross-lingual tasks. The central difference to our other embedding variants lies in the direct training on sentence data.

Table 2. F1 scores per feature set and preprocessing steps (l = lowercase, s = stopwords, p = punctuation, st = stemmer)

Feature set	Preprocessing	F1 (micro)	F1 (macro)
WZ16 baseline	Not available	0.66	Not available
WZ16 oracle condition	Not available	**0.88**	Not available
Unigrams	-	0.67	0.62
	l	**0.70**	0.65
	l, s, p	0.68	0.63
	l, s, p, st	0.68	0.64
	st	0.69	0.65
	l, st	0.69	0.65
Bigrams	l	0.59	0.51
Trigrams	l	0.49	0.25
Uni- and bigrams	l	0.69	0.63
Bi- and trigrams	l	0.58	0.48
Uni-, bi- and trigrams	l	0.68	0.61
fastText embeddings (300d)	-	0.71	0.67
	p	0.73	0.69
GloVe embeddings (200d)	-	0.60	0.55
	p	0.60	0.55
GloVe embeddings (300d)	-	0.61	0.56
	p	0.59	0.54
USE embeddings (512d)	-	0.77	0.73
	p	**0.78**	0.75

We implement the USE using its TensorFlow [1] module. Text data simply gets loaded into the module and it outputs an embedding with 512 dimensions.[5] As the encoder also can handle texts longer than single sentences it can be fruitfully utilized for our task.

5   Results

Results, i.e. micro and macro averaged F1 scores, are reported in Table 2. Consistent with WZ16, we only discuss micro averaged F1 scores. With our n-gram model we achieve an F1 score of 0.70, thereby beating the baseline of 0.66 that has been reported in WZ16. Our simplest model only including unigrams yields the best results. Furthermore, the choice of preprocessing steps has a large effect on the performance. While lower casing improves the results substantially, additionally removing stopwords and punctuation in fact decreases the evaluation scores. Stemming can have a positive effect if used without token removal but does not achieve best results.

Using more complex n-grams like bigrams, trigrams or their concatenated combinations does not outperform the simple unigram model. In fact, applying bigrams and trigrams considerably decreases F1 scores to 0.59 and 0.49, respectively. Only the combinations of uni- and bigrams and of uni-, bi- and trigrams yield results comparable to the unigram model, albeit with higher computational costs.

The word and sentence embeddings yield mixed results. While the highest F1 score of the fastText embeddings (0.73) is above the n-gram results, GloVe embeddings reach only low scores. Importantly, both 200- and 300-dimensional GloVe vectors yield similar results. The highest result of 0.78, however, is achieved using USE embeddings. For preprocessing no cleaning or normalization step is applied apart from punctuation removal.

6   Discussion and Outlook

The benefit of our work is twofold. First, we replicate the results of WZ16 by implementing our own processing pipeline using the Python language. The replication includes different preprocessing steps, n-gram feature extraction and supervised classification using an SVM. By applying basic preprocessing (lower casing) and using simple unigrams we are able to enhance the original results.

Second, we make use of different pre-trained word and sentence embeddings to enhance the performance even further. Importantly, the different embedding variants do not yield similar results. While fastText embeddings achieve comparable but slightly better results than the n-gram model, our GloVe vectors cannot compete. This is surprising as the 200-dimensional GloVe vectors have

---

[5] As the USE model has been trained exclusively for 512-dimensional vectors [7], we are unable to create 300-dimensional vectors that would have been more directly comparable to the fastText and GloVe vectors.

been pre-trained on Twitter data. The best results are achieved via the language-agnostic USE. With an F1 score of 0.78 we improve the original results of WZ16 by more than 0.1. Hence, by using sentence embeddings instead of n-grams we take a large step toward the potential result given by WZ16's oracle condition. Recall that this is based on manual explicit stance annotations and yields an F1 score of 0.88.

The question remains why different embedding variants lead to substantially different results. One potential cause of performance differences could lie in the diverging complexities of the vectors. While our 512-dimensional USE vectors yield best results, F1 scores seem to decrease with a reduction of vector dimensions. Lowest scores were achieved with the 200-dimensional GloVe vectors. This is not surprising if we assume that more complex embeddings can capture semantic content to a more fine-grained degree. Recall, however, that the usage of 300-dimensional GloVe vectors does lead to similar results as the 200-dimensional GloVe vectors, thus providing evidence that vector dimensions alone are unlikely to explain the result pattern that we report.

Another reason for the better results of USE embeddings could be the fact that they have been trained on sentences instead of words. This could lead to a better encoding of syntactic information. In contrast, one possible constraint of word embeddings is that only word information, or subword information, is encoded. One may also conclude that the averaging of word vectors in order to create a document vector cannot compete with direct training on segments of text that are larger than words.

Finally, we want to point out that we can only make limited assumptions regarding the generalization of our model. This is due to the focus of the corpus on one topic. While the large improvement of results driven by USE vectors may give confidence that they can be applied for other corpora as well, further research is needed to prove this assumption.

To conclude, while the results of our USE embeddings are promising, clearly more work is needed on the causes of performance differences. Our next step will be to move to German as our language of interest. Having used language-agnostic USE embeddings and fastText embeddings that have been trained in parallel with a huge amount of other languages enables us to directly compare both NLP pipelines and their performances.

Acknowledgements. We would like to thank Michael Wojatzki for sharing further details about their implementation with us. We would further like to thank the anonymous reviewers for their helpful comments.

References

1. Abadi, M., et al.: TensorFlow: large-scale machine learning on heterogeneous systems (2015). http://tensorflow.org/
2. Boltužić, F., Šnajder, J.: Back up your stance: recognizing arguments in online discussions. In: Proceedings of the First Workshop on Argumentation Mining, Baltimore, Maryland, pp. 49–58. Association for Computational Linguistics, June 2014. https://doi.org/10.3115/v1/W14-2107

3. Bosc, T., Cabrio, E., Villata, S.: DART: a dataset of arguments and their relations on twitter. In: Proceedings of the Tenth International Conference on Language Resources and Evaluation (LREC 2016), Portorož, Slovenia, pp. 1258–1263. European Language Resources Association (ELRA), May 2016

4. Bosc, T., Cabrio, E., Villata, S.: Tweeties squabbling: positive and negative results in applying argument mining on social media. In: Proceedings of the 6th International Conference on Computational Models of Argument, Potsdam, Germany, September 2016

5. Cabrio, E., Villata, S.: Combining textual entailment and argumentation theory for supporting online debates interactions. In: Proceedings of the 50th Annual Meeting of the Association for Computational Linguistics (Volume 2: Short Papers), Jeju Island, Korea, pp. 208–212. Association for Computational Linguistics, July 2012

6. de Castilho, R.E., Gurevych, I.: A broad-coverage collection of portable NLP components for building shareable analysis pipelines. In: Proceedings of the Workshop on Open Infrastructures and Analysis Frameworks for HLT, Dublin, Ireland, pp. 1–11. Association for Computational Linguistics and Dublin City University, August 2014. https://doi.org/10.3115/v1/W14-5201

7. Chidambaram, M., et al.: Learning cross-lingual sentence representations via a multi-task dual-encoder model. CoRR abs/1810.12836 (2018)

8. Daxenberger, J., Ferschke, O., Gurevych, I., Zesch, T.: DKPro TC: a Java-based framework for supervised learning experiments on textual data. In: Proceedings of 52nd Annual Meeting of the Association for Computational Linguistics: System Demonstrations, Baltimore, Maryland, pp. 61–66. Association for Computational Linguistics, June 2014. https://doi.org/10.3115/v1/P14-5011

9. Dusmanu, M., Cabrio, E., Villata, S.: Argument mining on Twitter: arguments, facts and sources. In: Proceedings of the 2017 Conference on Empirical Methods in Natural Language Processing, Copenhagen, Denmark, pp. 2317–2322. Association for Computational Linguistics, September 2017. https://doi.org/10.18653/v1/D17-1245

10. Gimpel, K., et al.: Part-of-speech tagging for Twitter: annotation, features, and experiments. In: Proceedings of the 49th Annual Meeting of the Association for Computational Linguistics: Human Language Technologies, Portland, Oregon, USA, pp. 42–47. Association for Computational Linguistics, June 2011

11. Grave, E., Bojanowski, P., Gupta, P., Joulin, A., Mikolov, T.: Learning word vectors for 157 languages. In: Proceedings of the International Conference on Language Resources and Evaluation (LREC 2018) (2018)

12. Grosse, K., González, M.P., Chesñevar, C.I., Maguitman, A.G.: Integrating argumentation and sentiment analysis for mining opinions from twitter. AI Commun. 28(3), 387–401 (2015)

13. Loper, E., Bird, S.: NLTK: the natural language toolkit. In: Proceedings of the ACL 2002 Workshop on Effective Tools and Methodologies for Teaching Natural Language Processing and Computational Linguistics, ETMTNLP 2002, Stroudsburg, PA, USA, vol. 1, pp. 63–70. Association for Computational Linguistics (2002). https://doi.org/10.3115/1118108.1118117

14. Moens, M.F., Boiy, E., Palau, R.M., Reed, C.: Automatic detection of arguments in legal texts. In: Proceedings of the 11th International Conference on Artificial Intelligence and Law, ICAIL 2007, pp. 225–230. ACM, New York (2007). https://doi.org/10.1145/1276318.1276362

15. Mohammad, S., Kiritchenko, S., Sobhani, P., Zhu, X., Cherry, C.: SemEval-2016 task 6: detecting stance in tweets. In: Proceedings of the 10th International Workshop on Semantic Evaluation (SemEval-2016), San Diego, California, pp. 31–41. Association for Computational Linguistics, June 2016. https://doi.org/10.18653/v1/S16-1003
16. Pedregosa, F., et al.: Scikit-learn: machine learning in Python. J. Mach. Learn. Res. **12**, 2825–2830 (2011)
17. Pennington, J., Socher, R., Manning, C.D.: GloVe: global vectors for word representation. In: Empirical Methods in Natural Language Processing (EMNLP), pp. 1532–1543 (2014)
18. Snajder, J.: Social media argumentation mining: the quest for deliberateness in raucousness. CoRR abs/1701.00168 (2017)
19. Stab, C., Gurevych, I.: Identifying argumentative discourse structures in persuasive essays. In: Proceedings of the 2014 Conference on Empirical Methods in Natural Language Processing (EMNLP), Doha, Qatar, pp. 46–56. Association for Computational Linguistics, October 2014. https://doi.org/10.3115/v1/D14-1006
20. Wojatzki, M., Zesch, T.: Stance-based argument mining - modeling implicit argumentation using stance. In: Proceedings of the KONVENS, pp. 313–322 (2016)

Towards Leveraging Backdoors
in Qualitative Constraint Networks

Michael Sioutis[1]([✉]) [iD] and Tomi Janhunen[1,2] [iD]

[1] Department of Computer Science, Aalto University, Espoo, Finland
{michael.sioutis,tomi.janhunen}@aalto.fi
[2] Tampere University, Tampere, Finland

Abstract. In this short paper we introduce the notions of backbones and backdoors in the context of qualitative constraint networks. As motivation for the study of those structures, we argue that they can be used to define collaborative approaches among SAT, CP, and native tools, inspire novel decomposition and parallelization techniques, and lead to the development of adaptive constraint propagators with a better insight into the particularities of real-world datasets than what is possible today.

Keywords: Qualitative constraints · Spatio-temporal reasoning ·
Local consistencies · Backdoors · Backbones

1 Introduction

Qualitative Spatial and Temporal Reasoning (QSTR) is a Symbolic AI approach that deals with the fundamental cognitive concepts of space and time in a qualitative, human-like, manner [7,12]. For instance, in natural language one uses expressions such as *inside*, *before*, and *north of* to spatially or temporally relate one object with another object or oneself, without resorting to providing quantitative information about these entities. QSTR provides a concise framework that allows for rather inexpensive reasoning about entities located in space or time and, hence, further boosts research and applications to a plethora of areas such as dynamic GIS [4], cognitive robotics [8], and deep learning [1,11]. Qualitative spatial or temporal information can be typically captured by a *qualitative constraint network* (QCN), i.e., a network of constraints corresponding to qualitative spatial or temporal relations between the respective kinds of variables.

Here, we introduce the notions of *backbones* and *backdoors* [21] in the context of QSTR, in order to facilitate the integration of QCNs into more generic paradigms such as SAT and CP on the one hand, but also motivate the further study of QCNs themselves in an effort to obtain a better understanding of their computational characteristics on the other hand. In short, a backbone in a given QCN represents the part of it that can only map to a single qualitative configuration (e.g., the relationship between two regions can only be such that one is contained inside the other), and a backdoor in a given QCN represents its

C. Benzmüller and H. Stuckenschmidt (Eds.): KI 2019, LNAI 11793, pp. 308–315, 2019.
https://doi.org/10.1007/978-3-030-30179-8_27

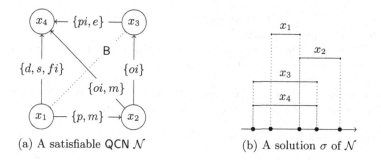

(a) A satisfiable QCN $\mathcal{N}$ (b) A solution σ of $\mathcal{N}$

Fig. 1. Figurative examples of QCN terminology using Interval Algebra; symbols p, e, m, o, d, s, and f correspond to the atoms *precedes*, *equals*, *meets*, *overlaps*, *during*, *starts*, and *finishes* respectively, with $\cdot i$ denoting the converse of $\cdot$ (note that $ei = e$)

intractable part for some local consistency (i.e., utilizing that consistency alone does not allow one to decide the satisfiability of the QCN). We argue that these notions can drive both theoretical and practical future research (see Sect. 4).

2 Preliminaries

A binary qualitative constraint language is based on a finite set B of *jointly exhaustive and pairwise disjoint* relations, called the set of *base relations* [13], that is defined over an infinite domain D. These base relations represent definite knowledge between two entities with respect to the level of granularity provided by the domain D; indefinite knowledge can be specified by a union of possible base relations, and is represented by the set containing them. The set B contains the identity relation Id, and is closed under the *converse* operation ($^{-1}$). The total set of relations 2^B is equipped with the usual set-theoretic operations of union and intersection, the converse operation, and the *weak composition* operation denoted by $\diamond$ [13]. For all $r \in 2^B$, $r^{-1} = \bigcup \{b^{-1} \mid b \in r\}$. The weak composition ($\diamond$) of two base relations $b, b' \in$ B is defined as the smallest (i.e., strongest) relation $r \in 2^B$ that includes $b \circ b'$, or, formally, $b \diamond b' = \{b'' \in B \mid b'' \cap (b \circ b') \neq \emptyset\}$, where $b \circ b' = \{(x, y) \in D \times D \mid \exists z \in D \text{ such that } (x, z) \in b \wedge (z, y) \in b'\}$ is the (true) composition of b and b'. For all $r, r' \in 2^B$, $r \diamond r' = \bigcup \{b \diamond b' \mid b \in r, b' \in r'\}$.

As an illustration, consider the well-known qualitative temporal constraint language of Interval Algebra (IA), introduced by Allen in [2]. IA considers time intervals (as temporal entities) and the set of base relations B = $\{e, p, pi, m, mi, o, oi, s, si, d, di, f, fi\}$ to encode knowledge about the temporal relations between intervals on the timeline; the symbols are explained in the caption of Fig. 1. Specifically, each base relation represents a particular ordering of the four endpoints of two intervals on the timeline, and e is the identity relation Id. The problem of representing and reasoning about qualitative information can be modeled as a *qualitative constraint network*, defined in the following manner:

Definition 1. *A qualitative constraint network (QCN) is a tuple (V, C) where:*

- $V = \{v_1, \ldots, v_n\}$ is a non-empty finite set of variables, each representing an entity of an infinite domain D;
- and C is a mapping $C : V \times V \to 2^B$ such that $C(v,v) = \{Id\}$ for all $v \in V$ and $C(v,v') = (C(v',v))^{-1}$ for all $v,v' \in V$.

An example of a QCN of IA is shown in Fig. 1a; for clarity, converse relations as well as Id loops are not mentioned or shown in the figure.

Definition 2. Let $\mathcal{N} = (V,C)$ be a QCN, then:

- a solution of $\mathcal{N}$ is a mapping $\sigma : V \to D$ such that, $\forall(u,v) \in V \times V$, $\exists b \in C(u,v)$ such that $(\sigma(u), \sigma(v)) \in b$ (see Fig. 1b);
- the constraint graph of $\mathcal{N}$ is the graph (V,E) with $\{u,v\} \in E$ iff $C(u,v) \neq B$;
- given a subset $S \subseteq V \times V$, a refinement $\mathcal{N}_S$ of $\mathcal{N}$ with respect to S is a QCN (V,C') such that $\forall(u,v) \in S$ we have $C'(u,v) \subseteq C(u,v)$; if in addition $|C'(u,v)| = 1$ $\forall(u,v) \in S$, then the refinement $\mathcal{N}_S$ is called atomic.

Let us further introduce the following operation that substitutes $C(v,v')$ with $r \in 2^B$ in a given QCN: given a QCN $\mathcal{N} = (V,C)$ and $v,v' \in V$, we have that $\mathcal{N}_{[v,v']/r}$ with $r \in 2^B$ yields the QCN $\mathcal{N}' = (V,C')$ defined by $C'(v,v') = r$, $C'(v',v) = r^{-1}$ and $\forall(u,u') \in (V \times V) \setminus \{(v,v'),(v',v)\}$, $C'(u,u') = C(u,u')$.

3   Backbones and Backdoors in QCNs

In this section we introduce the notions of backbones and backdoors in QCNs. In essence, these notions mirror the respective ones defined in [21] for classical (finite-domain) constraint programming; however, in our context the definitions that we provide are quite different from a technical point of view, in that they involve the constraints of QCNs rather than their variables, and the backdoors particularly are tied to local consistencies instead of *sub-solvers* (cf. [21]).

Given a QCN, a set of constraints (which we simply represent by the set of pairs of variables they constrain) is called a backbone in that QCN, if there is a unique atomic refinement with respect to the constrained pairs of variables such that the QCN is satisfiable. Formally, a backbone is defined as follows:

Definition 3. Given a QCN $\mathcal{N} = (V,C)$, a subset $S \subseteq V \times V$ is a backbone in $\mathcal{N}$ iff there exists a unique atomic refinement $\mathcal{N}_S$ of $\mathcal{N}$ such that $\mathcal{N}_S$ is satisfiable.

Clearly, if a QCN $\mathcal{N} = (V,C)$ has only one solution, then the entire set $V \times V$ is a backbone in and of itself. In addition, every QCN has a unique largest backbone (if any at all). A backbone should be contrasted with a set of *frozen constraints*, in the sense defined in [6]; in particular, a frozen constraint is a kind of a hard constraint that pertains to the background knowledge of a given problem. For example, a program may need to be compiled before its execution, which would pose a frozen, fixed, constraint that would not be subject to revision.

Next, we introduce the notion of backdoors. As opposed to backbones, backdoors are defined with respect to some (local) consistency; when a backdoor set of constraints in a given QCN is properly instantiated, the consistency can be utilized to decide the satisfiability of that QCN. We view a consistency $\stackrel{\phi}{G}$, where ϕ is some operation (such as the *weak composition* operation) and G a graph, as a predicate on QCNs, i.e., a function that receives an input QCN and returns true or false depending on whether $\stackrel{\phi}{G}$ holds on that QCN or not respectively. Given a consistency $\stackrel{\phi}{G}$, a subset $\mathcal{R} \subseteq 2^{\mathsf{B}}$ is said to be *tractable* for $\stackrel{\phi}{G}$ if $\stackrel{\phi}{G}$ is complete for deciding the satisfiability of any QCN defined over $\mathcal{R}$ with respect to some graph G. We require that a consistency is *well-behaving* (cf. [5]), as the notion of a backdoor would be overly complicated to define (and utilize) otherwise.

Definition 4. *A consistency $\stackrel{\phi}{G}$ is* well-behaving *iff for any QCN $\mathcal{N} = (V, C)$ and any graph $G = (V, E)$ the following properties hold:*

- *there exists a unique $\subseteq$-maximal $\stackrel{\phi}{G}$-consistent sub-QCN of $\mathcal{N}$, denoted by $\stackrel{\phi}{G}(\mathcal{N})$ and referred to as the $\stackrel{\phi}{G}$-closure of $\mathcal{N}$ with respect to G (Dominance);*
- *$\stackrel{\phi}{G}(\mathcal{N})$ is equivalent to $\mathcal{N}$ (Equivalence).*

Now we are ready to formally define a backdoor, and a stronger variant of it called a *strong* backdoor as well.

Definition 5. *Given a QCN $\mathcal{N} = (V, C)$, a subset $S \subseteq V \times V$ is a backdoor (resp. strong backdoor) in $\mathcal{N}$ for a well-behaving consistency $\stackrel{\phi}{G}$ iff for some (resp. every) atomic refinement $\mathcal{N}_S$ of $\mathcal{N}$ we have that $\stackrel{\phi}{G}(\mathcal{N}_S)$ is defined over a tractable subset of relations $\mathcal{R} \subseteq 2^{\mathsf{B}}$ for $\stackrel{\phi}{G}$.*

Additionally, we can identify the notion of a minimal (strong) backdoor, defined as follows:

Definition 6. *Given a QCN $\mathcal{N} = (V, C)$, a backdoor (resp. strong backdoor) S in $\mathcal{N}$ for a well-behaving consistency $\stackrel{\phi}{G}$ is* minimal *iff there exists no backdoor (resp. strong backdoor) S' in $\mathcal{N}$ for $\stackrel{\phi}{G}$ such that $S' \subset S$.*

Fundamentally, a backdoor in a given instance for some consistency constitutes the *hard* part of that instance with respect to that consistency, in the sense that, once that part is dealt with, simply enforcing the consistency in the instance allows deciding its satisfiability.

Example. We present here a detailed example that illustrates the aforementioned notions of backbones and backdoors.

First, we recall the definition of $\stackrel{\diamond}{G}$-consistency, which is a fundamental and widely used well-behaving local consistency for reasoning with QCNs (cf. [17]) that entails consistency for all triples of variables in a given QCN $\mathcal{N}$ that correspond to three-vertex cycles (triangles) in an accompanying graph G.

Definition 7. *Given a QCN $\mathcal{N} = (V, C)$ and a graph $G = (V, E)$, $\mathcal{N}$ is said to be $\stackrel{\diamond}{G}$-consistent iff $\forall \{v_i, v_j\}, \{v_i, v_k\}, \{v_k, v_j\} \in E$ we have that $C(v_i, v_j) \subseteq C(v_i, v_k) \diamond C(v_k, v_j)$.*

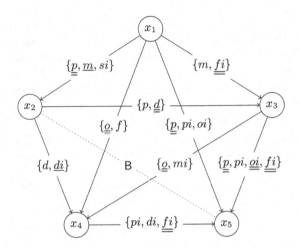

Fig. 2. A QCN $\mathcal{N}$ of Interval Algebra where the underlined base relations are not present in $^{\diamond}_G(\mathcal{N})$, and the double-underlined base relations are additionally not present in $^{\bullet U}_G(\mathcal{N})$; G is the constraint graph of $\mathcal{N}$, i.e., the graph that results by removing edge $\{x_2, x_5\}$ from the complete graph on $\{x_1, x_2, x_3, x_4, x_5\}$, and is chordal

If G is the complete graph on the variables of a given QCN, then $^{\diamond}_G$-consistency becomes identical to $\diamond$-consistency [17], and, hence, $\diamond$-consistency can be seen as a special case of $^{\diamond}_G$-consistency.

Next, we recall the definition of $^{\bullet U}_G$-consistency, which is a well-behaving local consistency that is strictly stronger than any of the known practical consistencies and is based on the idea of partitioning a constraint into *singleton relations* [20].

Definition 8. *Given a* QCN *$\mathcal{N} = (V, C)$ and a graph $G = (V, E)$, $\mathcal{N}$ is said to be $^{\bullet U}_G$-consistent iff $\forall \{v, v'\} \in E$, $\forall b \in C(v, v')$, and $\forall \{u, u'\} \in E$ we have that $\exists b' \in C(u, u')$ such that $b \in C'(v, v')$, where $(V, C') = ^{\diamond}_G(\mathcal{N}_{[u,u']/\{b'\}})$.*

Given either of the above consistencies, the subset $\mathcal{H}_{IA}$ of the relations of Interval Algebra is tractable for those consistencies; that subset contains exactly those relations that are transformed to propositional Horn formulas when using the propositional encoding of Interval Algebra [16]. Further, that tractability property is maintained with respect to any chordal supergraph of the constraint graph of a given QCN [3].

We proceed with the description of our detailed example. Consider the QCN $\mathcal{N}$ of Interval Algebra shown in Fig. 2, along with its accompanying graph G described in the caption. Initially, it can be verified that every constraint that corresponds to some edge in G is defined by a relation that does not belong to the tractable subset of relations $\mathcal{H}_{IA}$ of Interval Algebra; there are 9 such constraints. After the application of $^{\diamond}_G$-consistency on $\mathcal{N}$, the relations corresponding to constraints $C(x_1, x_2)$ and $C(x_2, x_4)$ are refined to $\{p, si\}$ and $\{d\}$ respectively, with the latter now belonging to $\mathcal{H}_{IA}$. At this point we can recognize the set $\{(x_1, x_2), (x_1, x_3), (x_1, x_4), (x_1, x_5), (x_2, x_3), (x_3, x_4), (x_3, x_5), (x_4, x_5)\}$ as a strong backdoor in $\mathcal{N}$ for $\overset{\diamond}{_G}$-consistency, since any atomic refinement of the corresponding relations will result in $\overset{\diamond}{_G}(\mathcal{N})$ being defined over $\mathcal{H}_{\mathsf{IA}}$. Upon closer inspection we can identify the set $\{(x_1, x_2), (x_4, x_5)\}$ as a minimal strong backdoor in $\mathcal{N}$ for $\overset{\diamond}{_G}$-consistency; indeed, any atomic refinement of the corresponding relations will result in $\overset{\diamond}{_G}(\mathcal{N})$ being defined over $\mathcal{H}_{\mathsf{IA}}$. The singleton $\{(x_4, x_5)\}$ is a backdoor, since there exists an atomic refinement such that $\overset{\diamond}{_G}$-consistency can be used to detect the unsatisfiability of the refined QCN, namely, that of $C(x_4, x_5)$ to $\{fi\}$. After the application of $\overset{\bullet^{\cup}}{_G}$-consistency on $\mathcal{N}$, the relations corresponding to constraints $C(x_1, x_2)$, $C(x_1, x_3)$, $C(x_1, x_4)$, $C(x_1, x_5)$, $C(x_2, x_3)$, $C(x_3, x_4)$, $C(x_3, x_5)$, and $C(x_4, x_5)$ are refined to $\{si\}$, $\{m\}$, $\{f\}$, $\{pi, oi\}$, $\{p\}$, $\{mi\}$, $\{pi\}$, and $\{pi, di\}$, respectively, with all relations except the one corresponding to constraint $C(x_4, x_5)$ now belonging to $\mathcal{H}_{\mathsf{IA}}$. In fact, at this point we can recognize the set $\{(x_1, x_2), (x_1, x_3), (x_1, x_4), (x_2, x_3), (x_2, x_4), (x_3, x_4), (x_3, x_5)\}$ as a backbone in $\mathcal{N}$. Regarding strong backdoors in $\mathcal{N}$ for $\overset{\bullet^{\cup}}{_G}$-consistency, the only choice is the singleton $\{(x_4, x_5)\}$, which is minimal.

In the aforementioned example the use of $\overset{\bullet^{\cup}}{_G}$-consistency made identifying the largest backbone and a minimal strong backdoor in $\mathcal{N}$ for $\overset{\bullet^{\cup}}{_G}$-consistency effortless; however, it is not expected that this will generally be the case.

4   Discussion

In this section we discuss some of the ways in which the notions of backbones and backdoors can be exploited and gain impact in the field of QSTR.

Satisfiability Modulo Theories (SMT). Over the past years SAT encodings of QCNs have been proposed that are very successful in tackling the hardest of instances, see for example the work in [10]. However, a disadvantage of such encondings is that they generally do not scale well compared to native QSTR tools because they are proportional (to some extent) to the number of variable triples in a given QCN, see for instance the experimental analysis in [10, Section 6.4] and [9, Section 5]. The identification of a backdoor in a given QCN for some consistency and parts of a potential backbone, could inspire SMT approaches where the partial backbone along with the rest of the tractable part of the QCN would be dealt with by use of a native QSTR tool, and the hard part, the backdoor, would be treated by an off-the-shelf SAT solver. Further, such combination of theories could occur lazily by allowing each of the involved decision procedures to act as a referee upon the other one at each step of the reasoning process.

Decomposition and Parallelization Techniques. A potential backbone in a QCN can allow for partitioning its constraint graph into simpler to solve instances, perhaps even independently of one another, in parallel; for example, we can imagine the case where a QCN can be viewed as two overlapping instances whose common constraints form a local backbone. In the same vein, exposing a (strong) backdoor in a given QCN with respect to some local consistency, allows for defining search space splitting approaches, i.e., approaches based on dividing the search space of the QCN into disjoint subspaces to be explored in parallel [15].

Adaptive Constraint Propagators. *Real-world spatio-temporal datasets* that have been studied in the literature tend to be different from synthetic ones, in that they are usually large-scale and composed of a substantial tractable part for even the weakest of local consistencies [14,18,19]; thus, it would be perfectly appropriate to coin the phrase "one consistency does not fit all". The use of backbones and backdoors could help us to understand and quantify in a better manner the (hidden) structural differences between real-world and synthetic datasets, and lead to the definition and implementation of generic algorithms that would adapt themselves to the diverse computational characteristics of the given instance. Furthermore, such notions could be used for establishing heuristics that would guide search in backtracking algorithms more fruitfully.

References

1. Alirezaie, M., Längkvist, M., Sioutis, M., Loutfi, A.: Semantic referee: a neural-symbolic framework for enhancing geospatial semantic segmentation. Semant. Web (2019, in press)
2. Allen, J.F.: Maintaining knowledge about temporal intervals. Commun. ACM **26**, 832–843 (1983)
3. Amaneddine, N., Condotta, J.F., Sioutis, M.: Efficient approach to solve the minimal labeling problem of temporal and spatial qualitative constraints. In: IJCAI (2013)
4. Bhatt, M., Wallgrün, J.O.: Geospatial narratives and their spatio-temporal dynamics: commonsense reasoning for high-level analyses in geographic information systems. ISPRS Int. J. Geo-Information **3**, 166–205 (2014)
5. Condotta, J.F., Lecoutre, C.: A class of $\frac{\diamond}{f}$-consistencies for qualitative constraint networks. In: KR (2010)
6. Condotta, J.-F., Ligozat, G., Saade, M.: Eligible and frozen constraints for solving temporal qualitative constraint networks. In: Bessière, C. (ed.) CP 2007. LNCS, vol. 4741, pp. 806–814. Springer, Heidelberg (2007). https://doi.org/10.1007/978-3-540-74970-7_58
7. Dylla, F., et al.: A survey of qualitative spatial and temporal calculi: algebraic and computational properties. ACM Comput. Surv. **50**, 7:1–7:39 (2017)
8. Dylla, F., Wallgrün, J.O.: Qualitative spatial reasoning with conceptual neighborhoods for agent control. J. Intell. Robotic Syst. **48**, 55–78 (2007)
9. Glorian, G., Lagniez, J.-M., Montmirail, V., Sioutis, M.: An incremental SAT-based approach to reason efficiently on qualitative constraint networks. In: Hooker, J. (ed.) CP 2018. LNCS, vol. 11008, pp. 160–178. Springer, Cham (2018). https://doi.org/10.1007/978-3-319-98334-9_11
10. Huang, J., Li, J.J., Renz, J.: Decomposition and tractability in qualitative spatial and temporal reasoning. Artif. Intell. **195**, 140–164 (2013)
11. Krishnaswamy, N., Friedman, S., Pustejovsky, J.: Combining deep learning and qualitative spatial reasoning to learn complex structures from sparse examples with noise. In: AAAI (2019)
12. Ligozat, G.: Qualitative Spatial and Temporal Reasoning. Wiley, Hoboken (2013)

13. Ligozat, G., Renz, J.: What is a qualitative calculus? A general framework. In: PRICAI (2004)
14. Long, Z., Sioutis, M., Li, S.: Efficient path consistency algorithm for large qualitative constraint networks. In: IJCAI (2016)
15. Martins, R., Manquinho, V.M., Lynce, I.: An overview of parallel SAT solving. Constraints **17**, 304–347 (2012)
16. Nebel, B.: Solving hard qualitative temporal reasoning problems: evaluating the efficiency of using the ORD-horn class. Constraints **1**, 175–190 (1997)
17. Renz, J., Ligozat, G.: Weak composition for qualitative spatial and temporal reasoning. In: van Beek, P. (ed.) CP 2005. LNCS, vol. 3709, pp. 534–548. Springer, Heidelberg (2005). https://doi.org/10.1007/11564751_40
18. Sioutis, M., Condotta, J., Koubarakis, M.: An efficient approach for tackling large real world qualitative spatial networks. Int. J. Artif. Intell. Tools **25**, 1–33 (2016)
19. Sioutis, M., Long, Z., Li, S.: Leveraging variable elimination for efficiently reasoning about qualitative constraints. Int. J. Artif. Intell. Tools **27**, 1860001 (2018)
20. Sioutis, M., Paparrizou, A., Condotta, J.: Collective singleton-based consistency for qualitative constraint networks: theory and practice. Theor. Comput. Sci. (2019, in press)
21. Williams, R., Gomes, C.P., Selman, B.: Backdoors to typical case complexity. In: IJCAI (2003)

GAN Path Finder: Preliminary Results

Natalia Soboleva[1,2(✉)] [ID] and Konstantin Yakovlev[1,2] [ID]

[1] National Research University Higher School of Economics, Moscow, Russia
nsoboleva@edu.hse.ru, kyakovlev@hse.ru
[2] Federal Research Center "Computer Science and Control"
of Russian Academy of Sciences, Moscow, Russia
yakovlev@isa.ru

Abstract. 2D path planning in static environment is a well-known problem and one of the common ways to solve it is to (1) represent the environment as a grid and (2) perform a heuristic search for a path on it. At the same time 2D grid resembles much a digital image, thus an appealing idea comes to being – to treat the problem as an image generation task and to solve it utilizing the recent advances in deep learning. In this work we make an attempt to apply a generative neural network as a path finder and report preliminary results, convincing enough to claim that this direction of research is worth further exploration.

Keywords: Path planning · Machine learning ·
Convolutional neural networks · Generative adversarial networks

1 Introduction

Grids composed of blocked and free cells are commonly used to represent static environment of a mobile agent. They appear naturally in game development [22] and are widely used in robotics [4, 24]. When the environment is represented by a grid, heuristic search algorithms, e.g. A* [11], are typically used for path planning. These algorithms iteratively explore the search space guided by a heuristic function such as Euclidean or octile distance. When the obstacles are present on the way such guidance leads to unnecessary exploration of the areas surrounding the obstacles. This issue can be mitigated to a certain extent by weighting the heuristics [2], using random jumps [15] or skipping portions of the search space exploiting the grid-induced symmetries [10]. At the same time, having in mind, that grids resemble digital images a lot and recently convolutional neural networks demonstrate tremendous success various image processing tasks, an orthogonal idea can be proposed – to plan entirely in the image domain using the state-of-the-art deep learning techniques thus avoiding the unnecessary state-space exploration by construction. In this work we leverage this idea and report preliminary results on path finding as image generation. We describe generative adversarial net that generates a path image in response to context input, i.e. image of the grid-map with start and goal. We demonstrate empirically that the proposed model can successfully handle previously unseen instances.

C. Benzmüller and H. Stuckenschmidt (Eds.): KI 2019, LNAI 11793, pp. 316–324, 2019.
https://doi.org/10.1007/978-3-030-30179-8_28

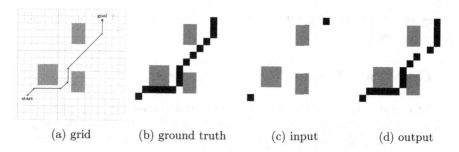

| (a) grid | (b) ground truth | (c) input | (d) output |

Fig. 1. (a) A 16×16 grid and a path on it; (b) corresponding image; (c) image-input for the generator; (d) image-output of the generator. For (b), (c), (d) image pixels are depicted as squares for illustrative purposes.

2 Related Work

The line of research that is most relevant to our work is deep learning (DL) for path/motion planning. A wide variety of works, e.g. [3,5], are focused on motion planning for manipulators. Unlike these works we are interested in path planning for mobile agents. DL approaches to navigation in 3D environment, that rely on the first-person imagery input, are considered in [9,16,25]. In contrast to these papers we focus on 2D path finding when a top-down view, i.e. a grid-map, is given as the input. In [23] such a task was considered, among the others, when the Value Iterations Networks (VINs) were presented. Evaluation was carried out on 16×16 and 28×28 grids. We are targeting larger maps, i.e. 64×64 grids. In [14] it was shown that VINs are "often plagued by training instability, oscillating between high and low performance between epochs" and other drawbacks. Instead Gated Path Planning Networks (GPPNs) were proposed but, again, the evaluation was carried out only on grids of size 15×15 and 28×28. The most recent work on VINs [21] proposes a pathway to use them on larger maps via abstraction mechanism, value iteration network is applied to 8×8 feature maps. Unlike VINs or other approaches based on reinforcement learning (e.g. [18]), this work (i) is not rooted in modeling path planning with Markov decision process, (ii) considers quite large grids, i.e. 64×64, as the indecomposable input.

3 Problem Statement

Consider a 2D grid composed of blocked and unblocked cells with two distinguished cells – start and goal. The path on a grid is a sequence of adjacent unblocked cells connecting start and goal[1] – see Fig. 1a. The task of the path planner is to find such path. Often the length of the path is the cost objective to be minimized, but in this work we do not aim at finding shortest paths.

Commonly the task is solved by converting the grid to the undirected graph and searching for a path on this graph. Instead we would like to represent the

---

[1] We are assuming 8-connected grids in this work.

grid as an image and given that image, generate a new one that implicitly depicts the path – see Fig. 1.

4   GAN Path Finder

Grid-to-Image Conversion. To convert the grid to an image we use a straight-forward approach: we distinguish 3 classes of the cells, – free, blocked and path (incl. start and goal), and assign a unique color to each of them. Although, we do not use loss functions based on the pixel-distance later on, we intuitively prefer this distance to be maximal between the free pixels and the path pixels. Thus, the free cells become the white pixels of the grayscale image, path cells (including start and goal) – black, blocked cells – gray (as depicted on Fig. 1b–d).

Types of Images. 3 types of images depicting grids and paths are to be distinguished. First, the image that depicts the grid with only start and goal locations – see Fig. 1c. This is the input. Second, the generated image that is the output of the neural network we are about to construct – see Fig. 1d. Third, the ground truth image that is constructed by rendering the input image with the A* path on it – see Fig. 1a. Ground truth images are extensively used for training, i.e. they serve as the examples of how "good" images look like. At the same time, from the path-finding perspective we should not penalize the output images that differ from the corresponding ground-truth image but still depict the correct path from start to goal. We will cover this aspect later on.

Architectural Choices. Convolutional neural networks (CNNs) [13] are the natural choice when it comes to image processing tasks. As there may exist a few feasible paths on a given grid we prefer to use Generative Adversarial Nets (GANs) [6] for path planning as we want our network to learn some general notion of the feasible path rather than forcing it to construct the path exactly in the same way that the supervisor (e.g. A*) does. GAN is composed of 2 sub-networks – generator and discriminator. Generator tries to generate the path-image, while discriminator is the classifier that tries to tell whether the generated image is "fake", i.e. does not come from the distribution of ground-truth images. Both these networks are the CNNs that are trained simultaneously.

   In this work we are, obviously, not interested in generating the images that depict some random grid with a correct path on it, but rather the image that depicts the solution of the given path finding instance (encoded as the input image). That leads us to the so-called conditional GANs (cGANs) [17]. Conditioning here means that the output of the network should be conditioned on the input (and not just generated out of the random noise as in vanilla GANs). We experimented with two prominent cGAN architectures – Context Encoders [19] and pix2pix [12]. CE – is the model that is tailored to image inpainting, i.e. filling the missed region of the image with the pixels that look correct. In our case we considered all the free-space pixels as missing and make CE inpaint them.

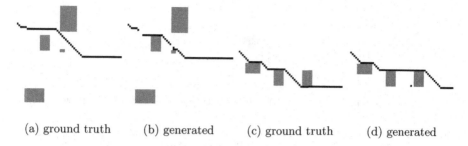

(a) ground truth   (b) generated   (c) ground truth   (d) generated

Fig. 2. Examples of the generated solutions, for which the MSE metric is not consistent, as the generated paths do not match ground truth, but are still feasible.

Pix2pix is a more general cGAN that is not tailored to particular generation task but rather solves the general "from pixels to pixels" problem. In path finding we want some free pixels become path pixels. We experimented with both CE and pix2pix and the latter showed more convincing results, which is quite foreseeable as pix2pix is a more complex model utilizing residual blocks. Thus, we chose pix2pix as the starting point for our model.

Generator. The general structure of generator is borrowed from pix2pix [12]. The difference is that in original work authors suggested two slightly different types of generator: the one with separated encoder/decoder parts with residual blocks in the bottleneck and the one utilizing skip-connections through all layers following the general shape of a "U-Net" architecture [20]. We experimented with both variants and the latter appeared to be more suitable for the considered task.

Original pix2pix generator's loss function is the weighted sum of two components. The first component penalizes generator based on how close the generated image is to the ground truth one, the second one – based on the discriminator's response (adversarial loss). We kept the second component unchanged while modified the first one to be the cross-entropy rather then the L1 pixel-distance. The rationale behind this is that in the considered case we prefer not to generate a color for each pixel but rather to classify whether it belongs to "free", "blocked", "path" class. This turned to provide a substantial gain in the solution quality.

Discriminator. The task of the discriminator is to detect whether the generated image comes from the distribution of the ground-truth images or not. We opt to focus discriminator only on the path component of the image, i.e. to train it to detect fake paths, thus we modify the input of the discriminator to be one-channel image which contains path pixels only. Such a "simplification" is evidently beneficial at the learning phase as otherwise the discriminator's loss is converging too fast and have no impact on the loss of the generator (see Fig. 3 on the left). Another reason for the discriminator to be focused on the path

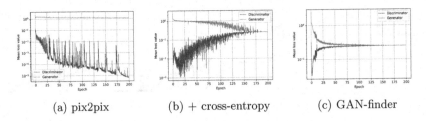

(a) pix2pix   (b) + cross-entropy   (c) GAN-finder

Fig. 3. Generator and Discriminator losses (in blue and orange respectively) on the grids with 20% of rectangular obstacles. (Color figure online)

apart from obstacles is that the displacements of path pixels (e.g. putting them inside the obstacles) is penalized by the supervised part of the generator (i.e., via cross-entropy loss) thus the discriminator should rather detect how well the sequence of cells resembles the path pattern in general (are all cell adjacent, are there no loops/gaps etc.). Such an approach also naturally aligns with the idea that there may exist a handful of equivalent and plausible (and even optimal) paths from start to goal while the ground truth image depicts only one of them.

In contrast to [12] we achieved the best performance when training discriminator un-conditionally (without using input image as a condition). Implementing gradient penalty using Wasserstein distance [8] for training the discriminator also yields better results.

Image Post-processing. To make sure that all obstacles remain at their places we transfer all blocked pixels from the original image to the generated one. Another technique we opt to use is gap-filling. We noticed that often a generated path is missing some segments. We use Bresenham line-drawing algorithm [1] to depict them. If the line segment is drawn across the obstacle, the gap remains.

Success Metrics. In the image domain one of the most common metrics used to measure how well the model generates images is per-pixel mean-squared error (MSE). Path finding scenario is different in a sense that generated path pixels may be put to the other places compared to the ground truth image, thus MSE will be high, although the result is plausible, as it simply depicts some alternative path – see Fig. 2. We have already accounted for that fact when forced the discriminator to focus on the path structure in general rather than on the path pixels to be put precisely to the same places as on the ground truth image. We now want to account for it at test time so we introduce an additional metric called "gaps" which measures how many gaps are present in the generated path before post-processing. Finally, after the gaps are attempted to be removed we count the result as the "success" in case there are none of them left and the path truly connects start with goal (thus the path finding instance is solved).

Table 1. Success metrics on different types of data.

	20% density			30% density			Random		
	MSE	Gaps	Success	MSE	Gaps	Success	MSE	Gaps	Success
pix2pix [12]	0.0336	19.54	65%	0.13	27.22	57%	0.2	27.56	32%
GAN-finder	0.014	1.4916	91.4%	0.164	2.71	73.1%	0.045	3.142	65.1%

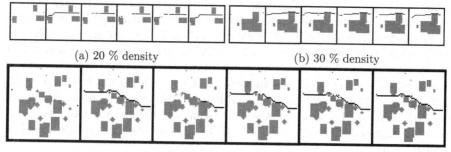

    (a) 20 % density   (b) 30 % density

(c) Random data evaluation

Fig. 4. From left to right: (1) input, (2) ground truth, (3) baseline pix2pix, (4) pix2pix using cross-entropy, (5) GAN-finder output, (6) GAN-finder output post-processed.

5 Experimental Evaluation

Dataset. We evaluated the proposed GAN on the 64×64 grids, representing outdoor environments with obstacles, as those types of grids were used in previous research on application of deep learning techniques to path finding (see [14,23] for example). Start was always close to the left border, goal – to the right (as any grid can be rotated to fit this template). We used two approaches to put obstacles. In the first approach, rectangular obstacles of random size and orientation were put to random positions on the grid until obstacle density reached 20% (we also used maps with 30% for the evaluation but not learning). In the second approach, obstacles of rectangular, diamond and circular shape of random size were put to the map until the random obstacle density in the interval [0.05; 0.5] was reached. The total size of each dataset was 50000, divided into train – 75%, test – 15% and validation – 10%. For each input we built a ground-truth image depicting $A*$ path.

Evaluation. Figure 3 illustrates the training process for (a) baseline pix2pix GAN, (b) pix2pix trained with cross-entropy and (c) GAN-finder. It is clearly seen that GAN-finder converges much faster and in a more stable fashion. The examples of the paths found by various modifications of the considered GANs are shown in Fig. 4.

Success metrics for the 20% density maps (test part of the dataset) are shown in Table 1 on the left. We also evaluated the trained model on the 30% density maps (maps with such density were not part of the training) – results are shown in Table 1 in the middle. Observing these results, one can claim that GAN-finder adapts well to the unseen instances with the same obstacle density (success rate exceeds 90%). It is also capable to adapt to the unseen instances of higher obstacle density. Although in this case success rate is notably lower (around 73%), it does not degrade to near zero values, which means that the model has indeed learned some general path finding techniques. One may also notice that GAN-finder significantly reduces the number of gaps (up to an order of magnitude), compared to baseline. The results achieved on the random dataset are shown in the right column of the Table 1. Again GAN-finder is performing much better than the baseline. At the same time, success rate is now lower compared to 20% density maps. We believe this is due to the more complex structure of the environments. One possible way to increase the success rate in this case might be to use more samples for training, another – to use attention/recurrent blocks as in [7]. Overall, the results of the evaluation are convincing enough to claim that the suggested approach, i.e. using GANs for path planning, is worth further investigation.

6   Conclusion and Future Work

In this work we suggested the generative adversarial network – GAN-finder – capable of solving path finding problems via image generation. Obtained results, being preliminary in nature, demonstrate that the suggested approach has a potential for further development as clearly the neural net has learned certain path finding basics. We are planning to extend this work in the following directions.

First, we want to study GAN-finder behaviour in more complex domains (e.g. the ones populated with complex-shaped obstacles, with highly varying obstacle densities etc.). As well we need to fairly compare our method with the other learning-based approaches such as Value Iteration Networks [23].

Second, we wish to further enhance the model to make it more versatile tool suitable for path planning. One of such enhancements is modifying the generator's loss in correlation with the idea of multiple possible paths from start to goal. E.g., we can ignore path pixels when computing cross-entropy loss but introduce an extra semi- or non-supervised loss component for them in addition to (or completely substituting) the discriminator's feedback. Another appealing option is to add attention/recurrent blocks to the model. This will provide a capability to successively refine the path in complex domains, e.g. the ones densely populated with the obstacles of non-trivial shapes. This also might help in scaling to large maps.

Finally, we can use GAN-finder not just as a path planner on it's own, but rather as a complimentary tool for the conventional and well-established heuristic search algorithms, e.g. A*, providing them with a more informed heuristics.

Acknowledgements. This work was supported by the Russian Science Foundation (Project No. 16-11-00048).

References

1. Bresenham, J.E.: Algorithm for computer control of a digital plotter. IBM Syst. J. **4**(1), 25–30 (1965)
2. Ebendt, R., Drechsler, R.: Weighted A* search - unifying view and application. Artif. Intell. **173**(14), 1310–1342 (2009)
3. Eitel, A., Hauff, N., Burgard, W.: Learning to singulate objects using a push proposal network. In: Proceedings of the International Symposium on Robotics Research (ISRR 2017), Puerto Varas, Chile (2017)
4. Elfes, A.: Using occupancy grids for mobile robot perception and navigation. Computer **22**(6), 46–57 (1989)
5. Finn, C., Levine, S.: Deep visual foresight for planning robot motion. In: Proceedings of the 2017 IEEE International Conference on Robotics and Automation (ICRA 2017), pp. 2786–2793 (2017)
6. Goodfellow, I., et al.: Generative adversarial nets. In: Advances in Neural Information Processing Systems, vol. 27, pp. 2672–2680 (2014)
7. Gregor, K., Danihelka, I., Graves, A., Rezende, D.J., Wierstra, D.: Draw: a recurrent neural network for image generation. In: Proceedings of the 32nd International Conference on Machine Learning (ICML 2015) (2015)
8. Gulrajani, I., Ahmed, F., Arjovsky, M., Dumoulin, V., Courville, A.: Improved training of Wasserstein GANs. In: Proceedings of the 31st International Conference on Neural Information Processing Systems, NIPS 2017, pp. 5769–5779. Curran Associates Inc., Red Hook (2017)
9. Gupta, S., Davidson, J., Levine, S., Sukthankar, R., Malik, J.: Cognitive mapping and planning for visual navigation. In: Proceedings of the 30th IEEE Conference on Computer Vision and Pattern Recognition (CVPR 2017) (2017)
10. Harabor, D., Grastien, A.: Online graph pruning for pathfinding on grid maps. In: Proceedings of the 25th AAAI Conference on Artificial Intelligence (AAAI 2011), pp. 1114–1119 (2011)
11. Hart, P.E., Nilsson, N.J., Raphael, B.: A formal basis for the heuristic determination of minimum cost paths. IEEE Trans. Syst. Sci. Cybern. **4**(2), 100–107 (1968)
12. Isola, P., Zhu, J.Y., Zhou, T., Efros, A.A.: Image-to-image translation with conditional adversarial networks. In: 2017 IEEE Conference on Computer Vision and Pattern Recognition (CVPR), pp. 5967–5976 (2017)
13. Krizhevsky, A., Sutskever, I., Hinton, G.E.: Imagenet classification with deep convolutional neural networks. Commun. ACM **60**, 84–90 (2012)
14. Lee, L., Parisotto, E., Chaplot, D.S., Xing, E., Salakhutdinov, R.: Gated path planning networks. In: Proceedings of the 25th International Conference on Machine Learning (ICML 2018), pp. 2953–2961 (2018)
15. Likhachev, M., Stentz, A.: R* search. In: Proceedings of the 23rd AAAI Conference on Artificial Intelligence (AAAI-2008) (2008)
16. Mirowski, P., et al.: Learning to navigate in cities without a map. In: Advances in Neural Information Processing Systems, pp. 2419–2430 (2018)
17. Mirza, M., Osindero, S.: Conditional generative adversarial nets. CoRR abs/1411.1784 (2014). http://arxiv.org/abs/1411.1784
18. Panov, A.I., Yakovlev, K.S., Suvorov, R.: Grid path planning with deep reinforcement learning: preliminary results. Procedia Comput. Sci. **123**, 347–353 (2018)
19. Pathak, D., Krähenbühl, P., Donahue, J., Darrell, T., Efros, A.A.: Context encoders: feature learning by inpainting. In: 2016 IEEE Conference on Computer Vision and Pattern Recognition (CVPR), pp. 2536–2544 (2016)

20. Ronneberger, O., Fischer, P., Brox, T.: U-Net: convolutional networks for biomedical image segmentation. In: Navab, N., Hornegger, J., Wells, W.M., Frangi, A.F. (eds.) MICCAI 2015. LNCS, vol. 9351, pp. 234–241. Springer, Cham (2015). https://doi.org/10.1007/978-3-319-24574-4_28
21. Schleich, D., Klamt, T., Behnke, S.: Value iteration networks on multiple levels of abstraction. In: Proceedings of Robotics: Science and Systems (RSS-2019) (2019)
22. Sturtevant, N.R.: Benchmarks for grid-based pathfinding. IEEE Trans. Comput. Intell. AI Games **4**(2), 144–148 (2012)
23. Tamar, A., Wu, Y., Thomas, G., Levine, S., Abbeel, P.: Value iteration networks. In: Advances in Neural Information Processing Systems 29 (NIPS 2016), pp. 2154–2162 (2016)
24. Thrun, S.: Learning occupancy grid maps with forward sensor models. Auton. Robots **15**(2), 111–127 (2003)
25. Zhu, Y., et al.: Target-driven visual navigation in indoor scenes using deep reinforcement learning. In: 2017 IEEE International Conference on Robotics and Automation (ICRA 2017), pp. 3357–3364 (2017)

InformatiCup Competition 2019: Fooling Traffic Sign Recognition

Marcus Soll[(⊠)]

Universität Hamburg, Vogt-Koelln-Str. 30, 22527 Hamburg, Germany
2soll@informatik.uni-hamburg.de
https://www.uni-hamburg.de/

Abstract. Neural networks are used more and more in critical areas such as autonomous driving. In such cases, their limitations might cause dangerous situations. Researchers were able to show that such limitations enable attacks on systems containing neural networks, which are even possible in real world scenarios. For example, a state-of-the-art network might misclassify modified traffic signs. Other researchers have shown that modern car assistants can easily be fooled to drive the car into the wrong lane on a street.

The InformatiCup is a collegiate computer science competition in Germany, Switzerland and Austria for all students, with tasks based on real world problems. This year's task is based on the above mentioned problem. To demonstrate this problem and to motivate students for experimenting with neural networks, participants were asked to generate fooling images for a traffic sign classifying neural network without having direct access to the network. The images should not be recognisable by humans as traffic signs, but be classified as such with a high confidence by the neural network.

Keywords: Fooling images · Neural network · Competition

1 Motivation

Imagine driving an autonomous car down a road. You pass a sticker with some weird signs (such a scene might appear as shown in Fig. 1). Suddenly, your car stops in the middle of the road because your car has identified the sticker as a "No through traffic" sign. This way, fooling images lead to dangerous situations.

The troubling thing is that similar attacks have already been shown in practice. For example, Eykholt et al. [4] were able to let neural networks misclassify traffic signs by slightly modifying them. The Tencent Keen Security Lab [14] was able to mislead a Tesla car into the wrong lane by simply placing coloured dots on the road.

To get more insights into fooling images, the participants got the task of creating these images against a target network. The hope was that students can be motivated into experimenting with neural networks through this task.

© Springer Nature Switzerland AG 2019
C. Benzmüller and H. Stuckenschmidt (Eds.): KI 2019, LNAI 11793, pp. 325–332, 2019.
https://doi.org/10.1007/978-3-030-30179-8_29

Fig. 1. Example of a fooling image on the road, which might be classified as a "No through traffic" sign.

2   InformatiCup

The InformatiCup[1] (established 2005) is a yearly computer science competition held by the Gesellschaft für Informatik[2] for students in all branches of study in Germany, Switzerland and Austria. It offers prize money to the winning team as well as prizes for the best teams.

The topics are oriented on real world problems. Past topics include, for example, harvesting strategies for manganese nodules or the prediction of fuel prices.

The InformatiCup is a competition with a holistic approach, where the whole solution is important and not only the programming or simply the quality of the results. The judgement is based on the following criteria:

- the theoretical background of the solution
- quality of programming (including software architecture and quality management)
- presentation
- quality of the result (e.g. accuracy)
- user manual
- additions by the teams (like graphical user interfaces)

The InformatiCup is well recognised in the industry and some tasks have even contributed to research [11,12].

3   Background: Fooling Images

In recent research it was shown that neural networks, despite showing high accuracy for many tasks including images classification [7], are susceptible to malicious input. Most research focuses on so called *adversarial examples* [1]. In these

---

[1] https://gi.de/informaticup/
[2] https://gi.de/

examples, noise is added to a correctly classified image to make neural networks misclassify it, while at the same time the change should not be detectable by humans.

Another approach was taken by Nguyen et al. [8] and followed by Soll [10]. In contrast to adversarial examples, *fooling images* are not created from existing images. Instead, they are created artificially and are classified by neural networks with high confidence, while not being recognisable by humans.

4   Task Description

The task of the InformatiCup 2019 was to develop a software solution that is able to generate fooling images for a provided neural network for at least five different traffic signs. All generated images must be classified as a traffic sign by the neural network with at least 90% confidence. There were no requirements of a specific traffic sign, which allowed untargeted attacks. Some examples of possible solutions (generated by the jury) can be seen in Fig. 2.

blocks	bubbles	pixel clouds	rectangles

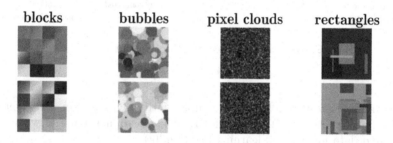

Fig. 2. Examples of fooling images created by the organisers of the competition. All are classified as a "Vorfahrt" sign (priority traffic sign) with at least 90% confidence by the target network. All images are 64 × 64 pixels in size.

To make the task harder, several limitations were put in place for the participants:

- The participants had no direct access to the network. Instead, a Web API had to be used.
- The neural network architecture was unknown to the participants.
- Each team was restricted to only 60 requests per minute. This was checked by providing each team a unique API key.
- The number of output classes was not provided to the participants, although the dataset was known.
- Only the top 5 classification results were returned.

In addition to the software solution, teams had to turn in a paper describing the theoretical background, the software design decisions and a result discussion.

A user manual was required, which could be part of the paper or a separate paper. The best teams had to present their solution to a jury consisting of members from industry and academia.

4.1   Neural Network Used

For the task, a simple single-layer neural network (see Fig. 3) was trained on *The German Traffic Sign Recognition Benchmark* [13]. The input of the network was an image with 32 × 32 pixels. In an attempt to reduce the susceptibility of the neural network against fooling images, several measures were taken:

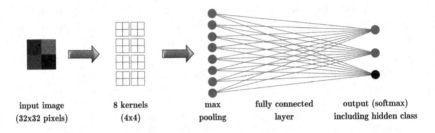

input image   8 kernels   max   fully connected   output (softmax)
(32x32 pixels)   (4x4)   pooling   layer   including hidden class

Fig. 3. Schema of neural network architecture.

1. The architecture was deliberately simple, with only one layer and eight kernels. This was to keep the Vapnik-Chervonenkis-dimension and with it the required data for optimal learning low (see [6]).
2. In addition to the provided images in the dataset, additional images were generated and used as a hidden class (i.e. not visible to the participants) in the training (see Fig. 4). The goal was to make the network more robust to certain changes. These images include:
   - Images with a single colour to counter background detection
   - Images with random circles to counter the shape of the traffic signs
   - Images with random noise to counter reaction to noise
3. The network was trained on a low number of epochs (five) to counter overfitting.

With all those measurements, the network reached an accuracy of about 85%. Although the accuracy might not be as high as desired, it seemed suitable enough for the competition.

To ensure that the network is not easily fooled, a dataset of 38 images (including 10 random noise images) was tested against the neural network, of which none was detected as a traffic sign.

random circles   **random colour**   **random noise**

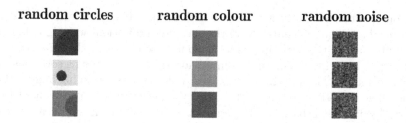

Fig. 4. Examples of images added as a hidden class to the trainings set to reduce the susceptibility against fooling images. (Color figure online)

4.2   Network Interface

For the communication with the neural network, two interfaces were provided.

Website: Through a website, a single image could be classified. A view on the website is shown in Fig. 5.

(a) A single image can be uploaded with   (b) Example feedback of the website.
a valid API key.

Fig. 5. Website as an interface to the neural network.

Web API: A HTTP POST-Request in the encoding *multipart/form-data* containing the API key and the image could be sent to an endpoint. If the request is valid, a JSON object containing the top five prediction and the corresponding confidence values is returned.

5   Analysis of the Competition

In this year's competition, 46 teams from all over Germany registered for the competition. Out of those, 30 teams turned in a working final solution, which were all graded by a jury from both industry and academia. Out of those, five teams advanced to the final round and presented their solutions. The results (including links to repositories of the student solutions) can be found on GitHub[3].

This year's competition not only had the highest number in solutions turned in (for comparison, the InformatiCup 2018 had a total of 17 teams turning in

---

[3] https://github.com/InformatiCup/InformatiCup2019/blob/master/results/
README.md

solutions), but also the solutions were of high quality. This shows that the interest in artificial intelligence/neural networks and their limitations was high. This was also confirmed by the participants in personal discussions at the final round.

The participating teams turned in a wide variety of different solutions. The winners combined methods from recent research to generate fooling images: They trained a new substitution model based on the feedback from the Web API plus the provided dataset (based on Papernot et al. [9] with slight modifications) and applied state-of-the-art methods from adversarial examples research on the new model (Modified attack of Carlini and Wagner [2] as well as Eykholt et al. [4]).

The team in second place provided two solutions:

- Based on an initial image (e.g. black background), the image is divided into blocks with a user defined size. For each block (in random order), the effect of the different colours is analysed. The colour variant with the highest confidence is chosen for that block. The algorithm ends when the target confidence is reached.
- Similar to the winning team, the team trained a substitution model (based on Papernot et al. [9]). For this, they used 1000 randomly chosen images of the dataset for training (100 for the test set), and used the Jacobian-based Data Augmentation [9] for training. They then used the Momentum-based iterative Fast Gradient Sign Method [3] for generating fooling images (either targeted for a specific sign or untargeted).

The team in third place used genetic algorithms [5,15] for creating untargeted fooling images, however they omitted the recombination phase of the genetic algorithm and only used mutation. Starting on a user provided image, they implemented different mutation methods (all controlled by variables modifiable by the user):

- Set a percent of pixels to a random colour.
- Draw circles (either filled or unfilled) on the image.
- Draw rectangles (either filled or unfilled) on the image.
- Draw multiple polygons (always filled) on the image in a way that results in rotationally symmetrical placement of the polygons.
- Divide the image into a grid of blocks and slightly stain the different blocks with random colours (keeping the original image visible if desired).

Besides the three approaches described here, many more solutions were turned in with vastly different approaches. However, it is not in the scope of this paper to describe all approaches in detail.

6   Conclusion

Neural networks are widely used. However, their limitations - like fooling images - are not understood well. The InformatiCup used this as a topic of this year's competition, where participants should generate fooling images for a traffic sign classifying neural network. With 30 solutions from all over Germany, this year's competition has motivated students to look into neural networks. The InformatiCup will be continued in 2020.

Acknowledgments. I would like to thank all organisers, jury and participants of the InformatiCup 2019 competition organised by the "Gesellschaft für Informatik". A special thanks goes to the sponsors of the event: Amazon, PPI AG, Netlight, Volkswagen, TWT GmbH Science & Innovation and GitHub. Further thanks goes to the AutoUni Wolfsburg for hosting the final presentation.

References

1. Akhtar, N., Mian, A.: Threat of adversarial attacks on deep learning in computer vision: a survey. IEEE Access **6**, 14410–14430 (2018). https://doi.org/10.1109/ACCESS.2018.2807385
2. Carlini, N., Wagner, D.: Towards evaluating the robustness of neural networks. In: 2017 IEEE Symposium on Security and Privacy (SP), pp. 39–57, May 2017. https://doi.org/10.1109/SP.2017.49
3. Dong, Y., et al.: Boosting adversarial attacks with momentum. In: 2018 IEEE Conference on Computer Vision and Pattern Recognition, CVPR 2018, Salt Lake City, UT, USA, 18–22 June 2018, pp. 9185–9193 (2018). https://doi.org/10.1109/CVPR.2018.00957
4. Eykholt, K., et al.: Robust physical-world attacks on deep learning visual classification. In: 2018 IEEE/CVF Conference on Computer Vision and Pattern Recognition, pp. 1625–1634, June 2018. https://doi.org/10.1109/CVPR.2018.00175
5. Gerdes, I., Klawonn, F., Kruse, R.: Evolutionäre Algorithmen: Genetische Algorithmen – Strategien und Optimierungsverfahren – Beispielanwendungen. Vieweg+Teubner Verlag, Wiesbaden (2004). https://doi.org/10.1007/978-3-322-86839-8
6. Harman, G., Kulkarni, S.: Statistical learning theory as a framework for the philosophy of induction. In: Bandyopadhyay, P.S., Forster, M.R. (eds.) Philosophy of Statistics. Handbook of the Philosophy of Science, vol. 7, pp. 833–847. North-Holland, Amsterdam (2011). https://doi.org/10.1016/B978-0-444-51862-0.50027-7. http://www.sciencedirect.com/science/article/pii/B9780444518620500277
7. Liu, W., Wang, Z., Liu, X., Zeng, N., Liu, Y., Alsaadi, F.E.: A survey of deepneural network architectures and their applications. Neurocomputing **234**, 11–26 (2017). https://doi.org/10.1016/j.neucom.2016.12.038. http://www.sciencedirect.com/science/article/pii/S0925231216315533
8. Nguyen, A., Yosinski, J., Clune, J.: Deep neural networks are easily fooled: High confidence predictions for unrecognizable images. In: 2015 IEEE Conference on Computer Vision and Pattern Recognition (CVPR), pp. 427–436, June 2015. https://doi.org/10.1109/CVPR.2015.7298640
9. Papernot, N., McDaniel, P., Goodfellow, I., Jha, S., Celik, Z.B., Swami, A.: Practical black-box attacks against machine learning. In: Proceedings of the 2017 ACM on Asia Conference on Computer and Communications Security, ASIA CCS 2017, pp. 506–519. ACM, New York (2017). https://doi.org/10.1145/3052973.3053009
10. Soll, M.: Fooling deep neural networks using Cuckoo Search. Technical report, University of Hamburg, February 2016. https://doi.org/10.13140/RG.2.1.1402.7760
11. Soll, M., Naumann, P., Schöning, J., Samsonov, P., Hecht, B.: Helping computers understand geographically-bound activity restrictions. In: Proceedings of the 2016

CHI Conference on Human Factors in Computing Systems, CHI 2016, pp. 2442–2446. ACM, New York (2016). https://doi.org/10.1145/2858036.2858053

12. Soll, M., Vosgerau, M.: ClassifyHub: an algorithm to classify GitHub repositories. In: Kern-Isberner, G., Fürnkranz, J., Thimm, M. (eds.) KI 2017. LNCS (LNAI), vol. 10505, pp. 373–379. Springer, Cham (2017). https://doi.org/10.1007/978-3-319-67190-1_34

13. Stallkamp, J., Schlipsing, M., Salmen, J., Igel, C.: Man vs. computer: Benchmarking machine learning algorithms for traffic sign recognition. Neural Netw. **32**, 323–332 (2012). https://doi.org/10.1016/j.neunet.2012.02.016. http://www.sciencedirect.com/science/article/pii/S0893608012000457. Selected Papers from IJCNN 2011

14. Tencent Keen Security Lab: Experimental security research of tesla autopilot. Technical report, Tencent Keen Security Lab (2019)

15. Weicker, K.: Evolutionäre Algorithmen. Springer Fachmedien Wiesbaden, Wiesbaden (2015). https://doi.org/10.1007/978-3-658-09958-9

The Higher-Order Prover Leo-III
(Extended Abstract)

Alexander Steen[1]([✉])(iD) and Christoph Benzmüller[2](iD)

[1] FSTC, University of Luxembourg, Esch-sur-Alzette, Luxembourg
alexander.steen@uni.lu
[2] Department of Maths and Computer Science, Freie Universität Berlin,
Berlin, Germany
c.benzmueller@fu-berlin.de

Abstract. Leo-III is an automated theorem prover for extensional type theory with Henkin semantics. It also automates various non-classical logics, e.g., almost every normal higher-order modal logic is supported. In this extended abstract, the features of Leo-III are surveyed.

This is an abstract of the homonymous paper accepted at the 9th International Joint Conference on Automated Reasoning (IJCAR 2018), see doi: 10.1007/978-3-319-94205-6_8.

1 Introduction

Leo-III is an automated theorem prover (ATP) for extensional type theory (also referred to as *classical higher-order logic*, HOL) with Henkin semantics and choice. The system is implemented in Scala, open-source and freely available under a BSD license.[1] It is the successor of the LEO-II prover [7], whose development significantly influenced the build-up of the TPTP THF infrastructure [21] for higher-order reasoning. The full details on Leo-III are presented in [18].

The logical formalisms supported by Leo-III include HOL as its primary target language, but also first-order and propositional logic. As input formats, Leo-III supports all common TPTP [20,21] dialects (CNF, FOF, TFF, THF) as well as the polymorphic variants TF1 and TH1 [10,16]. The prover returns results according to the standardized SZS ontology and additionally produces a TSTP-compatible (refutation) proof certificate, if a proof is found. Furthermore, Leo-III natively supports reasoning for almost every normal higher-order (HO) modal logic, including (but not limited to) logics **K**, **D**, **T**, **S4** and **S5** with constant, cumulative or varying domain quantifiers and both global and local notions of consequence [9]. In a recent evaluation study of 19 different first- and higher-order ATP systems, Leo-III was found the most versatile (in terms of supported logic fragments) and best performing ATP system overall [12].

---

[1] See the Leo-III project at GitHub: http://github.com/leoprover/Leo-III.

The work was supported by the German National Research Foundation (DFG) under grant BE 2501/11-1 (Leo-III).

C. Benzmüller and H. Stuckenschmidt (Eds.): KI 2019, LNAI 11793, pp. 333–337, 2019.
https://doi.org/10.1007/978-3-030-30179-8_30

$$\frac{\mathcal{C} \vee [l \simeq r]^{\text{tt}} \qquad \mathcal{D} \vee [s \simeq t]^{\alpha}}{\mathcal{C} \vee \mathcal{D} \vee [s[r]_{\pi} \simeq t]^{\alpha} \vee [s|_{\pi} \simeq l]^{\text{ff}}} \ (\text{Para}) \qquad \frac{\mathcal{C} \vee [l \simeq r]^{\alpha} \vee [s \simeq t]^{\alpha}}{\mathcal{C} \vee [l \simeq r]^{\alpha} \vee [l \simeq s]^{\text{ff}} \vee [r \simeq t]^{\text{ff}}} \ (\text{EqFac})$$

$$\frac{\mathcal{C} \vee [X_{\overline{\tau_i} \to o} \ \overline{t^i_{\tau_i}}]^{\alpha} \qquad p \in \mathcal{GB}^{\{\neg, \vee\} \cup \{\Pi^\tau, =^\tau | \tau \in \mathcal{T}\}}_{\overline{\tau_i} \to o}}{(\mathcal{C} \vee [X_{\overline{\tau_i} \to o} \ \overline{t^i_{\tau_i}}]^{\alpha})\{X/p\}} \ (\text{PS})$$

Fig. 1. Primary inferences of Leo-III's underlying calculus EP. *Technical notes:* $s \simeq t$ denotes an HO equation, where $\simeq$ is assumed to be symmetric. A literal ℓ is a signed equation, written $[s \simeq t]^{\alpha}$ where $\alpha \in \{\text{tt}, \text{ff}\}$ is the polarity of ℓ. Literals of form $[s_o]^{\alpha}$ are a shorthand for $[s_o \simeq \top]^{\alpha}$. A clause $\mathcal{C}$ is a multiset of literals, denoting its disjunction. For brevity, if $\mathcal{C}, \mathcal{D}$ are clauses and ℓ is a literal, $\mathcal{C} \vee \ell$ and $\mathcal{C} \vee \mathcal{D}$ denote the multi-union $\mathcal{C} \cup \{\ell\}$ and $\mathcal{C} \cup \mathcal{D}$, respectively. $s|_{\pi}$ is the subterm of s at position π, and $s[r]_{\pi}$ denotes the term that is created by replacing the subterm of s at position π by r.

Related ATP Systems. Next to the LEO prover family [3,7,19], there are further HO ATP systems available: This includes TPS [1] as one of the earliest systems, as well as Satallax [13], cocATP [8], agsyHOL [17] and the higher-order model finder Nitpick [11]. Related modal logic provers are still restricted to propositional or first-order logics only [5,15,22].

Higher-Order Logic. HOL as addressed here has been proposed by Church, and further studied by Henkin, Andrews and others, cf. [2,4] and the references therein. It provides lambda-notation, as an elegant and useful means to denote unnamed functions, predicates and sets (by their characteristic functions). In the remainder a notion of HOL with Henkin semantics and choice is assumed.

Higher-Order Paramodulation. Leo-III extends the complete, paramodulation based calculus EP with practically motivated, heuristic inference rules [18]. The primary inferences of EP, displayed in Fig. 1, are paramodulation (Para), equality factoring (EqFac) and primitive substitution (PS).

2   Modal Logic Reasoning

Modal logics have many relevant applications in computer science, artificial intelligence, mathematics and computational linguistics. They also play an important role in many areas of philosophy, including ontology, ethics, philosophy of mind and philosophy of science. Many challenging applications, as recently explored in metaphysics, require FO or HO modal logics (HOMLs). The development of ATPs for these logics, however, is still in its infancy.

Leo-III is addressing this gap. In addition to its HO reasoning capabilities, it is the first ATP that natively supports a very wide range of normal HOMLs. To achieve this, Leo-III internally implements a shallow semantical embeddings approach [6,14]. The key idea in this approach is to provide and exploit faithful mappings for HOML input problems to HOL that encode its Kripke-style semantics. An example is as follows:

A The user inputs a HOML problem in a suitably adapted TPTP syntax, e.g.

```
thf(1,conjecture,( ! [P:$i>$o,F:$i>$i, X:$i]: (? [G:$i>$i]:
     (($dia @ ($box @ (P @ (F @ X)))) => ($box @ (P @ (G @ X))))))).
```

which encodes $\forall P_{\iota\to o}\forall F_{\iota\to\iota}\forall X_\iota\exists G_{\iota\to\iota}(\Diamond\Box P(F(X)) \Rightarrow \Box P(G(X)))$, with $box and $dia representing the (mono-)modal operators. This example formula (an instance of a corollary of Becker's postulate) is valid in **S5**.

B In the header of the input file the user specifies the logic of interest, say **S5** with rigid constants, constant domain quantifiers and a global consequence relation. For this purpose the TPTP language has been suitably extended:[2]

```
thf(simple_s5, logic, ($modal := [
     $constants := $rigid, $quantification := $constant,
     $consequence := $global, $modalities := $modal_system_S5 ])).
```

C When being called with this input file, Leo-III parses and analyses it, automatically selects and unfolds the corresponding definitions of the semantical embedding approach, adds appropriate axioms and then starts reasoning in (meta-logic) HOL. Subsequently, it returns SZS compliant result information and, if successful, also a proof object just as for standard HOL problems.

Leo-III supports (but is not limited to) FO and HO extensions of the well known modal logic cube. When taking the different parameter combinations into account (constant/cumulative/varying domain semantics, rigid/non-rigid constants, local/global consequence relation, and further semantical parameters) this amounts to more than 120 supported HOMLs.[3] The exact number of supported logics is in fact much higher, since Leo-III also supports multi-modal logics in such a way that the properties of each integrated modal operator can be specified individually. Also, user-defined combinations of rigid and non-rigid constants and different quantification semantics per type domain are possible.

3   Summary

Leo-III is a state-of-the-art higher-order reasoning system offering many relevant features and capabilities. Due to its wide range of natively supported classical and non-classical logics, which include polymorphic higher-order logic and numerous first-order and higher-order modal logics, the system has many topical applications in computer science, AI, maths and philosophy.

An evaluation on heterogeneous benchmark sets shows that Leo-III is one of the most effective HO ATP systems to date [12,18], and it also plays a pivotal role in the ongoing extension of the TPTP library and infrastructure to support modal logic reasoning.

References

1. Andrews, P.B., Brown, C.E.: TPS: a hybrid automatic-interactive system for developing proofs. J. Appl. Log. **4**(4), 367–395 (2006). https://doi.org/10.1016/j.jal.2005.10.002

---

[2] Cf. http://www.cs.miami.edu/~tptp/TPTP/Proposals/LogicSpecification.html.
[3] Cf. [14, §2.2]; we refer to the literature [9] for more details on HOML.

2. Benzmüller, C., Andrews, P.: Church's type theory. In: Zalta, E.N. (ed.) The Stanford Encyclopedia of Philosophy. Metaphysics Research Lab, Stanford University, Stanford (2019). https://plato.stanford.edu/entries/type-theory-church/

3. Benzmüller, C., Kohlhase, M.: System description: LEO – a higher-order theorem prover. In: Kirchner, C., Kirchner, H. (eds.) CADE 1998. LNCS, vol. 1421, pp. 139–143. Springer, Heidelberg (1998). https://doi.org/10.1007/BFb0054256

4. Benzmüller, C., Miller, D.: Automation of higher-order logic. In: Siekmann, J.H. (ed.) Computational Logic, Handbook of the History of Logic, vol. 9, pp. 215–254. Elsevier, Amsterdam (2014). https://doi.org/10.1016/B978-0-444-51624-4.50005-8

5. Benzmüller, C., Otten, J., Raths, T.: Implementing and evaluating provers for first-order modal logics. In: Raedt, L.D., et al. (eds.) ECAI 2012. Frontiers in AI and Applications, vol. 242, pp. 163–168. IOS Press, Montpellier (2012). https://doi.org/10.3233/978-1-61499-098-7-163

6. Benzmüller, C., Paulson, L.C.: Multimodal and intuitionistic logics in simple type theory. Log. J. IGPL **18**(6), 881–892 (2010). https://doi.org/10.1093/jigpal/jzp080

7. Benzmüller, C., Sultana, N., Paulson, L.C., Theiss, F.: The higher-order prover LEO-II. J. Autom. Reason. **55**(4), 389–404 (2015). https://doi.org/10.1007/s10817-015-9348-y

8. Bertot, Y., Castéran, P.: Interactive Theorem Proving and Program Development - Coq'Art: The Calculus of Inductive Constructions. Texts in Theoretical Computer Science an EATCS Series. Springer, Heidelberg (2004). https://doi.org/10.1007/978-3-662-07964-5

9. Blackburn, P., van Benthem, J.F., Wolter, F.: Handbook of Modal Logic, vol. 3. Elsevier, Amsterdam (2006)

10. Blanchette, J.C., Paskevich, A.: TFF1: the TPTP typed first-order form with rank-1 polymorphism. In: Bonacina, M.P. (ed.) CADE 2013. LNCS (LNAI), vol. 7898, pp. 414–420. Springer, Heidelberg (2013). https://doi.org/10.1007/978-3-642-38574-2_29

11. Blanchette, J.C., Nipkow, T.: Nitpick: a counterexample generator for higher-order logic based on a relational model finder. In: Kaufmann, M., Paulson, L.C. (eds.) ITP 2010. LNCS, vol. 6172, pp. 131–146. Springer, Heidelberg (2010). https://doi.org/10.1007/978-3-642-14052-5_11

12. Brown, C., Gauthier, T., Kaliszyk, C., Sutcliffe, G., Urban, J.: GRUNGE: a grand unified ATP challenge. In: Fontaine, P. (ed.) Proceedings of the 27th International Conference on Automated Reasoning (2019, to appear). Preprint: arXiv:1903.02539 [cs.LO]

13. Brown, C.E.: Satallax: an automatic higher-order prover. In: Gramlich, B., Miller, D., Sattler, U. (eds.) IJCAR 2012. LNCS (LNAI), vol. 7364, pp. 111–117. Springer, Heidelberg (2012). https://doi.org/10.1007/978-3-642-31365-3_11

14. Gleißner, T., Steen, A., Benzmüller, C.: Theorem provers for every normal modal logic. In: Eiter, T., Sands, D. (eds.) LPAR-21, 21st International Conference on Logic for Programming, Artificial Intelligence and Reasoning. EPiC Series in Computing, Maun, Botswana, 7–12 May 2017, vol. 46, pp. 14–30. EasyChair (2017). https://doi.org/10.29007/jsb9

15. Hustadt, U., Schmidt, R.A.: MSPASS: modal reasoning by translation and first-order resolution. In: Dyckhoff, R. (ed.) TABLEAUX 2000. LNCS (LNAI), vol. 1847, pp. 67–71. Springer, Heidelberg (2000). https://doi.org/10.1007/10722086_7

16. Kaliszyk, C., Sutcliffe, G., Rabe, F.: TH1: the TPTP typed higher-order form with rank-1 polymorphism. In: Fontaine, P., Schulz, S., Urban, J. (eds.) Proceedings of the 5th Workshop on Practical Aspects of Automated Reasoning. CEUR Workshop Proceedings, vol. 1635, pp. 41–55 (2016). CEUR-WS.org

17. Lindblad, F.: A focused sequent calculus for higher-order logic. In: Demri, S., Kapur, D., Weidenbach, C. (eds.) IJCAR 2014. LNCS (LNAI), vol. 8562, pp. 61–75. Springer, Cham (2014). https://doi.org/10.1007/978-3-319-08587-6_5

18. Steen, A.: Extensional paramodulation for higher-order logic and its effective implementation Leo-III, DISKI, vol. 345. Akademische Verlagsgesellschaft AKA GmbH, Berlin, September 2018. Dissertation, Freie Universität Berlin, Germany

19. Steen, A., Benzmüller, C.: The higher-order prover Leo-III. In: Galmiche, D., Schulz, S., Sebastiani, R. (eds.) IJCAR 2018. LNCS (LNAI), vol. 10900, pp. 108–116. Springer, Cham (2018). https://doi.org/10.1007/978-3-319-94205-6_8

20. Sutcliffe, G.: The TPTP problem library and associated infrastructure - from CNF to TH0, TPTP v6.4.0. J. Autom. Reason. **59**(4), 483–502 (2017)

21. Sutcliffe, G., Benzmüller, C.: Automated reasoning in higher-order logic using the TPTP THF infrastructure. J. Formaliz. Reason. **3**(1), 1–27 (2010). https://doi.org/10.6092/issn.1972-5787/1710

22. Tishkovsky, D., Schmidt, R.A., Khodadadi, M.: The tableau prover generator MetTeL2. In: del Cerro, L.F., Herzig, A., Mengin, J. (eds.) JELIA 2012. LNCS (LNAI), vol. 7519, pp. 492–495. Springer, Heidelberg (2012). https://doi.org/10.1007/978-3-642-33353-8_41

Personalized Transaction Kernels
for Recommendation Using MCTS

Maryam Tavakol[1,2]([envelope]), Tobias Joppen[3], Ulf Brefeld[1], and Johannes Fürnkranz[3]

[1] Machine Learning Group, Leuphana Universität Lüneburg, Lüneburg, Germany
brefeld@leuphana.de
[2] Artificial Intelligence Group, TU Dortmund, Dortmund, Germany
maryam.tavakol@cs.tu-dortmund.de
[3] Knowledge Engineering Group, TU Darmstadt, Darmstadt, Germany
{tjoppen,juffi}@ke.tu-darmstadt.de

Abstract. We study pairwise preference data to model the behavior of users in online recommendation problems. We first propose a tensor kernel to model contextual transactions of a user in a joint feature space. The representation is extended to all users via hash functions that allow to effectively store and retrieve personalized slices of data and context. In order to quickly focus on the relevant properties of the next item to display, we propose the use of Monte-Carlo tree search on the learned preference values. Empirically, on real-world transaction data, both the preference models as well as the search tree exhibit excellent performance over baseline approaches.

Keywords: Preference learning · Tensor kernel · Personalization · MCTS

1 Introduction

Understanding user behavior is essential in many recommendation tasks involving implicit feedback. Several approaches aim at capturing characteristic traits of users by analyzing data ranging from atomic user actions, such as clicks and purchases, to their entire navigation patterns. However, a reliable analysis of navigation patterns requires regular (and possibly frequent) visits of the same user, but for the vast majority of users, the available data is very limited, because purchases are generally rare events, and user clicks do not per se express an interest in an item. Maintaining an individual model for every user bears another caveat; besides retrieval and maintenance costs, again only heavy hitters will really benefit from such an approach. Therefore, there is a great need for techniques that leverage all available data so that *every* user benefits, irrespectively of the available amount of data.

In this paper, we explore a tree search approach with pairwise preference data to study the behavior of users in online recommendation problems. We

---

M. Tavakol and T. Joppen—Have contributed equally.

© Springer Nature Switzerland AG 2019
C. Benzmüller and H. Stuckenschmidt (Eds.): KI 2019, LNAI 11793, pp. 338–352, 2019.
https://doi.org/10.1007/978-3-030-30179-8_31

propose to use qualitative feedback in the form of pairwise preferences as the lever. Preference data have often served as a reliable source of information, and preference learning can be used to reveal the true interests of a user from such data [8,10]. However, preferences highly depend on the context of the user. We use results from tensor theory to propose a transaction kernel that maps multiple data sources into a joint feature space (e.g., the user's click history, context, demographics, etc.). Hash functions augment data from other users into this space such that user slices can be efficiently stored and retrieved. The kernel can be extended to pairwise preference data, so that a preference learning algorithm such as SVM^{rank} [12] can be used to obtain personalized preference models.

Furthermore, we introduce an online search technique to recommend the most relevant items to the actual user and context. It relies on the personalized preference models as a utility function, which needs to be maximized in order to identify the optimal items, i.e., those items that are most likely to be clicked on by the user in a given context according to the learned model. A naïve approach for computing the a recommendation is to exhaustively search over all possible items and to return the one with the maximum value. An anytime version of this algorithm returns the product with the highest value among those that have been seen so far. To improve this, we suggest to employ a variant of Monte Carlo tree search (MCTS), which allows to quickly focus on items with desirable features. Our results show that the MCTS variant returns better recommendations in cases where the number of sampled products is limited.

We start our paper with a brief review of related work. Section 3 then formalizes the problem setting and describes our approach for learning contextual and personalized user models from preference data. This is then followed by the description of our informed sequential search technique using MCTS in Sect. 4. Finally, Sect. 5 reports on empirical results, and Sect. 6 concludes.

2 Related Work

Personalized recommender systems range from collaborative filtering [11,20] and matrix factorization [15], to contextual and session-based approaches [16,26,29]. Recommender systems leverage quantitative feedback either in form of explicit ratings or implicit views to retrieve items of interest to the user.

An alternative viewpoint constitutes scenarios that are based on feedback in form of user preferences [10]. Preference learning describes a family of learning problems where the target information is not necessarily given, but preferences between options are known; the task is to predict an ordering between these options [8]. One can distinguish between object ranking problems [13], and label ranking problems [28]. Both problems can be approached in different ways. We formalize our problem as an object ranking task, which we address by learning an underlying utility function. Thus, we learn a personalized preference model using SVMs, in a similar fashion to Joachims [12], who effectively utilizes an SVM to learn a ranking function for click-through data, and Chapelle and Keerthi [5] who present an efficient method to speed up the algorithm. The use of SVMs facilitates the use of the kernel trick for dealing with non-linearities. Kernel methods have been successfully employed for top-N recommendation using, for instance, Gaussian processes [27] or contextual bandits [25].

In this paper, we benefit from tensor kernels to express the conjugation of different feature representations (or contexts) via tensor products [7], which have—both as an explicit feature mapping and kernel function—been previously employed for feature selection in classification tasks [3,4,24]. Oyama and Manning [18] propose a tensor kernel to conjugate features of example pairs for learning pairwise classifiers. Tensors are additionally used for relation extraction in unstructured natural language parsing [32]. The idea of joint feature maps using tensor product is further utilized in recommendation, where Basilico and Hofmann [1] present a collaborative-based kernel method over user-item pairs for rating prediction. Instead, we use hash functions for learning user-specific models, and empirically show that our approach significantly outperforms their algorithm yet with a much faster computation.

Hashing functions are introduced by Shi et al. [22] for sparse projections in multi-class classification tasks, and are originally known as *Count Sketch* [6]. Weinberger et al. [31] propose a hashing trick for large-scale multi-task learning, where all tasks are mapped into a joint hash space. Together with tensor products, Pham and Pagh [19] apply hashing as a random feature mapping to approximate polynomial kernels in large-scale problems with bounded error. They exhibit the tensor product feature space as an equivalent to polynomial kernels, and propose an efficient way to project the data into a lower dimension without explicitly computing the tensor products. Subsequently, Wang et al. [30] exploit randomized tensors to efficiently perform implicit tensor decomposition for latent topic modeling.

Our learned model is used in an MCTS framework to sample near-optimal products for online recommendation. MCTS is an anytime tree search algorithm for sequential decision making [2,14] which became very popular due to its great success in game playing domains such as Go [23] but has also previously been employed in recommendation problems: Liebman et al. [17] propose MCTS for playlist recommendation and develop alternative backup strategies to increase convergence speed, and Gaudel and Sebag [9] deploy MCTS in feature selection for recommendation tasks.

3   Informed Sampling from Personalized Preferences

3.1   Preliminaries

We study transaction scenarios in which users, represented by their user ID $u \in \mathbb{U}$, click on a product $\mathbf{p} \in \mathbb{P}$. The context of the click (e.g., the sequence of previous clicks, the day and time, etc.) is captured by $\mathbf{s} \in \mathbb{S}$. We aim to understand why user u in context $\mathbf{s}$ clicks on item $\mathbf{p}$ and not on some other presented item $\mathbf{p}'$, and to turn this understanding into a recommender system that shows interesting new items to users depending on their context. Thus, our basic information entities are triples $\mathbf{x}_i = (\mathbf{p}_i, u_i, \mathbf{s}_i)$ representing an item that was shown to user in a certain context.

Note that some scenarios may provide additional data sources such as user profile data, shipping and billing addresses, additional information on items, user friendship graphs, or further demographics. In general, we thus assume the existence of m different data sources, $\mathcal{X} = \{\mathbb{X}^1, \ldots, \mathbb{X}^m\}$ where each source adds some piece of information to the problem. We first consider the generalized problem of merging the m sources into a personalized joint representation before we incorporate preferences and learn a utility function that can be used together with MCTS.

3.2 Transaction Kernels

Tensor Kernels. In order to completely capture the interlace properties of data sources, $\{\mathbb{X}^1, \ldots, \mathbb{X}^m\}$, we define the mapping ψ^t as the tensor product of their respective vector spaces. The tensor product of two vector spaces V and V' is again a vector space $V \otimes V'$ [7]. Let $\mathbf{v} = \{v_1, v_2, \ldots, v_k\}$ and $\mathbf{v}' = \{v'_1, v'_2, \ldots, v'_{k'}\}$ be the basis systems of V and V', respectively. Their tensor product space is spanned by a basis that contains all pairs (v_i, v'_j). For instance, if $\mathbf{v} = \{v_1, v_2, v_3\}$ and $\mathbf{v}' = \{v'_1, v'_2\}$, the tensor product $\mathbf{v} \otimes \mathbf{v}'$ is $\{v_1 v'_1, v_1 v'_2, v_2 v'_1, v_2 v'_2, v_3 v'_1, v_3 v'_2\}$. Applying this to our setting results in a mapping ψ^t on $\mathbf{x} \in \mathcal{X}$ which is given by

$$\psi^t(\mathbf{x}) = \psi^t(\mathbf{x}^1, \ldots, \mathbf{x}^m) = \mathbf{x}^1 \otimes \ldots \otimes \mathbf{x}^m. \tag{1}$$

Let $n_1, \ldots, n_m$ be the dimensions of the feature spaces, $\forall \mathbf{x}, \mathbf{z} \in \mathcal{X}$ we derive

$$\langle \psi^t(\mathbf{x}), \psi^t(\mathbf{z}) \rangle = \sum_{i=1}^{n_1} \sum_{j=1}^{n_2} \ldots \sum_{l=1}^{n_m} (x_i^1 x_j^2 \ldots x_l^m)(z_i^1 z_j^2 \ldots z_l^m)$$

$$= \sum_{i=1}^{n_1} \sum_{j=1}^{n_2} \ldots \sum_{l=1}^{n_m} x_i^1 z_i^1 x_j^2 z_j^2 \ldots x_l^m z_l^m$$

$$= \langle \mathbf{x}^1, \mathbf{z}^1 \rangle \langle \mathbf{x}^2, \mathbf{z}^2 \rangle \ldots \langle \mathbf{x}^m, \mathbf{z}^m \rangle.$$

Thus, the *tensor kernel* k^t is obtained by multiplying the corresponding inner products between the spaces

$$k^t(\mathbf{x}, \mathbf{z}) = \prod_{r=1}^{m} \langle \mathbf{x}^r, \mathbf{z}^r \rangle. \tag{2}$$

The tensor product features are equivalent to the product of kernels for all domains in case of linear kernel [24]. Note that the proposed kernel possesses an explicit representation given in Eq. (1) that may be useful in large-scale tasks with small dimensionalities.

Personalized Kernels. As we mentioned in Sect. 3.1, we consider the user IDs a source of information. However, tensor products of such terms with other views act as normal inner products that do not affect the learning process in a meaningful way. We thus propose a hashed feature mapping ψ^p on top of the tensor product ψ^t to remedy this limitation. Given two hash functions $g : \mathbb{N} \to \{1, \ldots, d\}$ and $\gamma : \mathbb{N} \to \{-1, +1\}$ the hashed feature map ψ^p is defined as

$$\psi_i^p(\mathbf{x}) = \sum_{j:g(j)=i} \gamma(j) x_j \tag{3}$$

where d is the hash size and the binary hash γ is used to remove the bias inherent in the hash kernel (cf. also [31]). Consequently, the obtained hashing function gives rise to the *personalized kernel* k^p

$$k^p(\mathbf{x}, \mathbf{z}) := \langle \psi^p(\psi^t(\mathbf{x})), \psi^p(\psi^t(\mathbf{z})) \rangle. \tag{4}$$

The presence of a user ID automatically leads to a user-specific representation without the need to maintain an individual model for every user. Hence, the personalized kernel individually hashes all data sources into user slices and allows to control the dimensionality of the resulting feature space via the number of bits in the hash function. Moreover, the length of the hashed vector is preserved with high probability in the new space [31].

Collective Kernels. A substantial problem of personalized systems is to cope with cold start situations. Usually, for many users in the system no or too few transactions are available, which leads to inaccurate personalized models. Borrowing ideas from Tavakol and Brefeld [25] and Weinberger et al. [31], we propose an additional collective kernel that stores all user data in a single slice to account for users and contexts with limited data. Therefore, the *collective kernel* function k^c simply discards the user IDs from the tensor products and is thus given by

$$k^c(\mathbf{x}, \mathbf{z}) := \langle \psi^p(\psi^t(\mathbf{x} \setminus u)), \psi^p(\psi^t(\mathbf{z} \setminus u)) \rangle. \tag{5}$$

Combining Personalized and Collective Kernels. We propose to combine the personalized and the collective kernels into a single kernel function to have the best of the two worlds. Every user has their own individual model with all data created by that user and whenever that information is insufficient, the collective part of the kernel may help out. Given the union operation $\cup$, the combined feature map ψ^{pc} is given by

$$\psi^{pc}(\mathbf{x}) = \psi^p\Big(\psi^t(\mathbf{x}) \cup \psi^t(\mathbf{x} \setminus u)\Big). \tag{6}$$

This leads to the *personalized and collective kernel* k^{pc},

$$k^{pc}(\mathbf{x}, \mathbf{z}) := \langle \psi^{pc}(\mathbf{x}), \psi^{pc}(\mathbf{z}) \rangle. \tag{7}$$

Table 1. Exemplary feature mappings

Collective	Personalized	Personalized+Collective
red::white		red::white
red::women		red::women
red::shoes		red::shoes
...		...
Adidas::sneakers		Adidas::sneakers
Adidas::Nike		Adidas::Nike
	u-742::red::white	u-742::red::white
	u-742::red::women	u-742::red::women
	u-742::red::shoes	u-742::red::shoes
	...	...
	u-742::Adidas::sneakers	u-742::Adidas::sneakers
	u-742::Adidas::Nike	u-742::Adidas::Nike

Example. As a result, three models are considered: a collective model, a personalized model, and a personalized+collective model. Note that the former learns the same parameters for all the users. To shed light on the characteristic traits of the proposed kernels, we showcase their feature spaces on the example of a user u-742 with context $\mathbf{s} =$ red, women, shoes, sneakers, Adidas currently viewing an item $\mathbf{p} =$ white, women, shoes, sneakers, Nike. Table 1 shows the resulting features for the collective, personalized, and personalized+collective feature maps where the tensor product is represented as the concatenation of the corresponding features. Note that we ignore the hash functions for a moment, which would map the resulting strings to numbers.

Preference-Based Transaction Kernels. Finally, to leverage pairwise preference data for the recommendation scenarios, we consider user preferences of the form $\{\mathbf{p}_i \succ \mathbf{p}'_i \mid u_i, \mathbf{s}_i\}_{i=1}^n$, indicating that user u_i prefers item $\mathbf{p}_i$ over $\mathbf{p}'_i$ in context $\mathbf{s}_i$. Every preference is translated into $\mathbf{x}_i = (\mathbf{p}_i, u_i, \mathbf{s}_i)$ and $\mathbf{x}'_i = (\mathbf{p}'_i, u_i, \mathbf{s}_i)$. Note that additionally available data sources are simply appended in the representation. Using a linear model with parameters $\boldsymbol{\theta}$, we thus obtain

$$\mathbf{x}_i \succ \mathbf{x}'_i \Leftrightarrow \boldsymbol{\theta}^\top \psi^{pc}(\mathbf{x}_i) \geq \boldsymbol{\theta}^\top \psi^{pc}(\mathbf{x}'_i) \Leftrightarrow \boldsymbol{\theta}^\top \left(\psi^{pc}(\mathbf{x}_i) - \psi^{pc}(\mathbf{x}'_i) \right) \geq 0. \quad (8)$$

After certain transformations, the representer theorem [21] allows to rewrite the primal parameters as

$$\boldsymbol{\theta} = \sum_j \alpha_j \left(\psi^{pc}(\mathbf{x}_j) - \psi^{pc}(\mathbf{x}'_j) \right)$$

for dual variables α_j. Plugging this result back into Eq. (8) shows that all data-driven parts are of the form

$$\left\langle \psi^{pc}(\mathbf{x}_i) - \psi^{pc}(\mathbf{x}'_i), \psi^{pc}(\mathbf{x}_j) - \psi^{pc}(\mathbf{x}'_j) \right\rangle.$$

Expanding the term yields

$$\langle \psi^{pc}(\mathbf{x}_i), \psi^{pc}(\mathbf{x}_j) \rangle - \langle \psi^{pc}(\mathbf{x}_i), \psi^{pc}(\mathbf{x}_j') \rangle - \langle \psi^{pc}(\mathbf{x}_i'), \psi^{pc}(\mathbf{x}_j) \rangle + \langle \psi^{pc}(\mathbf{x}_i'), \psi^{pc}(\mathbf{x}_j') \rangle,$$

and using Eq. (7) leads to the desired *preference-based transaction kernel* that is given by

$$k(\mathbf{x}_i \succ \mathbf{x}_i', \mathbf{x}_j \succ \mathbf{x}_j') = k^{pc}(\mathbf{x}_i, \mathbf{x}_j) - k^{pc}(\mathbf{x}_i, \mathbf{x}_j') - k^{pc}(\mathbf{x}_i', \mathbf{x}_j) + k^{pc}(\mathbf{x}_i', \mathbf{x}_j').$$

Note that in the experiments, we also evaluate the other proposed kernels, k^p and k^c, as well. The kernel can be plugged into a binary support vector machine or any other kernel machine. In case of the former, every preference encodes a positive example which renders the problem a binary ranking task. Note that thresholds cancel out in Eq. (8); hence, the optimal hyperplane has to pass through the origin.

4   Informed Sampling Strategies

To recommend an item to a user u in a given context $\mathbf{s}$, we need to maximize the utility over all products $\mathbf{p}_i \in \mathbb{P}$. In many tasks with only a small set of items and a fast utility function, a complete enumeration, i.e., an evaluation of every possible product, may be feasible to find the best-rated item within $\mathcal{O}(|\mathbb{P}|)$. However, in real applications, the size of item set is very large, and an efficient technique is required for online recommendation. We present a variant of MCTS for reducing the search space and efficiently finding the (near-) optimal candidates.

Thus, we aim to minimize the computational costs for evaluating the utilities of the items while still obtaining a reasonable approximation of the optimum. One way to minimize the costs is to limit the number of examples under consideration, which implies a trade-off between the utility value of the returned optimal product and the number of items considered. In other words, we strive for finding near-optimal products while visiting a bounded number of items. For this purpose, we incrementally build up a search tree.

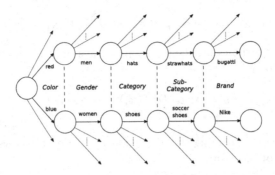

Fig. 1. The structure of search tree used by MCTS with five categorical layers.

Structure of the Search Tree. Every product is characterized by a set of five categorical features: color, gender, category, sub-category, and brand. Figure 1 illustrates the search tree for this task which is constructed in a way such that each layer of the tree corresponds to one categorical feature. The actions/arcs between two layers correspond to values of this feature, e.g., setting the color of a product to blue. Therefore, a trajectory starting from the root node first chooses a value for feature 1, followed by a value for feature 2 and so on. At the leaf nodes of the tree, all five features have been assigned that leads to a complete item description, and can be used with the current user and context to query its utility value. We ensure that each leaf node corresponds to a real product. As an example, choosing action shoes in depth 3 sets the third feature of the product to shoes, making shirts an illegal action at depth 4.

Monte-Carlo Tree Search. MCTS is an online search algorithm to explore the state space and find the optimal states for a given utility function. Its key idea is to incrementally construct an asymmetric partial search tree, guided by the estimates for the encountered actions [14]. The tree is expanded deeper in branches with most promising actions, so that less time is spent on evaluating less promising ones. In our setting, the nodes correspond to product features and the leaves are the products to recommend. Thus, products with more promising features will be more likely to be sampled than products with uninteresting features. MCTS is an anytime algorithm, i.e., the algorithm can be stopped at any time and will provide the best result encountered up to that point.

The algorithm consists of four consecutive steps, which are iterated for each new example [2]. The *selection step* follows a path through the tree until a leaf is reached. The *expand step* adds a child of this node to the partial tree. Unless this leaf is already a terminal state in the search space (in our case a product with all features), Monte-Carlo sampling is used to sample a random terminal state below the current leaf (the *rollout step*). The value of this terminal state, in our case the utility value of the sampled product, is then propagated back through all nodes up to the root node (the *backpropagation step*). These backed up values in the nodes are further used in the next selection step.

Upper Confidence Bounds on Trees. In the selection step, the next node to expand can be selected in many different ways. We use Upper Confidence Tree (UCT) [14], which treats each node as a bandit problem. More precisely, in each node, it selects the action that maximizes the term

$$i = \arg\max_j \left(\bar{v}_j + 2 \cdot \lambda \sqrt{\frac{2 \ln n}{n_j}} \right), \tag{9}$$

where $\bar{v}_j$ is the average value propagated through the j-th node, n_j is the number of times a value has been propagated through this node, while n is the number of times a value has been propagated through its parent node. Parameter λ trades off two terms in this formula, which correspond to exploitation (focusing on the best parts of the tree) and exploration (focusing on unexplored parts of the tree).

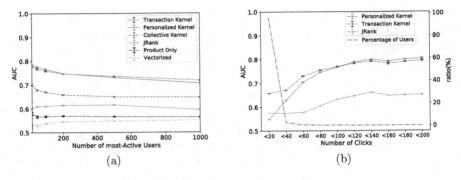

Fig. 2. AUC values for (a) SVMs with different kernels vs. baseline, (b) various click distribution of users.

Algorithmic Modifications. Once a leaf node with high value is found and added to the partial search tree, it is very likely that MCTS will visit that node again to get a better estimation. For most applications of MCTS, this is a desired behavior. However, in our setting, a recently evaluated item does not necessarily need to be re-evaluated, since its value remains the same (deterministic setting). Hence, we remove actions/arcs from the search tree if all products reachable from this edge have already been evaluated in a previous iteration. In this way, we ensure that products are sampled at most once, but the search nevertheless focuses on products which match the important properties in the higher levels of the tree. To select the best product, we do not consider the most frequently visited actions, as the base MCTS algorithm would do, but keep track of the top encountered items with respect to the utility value. Although we only consider recommendations for the best product in this paper, the framework can be easily extended to do top-k recommendations.

5   Empirical Study

We conduct our experiments on a real-world dataset from Zalando, a large European online fashion retailer. The data contains pairwise preferences of ∼680k users on ∼16k items in ∼3.5 m total transactions. A transaction occurs when a user prefers an item over another item, any other click data is ignored. Additionally, every item is characterized by a set of five categorical features: color, gender, category, sub-category, and brand. The evaluation of our proposed approach is twofold: firstly we study the how well a model of the users' preferences can be learned, and secondly, the efficiency of finding optimal items from the feature-based search tree is explored.

5.1   Performance of Preference Model

The pairwise preference model is obtained by training a support vector machine with the proposed transaction kernel. To assess the quality of the latter, we run

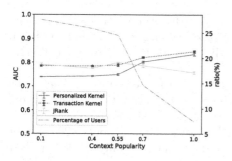
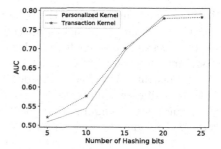

Fig. 3. AUC over context popularity.   **Fig. 4.** Influence of different hash sizes.

the SVM with different feature representations, i.e., kernels, and compare their performance. The preferences are further converted to both positive and negative examples to have a balanced dataset. Additionally, the features are represented as the unmodified *string* attributes of products for the hash function as shown in Table 1 with a hash size of 2^{17}. SVM trade-off parameters are optimized by model selection techniques.

The simplest feature representation in our experiment uses the five attributes of the products and discards user or context features. That is, $\psi(\mathbf{p}, u, \mathbf{s}) = \mathbf{p}$, where the features are one-hot encoded. We refer to this representation as "product only". A second baseline concatenates all available features into a single vector. Since the user ID is hardly an informative quantity, we replace it by clicking frequencies of item categories to form a feature vector for users. The frequencies are computed on historic data, and the final representation is given by $\psi(\mathbf{p}, u, \mathbf{s}) = [\mathbf{p}; freq_{cat}(u); \mathbf{s}]$. We refer to this representation as "vectorized". We include the collective kernel and the personalized kernel as special cases of the transaction kernel in our experiments. We also compare the performances with JRank [1], as another kernel-based recommendation approach which is based on collaborative filtering view to predicts ordinal ratings; this corresponds to learning a binary ranking in our scenario.

Figure 2(a) shows AUC values obtained by a 10-fold cross-validation for the different models. The users on the x-axis are ordered from left to right according to their click frequencies. The results clearly demonstrate that the information encoded in the baselines "product only" and "vectorized" is not sufficient to accurately learn the preferences. The poor performance of JRank is caused by the sparsity of the data as well as cold start situations. JRank tries to remedy cold start issues by incorporating attributes of users and items into the model; however, compared to including the short-term context as in our model, there is only little to incorporate for JRank. Furthermore, the correlation kernel in JRank depends on collaborative information extracted from the user-item matrix which is too sparse in the problem to capture accurate correlations between users and items. The collective kernel alone also does not perform well. The reason for this lies in the choice of the users. Since all users expressed many preferences, they left enough data for the personalized kernel to capture their characteristic traits.

However, at about rank 200, the performance of the transaction kernel increases over the personalized kernel as the collective kernel kicks in. The users with 200 to 1000 clicks clearly benefit, if only slightly, from the inclusion of the collective model into the transaction kernel.

To illustrate this effect, consider Fig. 2(b) which uses all data. The x-axis shows the different numbers of clicks of the users together with the distribution. Simultaneously, the figure shows the AUC of the transaction and the personalized kernel (y-axis on left side). In terms of AUC, users who have about 120 clicks or more are better off with a purely personalized model that is only trained on their data alone. However, the red curve shows that these users are only a vanishing minority of all users. The distribution of clicks clearly follows an exponential law where the majority of users have only one or two dozens of clicks. For them, the transaction kernel leverages the collective kernel so that the majority benefits, even though they have only little data to share. On the other side of the scale, the heavy hitters do not loose too much in terms of AUC if the transaction kernel is used. This renders that the proposed approach provides the best representation in this study. Note that the two left-most points of the figure involve data at large scales and the first cross validation fold for JRank took more than ≈ 30 days. We thus resort to showing only the results of this first fold.

Figure 3 draws a similar picture for context popularity instead of user clicks. We randomly choose a smaller subset of data for this experiment to evaluate the baseline in a reasonable amount of time, which leads to an overall higher AUC in all the approaches. The figure confirms that the more popular the context, the better the performance of the transaction kernel. In addition, popular contexts are rare, and again the majority of users create new and unseen contexts. However note that the transaction kernel clearly outperforms the personalized kernel for all contexts. JRank does not rely on any context related information and is more or less unaffected by context popularity.

We also investigate the effect of the size of the hashing function. Figure 4 shows the results for data from the 200 most active users. The more bits are used, the larger the resulting hashed space. Smaller numbers of bits lead to collisions that introduce noise into the representation as the mapping is no longer one-to-one but one-to-many.

5.2   Performance of Informed Sampling

We compare the performance of our MCTS-based sampling to alternative search strategies. In particular, we use *random subset exhaustion* (RSE) and *greedy stochastic search* (GSS) as the baselines. RSE is a simple way to approximate the optimal element of a countable set without taking any structure into account. Given a fixed limit on the number of products that can be tested, it takes a random sample of the given size and exhaustively determines the best discovered item in this sample. GSS explores the search tree in a greedy fashion. We first randomly initialize a product, and then explore a stochastic neighborhood of this product. This neighborhood is formed by sampling a fixed number of h products, where half of them are randomly selected among those that differ only in brand

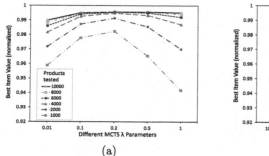
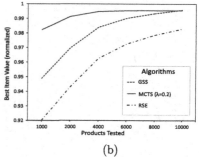

(a)   (b)

Fig. 5. Performance of MCTS (a) w.r.t. different parameters, and (b) compared to baseline methods.

(distance $d = 2$ edges in the tree of Fig. 1), one quarter of the products differ in brand and subcategory ($d = 4$), and, in general, $1/d$ percent of the products in the neighborhood are randomly selected among those with distance d. Then, all products among the h products in this neighborhood are evaluated and the search continues with the best one among those.

We run the experiments on four randomly selected users (three existing users and one new), using 50 randomly selected items as contexts, yielding 200 user-context pairs. For MCTS and GSS, the reported results are averages over 50 runs, for RSE, we show the average over all possible subsets. We first evaluate the performance of the proposed method for various values of λ that we choose from $\{0.01, 0.1, 0.2, 0.5, 1\}$. Figure 5(a) shows that the value of $\lambda = 0.2$ achieves the best result for different numbers of tested products.

We further evaluate the performance of the MCTS approach compared to the baselines. Figure 5(b) shows the average value for the best found product for different numbers of tested items. The results confirm that informed sampling via MCTS outperforms RSE for the same number of products for all maximum sample sizes. The advantage can be observed for all settings of the parameter λ, but the magnitude of the advantage varies. The performance of GSS lies between RSE and MCTS until 10,000 products, and then starts to slightly outperform MCTS with an average value of over 99.5%. The parameter value of $\lambda = 0.2$ performs the best over all numbers of items considered. It is not surprising that this value favors exploitation, since our algorithmic modifications of MCTS already enforces some exploration.

In Fig. 6, we show a more detailed analysis for a single product (hand-picked as a representative case). The values of the best found item are shown for different users and different parameter settings. For all selected users, MCTS with $\lambda = 0.2$ finds a better product within 2,000 products than RSE does within 10,000 products. There are extreme cases such as User 4, a new user without training data, where MCTS is able to find the best rated item very quickly. For User 2, a bad choice for MCTS, the parameter λ shows a worse performance than RSE, but this is a rare case. In summary, MCTS is able to find near-optimal products

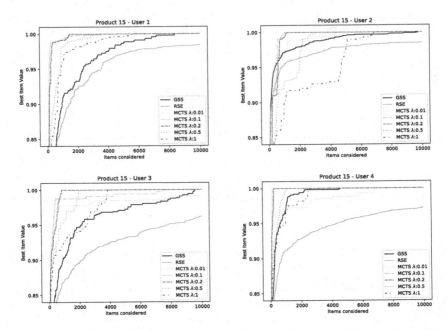

Fig. 6. Given one product and four users (user 4 is a new user), different MCTS parameters, GSS and RSE are tested.

using a considerably lower number of samples than GSS or RSE. However, this reduction in the number of tested products comes with higher computational costs. Therefore, the choice of sampling strategy depends on the problem at hand.

6   Conclusion

In this paper, we presented an effective and efficient preference-based learning approach to model personalized interests of users in contextual settings. We devised transaction kernels from pairwise preference data that combine theories from tensor products with hashing functions to capture individual as well as collective user preferences. The kernel functions were used in training a preference model via support vector machines to predict the utility of various products for a given user and context. Subsequently, we proposed the use of Monte Carlo tree search for efficiently retrieving near-optimal items for the purpose of online recommendation. Empirically, on a real-world transaction dataset, both the preference models as well as the search tree exhibited excellent performance over baseline approaches, in particular in cases where only a small number of products could be sampled.

Acknowledgements. We would like to thank Christian Wirth for contributing in our discussions and providing helpful ideas during the work. Tobias Joppen has been supported by the German Science Foundation (DFG).

References

1. Basilico, J., Hofmann, T.: Unifying collaborative and content-based filtering. In: Proceedings of the 21st International Conference on Machine Learning (ICML 2004), p. 9. ACM (2004)
2. Browne, C.B., et al.: A survey of Monte Carlo tree search methods. IEEE Trans. Comput. Intell. AI Games **4**(1), 1–43 (2012)
3. Cao, B., He, L., Kong, X., Philip, S.Y., Hao, Z., Ragin, A.B.: Tensor-based multi-view feature selection with applications to brain diseases. In: Proceedings of the IEEE International Conference on Data Mining (ICDM 2014), pp. 40–49 (2014)
4. Cao, B., Kong, X., Yu, P.S.: A review of heterogeneous data mining for brain disorder identification. Brain Inform. **2**(4), 211–233 (2015)
5. Chapelle, O., Keerthi, S.S.: Efficient algorithms for ranking with SVMs. Inf. Retr. **13**(3), 201–215 (2010)
6. Charikar, M., Chen, K., Farach-Colton, M.: Finding frequent items in data streams. In: Widmayer, P., Eidenbenz, S., Triguero, F., Morales, R., Conejo, R., Hennessy, M. (eds.) ICALP 2002. LNCS, vol. 2380, pp. 693–703. Springer, Heidelberg (2002). https://doi.org/10.1007/3-540-45465-9_59
7. Dullemond, K., Peeters, K.: Introduction to Tensor Calculus. University of Heidelberg (2010). http://www.e-booksdirectory.com/details.php?ebook=9967
8. Fürnkranz, J., Hüllermeier, E. (eds.): Preference Learning. Springer, Boston (2010). https://doi.org/10.1007/978-0-387-30164-8
9. Gaudel, R., Sebag, M.: Feature selection as a one-player game. In: Fürnkranz, J., Joachims, T. (eds.) Proceedings of the 27th International Conference on Machine Learning (ICML 2010), pp. 359–366. Omnipress, Haifa (2010)
10. de Gemmis, M., Iaquinta, L., Lops, P., Musto, C., Narducci, F., Semeraro, G.: Learning preference models in recommender systems. In: Fürnkranz and Hüllermeier [8], pp. 387–407
11. Hu, Y., Koren, Y., Volinsky, C.: Collaborative filtering for implicit feedback datasets. In: Proceedings of the 8th IEEE International Conference on Data Mining (ICDM 2008), pp. 263–272. IEEE (2008)
12. Joachims, T.: Optimizing search engines using clickthrough data. In: Proceedings of the 8th ACM SIGKDD International Conference on Knowledge Discovery and Data Mining, pp. 133–142. ACM (2002)
13. Kamishima, T., Kazawa, H., Akaho, S.: A survey and empirical comparison of object ranking methods. In: Fürnkranz and Hüllermeier [8], pp. 181–201
14. Kocsis, L., Szepesvári, C.: Bandit based Monte-Carlo planning. In: Fürnkranz, J., Scheffer, T., Spiliopoulou, M. (eds.) ECML 2006. LNCS (LNAI), vol. 4212, pp. 282–293. Springer, Heidelberg (2006). https://doi.org/10.1007/11871842_29
15. Koren, Y., Bell, R., Volinsky, C.: Matrix factorization techniques forrecommender systems. Computer **42**(8), 30–37 (2009)
16. Li, L., Chu, W., Langford, J., Schapire, R.E.: A contextual-bandit approach to personalized news article recommendation. In: Proceedings of the 19th International Conference on the World Wide Web (WWW 2010), pp. 661–670. ACM (2010)
17. Liebman, E., Khandelwal, P., Saar-Tsechansky, M., Stone, P.: Designing better playlists with Monte Carlo tree search. In: Proceedings of the 31st AAAI Conference on Artificial Intelligence (AAAI 2017), pp. 4715–4720 (2017)
18. Oyama, S., Manning, C.D.: Using feature conjunctions across examples for learning pairwise classifiers. In: Boulicaut, J.-F., Esposito, F., Giannotti, F., Pedreschi, D. (eds.) ECML 2004. LNCS (LNAI), vol. 3201, pp. 322–333. Springer, Heidelberg (2004). https://doi.org/10.1007/978-3-540-30115-8_31

19. Pham, N., Pagh, R.: Fast and scalable polynomial kernels via explicit feature maps. In: Proceedings of the 19th ACM SIGKDD International Conference on Knowledge Discovery and Data Mining, pp. 239–247. ACM (2013)

20. Sarwar, B., Karypis, G., Konstan, J., Riedl, J.: Item-based collaborative filtering recommendation algorithms. In: Proceedings of the 10th International Conference on the World Wide Web (WWW 2001), pp. 285–295. ACM (2001)

21. Schölkopf, B., Herbrich, R., Smola, A.J.: A generalized representer theorem. In: Helmbold, D., Williamson, B. (eds.) COLT 2001. LNCS (LNAI), vol. 2111, pp. 416–426. Springer, Heidelberg (2001). https://doi.org/10.1007/3-540-44581-1_27

22. Shi, Q., et al.: Hash kernels. In: Proceedings of the 12th International Conference on Artificial Intelligence and Statistics (AISTATS 2009), pp. 496–503. JMLR, Clearwater Beach (2009)

23. Silver, D., et al.: Mastering the game of Go with deep neural networks and tree search. Nature **529**(7587), 484–489 (2016)

24. Smalter, A., Huan, J., Lushington, G.: Feature selection in the tensor product feature space. In: Proceedings of the 9th IEEE International Conference on Data Mining (ICDM 2009), pp. 1004–1009. IEEE (2009)

25. Tavakol, M., Brefeld, U.: A unified contextual bandit framework for long- and short-term recommendations. In: Ceci, M., Hollmén, J., Todorovski, L., Vens, C., Džeroski, S. (eds.) ECML PKDD 2017. LNCS (LNAI), vol. 10535, pp. 269–284. Springer, Cham (2017). https://doi.org/10.1007/978-3-319-71246-8_17

26. Tavakol, M., Brefeld, U.: Factored MDPs for detecting topics of user sessions. In: Proceedings of the 8th ACM Conference on Recommender Systems, pp. 33–40. ACM (2014)

27. Vanchinathan, H.P., Nikolic, I., De Bona, F., Krause, A.: Explore-exploit in top-n recommender systems via Gaussian processes. In: Proceedings of the 8th ACM Conference on Recommender Systems, pp. 225–232. ACM (2014)

28. Vembu, S., Gärtner, T.: Label ranking algorithms: a survey. In: Fürnkranz and Hüllermeier [8], pp. 45–64

29. Wang, C., Blei, D.M.: Collaborative topic modeling for recommending scientific articles. In: Proceedings of the 17th ACM SIGKDD International Conference on Knowledge Discovery and Data Mining, pp. 448–456. ACM (2011)

30. Wang, Y., Tung, H.Y., Smola, A.J., Anandkumar, A.: Fast and guaranteed tensor decomposition via sketching. In: Advances in Neural Information Processing Systems, pp. 991–999 (2015)

31. Weinberger, K., Dasgupta, A., Langford, J., Smola, A., Attenberg, J.: Feature hashing for large scale multitask learning. In: Proceedings of the 26th International Conference on Machine Learning (ICML 2009), pp. 1113–1120. ACM (2009)

32. Zelenko, D., Aone, C., Richardella, A.: Kernel methods for relation extraction. J. Mach. Learn. Res. **3**(Feb), 1083–1106 (2003)

Author Index

Printed in the United States
By Bookmasters